Vistas

in Reading Literature

GREEN LEVEL
Red Level
Gold Level

Vistas
in Reading Literature

Green Level

Jacqueline L. Chaparro
Curriculum Coordinator, English Language Arts
San Diego County Office of Education,
San Diego, California

Mary Ann Trost
Specialist in Educational Materials for the
Middle Grades, Cleveland Heights, Ohio

McDougal, Littell & Company
Evanston, Illinois
New York   Dallas   Sacramento   Raleigh

Consultants

Joyce Allen, Teacher, Saint Cletus School, La Grange, Illinois

James Dedes, Teacher, Holmes Junior High School, Mount Prospect, Illinois

Richard H. Gray, Chairman, English Department, Enfield High School,
Enfield, Connecticut

Denis M. Hennessy, English Department, Delaware Academy,
Delhi, New York

Patricia West Jeffries, High school teacher and free-lance writer on basic
skills for the Memphis (Tennessee) City Schools.

Aramenta Kirkpatrick, Teacher, Warrensville Heights Junior High School,
Cleveland, Ohio

Neeta Lewis, Teacher, Richardson Junior High School, Richardson, Texas

Sandra J. Nash, Teacher, Beverly Hills Junior High School,
Huntington, West Virginia

Caroline P. Nelson, Teacher, Cloverdale Junior High School,
Montgomery, Alabama

Lois Samuels, Teacher, Chandler Junior High School, Chandler, Arizona

Mary Theis, S.S.S.F., Coordinator of Curriculum,
Archdiocese of Milwaukee, Milwaukee, Wisconsin

William H. Thomas, Curriculum Specialist, Mt. Diablo Unified
School District, Concord, California

Jeane S. Travis, Teacher, Griffin Middle School, Smyrna, Georgia

Virginia Vargas, Teacher, Berta Cabaza Middle School, San Benito, Texas

Van White, Department Chairman, English, Walker Junior
High School, La Palma, California

Frontispiece: *Inhabited Tree,* 1980, JUAN ROMERO. Photograph: Edmund Newman, Inc.

ISBN: 0–86609–940–9

Copyright © 1989, by McDougal, Littell & Company
Box 1667, Evanston, Illinois 60204
All rights reserved. Printed in the United States of America

89 90 / 15 14 13 12 11 10 9 8 7 6 5 4 3

CONTENTS

CHAPTER ONE
Legends and Other Tales 1

Science Fiction and Fantasy *285*

▬ *Chapter 4 Review* *310*

CHAPTER FIVE
Poetry *313*

Poems About Nature *320*

Poems About Sports   *345*

Poems About the Individual   *364*

Poems About America   *384*

CHAPTER SIX
Nonfiction

Autobiographies

Biographies

Personal Writings, Anecdotes, and Speeches

Essays

CHAPTER SEVEN
Drama

■ *Chapter 7 Review*   *590*

Handbook for Reading and Writing   *593*

Dear Student,

You are about to embark on an adventure—the adventure of reading fine literature. You will travel through time and space, visiting cities of the past and worlds of the future. You will meet fascinating characters who face exciting challenges. This book and your imagination will guide you.

Reading Literature will introduce you to a wide variety of literature. You will read stories, poems, plays, and works of nonfiction in their original forms. These works have been written by world-famous authors such as Anton Chekhov, Joan Aiken, Isaac Asimov, A. A. Milne, Langston Hughes, Rosemary Sutcliff, Carl Sandburg, and Alice Walker. Some of the works may make you laugh and others may make you cry. All of them should make you think.

Literature is your inheritance. Great writers of the past and present have left you a wealth of ideas, experiences, and feelings. Through reading, you can share and enjoy these riches.

Reading Literature can stretch your mind, sharpen your senses, and enrich your life. You will improve your reading, thinking, and vocabulary skills. You will discover how professional writers write, and you will learn to use a similar process for your own writing. Most of all, you will have the thrill of losing yourself in literature and finding there the wondrous challenge that is life.

Sincerely,
The Authors and Editors

CHAPTER ONE

Legends and Other Tales

Blue Corn Maiden, 1967, GILBERT ATENCIO (Wah Peen
meaning "Mountain of the Sacred Wind"). Photograph by
Patricia Janis Broder, Short Hills, New Jersey.

Reading Literature

Legends and Other Tales

A **legend** is a story about heroes and heroines and extraordinary events from the past. Legends, along with other tales, are part of **oral tradition.** That is, storytellers have passed on the stories from one generation to the next.

The History of the Legend

Legends start because people need to recall the past. Long after an important person dies, people talk about that person's actions and personal qualities. People also talk about the events and the problems that affect their history.

Most legends are based on facts. For example, Richard the Lion-Hearted did have many loyal followers. At the time of Robin Hood, the rich often did treat the English common people unjustly. When a story is repeated many times, some facts stay the same. However, the details of the story change. One teller might exaggerate the powers of a character. The next teller might add new details to make an event seem more exciting. Another teller might remember an old tale and include that in the story, too. Soon, the true story is blended with the exaggerations and additions. The new story is a legend—an account that mixes facts with imaginative details.

The Elements of Legends and Tales

Legends, like other tales, are stories. Therefore, they have the four major elements of any story: character, setting, plot, and theme.

Character. A **character** is a person or animal who takes part in a story. In a legend, the main character is generally an outstanding person who has unusual powers. Followers often join the hero or heroine to work against a powerful person or a force that is causing a problem.

Setting. The **setting** is the time and place of the action of a story. Usually the setting is introduced at the beginning. However, details about time and place are scattered throughout the story.

Plot. The **plot** is the series of events in a story. The plot of a legend centers on how the hero or heroine deals with a struggle, or **conflict.** In a legend, he or she must show courage or cleverness to win over or defeat the forces that are creating the problem.

Many legends include events that could not take place in the real world. For example, one hero in this chapter is carried down a mountain by two eagles.

Theme. The **theme** is the writer's message. In a legend or a tale, the theme often concerns a quality or a way of behaving that is admirable.

How to Read a Legend

When you read a legend or a tale, follow these guidelines:

1. Identify the setting. Does the story take place in the time of knights and castles? Is it set in a forest or a jungle?
2. Look for the problem that the hero or heroine faces.
3. Remember that legends are almost always larger than life. Enjoy the imaginings of storytellers who describe events that are impossible in everyday life.
4. Decide what the legend or tale tells you about the people who created it. Do they value courage, loyalty, patience, intelligence, or some other quality?

Comprehension Skills

Main Idea and Supporting Details

Every paragraph has a main idea. The **main idea** is the most important idea in the paragraph.

Read this paragraph about rats in Hamelin.

> <u>Hamelin, a little German town in the duchy of Brunswick, was overrun by rats.</u> They were so fierce and so numerous that they attacked the cats and drove the dogs out of the city. All kinds of traps were laid, but the rats just flipped them about. . . . The creatures were everywhere.   —Louis Untermeyer, "The Pied Piper of Hamelin: The Broken Bargain"

The main idea of a paragraph can be stated in a topic sentence. In the paragraph above, the topic sentence is underlined. Notice how the underlined sentence states the most important idea. The other sentences give details about how Hamelin was overrun by rats. All the supporting details tell about the main idea.

Some paragraphs do not have a topic sentence. Instead, the main idea is implied, or suggested, by the details. The detail sentences, though, still must relate to one main idea.

Important and Less Important Details

The main idea in a paragraph is developed through details. Some details are more important than others. Notice the details in this paragraph about the travels of Blondel, taken from "Richard the Lion-Hearted: Saved by a Song" by Louis Untermeyer.

> One evening in autumn he came to an unusually large castle in the middle of a wild forest. It had a grim look, dark and desolate. Two equally grim guards stood in front of the drawbridge.

The main idea of this paragraph is that Blondel discovered a castle in the middle of a forest. One important detail is the grim look of the place. Another important detail is that the castle was guarded.

Other details are not as important to the story. For example, the season does not matter much. Nor does the fact that the castle had a drawbridge. These details paint a more exact picture of what is happening, but they are not absolutely necessary for an understanding of the story. Notice that less important details sometimes are included in the same sentence with more important details.

Exercises: Understanding Main Idea and Details

A. What is the main idea of this paragraph?

Meanwhile, things were going badly in England, where Richard's absence had caused much confusion. There were rumors that the demand for ransom was a deception to get money for the German emperor and that Richard was really dead. His brother John robbed the treasury and plotted to seize the throne; the country was in a state of turmoil and anxiety. No one thought of clarifying the situation by finding out whether Richard was alive or dead. No one except Blondel de Nesle.   —Louis Untermeyer, "Richard the Lion-Hearted: Saved by a Song"

B. Read the following paragraph. Then match the items below.

Now he had taken Nassa, the fair daughter of the chief himself. Everyone loved this girl. She was known to be the kindest and most beautiful of all the girls in that countryside. It is no wonder that this Ballo should wish her for his wife. The marvel was that he could have stolen her out of her bed without waking the guards. But that he had done.   —Frances Carpenter, "The Six Horsemen"

1. States the main idea
2. Gives an important detail
3. Tells a less important detail

a. Everyone loved Nassa.
b. Ballo had taken Nassa.
c. The guards did not wake up.

$\mathcal{V}$ocabulary Skills

Context Clues

You do not always need a dictionary to figure out the meanings of unfamiliar words. Sometimes you can use context clues. The **context** of a word means the sentences and paragraphs surrounding the word. In this chapter, you will learn to use definition and restatement clues and synonyms and antonyms to unlock the meanings of words.

Definition and Restatement Clues. Sometimes the definition of a new word will be given directly. The definition may appear in the same sentence as the word or in a following sentence.

The man held a <u>pipe</u>. A pipe is a tube of wood or metal used as a musical instrument.

Other times a writer repeats the same idea in a slightly different way. This example from the story has a restatement clue.

He was not one to bring <u>enmity</u> to his people, to set one family against the other.

Key Words and Punctuation. Certain key words and punctuation marks tell you to look for definition or restatement clues. Here are some of these keys.

is	that is	in other words	parentheses	dash
or	who is	which is	comma	

Notice the key words and punctuation marks that signal context clues in these sentences.

1. A gale, <u>which is</u> a strong wind, blew the ships off course.
2. Blondel was a minstrel, a poet who was also a singer.
3. He looked into the abyss (<u>a</u> deep hole in the earth).

Synonyms and Antonyms. A **synonym** is a word that means almost the same thing as another word. Sometimes a synonym is used as a restatement clue.

> There was no way one could climb down the sheer rock wall, but Black Crow took his rawhide <u>lariat</u>, made a loop in it, put the <u>rope</u> around Spotted Eagle's chest under his armpits, and lowered him down.
>
> —Jenny Leading Cloud, "Spotted Eagle and Black Crow"

An antonym also can be a context clue. An **antonym** is a word that means the opposite of another word. Notice the underlined words in the following sentence. The second word gives you a clue to the meaning of the first.

> England was in <u>turmoil</u>, but Richard soon restored <u>order</u>.

In the example, *but* signals an antonym clue. Other key words include *although*, *however*, and *on the other hand*.

Exercises: Using Context Clues

A. For each underlined word, find the definition or restatement.

1. John was a <u>tyrant</u>. A tyrant is a cruel ruler.
2. All that you possess will be <u>forfeited</u>, that is, given up, to me.
3. Black Crow wore a <u>sash</u>, a type of scarf, around his waist.

B. For each sentence, identify the word that has been restated, the key words or punctuation that helped you find the restatement clue, and the meaning of the restated word.

1. A deeper meaning was concealed—hidden—in the song.
2. The mayor summoned, or called together, his councilors.
3. Spotted Eagle lived on the ledge with the eagle fledglings (young birds).

Richard the Lion-Hearted:
Saved by a Song

TRADITIONAL TALE
Retold by Louis Untermeyer

Is a hero always a great and powerful leader? As you read, decide who is the hero of this story. Think about the qualities that you admire in this hero.

Richard the First, a twelfth-century king, was a great English ruler. He was also Duke of Aquitaine and Normandy. Wars in Europe as well as the Crusades in the Holy Land kept him away from England during most of his reign. He was in the forefront of every battle he fought. When he wielded his huge battle-axe, none could withstand him. So fearless was he that he was known not merely as King Richard the Mighty but as Richard the Lion-Hearted. Enemies fled when he charged upon them shouting his battle cry, "God be with us!"

Richard had gone on the Third Crusade against the Saracens, hoping to drive them out of Jerusalem so that Christians could visit the holy places in safety. He had been aided by two other European kings, but he quarreled with his allies and grew to respect his enemies more than his friends. Saladin, king of Saracens, returned his respect and welcomed Richard as his guest. After mutual acts of courtesy and expressions of good will, a three-year truce was proposed.

"We of the East believe greatly in the number three," said Saladin. "It is a powerful number. Man is a threefold creature made of body, soul, and spirit, and the enemies of man are three: the world, the flesh, and the devil. Do you not believe so, you of the North?"

"It is so," replied Richard. "The Greeks taught us that man's life depends on the three fates, that nature is divided into three kingdoms—animal, vegetable, and mineral—and that there are three prime colors: red, yellow, and blue."

"That being true," said Saladin, "let us make our truce really binding. Let it be for three years, three months, three days, and three hours. And let us take an oath that nothing shall break such a truce."

Stories of the Emperors: Soliman Against the Christians, 15th century. Paris Bibliotèque de l'Arsenale. Photograph: Art Resource, New York.

The two leaders swore to keep the peace for that length of time and, if they were still friends, for the rest of their lives. Then Richard withdrew his troops from the Holy Land. He set sail for England by way of Cyprus, but a gale blew his ships off their course and drove them to Italy. Worse weather occurred when he resumed the journey. Storms overwhelmed the fleet with waves like battering rams, and knife-sharp winds tore the sails. After a grueling week, the boats lost contact with each other. King Richard's ship was thrown against a rocky coast and destroyed. His men were drowned, and he himself barely managed to survive.

After wandering for weeks, he found himself in the land of one of his worst enemies, Duke Leopold of Austria. He was recognized at once and captured. The Duke of Austria shut him up in a dungeon and then asked a huge ransom for his release. When Henry, Emperor of Germany, heard of this, he compelled Leopold to give up his prize. Instead of freeing Richard, Henry imprisoned him in one of his own castles and demanded a still more staggering ransom. So that no one would know where the King of England was hidden and attempt to rescue him, he was moved at various times from one secret stronghold to another.

Meanwhile, things were going badly in England, where Richard's absence had caused much confusion. There were rumors that the demand for ransom was a deception to get money for the German emperor and that Richard was really dead. His brother John robbed the treasury and plotted to seize the throne; the country was in a state of turmoil and anxiety. No one thought of clarifying the situation by finding out whether Richard was alive or dead. No one except Blondel de Nesle.

Blondel was a minstrel, a poet who was also a singer. He had been a boon companion to Richard in his youth. Richard and Blondel had spent many hours together making up tunes, matching rhymes, and composing songs on any subject that came to mind. It was Blondel who asked Richard's minister for permission to look for the king.

"But how do you expect to conduct so wild a hunt?" inquired the minister. "Where will you start?"

"I cannot tell you *how* until I begin," answered Blondel. "But I can tell you *where*. The demands for the ransom have come from Germany, so Germany is the most likely place to start."

"How many men will you require?" asked the minister.

"None," said Blondel. "I will go alone."

"You will, I hope, be well armed. What weapons will you need?"

"One weapon only," said Blondel, "if

you can call it that. I will take along my little hand harp. It will be all I need."

For three months Blondel wandered up and down Germany. He played his harp and sang his songs in taverns, inns, courtyards, and castles. He was always welcome, for people in every land delight to hear songs of war and wooing, of gallant deeds and lovely ladies, especially when they are sung as beautifully as Blondel sang them. He was offered large sums of money to remain in many a palace; he heard much gossip and was told many things in confidence. But never a word did he hear about King Richard.

One evening in autumn he came to an unusually large castle in the middle of a wild forest. It had a grim look, dark and desolate. Two equally grim guards stood in front of the drawbridge.

"Keep back," one of them said. "We make short work of spies."

"I am no spy," said Blondel. "I am a minstrel. I go from place to place to entertain lords and ladies. I am sure those inside would like to hear me."

"There is no one inside who cares for merrymaking," said the other guard. "Your eyes must be poor if you think this is a place for entertainment. It is not so much a castle as a prison."

"Indeed?" said Blondel. "I would not have suspected it."

"Yes," said the first guard, a note of pride coming into his voice. "It is one of the strongest prisons in Europe and one of the least known. And the curious part is this: it houses only one prisoner.''

"And who might that be?" Blondel asked eagerly. "Who has an entire prison to himself?"

"That we can't tell you," replied the second guard. "In fact, we ourselves don't know. All we know is that he must be someone very important, someone who has to be watched very carefully."

"Well," said Blondel. "That is very interesting. But, after all, it has nothing to do with me. If I cannot get a welcome here, I will try elsewhere. Before I go, perhaps you would like to hear a song."

"Go ahead," said the first guard. "A song never hurt anyone."

"Nor helped them, either," added the second. "But go ahead."

Blondel tuned his harp and began:

My lady sits within her bower;
*   She sings "alas" right dolefully:*
She lingers hour after hour
*   For her true lord. But where is he?*

Blondel paused. It was a song that he and King Richard had made up and sung together years ago. It had a new meaning now. Then another voice was added to his, completing the second stanza:

O tell my lady that the fates
*   Have kept her lord away from men;*
But patiently her lover waits
*   The day he can come home again.*

A twelfth-century signet ring of Richard I (1189–99). The British Museum, London.

The guards were startled to hear the second voice. They did not guess the meaning concealed in the song, but they were angry with themselves for having let the minstrel linger.

"That's enough!" shouted the guards. "On your way!"

Blondel went. But he had found what he had been seeking. He knew whose voice had answered him, and the captured king knew who had given him the message. The king also knew that Blondel had discovered where he had been hidden. He did not have to wait long to be freed.

Three months later his release was accomplished and he was brought back to England. More powerful than ever, King Richard restored his country to peace.

Louis Untermeyer (1885–1977) was a writer, a poet, and an editor. He was born in New York City. During the first twenty-three years of his career, he worked as a businessman and wrote mostly in the evenings. Then he resigned as vice-president of a jewelry company to write full-time. He edited several collections of poetry such as *Modern British Poetry* and *Modern American Poetry*. He also retold many traditional tales for modern readers.

Developing Comprehension Skills

1. Why do Richard and Saladin change from being enemies to being friends? How do they decide on the length of the truce?

2. How does Richard come to be in Henry's prison?

3. Read the paragraph in the second column on page 10 beginning "For three months. . . ." What is the main idea of the paragraph? List two important details.

4. What does Blondel do to find Richard? Could someone else have found him in the same way?

5. Who would you say is the hero of this legend: Richard or Blondel? Explain your answer.

Reading Literature: Legends

1. **Understanding Character.** Heroes of legends show qualities that are admired by the groups that created the legends. Which three of the following qualities does the teller of "Richard the Lion-Hearted" seem to admire in Blondel? Choose one of the qualities and tell how Blondel showed it.
   a. self-confidence
   b. courage in battle
   c. cleverness
   d. loyalty
   e. physical strength

2. **Identifying Setting. Setting** is both the time and the place of a story. "Richard the Lion-Hearted" has several settings: the Holy Land, a ship at sea, Austria, prisons in Austria and Germany, England, taverns and castles in Germany, one particular prison in Germany, and England again. List details that help you picture at least two of these settings. Which setting is described the most clearly?

3. **Studying Legends.** Legends and folk tales often tell about events that happen in threes. The legend about Richard gives several reasons why three is such a powerful number. Find this explanation. Then retell it in your own words.

4. **Recognizing Irony.** A writer can let the reader know more than a character in the story knows. The character thinks that one thing is true, but the reader knows that the opposite is true. When what appears to be true is not true at all, the writer is using **irony.**

On page 11, Blondel asks the guards if he may sing. Not knowing his real purpose, the guards agree:

"Go ahead," said the first guard. "A song never hurt anyone."

"Nor helped them, either," added the second.

Explain how both guards are wrong.

Vocabulary

Using Context Clues. The underlined words in the following sentences were drawn from the story. The meaning of each word can be figured out using a definition or restatement clue. For each underlined word, write the definition of the word.

1. Wars in Europe kept King Richard away during most of his reign—his time in power.

2. The Duke of Austria shut Richard up in a dungeon and then asked for a huge ransom, the price asked for his release.

3. When Henry heard of this he compelled, or forced, Leopold to give up his prize.

4. There were rumors that the demand for ransom was a deception (trick) to get money for the German Emperor.

5. The guards were angry with themselves for having let the minstrel linger, or stay around.

6. More powerful than ever, King Richard restored, that is, brought back, peace to his country.

Study and Research

Finding Information in a Library. The legend about Richard the Lion-Hearted includes some historical facts. How can you find out which parts of the legend are true? Begin in your school or local library.

In the library, the nonfiction books are separated into smaller groups, according to their subjects. One system for grouping nonfiction books is the **Dewey Decimal System.** In this system, every nonfiction book is assigned to one of ten categories. Each category has a range of one hundred numbers between 0 and 999. When a book is assigned to a category, it is given a number within that range.

Some libraries use the **Library of Congress System** to group nonfiction books. In this system, one or two letters plus numbers are assigned to each book. The letters and numbers both indicate the subject of the book.

Use information posted in your library to answer the following questions. If necessary, ask a librarian for help.

1. Which system does your library use to number nonfiction books?

2. What are the major categories used in the system?

3. What range of numbers is used for books on the history of England in the time of Richard the Lion-Hearted?

Developing Writing Skills

Explaining Setting. Write a paragraph to answer: What information is given in the first seven paragraphs of the story?

Prewriting. List the events that happen to Richard in the first seven paragraphs. Make notes about the setting for each event.

Drafting. Write a topic sentence that summarizes what happens to Richard in the opening paragraphs of the story. Add details about each event and where it takes place.

Revising and Sharing. Share the draft of your paragraph with a partner. Discuss these points: Does the paragraph have a clear main idea? Does each detail help to develop that idea? Use your partner's comments to revise your paragraph.

The Pied Piper of Hamelin:
The Broken Bargain

TRADITIONAL TALE
Retold by Louis Untermeyer

How important is it to keep a promise? In this legend, a mayor's decision about keeping a bargain affects the lives of many people. Does the mayor make the right decision?

Everyone—or almost everyone—knows Robert Browning's poem, *The Pied Piper of Hamelin.* However, not many people know that the story was many hundred years old when this nineteenth-century poet rewrote it. When first told, it ran something like this:

Hamelin, a little German town in the duchy of Brunswick, was overrun by rats. They were so fierce and so numerous that they attacked the cats and drove the dogs out of the city. All kinds of traps were laid, but the rats just flipped them about. The creatures swarmed through the streets, broke into the houses, filled the attics, invaded the kitchens, sprang on the tables, and raced through the bedrooms. They were everywhere. Browning describes them:

Rats!
They fought the dogs, and killed the cats,
*   And bit the babies in the cradles,*
And ate the cheeses out of the vats,
*   And licked the soup from the cook's*
*   own ladles,*
Split open the kegs of salted sprats,
Made nests inside men's Sunday hats,
And even spoiled the women's chats,
*   By drowning their speaking*
*   With shrieking and squeaking*
In fifty different sharps and flats!

The townspeople complained bitterly. "What kind of a mayor have we got," they said, "who allows such a thing to happen! He sits in his elegant office, gazes out of the window, and does nothing about it!"

The mayor summoned his councilors, but they were no help. Day after day they met, but nothing they thought up had the slightest effect on the plague of rats. It grew worse every hour.

One summer morning—the records give the year as 1376—a tall, odd-looking stranger entered Hamelin and came straight to the town hall. Browning saw him this way:

> *His queer long coat from heel to head*
> *Was half of yellow and half of red;*
> *And he himself was tall and thin,*
> *With sharp blue eyes, each like a pin,*
> *And light loose hair, yet swarthy skin.*
> *No tuft on cheek nor beard on chin,*
> *But lips where smiles went out and in—*

> *There was no guessing his kith and kin.*
> *And nobody could enough admire*
> *The tall man and his quaint attire.*

The stranger advanced to the council table and spoke directly to the mayor.

"I hear," he said, "you are troubled with rats. I can help you, for I happen to be a rat-catcher. By means of a certain power—call it music or call it magic—I can rid your town of the pests that are such a plague to you. People call me the Pied Piper."

Pied Piper, 1909, MAXFIELD PARRISH. Palace Hotel, San Francisco.

The mayor looked up at the man and noticed that at the end of the stranger's red and yellow scarf there hung a small pipe, and the stranger's fingers kept twitching as though they wanted to be playing on it.

"Yes," continued the strange figure, "I have freed many cities of rats, as well as gnats and bats. I will do the same for you—" he paused for a moment and coughed gently, "only you will have to pay me a thousand guilders."

"A thousand guilders?" echoed the mayor. "Make it fifty thousand! If you can really clear Hamelin of rats, it will be well worth it."

The piper stepped into the street and played a shrill tune on his pipe. As he played, rats came tumbling out of the houses. It was as if an army were on the run, murmuring and muttering. The muttering grew to a grumbling, the grumbling to a mighty rumbling, and still the rats kept coming. Great rats, small rats, lean rats, tall rats, young rats, old rats, big rats, bold rats, rats of every size and color. They

ED PIPER

followed the piper wherever he went. Still playing, he led them to the river Weser. Into the river went the rats, and every single rat was drowned.

The piper returned to the city hall, and asked politely for his thousand guilders. The mayor looked blank.

"You must be joking," said the mayor. "Surely you wouldn't expect anyone to pay such a huge sum of money for getting rid of a few rats. Besides, the river did most of the work for you. A thousand guilders? Don't be silly. Come, take fifty."

The piper's face grew dark. "I don't drive bargains," he said. "I want the full payment agreed upon. If not, you will be sorry that you didn't keep your promise. See, I still have my pipe. And if you force me, I can play a different tune."

"What!" exclaimed the mayor angrily. "You dare to threaten me! The mayor of Hamelin is not to be insulted by a fool in crazy clothes! Do your worst! Blow on your pipe until you burst!"

The piper did not say another word. Instead he left the council room and stepped out into the street. Putting his lips to the pipe, he blew again. This time the sound was anything but shrill. It was sweet and low, a dreamy tune, full of delightful turns and twists, gentle and at the same time fun, promising all manner of marvelous things. As he played, there came a sound of little hands clapping and feet pattering, of small voices chattering, like chicks in a barnyard when corn and grain

are scattering. Out of the houses came boys and girls, flocking to the piper, tripping and skipping, following after the magic music with shouting and laughter.

People looked on in amazement. The mayor cried "Stop!" But the children paid no attention to anything or anyone except the piper. Singing and dancing, they followed him out of town.

This time the piper did not guide them toward the river but toward the hills. When they came to the Köppelberg, a side of this mountain opened as though it were a door and all the children—one hundred and thirty of them—trooped inside. Then the hill closed up again. Not one of these boys and girls was ever seen again.

It would never have been known what the piper's music promised, what was to be seen inside the hill, had it not been for one lame boy. He never tired of saying how dull it was in Hamelin without his playmates nor of telling what he remembered.

"Because of my lame foot," he said, "I was a little behind the others. We were all happy as on a holiday. We were all looking forward to the place the piper—I mean the piper's music—told us about. It was a land where all things were beautiful and all people were good. A dozen rivers flowed there, each with a different sweet flavor. The flowers were larger and lovelier than anywhere else on earth. The sparrows were not dull brown, as they are here, but brighter than peacocks. Dogs ran faster than deer and never barked. Bees had lost their sting. Horses were born with eagles' wings. No one was ever sad or sick, and anyone who came to the place with anything wrong—like a lame foot—was instantly cured. Just as I was about to catch up with the other children, the door in the side of the mountain closed, the music stopped, and I was left on the Köppelberg, alone."

All of this happened (or was believed to have happened) centuries ago. But still, they say, no one is allowed to play the pipe in Hamelin. Besides, they say that in Transylvania there lives a strange group of people who wear outlandish garments of red and yellow, and have names something like those of the families that once lived in Hamelin. Not one of them, they say, ever breaks a promise.

Developing Comprehension Skills

1. What complaint do the citizens of Hamelin have about their mayor? What is the mayor's reaction?

2. The second paragraph of the story and the first lines quoted from Browning's poem are both about the rats in Hamelin. Is the main idea of each passage the same? What are some details that develop each main idea?

3. What bargain does the mayor make with the piper?

4. Does the piper keep his part of the bargain? What reason does the mayor give for not keeping his part of the bargain?

5. Does the mayor seem to take seriously either the bargain or the piper's threat? Refer to the story to support your answer.

6. What happens to the children who follow the piper? How do the townspeople find out what happens?

7. Who are the strange people who wear clothes of red and yellow?

8. Do you admire everything the Pied Piper does? Do you think the storyteller wants you to admire the piper? Explain your answer.

Reading Literature: Legends

1. **Identifying Conflict.** The plot of a story always involves a **conflict,** or struggle. Describe the conflict between the mayor and the piper. What minor conflict between the mayor and the people of Hamelin leads up to the major conflict?

2. **Using a Time Line to Show Plot.** A **time line** is a way of showing the plot of a story. To make a time line, first draw a straight

line. Then make a dot on the line for each important event in the story.

first event   third event   last event

second event   fourth event

Next to each dot, write a few words describing an event. Complete this time line for "The Pied Piper of Hamelin."

a. Hamelin is overrun by rats.

b. A stranger offers to rid the town of the rats.

3. **Understanding the History of Legends.** The writer makes it clear that "The Pied Piper of Hamelin" is a legend with a long history. How old does the opening paragraph say that the legend is? What earlier written version of the legend does the writer of this version quote from?

Vocabulary

Using Context Clues. Read the following sentences about "The Pied Piper of Hamelin." Each underlined word can be understood using context clues. Identify the definition or restatement clue that you used to figure out the meaning of the word. Then write the definition.

1. Hamelin is a little German town in the duchy of Brunswick. A duchy is the land ruled by a prince or a duke.

2. The rats were so numerous that they attacked the cats. There were so many that they even drove the dogs out of the city.

3. The strange figure told the mayor that the price would be a thousand guilders. For this money, the piper would free the town of rats.

4. When the piper asked politely for his thousand guilders, the mayor looked at him blankly, without understanding.

5. The boy was behind the others because of his lame foot. In other words, he was unable to walk as well as the other children.

6. They say that in Transylvania there lives a strange group of people who wear outlandish garments of red and yellow. The same unusual clothes were worn by the Pied Piper.

Critical Thinking

Evaluating Realism. The events in the legend about Richard were realistic; that is, they were all possible. In "The Pied Piper of Hamelin," however, some of the most important events could not have happened. Think about each event listed here. Tell which events are realistic and which could not have happened.

1. Rats overrun a town.

2. The mayor and the council search for a solution to the rat problem.

3. A stranger says he can help.

4. The stranger asks for a thousand guilders as pay.

5. The mayor promises to pay what the man asks.

6. The stranger charms the rats with pipe music.

7. The mayor refuses to pay the piper.

8. The stranger threatens the mayor.

9. The stranger charms the children of the town with pipe music.

10. The children follow the piper into a mountain.

Speaking and Listening

Reading a Poem Aloud. Browning's poem "The Pied Piper of Hamelin" is meant to be read aloud. It uses rhyme, rhythm, and specific words to create vivid pictures of scenes and characters. Look up the complete Browning poem in your school or local library. Choose a section of the poem to read. Let your voice express the disgust, amazement, excitement, or longing that the passage creates. Practice speaking clearly so that your listeners will understand every word. Then present your reading to the group.

Developing Writing Skills

Writing a Description. Imagine that you live in Hamelin. Describe what life is like with the rats. If you wish, write your description as a letter to a friend in another town.

Prewriting. Decide if you will describe a single experience with a rat or the different ways the rats bother people. In either case, list words and phrases that picture the way the rats look and act, the noises they make, and the problems they cause.

Drafting. As you draft your description, remember to use *I* and *me*. Be sure to include a sentence that sets the scene.

Revising and Sharing. When you have finished drafting your description, put it aside for a while. Later, read the description aloud. Listen for places that can be improved by using a more exact word or phrase. Make sure that your sentences read smoothly and are complete. You also might read the description to a friend.

Spotted Eagle and Black Crow

NATIVE AMERICAN LEGEND
Retold by Jenny Leading Cloud

The first two legends were from European peoples. This one is from Native Americans. As you read, ask yourself: What qualities are admired by both groups? What other qualities of heroes are shown in this legend?

This is a story of two warriors, of jealousy, and of eagles. This legend is supposed to have been a favorite of the great *Mahpiya Luta*—Chief Red Cloud of the Oglalas.

Many lifetimes ago, there lived two brave warriors. One was named *Wanblee Gleska*—Spotted Eagle. The other's name was *Kangi Sapa*—Black Crow. They were friends but, as it happened, they both loved the same girl, *Zintkala Luta Win*—Red Bird. She was beautiful, a fine tanner and quill-worker, and she liked Spotted Eagle best, which made Black Crow very jealous.

Black Crow went to his friend and said, "Let us, you and I, go on a war party against the Pahani. Let us get ourselves some fine horses and earn eagle feathers." Spotted Eagle thought this a good idea. The two young men purified themselves in a sweat bath. They got out their war medicine and their war shields. They painted their faces. They did all that warriors should do before a raid. Then they went against the Pahani.

Their raid was not a success. The Pahani were watchful. The young warriors got nowhere near the Pahani horse herd. Not only did they capture no ponies, but they even lost their own mounts, because, while they were trying to creep up to their enemies' herd, the Pahani found their horses. The two young men had a hard time getting away on foot because their enemies were searching for them everywhere. At one time, they had to hide themselves in a lake, under the water, breathing through long, hollow reeds which were sticking up above the surface. They were so clever at hiding themselves that the Pahani finally gave up searching for them.

The young men had to travel home on foot. It was a long way. Their moccasins were tattered, their feet bleeding. At last they came to a high cliff. "Let us go up there," said Black Crow, "and see whether our enemies are following us."

They climbed up. They could see no one following them; but on a ledge far below them, halfway down the cliff, they spied a nest with two young eagles in it. "Let us at least get those eagles," Black Crow proposed. There was no way one could climb down the sheer rock wall, but Black Crow took his rawhide lariat, made a loop in it, put the rope around Spotted Eagle's chest under his armpits, and lowered him down. When his friend was on the ledge with the nest, Black Crow said to himself, "I will leave him there to die. I will come home alone, and then Red Bird will marry me." And he threw his end of the rawhide thong down and left without looking back and without listening to Spotted Eagle's cries of what had happened to the lariat and Black Crow.

Spotted Eagle cried in vain. He got no answer, only silence. At last it dawned on him that his companion had betrayed him, that he had been left to die. The lariat was much too short for him to lower himself to the ground; there was an abyss of two hundred feet yawning beneath him. He was left with the two young eagles screeching at him, angered that this strange, two-legged creature had invaded their home.

Black Crow came back to his village. "Spotted Eagle died a warrior's death," he told the people. "The Pahani killed him." There was loud wailing throughout the village because everybody had liked Spotted Eagle. Red Bird grieved more than the others. She slashed her arms with

Brulé Sioux shield with feather decoration.
Museum of the American Indian, Heye Foundation, New York City.

a sharp knife and cut her hair to make plain her sorrow to all. But in the end she became Black Crow's wife, because life must go on.

But Spotted Eagle did not die on his lonely ledge. The eagles got used to him. The old eagles brought plenty of food—rabbits, prairie dogs, or sage hens—and Spotted Eagle shared this raw meat with the two chicks. Maybe it was the eagle medicine in his bundle, which he carried on his chest, that made the eagles accept him. Still, he had a very hard time on that ledge. It was so narrow that, when he wanted to rest, he had to tie himself with the rawhide thong to a little rock sticking out of the cliff, for fear of falling off the ledge in his sleep. In this way he spent a few very uncomfortable weeks; after all, he was a human being and not a bird to whom such a crack in the rock face is home.

At last the young eagles were big enough to practice flying. "What will become of me now?" thought the young warrior. "Once these fledglings have flown the nest for good, the old birds won't be bringing any more food up here." Then he had an inspiration. "Perhaps I will die. Very likely I will die. But I will try it. I will not just sit here and give up." He took his little pipe out of the medicine bundle and lifted it to the sky and prayed, "*Wakan Tanka, onshimala ye. Great Spirit, pity me. You have created man and his cousin, the eagle. You have*

given me the eagle's name. I have decided to try to let the eagles carry me to the ground. Let the eagles help me, let me succeed."

He smoked and felt a surge of confidence. He grabbed hold of the legs of the two young eagles. "Brothers," he told them, "you have accepted me as one of your own. Now we will live together or die together. *Hokahay.*" And he jumped off the ledge. He expected to be shattered on the ground below, but with a mighty flapping of wings the two young eagles broke his fall and all landed safely. Spotted Eagle said a prayer of thanks to the Ones Above. He thanked the eagles, telling them that one day he would be back with gifts and have a giveaway in their honor.

Spotted Eagle returned to his village. The excitement was great. He had been dead and had come back to life. Everybody asked him how it happened that he was not dead, but he would not tell them. "I escaped," he said, "and that is all." He saw his love married to his treacherous friend, but he bore it in silence. He was not one to bring enmity to his people, to set one family against the other. Besides, what happened could not be changed. Thus he accepted his fate.

A year or so later, a great war party of Pahani attacked his village. The enemy outnumbered them tenfold, and there was no chance of victory for Spotted Eagle's band. All the warriors could do was to fight a slow rear-guard action, which would give the women, children, and old folks a chance to escape across the river. Guarding their people this way, the few warriors at hand fought bravely, charging the enemy again and again, making them halt and regroup. Each time, the warriors retreated a little, taking up a new position on a hill, or across a gully. In this way they could save their families.

Showing the greatest courage, exposing their bodies freely, were Spotted Eagle and Black Crow. In the end they alone faced the enemy. Then, suddenly, Black Crow's horse was hit by several arrows in succession and collapsed under him. "Brother, forgive me for what I have done," he cried to Spotted Eagle. "Let me jump up on your horse behind you."

Spotted Eagle answered, "You are a Fox. Pin yourself and fight. Then, if you survive, I will forgive you; and if you die, I will forgive you also."

What Spotted Eagle meant was this: Black Crow was a member of the Fox Warrior Society. The braves who belong to it sing this song:

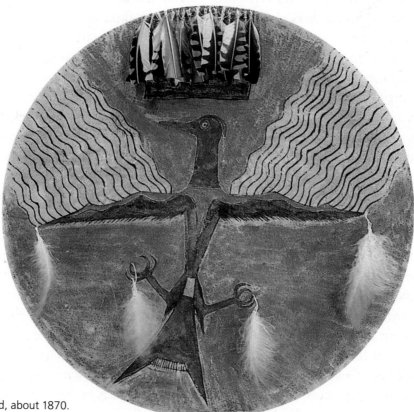

Lakota Sioux shield, about 1870.
Denver Art Museum.

I am a Fox.
If there is anything daring,
If there is anything dangerous to do,
That is a task for me to perform.
Let it be done by me.

Foxes wear a long, trailing sash, decorated with quillwork, which reaches all the way to the ground even when the warrior is on horseback. In the midst of battle, a Fox will sometimes defy death by pinning his sash to the earth with a special wooden pin, or with a knife or arrow. This means: I will stay here, rooted to this spot, facing my foes, until someone comes to release the pin, or until the enemies flee, or until I die.

Black Crow pinned his sash to the ground. There was no one to release him, and the enemy did not flee. Black Crow sang his death song. He was hit by lances and arrows and died a warrior's death. Many Pahani died with him.

Spotted Eagle had been the only one to see this. He finally joined his people, safe across the river. The Pahani had lost all taste to follow them there. "Your husband died well," Spotted Eagle told Red Bird. After some time had passed, Spotted Eagle married Red Bird. And much, much later he told his parents, and no one else, how Black Crow had betrayed him. "I forgive him now," he said, "because once he was my friend, and because he died like a warrior should, fighting for his people, and also because Red Bird and I are happy now."

After a long winter, when spring came again, Spotted Eagle told his wife, "I must go away for a few days to fulfill a promise. I must go alone." He rode off by himself to that cliff. Again he stood at its foot, below the ledge where the eagles' nest had been. He pointed his sacred pipe to the four directions, down to Grandmother Earth and up to the Grandfather, letting the smoke ascend to the sky, calling out: "*Wanblee, misunkala.* Little eagle brothers, hear me."

High above him in the clouds appeared two black dots, circling. These were the eagles who had saved his life. They came at his call, their huge wings spread majestically, uttering a shrill cry of joy and recognition. Swooping down, they alighted at his feet. He stroked them with a feather fan, and thanked them many times, and fed them choice morsels of buffalo meat, and fastened small medicine bundles around their legs as a sign of friendship, and spread sacred tobacco offerings around the foot of the cliff. Thus he made a pact of friendship and brotherhood between *Wanblee Oyate*—the Eagle Nation—and his own people. After he had done all this, the stately birds soared up again into the sky, circling motionless, carried by the wind, disappearing into the clouds. Spotted Eagle turned his horse's head homeward, going happily back to Red Bird.

Developing Comprehension Skills

1. What reason does Black Crow give for going on a war party against the Pahani?

2. Make a time line showing the major events in this story. Include at least six events.

3. The paragraph on page 24 beginning "But Spotted Eagle did not die . . ." tells about Spotted Eagle's life on the ledge. What main point is made about his life there? List important details that develop this main idea.

4. Explain the reason behind each of these actions.
   a. Black Crow abandons Spotted Eagle on the eagles' ledge.
   b. Red Bird marries Black Crow.
   c. Black Crow pins his sash to the ground and fights until he dies.
   d. Spotted Eagle tells only his parents of Black Crow's actions.

5. Which events in this legend could not have happened? Do you think "Spotted Eagle and Black Crow" is more realistic or less realistic than "The Pied Piper of Hamelin"?

Reading Literature: Legends

1. **Studying Legends.** Legends reflect the beliefs and practices of the culture from which they come. Explain how one of the following events reflects the Oglala culture: Red Bird's reaction to the news of Spotted Eagle's death; Spotted Eagle's escape from the ledge; Black Crow's final battle; Spotted Eagle's gift of medicine bundles to the young eagles.

2. **Identifying Conflict.** A story always has a main **conflict,** or struggle. It also may have one or more less important conflicts. A conflict may be between two characters or between a character and a force of nature. Which person is Spotted Eagle in conflict with? What force of nature must he struggle with? Which conflict is the main conflict in the legend?

3. **Recognizing Theme.** The **theme** of a story is the writer's message. In a legend, the theme may be developed through a character who has qualities that the storyteller wants listeners to admire. Which character in "Spotted Eagle and Black Crow" do you think is most worthy of being admired? What qualities of this character are emphasized?

Vocabulary

Learning Meaning from Context. Sometimes you can figure out the meaning of a difficult word by trying to understand the important idea of the sentence or paragraph in which the word is found. From this wide context, you can infer, or understand, the meaning of the unknown word.

Read these sentences from "Spotted Eagle and Black Crow." For each underlined word, choose the definition that best fits the sentence. Write the letter of your answer on a sheet of paper.

1. There was no way one could climb down the <u>sheer</u> rock wall. . . .
   a. very steep   c. shiny
   b. beautiful   d. flat

2. Spotted Eagle cried <u>in vain</u>. He got no answer, only silence.
   - a. too softly
   - b. too loudly
   - c. unkindly
   - d. without success

3. At last it dawned on him that his companion had <u>betrayed</u> him, that he had been left to die.
   - a. felt sorry for
   - b. deceived
   - c. forgiven
   - d. become angry with

4. Red Bird <u>grieved</u> more than the others. She slashed her arms with a sharp knife and cut her hair to make plain her sorrow to all.
   - a. felt sorrow
   - b. smiled shyly
   - c. showed no feeling
   - d. lost interest

5. Foxes wear a long, trailing <u>sash</u>, decorated with quillwork, which reaches all the way to the ground even when the warrior is on horseback.
   - a. armband
   - b. strip of cloth
   - c. headband
   - d. piece of armor

Speaking and Listening

Comparing Rhythms. Each legend you have read has a slightly different rhythm. **Rhythm** results from the pattern created by things such as the lengths of sentences and the repetition of words and phrases. For example, the rhythm of a paragraph made up of long sentences is likely to be slow and smooth. A series of very short sentences can have a choppy rhythm.

Do the following exercise in small groups. Take turns reading aloud the passages listed here. Then discuss what you heard. Did each of the passages have a different rhythm? What kind of pattern was created by sentence length or by repetition in each passage? What adjectives describe the rhythm that you hear as you read each passage?

1. "Richard the Lion-Hearted," pages 9–10; three paragraphs beginning with "After wandering for weeks" through "to look for the king."

2. "The Pied Piper of Hamelin," page 15; two paragraphs beginning with "Hamelin, a little German town," through "and does nothing about it!"

3. "Spotted Eagle and Black Crow," pages 24–25; two paragraphs beginning with "Spotted Eagle returned to his village" through "they could save their families."

Developing Writing Skills

Comparing Characters. In this legend, both Spotted Eagle and Black Crow show courage. However, the legend suggests that courage is not enough to make a good warrior into a hero. What qualities does Spotted Eagle show that suggest he is a better person than Black Crow? Answer in one paragraph.

Prewriting. Begin by planning your answer. For each warrior, list actions that show good qualities. Then list actions that suggest bad qualities or weaknesses.

Drafting. Write a topic sentence that tells what makes Spotted Eagle more heroic than Black Crow. Support your main idea by giving details about each warrior. Draw the examples from the lists you made.

Revising and Sharing. As you work on revising your draft, be sure that you have clearly stated your main idea and that your support includes a point about each of the two warriors. Take out any sentences that do not develop the main idea.

Revenge in Trade for a Wife, 1982, RANDY LEE WHITE. The Philbrook Museum of Art, Tulsa, Oklahoma.

The Six Horsemen

WEST AFRICAN LEGEND
Retold by Frances Carpenter

As you read, think about whether Fadebi could have succeeded without the help of his followers. Do you think he still should be considered a hero?

"The chief's daughter is gone!"
"Nassa has been kidnaped by Ballo, the Robber."

The news spread through the Hausa towns. People shook their heads with dismay. All knew this Ballo, the chief of a neighboring tribe. They called him "The Robber" because he often carried off a camel or a horse from right under their eyes.

Now he had taken Nassa, the fair daughter of the chief himself. Everyone loved this girl. She was known to be the kindest and the most beautiful of all the girls in that countryside. It is no wonder that this Ballo should wish her for his wife. The marvel was that he could have stolen her out of her bed without waking the guards. But that he had done.

The chief, father of Nassa, was beside himself with sadness. "I offer my daughter as bride to any good young man of our tribe who shall bring her home safe and sound. Half of my riches shall be their wedding gift."

Like autumn leaves in a storm, this promise was carried through the Hausa towns. And it came to the ears of a certain young prince. He was, himself, the son of a chief. Fadebi, he was called. And he was well known for his brave deeds.

"I will bring back the chief's daughter," Fadebi declared. He had seen Nassa. He admired her. Indeed, he was already in love with her. He saddled his fastest mare, and he galloped away toward the strong fortress where Ballo had shut up the girl.

Fadebi had not ridden far before he met another traveler. After the custom on the highroad, the two reined in their steeds to give each other greeting.

"Allah give thee peace!" they said. And when Fadebi was asked where he was going, he replied bravely: "I go to find Nassa, daughter of our chief. She is shut up in the fortress of Ballo, the Robber."

The other horseman shuddered. Everyone feared Ballo in that part of Africa. His fortress of mud bricks was strong. His soldiers were as cruel as he was himself.

"You should not go alone," the horseman cried. "You should have a companion to help you. I'll give you my help." He, too, was young, and he, too, liked adventure.

"Two are always better than one," Fadebi agreed. "Come along if you wish." So the two horsemen rode on together.

It was not long before they met a third traveler. And when that one heard the story of their bold errand, he also wanted to join them.

"If two are better than one, then three are better than two, I suppose." Fadebi gave his consent. And he did likewise to three other young horsemen whom they met on the highroad.

They were now a company of six. Their horses' hoofs made a clatter as they galloped over the land. With Fadebi in the lead, they swam their horses across the river that divided their country from that of Ballo, the Robber.

In the town on the other side of this river, they found shelter for the night in a small inn. The young woman who served their evening meal gave them news of fair Nassa.

"I know the girl well," she said. "Each morning I go into Ballo's fortress to dress the hair of his wives. Nassa is the prettiest of them all. But she also is the saddest. My heart aches when I see her tears. If I could, I would set her free."

Thus, Fadebi found out that even the people of Ballo's own tribe hated his cruelty.

"My father is rich, girl," Fadebi said to the hairdresser. "You shall have a bolt of fine cloth if you will do a service for me. Another bolt will come with it if no one finds out that I come from Nassa's land." The girl nodded consent, and Fadebi continued.

"Tell Nassa I come from her father. I will bring her out of her prison. But she must help me find the way in."

Next morning, while the girl from the inn went to the fortress, Fadebi called his five companions around him. "You have offered your help," he said. "Pray tell me what each one of you can do best. If we succeed and I marry the chief's daughter, you shall have your rewards."

"I have great wisdom," said the first horseman. "There is no question on earth that I cannot answer."

"I can see into the future," the second horseman declared. "I know what is to happen before the time comes."

"I can dig a long tunnel in the wink of an eye." The third one was speaking now. And the fourth then cried out, "I can build a large boat before anyone knows I have begun it."

"As for me," said the fifth horseman, "I have a strong JuJu. With my magic I can change myself into any form I wish to take on."

You can know by these words that the six horsemen lived in the fairy-tale times of long ago.

Carved ivory equestrian figure from the Oyo area.
Private Collection. Photograph: Pace Gallery, New York City.

At that very moment, in the fortress of Ballo, the Robber, the hairdresser was combing Nassa's long black hair. She was whispering Fadebi's message into the girl's listening ear.

"A handsome young man is this Fadebi who has come here from your father," she was saying. "He promises to get you out of this prison, if you will tell him how he may make his way into the fort."

Nassa was quiet until the hairdresser had finished combing her hair. Then, without speaking a word, she put into the girl's hands three little bundles.

The hairdresser hastened to hide them under her brushes.

"Will Fadebi know how to use them?" she asked. The chief's daughter nodded her head.

Fadebi, too, was puzzled when he opened the three bundles. In one there was a fig leaf. A strange leaf it was, like none the young man ever had seen. In the second bundle there was a bone, with bits of meat still upon it. And in the third, there was only a bunch of green grass.

"What am I to do with this fig leaf, this bone, and these blades of grass?" He turned to his companion who had said he could answer all questions.

"It is quite simple," the wise young fellow nodded his head. "The leaf is from the tree that reaches up to Nassa's window. The bone is for the watchdog at the foot of the tree, so that he shall not bark. And when the Robber's horse, who is tied there, is about to whinny a warning to his master, this green grass will stop his cry."

This young man truly had wisdom. For that night, when the moon rose, Fadebi climbed over the garden wall. It was easy to find the tree with the strange leaf. Before the watchdog could bark, the bone was in his mouth. And before the Robber's horse could make even one whinny, it was munching the grass.

Without trouble, Fadebi went up the tree and in through the open window where Nassa was waiting. With sweet words he told her of her father's promise that she should marry that young man who would bring her home safe and sound. He spoke of how he would love her and how happy they would be. They talked and they talked as they waited for a dark cloud to cover the moon, so that they could get away without being seen.

Although they spoke softly, the watchful chief, Ballo, heard them as he walked in the garden. And at once he called for the guards.

"A strange man is with Nassa! I have heard his voice. He must not escape. Beat the drums! Call all the people! I have work for them to do."

When all the town was wakened, Ballo, the Robber gave his commands. "A thief is in my fortress. You shall see it for yourselves. Lift off its roof. Take first one tile, then another, so that he may not leap through. Then take down its walls, one mud brick at a time. The stranger cannot

run away with so many of us in wait for him."

The people began the work. In the crowd, looking on, were the young hero's five companions.

"Our friend is in trouble," whispered the One-who-knew-what-was-going-to-happen-before-the-time. "Ballo means to kill him. I see it all clearly. We must find some way to get Fadebi and Nassa out of the fort."

Then the One-who-could-dig-a-long-tunnel-in-the-wink-of-an-eye began to work on the opposite side of the fortress. In the ground at the back, out of sight of the crowd, he dug and he dug. Before anyone knew it, Fadebi and Nassa had crept out through his tunnel. Their horses were waiting. With Nassa riding behind him on his swift mare, Fadebi led the way out of the Robber's town.

Meanwhile, the roof of the fortress had been taken off, tile after tile. Its walls were coming down, one brick at a time. But no stranger was there. Gone, too, was Ballo's pretty prisoner, Nassa. Ballo flew into a rage, "My horse! Bring me my horse!"

Ballo was soon in the saddle. With soldiers riding behind him, he was galloping across the land after Fadebi and Nassa.

It was the river that slowed up the six fleeing young horsemen. They heard clearly the hoofbeats of their pursuers. They feared they would never be able to swim across the river in time.

Then it was the turn of the One-who-could-build-a-large-boat-in-a-jiffy. Before Ballo could come up with them, the six horsemen and the chief's daughter were safe in a huge vessel out in the stream. It was so big that their horses, too, were aboard.

Ballo leapt from his steed and threw himself into the river. With flashing arms and legs he swam like a big fish, trying to catch up with the boat. He might have succeeded if Fadebi's fifth companion had not remembered his JuJu. By its strong magic, he turned himself into a giant eagle. White as a cloud was this eagle. Larger than an elephant! So strong was the great bird that it could lift the boat high up into the air. Its passengers were well out of Ballo's reaching hands.

When they were set safely down on the other side of the river, the man's JuJu worked once more. It changed the giant eagle into a huge crocodile, with rows of teeth as big as an elephant's tusk. With one bite, that crocodile made an end of Ballo, the Robber. Never again would he trouble the chief's gentle daughter.

Her father rejoiced to have Nassa again at home, safe and sound. He gladly kept his promise to the young man who had saved her.

The wedding feast was splendid. The five horsemen who had helped Fadebi were the most honored guests. Each one of them went home with five handsome horses as his reward.

Frances Carpenter (*1890–1972*) was the daughter of a well-known geographer. Her father traveled the world and often brought his family along. Frances Carpenter used information gathered on those trips as background for much of her writing. Two of her popular collections of folk tales are *Tales of a Chinese Grandmother* and *African Wonder Tales.*

Developing Comprehension Skills

1. Identify who or what is named by each of these words:

   a. Ballo   b. Hausa   c. Nassa   d. JuJu

2. Nassa is rescued through the help of the six horsemen and of the hairdresser. Tell what part each plays in the rescue.

3. Reread the paragraph beginning "Without trouble. . . ." Below are listed three ideas from that paragraph. Decide which is the main idea, which is an important detail, and which is a less important detail that was included to make the paragraph more interesting.

   a. Fadebi uses sweet words.
   b. Fadebi gets into Nassa's room and explains his mission.
   c. Fadebi and Nassa wait for a dark cloud to cover the moon.

4. How much credit should Fadebi get for saving Nassa? How much does the rescue depend on others?

5. Would you say this legend is closely based on something that really happened? In your answer, list the major events and tell which of them could really have happened.

Reading Literature: Legends

1. **Recognizing Elements of Legends.** The Pied Piper carried enchantment in his pipe. Spotted Eagle carried eagle medicine in his bundle. Which of the six horsemen has a magic object? What power does it have?

   Look at the storyteller's comment to the audience on page 31 that begins "You can know by these words. . . ." Does the storyteller accept magic as something that might really happen?

2. **Understanding Character.** Does each character in "The Six Horsemen" combine both good and bad qualities, or is it clear who is good and who is bad? Do the characters seem to change or grow, or do they stay the same? Support your answers with examples.

3. **Identifying Conflict.** What is the main conflict, or struggle, in "The Six Horsemen"? In what ways is the conflict like that in "Richard the Lion-Hearted"?

4. **Understanding Setting.** In "The Six Horsemen," scattered details give clues about the time and the place in which the story is set. Look for details to answer these questions about the setting: In what part of the world does the story take place? What kind of ruling system did the Hausa have? What kinds of animals could be found among the Hausa? What did the Hausa use to build fortresses?

Vocabulary

Examining Context. You cannot always figure out the meaning of an unfamiliar word by using context clues. At times, you will have to look up the meaning of the word. You might look it up in the glossary of the book you are reading. A **glossary** is an alphabetical list of words and their definitions given at the back of a book. If the glossary does not list the word or if the book does not have a glossary, then look up the word in a dictionary.

Read each of the following sentences. Try to figure out the meaning of the underlined word by using context clues. If there is a context clue, write the definition. If there is no clue, write *No clue—use dictionary*.

1. Fadebi saddled his fastest mare and galloped toward the <u>fortress</u>.

2. The six horsemen and the chief's daughter were safe in a huge <u>vessel</u>, or boat, in the stream.

3. Fadebi gave his <u>consent</u>—that is, he approved—and the third traveler joined them.

4. The hoofbeats of their <u>pursuers</u> could be heard easily.

Study and Research

Finding Information in a Library. The **card catalog** is an alphabetical file that lists every book in a library. This file is kept in a cabinet of narrow drawers. For each nonfiction book the catalog usually contains three cards: a title card, an author card, and a subject card. In some libraries, the same information is put into the computer system.

If you want to find a nonfiction book, you first look it up in the card catalog or search for it on a computer terminal. You can look for the title, the author, or the subject. Once you find the number of the book, you can look for the book on the shelves.

Find out if your school or local library has any books that give historical background for one of the legends in this chapter. For example, you might look up Hausa or King Richard the Lion-Hearted. Then find on the shelves at least one of the books listed in the catalog. On a sheet of paper, write the title, author, and number of the book you found.

Developing Writing Skills

Defining a Hero. In one paragraph, explain whether you think Fadebi is a true hero.

Prewriting. Think about what makes a true hero. Consider points such as these: What qualities must a human have to be a hero? Must a hero defeat an evil power or person? Must a hero succeed in overcoming the forces he struggles against? Does a true hero depend mostly on himself, or can a hero depend on others? Reread "The Six Horsemen" and take notes on how well Fadebi fits your idea of a hero.

Drafting. Be sure that you state clearly your definition of a hero. Include examples to show how Fadebi does or does not show these qualities.

Revising and Sharing. Share your draft with another student. After that student reads your paragraph, ask him or her to try to explain your definition of a true hero. Then discuss whether you made a good case for saying that Fadebi is or is not a true hero.

The Sacred Drum of Tepozteco

MEXICAN LEGEND
Retold by M. A. Jagendorf and R. S. Boggs

A wise king wishes to be honored for what he is, not for what he wears. How does he make his point?

Long ago, in the valley of Tepoztlán (tā pōs tlän´), a valley in Mexico where there is much copper, Tepozteco was born. He was born to be different from other children, for he was destined to be a god.

In a short time he was a fully grown man, rich in wisdom and great in strength and speed. He could hunt better than other men, and he gave counsel that brought success.

So the people made him king. And as he grew in wisdom and understanding and strength, they worshiped him and made him a god.

He was known for his virtues even to the farthest corners of his kingdom, and he was loved and respected by all. The other kings feared him, although they never dared to say so.

One day the king of Tlayacapan (t lä-yä kä´ pän) asked Tepozteco to come to a great feast to be given in his honor. Other kings and nobles and men of strength were also invited.

The king told his cooks to prepare food such as had never been eaten before. He had new dishes painted in bright colors, and he ordered new blankets of lovely designs.

And the most beautiful blanket of all was to be for Tepozteco to sit upon. This was to be a feast of feasts.

On the appointed day, the kings and nobles arrived wearing their richest robes and jewels of jade and gold. It was a wonderful sight to see the great company seated on the many-colored mats, with the richly painted dishes before them. All around were beautiful servants ready to bring the fine food.

They sat and they sat. They were waiting for the great guest, Tepozteco.

They waited and they waited. After a long time they heard the *teponaztli* (tā pō näs′ tlē), the drum that always announced the coming of Tepozteco.

Soon he was seen, approaching with his followers. But he was not dressed for the feast. He was dressed in hunting clothes, with an ocelot skin thrown over his shoulders and weapons in his hands. His followers also were dressed in hunting clothes.

The king and his guests looked at them in silent surprise. Then the king spoke.

"Noble Tepozteco," he said, "you have put shame on me and my land and my guests. This feast was in your honor, and we came properly dressed to honor you, but you have come in your hunting clothes and not in your royal garments."

Tepozteco looked at the king and his company and did not say a word. For a long time he was silent. Then he spoke.

"Wait for me. I shall soon return in my royal clothes."

Then he and his followers vanished into the air like a cloud.

Again the company waited a long time, and finally the drum of Tepozteco was heard once again. Suddenly the whole company saw him.

He was alone, dressed more beautifully than anyone there. He was all covered with gold. From his shoulders hung a mantle in colors that gleamed more richly than birds in the sunlight. His headdress was of the most brilliant quetzal feathers

Nezahualcoyotl, Ruler of Texcoco, in Feathered Costume, about 1582. Bibliotheque Nationale, Paris.

ever seen. Gold bands bound his arms and jade beads encircled his neck. In his hand he held a shield studded with jewels and richly colored stones.

The king and his company were greatly pleased at the sight.

"Now you are dressed in a manner befitting this noble gathering in your honor. Let the food be served."

Tepozteco did not answer. He seated himself on a mat, and the food was served by beautiful maidens. Everyone ate except Tepozteco, who took the dishes and poured his food on his mantle.

Everyone stopped eating and looked at the guest of honor in surprise.

"Why do you do this?" asked the king.

"I am giving the food to my clothes, because it was they, not I, that you wanted at your feast. I was not welcome here in whatever clothes I chose to wear. Only when I came in these, my feast-day clothes, were you pleased. Therefore this feast is for them, not for me."

"Leave my palace," said the king sharply.

Tepozteco rose and left.

When he had gone, a great cry of anger rose from all the guests.

"He is not fit to live among us," they cried. "We must destroy him!"

Everyone agreed to this, and the kings and nobles gathered a great army of warriors and marched on Tepoztlán.

Tepozteco knew he could not do battle against this great army, for his soldiers were too few. So he went up on the Montaña del Aire—the Mountain in the Air—where a vast temple had been built for him by his people.

There he stood, drawn up to his full height, almost reaching the sky. He raised his hands and waved them in all directions. The earth quaked and trembled and roared. Trees fell and rocks flew in every direction. Masses of earth rose into the air. Everything fell on the army that had come to destroy Tepozteco and his people, and the enemy was wiped out.

The temple of Tepozteco still stands on that mountain, and at night, when the wind screams through the canyons that the earthquake created along the Montaña del Aire, one can hear the sacred drum of Tepozteco, telling his people he is still there to guard and protect his city.

Developing Comprehension Skills

1. What makes Tepozteco different from others?

2. What preparations does the king of Ilayacapan make for the feast in honor of Tepozteco? Does Tepozteco go to the same trouble to get ready for the feast?

3. What is the main idea of the paragraph on page 38 beginning "He was alone. . . ." List three important details that support the main idea.

4. What makes the king of Ilayacapan and his guests angry at Tepozteco? Do you think they have good reason for being so angry?

Reading Literature: Legends

1. **Recognizing Theme.** When Tepozteco explains why he poured food on his mantle, he is stating the **theme,** or message, of this legend. Restate the theme in your own words.

2. **Identifying Setting.** The opening sentence of the legend gives some information about the setting, the time and place of the action. Find other details about the geographical setting, such as the name of the nearby mountain range.

3. **Recognizing Elements of Legends.** Some legends credit a hero rather than nature with an event such as a flood or earthquake. What event does "The Sacred Drum of Tepozteco" explain?

Vocabulary

Recognizing Antonyms as Context Clues. You can sometimes figure out the meaning of an unfamiliar word if you notice a word in context that is opposite in meaning. Such a word is called an **antonym.** An antonym may be found in the same sentence or in a nearby sentence. It is usually in the same position in the sentence as the unfamiliar word. Study this example.

This lion cub is not <u>vicious</u>. He is <u>gentle</u>.

The opposite of *vicious* is *gentle.*

Read the following sentences about the legends you have read. Find the antonym for each underlined word. Write the word and its antonym.

1. Richard quarreled with his <u>allies</u> but grew to respect his enemies.

2. The <u>outlandish</u> clothes of the piper looked very different from the ordinary fashions worn by the people of Hamelin.

3. The six horsemen saved the <u>gentle</u> Nassa from the violent Ballo, the Robber.

4. The king considered hunting clothes unsuitable for the party; he thought Tepozteco's feast-day clothes were much more <u>befitting</u>.

5. Tepozteco knew he could not win a battle with the <u>vast</u> army of his enemies, for his own troop was too small.

Study and Research

Using an Atlas. An **atlas** is a collection of maps. Every atlas includes an index that lists all the countries shown on the maps. The index tells which countries are shown on the different maps. The index also includes information about the cities indicated on the maps.

To find the atlases in a library, begin with the card catalog. Start with the heading *Atlas.* Listed under this heading will be all the atlases in the library.

Make a list of the atlases owned by your school or local library. Locate one atlas and write its title and call number. Then use the index to find and note where in the atlas is a map for each of these places: Africa; England; Hamelin, Germany; and Mexico. Finally, look up the map of Mexico and write the names of three mountain ranges.

Developing Writing Skills

Writing a Story. Write a story of your own that teaches the importance of respecting others for who they are, rather than for what they wear or look like. Use the legend of Tepozteco as a model for your story.

Prewriting. Decide on the kind of character and the situation you want to build your story around. Who will be the main character? Will the story be set in modern times or in a long-ago world? What kind of situation will the main character be involved in? Will others accept the lesson from the hero, or will there be a battle, as in "The Sacred Drum of Tepozteco"? Organize your thinking by making notes for each heading: setting, characters, conflict, ending.

Drafting. As you begin, give some clue to the setting. Use dialogue to make your story more lively. Add to or change your prewriting notes if necessary.

Revising and Sharing. Allow some time between finishing your draft and revising. Then read critically to see if you can sharpen your description of the setting or the characters' clothing and actions. Before turning in your final copy, proofread for mistakes in capitalization, punctuation, and spelling.

The number three is used again and again in tales. How is it important in this story?

Lazy Peter and His Three-Cornered Hat

PUERTO RICAN TALE
Retold by Ricardo E. Alegría and translated by Elizabeth Culbert

This is the story of Lazy Peter, a shameless rascal of a fellow, who went from village to village making mischief.

One day Lazy Peter learned that a fair was being held in a certain village. He knew that a large crowd of country people would be there selling horses, cows, and other farm animals and that a large amount of money would change hands. Peter, as usual, needed money, but it was not his custom to work for it. So he set out for the village, wearing a red three-cornered hat.

The first thing he did was to stop at a stand and leave a big bag of money with the owner, asking him to keep it safely until he returned for it. Peter told the man that when he returned for the bag of money, one corner of his hat would be turned down, and that was how the owner of the stand would know him. The man promised to do this, and Peter thanked

him. Then he went to the drugstore in the village and gave the druggist another bag of money, asking him to keep it until he returned with one corner of his hat turned up. The druggist agreed, and Peter left. He went to the church and asked the priest to keep another bag of money and to return it to him only when he came back with one corner of his hat twisted to the side. The priest said fine, that he would do this.

Having disposed of three bags of money, Peter went to the edge of the village where the farmers were buying and selling horses and cattle. He stood and watched for a while until he decided that one of the farmers must be very rich indeed, for he had sold all of his horses and cows. Moreover, the man seemed to be a miser who was never satisfied but wanted, always, more and more money. This was Peter's man! He stopped beside him. It was raining, and, instead of keeping his hat on to protect his head, he took it off and wrapped it carefully in his cape, as though it were very valuable. It puzzled the farmer to see Peter stand there with the rain falling on his head and his hat wrapped in his cape.

After a while he asked, "Why do you take better care of your hat than of your head?"

Peter saw that the farmer had swallowed the bait. Smiling to himself, he said that the hat was the most valuable thing in all the world and that was why he took care to protect it from the rain. The farmer's curiosity increased at this reply, and he asked Peter what was so valuable about a red three-cornered hat. Peter told him that the hat worked for him. Thanks to it, he never had to work for a living because, whenever he put the hat on with one of the corners turned over, people just handed him any money he asked for.

The farmer was amazed and very interested in what Peter said. As money-getting was his greatest ambition, he told Peter that he couldn't believe a word of it until he saw the hat work with his own eyes. Peter assured him that he could do this, for he, Peter, was hungry, and, since he had no money with which to buy food, the hat was about to start working.

With this, Peter took out his three-cornered hat, turned one corner down, put it on his head, and told the farmer to come along and watch the hat work. Peter took the farmer to the stand. The minute the owner looked up, he handed over the bag of money Peter had left with him. The farmer stood with his mouth open in astonishment. He didn't know what to make of it, but of one thing he was sure— he had to have that hat!

Peter smiled and asked if he was satisfied, and the farmer said yes, he was. Then he asked Peter if he would sell the hat. This was just what Lazy Peter wanted, but he said no, that he was not interested in selling the hat because, with it, he never had to work and he always had money. The farmer said he thought that was unsound reasoning because thieves could easily steal a hat. Wouldn't it be safer to invest in a farm with cattle? So they talked, and Peter pretended to be impressed with the farmer's arguments. Finally he said yes, that he saw the point. If the farmer would make him a good offer, he would sell the hat. The farmer, who had made up his mind to have the hat at any price, offered a thousand pesos. Peter laughed aloud and said he could make as much as that by just putting his hat on two or three times.

As they continued haggling over the price, the farmer grew more and more determined to have that hat until, finally, he offered all he had realized from the sale of his horses and cows—ten thousand pesos in gold. Peter still pretended not to be interested, but he chuckled to himself, thinking of the trick he was about to play on the farmer. All right, he said, it was a deal. Then the farmer grew cautious and told Peter that, before he handed over the ten thousand pesos, he would like to see the hat work again. Peter said that was fair enough. He put on the hat with one of the corners turned up and went with the farmer to the drugstore. The moment the druggist saw the turned-up corner, he handed over the money Peter had left with him. At this the farmer was convinced and very eager to set the hat to work for himself. He took out a bag containing ten thousand pesos in gold and was about to hand it to Peter, when he had a change of heart and thought better of it. He asked Peter please to excuse him, but he had to see the hat work just once more before he could part with his gold. Peter said that that was fair enough, but now he would have to ask the farmer to give him the fine horse he was riding as well as the ten thousand pesos in gold. The farmer's interest in the hat revived, and he said it was a bargain!

Lazy Peter put on his hat again and doubled over one of the corners. He told the farmer that, since he still seemed to have doubts, this time he could watch the hat work in the church. The farmer was delighted with this. His doubts were stilled, and he fairly beamed thinking of all the money he was going to make once that hat was his.

They entered the church. The priest was hearing confession, but when he saw Peter with his hat, he said, "Wait here, my son." He went to the sacristy and returned the bag of money Peter had left with him. Peter thanked the priest, then knelt and asked for a blessing before he left. The farmer had seen everything and was fully convinced of the hat's magic powers. As soon as they left the church, he gave Peter the ten thousand pesos in gold and told him to take the horse, also. Peter tied the bag of pesos to the saddle, gave the hat to the farmer, begging him to take good care of it, spurred his horse, and galloped out of town.

As soon as he was alone, the farmer burst out laughing at the thought of the trick he had played on Lazy Peter. A hat such as this was priceless! He couldn't wait to try it. He put it on with one corner turned up and entered the butcher shop. The butcher looked at the hat, which was very handsome indeed, but said nothing. The farmer turned around, then walked up and down until the butcher asked him what he wanted. The farmer said he was waiting for the bag of money. The butcher laughed aloud and asked if he were crazy. The farmer thought that there must be something wrong with the way he had folded the hat. He took it off and doubled another corner down. But this had no effect on the butcher. So he decided to try it out some other place. He went to the Mayor of the town.

The Mayor, to be sure, looked at the hat but did nothing. The farmer grew desper-

San Juan: La Plaza del Mercado, 1958, LUIS CAJIGAS, Art Museum of Ponce, Puerto Rico, Louis Ferré Foundation.

ate and decided to go to the druggist who had given Peter a bag of money. He entered and stood with the hat on. The druggist looked at him but did nothing.

The farmer became very nervous. He began to suspect that there was something very wrong. He shouted at the druggist, "Stop looking at me and hand over the bag of money!"

The druggist said he owed him nothing, and what bag of money was he talking about anyway? As the farmer continued to shout about a bag of money and a magic hat, the druggist called the police. When

they arrived, he told them that the farmer had gone out of his mind and kept demanding a bag of money. The police questioned the farmer, and he told them about the magic hat he had bought from Lazy Peter. When he heard the story, the druggist explained that Peter had left a bag of money, asking that it be returned when he appeared with a corner of his hat turned up. The owner of the stand and the priest told the same story.

And I am telling you, the farmer was so angry that he tore the hat to shreds and walked home.

Ricardo E. Alegría (*born 1921*) lives and writes in his native city, San Juan, Puerto Rico. His collection of Puerto Rican folk tales, *The Three Wishes,* is well known. Alegría directs the Center of Advanced Studies of Puerto Rico and the Caribbean. He also has taught history at the University of Puerto Rico.

Developing Comprehension Skills

1. At the beginning of the story, Lazy Peter asks three people to keep three bags of money. Describe two other sets of events in which a similar action is repeated three times. Which set of events does the story-teller spend the most time developing?

2. Peter spends some time watching the farmers at the market before picking the man to try his trick on. What kind of person is Peter looking for? How does Peter take advantage of the farmer's weakness?

3. What first makes the farmer think that the hat may be valuable? What leads him to be sure it is worth a great deal of money?

4. Reread the paragraph on page 44 that begins "As soon as he was alone. . . ." Below are listed three ideas from that para-

graph. Identify the main idea, an important detail, and a less important detail.

   a. The farmer folds up the corner of his hat.
   b. The farmer walks up and down in the shop.
   c. The farmer tries without success to get money from the butcher.

5. Are there any events in this tale that could not really happen? How likely is it that someone would fall for Peter's trick?

Reading Literature: Tales

1. **Comparing Characters.** Lazy Peter, Blondel, and the first horseman are all clever. Do they use their cleverness in the same way? Which characters do you admire? Why?

2. **Identifying Theme.** The **theme,** or message, of a legend or tale can sometimes be stated as advice. For example, the theme of "The Six Horsemen" might be stated "Cooperation will bring success." The theme of "The Sacred Drum of Tepozteco" could be "Don't measure worth by outward appearances." How would you state the theme of "Lazy Peter and His Three-Cornered Hat"?

3. **Analyzing Conflict.** In many legends, **conflict** arises from a problem that a villain, or bad character, creates. For example, both King Richard and Nassa are captured by enemies and must be freed. Spotted Eagle must rescue himself from Black Crow's treachery. How is the conflict in "Lazy Peter and His Three-Cornered Hat" different?

4. **Recognizing Elements of Tales.** Identify the ways that the number three is used in this tale. Then answer these questions: Would Peter have been as likely to trick the farmer if he had arranged to pick up only two bags of money? Would the story be more interesting or would it only be longer if Lazy Peter had left a fourth bag of money with someone?

Vocabulary

Recognizing Context Clues. Read the following sentences or groups of sentences. On a sheet of paper, write this information about each underlined word:

   a. the definition of the word
   b. whether you used a *definition or restate-ment clue,* a *synonym,* or an *antonym* to help you figure out the meaning of the word

1. Lazy Peter <u>disposed</u> of, or got rid of, three bags of money.

2. The farmer seems to be a <u>miser</u> who is never satisfied but always wants more and more money.

3. Seeing the bag of money was such a surprise, the farmer stood with his mouth open in <u>astonishment</u>.

4. The farmer offered a thousand <u>pesos</u>, Spanish coins, for the hat.

5. The farmer said Peter used <u>unsound</u> thinking because thieves could easily steal a hat. He asked if it wouldn't be more reasonable to invest in a farm with cattle.

Critical Thinking

Classifying Legends and Tales. There are many different ways to classify, or group, the stories in this chapter. For example, you might make one list of the stories that include rulers and another of stories that use a pattern of three. The same story may be classified in more than one group. For example, "Richard the Lion-Hearted" is about a ruler and uses a pattern of three.

Choose three classifications in which to group the stories. Then decide on the stories that fit in each category. You can use the classifications already given as well as others such as "Stories about heroes with unusual powers" or "Stories about events that could not happen."

Speaking and Listening

Retelling a Tale. Prepare to tell the story of "Lazy Peter and His Three-Cornered Hat" to a group of younger students. First, read the story several times until you know the order in which things happen. If you like, take notes that will help you remember the events.

Next, practice telling the story. Use simple words that your audience will understand. Make up speeches that Lazy Peter and the other characters might say to each other. Try to make their voices sound different from one another and different from the storyteller. If you can find or make a three-cornered hat, practice showing how Peter used it throughout the tale.

Finally, tell the story to a group. Remember to look directly at your listeners. If your listeners start to laugh, remember to pause until they can hear your next words.

Developing Writing Skills

Presenting an Opinion. Does Lazy Peter wrongfully take the farmer's money? Or would you say the farmer cheats himself by letting his greed rule over common sense? Give your opinion in one paragraph.

Prewriting. Reread the story to make sure you are clear about what Peter does and what the farmer does. Form your opinion about Lazy Peter's actions. Note the points in the story that support your opinion.

Drafting. Write a topic sentence in which you state your opinion. Write sentences that state at least two points in support of your opinion. Include references to the story.

Revising and Sharing. Carefully examine your arguments. Remember, an effective argument does not simply say the same general thing again and again. Rather, it gives an opinion and then backs up the opinion with solid reasons.

From

The Chronicles of Robin Hood:
How Marian Came to the Greenwood

ROSEMARY SUTCLIFF

Robin Hood, a hero of medieval legends, led a band of outlaws in Sherwood Forest. Why does the noble Marian join the outlaws?

Robin Hood is said to have lived in the time of King Richard the Lion-Hearted. When Richard fought in the Crusades, greedy landlords often unjustly accused farmers of wrongdoing and then took their lands. Robin Hood was outlawed in this way by Lord Fitzwater. Robin hid in the safety of the large forest, or Greenwood, near Sherwood. Any greedy lord who traveled in the forest risked being stopped by Robin's band. The outlaws would take the landlord's riches and use them to help the poor.

In their caves at Dunwold Scar the outlaws sat or sprawled around the fire. The spitting pine logs burned with clear red and saffron flames, sending up thick, curling feathers of smoke that found their way out through a cranny in the rocks overhead. Outside, the cold February rain drenched down, turning the forest tracks into icy quagmires and every leaf on the holly bushes to a spouting water-chute. But within the great central cave of the many that honeycombed the sandstone scar, there was warmth and shelter, dry sand underfoot and warm, high-piled bracken for bedding, and the saffron flicker of firelight on the faces of the men and hounds gathered about the rude hearth.

Scarcely a man sat idle, for there were always many tasks to be attended to when ill weather closed the roads and hunting trail alike. Some of them were making new clothes or mending old ones. Others were refurbishing their weapons. Will Scarlet was building himself a short birding bow. Little John, with a pot of glue heating in the fire beside him, was mending his fishing tackle. Robin himself was burnishing the red rust-blotches from his steel cap.

As they worked, the outlaws talked among themselves and to their guests—for they had guests that day, as they often did in bad weather—a quiet palmer who had been found trudging along the sodden highway by Will-the-Bowman; a burly man-at-arms with a damaged knee that needed resting; and last, but assuredly not least, a very small man with a snub-nose and sloe-black eyes set very wide apart in his tanned face, who now sat

Cover design for *Robin Hood*, 1917, N. C. WYETH. The New York Public Library, Central Children's Room, Donnell Library Center. Photograph: Brandywine River Museum, Chadds Ford, Pennsylvania.

in his shirt and scarlet hose, holding out a tattered parti-colored surcoat to dry before the fire. He had pushed his fantastic red and yellow fool's cap back from his forehead, and every time he moved his head to look from one speaker to another, the tiny silver bells along the flaunting cockscomb rang very sweetly. He seemed a quiet little man, and though he sat there fully an hour, he had scarcely spoken. Yet his face was alight with interest, and his bright black eyes flickered ceaselessly from face to face of all the outlaws scattered around the fire.

Presently Ket-the-Smith turned to him, saying: "Now, Master Fool, how about a song? A song of love, or a song of battle— who cares, so long as it be a merry one?"

The little man shook his head and laughed. "I am no minstrel, to sing you songs. A juggler am I, and my name is Peterkin. But if you are minded to see some juggling, the best juggling in all the North Country. . . ."

"Lads!" cried Ket, looking round about him. "Here is Peterkin the Juggler. He says he will juggle for us. Shall we take him at his word?"

"Yes," cried the outlaws, "let us have some juggling! Begin, Master Juggler— up with you, and begin!"

Work was laid aside and every man settled himself more comfortably, turning to face the little juggler, who first wriggled into his red and yellow surcoat, and then, getting up, opened his ragged bundle and delved inside it. Bright balls of painted wood rolled out onto the floor—the green of a breaking wave, the scarlet of a corn-poppy, the gold of saffron cake, the blue of the Madonna's mantle. Two or three little bright daggers spilled out after them, and he gathered them up and turned to face his eager audience.

Then an odd change seemed to come over Peterkin the Juggler. He was no longer a ridiculous little man—for a little while he was beautiful. The firelight flickered over his thin figure in its fantastic garments as he tossed up ball after ball, seemingly without any thought of the matter, until there were eight of them shuttling backward and forward above his head. Sometimes they seemed a continuous many-colored arc. Sometimes they would separate, and for an instant the firelight would pick out a ball of blue or crimson or bright gilt, or the sparkling blade of a little dagger.

The outlaws watched him, entranced. The palmer forgot his beads, and the man-at-arms his aching knee. When at last he made an end, the great cave echoed and re-echoed with their roar of approval.

Smiling to himself, Peterkin sat down again and returned the bright baubles to his bundle. "It be all in the knack," he said, almost apologetically.

Then Robin spoke for the first time. "It is a knack worth having, Friend Peterkin."

"Oh aye! It earns me my bread and

meat, and it gives pleasure to many—most of all to me."

"Yet it must be a hard life in the winter."

"Why, there are worse," said the little man comfortably. "I ply my trade in rich men's halls and village ale-houses, and I seldom want for my supper and a warm place to sleep—and there is always the spring coming, and the country fairs. Sometimes I juggle at weddings, too. I should be on my way to a wedding now. . . ."

He broke off and cast a questioning glance at the gray curtain of rain beyond the entrance of the cave. Seeing this, Robin said: "It is cruel weather for traveling. Have you far to go to this wedding?"

"A matter of twenty miles or so—to Malaset, over beyond Locksley. The wedding is not until the day after tomorrow, but the guests will most likely have gathered by now, and there will be many of them, for 'tis a lordling's daughter that is being wed to a knight."

"Her name, man—her name!" cried Robin harshly, and he sprang to his feet.

Peterkin the Juggler looked up in surprise. "I have not heard her name, but she is daughter to Lord Robert Fitzwater of Malaset."

"Do you know who is the bridegroom?"

"Aye, that I do know. He is Sir Roger of Doncaster: a covetous young villain, if ever there was one, and no fit mate for any woman. And this I have heard," added Peterkin slowly, "that in this marriage she does not follow her own heart."

Robin turned away without a word, and went and stood in the opening of the cave, staring blindly out at the downpour.

So Marian was to be married, and to Roger of Doncaster—that smooth-faced young coxcomb, whose name had already begun to have an ugly sound in the ears of the country folk. And she was being forced into the marriage. Even if the little juggler had not said as much, Robin would have known that she did not follow her own heart. She was his, his dear Marian, alone and frightened in the power of that old tyrant, her father. He swung round to the juggler.

"You say the wedding is not until the day after tomorrow?"

Peterkin nodded. Every outlaw in the place was silent, watching their leader.

"Peterkin," said Robin, "I shall go with you to that wedding. Do you not think I shall make a fine minstrel?" And without even noticing the surprised bewilderment on the faces of his band, he strode across to the mouth of one of the inner caves which opened from the main one, and disappeared inside.

The inner cave was one of the brotherhood's treasure-stores, and when Robin came back a few minutes later, he carried a lute and a rich suit of clothes which had been taken only a few days before from the baggage of a young nobleman on the Nottingham road. One leg of the silken hose was green, the other violet. The tight-fitting surcoat was parti-colored in the same bright hues, and the wide, fantastically dagged sleeves were lined with rose-color, while rose-color also lined the hood of crimson velvet. Robin settled down by the fire again, with the exquisite garments across his knees. Taking woodash, staining lichen, and a sharp stone, he set to work to wreck them.

While he worked, he spoke to his followers: "Lads, you'll be thinking that I am out of my wits; but listen to me. You know, all of you, what manner of man is Sir Roger of Doncaster. And the lady who is to be wed to him in two days time—against her will, as you have heard the juggler say—is my own dear lady. I have neither seen her nor spoken with her since I was proclaimed wolfshead, for the Greenwood is no life for a woman. But now it seems that there are worse things than the Greenwood, and so tomorrow I am going to bring her away."

"We will come with you!" cried Little John.

"Aye, we'll come with you, Master!" cried the others.

On the opposite side of the fire a boy sat forward with a jerk, his face alight with eagerness and his eyes shining. Gilbert Shuttleworth—or Gilbert-of-the-White-Hand, as the others had nicknamed him because of his appearance—had good cause to hate Sir Roger of Doncaster,

whose serf he had been. It was only a few months since his father, forced to work in the fields with the marsh fever upon him, and then flogged for skimping his work, had died of the flogging. Gilbert had fled to join the outlaws after that, but he had neither forgotten nor forgiven, and his eagerness to pay a little of the debt leaped in his eyes as he exclaimed: "Let *me* come with you, Master Robin."

"You shall come," Robin said kindly. He looked round on all of them. "Twenty of you shall follow me as far as the edge of Locksley Chase, but from there I go alone—save for Peterkin here, if he is not afraid to come with me?"

Peterkin shook his head until the bells

Robin Meets Maid Marian, 1917, N. C. WYETH. New York Public Library, The Central Children's Room, Donnell Library Center. Photograph: Brandywine River Museum, Chadds Ford, Pennsylvania.

on his fool's cap rang sweet and shrill. "I be small in body and a man of peace," said he in his slow, pleasant voice, "but I have my little knives, and I be no coward, Master."

Next morning, in the gray dawn, two figures emerged from the creeper-hidden entrance to one of the caves, and struck away through the forest in the direction of the Nottingham to Sheffield road. One of them was the little juggler; the other was a tall, tatterdemalion minstrel who bore only a very slight resemblance to the outlaw Robin Hood. He wore the stained and tattered remnants of what had once been a fine surcoat and hose of green and violet silk, and a hood of threadbare crimson velvet. He had stained his already brown skin to a gipsyish darkness with walnut juice. His hair was greased and flattened down beneath a fillet of twisted silk, and by careful use of a razor he had thinned his thick, level eyebrows, altering their shape and giving them a devilish upward quirk at the outer corners. He carried a ribboned lute, but there was a serviceable broadsword at his hip and a dented buckler at his back—for in those days there was nothing unusual in a minstrel going armed against robbers on the lonely roads.

"I suppose you *can* sing?" asked Peterkin presently, as they went along.

"Well enough," replied Robin briefly, and broke into song in a pleasant voice, accompanying himself on the lute. But after a few bars he fell silent again, and the two walked on without a word between them.

A mile behind them followed Will Scarlet and a score of the outlaw band, moving among the trees, silent and unseen in their winter brown, each man with bowstave in hand and well-filled quiver on hip.

On went Robin and Peterkin, the one striding, the other trotting along the highway, through a world that was clearwashed after the rain of the day before and blithe in the early sunshine. The puddles in the deeply rutted road reflected the blue sky and the small white clouds. Though it was still winter, spring was in the air. The bare twigs of the forest were flushing purple with rising sap, and small birds were beginning to whisper the songs they would sing later in the year. Surely, thought Robin, on such a day as this all must go well and have a happy ending.

It was evening when they came at last down the long road through Locksley Village, and Robin looked about him with fondness at the little cottages crowding together in the dusk around their squat church tower.

On they went into the gathering darkness of the open dale beyond, where the road curved beside Locksley Chase, through the tiny hamlet of Malaset and out again to the last broad tongue of the Chase that reached down towards the road. Then at last they saw the great castle close before them, its buttressed keep standing dark against the primrose after-glow.

Standing hidden among the trees, the two men saw there were lights in the Gate House and a great coming and going across the moat-causeway. Evidently some important wedding guest had just arrived, and his baggage animals had got mixed up with a donkey bringing in vegetables for the household.

Robin Hood waited until the causeway was clear again. Then he laughed softly in his throat and, twanging his lute, strode forward from the shelter of the trees and down towards the castle, with Peterkin the Juggler trotting beside him. The men-at-arms at the gate passed them through without a second thought, for a wedding always drew plenty of such folk: jugglers, tumblers, minstrels, and sword-dancers, and the guests within would no doubt be glad of entertainment.

The outer bailey was in darkness, save for the swinging light of a lantern as a groom hurried towards the stables, and empty save for a little page exercising two greyhounds in leash. But the inner bailey, when they reached it, was filled with light and bustle as servants, scullions, men-at-arms, and young squires hurried hither and thither about the business of the great castle and the wedding which was to take place on the morrow.

Swiftly Robin and Peterkin threaded their way through the throng and so came to the doorway of the great hall. The doors stood open and yellow light flowed down the steps and out into the hurry-scurry of the bailey. They asked permission of none—for on such an occasion as this no permission was needed—but strode boldly into the hall, Robin strumming his lute, and the bells on Peterkin's cap jingling as they went.

The steward's men were already ushering the company to their places at the long tables. The golden light shimmered on silks and velvets and rich brocades in all the colors of the rainbow, dagged sleeves swung and long skirts trailed across the rush-strewn floor, jewels flashed and gold-work sparkled, as the knights and ladies moved about. There were lights everywhere: torches flared along the painted walls, waxen candles glimmered crocus-flamed all down the long tables, and the great fire on the central hearth shed a leaping radiance over the floor and the hounds which lay there waiting for scraps from the tables.

Peterkin bowed with a flourish to the company. "Good e'en to you, Gentles all," said he and went swinging up the hall towards the raised dais at the farther end, whereon stood the high table.

Robin followed him, plucking gently at his lute as though he had not a care in the world. But all the time he glanced about him in search of Marian.

He saw Lord Fitzwater already seated at the high table—paunchy, old, and ill humored. He saw the bridegroom in the place of honor, clad in the flashing green of a dragonfly and playing with the great ruby on his finger—a very exquisite young gallant. But cruelty showed in the lines of his red mouth and the coldness of his dark eyes. A little farther along the table Robin recognized the scarred face of Sir Hugh de Staunton, a kinsman of Marian, and judged by the grimness of the young knight's look that he had little liking for the match. The hall seemed full to overflowing with knights and ladies, little scurrying pages and portly stewards; but of Marian there was as yet no sign.

Next moment Peterkin had mounted the dais and leapt upon the damask-covered table, where he capered among the silver dishes and starry candles, without so much as oversetting a goblet or disturbing the longest feather in the spread tail of the roast peacock which had just been set upon the board.

Heads turned to watch him as he tossed up his daggers, the bright baubles gleaming in the torchlight. The noise of many voices softened away, and even the old lord turned in his chair to watch for a few moments. But all was not well in the great hall. There was a growing uneasiness, and knights and ladies were beginning to whisper to each other all down the length of it and turn often to glance at the door of the women's quarters, through which Marian should by now have come. The nobles at the high table looked at each other with raised brows. Lord Fitzwater had begun to scowl and to drum upon the table with his fat old fingers, while Sir Roger had ceased to play with his ruby and was biting his fingers in an agony of impatience.

Robin had put back his hood and was sitting on the edge of the dais, strumming his lute. He dared not seem to be watching the door of the women's quarters, but he could see it out of the corner of his eye, and he too was waiting for Marian to appear. He had no plan, save to get word with her; what came after must be left to the moment. If it were possible he would get her away during the night, none knowing of her flight. If not, he had his broadsword and Peterkin his daggers. Hugh de Staunton had ever been a good friend to Marian and could be counted on to draw his sword on her behalf if it came to fighting, and the little band of outlaws was waiting little more than a bowshot from the castle walls.

More and more huge dishes were being borne in from the kitchens: smoking pies, roast joints still on the spits, swans and peacocks with their feathers still upon them. The tables were laden with rich food, and the company waiting to begin, and still Marian had not come.

Peterkin finished his act, as though he had not noticed that anything was amiss, but when he leaped down from the table to Robin's side, he whispered: "Your lady is taking her time, it seems."

"Poor lass!" muttered Robin, not ceasing to strum his lute. There was no need for him to sing as yet, for already two tumblers in rags of green and crimson were tying themselves in knots for the amusement of the company. He was glad of this, for he was in no mood for song just then.

Suddenly the old lord let out a roar like an enraged bull and banged both fists upon the table until the drinking vessels jumped and clattered. Humfrey, the chief steward, hurried to him and was sent trundling off as fast as his short legs would carry him, to fetch the Lady Marian. The guests looked at one another, and a bleak silence descended on the long hall, which had been so lively a little while before.

Then they heard running footsteps, and the tapestry over the doorway was dragged aside to reveal the steward, panting and wild of eye, with the white-faced womenservants behind him. "My Lord!" he cried. "Oh my Lord, the Lady Marian is *gone!*"

"*Gone?*" shouted Fitzwater, lurching to his feet. But the bridegroom had already sprung up with an oath, and catching the unlucky steward by the neckband of his tunic, shook him like a rat.

All down the long hall a babble of voices had broken out; but Robin could hear the stammering voice of one of the maids telling how the steward had sent her to fetch her mistress, and how she had found the bower empty. And he could hear Fitzwater shouting that the castle must be searched, the gate-guard questioned, and his daughter instantly found. It seemed that everyone was shouting now, everyone running to and fro; and in the uproar Robin and Peterkin slipped away.

When the two came to the gate-house, the men-at-arms at the gate were explaining to an agitated squire that no lady, let alone their own lady, had passed through the gate since *they* had been on duty. Robin strode blithely past them, calling out: "Seemingly there will be no wedding here tomorrow, unless you can catch the bride!" But his face was grim and haggard in the light of the guard-room door.

A few minutes later they were safely across the causeway and on the open turf beyond. As they headed for the dark bulk of the Chase, Robin spoke quietly to his companion: "It seems that you have had a bootless journey, friend Peterkin. Will you make for the village ale-house now? Or will you come with me and the rest of our party to search for my lady?"

"I do not like to turn my back upon a venture before it is ended," said Peterkin slowly. "I will go with you to search for your lady. And when we have found her, I shall go with you still—if you will have me."

"Certainly we will have you."

So Peterkin joined the Outlaw Brotherhood.

Among the first trees of the Chase they found the little band waiting. Will Scarlet's voice whispered out of the darkness:

"What news?"

"She has gone," Robin answered dully. The men crowded round him, scarcely visible in the crowding shadows, and briefly he told them what had happened. "Lads," he finished, "we must find my lady before harm comes to her, or she is retaken by her father or that devil—Roger of Doncaster!"

"We will find her, Master, never fear," came the answer from the darkness around him; and Robin's heart warmed towards his men as he gave them their orders.

Robin Hood and His Companions Lend Aid to Will o' th' Green from Ambush, 1917, N. C. WYETH. Oil on canvas, illustration for *Robin Hood* by Paul Creswick, David McKay, 1917. Collection of the New York Public Library, Central Children's Room, Donnell Library Center.

Diggery he sent off hot-foot to Kirklees Nunnery, for he thought perhaps Marian, knowing that Ursula, his kinswoman, was a nun there, had gone to her for shelter. He sent Gilbert off on the same errand to Sir Hugh de Staunton's manor, over towards the Peak, and bade him search for her also on the road, since it was hardly likely that she would reach the manor that night.

But though she might have gone to either of these two, Robin knew in his heart that she was far more likely to have gone eastward into Sherwood or Barnesdale, seeking him, and he portioned out his men accordingly. This man was to watch the Nottingham road; this man to watch the track from Doncaster; a party to cut south through the forest towards Sheffield; another, under Will Scarlet, to search the southern skirts of Barnesdale. So he divided the forest among searchers in a wide curve about the eastern sides of Locksley.

Finally, he sent Roger Lightfoot, the swiftest runner of them all, speeding back through the forest to Dunwold Scar, to rouse out the rest of the band. The score of men split up into their separate parties and melted into the darkness. Robin Hood was left standing alone among the stately trees of Locksley Chase, where so often he had walked and ridden with Marian.

Where was she now, he wondered? Was she safe? The forest, which was a familiar friend to him, would be full of danger to a defenseless girl who did not know its ways. And how desperate and afraid she must have been, before she made up her mind to run away. Robin dropped his ribboned lute on the turf and, turning on his heel, plunged away into the darkness.

By the following dawn the whole outlaw band—save for a few under the captaincy of Little John, who were to remain at the Scar in case Marian should find her way there—were out and scouring the forest from Nottingham to Barnesley; but all that day they searched without success, and Robin with them.

Diggery and Gilbert returned from their errands with word that Marian had not gone either to the nunnery or her kinsman's manor, and the day drew on to evening. Robin had not rested, and scarcely eaten, since the search began. Nor did he rest the following night, but still walked the forest deer-paths in the moonlight, his bedraggled finery more stained and tattered than before, his face haggard beneath his hood.

Dawn found him following a narrow track between the little villages of Sheffield and Worksop, not many miles from Dunwold Scar. It was a quiet dawn, giving promise of a glorious day later. But Robin, usually so alive to the beauty of the forest, did not see the shreds of mist among the trees, nor the lengthening catkins on the hazel sprays. On he went, moving wearily down the track, for he was very tired. As he rounded the corner into a broad ride among the trees, he saw a figure seated on a fallen tree-trunk some twenty yards from him. The light was still bad, but he could see that it was a stripling boy in a rough tunic and great-hooded capuchin, who sat with elbows on knees and head sunk in cupped hands, a broadsword at his side and a round buckler lying on the turf at his feet.

Robin halted for a moment and then went on. He took no particular pains to be silent, and a moment later a twig snapped sharply under his foot. Instantly the boy snatched up his buckler and, springing up, stood like some wild thing at bay. Robin could not see the face in the shadow of the great hood, but he liked the boy's speed and his look of defiance and called out to him, kindly enough: "Nay, my little game-cock, I mean you no harm."

For answer, the boy gave an odd, short cry and, drawing his sword, made straight at Robin, shield up, blade raised to strike. Then Robin laughed grimly and, drawing his own sword, stepped forward to meet him.

They met, shield to shield, and their blades rang together. The boy was as quick on his feet as a wild cat, and as fierce; but he was no match for Robin, though the outlaw fought only on the defensive, contenting himself with warding off the blows aimed at him. At last, growing tired of the fight, Robin brought up his blade with a flash, and beat his assailant's sword from his hand. The weapon flew wide, to land with a thud on the grass some way off. And then a strange thing happened, for the brave swordsman dropped his buckler, and sinking down upon the turf, held out imploring hands, and begged in a girl's voice: "Mercy! Have mercy, good sir, and let me go away!"

For a long moment Robin remained staring down at the bowed figure, then he cast down his own sword and, stooping suddenly, put back the clumsy hood.

Long golden-brown hair flowed out over his hands, and next moment he had his lady in his arms. She had known him at the moment when he bent over her to put back her hood, and with a little glad cry she laid her head against his breast like a tired child.

"Sweetheart," he said at last, "what possessed you to do such a mad thing?"

"Why, I am not such a poor swordsman after all," said Marian, between tears and laughter. "For you taught me yourself, Robin, long ago in Locksley Chase. And how was I to know you in those clothes? And when you came upon me so suddenly, I was afraid."

"And so you attacked me because you were afraid, my valiant lady?" said Robin gently. "And as for these clothes: I put them on to play the minstrel at your wedding, meaning to bring you away to the Greenwood. But you had already flown—

and I have been searching for you ever since."

"Oh, Robin, if I had only known! But I had no one to counsel me. I have been so unhappy since you were proclaimed an outlaw. I have had no word from you in all these years, and I did not know how to get a message to you when my father chose a husband for me and I was in need of your help. So at last I stole some food and a broadsword and took one of the scullions' Sunday clothes, and came to look for you."

"Dear love," said Robin gravely, "I have sent you no word in all these years because I thought it best that you should forget me—wolfshead as I am. But now that you have come to me, why, Friar Tuck shall wed us this very day."

So they set out for Dunwold Scar, walking hand in hand, and as blithe as birds on a tree, though both of them were very weary. And as they went, they talked together joyously, for they had many things to say to each other after the years they had been parted.

The sun was yet low in the blue sky of early morning when they came into the long forest-ride below the caves of the Scar, and the few outlaws who had been left there were moving about, collecting arrows and unstringing bows after the morning's target practice. They came running to their leader—then, seeing his companion, checked a little shamefacedly, uncertain how to greet a lady (for Marian's long hair still streamed loose about her shoulders and her face was no longer shadowed by her hood).

Robin saw their uncertainty and called his tall lieutenant out from the others. "Little John," said he, "this is my dear lady."

Little John came forward and dropped on one knee before Marian, raising to his lips the hand which she held out to him. She looked down at him very kindly, saying: "So you are Little John? I have heard much of you already, though 'tis scarcely two hours since Robin found me."

Little John flushed with pleasure beneath his tan and from that moment was her staunch friend and devoted slave.

Then came the others, one by one, to bend the knee to her. Marian turned from one to another, gravely, as Robin told her their names. Lastly came the gigantic friar, with his ban-dogs thrusting around him as usual. He took her hand, very kindly, in his, while the dogs stood round with stiff legs and quivering noses. They were enough to scare any maid, those great hounds, and Little John would have whistled them off; but Marian was used to dogs, and of a good courage, and she held out her hands to them, speaking to them softly. With pricked ears they came forward to sniff at her hands; the pack leader began to wag his tail, Orthros whined deep in his throat. They had accepted her into the band.

Robin turned away and, calling out

three of his men, sent them off: Roger Lightfoot southward, George-a-Green westward, and Hob-o'-the-Hoar-Oak to the north, to begin the recall of his scattered band from their search.

"And now," cried he, as the three men sank into the forest in their different directions, "food, Little John! Food—and a great deal of it!"

So Marian and Robin sat down side by side on the soft turf below the caves: he still in his bedraggled minstrel's finery, she in the scullion's Sunday clothes; and Little John brought them cold venison and manchet bread in a napkin of fine linen. They ate hungrily, while in the glade before them the outlaws continued with their daily tasks—though they often paused to glance aside at the lady.

The pale February sunshine dappled the turf, where the tiny green rosettes of the primroses were beginning to uncurl. The little brook which ran down one side of the glade sparkled between its rushy banks. A robin sang his heart out from the topmost branch of an oak tree, and in all broad Sherwood there were no happier people than Maid Marian and Robin Hood.

Photograph by Mark Gerson

Rosemary Sutcliff (*born 1920*) lives in England. She is well known as a writer of stories for young people. Many of her stories help her readers imagine people who lived long ago. For example, *Warrior Scarlet* is about a crippled boy in England during the Bronze Age, sometime between 2500 and 650 B.C. Besides writing many novels, she has retold the legends of King Arthur and Robin Hood.

Developing Comprehension Skills

1. What setting is described at the beginning of the story? Include the time of year, weather, and location.

2. What upsetting news does Peterkin the Juggler bring to Robin Hood?

3. What preparations does Robin make to go to Lord Fitzwater's hall? Why does he do these things?

4. Does the wedding feast seem like a happy, festive event? Give examples to support your answer.

5. Who is the "stripling boy" who attacks Robin? At what point does Robin realize the attacker's true identity? At what point did you know the attacker's identity?

6. Are there any events in this story that could not have happened? Do the descriptions picture things as they might really have been, or do they suggest a fairy-tale world? Explain your answers.

Reading Literature: Legends

1. **Studying Description.** Reread the description on page 51 of Peterkin juggling for Robin and his men. What was the effect of Peterkin's act? Find at least three details that help you picture specific colors and actions.

2. **Analyzing Plot.** The **plot** of a longer story can be made up of closely related episodes. An **episode** is an event that takes place in one location and time. For example, the first episode in "How Marian Came to the Greenwood"—Peterkin juggling for Robin Hood and his men—takes place on a rainy February day in Robin's cave at Dunwold Scar. Identify one other episode that involves a large gathering. What third episode shows Robin and Marian together?

3. **Comparing Characters.** Robin Hood and Blondel are two heroes associated with England in the time of Richard the Lion-Hearted. Think about how well the following qualities and actions apply to each hero:

   a. loyal
   b. determined to rescue someone he loves and respects
   c. clever in making plans
   d. takes risks to help someone
   e. succeeds in rescuing someone.

   Are there any qualities that one seems to show more than the other? Based on the two stories in this chapter, does one seem to be more of a hero than the other?

Vocabulary

Using Context to Learn Meaning. Not all difficult words can be defined using context clues such as restatements, synonyms, or antonyms. Sometimes you do need to consult a dictionary or glossary. Other times you can infer some idea of what the word means from the sentence that includes the word. Here is an example.

The little juggler wriggled into the damp red and yellow surcoat that he had been trying to dry before the fire.

This sentence makes it clear that a *surcoat* is something that can be put on and can be dried. You can guess that a surcoat is a piece of clothing.

Carefully read these sentences taken from "How Marian Came to the Greenwood." Then decide which of the definitions best fits the underlined word.

1. Robin himself was <u>burnishing</u> the red rust-blotches from his steel cap.

   a. admiring   c. counting
   b. polishing   d. building

2. The outlaws watched him, <u>entranced</u>. The palmer forgot his beads, and the man-at-arms his aching knee.

   a. carelessly   c. fascinated
   b. in anger   d. scornful

3. So Marian was to be married, and to Roger of Doncaster—that smooth-faced young <u>coxcomb</u>, whose name had already begun to have an ugly sound in the ears of the country folk.

   a. handsome prince
   b. hero
   c. undesirable person
   d. singer

4. Next morning, in the gray dawn, two figures <u>emerged</u> from the creeper-hidden entrance to one of the caves, and struck away through the forest in the direction of the Nottingham to Sheffield road.

   a. came out   c. looked
   b. stayed hidden   d. questioned

5. The outer <u>bailey</u> was in darkness, save for the swinging light of a lantern as a groom hurried towards the stables, and empty save for a little page exercising two greyhounds in leash.

   a. forest
   b. mountainous area
   c. open area in a castle
   d. bedroom

6. . . . he <u>capered</u> among the silver dishes and starry candles, without so much as oversetting a goblet or disturbing the longest feather in the spread tail of the roast peacock.

   a. trampled   c. walked slowly
   b. danced   d. stood

7. The tables were <u>laden</u> with rich food, and the company waiting to begin. . . .

   a. empty   c. hidden
   b. stained   d. filled

Critical Thinking

Recognizing Slanted Writing. Writers can create a good or bad impression of a character through word choice. Reread the description of the feast inside the Great Hall at Lord Fitzwater's castle. List the adjectives used to describe Lord Fitzwater and Roger of Doncaster. Do these words create a good or bad impression? Imagine that the first sentence describing Lord Fitzwater read:

He saw Lord Fitzwater already seated at the high table—plump, elderly, and upset.

Explain how the difference in vocabulary affects your impression.

Developing Writing Skills

1. **Rewriting a Legend.** Rewrite one episode of the story so that the event can be understood by a second or third grader.

    Prewriting. Choose an episode, reread it, and list the details that your version must include.

    Drafting. Draft your story, using your list of details. Use simple words and short sentences.

    Revising and Sharing. When you have finished your draft, read it to a younger student. Ask your listener a few questions to make sure that you have covered the main points and used simple language.

2. **Analyzing Setting.** Write a paragraph comparing the setting at the beginning of the story with the setting at the end. Begin by rereading the descriptions of the settings. Then make up a chart comparing details of the settings. Include such categories as weather, location (indoor or outdoor), and mood (pleasant or unpleasant).

    Write a topic sentence that states how the settings at the beginning and the ending compare or contrast. Refer to your chart and to the text as you develop your main idea. As part of your revision, make sure that every sentence in the paragraph develops the main idea.

Chapter 1 Review

Using Your Skills in Reading Legends

The following paragraph is from a legend about Roland, a knight. Tell in your own words what you learn about him in this paragraph. What do you find out about him from the description of his armor? Is the setting of the legend long ago or today's world?

> Some of Roland's ancestors were the noblest heroes the world had ever seen. The blood of heroes flowed in the lad's veins. Of all the knights and warriors in Charlemagne's kingdom, Roland was the bravest and most skillful. When he reached manhood, he was given suitable armor for the knight of a king. His helmet was made of steel and inlaid with pearls, and engraved on it were battle scenes. His shield was made of copper and gold.

Using Your Comprehension Skills

The following paragraph describes the legendary hero you will read about in Chapter 2. Read the paragraph. Then state the main idea of the paragraph. Also, identify an important detail that supports the main idea.

> King Arthur was considered a great leader in battle. He never stayed safely behind until victory was certain. No matter how fierce the enemy, Arthur rode straight for the thickest part of the battle. Waving his sword, Excalibur, Arthur inspired even the youngest and most frightened of his knights to great deeds.

Using Your Vocabulary Skills

The following sentences are from "The Legend of King Arthur," which you will read in Chapter 2. Use context clues to determine the meaning of each underlined word. Tell the meaning of the word in your own words. Then tell whether you figured out the meaning from a direct context clue such as a definition or restatement, synonym, or antonym, or inferred the meaning from the general context of the sentence.

1. At first, Arthur had a <u>multitude</u> of enemies, but he had only a few supporters.

2. For many months, Lancelot <u>isolated</u> himself in the forests. He avoided all human contact.

3. When Arthur returned to his <u>lodgings</u>, he found the inn empty and locked.

4. Then Arthur's foster father <u>revealed</u> the secret of Arthur's birth. He told the boy that Merlin had arranged for Sir Ector to raise him, but his real father was King Uther Pendragon.

5. When Joseph arrived in England, he brought with him the cup Jesus had used at the Last Supper. The cup was called the <u>Holy Grail</u>.

Using Your Study and Research Skills

The following questions can be answered through the information available in a library. Read each question. For each question, tell how you would use the card catalog to locate information.

1. Who was the father of Richard the Lion-Hearted?

2. What was the major export of the city of Nottingham during the Middle Ages?

3. What other legends has Rosemary Sutcliff retold?

Using Your Writing Skills

1. Choose one of the legends you have read in this chapter. In one paragraph identify which of these elements of a legend can be found in the story:
   a. a powerful hero or heroine;
   b. a powerful evil character;
   c. an unbelievable event or events.

2. Create your own hero or heroine. Decide on one admirable quality for which your character will be known. Write a one-paragraph description of this character. Be sure to describe the character's appearance as well as his or her most admirable quality.

CHAPTER TWO

The Legend of King Arthur

It Hung Upon a Thorn, and There He Blew Three Deadly Notes, 1917, N.C. WYETH. Private Collection.
Photograph: Brandywine River Museum, Chadds Ford, Pennsylvania.

Reading Literature

The Legend of King Arthur

Among the world's best-loved legends are stories of King Arthur of Britain and his noble knights of the Round Table. Together, these stories are known as the Arthurian legend.

The History of the Arthurian Legend

Like most legends, the legend of King Arthur is probably based on fact. Long ago, a people called the Celts lived in Britain. In the fifth and sixth centuries, Britain was invaded by the Angles, Saxons, and Jutes from Germany. Arthur is believed to have been a Celtic chief who fought against the invading tribes. Eventually he was killed in battle.

After Arthur's death, some of his followers fled to Wales and others to Brittany in France. These Celtic people became the great storytellers of Europe. In their stories, they told of Arthur's courage and his wish to keep his people united. As time went on, the storytellers wove more magic into their tales.

Later during the Middle Ages—the age of knighthood—the Arthurian legend changed. Arthur and his followers were pictured as knights. Their courage, honesty, and courtesy were presented as models for others to follow. More and more details were added to the legend. For example, a French writer invented the Round Table, where Arthur's knights sat in perfect equality.

In 1470, Sir Thomas Malory of England combined many French and British poems and stories about Arthur in *Morte d'Arthur*. In the nineteenth century, Alfred, Lord Tennyson of England, wrote a stirring series of poems, *Idylls of the King,* based on this legend. Many retellings of the Arthurian legend have appeared in the twentieth century. Among them are T. H. White's *The Once & Future King,* Mary Stewart's *The Crystal Cave,* and the musical play *Camelot.*

The Elements of the Arthurian Legend

Characters. A **character** is a person or animal who takes part in the action of a work of literature. The stories in the Arthurian legend contain many characters. Besides Arthur and his wife Guinevere, famous knights such as Lancelot, Gawaine, and Galahad appear. The mysterious figures of Merlin and Morgan Le Fay add elements of magic. Often, these characters are not presented realistically. Instead, they are symbols of qualities such as loyalty, purity, and greed.

Setting. The **setting** is the time and place of the action of a story. The legend pictures Arthur and his friends as knights. In reality, the age of knighthood came hundreds of years after Arthur may have lived. To enjoy the story, ignore that fact and imagine knights in armor and ladies in flowing gowns.

Plot. **Plot** is the sequence of events in a story. Many stories were combined to make the Arthurian legend. The version you will read, based on Malory's *Morte d'Arthur,* is a combination of shorter stories. Each story has its own plot.

How to Read the Arthurian Legend

1. Notice all the ways in which King Arthur shows his goodness and courage. By studying Arthur, you can understand why this legend has survived for so long.
2. Read each name carefully the first time it appears. Especially important are Merlin, Morgan Le Fay, and Mordred.
3. Appreciate the way this legend takes you into a magical world.

Comprehension Skills

Inferences and Outcomes

Sometimes writers do not directly state facts or ideas. The reader then must look for evidence on which to base conclusions about the events and the characters. An **inference** is a conclusion reached through logical reasoning.

A good reader, like a good detective, thinks about the facts. Instead of making wild guesses, the reader selects details from the story to use as clues. Notice how the following inference about Arthur is based on details from the story.

You know these facts:

1. Only the true king can pull the magic sword from the stone.
2. Many people try to pull the sword out, but they fail.
3. Arthur pulls the sword from the stone easily.

You make this inference: Arthur is the true king.

What evidence should you look for as you read a story? Here are some questions that will help you uncover the clues you need to make reasonable inferences.

1. **Character.** What details about the character's appearance suggest the kind of person he or she is? Is there evidence that the character changes during the story? What do other characters say about this character? How does the character treat others? What clues help you understand why the character acts as he or she does?
2. **Setting.** When and where do the events take place? What details help you create a picture of the setting in your mind? How does the setting affect what happens in the story?
3. **Theme.** What qualities might the characters stand for? What details suggest a message about human experience?

Predicting Outcomes

One of the pleasures of reading a good story is predicting what will happen. Good readers base their predictions on evidence. Details about characters, plot, and setting will help you predict what might take place.

Study this model for predicting outcomes.

You know these facts:

1. Arthur's magic sword helps him keep his power.
2. Merlin often helps Arthur when problems arise.
3. Arthur's magic sword breaks while Merlin watches.

Given this information, you can predict that Merlin probably will help Arthur get a new magic sword.

Exercise: Making Inferences and Predictions

The following paragraphs are from "The Legend of King Arthur." They tell what happens when Sir Kay sends Arthur for a sword.

Arthur yanked the magic sword from the stone. Then he hurried back to Sir Kay with the borrowed sword.

As soon as he saw the sword, Sir Kay knew where it had come from. He grabbed it, ran to his father, and said, "Sir! Look! I have the sword from the stone, so I must be the rightful King of England!"

Which of the following inferences are reasonable, given the details in the paragraphs?

1. Sir Kay is the rightful King of England.

2. Sir Kay is not very honest.

3. Arthur is handsome.

4. Arthur has no time to lose.

Predict whether or not Sir Kay will become King of England. When you read Part One of the legend, see if your prediction is correct.

$\mathcal{V}$ocabulary Skills

Word Parts

Words in the English language are formed in many ways. One way is by adding a beginning or an ending to a **base word.** A word part added to the beginning of a base word is called a **prefix.** A word part added to the end of a base word is called a **suffix.**

Prefix	+	**Base Word**	=	**New Word**
re-	+	use	=	reuse

Base Word	+	**Suffix**	=	**New Word**
care	+	*-ful*	=	careful

Adding a prefix or a suffix to a base word makes a new word with a different meaning. Study the following list of prefixes and suffixes. What is the meaning of each new word?

Prefixes	**Meaning**	**New Words**
re-	again	retake
mis-	wrong or wrongly	miscount
dis-	the opposite of	displease
in-, im-, ir-, il-, and *un-*	not	inactive, immortal, irresistible, illegal, unnecessary

Suffixes	**Meaning**	**New Words**
-ness	the quality of or state of being	goodness
-less	without	hopeless
-ful, -ous	full of or having	wonderful, dangerous

Word Parts from Greek and Latin

Some English words are based on Latin or Greek words. For example, the words *cyclone* and *motorcycle* come from the Greek word *kyklos,* meaning "wheel." Also, many English words contain prefixes and suffixes from Greek and Latin. Knowing the meanings of the word parts will help you understand the English words that they are part of.

Greek	Latin	Meaning	Examples
mono-	*uni-*	one	monotone, unicycle
di-	*bi-, duo-*	two	dialogue, bicycle, duet
tri-	*tri-*	three	triangle
deca-	*deci-*	ten	decade, decimal
poly-	*multi-*	many	polygon, multitude
hemi-	*semi-, hemi-*	half	semiannual, hemisphere
pan-	*omni-*	all	panorama, omnipresent
-ology		science of	zoology

Exercises: Using Word Parts

A. In each sentence, find a word with a prefix or suffix from page 74. Identify each word part and tell what the word means.

1. One seat at the Round Table was called the "Seat Perilous."
2. Merlin could vanish and reappear by magic.
3. The punishment for being disloyal was death.

B. Use the chart of Greek and Latin word parts. Answer these questions.

1. How many colors are there in a <u>tricolored</u> flag?
2. If <u>lateral</u> means "sided," what does <u>multilateral</u> mean?
3. If <u>cornu</u> is the Latin word for "horn," how many horns does a <u>unicorn</u> have?

The Legend of King Arthur: Part One

A retelling of Morte d'Arthur
by Sir Thomas Malory

This part of the legend tells how the young Arthur gained the throne and formed his court. Whom did Arthur trust? Why? Why did others trust Arthur? As you read, look for clues to these answers.

Centuries ago, when Uther Pendragon reigned as King of England, he and his wife Igraine had a son named Arthur. Uther's close aide, the magician Merlin, foresaw that Arthur would need special training. Therefore, he talked the King into keeping the birth of his son secret. At Merlin's urging, Uther sent his baby son away. Safe from the dangers and distractions of court life, Arthur could learn the ways of knighthood.

Merlin took Arthur to Sir Ector and his wife to raise, along with their own son Kay. Together the boys trained to become knights.

While Arthur was still a young boy, King Uther Pendragon became seriously ill. Merlin asked him, "Do you wish Arthur to become king after your death?"

The King replied, "Yes, the throne is his by right of birth."

Shortly after that, Uther died. His enemies began to take over his lands and there was much unrest. When Merlin saw this, he went to the Archbishop of Canterbury. He suggested that a call be issued to all the lords of the kingdom. He asked that the lords gather on Christmas Eve in a church in London. There they could search for a sign that would show who should be the next King of England.

When they assembled, everyone was amazed. In the churchyard they found a large block of marble. In the marble was a steel anvil with a sword driven into it. Gold letters on the sword read: "Whoever pulls this sword out of the stone and anvil is the King of England by right of birth."

Immediately, several knights tried to pull the sword out of the stone. No matter how hard they tried, no man could even budge it. The sword in the stone was left in the churchyard, a challenge to all.

On New Year's Day, there was to be a tournament of jousts and matches in the fields outside London. Each man would test his strength and skill against each of the others. Sir Ector brought Sir Kay,

recently knighted, and Arthur to witness this great event. On New Year's Eve, the three arrived in London and found an inn at which to stay. The next day they rode out to the site of the tournament.

When they arrived at the field, Sir Kay realized he had forgotten his sword. He asked Arthur to ride back to their lodgings in town and get it for him.

Arthur found the inn empty and locked. Upset, he remembered the sword and anvil he had seen as he had ridden past the church. He rode back quickly and, without stopping to read the inscription, yanked the sword from the stone. Then he hurried back to Sir Kay with the borrowed sword.

As soon as he saw the sword, Sir Kay

knew where it had come from. He grabbed it, ran to his father, and said, "Sir! Look! I have the sword from the stone, so I must be the rightful King of England!"

Sir Ector took his son and Arthur to the church. There he demanded that Sir Kay tell the truth. Unwilling to lie in a holy place, Sir Kay admitted that Arthur had brought the sword to him. Sir Ector questioned Arthur, and then pondered things over in his mind. At last he told Arthur, "Now I know you must be the rightful King of England."

Arthur asked, "But, sir, how can this possibly be?"

First, Sir Ector explained the magic of the sword in the stone. Only the man fit to be the next King of England would have the power to draw that sword out of the stone. Then Arthur's foster father revealed the secret of Arthur's birth. He told the boy that Merlin had arranged for Sir Ector to raise him, but his real father was King Uther Pendragon.

Arthur declared, "You, Sir, and your wife have raised me from my birth. I owe you love and honor for all you have done for me."

Sir Ector replied, "Arthur, I ask only one thing of you when you become King of England. Make Sir Kay the keeper of all your lands."

Arthur was mightily surprised at this news of his birthright and at the thought that he should be king. Yet something inside him told him what to do and say. Without hesitation he answered, "Sir, your wish is granted. Sir Kay shall retain his office as long as he and I shall live."

Sir Ector took Arthur to the Archbishop. He pointed out the magic sword in Arthur's hands and explained how Arthur had drawn it from the stone. As the word spread, onlookers hurried from the tournament fields to the church. The crowds watched Arthur put the sword back into the stone. Several knights and barons tried to pull the sword out again. Over and over they tried, but no one could do so. Finally, Arthur stepped up to the stone once more. Effortlessly, he slid the sword out and raised it before all the people.

Many knights were angry that a mere boy could accomplish this feat. They convinced the Archbishop that many more knights deserved a chance to draw the sword. Several times over the next few months, nobles and knights gathered so that all might have an opportunity to pull the sword from the stone. Still, none could do so except Arthur.

Finally, the people cried, "We will wait no longer. We want Arthur for our king. We will fight anyone who opposes him."

Then the knights accepted Arthur despite his youth. He was immediately declared a knight. Shortly after that, Sir Arthur was officially crowned King of England.

As soon as he took office, the young

king promised to right the wrongs that had been committed since his father's death. The people's hearts were filled with joy. Once again peace and justice would rule the land.

Excalibur

After he was made king, Arthur decided to give a great feast. He sent messengers out with gifts for all the kings of the neighboring counties. He dressed in his finest clothes and waited for their arrival.

However, when his messengers returned they brought back his gifts. They told him that the neighboring kings had refused the presents. They had called Arthur a boy of low birth. They did not recognize his right to rule as king. In fact, they were on their way to take Arthur's lands away from him.

Alarmed, Arthur gathered an army of men to help him. He and his five hundred followers gathered supplies and went into a strong castle.

When the rivals came, Arthur and his men withstood a siege that lasted for fifteen days. Then Merlin made his way into the camp of Arthur's enemies. The leaders recognized Merlin and asked him, "Why has a young boy like Arthur been made king?"

Merlin told them how Sir Ector had raised Arthur, but that Arthur's father actually was King Uther Pendragon and the throne was his by right of birth. He convinced some of the leaders of Arthur's claim to the throne. Others, however, laughed at Merlin.

"Even if your story is true," they said, "the boy Arthur hasn't proved himself. He must show by victories that he deserves to be our king."

Merlin warned them, "It would be good for you to accept him and end this resistance. Even if there were ten times as many of you as there are now, you would never defeat Arthur."

"Should we be afraid of this dream-reader?" King Lot, one of the leaders, mocked Merlin.

At that, Merlin vanished. He reappeared before King Arthur, inside his fortress.

"Begin the attack," Merlin told Arthur. "They won't listen to reason. But be careful. The fighting will be fierce. Do not use the sword you have acquired by magic until you have no choice. Then do your best with it."

Arthur immediately mounted his horse and led his men out of the castle. They fiercely attacked the enemy camp. Arthur was always at the front of the battle, doing marvelous deeds of arms. In the thick of the fighting, his horse was killed beneath him. King Lot came upon Arthur just then. To save himself, Arthur drew his magic sword. It was so bright that it blinded Lot and his men. They turned and ran, leaving Arthur the victor.

Now that he had established himself as a leader, Arthur relaxed by going out hunting. In the forest, he came across a knight who insisted on fighting him. They were both strong and skillful swordsmen. For a long time the fight was even, each man giving and taking wounds. Then the two swords smashed together, and King Arthur's magic sword broke in two. The strange knight was about to kill Arthur. Suddenly Merlin arrived. He quickly put an enchantment on the knight, who fell to the ground in a deep sleep.

"What have you done, Merlin?" Arthur cried. "Have you killed this good knight by your crafts? He was the bravest and strongest knight I have ever come across! I would have wanted him to fight under me."

"Don't worry," Merlin assured him. "He's in better health now than you are. He will wake soon. In the future he will do you much good service."

For three days King Arthur rested from the fight. Then he became worried because he had no sword.

"Come with me," Merlin said. "I will take you to one."

Merlin led Arthur to a wide lake. At the center of the lake was an arm reaching up out of the water. Its hand held up a sword encased in a sheath.

"Look," said Merlin. "That is the sword I spoke of. And here comes the Lady of the Lake. Speak courteously to her, and she will give you a sword."

"Fair Lady," Arthur asked the Lady of the Lake, "what sword is this which an arm holds above the water? I wish to have that sword because I no longer have my own."

"The sword is mine," said the Lady. "You may have it, if you will give me a gift when I ask for it."

Arthur agreed. The Lady pointed out a barge that Arthur could use. He rowed across the lake. When he reached the arm, he grasped the sword by the handle. The arm slowly went back under the water.

When Arthur returned to the shore, Merlin told him, "Your sword is called Excalibur. Keep it close to you as long as you live."

As they rode back to court, Merlin

asked Arthur, "Which do you like better, the sword or the sheath?"

Arthur answered, "The sword, of course."

"The sheath is far more valuable than the sword," said Merlin. "While you wear it, you will lose no blood, even if you are badly wounded. Always keep it nearby."

From that day on, Arthur felt more capable of fighting against his enemies. He began to have a large following who recognized him as a good and strong leader.

Arthur and Guinevere

Once Arthur began to get his kingdom in order, he decided it was time to marry. He consulted with Merlin.

"Have you seen anyone fit to be the Queen?" Merlin asked.

"Yes," said Arthur. "The most beautiful woman I have ever seen is Guinevere, the daughter of King Leodegrance. She is the woman I wish to marry."

Merlin wasn't happy about Arthur's choice. With his gift of foresight, he knew that Guinevere would love another as well as Arthur. Merlin advised Arthur, "She is not the woman I would have chosen for you. I could find you a woman who would make you even happier."

Arthur answered, "No. I want only Guinevere for my wife. Go and settle matters for me with her father."

King Leodegrance had been an ally of Arthur's father. For his wedding present,

Uther Pendragon had sent Leodegrance an enormous round table. The table was so large that one hundred and fifty knights could sit around it.

King Leodegrance was very happy that Arthur wanted to marry his daughter. He told Merlin, "Arthur does not need any more lands. I will give him the finest gift I can offer him. I will give him the Round Table that his father gave to me long ago."

With the Round Table went one hundred knights who would help Arthur to make decisions and protect his lands. Still, there were fifty empty seats to be filled.

Merlin, Guinevere, and the Knights of the Round Table set off for Arthur's castle at Camelot. When Arthur saw Guinevere, she looked even more beautiful than he had remembered her. He was delighted with the gift of the Round Table and the hundred knights. These were men of maturity and experience whom he could count on.

Arthur set a high standard for his knights. He declared that the knights of the Round Table could not fight each other and could not start battles just to gain power or riches. Instead, they were to protect people in need, including the poor. They were to guard the kingdom against dangers from lawbreakers within the country and enemies outside the borders. They must always show courage and courtesy.

In order that the empty seats of the Round Table would be filled, a custom was established. The feast of Pentecost came in early summer, the seventh Sunday after Easter. Every year at this time more knights would be added to the Round Table, as they proved themselves worthy of this great honor. When a new knight sat in one of the seats, the seat was magically labeled with his name in letters of gold. One seat, called "Seat Perilous," was left empty. If anyone unworthy sat there, he would be destroyed.

When Guinevere became Arthur's queen, she was overwhelmed by the splendor of Arthur's kingdom. She quickly established herself in his court, and his knights became devoted to her. Her love for Arthur, and Arthur's love for her, grew steadily.

In the meantime, Merlin also fell in love. The lake in which Arthur had found his sword, Excalibur, also held a great rock. Underneath the great rock was a palace. The Lady of the Lake lived there. One day she cast her spell and persuaded Merlin to come and live with her. That was the last time anyone ever saw Merlin the magician.

Developing Comprehension Skills

1. What is Arthur's relationship to each of the following: Uther Pendragon, Sir Kay, King Lot, Guinevere?

2. Three episodes in this selection involve swords. What happens in each episode?

3. At first, the kings of the neighboring counties oppose Arthur. Name two of their objections against him. Then tell at least two ways in which Arthur proves his right to be king.

4. Based on what you know so far, predict whether Arthur will rule well once Merlin is gone. What evidence did you use for your prediction?

5. How does the kingdom benefit from the standards Arthur sets for his knights? What might the kingdom have been like if Arthur had encouraged the knights to seek wealth and power? Explain.

Reading Literature: The Legend of King Arthur

1. **Studying Plot.** Put in order the following five events from Part One.

   a. Arthur defeats King Lot in battle.
   b. Merlin suggests that Arthur be raised by Sir Ector.
   c. Arthur marries Guinevere and receives the gift of the Round Table.
   d. Merlin disappears and is not heard from again.
   e. Arthur pulls the sword from the stone.

2. **Interpreting Character.** After Arthur draws the sword from the stone, Sir Ector tells him about his real father, Uther Pen-dragon. Arthur immediately declares, "I owe you love and honor for all you have done for me," and promises to make Sir Kay the keeper of his lands. What can you infer about Arthur's character from these statements? That is, what do these statements tell you about the kind of person Arthur is?

   Choose one other incident and tell what you can infer about Arthur from it.

3. **Understanding Setting.** The **setting** is the time and place of the action of a story. "The Legend of King Arthur" is set in a world that seems magical and mysterious. What details about the setting and the events give you a sense of magic and mystery?

Vocabulary

Using Word Parts from Greek and Latin. Examine the list below. Note the meaning of each Greek and Latin word and word part listed. Then read the numbered sentences. The underlined word in each sentence includes one or more of the words or word parts in the list. Using the information in the list and the context clues in each sentence, write the meaning of each underlined word.

mono-, uni-	one	*omni-*	all
bi-	two	*scientia-*	knowledge
multi-	many	*archein*	to rule
hemi-	half		

1. Arthur wanted to <u>unite</u> all of England under his rule.

2. His enemies led a <u>multitude</u> against Arthur's men.

3. Because Merlin could foresee events, some people thought he was <u>omniscient</u>.

4. The government of England has been a <u>monarchy</u> for about 1200 years.

5. Did Arthur draw the sword from the stone <u>bimanually</u>, or did he use only one hand?

Study and Research

Using an Encyclopedia. A general encyclopedia contains articles on many topics. The articles, arranged alphabetically, often fill several books, or volumes. The encyclopedia **index** lists the titles of the articles and tells the volume and page where you will find each article. The index is often found in a single volume. Sometimes one article discusses several related topics. The title of the article may name only one of the topics. The other related topics are also listed in the index as separate entries.

In your school or local library, choose one set of encyclopedias. Look up the following names and terms in that encyclopedia. Find out which names and terms are titles of separate articles and how long each article is. Find out which names and terms are discussed only under other titles. Use the index to help you.

Arthur or King Arthur	Guinevere
Round Table	Merlin
Arthurian Legend	Knighthood
Lady of the Lake	Camelot
Uther Pendragon	

Developing Writing Skills

1. **Describing a Character.** In one paragraph, give your impression of Merlin the magician.

    Prewriting. Jot down notes about Merlin's special abilities and qualities.

    Drafting. Begin your draft with a sentence that states your impression of Merlin. In the draft, include details from the story that support this impression.

    Revising and Sharing. Work in small groups for revising. Begin by having each person read his or her draft aloud. Then discuss the details used in each paragraph. After the discussion, revise your draft. Add details if necessary. Proofread the final copy.

2. **Describing Action.** Imagine you are present when young Arthur successfully draws the sword from the stone. Write an eyewitness account of what happens. Complete the stages in the process of writing: prewriting, drafting, and revising and sharing. If you need help, refer to the Guidelines for the Process of Writing on page 623 in the handbook.

The Legend of King Arthur: Part Two

A retelling of Morte d'Arthur
by Sir Thomas Malory

Lancelot, Tristram, and Galahad are three of the bravest and noblest of King Arthur's knights. Each faces a different challenge. What qualities enable each knight to meet his challenge?

These are the stories of three of the most respected of King Arthur's knights.

Sir Lancelot

One of the finest and bravest knights of King Arthur's court was a young man named Lancelot. He became Arthur's closest friend. Earlier in his life, he had met Guinevere at her father's castle and had fallen in love with her. Now that she was King Arthur's wife, he kept his love for her in his heart and tried to avoid her in the court.

Lancelot fought valiantly in battles. No one could win over him. One night he was attacked by four knights. He killed two and the other two fled in terror.

Later, he discovered Sir Kay in the midst of a battle. He fought off the three attackers easily. Then he exchanged horses and armor with Sir Kay, so that Sir Kay could ride home in safety.

Lancelot was often pursued by the ladies of the court. Since none of them seemed to him as beautiful as Guinevere, he had no time for them. Once, Arthur's sister, Morgan Le Fay, found Lancelot asleep in a forest. She cast a spell on him and had him transported to her castle. When he woke up, four women were standing over him. They told him they knew his heart belonged to Guinevere, but he must choose one of them for his wife or face death in prison.

After thinking it over, Lancelot declared, "I choose to die rather than to have one of you as my wife. As for Guinevere, she is faithful to her husband."

Very discouraged and knowing they were defeated, the four women let Lancelot go on his way. When his friends at the court heard this story, they respected him even more.

By this time, Guinevere had learned of

Lancelot's love for her. She had no desire to leave King Arthur or to offend him. Still, she enjoyed the fact that the finest knight in all the court would love no woman but her. She became jealous if she heard any rumor that Lancelot had paid attention to anyone else.

Once she believed that Lancelot had fallen in love with the lady Elaine, daughter of King Pelleas. Furious with Lancelot, Guinevere insulted him, calling him a traitor. "Leave the court immediately!" she demanded. "And never again come into my sight!"

Filled with sorrow, Lancelot went mad and fled to the countryside. Guinevere soon regretted her angry words. She sent messengers to find him, but he could not be found anywhere.

For many months, Lancelot isolated himself in the forests and lived like an animal. He survived by eating fruits and berries. He avoided all human contact. When he at last went into a town, he could not remember who he was. The people of the town, feeling sorry for the crazy man, gave him enough food to survive.

Finally, Elaine happened to see this crazy person, and she recognized Lancelot. As he slept, her knights carried him to a tower. When he awoke, Lancelot thought that Elaine was Guinevere.

In the tower was hidden the most precious object in all England. Hundreds of years before, Joseph of Arimathea had come to England. This was the man who had given his tomb to the Apostles for the burial of Jesus. When Joseph arrived in England to spread the Gospel, he brought with him the cup Jesus had used at the Last Supper. This cup was called the Holy Grail. Joseph left the Grail in the keeping of a good family.

After a time the people of England fell into evil habits. They were no longer worthy to see the Holy Grail. From then on, the Grail was hidden in the tower of the good family with whom it had been left.

As Lancelot lay near the Grail, he was cured of his madness. He was ashamed of what he had done while out of his mind.

Elaine wanted him to marry her, but Lancelot would not listen. As soon as he heard that Guinevere wanted him back in court, he returned to Camelot.

Sir Tristram

Another of King Arthur's knights was named Tristram. His name meant "sorrowful birth." He got his name from his mother shortly before she died. Tristram's mother had heard that her husband, King Melodius, had unjustly been thrown into prison. She set off to help him and died from exposure to the cold on a winter's night. The next day, King Melodius was freed. He returned home to find that his son had been born and his wife had died.

Seven years later, King Melodius married again. His new wife became jealous of Tristram and decided to poison him. By mistake, one of her own sons drank the potion and died.

When Melodius heard about this, he condemned his wife to be burned at the stake as a traitor. Tristram begged for her life to be spared. He could not accept the severity of this punishment. The king agreed, but sent his son off for his own safety to learn the ways of knighthood.

Tristram left for France. There he learned to play beautiful music on the harp. He also learned to fight bravely, and he became a knight.

Tristram returned home to Cornwall to help King Mark, his uncle, defend the kingdom. When he was fighting with the Irish Sir Marhaus, Tristram thrust his sword into his opponent's skull. Tristram's sword was chipped, and the chip stayed in Marhaus's skull. Sir Marhaus went home to Ireland to die.

Tristram had been wounded seriously in this fight. He boarded a ship, intending to go in search of a doctor who could heal him. Strong winds drove the ship to Ireland. There he was given hospitality by King Anguish. Tristram fell in love with Anguish's daughter, Isoud.

One day a servant noticed Tristram's broken sword. It matched the piece that had killed Isoud's uncle, Sir Marhaus. Tristram was asked to leave King Anguish's house immediately. Before he left, he pledged his love for Isoud. She promised to keep her love for him, too.

On his return home, Tristram talked constantly of the fair maiden Isoud. King Mark grew jealous of Tristram and decided to marry Isoud himself.

To overcome his grief at the marriage, Tristram plunged into his duties as a knight. Once he saved a knight from being killed by two enemies and discovered that it was King Arthur he had rescued.

In gratitude, Arthur awarded Tristram a seat at his Round Table. There the knight became well known and loved. The knights and ladies of Camelot appreciated his gift for music.

Later, King Mark traveled to Camelot with two knights. He planned to surprise and kill Tristram. However, when he told his plan to the knights, they rejected it in horror. Then they told King Arthur of Mark's treachery. Arthur quickly had Mark arrested.

Brought before King Arthur, Mark confessed his crime. Arthur forgave him this time. However, he warned Mark that if he tried again to harm Tristram, he would be severely punished. Mark agreed to leave Tristram alone and returned to Cornwall.

Trying to forget Isoud, Tristram went to Brittany in search of adventure. There he fought bravely for King Hoel. In gratitude, the king offered to Tristram marriage with his daughter, another Isoud. She was known as Isoud of the White Hands.

By now, Tristram realized that he was never to win his first love. He liked Isoud of the White Hands well enough, and he decided to marry her. They lived happily for a while, until Tristram was badly wounded in another battle. Despite the loving care of his wife, Tristram grew weaker and weaker.

Tristram remembered how badly wounded he had been when he had landed in Ireland. He remembered how Isoud, his first love, had nursed him to health. He asked his wife to send for her. Perhaps, he reasoned, she might bring him back to health again.

At first, Isoud of the White Hands agreed. She sent messengers to Cornwall to ask Isoud to come and help. If Isoud agreed to come, the ship was to return bearing white sails. If Isoud refused, the ship was supposed to use black sails.

After the ship with the messengers left, Tristram's wife began to worry. What was to stop her husband from falling in love once more with the first Isoud?

When she saw the ship return with white sails, Isoud of the White Hands made up her mind. She went to her husband where he lay ill. She told him that the ship had returned with black sails. Tristram turned away sorrowfully.

"Alas, my beloved," Tristram sighed,

"we shall never see each other again."
Then he died.

When the ship landed, Isoud heard the terrible news. She was led to Tristram's bedroom. There she, too, died of grief.

The bodies of Tristram and Isoud were returned to Cornwall. King Mark sadly buried them in his own chapel.

Sir Galahad

Throughout the years, the seat at the Round Table called "Seat Perilous" had remained empty. Finally, a man came to court who was worthy to sit there.

A young man named Galahad, the son of Elaine and Lancelot, had been raised by nuns in a quiet cloister. He had been taught wisdom, understanding, and purity of heart. Now that Galahad had become a young adult, he had been sent out to learn the ways of knighthood.

It was the feast of Pentecost, and the knights were waiting for one of the seats at the Round Table to be filled.

A squire came into the court and told the knights that he had seen a great red stone with a sword stuck in it floating on the river. Immediately, they all rushed out to the river to see if they could capture the sword. When they got there, not one man could do so. Disappointed, they returned to the court.

Later, when they were again seated at the Round Table, an old man led a young man into the room. In the young man's hand was the sword from the red rock in the river. Amazed, they watched the old man lead this young man to the Table. He led the youth to the "Seat Perilous," but now the words read, "This is the seat of Sir Galahad, the high prince." King Arthur remembered how he, too, had pulled a sword from a stone. From that moment on, Sir Galahad was treated with the greatest honor and respect.

At this same season, a vision appeared to the knights as they sat at the Round Table. There was a bright light and a clap of thunder. Then the Holy Grail, covered so that no one could see it, appeared at one end of the hall. It passed before all the knights and disappeared. After a moment Sir Gawaine stood up.

"I make a holy vow," he declared. "I am starting now on a search for the Holy Grail. I will not return until I have succeeded in finding it."

All the knights knew that only a man of pure heart could see this holy vessel. In spite of this, each one of them wanted to be the first person to see it.

Every Knight of the Round Table took up the challenge to search for the Holy Grail. King Arthur's heart was filled with sadness. He knew his Round Table would never be the same. Many knights would never return from this quest.

Galahad rode off unarmed. He had no shield to protect himself. While he was riding, he saw a white abbey. When he stopped there, a white knight told him, "Here is a shield which only you, sir, are fit to wear. Take it and ride in safety."

As Galahad rode on, he discovered the Castle of Maidens. He wounded and chased away seven knights who were barring his entrance to it. Once inside, Galahad set free hundreds of people who had been imprisoned there by the seven wicked knights he had just fought.

As he traveled on, Galahad stopped at a hermitage to share a meal with an old man who lived there. A woman came to the door and asked for him by name.

"Galahad, come with me. I will show you the greatest vision you have ever seen."

She led Galahad to a ship. He with two of his friends, Sir Bors and Sir Percival, sailed to a castle in the city of Sarras.

When they arrived, Galahad was met by the vision of Joseph of Arimathea. Joseph told Galahad that he would take him to see the Holy Grail. Galahad entered the holy place in fear and trembling. He knew that he would not survive once he had seen the vision. He also knew it would be the greatest vision he had ever seen. When he saw the Holy Grail, he fell on his knees

in a state of rapture and happiness. Galahad felt his life had now been fulfilled.

He came out, briefly, to say farewell to his friends. Before their eyes, they saw Galahad's soul carried up into the heavens. With him went the Holy Grail.

After this remarkable experience, Sir Bors entered a holy hermitage. Sir Percival returned to King Arthur's court to recount the amazing story.

Now that the search for the Holy Grail had ended, the remaining knights returned to the Round Table. King Arthur was overjoyed at their return.

Developing Comprehension Skills

1. How does Lancelot feel about Guinevere? How do these feelings affect his actions?

2. Do you think that Lancelot will ever fall in love with someone other than Guinevere? Explain the reasons for your prediction.

3. Tristram's uncle, Sir Mark, wants to marry Isoud after he finds out that Tristram loves her. What inferences can you draw from this?
   a. Sir Mark is brave and gallant.
   b. Sir Mark is jealous of Tristram.
   c. Sir Mark loves Isoud and does not want to hurt Tristram.
   d. Sir Mark cares only about himself.

4. Why does King Anguish order Tristram to leave his house? What evidence upsets him? What conclusion does he draw?

5. What is the Holy Grail? How did it come to be in England?

6. Only Sir Galahad sees the vision of the Holy Grail. What qualities make Galahad worthy of this vision?

7. Which of the three knights described in this section seems most appealing to you? Explain your choice.

Reading Literature: The Legend of King Arthur

1. **Examining Character.** Lancelot, Tristram, and Galahad are three of the greatest knights of the Round Table. What qualities do all three share? Does each knight seem to represent a special quality? Give evidence for your conclusions.

2. **Studying Plot.** Choose one episode in Part Two and make a time line for it. Include a dot on the time line for each important event involving the hero.

3. **Understanding Conflict. Conflict** is a struggle between opposing forces. Two

episodes in Part Two concern the conflict between love for a lady and loyalty to a leader. Tell who is involved in each conflict. Does each knight act honorably? How does each conflict end?

Vocabulary

Using Prefixes and Suffixes to Determine Word Meaning. Each of the following sentences includes a word built from a base word and one of the prefixes and suffixes on page 74. Identify the word, separate its base word from its prefix or suffix, and tell what the word means.

1. "It [the Holy Grail] passed before all the knights and disappeared."

2. "Furious with Lancelot, Guinevere insulted him, calling him a traitor."

3. "King Arthur's heart was filled with sadness."

4. "Arthur was always at the front of the battle, doing marvelous deeds of arms."

5. "As Lancelot lay near the Grail, he was cured of his madness."

Study and Research

Comparing Encyclopedias. Most school and local libraries have different sets of encyclopedias. One encyclopedia may provide more information on one topic, while another encyclopedia may tell more about a different topic.

Look up these topics in at least two encyclopedias. Compare the information given by the different encyclopedias. Which encyclopedia provides more information about the topic? Which encyclopedia has more pictures, charts, and maps? Which one looks easier to read and understand?

> Arthur *or* King Arthur
> Knights *or* Knighthood
> Legends
> Britain, Great Britain, *or* United
>   Kingdom

Speaking and Listening

Reading Formal Language. In many versions of the Arthurian legend, the language used by the characters is more formal than everyday speech. Read the following passage, based on a speech from Malory's *Morte d'Arthur.* In the speech, Sir Ector begs Lancelot to return with him to court. Practice until you can read the words smoothly, clearly, and with expression. Then read the passage to one or more classmates.

> "Sir," said Sir Ector, "I am your brother, and you are the man in the world that I love most. And if I understand that returning would disgrace you, you may know I would never advise you to do so. But King Arthur and all his knights, and in especial Queen Guinevere, make such sadness and sorrow for you that it is a marvel to see and hear. And you must remember the great worship and renown that you have, how you have been more spoken of than any other knight that is now living, for there is none that bears the name now but you and Sir Tristram. And therefore, brother," said Sir Ector, "make you ready to ride to the court with us."

Developing Writing Skills

Comparing Characters. Both Mark and Isoud of the White Hands try to keep Tristram and the first Isoud apart. In your view, who did the greater wrong, Mark or Isoud of the White Hands? In a paragraph, explain your opinion.

Prewriting. Review what Mark and Isoud of the White Hands did to keep Tristram and the first Isoud apart. List the reasons for their actions. Jot down notes on who you think did the greater wrong.

Drafting. Begin your draft by stating your opinion. Your opinion should be based on your inferences, or conclusions, about the characters of Mark and Isoud of the White Hands.

Revising and Sharing. Read your draft to a classmate. Then ask: "Have I stated my opinion clearly? Have I given solid reasons for reaching my conclusion? Does my explanation include details from the story as evidence?"

The Legend of King Arthur: Part Three

A retelling of Morte d'Arthur
by Sir Thomas Malory

King Arthur loves his queen. He values the trust and friendship of his knights also. What happens when he must choose between wife and friends?

Spring was at hand, so Queen Guinevere decided to go "a-Maying." She and ten of her knights went out, unarmed, to pick the lovely flowers from the fields.

Sir Meliagrance, who had fallen in love with the Queen, seized this opportunity to strike. He rode out into the field to capture the Queen. When he declared his love and asked her to come with him, she responded angrily. She told him she would rather cut her throat than go with him. However, when his men began attacking her unarmed knights, she agreed to go with him if her knights could go, too.

When they arrived at Meliagrance's castle, Queen Guinevere waited for her chance. Then she sent a secret message to Sir Lancelot telling him of her plight. Lancelot set out immediately. While he was still at a distance, Meliagrance's men shot his horse from under him. Lancelot walked a long way, hampered by his heavy armor. Then he borrowed a woodsman's cart to ride the rest of the way.

When he finally arrived at the castle, Lancelot shouted to Meliagrance that the "knight of the cart" had come to fight. Meliagrance, knowing he couldn't win against Lancelot, begged and obtained mercy from the Queen. Lancelot, greatly disappointed that he couldn't fight with Meliagrance, rode away with Guinevere and delivered her safely home.

The Breakup of the Round Table

Two of King Arthur's nephews, Sir Mordred and Sir Agravaine, hated Queen Guinevere. They knew their words would be much more powerful than their swords. Therefore, they began to plant vicious rumors about the love Queen Guinevere felt for Sir Lancelot.

Together, they set a trap for Lancelot. They arranged for King Arthur to stay out

hunting one night. Then they hid outside Guinevere's chamber. As they had hoped, Lancelot came to visit the queen. As soon as he entered her room, they pounded on the door.

"Come out, traitor," they cried.

Lancelot had no choice. He had to open the door to try to escape. When he did so, the fight began.

Lancelot wounded Mordred. He killed Agravaine and the other knights. Finally, he escaped. Mordred rushed to tell King Arthur about Lancelot's disloyalty and his killing of the knights.

King Arthur's heart was broken. He could no longer trust his queen or his good friend Lancelot. They must both be punished.

One of Arthur's nephews, Sir Gawaine, was a good friend of Lancelot. He argued in Lancelot's defense. "Lancelot has defended the queen several times," Gawaine pointed out. "Perhaps she called him to her chamber to reward him. And perhaps she feared the rumors that would start if he were seen visiting her. That may be why she called him at night, when she thought no one was about.

"Lancelot is your best friend, your finest knight. You must believe that he and your queen wish you no harm."

Still, Mordred argued strongly against Gawaine. "They have loved each other for a long time. Everyone knows it!"

At last, Mordred convinced Arthur that Guinevere was guilty. Sorrowfully, the king sentenced Guinevere to be burned at the stake for treason.

Just as the wood piled about Guinevere was to be set afire, Lancelot rushed in with his forces and saved the queen. He rode off with her to his castle, Joyous Gard. In the chaos of the fight and the escape, Lancelot unknowingly killed two brothers of his friend Sir Gawaine.

When Gawaine heard that news, his friendship turned to vengeful hatred.

Hearing all that had taken place, King Arthur arrived with his men to lay siege on Lancelot's castle. For fifteen weeks Lancelot kept his men inside, refusing to fight Arthur.

At last Arthur stood before Lancelot's castle and called to him, "Come forth, if you dare, and fight me!"

"I cannot fight my king, the man who made me a knight," Lancelot replied.

"I am no longer your king! I am your enemy! You have killed my men and stolen my queen."

"I never wanted to hurt your men. They forced me to, in order to save myself. And how could I let your innocent queen die because of me! I had fought to defend her often enough before. I am heartily willing to return her to you. She is here only for her safety. She is true to you. Take her back, I beg you, and end this needless war."

Arthur weakened. He wanted to believe his old friend. Yet, Sir Gawaine remembered his dead brothers.

"Liar! Traitor! Killer!" Gawaine yelled. "I will forever make war against you!"

"I repent of your brothers' deaths," Lancelot said. "I will do whatever penance you ask."

Gawaine would not listen. Angrily he reminded Arthur of all the evidence against Lancelot and Guinevere. He pointed out the damage they had caused to the Round Table. Arthur once again resolved to fight Lancelot, and he broke off discussions with him. Sadly, Lancelot told his men that they could leave the castle to fight. He ordered them, however, not to harm his friends Arthur and Gawaine.

For the next several days, the fighting was hard and bloody. Several times Lancelot came upon Arthur and Gawaine. Each time he held back from killing either man. When he saw his own men attacking his old friends, he stepped in to save Arthur and Gawaine.

Hundreds of knights were killed on both sides. The number of deaths became so great that the Pope decided to intervene. He issued a decree that Arthur must take back Queen Guinevere and that peace must once again exist between King Arthur and Sir Lancelot.

Lancelot sent word to King Arthur that he would personally deliver the queen back to the court. The queen's ladies and knights arrived riding in a procession, all dressed in the finest green velvet. Behind them rode Lancelot and Guinevere, dressed in robes of white. They dismounted and knelt before the king. All who stood by wept.

Lancelot addressed the king in his finest words. He repeated what he had said before the battle. He blamed all the trouble on lies and swore unending loyalty to Arthur. Once more he asked that their friendship begin anew.

Gawaine, at Arthur's side, answered first. "The king may do as he pleases," Gawaine said bitterly, "but I will never forgive you."

"I am taking back Guinevere as my queen only because the Pope has commanded me to do so," Arthur stated wearily. "As for you, I will not fight you. But you must leave Camelot at once, forever."

Lancelot, hearing these words, turned and rode away. He bent his head in the deepest sorrow he had ever known.

Feeling he had lost everything, Lancelot called his knights together. He told them about his banishment from King Arthur's court. They cried, "We will remain with you forever. Wherever you go, we go."

Lancelot felt comforted. Together, he and his knights sailed for France. When they arrived, they were well accepted. Their reputation for helping the poor and downtrodden had preceded them.

Sir Mordred

Even though Lancelot had declared his sorrow at killing Gawaine's brothers, Gawaine was not satisfied with Lancelot's banishment. He continued to stir up King Arthur to take revenge. Despite the Pope's order, Arthur decided to take up the fight with Lancelot once again.

Before leaving for France, King Arthur gave his nephew Mordred complete charge of his kingdom and power to rule over his affairs.

Lancelot, hearing of Arthur's and Gawaine's arrival in France, sent a message to them, begging for peace. They would not hear of it, and the siege began again.

Both sides were equally matched. Hundreds were again killed in battle. Lancelot seriously wounded Gawaine. The battle raged on for months.

In the midst of the fighting, King Arthur received word that Sir Mordred had taken over all his lands in England. Mordred had ordered his men to write from abroad proclaiming that King Arthur had been killed. He had persuaded the Archbishop to crown him king. Now he was planning to make Guinevere his queen.

Guinevere had reluctantly agreed to Mordred's demands, but she first made a special request. She asked to travel to London to buy a new wardrobe. Mordred agreed. Once in the city, Guinevere locked herself up in the Tower of London to protect herself from Mordred.

King Arthur and his men left the siege in France and quickly returned to England. Mordred and his men attacked them as they left their ships. Sir Gawaine, not fully recovered from the wound Lancelot had given him in France, was again wounded seriously. Arthur found him lying half-dead. The king mourned, "Are you going to leave me too? You and Lancelot were my best knights. Will I lose you both? In you two I most had my joy. Losing you, I will lose all joy in life."

Sir Gawaine, realizing death was near, at last regretted his actions.

"I see now," he said, "that my willfulness has caused this disaster. If I had forgiven Lancelot, you and he would have come to terms. Then he would have been at your side, and this war with Mordred would never have begun. And now you will miss Lancelot."

Then Gawaine asked for ink and paper. He wrote a letter to Lancelot, asking his forgiveness for the pain he had caused. He begged Lancelot to come to Arthur's aid. Then he took his last breath.

The End of the Round Table

On the next morning, Arthur's army took the field against Mordred's. Many were slain, but at the end Mordred fled. Arthur took several days to have the dead buried and to let the wounded recover. Then he set a date to meet Mordred again.

The night before the battle, Arthur had a strange dream. In the dream Gawaine appeared to him.

"I advise you," Gawaine said, "in no way should you go to battle tomorrow. If you fight tomorrow, you will cause your own death and the death of many others. Postpone the battle for a month. By then Lancelot will arrive and slay Mordred."

Then Gawaine vanished.

Arthur told his councilors about his dream. He asked them to make a treaty with Mordred. In order to postpone the battle, he would agree to any conditions.

The councilors arranged the treaty. All that was left was for Arthur and Mordred to meet to complete the arrangements. Each was to bring fourteen men.

Before going to the meeting, Arthur warned his men, "I don't trust my nephew. This may be a trap. If any sword is drawn, strike immediately." Mordred gave his men the same message.

While they were negotiating, a snake crawled onto a knight's foot and bit him. Without thinking, the knight pulled his sword and struck at the snake. With that movement, fighting broke out at once.

The battle raged all day. Hundreds of men were killed. At the end, King Arthur had only two knights left, Sir Lucan and Sir Bedivere. Sir Mordred stood alone.

"Look, Sir Lucan," Arthur cried, "there is the man who has caused all this woe. Give me my spear."

"Sir," Lucan argued, "remember your dream. Leave him alone. We can finish this tomorrow."

Arthur ignored the warning. He shouted to Mordred, "Even if this is the end of me, I will not leave this life without killing such a traitor as you are, Mordred."

With that, Arthur grabbed his spear and ran at Mordred. The spear passed into Mordred and through his body. Mordred knew he was dying. Despite the spear, he pushed himself closer to Arthur and brought his sword down on Arthur's helmet. The blow was so strong that it cut through the helmet and into Arthur's head. Then Mordred fell dead.

Sir Lucan and Sir Bedivere carried Arthur to a chapel near the lake to recover. Arthur said to Bedivere, "Take my sword, Excalibur, and throw it into the water. Then tell me what you see."

Twice Sir Bedivere pretended to do so, each time returning and saying nothing had happened. Arthur said to him, "Would you betray me at the very end? Do as I say!"

Bedivere finally threw the sword into the water. As soon as he did so, an arm and a hand reached out of the water, grabbed the sword, shook it three times, and vanished with the sword underneath the water.

Arthur was greatly relieved when he heard the report. "Now," he said, "take me to the waterside."

When Sir Bedivere carried him there, they found a small barge on the lake. In the boat were Arthur's sister, Morgan Le Fay, and two other women. The women took Arthur into the boat and rowed him across the lake.

Sir Bedivere cried, "My lord Arthur, what will become of me? You are leaving me alone among my enemies!"

"Comfort yourself," Arthur replied. "Do as well as you can by yourself, for in me there is nothing left to trust. I am going to the valley of Avalon. If you never hear of me again, pray for my soul."

The next morning, Sir Bedivere discovered a chapel with a freshly-dug grave outside it. The hermit who lived at the chapel said that during the night several women had brought to him the body of a warrior to be buried.

Bedivere knew that the warrior must have been King Arthur. He decided to stay in this chapel and spend the rest of his life in prayer and fasting.

Lancelot and Guinevere

The news finally reached Lancelot that Sir Mordred had been crowned King of

England and would not allow Arthur to return. He also heard that Guinevere had locked herself up in the Tower of London for safety.

Quickly, Lancelot gathered his men and returned to England. In the meantime, Guinevere, learning that Arthur had been killed, fled to the peace and quiet of a convent in Almesbury.

Arriving in England, Lancelot learned about King Arthur's death. He set out to search for Guinevere. He finally found her in the cloister where she was living.

When Guinevere saw Lancelot, she cried, "Lancelot, because of us, a good king and thousands of knights have been killed. We must never see each other again. I will stay here and live a life of prayer. You must leave at once."

Lancelot left, greatly saddened, knowing that he, too, must find peace. As he rode along, he heard a bell ringing from a chapel. There he found Sir Bedivere and vowed to spend the rest of his life at the chapel with his friend and the hermit who had buried Arthur.

Six years went by. One day Lancelot received a sad message. Guinevere had died, leaving a note for Lancelot. She asked that he bury her beside her husband, King Arthur. Lancelot obeyed her request and brought her body back to the chapel.

There, he and the others buried Guinevere in a grave next to that of Arthur. Losing all interest in life, Lancelot grieved for the death of his king and his queen. He sorrowed for his part in the destruction of their kingdom.

And there, in six weeks, Lancelot died. His body was carried to his castle, Joyous Gard, as he had requested. At last he would rest in peace.

> **Sir Thomas Malory** *(?–1471?)* retold stories about King Arthur and his knights in his masterpiece *Morte d'Arthur.* William Caxton printed the first edition of this book in 1485. The facts of Malory's life are uncertain. Some scholars believe that he grew up in Warwickshire in England. Later, he may have spent many years in prison. For more than five hundred years, his retelling of the Arthurian legend has inspired writers and artists.

Developing Comprehension Skills

1. Reread the opening episode of Part Three. Which one of the following inferences is based on the facts?
   a. Meliagrance has no respect for the standards that Arthur has set for his knights.
   b. Meliagrance is a fearless fighter.
   c. Meliagrance's love for the queen is noble and strong.
   d. Meliagrance never attacks unarmed knights.

2. Make a time line showing the end of King Arthur's reign. Begin with Mordred's setting the trap for Lancelot and Guinevere. Show all the important events. Be sure to include Arthur's major decisions.

3. Tell the reason for each of these events:
   a. Gawaine's friendship for Lancelot turns to hate.
   b. King Arthur stops fighting Lancelot in France and returns to England.
   c. Guinevere locks herself in the Tower of London.
   d. Bedivere throws Excalibur into the lake.

4. After Arthur's death, why does Guinevere tell Lancelot that they must never see each other again?

5. If you were Arthur, what would you have done to save the kingdom? Explain.

Reading Literature: The Legend of King Arthur

1. **Interpreting Characters.** In Part Two, the characters of Lancelot, Tristram, and Galahad stand for human qualities. In Part Three, however, some of the characters are drawn more fully. Arthur, Lancelot, and Gawaine all have good and bad qualities. Choose one of these characters. Describe both the good and bad qualities of this character. Tell whether you think the character is believable—that is, whether he resembles a real person.

2. **Studying Plot.** Part Three begins with Lancelot's rescue of the Queen and ends with the deaths of Guinevere and Lancelot. List in order the important events that take place between these two episodes.

3. **Understanding Theme.** The **theme** is the message of a work of literature. Part Three deals with the demands of friendship. Review what Arthur does to keep both of his friends, Lancelot and Gawaine. Reread Arthur's statements to his friends, particularly to the dying Gawaine. What message about friendship do you find in this legend?

Vocabulary

Forming Words with Prefixes and Suffixes. In each of the numbered sentences a word is missing. A prefix or suffix from page 74 must be added to the base word, given in parentheses. Read the sentence. Choose the prefix or suffix that will change the base word into a word that will complete the sentence correctly. On a sheet of paper, write the new words.

1. Guinevere caused problems when she acted in a __(thought)__ manner.
2. It was __(legal)__ for a knight to visit the queen alone.
3. Despite his __(sorrow)__ life, Tristram often brought music and pleasant moments to the people of the court.
4. Galahad was noted for his __(truthful)__ and other virtues.
5. Merlin accomplished by magic many tasks that were considered __(possible)__ .

Critical Thinking

Recognizing Generalizations. Imagine that you are discussing the Arthurian legend with two other people. One of them states that all knights were braver than modern soldiers. The other person claims that all modern soldiers are braver than the knights.

Each of these statements is a generalization. A **generalization** is a statement that describes all the items in a certain category. Some generalizations are always true; for example, "all triangles have three sides." Other generalizations are true only in certain cases. A generalization that is not always true is called a **faulty generalization.** An example is this statement: "Bike riders are careless in traffic." It is true that some bike riders disobey traffic rules. However, other cyclists follow the rules carefully.

Some faulty generalizations can be corrected. For example, limiting the generalization about cyclists would make it true: "Some bike riders are careless in traffic."

Examine the two statements about knights and modern soldiers. Why are they faulty generalizations? How could you make them accurate?

Study and Research

Finding Reference Sources. A general encyclopedia contains articles on many topics. There are also encyclopedias in fields such as history, science, literature, and art. A school or public library will have these encyclopedias and other reference books too.

Look through the reference section at your school or local library. List any reference books that give information about either *Morte d'Arthur* or Sir Thomas Malory. Write both the title and the author(s) or editor(s) of each reference book.

Speaking and Listening

Interpreting Legends. As you learned, the Arthurian legend was handed down by Celtic storytellers. Imagine that you are a storyteller. Prepare to tell the episode of the knight of the cart or the episode of the end of the Round Table.

Reread the episode several times, and then list the events that you will tell. Next, plan the details that you will give your audience. Ask yourself questions such as these: "What details will help the audience understand the way things happen? What details will show how cowardly Meliagrance is, or how funny it is to see a noble knight in a humble cart?" Include dialogue as part of your story. Change your voice to show different speakers. Rehearse your story so that your delivery will be smooth. Finally, tell your story to the class or to a small group.

Developing Writing Skills

1. **Presenting an Opinion.** In a paragraph, explain who you think was most responsible for the ruin of King Arthur's court. Give reasons to support your opinion.

   Prewriting. First, list each key name and jot down what he or she did to destroy the court. Then answer the following questions: Was there a time when a different decision by Lancelot, Gawaine, Mordred, Guinevere, or Arthur could have saved the kingdom? Who is most responsible for the downfall? Jot down reasons to back up your ideas.

   Drafting. Use your notes as you work on your draft. State your opinion. Then present and explain your reasons.

   Revising and Sharing. Work with a partner as you revise your draft. Discuss the following points: "Is the opinion stated

clearly? Do the reasons given support the opinion? Is the explanation clear?" Then prepare a final copy of your draft and proofread it.

2. **Extending a Legend.** In the first episode of Part Three, Guinevere saves her unarmed knights but must wait for Lancelot to rescue them from Sir Meliagrance. Write a new ending to this episode. Have Guinevere outwit Meliagrance and free herself and her knights. However, do not use any modern inventions in your new legend. The characters and the setting should remain as described in the original legend. Complete the stages in the process of writing: prewriting, drafting, revising, and sharing. For help, refer to the Guidelines for the Process of Writing on page 623 in the handbook.

Chapter 2 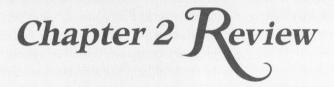 Review

Using Your Skills in Reading the Legend of King Arthur

Read the following paragraph from this chapter. Identify the characters, tell the setting, and point out what is magical in the events.

> Now that he had established himself as a leader, Arthur relaxed by going out hunting. In the forest, he came across a knight who insisted on fighting him. They were both strong and skillful swordsmen. For a long time the fight was even, each man giving and taking wounds. Then the two swords smashed together, and King Arthur's magic sword broke in two. The strange knight was about to kill Arthur. Suddenly Merlin arrived. He quickly put an enchantment on the knight, who fell to the ground in a deep sleep.

Using Your Comprehension Skills

Read the following paragraph from a short story by William Saroyan in Chapter 4. From the information given by the speaker, do you think he is ashamed or proud of his background? How can you tell?

> We were poor. We had no money. Our whole tribe was poverty-stricken. Every branch of the Garoghlanian family was living in the most amazing and comical poverty in the world. Nobody could understand where we ever got money enough to keep food in our bellies, not even the old men of the family. Most important of all, though, we were famous for our honesty. We had been famous for our honesty for something like eleven centuries, even when we had been the wealthiest family in what we liked to think was the world.

Using Your Vocabulary Skills

The following paragraph contains five words that have Greek or Latin word parts listed on page 75. Read the paragraph and locate those five words. Review the information on the chart on page 75. Then use that information and the context clues in the paragraph to define each word. If you cannot determine the meaning of a word from context, use a dictionary.

It was common knowledge around King Arthur's court that Merlin, the multi-talented magician, was a very special person. He was thought to have a monopoly on magic. He alone knew how to cast spells. His powers were so great that he seemed almost omnipotent. King Arthur knew that, even if he searched for a decade, he would never find another person like Merlin. Merlin was unique.

Using Your Skills in Study and Research

Imagine that you want to locate drawings of King Arthur and the knights and ladies of this legend. Describe the steps you would follow in using an encyclopedia. What help would the index provide?

Using Your Writing Skills

Choose one of the writing assignments below. Follow the stages in the process of writing.

1. Choose a magical event from "The Legend of King Arthur." Explain why the magical event appears believable. To support your explanation, tell the details that make the event seem possible. Think about the ways in which characters react to the event. Tell how their reactions help make the magic seem realistic.

2. Write another episode for any character in this legend. The episode should reveal the qualities that the character has. For example, you might "test" the goodness of a knight by having him tempted by a rich enemy of the king. Be sure to include details that describe the setting.

CHAPTER THREE

How Writers Write

Mimosa, 1945-51, HENRI MATISSE.
Ikeda Museum of 20th Century Art, Japan.

Using the Process of Writing

Good writing is the result of a process. It begins when the writer looks for a subject to write about. It ends after the writer has written something to share with the reader. In this section, you will read about these stages in the process of writing:

prewriting   revising

drafting   sharing

Morning Light, 1916, OSCAR BLUEMNER. Hirshhorn Museum and Sculpture Garden, Smithsonian Institution, Washington, D.C.

Understanding the Process of Writing

Picture yourself listening to a skilled guitarist at your first concert. You like the music but understand only a little about it. Soon, however, you start taking guitar lessons and learn some techniques. Then you attend another concert given by the same guitarist. Probably, your second concert will be a richer experience. You will get more out of the music because you will appreciate some of the techniques used by the guitarist.

Reading a writer's work is somewhat like listening to a guitarist. Knowing what to listen for helps you appreciate the quality of the guitarist's performance. Knowing what to look for in a writer's work helps you appreciate the quality of the writing.

In this chapter, you will read about how writers make their writing clear, lively, and smooth. Then you can practice some of their techniques. The more you learn about writing, the more you will get out of your reading.

Stages in the Process of Writing

Generally writers do not turn out finished work on the first try. Instead, writers work hard and long at their writing. Different writers use different methods. Still, most writers find that their writing develops through four stages, called the **process of writing:**

> **prewriting,** or planning the writing
> **drafting,** or doing the writing
> **revising,** or improving the writing
> **sharing,** or giving the writing to others

This process is not a rigid step-by-step description. Sometimes, writers repeat certain stages before moving ahead. For example, in revising a draft, a writer may decide to do more planning. This planning, in turn, leads to more drafting and still more revising. The stages can overlap.

Prewriting

The first stage of the process of writing is called **prewriting.** During this stage, writers plan their work before drafting it on paper or entering it in a word processor. Before you write, complete these steps:

Choose a subject. Often, an assignment will tell you what to write about. Sometimes, though, you must choose your own subject. To do so, ask yourself some questions. What interests you? Do you know a great deal about one thing? Would you like to learn more about something else? List any ideas that come to mind, and then go over them. Choose the idea that you find most appealing. This idea is your subject for writing.

Jean Craighead George, who writes books about the wilderness, gathers ideas from daily experience.

> Ideas for my stories come from memories of my childhood, from events that happen to the people I love, live, and work with— and from reading. I mean all reading—ads, books, magazines, newspapers, scientific journals, trashy stuff, classics, my children's homework, postcards, even legal papers. Ideas do not come out of thin air.

Select a form. After choosing a subject, you should select the form for your writing. Often, an assignment will specify the form, requiring that you write an autobiography or perhaps a poem. Sometimes, however, the choice is yours. Then you must ask yourself what you want to do with the subject. Do you want to write about characters and events? If so, you might select the short story as the form. Do you have a new or interesting idea? You might want to share your idea in a poem or in an essay. Let your purpose guide you in selecting the form.

Limit the subject. The next step is to narrow the subject to a topic, or one guiding idea. To do so, ask these questions: Which aspects of the subject can you cover? Which aspect do you most want to cover? That aspect will be the topic for writing. Suppose that you have chosen hockey as the subject and the short story as the form. Then you might narrow the subject by choosing this topic: the courage of a hockey player. Your short story will treat this guiding idea.

Consider the audience. After choosing the topic, think about those who will read your writing. After all, you are writing to be read. Suppose that the topic is the courage of a hockey player. Ask yourself, who will read your work? your classmates and teachers? readers of the local paper? professional hockey players? young children? For each group you must tailor the writing differently. For those unfamiliar with the game, you would probably provide more background information. For experienced players, on the other hand, you might write about the finer points of the game.

Later, in drafting your work, you must again consider the needs of your readers. For young readers, for example, you probably would use short words and sentences.

Once writer Mary Lewis has her topic, she targets her audience.

> When a story idea seems to be a good one, I next must think of exactly what age group I am going to write it for. The age group must be more definite than just for children. I write the story for children of one special age and then try to make the story interesting also for children who are a few years younger or older.

Gather supporting information. Now you can begin to gather information about the topic. First, write down what you already know. Then, list questions that you want to answer. Use several resources to find the answers needed. You can gather, or glean, information from books, newspapers, and magazines. You might also interview people who know something about the topic. Take notes as you gather the information.

Frank Bonham, who has written several westerns, gives this advice: "Take notes—notes on anything you might possibly need later. Never trust your memory." In researching a book, he gleans information from several sources.

> For a book I wrote about dolphins, I read all I could find about these delightful animals in books and scientific journals. I visited them at Marineland. Then I talked to marine biologists. I talked, finally, to tuna fishermen who find the tuna by spotting schools of dolphins feeding on the fish.

Organize your ideas. Read over the details that you have gathered. Some will be useful; others, not. Cross out details that seem unrelated to the topic. You may have gathered much interesting information on a slightly different topic. If so, you may choose to keep this information and shift the focus of the topic.

Next, organize the details that you want to keep. Choose the order that makes sense. In stories, the details usually are arranged in time order. In descriptions, the details often are arranged according to the order in which you might notice them.

Carol Ryrie Brink wrote *Caddie Woodlawn,* a book based on her grandmother's childhood adventures. In organizing her information, the writer began to see connections.

> My grandmother had told me many stories of her childhood. I had to sort them out in my mind and decide which things were most important, where natural climaxes should come, and how one story could be woven into another so that they made a unified whole.

As you organize your ideas, you may discover that you need more information. If so, do more research to find what you need.

Some writers organize their details in outlines. For instance, Matt Christopher, writer of sports books, outlines an entire book before writing it.

> Working with sheets of paper containing the scenes of my proposed book, I begin my outline, writing chapter after chapter, usually about half a page in length.

Marguerite Henry, writer of books about horses, has her own way of organizing her details.

> Conventional outlines are not for me. I construct a kind of skeleton skyscraper which foretells the story as visibly as steel girders and beams give promise of the building to come. This framework tells me more, in one glance, than all the *I, II, III*'s and *a, b, c*'s of a normal outline.

When you are the writer, you can choose the method of organizing details that will work best for you.

Drafting

Drafting means putting sentences on paper or typing them into a word processor. In writing a first draft, try to get your ideas down in sentences. Don't worry about errors in spelling and punctuation. You can correct them later when you revise your draft. Now is the time to try out words and phrases, cross out ideas, and add details. Follow your plan as a guide, but use other good ideas that may come to you while writing. You will find it helpful to skip lines on the draft to leave room for changes.

Of course, facing a blank sheet of paper can be scary. Still, all writers have to cope with that fear. One way is to plunge in and get something on paper. William Faulkner, who won the Nobel Prize in literature, offers this advice.

> Get it down. Take chances. It may be bad, but it's the only way you can do anything really good.

Pura Belpré, who was a storyteller and writer, wrote her first drafts quickly.

> I write my first draft by hand and always in pencil. I do it just as soon as I finish doing the research, and I am careful that I have covered everything that is needed for the story. Drafting quickly is important so that the freshness of the material is not lost.

Revising

Just because you wrote it doesn't mean it's good.
　　　　　　　　—Frank Bonham

Revising gives you another chance to get your ideas and words just right. Take advantage of the opportunity. To begin revising, read what you have written and ask these questions:

1. Is the topic developed? Are there unnecessary details? Should details be added?
2. Is the organization clear?
3. Is the writing interesting?
4. Are the words exact?

On your draft, mark any changes. Cross out the words you want to drop. Write in the words you want to add. If your paper becomes too messy, recopy it. If you are using a word processor, you can revise the draft on the screen.

Experienced writers know the importance of revising. They develop their own techniques to improve their writing. Glenn O. Blough, writer of books about nature, tries to look at his work from a different angle.

> Sometimes words seem stubborn and don't say what we have in mind. So we try again and sometimes again and again. Having someone else read what we have written often helps. So does leaving it alone for a while and then coming back to give it another try. Both of these help us find a "fresh" look. Reading it aloud, or sometimes just telling it as though you were talking to someone, helps in rewriting.

Holling C. Holling, who writes westerns, tries to improve his draft in at least three ways.

> In rewriting, I add details here and there, rearrange sentences for more directness, and where a sentence is long, shorten it or turn it into two sentences.

By the end of that winter it was clear ~~to everyone~~ that Barry was the best rescue dog ~~the monks had ever had.~~ *when it was snowing,* ~~In a snow storm~~ Barry was the first to find people buried under the snow. He was the fastest ~~at~~ *to* dig~~ging~~ them free. He worked *the* hardest, *to* ~~at~~ warm~~ing~~ them up. Sometimes, ~~after~~ the other dogs gave up~~,~~ *But* Barry went on licking a frozen face until ~~finally~~ there was *some* movement~~,~~ a moan, ~~an opening eye.~~ Then the great dog grew wild with joy.

Years passed. Werner grew tall and thin. *Now* ~~He~~ ~~put aside his school books and~~ gave all of his time to the dogs. He worked with Bro~~v~~*th*er Luigi every day~~.~~ *He fed* ~~feeding~~ the dogs, playing *ed* with them, *and helped* train~~ing~~ the pups. He was completely happy.

When ~~In 1806~~ Barry was six years old, ~~and~~ Werner was eighteen. *That* ~~It~~ was the most terrible winter ~~ever~~ *the monks had known* ~~to strike the mountains.~~ Rescue trips were made every day. Half of the *monastery* dogs ~~in the monastery~~ died that winter, trying to save the travelers' lives. Almost half of the monks died in icy traps as they went about their rescues.

One night in March, Werner and Barry were walking slowly up the trail toward home. Werner's face was stiff with cold, ~~and~~ even Barry seemed tired. It had been a terrible winter for both of them.

Author Lynn Hall shows how she corrected a page of her manuscript while writing the story *Barry, the Bravest St. Bernard.* Kerlan Collection, the University of Minnesota.

Ann Petry, who wrote a biography of Harriet Tubman, listens especially to the sounds of her sentences.

> I read my drafts with a critical ear. I test every sentence for meaning and for sound. I keep testing the book as I type. I'm a noisy writer. I mumble as I work because I have to find out how a sentence sounds when read aloud.

"Revise!" urges writer Frank Bonham. "Only the sculptor has the disadvantage of being stuck forever with what he has chipped out."

Proofreading. After you have revised your writing, reread your marked-up draft. Look for and correct errors in grammar, spelling, punctuation, and usage. Use a dictionary and a grammar book to help you.

Preparing the final copy. Write or type your draft for the last time. Remember to include the changes and corrections marked on the previous draft. If you are using a word processor, call up the draft, check it on the screen, and then have the draft printed out. Then proofread the final copy.

Sharing

Professional writers share their work. Their audience may number in the millions. Your audience is smaller, but just as important. Share your writing with your family, friends, and teachers—with anyone interested in the topic. Give them work of the highest quality.

Practicing the Process of Writing

When you write, use the methods in this chapter. Also, refer to the Guidelines for the Process of Writing in the Handbook for Reading and Writing. There you will find models for writing and suggestions for applying the process of writing.

Using the Sounds of Language

Words have both sounds and meanings. Writers use sound to reinforce meaning. In this section, you will read about these uses of sound:

alliteration   rhyme   rhythm   onomatopoeia

The Blue Guitar, 1982, DAVID HOCKNEY. Pantechnicon, London.

Alliteration

> **Alliteration** is the repetition of consonant sounds at the beginnings of words.
>
> Example: <u>r</u>ough and <u>r</u>eady

Alliteration in Prose. In everyday speech, you sometimes use alliteration. Phrases such as "tried and true" and "making a mountain out of a molehill" contain alliteration. So do comparisons such as "hungry as a horse" and "green as grass." In tongue twisters some beginning consonants are also repeated: "She sells seashells by the seashore."

Writers of prose sometimes use alliteration to give force to certain words to emphasize ideas, or to create rhythms. Here is an example. Notice how the use of repeated consonants adds a gentle rhythm.

> The silver rocket <u>l</u>ay in the <u>l</u>ight of the moon. And <u>b</u>eyond the rocket stood the yellow <u>l</u>ights of his home, a <u>b</u>lock away, <u>b</u>urning warmly.
> —Ray Bradbury, "The Rocket"

Alliteration in Poetry. Poets also use alliteration for emphasis. In this example, look for the repeated <u>t</u>'s, <u>c</u>'s, and <u>s</u>'s. This repetition reinforces the idea of the rise and fall of the waves.

> The tide rises, the tide falls,
> The twilight darkens, the curlew calls;
> Along the sea-sands damp and brown
> The traveler hastens toward the town,
>   And the tide rises, the tide falls.
> —Henry Wadsworth Longfellow, "The Tide Rises, the Tide Falls"

Sometimes the use of alliteration adds a comic touch, as in the following tongue twister.

Gazelle

O gaze on the graceful gazelle as it grazes
It grazes on green growing leaves and on grasses
On grasses it grazes, go gaze as it passes
It passes so gracefully, gently, O gaze!
—Mary Ann Hoberman

Exercises: Using Alliteration

A. Each of the following examples contains alliteration. Identify the consonant sounds repeated at the beginnings of words.

1. The hurrying hoof-beats of that steed,
   And the midnight message of Paul Revere.
                        —Henry Wadsworth Longfellow, "Paul
                        Revere's Ride"

2. There once was a witch of Willowby Wood,
   and a weird wild witch was she.
                        —Rowena Bennett, "The Witch of
                        Willowby Wood"

3. He sprang through the sleeping camp and in swift silence dashed through the woods.
                        —Jack London, *The Call of the Wild*

4. They climbed higher on the hill, cutting the briers and brushes and tree branches and stacking them neatly into piles.
                        —Jesse Stuart, "The Clearing"

B. Write three sentences containing alliteration. In each sentence, repeat a consonant sound at the beginnings of words at least three times.

Rhyme

> **Rhyme** is the repetition of sounds at the ends of words.
>
> Example: Listen, my children, and you shall hear
> Of the midnight ride of Paul Revere.
> —Henry Wadsworth Longfellow, "Paul Revere's Ride"

Rhyme in Prose.   Writers of prose seldom use rhyme. Once in a while, though, they use it for a special effect. For example, in the following proverb, the rhyme makes the words catchy.

Early to bed and early to rise, makes a man healthy, wealthy, and wise.   —John Clarke, *Paroemiologia*

Rhyme in Poetry.   Sometimes in poems one rhyming word comes within a line.

The splendor falls on castle walls.
—Alfred, Lord Tennyson, "The Splendor Falls"

More often the rhyming words are found at the ends of lines. The lines may come one after another.

Dreaming of honeycombs to share
With her small cubs, a mother bear
Sleeps in a snug and snowy lair.   —Harry Behn, "Waiting"

In the next example, the first and third lines rhyme. So do the second and fourth lines.

All day the snow fell on that Eastern town
With its soft, pelting, little endless sigh
Of infinite flakes that brought the tall sky down
Till I could put my hands in the white sky.
—Stephen Vincent Benét, *John Brown's Body*

In this poem which lines rhyme?

Whose woods these are I think I know.
His house is in the village though;
He will not see me stopping here
To watch his woods fill up with snow.
                    —Robert Frost, "Stopping by Woods on a
                              Snowy Evening"

In a poem the **rhyme scheme** is the pattern of rhymes at the ends of lines. You can chart this pattern by using letters to show which lines end with the same sounds. Use a different letter of the alphabet to stand for each different sound. Here is an example.

I never saw a Moor,   *a*
I never saw the Sea;   *b*
Yet know I how the Heather looks,   *c*
And what a Billow be.   *b*
                    —Emily Dickinson, "I Never Saw a Moor"

Notice that the second and fourth lines rhyme. Therefore, the same letter is used for both lines.

Here are the rhyme schemes for the other examples.

"Waiting"	"John Brown's Body"	"Stopping by Woods"
a	*a*	*a*
a	*b*	*a*
a	*a*	*b*
	b	*a*

Exercises: Using Rhyme

A. Read the lines from "The Tide Rises, the Tide Falls" by Longfellow on page 118. Write the rhyme scheme for the lines.

B. For each of the words below, write several rhyming words. Then, write a two-line or four-line poem using some of the rhyming words. Use any rhyme scheme you like.

moon   tree   skate   ball   race   money

Rhythm

Rhythm is the pattern of stressed and unstressed syllables in a sentence or line of poetry. To chart the pattern, mark each syllable with one of these signs:

/ for stressed syllables
⌣ for unstressed syllables

Example: 'Twas brillig, and the slithy toves
Did gyre and gimble in the wabe;

—Lewis Carroll, "Jabberwocky"

Rhythm in Prose. Rhythm can reinforce meaning in a sentence. In the following example, the rhythm suggests the crashing of the waves.

The wind was howling up from the sea, beating the waves against the wharves. —Esther Forbes, *Johnny Tremain*

Sometimes writers use the rhythm of entire paragraphs to suggest feelings to the reader. In the following example, the rhythm helps to give a feeling of growing excitement.

They had drums among the Indians, the Chinese, the Egyptians, thousands of years ago. And the words of their poetry move along like drum-beats, keeping time, now fast, now slow, drumming easy and slow at the opening of a war dance, drumming faster and faster, wild and furious, till it is so swift only the best-trained warriors can stand the speed of the dance that is drummed.

—Carl Sandburg, *Early Moon*

Rhythm in Poetry. In many poems the overall rhythm is regular. Any change in the rhythm gives force to certain words. As you read the following lines, listen for the change in rhythm.

‿ / ‿ / ‿ / ‿ / ‿ /
I'm going out to clean the pasture spring;
‿ / ‿ / ‿ / ‿ / ‿ /
I'll only stop to take the leaves away
‿ / ‿ / ‿ / ‿ / ‿ /
(And wait to watch the water clear, I may):
‿ / ‿ / ‿ / ‿ / / /
I shan't be gone long. — You come too.

—Robert Frost, "The Pasture"

The rhythm in the first three lines is regular. By changing this pattern, the poet adds force to the last three words. The invitation to the reader is strong and clear.

Exercises: Using Rhythm

A. Read this sentence. Then mark the stressed and unstressed syllables.

It was the best of times, it was the worst of times.

—Charles Dickens, *A Tale of Two Cities*

B. Read this paragraph aloud a few times. Describe the rhythm and the feeling that it gives you.

"Bang! I deliver your packages, pick up packages, bring you coffee, burn your trash, run to the post office, telegraph office, library! You'll see twelve of me in and out, in and out, every minute."

—Ray Bradbury, "The Sound of Summer Running"

C. Copy these lines. Mark the stressed and unstressed syllables.

Jake Hanson runs a fix-it shop.
He says he fixes anything
By mending what you break or drop
With wire or nails or glue or string.

—Kaye Starbird, "Jake Hanson"

Onomatopoeia

> **Onomatopoeia** is the use of words to imitate sounds.
>
> Examples: bang, thump, whizz

Onomatopoeia in Prose. Sometimes writers invent words to imitate sounds. In the following example, the writer imitates the sounds made by machine guns and by flame throwers.

> The pounding of the cannon increased; there was the rat-tat-tatting of machine guns, and from somewhere came the menacing pocketa-pocketa-pocketa of the new flame throwers.
>> —James Thurber, "The Secret Life of Walter Mitty"

Onomatopoeia in Poetry. Poets use this technique to create "sound pictures" for the reader. In the following example, the words *fizzed* and *hissed* imitate sounds made by fireworks.

> A white sky bomb fizzed on a black line.
> A rocket hissed its red signature into the west.
>> —Carl Sandburg, "Fourth of July Night"

Exercises: Using Onomatopoeia

A. In the following sentences, which words imitate sounds?

1. The bells in the steeples cling-clanged, telling people it was time to be up and about.   —Esther Forbes, *Johnny Tremain*
2. The tuba oomphs, the flutes tweet-tweet;
   >> —William Cole, "Here Comes the Band"

B. Write three sentences using words that imitate sounds. You might imitate the sounds made by animals, tools, or musical instruments.

Using Figures of Speech

Figurative language is a special way of using words. Writers use figurative language to go beyond the meaning of words. Figurative language includes the following figures of speech.

simile   metaphor   personification   hyperbole

The Starry Night, 1889, VINCENT VAN GOGH.   Oil on canvas, 29" x 36¼". Collection The Museum of Modern Art, New York City, Acquired through the Lillie P. Bliss Bequest.

Simile

A **simile** is a comparison using *like* or *as*.

Examples: The star is like a diamond in the sky.
The dancer was as graceful as a cat.

Similes in Prose. Writers use similes to suggest meaning. Similes can also help you see things in new ways. A good simile might make you say, "That's exactly what it's like! I never thought of it that way before."

Writers try to make their similes fresh and original. Similes used too often can become **clichés.** For example, comparisons such as "old as the hills" or "big as a house" are worn out. They no longer create striking pictures.

In the following samples, look for the two things that are compared. What do they have in common?

A pale smile, like a gleam of cold sun on a winter's evening, passed over the old man's face.
—J.R.R. Tolkien, *The Return of the King*

The children pressed to each other like so many roses, so many weeds, intermixed, peering out for a look at the hidden sun.
—Ray Bradbury, "All Summer in a Day"

Similes in Poetry. Poets often use similes to create pictures for the imagination. In the following poem, for example, the writer compares trees to pencil strokes.

Scene
Little trees like pencil strokes
black and still
etched forever in my mind
on that snowy hill.   —Charlotte Zolotow

In the following lines, to what does the writer compare the future? What does this comparison tell you about how the speaker views the future?

> The days of our future stand before us
> Like a row of little lighted candles—
> Golden, warm, and lively little candles.
>
> —C. P. Cavafy, "Candles," *translated by* Rae Dalven

Exercises: Using Simile

A. For each example, tell the two things being compared. Then tell the additional meaning that each simile suggests.

1. I wandered lonely as a cloud
   That floats on high o'er vales and hills,
   > —William Wordsworth, "I Wandered Lonely as a Cloud"

2. The fence had lost many of its pickets and stood propped against the tangle like a large comb with teeth missing.
   > —Elizabeth Enright, "Nancy"

3. Black snake! Black snake!
   Curling on the ground,
   Rolled like a rubber tire,
   Ribbed and round.
   > —Patricia Hubbell, "The Black Snake"

B. Write three similes. If you wish, use some of these beginnings.

1. The engine sounded as noisy as _____.
2. The wind was like _____.
3. The cake tasted like _____.
4. The water in the pool looked like _____.

Metaphor

> A **metaphor** is an indirect comparison between two unlike things that have something in common.
>
> Example: The stars are candles in the sky.

In the example above, stars and candles are compared. Notice that a metaphor does not contain the words *like* or *as*.

Metaphors in Prose. Writers use metaphors to create vivid pictures for the imagination. In the following sentence, the writer uses the metaphor "snowstorms of torn paper."

> The air was filled with snowstorms of torn paper; strangers hugged each other in the streets. The war was over.
> —Alice Dalgliesh, *The Silver Pencil*

The reader must figure out that "snowstorms of torn paper" describes confetti. The writer suggests a comparison between them. The metaphor creates the picture of a multitude of white specks falling to the ground.

Read the following sentence. Which metaphor describes the grass? the flowers? For each metaphor, describe the picture that the writer creates in your imagination.

> Now and then Tom and Huck came upon snug nooks carpeted with grass and jeweled with flowers.
> —Mark Twain, *The Adventures of Tom Sawyer*

Metaphors in Poetry. Poets try to make every word count. Therefore, they often use metaphors to create brief, yet striking, descriptions. Read the following lines from a poem called "Steam Shovel." In them, the poet develops one metaphor in several lines.

What do a steam shovel and a dinosaur have in common? Which words develop the comparison?

> The dinosaurs are not all dead.
> I saw one raise its iron head
> To watch me walking down the road
> Beyond our house today.
> Its jaws were dripping with a load
> Of earth and grass that it had cropped.
> It must have heard me where I stopped,
> Snorted white steam my way,
> And stretched its long neck out to see,
> And chewed, and grinned quite amiably.
>
> —Charles Malam, "Steam Shovel"

Exercises: Using Metaphor

A. Point out the metaphors in the following quotations. What two things are compared? How are they alike?

1. The bones of the sea
   are on the shore,
   shells
   curled into the sand.   —Lilian Moore, "Shells"

2. All the world's a stage,
   And all the men and women merely players.
   —William Shakespeare, *As You Like It*

3. The goofy moose, the walking house-frame,
   Is lost
   In the forest.   —Ted Hughes, "Mooses"

B. Write three sentences containing metaphors. Remember that the words *like* or *as* are not found in metaphors. These questions will start you thinking.

1. To what can you compare your school when the dismissal bell rings?

2. To what can you compare snow?

3. To what can you compare a rocket?

Personification

> **Personification** is the technique of giving human qualities to an object, animal, or idea.
>
> Examples: The train whistle screamed.
> The hail tap-danced on the roof.

Personification in Prose. Personification, like other figures of speech, creates a picture in the reader's mind. In the following example, the writer pictures a city as one person waking up.

Boston slowly opened its eyes, stretched, and woke.
—Esther Forbes, *Johnny Tremain*

In the following example, the use of personification helps the reader imagine the sounds made by glaciers.

The ice talked, grinding its teeth, sending out every now and then a singing crack.   —Norah Burke, "Polar Night"

Personification in Poetry. In the following lines, the writer personifies Chicago. Which human jobs does the city do? Which words help you picture the city as a worker, mighty and muscular?

Hog Butcher for the World,
Tool Maker, Stacker of Wheat,
Player with Railroads and the Nation's Freight Handler;
Stormy, husky, brawling,
City of the Big Shoulders:
—Carl Sandburg, "Chicago"

In the next example, in what way do the telephone poles resemble humans?

The telephone poles
have been holding their
arms out a long time now.

> —Donald Justice, "Crossing Kansas by
> Train"

Exercises: Using Personification

A. In each example, tell what is pictured as human. Explain in what way or ways it resembles a human.

1. On all sides, green-clad mountains gazed down upon us.
> —Edwin Way Teale, *Journey into Summer*

2. Ten thousand daffodils saw I at a glance,
Tossing their heads in sprightly dance.
> —William Wordsworth, "Daffodils"

3. The wind stood up, and gave a shout;
He whistled on his fingers, and
Kicked the withered leaves about,
And thumped the branches with his hands.
> —James Stephens, "The Wind"

B. Use personification to describe the things listed below. Suggest some action or attitude in which the thing resembles a human being.

1. a mailbox
2. an apple tree bearing fruit
3. a radio

Hyperbole

> **Hyperbole** is an exaggeration for emphasis.
>
> Example: It was so hot, you could fry an egg on the sidewalk.

Hyperbole in Prose. Tall tales and folk humor contain many examples of hyperbole. In the following example, the exaggeration creates a funny picture.

> There is a man nearby whose feet are so large that, when it rains, he lies down and uses them as umbrellas.

Hyperbole also can help make a description exciting. In the following sentence, for example, the writer creates excitement by exaggerating the speed of a swing.

> The swing accelerated ever more wildly: soon it would take off entirely, depart from its hinges, fly through the air, burn a hole through the sky!
> —Elizabeth Enright, "Nancy"

Hyperbole in Poetry. Poets may also exaggerate for emphasis. What words exaggerate the strength of the batter's swing in the first example? the size of the dead man in the second example?

> And now the pitcher holds the ball, and now he lets it go,
> And now the air is shattered by the force of Casey's blow.
> —Ernest Lawrence Thayer, "Casey at the Bat"

> A hundred strong men strained beneath his coffin
> when they bore him to his grave.   —Gordon Parks, "The Funeral"

Exercises: Using Hyperbole

A. Tell which of the following excerpts contain hyperbole. Explain your answers.

1. I shall be saying this with a sigh
   Somewhere ages and ages hence,

   —Robert Frost, "The Road Not Taken"

2. It was hot. Only the black ants didn't feel it, and they would be happy in a furnace. — "Arap Sang and the Cranes," *retold by* Humphrey Harman

3. Mr. Johansen was a gentle, white-haired, elderly man; he walked slowly with a slight stoop and had a kindly, sad face with large, dark eyes.   —Joan Aiken, "The Serial Garden"

4. Some people say Paul Bunyan wasn't much taller than an ordinary house. Others say he must have been a lot taller to do the things he did, like sticking trees into his pockets and blowing birds out of the air when he sneezed.

   —Adrien Stoutenburg, "Paul Bunyan and Babe, the Blue Ox"

B. Write at least three hyperboles to complete each sentence.

1. My bedroom is so messy that _____.

2. Our car is so small that _____.

3. The speaker talked so long that _____.

Gaze, 1985–1986, ROBERT HUDSON.
Allan Frumkin Gallery, New York City.

Chapter 3 Review

Understanding the Process of Writing

Read the following statements. To which stage or stages in the process of writing—prewriting, drafting, revising, or sharing—does each statement refer?

1. I read the manuscript aloud to myself and discover awkward words or phrases that had escaped me when I read them silently. In the final draft I have been known to spend several hours working over one page, or sometimes one paragraph, in order to get it as close to what I am trying to create as possible.

   —Robert M. McClung

2. Many writers find it useful to keep a notebook. In my own, I keep ideas for plots, characters observed from real life, scenes, scraps of speeches, even single phrases that flash into the mind.

   —Geoffrey Trease

3. I do not worry about length or the order in which the material is written down. Neither do I worry about incomplete sentences, spelling, or grammar....This first draft is like an artist's quick sketch of a landscape or a figure.

   —Ann Petry

4. Inescapably, this reader exists—the same as ourselves; the reader who is also a user of imagination and thought. This reader picks up a story, maybe our new story, and behold, sees it fresh, and meets it with a storehouse of hope and interest.

   —Eudora Welty

5. I usually spend a very long time thinking about it. Sometimes years. You know when you are able to write it. The work goes in before you start, really. You can have variations of the pattern, but the whole book must be there.

   —Doris Lessing

6. The wastepaper basket is the writer's best friend.

— Isaac Bashevis Singer

Understanding the Sounds of Language

Read each of the following samples. In the poem, point out examples of onomatopoeia, alliteration, and rhyme. Next, mark the stressed and unstressed syllables in the last line. In the prose excerpt, point out examples of alliteration.

Puppy

Catch and shake the cobra garden hose.
Scramble on panicky paws and flee
The hiss of tensing nozzle nose,
Or stalk that snobbish bee.

The back yard world is vast as park
With belly-tickle grass and stun
Of sudden sprinkler squalls that arc
Rainbows to the yap yap sun.

— Robert L. Tyler

It was a beautiful afternoon. The street was very high with elms. The light that came through their roof of leaves was green and trembling like light water. Fiona became a little crab crawling among the roots of seaweed. The parked cars were fishes which would eat her up, danger was everywhere. . . .

The houses sat back from their green laps of lawn, silent and substantial, regarding her like people wearing glasses.

— Elizabeth Enright, "Nancy"

Understanding Figures of Speech

Reread the above selections. In each, point out examples of simile, personification, and metaphor.

CHAPTER FOUR

Short Stories

The Trodden Weed, 1951, ANDREW WYETH.
Private Collection.

Reading Literature

Short Stories

A **short story** is a form of writing that tells a story and that can be read at one sitting. Usually the story is about an important event in the life of one character. Short stories are **fiction.** They tell about something that did not really happen. However, many short stories present possible events. They also present characters who act and feel like real people.

The History of the Short Story

Stories have been told since the beginning of time. As writing developed, so did written stories. Brief tales were written down in Egypt as early as 3000 B.C. However, it was not until sometime in the 1800's that great writers in different parts of the world became interested in the short story. Instead of retelling an old tale, these writers made up their own stories. Each writer used his or her own approach. Some wrote exciting adventures. Others showed characters working out everyday problems. Still others made fantasy worlds.

The Elements of a Short Story

The main elements of a short story are character, setting, plot, and theme. You have studied these elements already. Now you will learn more about the parts of a plot.

Plot. The following terms explain what happens in a plot and why.

Exposition. This comes at the beginning of the story. You meet the characters, learn about the setting, and see the beginning of a **conflict,** or struggle.

Rising Action. The struggle grows stronger.

Climax. This is the most exciting point in the story. It is the turning point.

Falling Action. Events move toward the end of the story.

Resolution. The story is brought to an end.

Point of View. The person who tells a story is called the **narrator.** In a short story, the writer can choose either the first-person or the third-person point of view.

In the **first-person point of view,** the story is told by a character in the story. The narrator uses the pronouns *I* and *we.* The reader learns only as much as the narrator can see or hear.

A story told by an outsider who is not part of what is happening is told from the **third-person point of view.** The narrator uses *he, she,* or *they.* In some cases, the narrator knows everything that happens, and what the characters are thinking. Such stories are written from the **omniscient,** or all-knowing, third-person point of view. In other stories, the third-person narrator tells only what one character sees and thinks. These stories are written from a **limited** third-person point of view. The narrator may be either a main or minor character.

How to Read a Short Story

1. Read carefully. Your understanding of the story depends on what you can infer as well as what is directly said.
2. Decide who is telling the story. Does the narrator take part in the action? Is the narrator outside the story? If so, does he or she know everything or only a limited amount?
3. Keep track of what happens and why it happens.

Comprehension Skills

Relationships

A story makes sense when you can see how events and characters are connected. If you don't look for connections, you may not understand what happens.

Finding Relationships Among Events

Sometimes the writer clearly tells how one event is related to another. Often, though, you must use details to help you figure out the relationship. Two important relationships to watch for are time order and cause and effect.

Time Order. **Time order** refers to the sequence, or order, of events in a story: what happens first, second, third, and so on. In some stories, the plot follows the real order of events. In others, the plot moves from present to past to present again. Certain words can give clues about the time order. Some of these words are *after, before, finally, then, now, soon, next,* and *at last.*

Cause and Effect. Often events in a story are related through **cause and effect.** Something that happens early in the story leads to something that happens later. The early event is a **cause.** The later one is an **effect.**

Cause ————————→ Effect
The boy's shoes were worn out.   <u>Therefore</u>, he got a new pair.

Notice the underlined word in the second sentence. *Therefore* is a key word that points to cause and effect. Other key words are *because, so, for this reason, since,* and *that is why.*

You will not always find a key word. Often you will have to figure out how one event causes another.

Finding Relationships Among Characters

Characters may be friends, enemies, relatives, or people thrown together by chance. The characters may be alike or they may be different. How the characters relate is closely connected to the conflict in a story. The resolution of the conflict comes from changes in the characters.

Exercise: Understanding Relationships

Read the following passage from "The Long Way Around" by Jean McCord. Then answer the questions.

> My mother had died two years before when I was twelve, and even though I knew better, sometimes in the middle of the night, I'd wake up in a terrible fear and to comfort myself back to sleep I'd whisper into the pillow, "She's only gone away on a trip. And she'll be back." In the morning I had to face my own lie.
>
> My father had married again last year, and though my two little brothers, Jason and Scott, called this new woman "Mother," my father told me I didn't have to do so. I called her Alice even though sometimes it felt strange to call a grown woman by her first name.

1. Tell what happened two years before this story takes place. What happened one year before?

2. What causes the narrator to whisper that her mother is only gone on a trip?

3. What is the relationship between the narrator and Jason and Scott? between the narrator and Alice? Does the narrator seem to feel close to Alice?

*V*ocabulary Skills

Using Context Clues

As you learned in Chapter One, the **context** of a word is the sentence or group of sentences in which a word appears. Sometimes you will use the general context—the words and ideas in the whole sentence or paragraph—to infer the meaning of a word. At other times you will use context clues such as the four explained here.

Example Clues. An example in the sentence may point to the meaning of an unfamiliar word. Some key words and phrases are *for example, for instance, one kind, like, as, as if, such as, and other,* and *especially.*

> She received [the package] apathetically, almost with dislike, as if she would prefer not to be bothered by this tiresome gift ceremony.
> —Joan Aiken, "The Gift-Giving"

From this example clue, you can guess that *apathetically* means "without interest." The key phrase is *as if.*

Comparison Clues. A sentence may state a comparison that is a clue to the meaning of a word. Some key words and phrases to look for are *in addition to, also, too, moreover, besides, another, both, and all,* and *the same.*

> Besides being dejected at the loss of the necklace, she was also unhappy that there would be no further parties.
> —Guy de Maupassant, "The Necklace"

Besides and *also* signal a comparison. The comparison helps you see that *dejected* means the same as *unhappy.*

Contrast Clues. You sometimes can understand an unfamiliar word if you know its opposite. A contrast clue tells you that two words have opposite meanings. Key words are *although, but, however, on the other hand, unlike, instead, different from, in contrast,* and *not the same.*

> Instead of being delighted, as her husband had hoped, she threw the invitation spitefully upon the table.
> —Guy de Maupassant, "The Necklace"

The sentence makes it clear that someone who acts *spitefully* is not happy. The person is being angry and mean. The key word in this sentence is *instead*.

Words in a Series. Sometimes details are given in a series of words as in this sentence: The yard had maples, oaks, pines, and beeches. If you didn't know the meaning of *beeches,* you could figure out that it is a kind of tree.

> The salesperson opened the cabinet. He showed his customer the necklaces, bracelets, brooches, and rings.

You can guess that a *brooch* is a type of jewelry because all the other words in the series name jewelry.

Exercise: Using Context Clues

Use a context clue to figure out the meaning of each underlined word. Identify the key word or words that helped you discover the meaning.

1. The lawyer studied many subjects <u>zealously</u>, unlike the banker, who had lost his energy and confidence.
2. The circle of trees created an atmosphere of calm, stillness, and <u>tranquillity</u>.
3. Pineapples, tangerines, grapefruit, and <u>kiwis</u> are all in season now.
4. Grandmother treasured both the beautiful coat and the lovely <u>shawl</u>.

Great Classic Stories

The classic stories in this chapter were written between the late 1800's and the mid-1900's. Many of the details of daily life that these stories describe have changed. However, the feelings of love, fear, and longing that move the characters are just the same. The stories are classic because we can still enjoy them as did readers of long ago.

Spring Tryout, 1944, THOMAS HART BENTON. Charles H. MacNider Museum, Mason City, Iowa.

Hearts and Hands

O. HENRY

Have you ever unexpectedly met an old friend from your past? In this story, a man meets a woman he once knew. In the conversation that follows, what does he leave unsaid?

At Denver there was an influx of passengers into the coaches on the eastbound express. In one coach there sat a very pretty young woman dressed in elegant taste and surrounded by all the luxurious comforts of an experienced traveler. Among the newcomers were two young men, one of handsome presence with a bold, frank countenance and manner; the other a ruffled, glum-faced person, heavily built and roughly dressed. The two were handcuffed together.

As they passed down the aisle of the coach, the only vacant seat offered was a reversed one facing the attractive young woman. Here, the linked couple seated themselves. The young woman's glance fell upon them with a distant, swift disinterest; then with a lovely smile brightening her face and a tender pink tingeing her rounded cheeks, she held out a little gray-gloved hand. When she spoke, her voice, full, sweet, and deliberate, proclaimed that its owner was accustomed to speak and to be heard.

"Well, Mr. Easton, if you *will* make me speak first, I suppose I must. Don't you ever recognize old friends when you meet them in the West?"

The younger man roused himself sharply at the sound of her voice. He seemed to struggle with a slight embarrassment which he threw off instantly, and then clasped her fingers with his left hand.

"It's Miss Fairchild," he said, with a smile. "I'll ask you to excuse the other hand; it's otherwise engaged just at present."

He slightly raised his right hand, bound at the wrist by the shining "bracelet" to the left one of his companion. The glad look in the girl's eyes slowly changed to a bewildered horror. The glow faded from her cheeks. Her lips parted in a vague,

Hearts and Hands   145

relaxing distress. Easton, with a little laugh as if amused, was about to speak again when the other forestalled him. The glum-faced man had been watching the girl's expression with veiled glances from his keen, shrewd eyes.

"You'll excuse me for speaking, miss, but I see you're acquainted with the marshal here. If you'll ask him to speak a word for me when we get to the pen, he'll do it, and it'll make things easier for me there. He's taking me to Leavenworth prison. It's seven years they give for counterfeiting."

"Oh!" said the girl, with a deep breath and returning color. "So that is what you are doing out here? A marshal!"

"My dear Miss Fairchild," said Easton, calmly, "I had to do something. Money has a way of taking wings unto itself, and you know it takes money to keep step with our crowd in Washington. I saw this opening in the West, and—well, a marshalship isn't quite as high a position as that of ambassador, but——"

"The ambassador," said the girl, warmly, "doesn't call any more. He needn't ever have done so. You ought to know that. And so now you are one of these dashing Western heroes, and you ride and shoot and go into all kinds of dangers. That's different from the Washington life. You have been missed."

The girl's eyes, fascinated, went back, widening a little, to rest upon the glittering handcuffs.

"Don't you worry about them, miss," said the other man. "All marshals handcuff themselves to their prisoners to keep them from getting away. Mr. Easton knows his business."

"Will we see you again soon in Washington?" asked the girl.

"Not soon, I think," said Easton. "My butterfly days are over, I fear."

"I love the West," said the girl, irrelevantly. Her eyes were shining softly. She looked away out the car window. She began to speak truly and simply, without the gloss of style and manner: "Mamma and I spent the summer in Denver. She went home a week ago because Father was slightly ill. I could live and be happy in the West. I think the air here agrees with me. Money isn't everything. But people always misunderstand things and remain stupid——"

"Say, Mr. Marshal," growled the glum-faced man. "This isn't quite fair. I'm needin' a drink, and haven't had a smoke all day. Haven't you talked long enough? Take me to the smoker now, won't you? I'm half dead for a pipe."

The bound travelers rose to their feet, Easton with the same slow smile on his face.

"I can't deny a petition for tobacco," he said, lightly. "It's the one friend of the unfortunate. Good-bye, Miss Fairchild. Duty calls, you know." He held out his hand for a farewell.

"It's too bad you are not going East,"

Illustration from *The Railroad Book* by E. Boyd Smith. © 1913 the Fairfield County Council, Boy Scouts of America. © Renewed 1941. Reprinted by Permission of Houghton Mifflin Company, Boston.

she said, reclothing herself with manner and style. "But you must go on to Leavenworth, I suppose?"

"Yes," said Easton, "I must go on to Leavenworth."

The two men sidled down the aisle into the smoker.

The two passengers in a seat nearby had heard most of the conversation. Said one of them: "That marshal's a good sort of chap. Some of these Western fellows are all right."

"Pretty young to hold an office like that, isn't he?" asked the other.

"Young!" exclaimed the first speaker, "why—Oh! didn't you catch on? Say— did you ever know an officer to handcuff a prisoner to his *right* hand?"

O. Henry *(1862–1910)* was the pen name of William Sydney Porter. Before he became a famous writer, O. Henry worked as a store clerk, journalist, and bank teller. He served a prison term for bookkeeping irregularities at the bank, but always claimed innocence. O. Henry's stories usually have surprise endings. Two popular collections of his stories are *Of Cabbages and Kings* and *The Four Million.*

Developing Comprehension Skills

1. List the following events in time order.
   a. Miss Fairchild and Mr. Easton meet and speak on the train.
   b. Miss Fairchild and Mr. Easton become friends in Washington.
   c. Mr. Easton is arrested and convicted for counterfeiting.
   d. Miss Fairchild and Mr. Easton part for the last time.
   e. Mr. Easton goes West to seek his fortune.
   f. The marshal pretends to be the prisoner. With which event does the story begin? Which events took place in the past, before the action that is described in this story?

2. The title suggests the two different ways characters in the story are connected. Whose hands are linked together—what is the relationship between the two? Whose hearts seem to be connected in some way?

3. Describe the man who is the prisoner and the man who is the marshal. How do you know which is which? In reading the story, when did you find out?

4. In what way does the marshal show that he is a "good sort of chap"? Which person does he help more, Miss Fairchild or Mr. Easton? Explain your answer.

Reading Literature: Short Stories

1. **Understanding Exposition.** Many short stories open with **exposition.** That is, the first paragrapah or so gives the reader the background of the story. In the first paragraph of "Hearts and Hands," what do you learn about the main characters and the setting of the story?

2. **Studying a Surprise Ending.** O. Henry's stories often have surprise endings. The reader is expecting a certain outcome, but the actual ending is different. How is the ending of this story a surprise? What did you think was happening during the story? What was actually true?

3. **Recognizing Irony.** One kind of **irony** is a contrast between what is said and what is actually meant. In this story many of the remarks made by Mr. Easton to Miss Fairchild turn out to be ironic. Once you realize that Easton is the person going to jail, many of his comments take on a second meaning. For each of the following remarks by Mr. Easton, identify what Miss Fairchild thought he meant and then tell what second meaning can be understood.
   a. "I saw this opening in the West. . . ."
   b. ". . . it takes money to keep step with our crowd in Washington."
   c. "My butterfly days are over, I fear."
   d. "I must go on to Leavenworth."

Vocabulary

Recognizing the Meaning of Slang and Colloquialisms. One kind of **slang** refers to new words or words with new meanings that are used by a particular group. Two examples are *fencing* (selling stolen goods) and *on the lam* (hiding from the police). **Colloquialisms** are common phrases that occur in everyday conversation. Some examples are *rough* (difficult) and *clear up* (finish). Often you can figure out the meanings of these expressions by using context clues.

For each of the expressions below, reread the paragraph in which the expression is used and tell what the word or phrase means. Identify how the context suggests the meaning.

1. bracelet (page 145, paragraph 6)
2. pen (page 146, paragraph 1)
3. to keep step (page 146, paragraph 3)
4. catch on (page 147, paragraph 5)

Critical Thinking

Making Inferences. In this story the writer has his characters mention details that the reader must use to **infer**, or figure out, what is going on. Reread the story carefully to find details that support the following inferences:

1. Mr. Easton is the prisoner and the burly man is the marshal.
2. Miss Fairchild considers Mr. Easton attractive.
3. Although the marshal looks rough and dull, he is thoughtful of others and quick-thinking.

Developing Writing Skills

1. **Analyzing Cause and Effect.** Some of the events in this story happen by chance. Others come about because a character makes a deliberate choice to do or say something. After thinking about the events in the story, decide whether you think chance or deliberate choice is more important. In a brief paragraph state which you think is more important and give two or three examples.

   Prewriting. Make two columns, one headed *Chance* and the other headed *Deliberate Choice*. List each event that happens or is reported in the story under one of the two columns. Review the events in each column and decide whether you think chance or deliberate choice seems to be more important.

   Drafting. Write a topic sentence that states which cause you think is more important. You can write a statement such as "In 'Hearts and Hands' chance (*or* deliberate choice) is more important in causing the events of the story." Then give two or three examples from your list to support your statement.

   Revising and Sharing. In revising your paragraph, consider the following questions. Is the opening statement clear? Have you chosen examples that support your position? Do your examples include enough details?

2. **Writing a Conversation.** Imagine that the marshal in "Hearts and Hands" had not pretended to be the prisoner. Write a conversation Mr. Easton and Miss Fairchild might have had. How might the two characters feel toward each other? What might they say? As you write, use the characters' own words as much as possible. Try to use the style of speaking in the story. Follow the steps in the process of writing: prewriting, drafting, revising, and sharing. If you need help with the writing process, refer to the Guidelines for the Process of Writing on page 623 in the handbook at the back of the book.

Rikki-tikki-tavi

RUDYARD KIPLING

This story is about a series of battles in India. The warriors are not human beings but they do have human qualities. As you read, think about the qualities that make Nag a wicked villain and Rikki-tikki-tavi a hero.

This is the story of the great war that Rikki-tikki-tavi (rik′ē tik′ē tav′ē) fought single-handed, through the bathrooms of the big bungalow in Segowlee cantonment.[1] Darzee (där zē′) the Tailorbird helped him, and Chuchundra (chōō chun′drə) the Muskrat, who never comes out into the middle of the floor, but always creeps round by the wall, gave him advice, but Rikki-tikki did the real fighting.

He was a mongoose, rather like a little cat in his fur and his tail, but quite like a weasel in his head and his habits. His eyes and the end of his restless nose were pink. He could scratch himself anywhere he pleased with any leg, front or back, that he chose to use. He could fluff up his tail till it looked like a bottle brush, and his war cry as he scuttled through the long grass was *Rikk-tikk-tikki-tikki-tchk!*

One day, a high summer flood washed him out of the burrow where he lived with his father and mother, and carried him, kicking and clucking, down a roadside ditch. He found a little wisp of grass floating there, and clung to it till he lost his senses. When he revived, he was lying in the hot sun on the middle of a garden path, very draggled indeed, and a small boy was saying, "Here's a dead mongoose. Let's have a funeral."

"No," said his mother, "let's take him in and dry him. Perhaps he isn't really dead."

They took him into the house, and a big man picked him up between his finger and thumb and said he was not dead but half choked. So they wrapped him in cotton wool, and warmed him over a little fire, and he opened his eyes and sneezed.

"Now," said the big man (he was an

---

1. **Segowlee** (sē gou′lē) **cantonment**–A British army post in Segowlee, India.

Englishman who had just moved into the bungalow), "don't frighten him, and we'll see what he'll do."

It is the hardest thing in the world to frighten a mongoose, because he is eaten up from nose to tail with curiosity. The motto of all the mongoose family is "Run and find out," and Rikki-tikki was a true mongoose. He looked at the cotton wool, decided that it was not good to eat, ran all around the table, sat up and put his fur in order, scratched himself, and jumped on the small boy's shoulder.

"Don't be frightened, Teddy," said his father. "That's his way of making friends."

"Ouch! He's tickling under my chin," said Teddy.

Rikki-tikki looked down between the boy's collar and neck, snuffed at his ear, and climbed down to the floor, where he sat rubbing his nose.

"Good gracious," said Teddy's mother, "and that's a wild creature! I suppose he's so tame because we've been kind to him."

"All mongooses are like that," said her husband. "If Teddy doesn't pick him up by the tail, or try to put him in a cage, he'll run in and out of the house all day long. Let's give him something to eat."

They gave him a little piece of raw meat. Rikki-tikki liked it immensely; and when it was finished, he went out into the veranda and sat in the sunshine and fluffed up his fur to make it dry to the roots. Then he felt better.

"There are more things to find out about in this house," he said to himself, "than all my family could find out in all their lives. I shall certainly stay and find out."

He spent all that day roaming over the house. He nearly drowned himself in the bathtubs, put his nose into the ink on a writing table, and burned it on the end of the big man's cigar, for he climbed up in the big man's lap to see how writing was done. At nightfall he ran into Teddy's nursery to watch how kerosene lamps were lighted, and when Teddy went to bed, Rikki-tikki climbed up too. But he was a restless companion, because he had to get up and attend to every noise all through the night, and find out what made it. Teddy's mother and father came in, the last thing, to look at their boy, and Rikki-tikki was awake on the pillow.

"I don't like that," said Teddy's mother. "He may bite the child."

"He'll do no such thing," said the father. "Teddy is safer with that little beast than if he had a bloodhound to watch him. If a snake came into the nursery now——"

But Teddy's mother wouldn't think of anything so awful.

Early in the morning Rikki-tikki came to early breakfast in the veranda, riding on Teddy's shoulder, and they gave him banana and some boiled egg. He sat on all their laps one after the other, because every well-brought-up mongoose always hopes to be a house mongoose some day and have rooms to run about in; and Rikki-tikki's mother (she used to live in the general's house at Segowlee) had carefully told Rikki what to do if ever he came across white men.

Then Rikki-tikki went out into the garden to see what was to be seen. It was a large garden, only half cultivated, with bushes, as big as summer houses, of Marshal Niel roses, lime and orange trees, clumps of bamboos, and thickets of high grass. Rikki-tikki licked his lips. "This is a splendid hunting ground," he said, and his tail grew bottle-bushy at the thought of it; and he scuttled up and down the garden, snuffing here and there till he heard very sorrowful voices in a thornbush. It was Darzee the Tailorbird and his wife. They had made a beautiful nest by pulling two big leaves together and stitching them up the edges with fibers, and had filled the hollow with cotton and downy fluff. The nest swayed to and fro, as they sat on the rim and cried.

"What is the matter?" asked Rikki-tikki.

"We are very miserable," said Darzee. "One of our babies fell out of the nest yesterday and Nag (näg) ate him."

"H'm," said Rikki-tikki, "that is very sad—but I am a stranger here. Who is Nag?"

Darzee and his wife only cowered down in the nest without answering, for from the thick grass at the foot of the bush there came a low hiss—a horrid cold sound that made Rikki-tikki jump back two clear feet. Then inch by inch out of the grass rose up the head and spread hood of Nag, the big black cobra, and he was five feet long from tongue to tail. When he had lifted one-third of himself clear of the ground, he stayed balancing to and fro exactly as a dandelion tuft balances in the wind, and he looked at Rikki-tikki with the wicked snake's eyes that never change their expression, whatever the snake may be thinking of.

"Who is Nag?" said he. "*I* am Nag. The great God Brahm[2] put his mark upon all our people, when the first cobra spread his hood to keep the sun off Brahm as he slept. Look, and be afraid!"

He spread out his hood more than ever, and Rikki-tikki saw the spectacle mark on the back of it that looks exactly like the eye part of a hook-and-eye fastening. He was afraid for the minute, but it is impossible for a mongoose to stay frightened for any length of time; and though Rikki-tikki had never met a live cobra before, his mother had fed him on dead ones, and he knew that all a grown mongoose's business in life was to fight and eat snakes. Nag knew that too and, at the bottom of his cold heart, he was afraid.

"Well," said Rikki-tikki, and his tail began to fluff up again, "marks or no

---

2. **Brahm** (bräm)–The supreme god of the Hindu religion.

marks, do you think it is right for you to eat fledglings out of a nest?"

Nag was thinking to himself, and watching the least little movement in the grass behind Rikki-tikki. He knew that mongooses in the garden meant death sooner or later for him and his family, but he wanted to get Rikki-tikki off his guard. So he dropped his head a little, and put it on one side.

"Let us talk," he said. "You eat eggs. Why should not I eat birds?"

"Behind you! Look behind you!" sang Darzee.

Rikki-tikki knew better than to waste time in staring. He jumped up in the air as high as he could go, and just under him whizzed by the head of Nagaina (nə gī′nə), Nag's wicked wife. She had crept up behind him as he was talking, to make an end of him. He heard her savage hiss as the stroke missed. He came down almost across her back, and if he had been an old mongoose, he would have known that then was the time to break her back with one bite; but he was afraid of the terrible, lashing return stroke of the cobra. He bit, indeed, but did not bite long enough; and he jumped clear of the whisking tail, leaving Nagaina torn and angry.

"Wicked, wicked Darzee!" said Nag, lashing up as high as he could reach toward the nest in the thornbush. But Darzee had built it out of reach of snakes, and it only swayed to and fro.

Rikki-tikki felt his eyes growing red and hot (when a mongoose's eyes grow red, he is angry); and he sat back on his tail and hind legs like a little kangaroo, and looked all round him, and chattered with rage. But Nag and Nagaina had disappeared into the grass. When a snake misses its stroke, it never says anything or gives any sign of what it means to do next. Rikki-tikki did not care to follow them, for he did not feel sure that he could manage two snakes at once. So he trotted off to the gravel path near the house, and sat down to think. It was a serious matter for him.

If you read the old books of natural history, you will find they say that when the mongoose fights the snake and happens to get bitten, he runs off and eats some herb that cures him. That is not true. The victory is only a matter of quickness of eye and quickness of foot—snake's blow against mongoose's jump—and as no eye can follow the motion of a snake's head when it strikes, this makes things much more wonderful than any magic herb. Rikki-tikki knew he was a young mongoose, and it made him all the more pleased to think that he had managed to escape a blow from behind.

It gave him confidence in himself, and when Teddy came running down the path, Rikki-tikki was ready to be petted. But just as Teddy was stooping, something wriggled a little in the dust, and a tiny voice said: "Be careful. I am Death!" It was Karait (kə rīt′), the dusty brown snakeling that lies for choice on the dusty earth; and his bite is as dangerous as the cobra's. But he is so small that nobody thinks of him, and so he does the more harm to people.

Rikki-tikki's eyes grew red again, and he danced up to Karait with the peculiar rocking, swaying motion that he had inherited from his family. It looks very funny, but it is so perfectly balanced a gait that you can fly off from it at any angle you please, and in dealing with snakes this is an advantage.

If Rikki-tikki had only known, he was doing a much more dangerous thing than fighting Nag; for Karait is so small, and can turn so quickly, that unless Rikki bit him close to the back of the head, he would get the return stroke in his eye or his lip. But Rikki did not know. His eyes were all red, and he rocked back and forth, looking for a good place to hold. Karait struck out. Rikki jumped sideways and tried to run in, but the wicked little dusty gray head lashed within a fraction of his shoulder, and he had to jump over the body, and the head followed his heels close.

Teddy shouted to the house, "Oh, look here! Our mongoose is killing a snake." And Rikki-tikki heard a scream from Teddy's mother. His father ran out with a stick, but by the time he came up, Karait had lunged out once too far, and Rikki-tikki had sprung, jumped on the snake's back, dropped his head far between his forelegs, bitten as high up the back as he could get hold, and rolled away.

That bite paralyzed Karait, and Rikki-tikki was just going to eat him up from the tail, after the custom of his family at dinner, when he remembered that a full meal makes a slow mongoose; and if he wanted all his strength and quickness ready, he must keep himself thin. He went away for a dust bath under the castor-oil bushes, while Teddy's father beat the dead Karait.

"What is the use of that?" thought Rikki-tikki. "I have settled it all."

And then Teddy's mother picked him up from the dust and hugged him, crying that he had saved Teddy from death; and Teddy's father said that he was a providence, and Teddy looked on with big, scared eyes. Rikki-tikki was rather amused at all the fuss, which, of course, he did not understand. Teddy's mother might just as well have petted Teddy for playing in the dust. Rikki was thoroughly enjoying himself.

That night at dinner, walking to and fro among the wineglasses on the table, he might have stuffed himself three times over with nice things. But he remembered Nag and Nagaina, and though it was very pleasant to be patted and petted by Teddy's mother, and to sit on Teddy's shoulder, his eyes would get red from time to time, and he would go off into his long war cry of "*Rikk-tikk-tikki-tikki-tchk!*"

Teddy carried him off to bed and insisted on Rikki-tikki sleeping under his chin. Rikki-tikki was too well bred to bite or scratch, but as soon as Teddy was asleep, he went off for his nightly walk round the house; and in the dark he ran up against Chuchundra the Muskrat, creeping around by the wall. Chuchundra is a brokenhearted little beast. He whimpers and cheeps all the night, trying to make up his mind to run into the middle of the room. But he never gets there.

"Don't kill me," said Chuchundra, almost weeping. "Rikki-tikki, don't kill me!"

"Do you think a snake-killer kills muskrats?" said Rikki-tikki scornfully.

"Those who kill snakes get killed by snakes," said Chuchundra, more sorrowfully than ever. "And how am I to be sure that Nag won't mistake me for you some dark night?"

"There's not the least danger," said Rikki-tikki. "But Nag is in the garden, and I know you don't go there."

"My cousin Chua the Rat told me——" said Chuchundra, and then stopped.

"Told you what?"

"H'sh! Nag is everywhere, Rikki-tikki. You should have talked to Chua in the garden."

"I didn't—so you must tell me. Quick, Chuchundra, or I'll bite you!"

Chuchundra sat down and cried till the tears rolled off his whiskers. "I am a very poor man," he sobbed. "I never had spirit enough to run out into the middle of the room. H'sh! I mustn't tell you anything. Can't you *hear*, Rikki-tikki?"

Rikki-tikki listened. The house was as still as still, but he thought he could just catch the faintest *scratch-scratch* in the world—a noise as faint as that of a wasp walking on a windowpane—the dry scratch of a snake's scales on brick work.

"That's Nag or Nagaina," he said to himself, "and he is crawling into the bathroom sluice. You're right, Chuchundra; I should have talked to Chua."

He stole off to Teddy's bathroom, but there was nothing there, and then to Teddy's mother's bathroom. At the bottom of the smooth plaster wall there was a brick pulled out to make a sluice for the bath water, and as Rikki-tikki stole in by the masonry curb where the bath is put, he heard Nag and Nagaina whispering together outside in the moonlight.

"When the house is emptied of people," said Nagaina to her husband, "*he* will have to go away, and then the garden will be our own again. Go in quietly, and remember that the big man who killed Karait is the first one to bite. Then come out and tell me, and we will hunt for Rikki-tikki together."

"But are you sure that there is anything to be gained by killing the people?" said Nag.

"Everything. When there were no people in the bungalow, did we have any mongoose in the garden? So long as the bungalow is empty, we are king and queen of the garden; and remember that as soon as our eggs in the melon bed hatch (as they may tomorrow), our children will need room and quiet."

"I had not thought of that," said Nag. "I will go, but there is no need that we should hunt for Rikki-tikki afterwards. I will kill the big man and his wife, and the child if I can, and come away quietly. Then the bungalow will be empty, and Rikki-tikki will go."

Rikki-tikki tingled all over with rage and hatred at this, and then Nag's head came through the sluice, and his five feet of cold body followed it. Angry as he was, Rikki-tikki was very frightened as he saw the size of the big cobra. Nag coiled himself up, raised his head, and looked into the bathroom in the dark, and Rikki could see his eyes glitter.

"Now, if I kill him here, Nagaina will know; and if I fight him on the open floor, the odds are in his favor. What am I to do?" said Rikki-tikki-tavi.

Nag waved to and fro, and then Rikki-tikki heard him drinking from the biggest water jar that was used to fill the bath. "That is good," said the snake. "Now, when Karait was killed, the big man had a stick. He may have that stick still, but when he comes in to bathe in the morning he will not have a stick. I shall wait here till he comes. Nagaina—do you hear me?—I shall wait here in the cool till daytime."

There was no answer from outside, so

Rikki-tikki knew Nagaina had gone away. Nag coiled himself down, coil by coil, round the bulge at the bottom of the water jar, and Rikki-tikki stayed still as death. After an hour he began to move, muscle by muscle, toward the jar. Nag was asleep, and Rikki-tikki looked at his big back, wondering which would be the best place for a good hold. "If I don't break his back at the first jump," said Rikki, "he can still fight. And if he fights—O Rikki!" He looked at the thickness of the neck below the hood, but that was too much for him; and a bite near the tail would only make Nag savage.

"It must be the head," he said at last; "the head above the hood. And, when I am once there, I must not let go."

Then he jumped. The head was lying a little clear of the water jar, under the curve of it; and, as his teeth met, Rikki braced his back against the bulge of the red earthenware to hold down the head. This gave him just one second's purchase, and he made the most of it. Then he was battered to and fro as a rat is shaken by a dog—to and fro on the floor, up and down, and around in great circles, but his eyes were red and he held on as the body cart-whipped over the floor, upsetting the tin dipper and the soap dish and the flesh brush, and banged against the tin side of the bath.

As he held, he closed his jaws tighter and tighter, for he made sure he would be banged to death; and, for the honor of his family, he preferred to be found with his teeth locked. He was dizzy, aching, and felt shaken to pieces when something went off like a thunderclap just behind him. A hot wind knocked him senseless, and red fire singed his fur. The big man had been awakened by the noise, and had fired both barrels of a shotgun into Nag just behind the hood.

Rikki-tikki held on with his eyes shut, for now he was quite sure he was dead. But the head did not move, and the big man picked him up and said, "It's the mongoose again, Alice. The little chap has saved *our* lives now."

Then Teddy's mother came in with a very white face, and saw what was left of Nag, and Rikki-tikki dragged himself to Teddy's bedroom and spent half the rest of the night shaking himself tenderly to find out whether he really was broken into forty pieces, as he fancied.

When morning came, he was very stiff, but well pleased with his doings. "Now I have Nagaina to settle with, and she will be worse than five Nags; and there's no knowing when the eggs she spoke of will hatch. Goodness! I must go and see Darzee," he said.

Without waiting for breakfast, Rikki-tikki ran to the thornbush where Darzee was singing a song of triumph at the top of his voice. The news of Nag's death was all over the garden, for the sweeper had thrown the body on the rubbish heap.

"Oh, you stupid tuft of feathers!" said

Rikki-tikki angrily. "Is this the time to sing?"

"Nag is dead—is dead—is dead!" sang Darzee. "The valiant Rikki-tikki caught him by the head and held fast. The big man brought the bang stick, and Nag fell in two pieces! He will never eat my babies again."

"All that's true enough. But where's Nagaina?" said Rikki-tikki, looking carefully round him.

"Nagaina came to the bathroom sluice and called for Nag," Darzee went on, "and Nag came out on the end of a stick—the sweeper picked him up on the end of a stick and threw him upon the rubbish heap. Let us sing about the great, the red-eyed Rikki-tikki!" And Darzee filled his throat and sang.

"If I could get up to your nest, I'd roll your babies out!" said Rikki-tikki. "You don't know when to do the right thing at the right time. You're safe enough in your nest there, but it's war for me, down here. Stop singing a minute, Darzee."

"For the great, the beautiful Rikki-tikki's sake I will stop," said Darzee. "What is it, O Killer of the terrible Nag?"

"Where is Nagaina, for the third time?"

"On the rubbish heap by the stables, mourning for Nag. Great is Rikki-tikki with the white teeth."

"Bother my white teeth! Have you ever heard where she keeps her eggs?"

"In the melon bed, on the end nearest the wall, where the sun strikes nearly all day. She hid them there weeks ago."

"And you never thought it worthwhile to tell me? The end nearest the wall, you said?"

"Rikki-tikki, you are not going to eat her eggs?"

"Not eat exactly, no. Darzee, if you have a grain of sense you will fly off to the stables and pretend that your wing is broken, and let Nagaina chase you away to this bush. I must get to the melon bed, and if I went there now she'd see me."

Darzee was a feather-brained little fellow who could never hold more than one idea at a time in his head. And just because he knew that Nagaina's children were born in eggs like his own, he didn't think at first that it was fair to kill them. But his wife was a sensible bird, and she knew that cobra's eggs meant young cobras later on. So she flew off from the nest, and left Darzee to keep the babies warm, and continue his song about the death of Nag. Darzee was very like a man in some ways.

She fluttered in front of Nagaina by the rubbish heap and cried out, "Oh, my wing is broken! The boy in the house threw a stone at me and broke it." Then she fluttered more desperately than ever.

Nagaina lifted up her head and hissed. "You warned Rikki-tikki when I would have killed him. Indeed and truly, you've chosen a bad place to be lame in." And she moved toward Darzee's wife, slipping along over the dust.

"The boy broke it with a stone!"

shrieked Darzee's wife.

"Well! It may be some consolation to you when you're dead to know that I shall settle accounts with the boy. My husband lies on the rubbish heap this morning, but before night the boy in the house will lie very still. What is the use of running away? I am sure to catch you. Little fool, look at me!"

Darzee's wife knew better than to do *that,* for a bird who looks at a snake's eyes gets so frightened that she cannot move. Darzee's wife fluttered on, piping sorrowfully, and never leaving the ground, and Nagaina quickened her pace.

Rikki-tikki heard them going up the path from the stables, and he raced for the end of the melon patch near the wall. There, in the warm litter above the melons, very cunningly hidden, he found twenty-five eggs, about the size of a bantam's eggs, but with whitish skins instead of shells.

"I was not a day too soon," he said, for he could see the baby cobras curled up inside the skin, and he knew that the minute they were hatched they could each kill a man or a mongoose. He bit off the tops of the eggs as fast as he could, taking care to crush the young cobras, and turned over the litter from time to time to see whether he had missed any. At last there were only three eggs left, and Rikki-tikki began to chuckle to himself, when he heard Darzee's wife screaming.

"Rikki-tikki, I led Nagaina toward the

house, and she has gone into the veranda and—oh, come quickly—she means killing!"

Rikki-tikki smashed two eggs, and tumbled backward down the melon bed with the third egg in his mouth, and scuttled to the veranda as hard as he could put foot to the ground. Teddy and his mother and father were there at early breakfast, but Rikki-tikki saw that they were not eating anything. They sat stone-still, and their faces were white. Nagaina was coiled up on the matting by Teddy's chair, within easy striking distance of Teddy's bare leg; and she was swaying to and fro, singing a song of triumph.

"Son of the big man that killed Nag," she hissed, "stay still. I am not ready yet. Wait a little. Keep very still, all you three! If you move I strike, and if you do not move I strike. Oh, foolish people, who killed my Nag!"

Teddy's eyes were fixed on his father, and all his father could do was to whisper, "Sit still, Teddy. You mustn't move. Teddy, keep still."

Then Rikki-tikki came up and cried, "Turn round, Nagaina. Turn and fight!"

"All in good time," she said, without moving her eyes. "I will settle my account with you presently. Look at your friends, Rikki-tikki. They are still and white. They are afraid. They dare not move, and if you come a step nearer I strike."

"Look at your eggs," said Rikki-tikki, "in the melon bed near the wall. Go and look, Nagaina!"

The big snake turned half around, and saw the egg on the veranda. "Ah-h! Give it to me," she said.

Rikki-tikki put his paws on each side of the egg, and his eyes were blood-red. "What price for a snake's egg? For a young cobra? For a young king cobra? For the last—the very last of the brood? The ants are eating all the others down by the melon bed."

Nagaina spun clear round, forgetting

everything for the sake of the one egg. Rikki-tikki saw Teddy's father shoot out a big hand, catch Teddy by the shoulder, and drag him across the little table with the teacups, safe and out of reach of Nagaina.

"Tricked! Tricked! Tricked! *Rikk-tck-tck!*" chuckled Rikki-tikki. "The boy is safe, and it was I—I—I that caught Nag by the hood last night in the bathroom." Then he began to jump up and down, all four feet together, his head close to the floor. "He threw me to and fro, but he could not shake me off. He was dead before the big man blew him in two. I did it! *Rikki-tikki-tck-tck!* Come then, Nagaina. Come and fight with me. You shall not be a widow long."

Nagaina saw that she had lost her chance of killing Teddy, and the egg lay between Rikki-tikki's paws. "Give me the egg, Rikki-tikki. Give me the last of my eggs, and I will go away and never come back," she said, lowering her hood.

"Yes, you will go away, and you will never come back. For you will go to the rubbish heap with Nag. Fight, widow! The big man has gone for his gun. Fight!"

Rikki-tikki was bounding all round Nagaina, keeping just out of reach of her stroke, his little eyes like hot coals. Nagaina gathered herself together and flung out at him. Rikki-tikki jumped up and backward. Again and again and again she struck, and each time her head came with a whack on the matting of the veranda, and she gathered herself together like a watch spring. Then Rikki-tikki danced in a circle to get behind her, and Nagaina spun round to keep her head to his head, so that the rustle of her tail on the matting sounded like dry leaves blown along by the wind.

He had forgotten the egg. It still lay on the veranda, and Nagaina came nearer and nearer to it, till at last, while Rikki-tikki was drawing breath, she caught it in her mouth, turned to the veranda steps, and flew like an arrow down the path, with Rikki-tikki behind her. When the cobra runs for her life, she goes like a whiplash flicked across a horse's neck. Rikki-tikki knew that he must catch her, or all the trouble would begin again.

She headed straight for the long grass by the thornbush, and as he was running, Rikki-tikki heard Darzee still singing his foolish little song of triumph. But Darzee's wife was wiser. She flew off her nest as Nagaina came along, and flapped her wings about Nagaina's head. If Darzee had helped her, they might have turned her, but Nagaina only lowered her hood and went on. Still, the instant's delay brought Rikki-tikki up to her, and as she plunged into the rathole where she and Nag used to live, his little white teeth were clenched on her tail, and he went down with her—and very few mongooses, however wise and old they may be, care to follow a cobra into its hole.

It was dark in the hole; and Rikki-tikki

never knew when it might open out and give Nagaina room to turn and strike at him. He held on savagely, and stuck out his feet to act as brakes on the dark slope of the hot, moist earth.

Then the grass by the mouth of the hole stopped waving, and Darzee said, "It is all over with Rikki-tikki! We must sing his death song. Valiant Rikki-tikki is dead! For Nagaina will surely kill him underground."

So he sang a very mournful song that he made up on the spur of the minute; and just as he got to the most touching part, the grass quivered again, and Rikki-tikki, covered with dirt, dragged himself out of the hole leg by leg, licking his whiskers. Darzee stopped with a little shout. Rikki-tikki shook some of the dust out of his fur and sneezed. "It is all over," he said. "The widow will never come out again." And the red ants that live between the grass stems heard him, and began to troop down one after another to see if he had spoken the truth.

Rikki-tikki curled himself up in the grass and slept where he was—slept and slept till it was late in the afternoon, for he had done a hard day's work.

"Now," he said, when he awoke, "I will go back to the house. Tell the Coppersmith, Darzee, and he will tell the garden that Nagaina is dead."

The Coppersmith is a bird who makes a noise exactly like the beating of a little hammer on a copper pot. The reason he is always making it is that he is the town crier to every Indian garden, and tells all the news to everybody who cares to listen. As Rikki-tikki went up the path, he heard his "attention" notes like a tiny dinner gong, and then the steady *"Ding-dong-tock! Nag is dead—dong! Nagaina is dead! Ding-dong-tock!"* That set all the birds in the garden singing, and the frogs croaking, for Nag and Nagaina used to eat frogs as well as little birds.

When Rikki got to the house, Teddy and Teddy's mother (she looked very white still, for she had been fainting) and Teddy's father came out and almost cried over him; and that night he ate all that was given him till he could eat no more, and went to bed on Teddy's shoulder, where Teddy's mother saw him when she came to look late at night.

"He saved our lives and Teddy's life," she said to her husband. "Just think, he saved all our lives."

Rikki-tikki woke up with a jump, for the mongooses are light sleepers.

"Oh, it's you," said he. "What are you bothering for? All the cobras are dead. And if they weren't, I'm here."

Rikki-tikki had a right to be proud of himself. But he did not grow too proud, and he kept that garden as a mongoose should keep it, with tooth and jump and spring and bite, till never a cobra dared show its head inside the walls.

Rudyard Kipling *(1865–1936)* was born in India, of British parents. At the age of six, he was sent back to England for his schooling. Kipling later returned to India as a journalist and worked there for seven years. In his spare time he wrote stories and poems, which he published in England. In 1892 he married an American woman and moved to Vermont. Kipling continued to write nonsense stories, poetry, and longer works of fiction. *Just-So Stories* and *The Jungle Book* are two of his well-known books. He won a Nobel Prize in literature in 1907. This prize is an international award given once a year to an outstanding writer. It is one of the highest honors a writer can receive.

Developing Comprehension Skills

1. How does Rikki-tikki-tavi come to live at the bungalow? How does he learn about the cobras?

2. List the enemies Rikki-tikki fights and defeats, in the order in which the battles occur. Tell what caused each battle.

3. Explain the part that each of the following animals plays in helping Rikki-tikki defeat the snakes: Darzee, Darzee's wife, Chuchundra.

4. What effect does the news that the cobra eggs are about to hatch have on Rikki-tikki's plans? What effect does the sight of the last cobra egg have on Nagaina?

5. How does the attitude of Teddy's mother change toward Rikki-tikki in the course of the story? Does Teddy's father's view or Teddy's view of Rikki-tikki change?

6. What is more important to Rikki-tikki in his battles with his enemies—his physical strength or his strategy? Which of Rikki-tikki's battles do you think took the greatest courage?

Reading Literature: Short Stories

1. **Determining Point of View.** This story is told from the **third-person point of view.** The narrator is outside of the story. Does the narrator report actions or conversations that only one character could know? Or does the narrator seem to have more general knowledge? Which character's inner thoughts does the narrator report most completely? Give examples to support your answers.

2. **Understanding Character.** This story includes both human and animal characters. Whose thoughts, feelings, and actions are described in more detail—those of the humans or those of the animals?

   Tell which characters show the following qualities: curiosity and cleverness; cruelty and hatred; fear and sadness. Use examples from the story to support your answers.

3. **Examining Plot.** The following diagram shows how the plot of many short stories builds up to a high point and then back down to the resolution.

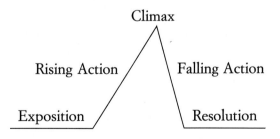

The following list gives events from the plot of this story. Put the events in time order. Then find the place for each event in the plot diagram. More than one event may belong in each part of the plot.

   a. Rikki-tikki meets Nag.
   b. Rikki-tikki fights Nag in the bathroom.
   c. Rikki-tikki comes to the bungalow.
   d. Rikki-tikki saves Teddy from Karait.
   e. Rikki-tikki kills Nagaina.
   f. Rikki-tikki saves Teddy from Nagaina.
   g. Rikki-tikki continues to keep the bungalow garden free from snakes.

4. **Evaluating Setting.** In some stories the **setting,** the time and place of the action, plays an important part in how and why events take place as they do. In other stories, the setting is of less importance. What is the setting of this story? Why is the country crucial to the plot? Would things happen differently if the bungalow did not have a garden? if the bath had modern pipes and running water instead of water jars and an open drain? Explain.

5. **Identifying Onomatopoeia.** The use of words that sound like what they describe is called **onomatopoeia.** For example, what does the main character get his name from? What words describe the noises that Chuchundra makes? the sound of Nag coming into the bathroom? the sound of Nagaina's head on the matting? the sound of the Copperbird?

Vocabulary

Using Context. Even if you are not familiar with some of the exact verbs that are used in this story, you can figure out what kind of movement is indicated by the rest of the context. For example, you may not know the verb *scuttled,* which describes Rikki-tikki's movements as he hunts in the garden. However, you know enough about how active and restless the mongoose is to guess that the word probably suggests a quick, hurried movement.

Use the context of the sentences and what you know about each of the characters to match each underlined verb with its definition. Show you have understood each word by using it in a sentence of your own.

1. "[Karait's] head lashed within a fraction of [Rikki-tikki's] shoulder. . . ."

2. "Nag coiled himself up, raised his head, and looked into the bathroom. . . ."

3. "[Darzee's wife] fluttered more desperately than ever."

4. "[Nagaina] was swaying to and fro, singing a song of triumph."

5. "[Rikki-tikki] jumped clear of the whisking tail. . . ."

a. to move from side to side
b. to quickly move or flap wings
c. to strike out with force
d. to make a quick, sweeping movement
e. to wind around in a circular shape

Critical Thinking

Classifying Characters. Rikki-tikki-tavi is clearly the main character in this story. Quite a few other characters play some part in the story as well. These characters can be grouped, or classified, in a number of ways. For example, some characters are human and some are animals. Several characters are enemies of Rikki-tikki. Another group is helped by Rikki-tikki, and still others help Rikki-tikki in his battle. Notice that one character may fit into several different groupings.

You can make a chart to classify the characters. Across the top, write at least four categories. On the left side, write the names of all the characters in the story. Draw lines as shown in the sample, and check the boxes that connect the characters with the correct categories.

	Animal	Human	Enemy	Helper	Helped
Rikki					
Nag					
Teddy					

Study and Research

Researching Facts. Some parts of "Rikki-tikki-tavi" could not happen in real life. For example, animals don't talk to each other. However, would a mongoose ever attack a cobra? What kinds of movements would each make in such a fight? Use your research skills to look up *mongoose* and *cobra* in an encyclopedia or a book on animal behavior. List the details about Rikki-tikki or Nag and Nagaina that are based on facts. Include points such as the physical appearance, the habits, and the movements of the animals.

Developing Writing Skills

1. **Describing Action.** No details are given about the fight to the death between Rikki-tikki and Nagaina. Write one to three paragraphs describing the fight in the rathole.

   Prewriting. Read over the fight scenes given in the story so that you are familiar with the way each animal defends and attacks. Then make one list of words and phrases you can use to describe the narrow, underground tunnel where the fight takes place. Draw up a second list of words and phrases that will help picture exactly how the two fighters move as they fight.

   Drafting. In your description, make clear how the setting of the rathole affects the fight. Decide if the tunnel will open out so that Nagaina will have a chance to turn and attack. Try to create suspense about how the fight will turn out.

   Revising and Sharing. Read your draft aloud to see where revisions can be made.

   Does your description include details that will let the reader imagine exactly what happened? Have you used exact verbs, adverbs, and adjectives? Would the description be clearer if you added clue words to indicate the order in which each stage of the fight took place? Does your description include enough details to make the setting clear?

   If you enjoy drawing, you might want to illustrate your final draft.

2. **Analyzing Characters.** Rikki-tikki is a hero because he defeats Nag and Nagaina. Are the cobras cruel, evil villains? Or do they have good reasons for their behavior? Write one or two paragraphs explaining your answer. Support your opinion with examples from the story. Follow the steps in the process of writing: prewriting, drafting, revising, and sharing. If you need help with the writing process, see the handbook at the back of the book.

The Bet

ANTON CHEKHOV

Think of how you have changed in the past five years. Then imagine spending three times as long alone. What might those years do to you? In this story, does the lawyer expect what happens to him?

It was a dark autumn night. The old banker was pacing from corner to corner in his room, recalling to his mind the party he had given in the autumn fifteen years before.

There had been many clever people at that party. There was much good talk. They talked, among other things, of capital punishment. The guests for the most part disapproved of it. They found it old-fashioned and evil as a form of punishment. They thought it had no place in a country that called itself civilized. Some of them thought that capital punishment should be replaced right away with life in prison.

"I don't agree with you," said the host. "In my opinion, capital punishment is really kinder than life in prison. Execution kills instantly; prison kills by degrees. Now, which is better? To kill you in a few seconds, or to draw the life out of you for years and years?"

"One's as bad as the other," said one of the guests. "Their purpose is the same, to take away life. The government is not God. It has no right to take a human life. It should not take away what it cannot give back."

Among the company was a young lawyer, a man about twenty-five. "Both are evil," he stated, "but if offered the chance between them, I would definitely take prison. It's better to live somehow than not to live at all."

"Nonsense!"

"It is so!"

"No!"

"Yes!"

The banker, who was then younger and more nervous, suddenly lost his temper. He banged his fist on the table. Turning to the young lawyer, he cried out:

"It's a lie! I bet you two million you couldn't stay in a prison cell, even for five years."

Two Bearded Men, 20th century, EMIL NOLDE. Milwaukee Art Museum Collection, Gift of Mrs. Harry Lynde Bradley.

"Do you mean that?" asked the young lawyer.

The banker nodded eagerly, his face an angry red.

"Then I accept your bet," the lawyer said simply. "But I'll stay not five years but fifteen."

"Fifteen! Fifteen!" cried the banker. He was now wild, as though he had already won the bet. "Done, then. The people here are our witnesses. I stake two million rubles. You stake fifteen years of your freedom."

So this foolish, senseless bet came to pass. At the time, the banker had too many millions to count. He was beside himself with joy. All through dinner he kept talking about the bet. He said to the lawyer jokingly, "Come to your senses, young man. It's not too late yet. Two million is nothing to me, but you stand to lose three or four of the best years of your life. I say three or four, not fifteen. You'll never stick it out longer than that, I can tell you. And they'll just be wasted years. Not the smallest coin do I give you if you leave earlier than fifteen years. Why, just think of it! My jail will have no bars, no locks. You'll be able to walk out of it any time you want to. That thought will be like poison to you. So you will walk out, I know that. Sooner or later, you will!''

Now the banker, pacing from corner to corner, recalled all this and asked himself, "Why did I make this bet? What's the good? The lawyer loses fifteen years of his life, and I throw away two million. That bet was a mistake. On my part, it was the foolishness of a well-fed man. On the lawyer's part, it was pure greed for gold.''

He remembered, further, what happened after the evening party. It was decided that the lawyer's ''prison'' would be in the garden wing of the banker's house. For fifteen years the lawyer was not to go through its door. He was not to see living people or to hear a human voice. He was not to receive letters or newspapers. Musical instruments, however, were to be permitted. He could also read books and write letters. Some other things, he could order. He had only to pass his order note through a special window. A guard would bring anything allowed.

Thus, the smallest details of the bet were discussed and settled. At twelve noon on November 14, 1870, the prison term began. It was to last until twelve noon on November 14, 1885. The lawyer must make no attempt to break the rules agreed upon. Any attempt to escape, even for two minutes, would free the banker from having to pay the two million.

The lawyer's first year, as far as it was possible to judge from his short notes, was one of suffering. He grew lonely and bored. From his wing, day and night, came the sound of the piano. Short, easy novels were his only reading—love stories, crime, and comedy.

In the second year, the piano was heard no more. The lawyer asked only for classics. By the fifth year, music was heard again. Guards who peeked into his room said that he yawned often and talked angrily to himself. Books he did not read now. Sometimes at night, he would sit down to write. He would write for a long time and then tear it all up in the morning. More than once, he was heard to weep.

In the second half of the sixth year, the prisoner began zealously to study languages, philosophy, and history. He fell on these subjects with hunger. The banker hardly had time to get books enough for him. In four years' time, about six hundred volumes were brought at his request. Later on, after the tenth year, the lawyer sat before his table and read only the New Testament. Then he went on to the history of religions.

During the last two years, the prisoner read a huge amount, quite haphazardly. He would ask for books on science. Then it would be Shakespeare. Notes used to come from him, asking at the same time for books on chemistry, religion, and medicine, as well as for a novel. He read as though he were swimming in a sea among broken pieces of wreckage. In his desire to save his life, he was eagerly grasping at one thing after another.

The banker recalled all this and thought, "Tomorrow at noon he receives his freedom. Under the agreement, I shall have to pay him two million. But if I pay, it's all over with me. I shall be ruined forever."

Fifteen years before, he had had too much money to count. Now, he did not know which he had more of, money or debts. He had gambled on the stock market—and lost. He had made business deals that turned sour. The fearless, proud man of business had become an ordinary person, trembling with worry about money.

"That cursed bet!" murmured the old man. "Why didn't the lawyer die? He's only forty years old. He will take all my money. He will marry and enjoy life. To him, I will look like an envious beggar, and he will say, 'Look, let me help you. After all, I owe my happiness to your money.' Oh, such shame!

"Ruin and shame," the banker went on. "No—it's too much. Too much for anyone. I must escape ruin and shame, even if he has to die—even if he has to die!"

The clock struck three. The banker stood, listening. In the house everyone was asleep, and he could hear only the frozen trees whining outside the windows. He put on his overcoat and went out of the house. The garden was dark and cold. It was raining. A damp wind argued with the noisy trees. Nearing the garden wing, he called the guard twice. There was no answer. "Good," the banker thought. Evidently the guard had taken shelter from the bad weather. The man was probably sleeping in the kitchen or greenhouse.

"If I have the courage to kill this man," thought the old banker, "the guard will get the blame."

In the darkness he groped for the door. It opened without a sound. In the prisoner's room, a candle was burning dimly. The prisoner sat by the table. Only his back, the hair on his head, and his hands were visible. Open books lay everywhere—on the table, on the two chairs, on the carpet.

Five minutes passed, and the prisoner never once stirred. "Probably asleep," thought the old banker. He stepped forward. Before him, at the table, sat a man unlike an ordinary human being. It was a skeleton, with tight skin, long curly hair like a woman's, and a shaggy beard. The face was yellow. The cheeks were sunken. The hands were so long and skinny that they were painful to look upon. His hair was already silvering with gray, and no one who looked at the thin, aging face would have believed that he was only forty years old. On the table before his bent head, lay a sheet of paper covered with tiny handwriting.

"Poor devil," thought the banker. "He's asleep and probably seeing millions in his dreams. I only have to throw this half-dead thing on the bed. Then I'll smother him in a moment with the pillow. But first, let's read what he has written."

His eyes dropped to the paper:

> *Tomorrow, at noon, I am to have my freedom. I shall have the right to mix with people. But before I leave this room, I want to say a few words to you. My conscience is clear, and I stand before God, who sees me. I declare to you that I despise all that your books call the blessings of the world.*
>
> *For fifteen years I have studied earthly life. In your books I hunted deer and sang songs. In your books I climbed Mt. Blanc. I saw from there how the sun rose in the morning. In your books I worked miracles, burned cities to the ground, preached new religions, conquered whole countries——*
>
> *Your books gave me wisdom. I know that I am cleverer than you all. You are mad and gone the wrong way. You worship things, not ideas. You take falsehood for truth and ugliness for beauty. So do I marvel at you. You have traded heaven for earth. I do not want to understand you.*
>
> *To show that I despise all that you live by, I give up the two million I once so desired. Can your money buy wisdom? No. I shall come out of here five minutes before noon tomorrow. I shall thus break our agreement.*

When he had read this, the banker kissed the head of the strange man. He began to weep. He went out of the wing. Never, not even after his terrible losses in the stock market, had he felt such hatred for himself. Back in his own room, he lay down on the bed. Tears of guilt kept him a long time from sleeping.

The banker slept late the next morning. About noon the poor guard came running to him. The prisoner had escaped! He had walked out into the garden! He had gone to the gate and disappeared!

The banker instantly went with his servants to the wing. Yes, the prisoner was gone. To avoid rumors, he picked up the note on the table. He made two neat folds. And on his return, he locked it in his safe.

Anton Chekhov *(1869–1904)* was a noted Russian playwright and short story writer. As a young doctor, he wrote short stories, which gradually made him well known. Later he began to write plays, which were performed at the Moscow Art Theater. His plays, such as *The Three Sisters, The Cherry Orchard,* and *Uncle Vanya,* are still popular and are considered important dramatic works.

Developing Comprehension Skills

1. What is being discussed at the party? What are the young lawyer's thoughts on the topic? the banker's thoughts? What happens as a result of the disagreement?

2. Tell what important event in the story takes place at each of the following times:
   a. an autumn night in 1870
   b. 12:00 noon on November 14, 1870
   c. 3:00 A.M. on November 14, 1885
   d. 11:55 A.M. on November 14, 1885

3. How do the lawyer's feelings about money change? What causes the change?

4. The bet grew out of an argument over which penalty is worse—capital punishment or life imprisonment. Do you think what the lawyer does and says in the end supports his argument in favor of life imprisonment?

5. What point do you think the lawyer wants to make by writing his letter and then leaving five minutes before the bet is up? Do you think it makes sense to make the point this way?

6. Do you think anyone would really suffer for fifteen years and then give up so much money at the very end to make a point?

Reading Literature: Short Stories

1. **Understanding Theme.** This story raises questions about the meaning of freedom. The lawyer in this story voluntarily gives up his own physical freedom. However, unlike most prisoners, he can choose to leave

his prison. Although he is not supposed to talk to anyone, the lawyer can choose to play music, read books, and write letters. Given the number of choices he can make, do you think the lawyer really experiences what it is like to be in prison?

Who seems freer at the end of the fifteenth year: the lawyer who chooses to do what he wants to do or the banker who is miserable because of money problems?

2. **Examining Flashback.** A **flashback** is a part of a story that interrupts the sequence of events to relate an earlier conversation, scene, or event. "The Bet" opens in 1885. What sentence opens the flashback? With what sentence does the story return to the night before November 14, 1885? How does the flashback focus attention on the conflict between the lawyer and the banker?

3. **Recognizing Character Development.** The banker changes from a confident, arrogant man, to an insecure, troubled person. Scattered through the story are passages that show him as he is at the time of the party and as he is fifteen years later. These passages show how he has changed. Here is an example:

Young Banker	Old Banker
At the time, the banker had too many millions to count. (page 169, column 2, paragraph 1)	"He will take all my money. He will marry and enjoy life. To him, I will look like an envious beggar. . . ." (page 171, column 1, paragraph 3)

Find at least two more descriptions of the young banker and two more of the old banker. Then find at least three descriptions of the lawyer when the bet is made and three of him at the end of his prison term.

Vocabulary

Completing Analogies. An **analogy** contains two pairs of related words. Each pair is related in the same way. Here are two examples:

a. Lion is to cat as wolf is to dog.

b. Tall is to short as pretty is to ugly.

In the first example, the relationship between *lion* and *cat* is that the lion is a wild animal and the cat is a tame animal in the same family. In the same way, the *wolf* and *dog* are wild and tame members of the same family.

In the second example, the words in each pair are opposites.

In an analogy question, you are given the first pair of words and must complete the second pair. First you must figure out the relationship between the first two words. Then you must identify the word that has the same relationship with the third word given. Here is an example:

Really is to actually as often is to _____.
many   carefully
frequently   terribly

The first two words are synonyms. Therefore, the missing word must be a synonym for *often*. If you remember the meaning of *often*, you will choose the answer *frequently*.

The following analogies use words from the selections in Chapters One, Two, and the first part of Chapter Four. Choose the word that completes each analogy. If necessary, refer to the glossary of this book or to a dictionary for help.

1. Wealth is to riches as friend is to _____.
   war   ally
   enemy   servant

2. Joy is to sadness as order is to _____.
   confusion   delight
   contempt   haven

3. Elegant is to queen as tattered is to _____.
   knight   beggar
   luxury   flag

4. Whimper is to cry as tap is to _____.
   defeat   scratch
   quote   blow

5. Raise is to lift as dismiss is to _____.
   rouse   shudder
   pace   banish

6. Despise is to adore as scorn is to _____.
   hassle   query
   treasure   fight

7. Up is to down as truth is to _____.
   fairness   falsehood
   accuracy   hope

Developing Writing Skills

Writing a Diary. Imagine that you are the lawyer in the story. Write a diary about the slow changes that take place in you over the fifteen years. For each of the following time divisions, write a one-paragraph or two-paragraph entry:

1. first year   4. tenth year

2. second year   5. fifteenth year

3. fifth year

Prewriting. Carefully reread the part of the story that describes the changes in the lawyer's behavior and reading habits during the fifteen years. Make notes about the kinds of interests and attitudes that each entry should suggest. Make up specific requests or observations the lawyer might make in each entry.

Drafting. Write the diary from the first-person point of view. Remember that you are the lawyer who has not communicated with anyone else since the bet began.

Revising and Sharing. Read over your draft. Does each entry suggest something that the lawyer has just read or is interested in? Do the entries show changes in thinking and personality? Do you think the handwriting should change as well? After revising your diary entries, share them with the class. Your teacher may want to use entries from several students to make a bulletin board display.

The Necklace

GUY DE MAUPASSANT

Have you ever wanted something badly that you believed would make you happy? Matilda thinks that a diamond necklace will bring her a night of pleasure. How do the jewels change her whole life?

She was one of those pretty, charming young ladies, born, as if through an error of destiny, into a family of clerks. She had no dowry, no hopes, no means of becoming known, appreciated, loved, and married by a man either rich or distinguished; and she allowed herself to marry a petty clerk in the office of the Board of Education.

She was simple, not being able to adorn herself, but she was unhappy, as one out of her class; for women belong to no caste, no race, their grace, their beauty and their charm serving them in the place of birth and family. Their inborn finesse, their instinctive elegance, their suppleness of wit, are their only aristocracy, making some daughters of the people the equal of great ladies.

She suffered incessantly, feeling herself born for all delicacies and luxuries. She suffered from the poverty of her apartment, the shabby walls, the worn chairs and the faded stuffs. All these things, which another woman of her station would not have noticed, tortured and angered her. The sight of the little Breton,[1] who made this humble home, awoke in her sad regrets and desperate dreams. She thought of quiet antechambers with their oriental hangings lighted by high bronze torches and of the two great footmen in short trousers who sleep in the large armchairs, made sleepy by the heavy air from the heating apparatus. She thought of large drawing rooms hung in old silks, of graceful pieces of furniture carrying bric-a-brac of inestimable value and of the little perfumed coquettish apartments made for five o'clock chats with most intimate friends, men known

---

1. **Breton** (bret′′n)–Her maid, a native of Brittany, a province in France.

Girl with a Hand Mirror, early 20th century, WILLIAM McGREGOR PAXTON. The Reading Public Museum and Art Gallery, Pennsylvania.

and sought after, whose attention all women envied and desired.

When she seated herself for dinner before the round table, where the tablecloth had been used three days, opposite her husband who uncovered the tureen with a delighted air, saying: "Oh! the good potpie! I know nothing better than that," she would think of the elegant dinners, of the shining silver, of the tapestries peopling the walls with ancient personages and rare birds in the midst of fairy forests. She thought of the exquisite food served on marvelous dishes, of the whispered gallantries, listened to with the smile of the Sphinx[2] while eating the rose-colored flesh of the trout or a chicken's wing.

She had neither frocks nor jewels, nothing. And she loved only those things. She felt that she was made for them. She had such a desire to please, to be sought after, to be clever and courted.

She had a rich friend, a schoolmate at

---

2. **smile . . . Sphinx** (sfiŋks)—The Sphinx is a famous Egyptian statue with the head of a man and the body of a lion. Its smile is mysterious and inscrutable.

the convent, whom she did not like to visit. She suffered so much when she returned. And she wept for whole days from chagrin, from regret, from despair and disappointment.

One evening her husband returned, elated, bearing in his hand a large envelope.

"Here," he said, "here is something for you."

She quickly tore open the wrapper and drew out a printed card on which were inscribed these words:

> *The Minister of Public Instruction and Madame George Ramponneau ask the honor of M. and Mme. Loisel's company Monday evening, January 18, at the Minister's residence.*

Instead of being delighted, as her husband had hoped, she threw the invitation spitefully upon the table, murmuring:

"What do you suppose I want with that?"

"But, my dearie, I thought it would make you happy. You never go out, and this is an occasion, and a fine one! I had a great deal of trouble to get it. Everybody wishes one, and it is very select; not many are given to employees. You will see the whole official world there."

She looked at him with an irritated eye and declared impatiently, "What do you suppose I have to wear to such a thing as that?"

He had not thought of that; he stammered, "Why, the dress you wear when we go to the theater. It seems very pretty to me."

He was silent, stupefied, in dismay, at the sight of his wife weeping. Two great tears fell slowly from the corners of her eyes toward the corners of her mouth; he stammered, "What is the matter? What is the matter?"

By a violent effort she had controlled her vexation and responded in a calm voice, wiping her moist cheeks, "Nothing. Only I have no dress and consequently I cannot go to this affair. Give your card to some colleague whose wife is better fitted out that I."

He was grieved but answered, "Let us see, Matilda. How much would a suitable costume cost, something that would serve for other occasions, something very simple?"

She reflected for some seconds, making estimates and thinking of a sum that she could ask for without bringing with it an immediate refusal and a frightened exclamation from the economical clerk.

Finally she said in a hesitating voice, "I cannot tell exactly, but it seems to me that four hundred francs ought to cover it."

He turned a little pale, for he had saved just this sum to buy a gun that he might be able to join some hunting parties the next summer, on the plains at Nanterre, with some friends who went to shoot larks up there on Sunday. Nevertheless, he answered, "Very well. I will give you four hundred francs. But try to have a pretty dress."

The day of the ball approached, and Mme. Loisel seemed sad, disturbed, anxious. Nevertheless, her dress was nearly ready. Her husband said to her one evening, "What is the matter with you? You have acted strangely for two or three days."

And she responded, "I am vexed not to have a jewel, not one stone, nothing to adorn myself with. I shall have such a poverty-laden look. I would prefer not to go to this party."

He replied, "You can wear some natural flowers. At this season they look very chic. For ten francs you can have two or three magnificent roses."

She was not convinced. "No," she replied, "there is nothing more humiliating than to have a shabby air in the midst of rich women."

Then her husband cried out, "How stupid we are! Go and find your friend Madame Forestier and ask her to lend you her jewels. You are well enough acquainted with her to do this."

She uttered a cry of joy. "It is true!" she said. "I had not thought of that."

The next day she took herself to her friend's house and related her story of distress. Mme. Forestier went to her closet with the glass doors, took out a large jewel case, brought it, opened it, and said: "Choose, my dear."

She saw at first some bracelets, then a collar of pearls, then a Venetian cross of gold and jewels and of admirable workmanship. She tried the jewels before the glass, hesitated, but could neither decide to take them nor leave them. Then she asked, "Have you nothing more?"

"Why, yes. Look for yourself. I do not know what will please you."

Suddenly she discovered in a black satin box a superb necklace of diamonds, and her heart beat fast with an immoderate desire. Her hands trembled as she took them up. She placed them about her throat, against her dress, and remained in ecstasy before them. Then she asked in a hesitating voice full of anxiety:

"Could you lend me this? Only this?"

"Why, yes, certainly."

She fell upon the neck of her friend, embraced her with passion, then went away with her treasure.

The day of the ball arrived. Mme. Loisel was a great success. She was the prettiest of all, elegant, gracious, smiling, and full of joy. All the men noticed her, asked her name, and wanted to be presented. All the members of the Cabinet wished to waltz with her. The Minister of Education paid her some attention.

She danced with enthusiasm, with passion, intoxicated with pleasure, thinking of nothing, in the triumph of her beauty, in the glory of her success, in a kind of cloud of happiness that came of all this homage and all this admiration, of all these awakened desires, and this victory so complete and sweet to the heart of women.

She went home toward four o'clock in the morning. Her husband had been half asleep in one of the little salons since midnight with three other gentlemen whose wives were enjoying themselves very much.

He threw around her shoulders the wraps they had carried for the coming home, modest garments of everyday wear, whose poverty clashed with the elegance of the ball costume. She felt this and wished to hurry away in order not to be noticed by the other women who were wrapping themselves in rich furs.

Loisel detained her. "Wait," said he. "You will catch cold out there. I am going to call a cab."

But she would not listen and descended the steps rapidly. When they were in the street they found no carriage, and they began to seek for one, hailing the coachmen whom they saw at a distance.

They walked along toward the Seine, hopeless and shivering. Finally they found on the dock one of those old nocturnal coupés that one sees in Paris after nightfall, as if they were ashamed of their misery by day.

It took them as far as their door in Martyr Street, and they went wearily up to their apartment. It was all over for her. And on his part he remembered that he would have to be at the office by ten o'clock.

Dancing in Town, 1883, PIERRE AUGUSTE RENOIR.
Musée d'Orsay, Paris. Photograph: Réunion des Musées Nationaux.

She removed the wraps from her shoulders before the glass for a final view of herself in her glory. Suddenly she uttered a cry. Her necklace was not around her neck.

Her husband, already half undressed, asked, "What is the matter?"

She turned toward him excitedly, "I have—I have—I no longer have Madame Forestier's necklace."

He arose in dismay, "What! How is that? It is not possible."

And they looked in the folds of the dress, in the folds of the mantle, in the pockets, everywhere. They could not find it.

He asked, "You are sure you still had it when we left the house?"

"Yes, I felt it in the vestibule as we came out."

"But if you had lost it in the street we should have heard it fall. It must be in the cab."

"Yes. It is probable. Did you take the number?"

"No. And you, did you notice what it was?"

"No."

They looked at each other, utterly cast down. Finally Loisel dressed himself again.

"I am going," he said, "over the track where we went on foot, to see if I can find it."

And he went. She remained in her evening gown, not having the force to go to bed, stretched upon a chair, without ambition or thoughts.

Toward seven o'clock her husband returned. He had found nothing.

He went to the police and to the cab offices and put an advertisement in the newspapers, offering a reward; he did everything that afforded them a suspicion of hope.

She waited all day in a state of bewilderment before this frightful disaster. Loisel returned at evening, with his face harrowed and pale, and had discovered nothing.

"It will be necessary," said he, "to write to your friend that you have broken the clasp of the necklace and that you will have it repaired. That will give us time to turn around."

She wrote as he dictated.

At the end of a week they had lost all hope. And Loisel, older by five years, declared, "We must take measures to replace this jewel."

The next day they took the box which had enclosed it to the jeweler whose name was on the inside. He consulted his books.

"It is not I, madame," said he, "who sold this necklace; I only furnished the casket."

Then they went from jeweler to jeweler, seeking a necklace like the other one, consulting their memories, and ill, both of them, with chagrin and anxiety.

In a shop of the Palais-Royal they found a chaplet of diamonds which seemed to them exactly like the one they had lost. It was valued at forty thousand francs. They could get it for thirty-six thousand.

They begged the jeweler not to sell it for three days. And they made an arrangement by which they might return it for thirty-four thousand francs if they found the other one before the end of February.

Loisel possessed eighteen thousand francs which his father had left him. He borrowed the rest.

He borrowed it, asking for a thousand francs of one, five hundred of another, five louis of this one and three louis of that one. He gave notes, made ruinous promises, took money of usurers and the whole race of lenders. He compromised his whole existence, in fact, risked his signature without even knowing whether he could make it good or not, and, harassed by anxiety for the future, by the black misery which surrounded him, and by the prospect of all physical privations and moral torture, he went to get the new necklace, depositing on the merchant's counter thirty-six thousand francs.

When Mme. Loisel took back the jewels to Mme. Forestier the latter said to her in a frigid tone, "You should have returned them to me sooner, for I might have needed them."

She did open the jewel box as her friend feared she would. If she should perceive the substitution, what would she think? What should she say? Would she take her for a robber?

Mme. Loisel now knew the horrible life of necessity. She did her part, however, completely, heroically. It was necessary to pay this frightful debt. She would pay it. They sent away the maid; they changed their lodgings; they rented some rooms under a mansard roof.

She learned the heavy cares of a household, the odious work of a kitchen. She washed the dishes, using her rosy nails upon the greasy pots and the bottoms of the stewpans. She washed the soiled linen, the chemises and dishcloths, which she hung on the line to dry; she took down the refuse to the street each morning and brought up the water, stopping at each landing to breathe. And, clothed like a woman of the people, she went to the grocer's, the butcher's and the fruiterer's with her basket on her arm, shopping, haggling to the last sou her miserable money.

Every month it was necessary to renew some notes, thus obtaining time, and to pay others.

The husband worked evenings, putting the books of some merchants in order, and nights he often did copying at five sous a page.

And this life lasted for ten years.

At the end of ten years they had restored all, all, with interest of the usurer, and accumulated interest, besides.

Mme. Loisel seemed old now. She had become a strong, hard woman, the crude woman of the poor household. Her hair badly dressed, her skirts awry, her hands red, she spoke in a loud tone and washed the floors in large pails of water. But sometimes, when her husband was at the office, she would seat herself before the window and think of that evening party of former times, of that ball where she was so beautiful and so flattered.

How would it have been if she had not lost that necklace? Who knows? Who knows? How singular is life and how full of changes! How small a thing will ruin or save one!

One Sunday, as she was taking a walk in the Champs Elysées to rid herself of the cares of the week, she suddenly perceived a woman walking with a child. It was Mme. Forestier, still young, still pretty, still attractive. Mme. Loisel was affected. Should she speak to her? Yes, certainly. And now that she had paid, she would tell her all. Why not?

She approached her. "Good morning, Jeanne."

Her friend did not recognize her and was astonished to be so familiarly addressed by this common personage. She stammered, "But, madame—I do not know—You must be mistaken."

"No, I am Matilda Loisel."

Her friend uttered a cry of astonishment, "Oh! my poor Matilda! How you have changed."

"Yes, I have had some hard days since I saw you, and some miserable ones—and all because of you."

"Because of me? How is that?"

"You recall the diamond necklace that you loaned me to wear to the minister's ball?"

"Yes, very well."

"Well, I lost it."

"How is that, since you returned it to me?"

"I returned another to you exactly like it. And it has taken us ten years to pay for it. You can understand that it was not easy for us who have nothing. But it is finished, and I am decently content."

Mme. Forestier stopped short. She said:

"You say that you bought a diamond necklace to replace mine?"

"Yes. You did not perceive it then? They were just alike."

And she smiled with a proud and simple joy. Mme. Forestier was touched and took both her hands as she replied.

"Oh, my poor Matilda! Mine were false. They were not worth over five hundred francs!"

Guy de Maupassant *(1850–1893)* was born in France. At an early age, de Maupassant was interested in writing. However, he served in the army and worked at a government job to earn money before becoming a successful writer. A famous French author, Gustave Flaubert, spent years helping de Maupassant perfect his writing. Before illness cut short his promising career, de Maupassant was known for his stories, among them "The Umbrella," "The Piece of String," and "The Necklace."

Developing Comprehension Skills

1. What kind of work is done by the members of Madame Loisel's family? What kind of work is done by the man she marries?

2. How does the kind of life Madame Loisel dreams of contrast with the life she has? How does she feel because of the difference between her dreams and reality?

3. Put the following quotations from the story in time order.

   a. "She washed the dishes, using her rosy nails upon the greasy pots and the bottoms of stewpans."

   b. "Instead of being delighted, as her husband had hoped, she threw the invitation spitefully on the table. . . ."

   c. "It took them as far as their door in Martyr Street, and they went wearily up to their apartment. It was all over for her."

   d. "The day of the ball arrived. Mme. Loisel was a great success. She was the prettiest of all, elegant, gracious, smiling, and full of joy."

4. Do Madame Loisel and her husband feel the same way about each other? Or does one of them seem to do more and care more for the other? Explain your answer.

5. What does Madame Loisel think she must have to go to the ball? Do you think these things were really necessary? Explain.

6. Do you think Madame Loisel deserves sympathy, either before or after the ball?

Reading Literature: Short Stories

1. **Relating Irony and the Surprise Ending.** One kind of **irony** is a contrast between what is expected and what actually happens. What do the Loisels, as well as the reader, assume about the value of the necklace throughout the story? At what point in the story do you, and Madame Loisel, find out the truth? What is ironic about

Madame Loisel's working to pay for the new necklace? Would the irony be as effective if the information came earlier?

2. **Identifying Point of View.** From what point of view is the story told: first-person, third-person omniscient, or third-person limited? Which character does the narrator focus on? Does the narrator seem to feel strongly critical or sympathetic toward that character? Or is the character presented objectively?

3. **Evaluating Exposition.** The first six paragraphs of the story describe the personality and social circumstances of Madame Loisel. Name one important quality of Madame Loisel's character that you learn from the exposition.

4. **Diagraming the Plot.** The plot diagram below shows the main events in three parts of "The Necklace." Tell what events belong in the climax and the falling action.

Vocabulary

Using Context Clues. You can figure out the meaning of unfamiliar words by using context clues such as contrast or words in a series. For each sentence taken from this story, write the definition of the underlined word. Then on a second line write (1) whether the context clue is a contrast or words in a series; and (2) the key words or punctuation that helped you figure out the meaning. Check the glossary or a dictionary to see if the meaning you wrote is correct.

1. "She suffered from the poverty of her apartment, the <u>shabby</u> walls, the worn chairs and the faded stuffs."

2. "And she wept for whole days from <u>chagrin</u>, from regret, from despair and disappointment."

3. "He was silent, <u>stupefied</u>, in dismay, at the sight of his wife weeping."

4. "By a violent effort she had controlled her <u>vexation</u> and responded in a calm voice, wiping her moist cheeks. . . ."

5. "He threw around her shoulders the wraps they had carried for the coming home, <u>modest</u> garments of everyday wear, whose poverty clashed with the elegance of the ball costume."

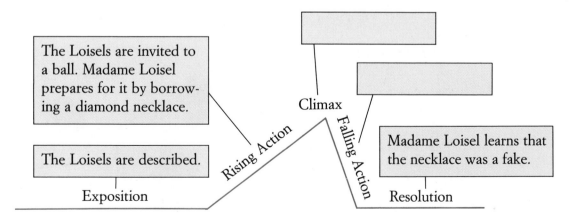

The Loisels are invited to a ball. Madame Loisel prepares for it by borrowing a diamond necklace.

The Loisels are described.

Exposition

Rising Action

Climax

Falling Action

Madame Loisel learns that the necklace was a fake.

Resolution

Developing Writing Skills

1. **Explaining an Opinion.** Mme. Loisel's circumstances change a great deal as the story develops. How much does Mme. Loisel herself change by the end of the story? Write two paragraphs explaining how much you think Mme. Loisel does or does not change.

   Prewriting. Make two lists: (a) ways in which Mme. Loisel changes and (b) ways in which Mme. Loisel does not change. Think about the details in each list. Think about her appearance, behavior, speech, and surroundings. Decide how much you think Mme. Loisel does or does not change.

   Drafting. Begin your composition with a topic sentence in which you state your opinion about Mme. Loisel. You might write something like "In 'The Necklace,' Mme. Loisel changes in several ways (*or* changes only slightly *or* does not change at all)." In the rest of your composition, give specific evidence from the story to support your opinion.

   Revising and Sharing. Choose a partner and read each other's paragraphs. Ask your partner the following questions: "Is the topic sentence clear? Are there enough details to support my opinion? Have I left out any important evidence?" Be prepared to discuss your opinion in class.

2. **Writing a Different Version of a Story.** Could a situation like the one in this story happen today? Write your own version of what happens when someone borrows a valuable object and then loses it. Follow the four steps in the process of writing: prewriting, drafting, revising, and sharing. When prewriting, make a plot outline showing the main events in your story. Be sure the reader will understand how the central conflict develops, what the climax is, and how the conflict is resolved.

The Summer of the Beautiful White Horse

WILLIAM SAROYAN

Do you have a relative who is a colorful character? How does Aram's cousin help make one summer unforgettable?

One day back there in the good old days when I was nine and the world was full of every imaginable kind of magnificence and life was still a delightful and mysterious dream, my cousin Mourad (moo′räd), who was considered crazy by everybody who knew him except me, came to my house at four in the morning and woke me up by tapping on the window of my room.

"Aram," he said.

I jumped out of bed and looked out the window.

I couldn't believe what I saw.

It wasn't morning yet but it was summer, and with daybreak not many minutes around the corner of the world it was light enough for me to know I wasn't dreaming.

My cousin Mourad was sitting on a beautiful white horse.

I stuck my head out of the window and rubbed my eyes.

"Yes," he said in Armenian. "It's a horse. You're not dreaming. Make it quick if you want to ride."

I knew my cousin Mourad enjoyed being alive more than anybody else who had ever fallen into the world by mistake, but this was more than even I could believe.

In the first place, my earliest memories had been memories of horses and my first longings had been longings to ride.

This was the wonderful part.

In the second place, we were poor.

This was the part that wouldn't permit me to believe what I saw.

We were poor. We had no money. Our whole tribe was poverty-stricken. Every branch of the Garoghlanian (gar′ə glän′yən) family was living in the most amazing and comical poverty in the world. Nobody could understand where we ever got money enough to keep us with food in our bellies, not even the old men of the family. Most important of all, though, we were famous for our honesty. We had been famous for our honesty for something like eleven centuries, even when we had been the wealthiest family in what we liked to think was the world. We were proud first, honest next, and after that we believed in right and wrong. None of us would take advantage of anybody in the world, let alone steal.

Consequently, even though I could *see* the horse, so magnificent; even though I could *smell* it, so lovely; even though I could *hear* it breathing, so exciting; I couldn't *believe* the horse had anything to do with my cousin Mourad or with me or with any of the other members of our family, asleep or awake, because I *knew* my cousin Mourad couldn't have *bought* the horse, and, if he couldn't have bought it he must have *stolen* it, and I refused to believe he had stolen it.

No member of the Garoghlanian family could be a thief.

I stared first at my cousin and then at the horse. There was a pious stillness and humor in each of them, which on the one hand delighted me and on the other frightened me.

"Mourad," I said, "where did you steal this horse?"

"Leap out of the window," he said, "if you want to ride."

It was true, then. He *had* stolen the horse. There was no question about it. He had come to invite me to ride or not, as I chose.

Well, it seemed to me stealing a horse for a ride was not the same thing as stealing something else, such as money. For all I knew, maybe it wasn't stealing at all. If you were crazy about horses the way my cousin Mourad and I were, it wasn't stealing. It wouldn't become stealing until we offered to sell the horse, which of course I knew we would never do.

"Let me put on some clothes," I said.

"All right," he said, "but hurry."

I leaped into my clothes.

I jumped down to the yard from the window and leaped up onto the horse behind my cousin Mourad.

That year we lived at the edge of town, on Walnut Avenue. Behind our house was the country: vineyards, orchards, irrigation ditches, and country roads. In less than three minutes we were on Olive Avenue, and then the horse began to trot. The air was new and lovely to breathe. The feel of the horse running was wonderful. My cousin Mourad, who was considered one of the craziest members of our family, began to sing. I mean, he began to roar.

Every family has a crazy streak in it somewhere, and my cousin Mourad was considered the natural descendant of the crazy streak in our tribe. Before him was our uncle Khosrove (käsh'rôv), an enormous man with a powerful head of black hair and the largest mustache in the San Joaquin Valley, a man so furious in temper, so irritable, so impatient that he stopped anyone from talking by roaring, "It is no harm; pay no attention to it."

That was all, no matter what anybody happened to be talking about. Once it was his own son Arak running eight blocks to the barber shop, where his father was having his mustache trimmed, to tell him their house was on fire. This man Khosrove sat up in the chair and roared, "It is no harm; pay no attention to it." The barber said, "But the boy says your house is on fire." So Khosrove roared, "Enough, it is no harm, I say."

My cousin Mourad was considered the natural descendent of this man, although Mourad's father was Zorab (zoo′räb), who was practical and nothing else. That's how it was in our tribe. A man could be the father of his son's flesh, but that did not mean that he was also the father of his spirit. The distribution of the various kinds of spirit of our tribe had been from the beginning capricious and vagrant.

We rode and my cousin Mourad sang. For all anybody knew we were still in the old country where, at least according to some of our neighbors, we belonged. We let the horse run as long as it felt like running.

At last my cousin Mourad said, "Get down. I want to ride alone."

"Will you let me ride alone?" I said.

"That is up to the horse," my cousin said. "Get down."

"The *horse* will let me ride," I said.

Horse with a Youth in Blue, 1905–1906, PABLO PICASSO. The Tate Gallery, London.

"We shall see," he said. "Don't forget that I have a way with a horse."

"Well," I said, "any way you have with a horse, I have also."

"For the sake of your safety," he said, "let us hope so. Get down."

"All right," I said, "but remember you've got to let me try to ride alone."

I got down and my cousin Mourad kicked his heels into the horse and shouted, *Vazire,* run. The horse stood on its hind legs, snorted, and burst into a fury of speed that was the loveliest thing I had ever seen. My cousin Mourad raced the horse across a field of dry grass to an irrigation ditch, crossed the ditch on the horse, and five minutes later returned, dripping wet.

The sun was coming up.

"Now it's my turn to ride," I said.

My cousin Mourad got off the horse.

"Ride," he said.

I leaped to the back of the horse and for a moment knew the worst fear imaginable. The horse did not move.

"Kick into his muscles," my cousin Mourad said. "What are you waiting for? We've got to take him back before everybody in the world is up and about."

I kicked into the muscles of the horse. Once again it reared and snorted. Then it began to run. I didn't know what to do. Instead of running across the field to the irrigation ditch, the horse ran down the road to the vineyard of Dikran Halabian (dik′rən hä läb′yän) where it began to leap over vines. The horse leaped over seven vines before I fell. Then it continued running.

My cousin Mourad came running down the road.

"I'm not worried about you," he shouted. "We've got to get that horse. You go this way and I'll go this way. If you come upon him, be kindly. I'll be near."

I continued down the road and my cousin Mourad went across the field toward the irrigation ditch.

It took him half an hour to find the horse and bring him back.

"All right," he said, "jump on. The whole world is awake now."

"What will we do?" I said.

"Well," he said, "we'll either take him back or hide him until tomorrow."

He didn't sound worried and I knew he'd hide him and not take him back. Not for a while, at any rate.

"Where will we hide him?" I said.

"I know a place," he said.

"How long ago did you steal this horse?" I said.

It suddenly dawned on me that he had been taking these early morning rides for some time and had come for me this morning only because he knew how much I longed to ride.

"Who said anything about stealing a horse?" he said.

"Anyhow," I said, "how long ago did you begin riding every morning?"

"Not until this morning," he said.

"Are you telling the truth?" I said.

"Of course not," he said, "but if we are found out, that's what you're to say. I don't want both of us to be liars. All you know is that we started riding only this morning."

"All right," I said.

He walked the horse quietly to the barn of a deserted vineyard, which at one time had been the pride of a farmer named

Fetvajian (fet va′jən). There were some oats and dry alfalfa in the barn.

We began walking home.

"It wasn't easy," he said, "to get the horse to behave so nicely. At first it wanted to run wild, but, as I've told you, I have a way with a horse. I can get it to want to do anything *I* want it to do. Horses understand me."

"How do you do it?" I said.

"I have an understanding with a horse," he said.

"Yes, but what sort of an understanding?" I said.

"A simple and honest one," he said.

"Well," I said, "I wish I knew how to reach an understanding like that with a horse."

"You're still a small boy," he said. "When you get to be thirteen you'll know how to do it."

I went home and ate a hearty breakfast.

That afternoon my uncle Khosrove came to our house for coffee. He sat in the parlor, sipping and remembering the old country. Then another visitor arrived, a farmer named John Byro, an Assyrian who, out of loneliness, had learned to

Edge Event XXVI, 1982, JOSEPH PICCILLO. Collection of Mrs. Glenn C. Janss.

speak Armenian. My mother brought the lonely visitor coffee, and he sipped and then at last, sighing sadly, he said, "My white horse which was stolen last month is still gone. I cannot understand it."

My uncle Khosrove became very irritated and shouted, "It's no harm. What is the loss of a horse? Haven't we all lost the homeland? What is this crying over a horse?"

"That may be all right for you, a city dweller, to say," John Byro said, "but what of my surrey? What good is a surrey without a horse?"

"Pay no attention to it," my uncle Khosrove roared.

"I walked ten miles to get here," John Byro said.

"You have legs," my uncle Khosrove shouted.

"My left leg pains me," the farmer said.

"Pay no attention to it," my uncle Khosrove roared.

"That horse cost me sixty dollars," the farmer said.

"I spit on money," my uncle said.

He got up and stalked out of the house, slamming the screen door.

My mother explained.

"He has a gentle heart," she said. "It is simply that he is homesick and such a large man."

The farmer went away, and I ran over to my cousin Mourad's house.

He was sitting under a peach tree, trying to repair the hurt wing of a young robin which could not fly. He was talking to the bird.

"What is it?" he said.

"The farmer, John Byro," I said. "He visited our house. He wants his horse. You've had it a month. I want you to promise not to take it back until I learn to ride."

"It will take you *a year* to learn to ride," my cousin Mourad said.

"We could keep the horse a year," I said.

My cousin Mourad leaped to his feet.

"What?" he roared. "Are you inviting a member of the Garoghlanian family to steal? The horse must go back to its true owner."

"When?" I said.

"In six months at the latest," he said.

He threw the bird into the air. The bird tried hard, almost fell twice, but at last flew away, high and straight.

Early every morning for two weeks my cousin Mourad and I took the horse out of the barn of the deserted vineyard where we were hiding it and rode it, and every morning the horse, when it was my turn to ride alone, leaped over grape vines and small trees and threw me and ran away. Nevertheless, I hoped in time to learn to ride the way my cousin Mourad rode.

One morning on the way to Fetvajian's deserted vineyard, we ran into the farmer John Byro who was on his way to town.

"Let me do the talking," my cousin Mourad said. "I have a way with farmers."

"Good morning, John Byro," my cousin Mourad said to the farmer.

The farmer studied the horse eagerly.

"Good morning, sons of my friends," he said. "What is the name of your horse?"

"*My Heart,*" my cousin Mourad said in Armenian.

"A lovely name," John Byro said, "for a lovely horse. I could swear it is the horse that was stolen from me many weeks ago. May I look into its mouth?"

"Of course," Mourad said.

The farmer looked into the mouth of the horse.

"Tooth for tooth," he said. "I would swear it is my horse if I didn't know your parents. The fame of your family for honesty is well known to me. Yet the horse is the twin of my horse. A suspicious man would believe his eyes instead of his heart. Good day, my young friends."

"Good day, John Byro," my cousin Mourad said.

Early the following morning we took the horse to John Byro's vineyard and put it in the barn. The dogs followed us around without making a sound.

"The dogs," I whispered to my cousin Mourad. "I thought they would bark."

"They would at somebody else," he said. "I have a way with dogs."

My cousin Mourad put his arms around the horse, pressed his nose into the horse's nose, patted it, and then we went away.

That afternoon John Byro came to our house in his surrey and showed my mother the horse that had been stolen and returned.

"I do not know what to think," he said. "The horse is stronger than ever. Better-tempered, too. I thank God."

My uncle Khosrove, who was in the parlor, became irritated and shouted, "Quiet, man, quiet. Your horse has been returned. Pay no attention to it."

© Layle Silbert

William Saroyan *(1908–1981),* the son of Armenian immigrants, grew up in Fresno, California. He loved to read and claimed that he had read every book in the public library. He never finished his formal education because family financial problems forced him to leave school at the age of fifteen. Saroyan's wide reading led to his career in writing. *The Human Comedy* and *The Time of Your Life* are two of his well-known works.

Developing Comprehension Skills

1. Find the following information. How old is the narrator? What time is it at the opening of the story? Where does the narrator live?

2. What is the relationship between Aram and Mourad? between Mourad and Uncle Khosrove? between John Byro and the two boys' families?

3. Why doesn't John Byro take the horse from Mourad and Aram when he meets the boys in the early morning? Do you think he knows that it is his horse? Does the relationship he has with the boys' families have any effect on his action? Explain.

4. Find phrases in the story that answer the following questions. How long had Mourad had the horse before Aram first saw it? How many weeks is Aram able to practice riding? How long after the boys meet John Byro on the road is the horse returned?

5. The narrator says that the events took place in his childhood when "life was still a delightful and mysterious dream." Do you think the boys would have acted the way they did if they were older—for example, if Mourad was eighteen and Aram fourteen? Would there be a difference in how much they wanted the horse or their ability to get one?

Reading Literature: Short Stories

1. **Recognizing Point of View.** Is this story told from the first-person or third-person point of view? What is the narrator's name? How does the point of view help you understand how the narrator feels about himself and his family?

2. **Examining Repetition.** Sometimes writers repeat words or ideas several times to create emphasis. Find the paragraph beginning "We were poor." What two points about the Garoghlanian family are emphasized through repetition?

   Later, Mourad says several times, "I have a way with a horse." What two variations of the phrase are used later in the story to help create a humorous effect? What other character is strongly associated with a phrase that he repeats?

3. **Identifying Conflict.** Aram feels that riding the white horse conflicts with an important family quality. What is this quality? What is the conflict that he feels? Does Mourad seem to feel the same conflict? How is the conflict settled?

Vocabulary

Using Context Clues. Each of the following sentences is based on "The Summer of the Beautiful White Horse." Use context clues to figure out the meanings of the underlined words. Identify the key word or words in each sentence that helped you figure out the meaning. Also, state what kind of context clue is given: example, comparison, contrast, or words in a series.

1. Aram was poor. Moreover, every branch of his family was poverty-stricken.

2. In Aram's tribe, the distribution of various kinds of spirit seemed capricious, not logical.

3. Mourad looked <u>pious</u>, as if he had done no wrong by taking the horse.

4. The horse was hidden in a barn and fed oats, corn, and <u>alfalfa</u>.

Study and Research

Using Reference Materials. Look up the entry *Armenia* in an encyclopedia. Read the article to answer the following questions. What country is Armenia part of today? During the late 1800's and early 1900's, what events forced thousands of Armenians to leave their homeland? What are some distinctive aspects of Armenian culture? Are any of these customs referred to in the story?

Developing Writing Skills

Writing an Exposition. Many people have faced at least one experience in which they want something so badly they have to find a way to get it. Write a two- to five-paragraph opening of a short story based on this kind of situation.

Prewriting. Even though you are not writing a complete story at this time, you need to have a clear idea of what will happen to write your exposition. Make a plan for the story that answers the following questions. Who will the main character be? What object will the character want? Where will the object be, and what ways does the character think of to get it? Will anyone else be involved? What time will the main action of the story take place? Are there any important details about setting that the reader would need to know?

Drafting. Make clear from what point of view the story is being told. In your paragraphs, suggest why the main character wants the object so badly. Give some indication of what strategies he or she might consider to get the object. Include some action and dialogue to show what the characters are like. Try to work in details of setting such as time and place.

Revising and Sharing. Trade drafts with a partner, and ask each other the following questions. "Is the point of view clear and consistent? Does the exposition identify the main character and the object that he or she is determined to get? Does the exposition show when and where the story takes place?"

The Sound of Summer Running

RAY BRADBURY

This story is about a boy and a pair of tennis shoes. Think about how you feel when you wear your favorite tennis shoes. How does the boy in this story feel about these shoes?

 Late that night, going home from the show with his mother and father and his brother Tom, Douglas saw the tennis shoes in the bright store window. He glanced quickly away, but his ankles were seized, his feet suspended, then rushed. The earth spun; the shop awnings slammed their canvas wings overhead with the thrust of his body running. His mother and father and brother walked quietly on both sides of him. Douglas walked backward, watching the tennis shoes in the midnight window left behind.

"It was a nice movie," said Mother.

Douglas murmured, "It was. . . ."

It was June and long past time for buying the special shoes that were quiet as a summer rain falling on the walks. June and the earth full of raw power and everything everywhere in motion. The grass was still pouring in from the country, surrounding the sidewalks, stranding the houses. Any moment the town would capsize, go down and leave not a stir in the clover and weeds. And here Douglas stood, trapped on the dead cement and the red-brick streets, hardly able to move.

"Dad!" He blurted it out. "Back there in that window, those Cream-Sponge Para Litefoot Shoes . . ."

His father didn't even turn. "Suppose you tell me why you need a new pair of sneakers. Can you do that?"

"Well . . ."

It was because they felt the way it feels every summer when you take off your shoes for the first time and run in the grass. They felt like it feels sticking your feet out of the hot covers in wintertime to let the cold wind from the open window blow on them suddenly and you let them stay out a long time until you pull them back in under the covers again to feel them, like packed snow. The tennis shoes felt like it always feels the first time every year wading in the slow waters of the creek and seeing your feet below, half an inch further downstream, with refraction, than the real part of you above water.

"Dad," said Douglas, "it's hard to explain."

Somehow the people who made tennis shoes knew what boys needed and wanted. They put marshmallows and coiled springs in the soles and they wove the rest out of grasses bleached and fired in the wilderness. Somewhere deep in the soft loam of the shoes the thin hard sinews of the buck deer were hidden. The people that made the shoes must have watched a lot of winds blow the trees and a lot of rivers going down to the lakes. Whatever it was, it was in the shoes, and it was summer.

Douglas tried to get all this in words.

"Yes," said Father, "but what's wrong with last year's sneakers? Why can't you dig *them* out of the closet?"

Well, he felt sorry for boys who lived in California where they wore tennis shoes all year and never knew what it was to get winter off your feet, peel off the iron leather shoes all full of snow and rain and run barefoot for a day and then lace on the first new tennis shoes of the season, which was better than barefoot. The magic was always in the new pair of shoes. The magic might die by the first of September, but now in late June there was still plenty of magic, and shoes like these could jump you over trees and rivers and houses. And if you wanted, they could jump you over fences and sidewalks and dogs.

"Don't you see?" said Douglas. "I just *can't* use last year's pair."

For last year's pair were dead inside. They had been fine when he started them out, last year. But by the end of summer, every year, you always found out, you always knew, you couldn't really jump over rivers and trees and houses in them, and they were dead. But this was a new year, and he felt that this time, with this new pair of shoes, he could do anything, anything at all.

They walked up on the steps to their house. "Save your money," said Dad. "In five or six weeks——"

"Summer'll be over!"

Lights out, with Tom asleep, Douglas lay watching his feet, far away down there at the end of the bed in the moonlight, free of the heavy iron shoes, the big chunks of winter fallen away from them.

"Reasons. I've got to think of reasons for the shoes."

Well, as anyone knew, the hills around town were wild with friends putting cows to riot, playing barometer to the atmospheric changes, taking sun, peeling like calendars each day to take more sun. To catch those friends, you must run much faster than foxes or squirrels. As for the town, it steamed with enemies grown irritable with heat, so remembering every winter argument and insult. *Find friends, ditch enemies!* That was the Cream-Sponge Para Litefoot motto. *Does the world run too fast? Want to catch up? Want to be alert, stay alert? Litefoot, then! Litefoot!*

He held his coin bank up and heard the faint small tinkling, the airy weight of money there.

Whatever you want, he thought, you got to make your own way. During the night now, let's find that path through the forest. . . .

Downtown, the store lights went out, one by one. A wind blew in the window. It was like a river going downstream and his feet wanting to go with it.

In his dreams he heard a rabbit running running running in the deep warm grass.

Old Mr. Sanderson moved through his shoe store as the proprietor of a pet shop must move through his shop where are kenneled animals from everywhere in the world, touching each one briefly along the way. Mr. Sanderson brushed his hands over the shoes in the window, and some of them were like cats to him and some were like dogs; he touched each pair with con-

cern, adjusting laces, fixing tongues. Then he stood in the exact center of the carpet and looked around, nodding.

There was a sound of growing thunder.

One moment, the door to Sanderson's Shoe Emporium was empty. The next, Douglas Spaulding stood clumsily there, staring down at his leather shoes as if these heavy things could not be pulled up out of the cement. The thunder had stopped when his shoes stopped. Now, with painful slowness, daring to look only at the money in his cupped hand, Douglas moved out of the bright sunlight of Saturday noon. He made careful stacks of nickels, dimes, and quarters on the counter, like someone playing chess and worried if the next move carried him out into sun or deep into shadow.

"Don't say a word!" said Mr. Sanderson.

Douglas froze.

"First, I know just what you want to buy," said Mr. Sanderson. "Second, I see you every afternoon at my window; you think I don't see? You're wrong. Third, to give it its full name, you want the Royal Crown Cream-Sponge Para Litefoot Tennis Shoes: 'LIKE MENTHOL ON YOUR FEET!' Fourth, you want credit."

"No!" cried Douglas, breathing hard, as if he'd run all night in his dreams. "I got something better than credit to offer!" he gasped. "Before I tell, Mr. Sanderson, you got to do me one small favor. Can you remember when was the last time you yourself wore a pair of Litefoot sneakers, sir?"

Mr. Sanderson's face darkened. "Oh, ten, twenty, say, thirty years ago. Why . . . ?"

"Mr. Sanderson, don't you think you owe it to your customers, sir, to at least try the tennis shoes you sell, for just one minute, so you know how they feel? People forget if they don't keep testing things. United Cigar Store man smokes cigars, don't he? Candy-store man samples his own stuff, I should think. So . . ."

"You may have noticed," said the old man, "I'm wearing shoes."

"But not sneakers, sir! How you going to sell sneakers unless you can rave about them and how you going to rave about them unless you know them?"

Mr. Sanderson backed off a little distance from the boy's fever, one hand to his chin. "Well . . ."

"Mr. Sanderson," said Douglas, "you sell me something and I'll sell you something just as valuable."

"Is it absolutely necessary to the sale that I put on a pair of the sneakers, boy?" said the old man.

"I sure wish you could, sir!"

The old man sighed. A minute later, seated panting quietly, he laced the tennis shoes to his long narrow feet. They looked detached and alien down there next to the dark cuffs of his business suit. Mr. Sanderson stood up.

"How do they *feel?*" asked the boy.

"How do they feel, he asks; they feel fine." He started to sit down.

"Please!" Douglas held out his hand. "Mr. Sanderson, now could you kind of rock back and forth a little, sponge around, bounce kind of, while I tell you the rest? It's this: I give you my money, you give me the shoes, I owe you a dollar. But, Mr. Sanderson, *but*—soon as I get those shoes on, you know what *happens?*"

"What?"

"Bang! I deliver your packages, pick up packages, bring you coffee, burn your trash, run to the post office, telegraph office, library! You'll see twelve of me in and out, in and out, every minute. Feel those shoes, Mr. Sanderson, *feel* how fast they'd take me? All those springs inside? Feel all the running inside? Feel how they kind of grab hold and can't let you alone and don't like you just *standing* there? Feel how quick I'd be doing the things you'd rather not bother with? You stay in the nice cool store while I'm jumping all around town! But it's not me really, it's the shoes. They're going like mad down alleys, cutting corners, and back! There they go!"

Mr. Sanderson stood amazed with the rush of words. When the words got going, the flow carried him; he began to sink deep in the shoes, to flex his toes, limber his arches, test his ankles. He rocked softly, secretly, back and forth in a small breeze from the open door. The tennis shoes silently hushed themselves deep in the carpet, sank as in a jungle grass, in loam and resilient clay. He gave one solemn bounce of his heels in the yeasty dough, in the yielding and welcoming earth. Emotions hurried over his face as if many colored lights had been switched on and off. His mouth hung slightly open. Slowly he gentled and rocked himself to a halt, and the boy's voice faded, and they stood there looking at each other in a tremendous and natural silence.

A few people drifted by on the sidewalk outside, in the hot sun.

Still the man and boy stood there, the boy glowing, the man with revelation in his face.

"Boy," said the old man at last, "in five years, how would you like a job selling shoes in this emporium?"

"Gosh, thanks, Mr. Sanderson, but I don't know what I'm going to be yet."

"Anything you want to be, son," said the old man, "you'll be. No one will ever stop you."

The old man walked lightly across the store to the wall of ten thousand boxes, came back with some shoes for the boy, and wrote up a list on some paper while the boy was lacing the shoes on his feet and then standing there, waiting.

The old man held out his list. "A dozen things you got to do for me this afternoon. Finish them, we're even Stephen, and you're fired."

"Thanks, Mr. Sanderson!" Douglas bounded away.

"Stop!" cried the old man.

Douglas pulled up and turned.

Mr. Sanderson leaned forward. "How do they *feel?*"

The boy looked down at his feet deep in the rivers, in the fields of wheat, in the wind that already was rushing him out of the town. He looked up at the old man, his eyes burning, his mouth moving, but no sound came out.

"Antelopes?" said the old man, looking from the boy's face to his shoes. "Gazelles?"

The boy thought about it, hesitated, and nodded a quick nod. Almost immediately he vanished. He just spun about with a whisper and went off. The door stood empty. The sound of the tennis shoes faded in the jungle heat.

Mr. Sanderson stood in the sun-blazed door, listening. From a long time ago, when he dreamed as a boy, he remembered the sound. Beautiful creatures leaping under the sky, gone through brush, under trees, away, and only the soft echo their running left behind.

"Antelopes," said Mr. Sanderson. "Gazelles."

He bent to pick up the boy's abandoned winter shoes, heavy with forgotten rains and long-melted snows. Moving out of the blazing sun, walking softly, lightly, slowly, he headed back toward civilization. . . .

© 1984 Jill Krementz

Ray Bradbury (*born 1920*) asked for a typewriter for his twelfth Christmas and has been turning out stories ever since. As a boy he liked adventure books, secret code rings, comics, and Saturdays at the movies. "I was in love with everything I did," he says. Most of Bradbury's writing is science fiction and fantasy. He has published more than a thousand short stories. Some are collected into books such as *The Martian Chronicles.* His novels *Fahrenheit 451* and *Something Wicked This Way Comes* were made into movies.

Developing Comprehension Skills

1. According to his father, could Douglas wear last year's shoes? According to Douglas, what is wrong with last year's shoes?

2. When might the magic in the new shoes die? When is there still plenty of magic?

3. Where and when does the first part of the story take place? What is the time, day of the week, and location of the second part? Is it clear how much time has passed between the two parts?

4. What does Mr. Sanderson do for a living? Is he young or old? How is he dressed? Is Mr. Sanderson interested only in making a sale? Explain your answers.

5. What are the two animals Mr. Sanderson asks about? What kinds of movements do these animals make? What sound does Mr. Sanderson remember?

6. Does this story describe something that could really happen? Do you think any real person feels as strongly about shoes as Douglas does?

Reading Literature: Short Stories

1. **Interpreting Description.** Descriptions can create an impression or show the effect something has on a character. Reread the paragraph on page 196 beginning "It was because they felt the way. . . ." Then read

the next paragraph beginning "Somehow the people. . . ." Find examples in both paragraphs of details that describe something you can see or feel. How do these descriptions create an impression of what sneakers mean to Douglas?

2. **Understanding Theme.** What meaning do the Litefoot shoes have for Douglas? What do the leather shoes represent to him? In what ways might summer have special meaning for young people rather than people the age of Douglas's father?

3. **Examining Point of View.** This story is told from the third-person point of view, meaning that the narrator is outside of the action. Is the point of view **limited,** with the narrator revealing the thoughts of only one character? Or is it **omniscient,** with the narrator revealing the thoughts of more than one character? How does the point of view in this story compare with that of "The Necklace"?

Vocabulary

Using Context Clues: Examples. Sometimes the meaning of a difficult word is suggested by an example. Notice how the technical term *refraction* is explained in the following sentence from the story.

> The tennis shoes felt like it always feels the first time every year wading in the slow waters of the creek and seeing your feet below, half an inch further downstream, with refraction, than the real part of you above water.

The example of refraction can help you understand the meaning of the word: the bending of a ray of light as it passes on a slant from air to water.

Use the examples to figure out the meanings of the underlined words in the following sentences. Record any key words that signal an example context clue.

1. Different animals were <u>kenneled</u> in different ways; for example, the dogs were in cages and the snakes were in glass cases.
2. He felt <u>detached</u>, as if he were someone who had nothing to do with the life going on around him.
3. The earth was <u>yielding</u>, like a mound of dough pressed by a finger.
4. He liked to do <u>limbering</u> exercises—neck rolls and other slow stretching movements that loosened his muscles.

Speaking and Listening

Reading Aloud. In many ways, this story is similar to poetry. The emphasis is more on creating a feeling than on the plot, and the descriptions include many images and comparisons. Above all, the sound of the language is important in creating the effect. Find a passage in which the rhythm of the language helps re-create a sense of flowing and movement. Practice reading the passage aloud. If possible, use a tape recorder to help yourself hear whether your voice is conveying the melody of the language.

Developing Writing Skills

1. **Writing a Description.** What is your favorite thing to wear? In one or two paragraphs describe this item and the enjoyable experiences you associate with it.

   Prewriting. Brainstorm with your classmates for ideas about items and experiences that you might write about. You might choose part of a uniform from a sport you enjoy, something you wore to a special outing, or an outfit you like to wear when you relax. Work on your own list of details about the item and the experiences that you want to describe.

   Drafting. Try to avoid a flat topic sentence such as "I like my baseball cap because it makes me think of my favorite sport." Instead, use comparisons and images that will create a specific impression.

   Revising and Sharing. Work with a partner on revising your description. Discuss how well the description makes someone else understand how you feel about the item. Look for ways to make images or comparisons more vivid or specific. After revising your description, share it with the class.

2. **Writing an Explanation.** A title often gives a clue about what is important in a story. For example, "The Necklace" names the object that is a major focus of the story. Write a paragraph explaining what you think the title "The Sound of Summer Running" means.

   Identify what kind of sound the title refers to and who or what makes the sound. Does the title identify an important object or character? Does it hint at the theme? Could the title have more than one meaning? As you develop your paragraph, follow the steps in the process of writing: prewriting, drafting, revising, and sharing. If you need help, refer to the handbook at the back of the book.

Great Modern Short Stories

The next set of short stories were all written in this century. Some are set in the distant past. Others are set in the future. Some are exciting adventure stories. Others emphasize feelings rather than plot. These stories are similar to the classics you have just read in one important way. Each story shows you how a character deals with a problem.

The City from Greenwich Village, 1922, JOHN SLOAN. National Gallery of Art, Washington, D.C., Gift of Helen Farr Sloan, 1970.

Reading Literature

More About Short Stories

The most important elements of a short story are character, setting, plot, and theme. On this page and the next, you will learn more about characters. You will also learn about the element of plot called *conflict* and about theme.

Characters. Characters can be either main or minor. The characters most involved in the conflict of a story are the **main characters.** Often a short story has only one main character, such as Matilda Loisel in "The Necklace." Her husband, her school friend, and others at the ball also take part in the story. These are **minor characters.** The story is not centered on them. Minor characters help carry out the action or show something about the main character.

Characterization. Characterization is the use of literary techniques to develop a character. A writer can create a character in at least three ways. One is by describing what the character looks like. A second is by telling what the character says. A third is by showing what he or she does. In "Hearts and Hands," the writer uses all these methods in presenting Miss Fairchild.

In some stories, the narrator shows the reader a character's thoughts and feelings. The narrator in "The Bet" uses this method of characterization for the banker.

Another method of characterization is to show how characters act with one another. At the end of "The Necklace," the reader understands how Matilda has changed when her friend does not know her.

Conflict. The plot of a short story describes some kind of difficulty that the main character faces. This central struggle is the **conflict**. There are two kinds of conflict.

In an **external conflict,** the struggle is between a character and some outside force. The outside force may be a difficult situation, a force of nature such as a storm, or even a supernatural force. In "Rikki-tikki-tavi" the conflict is between Rikki-tikki and the cobras. In "The Necklace," the outside force Matilda must defeat is the need to replace the diamonds.

In some stories, the conflict is an **internal conflict.** The struggle takes place within a character. In "The Summer of the Beautiful White Horse," Aram faces an internal conflict when he must choose between his love of horses and honoring his family's good name.

Theme. Every serious work of literature has a **theme,** or message, about life. Often the theme is not stated directly. Instead you have to figure out the main point. To do so, look over the story. What can you learn from the characters and from what happens to them? Can you understand more about the way people act or feel? Is there a lesson in the story about what a person should or should not do?

Not all readers will find the same themes in the same stories. Readers might find any of these messages in "The Necklace":

A thing may cost more than it is worth.
A short time of success does not always bring lasting happiness.
We do not always want what we get when we get what we want.

Southpaw

JUDITH VIORST

Do friends sometimes have conflicts that seem impossible to resolve? Watch the friends in this story work out their problem.

Dear Richard,

Don't invite me to your birthday party because I'm not coming. And give back the Disneyland sweat shirt I said you could wear. If I'm not good enough to play on your team, I'm not good enough to be friends with.

> Your former friend,
> Janet

P.S. I hope when you go to the dentist, he finds 20 cavities.

Dear Janet,

Here is your stupid Disneyland sweat shirt, if that's how you're going to be. I want my comic books now—finished or not. No girl has ever played on the Mapes Street baseball team, and as long as I'm captain, no girl ever will.

> *Your former friend,*
> *Richard*

P.S. I hope when you go for your checkup you need a tetanus shot.

Dear Richard,

I'm changing my goldfish's name from Richard to Stanley. Don't count on my vote for class president next year. Just because I'm a member of the ballet club doesn't mean I'm not a terrific ballplayer.

> Your former friend,
> Janet

P.S. I see you lost your first game, 28–0.

Dear Janet,

I'm not saving any more seats for you on the bus. For all I care you can stand the whole way to school. Why don't you forget about baseball and learn something nice like knitting?

> *Your former friend,*
> *Richard*

P.S. Wait until Wednesday.

Dear Richard,

My father said I could call someone to go with us for a ride and hot-fudge sundaes. In case you didn't notice, I didn't call you.

Your former friend,
Janet

P.S. I see you lost your second game, 34–0.

Dear Janet,

Remember when I took the laces out of my blue-and-white sneakers and gave them to you? I want them back.

Your former friend,
Richard

P.S. Wait until Friday.

Dear Richard,

Congratulations on your unbroken record. Eight straight losses, wow! I understand you're the laughingstock of New Jersey.

Your former friend,
Janet

P.S. Why don't you and your team forget about baseball and learn something nice like knitting, maybe?

Dear Janet,

Here's the silver horseback-riding trophy that you gave me. I don't think I want to keep it anymore.

Your former friend,
Richard

Girl Sitting by Mailbox, about 1965, JACK BEAL. Housatonic Museum, Bridgeport, Connecticut.

P.S. I didn't think you'd be the kind who'd kick a man when he's down.

Dear Richard,

    I wasn't kicking exactly. I was kicking *back.*

Your former friend,
Janet

P.S. In case you were wondering, my batting average is .345.

Dear Janet,

    Alfie is having his tonsils out tomorrow. We might be able to let you catch next week.

Richard

Dear Richard,

    I pitch.

Janet

Dear Janet,

    Joel is moving to Kansas and Danny sprained his wrist. How about a permanent place in the outfield?

Richard

Dear Richard,

    I pitch.

Janet

Dear Janet,

    Ronnie caught the chicken pox and Leo broke his toe and Elwood has these stupid violin lessons. I'll give you first base. That's my final offer.

Richard

Dear Richard,

    Susan Reilly plays first base, Marilyn Jackson catches, Ethel Kahn plays center field, I pitch. It's a package deal.

Janet

P.S. Sorry about your 12-game losing streak.

Dear Janet,

    Please! Not Marilyn Jackson.

Richard

Dear Richard,

    Nobody ever said that I was unreasonable. How about Lizzie Martindale instead?

Janet

Dear Janet,

    At least could you call your goldfish Richard again?

Your friend,
Richard

Judith Viorst *(born 1931)* is a poet and journalist. Most of her writing concerns the humorous side of everyday family life. Many of her ideas come from her own experiences as wife, mother, writer, and homemaker. Viorst writes poems and articles for magazines and newspapers. In 1970 she won an Emmy for a television script. Some of her most popular books for children are *Sunday Morning; Alexander and the Terrible, Horrible, No Good, Very Bad Day;* and *Rosie and Michael.*

Developing Comprehension Skills

1. Were Janet and Richard once good friends or just people who knew each other in school? Give three examples of what one or the other does to support your opinion.

2. When does Richard's attitude toward Janet start to change? Explain what causes the change. Does Richard accept Janet's viewpoint, do circumstances force him to change, or are both causes true?

3. What is the first team position Richard offers Janet? What position does Janet say she plays?

4. What agreement do Richard and Janet reach?

5. Janet explains her unfriendly comments to Richard by saying that she wasn't kicking a man when he was down, she was kicking *back*. What does she mean? Is there a real difference between "kicking a man when he is down" and "kicking back"? Is one more justified than the other? Be prepared to give reasons for your opinions.

Reading Literature: Short Stories

1. **Analyzing Conflict.** As you have learned, a **conflict** is a struggle between opposing forces. An **external conflict** is with an outside force or person. An **internal conflict** is within a character. The conflicts in this story are both internal and external. What two characters are in conflict? What internal conflict does each one face because of their disagreement? Which one of the two finds it harder to end both the internal and external conflicts? Explain.

2. **Examining Theme.** The **theme** is the message of a work of literature. Sometimes one story may suggest different themes. What message about stereotyping does this story suggest? Do you see any lesson about how to solve conflicts between friends?

Vocabulary

Recognizing Jargon and Specialized Vocabulary. People from a particular region or job may use words and terms that have a special meaning for that group. Such specialized vocabulary is known as **jargon.** Use your own knowledge of baseball, look in a dictionary, or consult someone who knows the game well to answer these questions about the baseball jargon in this story.

1. Is a southpaw right-handed or left-handed? What position does a southpaw usually play in baseball?

2. What does it mean to catch? to pitch?

3. What is a batting average? Is an average of .345 good or bad?

4. What is a place in the outfield? What two former players on the Mapes Street team played in the outfield?

Critical Thinking

Analyzing Stereotyping. Stereotyping occurs when one person judges what another is like or can do based on a simplified idea of an entire group. For example, in this story Richard has a stereotyped idea about girls. What idea does he have about what girls should not do? What facts does Janet explain that show the stereotype does not apply to her? What does Richard say is something nice for girls to learn? What stereotype does that remark suggest?

Developing Writing Skills

Telling a Story Through Letters. Think of a conflict or disagreement two good friends might have. You can make up a situation or use something that happened to you. Write two letters, one by each person, that show the two sides of the conflict.

Prewriting. Once you have decided on the conflict you want to write about, list what happened and who said what to create the conflict. Also note the ways in which each person misunderstood the other.

Drafting. As you write, remember that each letter should be limited to one person's viewpoint. Give some indication of how strong the friendship was before the conflict and whether one or both people would like to continue being friends. Try to create a sense of the personality of each writer. Feel free to use humor as the writer of "Southpaw" did.

Revising and Sharing. Have someone else read your set of letters. Make revisions based on his or her responses to these questions. "Is the conflict between the two letter writers clear? Are there enough details about how each one feels? Does the disagreement sound like one that might really take place? Do the two letter writers sound like different people? Are the letters written in the usual letter form?"

A Christmas Tree for Lydia

ELIZABETH ENRIGHT

Times are hard for Eddy's family at Christmas. They can't afford to buy the tree his little sister dreams of. Can Eddy keep her from being disappointed?

Lydia first learned about Christmas when she was one year old. Draped over her mother's shoulder she drooled and stared, and the lights of the Christmas tree made other lights in her large tranced eyes and in the glaze of spittle on her chin.

When she was two years old, she learned about Santa Claus. She paid very little attention to him then, but when she was three, she talked about him a lot, and they had some difficulty persuading her that he and the infant Jesus were not father and son. By the time she was four, she had come to accept him as one of the ordered phenomena that ruled her life, like daytime and nighttime: one seven o'clock for getting up and another seven o'clock for going to bed. Like praise and blame and winter and summer and her brother's right of seniority and her mother's last word. Her father did not exist in her field of magnitudes; he had been killed in Cassino[1] the winter she was born.

"Santa Claus will come," Lydia said and knew it was as true as saying tomorrow will come. "He will bring a Christmas tree. Big. With lights. With colors."

When she was four, her brother Eddy was nine and had long ago found out the truth concerning the matter. No note of illusion deceived his eye when he passed the street-corner Santas at Christmas time, standing beside their imitation chimneys, ringing their bells. He saw them for what they were. He saw how all their trousers bagged and their sleeves were too long, and how, above the false beards tied loosely on like bibs, their noses ran and their eyes looked out, mortal and melancholy.

---

1. **Cassino** (kə sē′nō)—A town in Italy that was the site of a fierce battle during World War II.

"You'd think the kid would catch on," Eddy said to his mother. "Gee, when you notice the differentness of them all."

Lydia believed in every one of them, from the bell-ringers on the street corners to the department-store variety who always asked the same questions and whose hired joviality grew glassy toward evening. She had faith in the monster idol in the store on Fourteenth Street which turned its glaring face from side to side and laughed a huge stony machinery laugh all day long, filling the region with sounds of compulsive derangement. For Lydia, the saint was ubiquitous, ingenious, capable of all, and looking into the different faces of his impersonators, she beheld the one good face she had invented for him.

"Eddy, don't you tell her now, will you?" his mother said. "Don't you dare to, now. Remember she's only four."

Sure, let the kid have her fun, thought Eddy, with large scorn and slight compassion. He himself remembered long-ago Christmas Eves when he had listened for bells in the air, and watched the limp shape of his sock hung up over the stove.

"How can he come in through the *stove,* Mum?"

"In houses like this, he comes in through the window. Go to sleep now, Eddy, like a good boy."

Eddy went to public school in the daytimes and Lydia went to a day nursery. Her mother called for her every evening on the way home from work. She was a thin dark young woman whose prettiness was often obscured by the ragged shadows of irritation and fatigue. She loved her children, but worry gnawed at her relations with them, sharpening her words and shortening her temper. Coming home in the evening, climbing up the stairs to the flat with one hand pressing the bags of groceries to her chest, and Lydia loitering and babbling, dragging on her other hand, she wished sometimes to let go of everything. To let go of Lydia, perhaps forever; to let go once and for all of the heavy paper grocery bags. It would be a savage happiness, she felt, to see and hear the catsup bottle smashed on the stairs, the eggs broken and leaking, and all the tin cans and potatoes rolling and banging their way downward.

They lived in a two-room flat with linoleum on the floor and a lively corrugated ceiling. In the daytime, from noon on, the rooms were hot with sunshine, but in the morning and at night they were as cold as caves unless the stove was going. The stove and the bathtub and the sink were all in the front room where Eddy slept. Sometimes at night the bathtub would gulp lonesomely, and the leaky tap of the sink had a drip as perfect in tempo as a clock.

Lydia and her mother slept in the back room, a darkish place, painted blue, with a big dim mirror over the bureau, and a window looking on to a shaft. The toilet was by itself in a little cubicle with a window also looking on to the shaft. When the chain was pulled, it was as though one had released a river genie. A great storming and rumbling rose upward through the pipes, shaking all the furniture in the flat, then there was a prolonged crashing of waters lasting for minutes, and at last the mighty withdrawal, thundering and wrathful, growing fainter at last, and still fainter, till silence was restored, docile and appeased.

Sometimes when Eddy was alone and the stillness got to be too much for him, he went into the water closet and pulled the chain just for the company of the noise.

He was often alone during the first part of his vacation. At noon, wearing his blue and grey Mackinaw and his aviator's helmet with the straps flying, he came stamping up the stairs and into the sun-flooded, crowded little flat. Humming and snuffling, he made his lunch: breakfast food, or huge erratic sandwiches filled with curious materials. When he was through, he always cleaned up: washed the bowl or dish and swept up the bread crumbs with his chapped hand. He had learned to be tidy at an early age and could even make his bed well enough to sleep in it.

In the afternoons and mornings he voyaged forth with Joey Camarda, and others, to the streets for contests of skill and wit. Sometimes they went to the upper reaches of the park with its lakes, bridges, battlegrounds, and ambushes. Or rainy days they tagged through the museums, shrill and shabby as sparrows, touching the raddled surfaces of meteorites without awe and tipping back their heads boldly to stare at the furious mask of Tyrannosaurus Rex.

"He isn't real. They made him out of pieces of wood, like," Joey said. "Men with ladders made him."

"He is, too, real," Eddy said. "He walked around and ate and growled and everything. Once he did."

"Naw, he wasn't real. Jeez, he *couldn't* be real. You'd believe anything. You'd believe in Santy Claus even."

Christmas and its symbols were more and more in their conversation as the time drew near. They speculated on the subject of possible gifts to themselves. Joey said his uncle was going to give him roller skates and a real Mauser rifle.

"It's one he got when he was in It'ly. What are you going to get, Eddy?"

Eddy said he thought he'd probably get a bike. It was just as likely that he would be given a bike as that he would be given the new moon out of the sky, but having made the statement, he went on to perfect it. He said that it would be a white bike with red trimming and a red piece of glass like a jewel on the back of it, and two raccoon tails floating from the handlebars.

"There's going to be two kinds of bells on the handlebars. One will be kind of a sireen."

"Will you let me ride on it sometimes,

Ed?"

"Sometimes," Eddy said.

That night he rode the bike all around the flat with the raccoon tails lying out on the speed-torn air. The taillight blazed like a red-hot ruby, and the siren was as terrible as human voice could make it.

"Watch me now, I'm taking a curve," shouted Eddy. "Eee-ow-oooo-eee. Just missed that truck by half an inch!"

Lydia sat safely on the bed in the back room questioning him as he flashed by.

"Is it a plane, Eddy?"

"No."

"Is it a car?"

"No."

"Is it a—is it a train?"

"No. Gosh, it's a bike. Look out now. I got to make that light. Eee-ow-ooo-eee!"

"Eddy, will you please for pity's sake *shut up!*" cried his mother. "I can't hear myself think even!"

Falls City, Nebraska, 1946, JOHN FALTER. Reprinted with Permission from *The Saturday Evening Post* © 1946 The Curtis Publishing Company, Indianapolis.

He came to a stop. "Gee, Mum, what are you cross about?"

She didn't look at him. She pushed the potatoes and onions around the frying pan with a fork. Then she shook salt over them, and spoke from a certain distance.

"Eddy, you kids don't get a tree this year."

"Heck, why not? What did we do? Why not?"

"I can't afford it, that's why!" she cried loudly, angry with him because she was hurting him. Then she lowered her voice. "They don't want me back at the store after Christmas, they told me today. They don't need me any more. I don't dare to get you any presents even but just things you have to have like socks and mittens." She looked at him. "Maybe some candy," she added.

A stinging hot odor arose from the frying pan to join the robust company of cooking smells from other flats on other floors: herring and chili and garlic and pork.

"Gee, Eddy, I'm scared to spend another cent. How do I know I'll get another job?"

"What are you going to tell Lydia? She talks about the Christmas tree all day long."

"She'll have to do without, that's all. Other people have to do without."

"But, gee, she talks about it all day long."

His mother threw down the fork and whirled on him.

"I can't *help* it, can I? My God, what am *I* supposed to do?"

Eddy knew better than to go on with it. He leaned against the sink and thought, and when they ate supper, he was kind and forebearing with Lydia who was both hilarious and sloppy. After a while his kindness became preoccupied like that of one who drinks secretly at a spring of inspiration, and when Lydia had gone to bed, he made a suggestion to his mother.

"I have an idea. If we put Christmas off for a few days, maybe a week, I can fix everything."

His mother, as he had expected, said no. It was this response on the part of his mother which was the starting point of all his campaigns, many of them successful. He leaned against the sink and waited.

"What good would it do? And anyway what would Lydia think!" she said.

"Tell her Santa Claus is late. Tell her we made a mistake about the day. She's too dumb to know the difference. Everyone's dumb when they're four."

"And anyway it seems kind of wrong."

"What would Jesus care if we put his birthday off for a couple of days?"

"Oh, Eddy, don't be silly. There won't be any more money than there is now."

"No, but I got an idea. Please, Mum, please. Please."

Eddy knew how to pester nicely. He had a quiet attentive way of looking and looking at one; of following one with his eyes and not saying anything, the request still shimmering all around him like heat-lightning. He waited.

His mother hung up the wet dishtowel and turned the dishpan upside down. She looked into the little mirror above the sink and looked away again. Then she sat down in the rocker and opened the tabloid newspaper.

"Oh, all *right*," she said. "For pity's sake, Eddy. What do you expect, a miracle?"

"Isn't there ever any miracles? Anyway I'm not thinking about a miracle, I'm thinking about something smart," Eddy said.

Christmas came, and for them it was a day like any other, except that their mother was at home. But it was easy to explain to Lydia that this was because her job at the store had ended for good, just as it was easy to explain Lydia's own absence from nursery school by the simple method of rubbing Vicks ointment on her chest. Eddy thought of that one, too.

"Gee, Eddy, I hope you know what you're doing," his mother said.

"I do know," Eddy said.

"You should at least tell *me* what you're going to do."

"It has to be a surprise for you, too," Eddy said, not so much because he wanted to surprise his mother as because he knew if he revealed his plan, he would come in contact with a "no" which none

of his stratagems could dissolve.

"It will be okay, Mum."

"And when is it to be, if I may ask?"

"On New Year's Day, I guess," Eddy said, and went in search of Joey Camarda, whose help he had enlisted.

On New Year's Eve, early, he shut Lydia and his mother into their room.

"No matter what noises you hear, you don't come out, see? Promise."

"But, Eddy, I don't think——"

"You promise."

"Well——" his mother conceded, and that was as good as promising. She went in and shut the door, and before the extraordinary sounds of toil and shuffling commenced in the hall, she was lost in the deep sleep of the discouraged: that temporary death which is free from all the images of fear or joy.

At midnight the city woke up and met the New Year with a mighty purring. In the streets people blew horns and shook things that sounded like tin cans full of pebbles. Lydia woke up too and thought that it was Santa Claus.

"I wanna get up, Mum. I wanna see him."

"You lay down this minute or he won't leave a single thing. He doesn't like for people to be awake when he comes," said her mother crossly, clinging to the warm webs of sleep.

But Lydia sat up for a while in her cot, rocking softly to and fro. Through the crack under the door came a fragrance she remembered well from Christmas a year ago, and the Christmas before that.

In the morning it was a long time before Eddy would let them out of their room.

"Eddy, it's cold in here," said his mother.

"I wanna see the tree, I wanna see the tree," chanted Lydia, half singing, half whining. "I wanna see the tree, I wanna see the tree."

"Heck, wait a minute," said Eddy.

"I wanna see the tree, I wanna see the tree," bayed Lydia.

There were sounds of haste and struggle in the next room.

"All right, you can come in now," said Eddy, and opened the door.

They saw a forest.

In a circle, hiding every wall, stood the Christmas trees; spare ones and stout ones, tall ones and short ones, but all tall to Lydia. Some still were hung with threads of silver foil, and here and there among the boughs the ornaments for a single tree had been distributed with justice. Calm and bright as planets they turned and burned among the needles. The family stood in a mysterious grove, without bird or breeze, and there was a deep fragrance in the room. It was a smell of health and stillness and tranquillity, and for a minute or two, before she had thought of the dropping needles and the general inconvenience of a forest in the kitchen, Eddy's mother breathed the smell full into her city lungs and felt within

herself a lessening of strain.

"Eddy, Eddy, how? How?"

"Me and Joe Camarda," Eddie whispered. "We went all around last night and dragged them out of gutters. We could of filled the whole entire house with them if we wanted to. Last night in here it was like camping out."

It had been like that. He had lain peacefully in his bed under the branches, listening to the occasional snowflake tinkle of a falling needle, and to the ticking of the leaky tap, hidden now as any forest spring.

"Eddy honey, look at Lydia."

Lydia still looked new from her sleep. She stood in her flannel nightgown with her dark hair rumpled and her eyes full of lights and her hands clasped in front of her in a composed, elderly way. Naturally a loud, exuberant girl, the noise had temporarily been knocked out of her.

"All the Christmas trees," she remarked gently.

"Gee," said Eddy. "Don't get the idea it's going to be this way every year. This is just because he was late, and it's instead of presents."

It was enough for Lydia, anyone could see that. In a way, it was enough for Eddy too. He felt proud, generous, and efficient. He felt successful. With his hands in his pockets he stood looking at his sister.

"All the Christmas trees," Lydia said quietly, and sighed. "All the Christmas trees."

Elizabeth Enright *(1909–1968)* was born in Chicago. She studied art in New York and Paris. At twenty she got her first job, doing illustrations for a fairy tale. Enright later tried writing and soon preferred it to drawing. Her second book, *Thimble Summer*, was awarded the Newbery Medal in 1939. The successful volumes that followed are still popular.

Developing Comprehension Skills

1. How old is Lydia at the time of the story? How old is Eddy? What does each of them think about Santa Claus?

2. What problems does Eddy's mother face?

3. What is Eddy doing when his mother shouts at him? Is she really angry at Eddy?

4. What plan does Eddy have to give Lydia a Christmas? Why doesn't he tell his mother what he is going to do?

5. At the end of the story we are told that the room of Christmas trees was enough to satisfy Lydia and that, "In a way, it was enough for Eddy too." What kind of satisfaction does Eddy get out of his project? Would he have gotten the same satisfaction if his mother had thought up and then carried out the plan? Explain.

Reading Literature: Short Stories

1. **Thinking About Conflict.** What force or problem do Eddy and his mother struggle with? Is the conflict internal or external?

2. **Analyzing Characterization.** A writer can develop a character by showing what the character says and does, by describing appearance, by telling thoughts and feelings, and by showing how others react to the character. Choose either Eddy or his mother and give examples of at least two techniques used to develop the character.

3. **Examining Mood. Mood** is the feeling created in the reader by a piece of writing. The mood may be sad, joyful, angry, or humorous. A writer can create mood through details. Read the descriptions of the street-corner Santas on pages 213–214. Do they seem like figures of magic and happiness? Or does the description make them seem depressing and sad? List three details that create the mood. Does the description of the department-store Santa two paragraphs later fit this mood?

Vocabulary

Using a Glossary. The underlined words in the following sentences from the story may be words that you are not familiar with. Look up each underlined word in the glossary at the back of this book. Write the definition of the word and use it in a sentence of your own.

1. ". . . she had come to accept him as one of the ordered phenomena that ruled her life. . . ." (page 213)

2. ". . . their eyes looked out, mortal and melancholy." (page 213)

3. "For Lydia, the saint was ubiquitous. . . ." (page 214)

4. "They speculated on the subject of possible gifts to themselves. . . ." (page 215)

Speaking and Listening

Reading Dialogue. The writer of this story often shows the action through dialogue, by having the characters speak back and forth in their own voices, without too much narrative. Work with a few classmates to do a dramatic reading of a passage of dialogue, such as a conversation between Eddy and his friends or between Eddy and his mother. Assign one person to be the narrator and one to be each speaker. Practice so that each reader pauses and changes his or her tone of voice as real speakers would. Notice how the dialogue helps to create characters that sound like real people.

Developing Writing Skills

Describing Character. Use the details given in this story as the basis for a paragraph describing Eddy, Lydia, or their mother.

Prewriting. Reread the story carefully. Take notes on details that show the characters' appearance and important qualities. You will find it helpful to review your notes for study question 2 in **Reading Literature.** When you have finished listing all the details, organize them in groups. Decide on the order in which you will present the groups.

Drafting. Follow the organization you decide on during prewriting. Support each statement you make about the character by showing something he or she says, does, or thinks in the story. Make clear connections between ideas.

Revising and Sharing. Form a group with other students who wrote a paragraph about the same character. Read each paragraph in turn and compare your interpretations of the character. Go back over your own draft to make sure that you have organized your presentation of the character in a way that builds a clear, accurate impression. Then do a final draft.

The Old Soldier

DOROTHY CANFIELD

The title of this story draws attention to one character. Is he the most important character? As you read, decide just who is the main character.

No matter how I set this story down, you will take it, I fear, as a fable. But it is not. It is as literally true as a local news item in your this-morning's newspaper. It happened up the state a ways from our town, "over the mountain," as we call that middle upland valley of Vermont.

For a long time, after the Revolution, the citizens of the little town of Sunmore had made a great day out of the Fourth of July. They seemed to hear, more clearly than some other towns, the very sound of the old Liberty Bell in Philadelphia as it rang out in joy over the signing of the Declaration of Independence. They had not at all forgotten what the Fourth meant. As the years went by, a set form grew up for the day's celebration. At dawn, the big boys fired off again and again the old cannon which stood on the village common. There was a meeting, about eleven in the morning, at the Town Hall, where people made speeches and sang patriotic songs. After that, a picnic lunch was eaten out on the green. If it rained, the lunch was eaten inside the Town Hall. Then, rain or shine, the procession formed to escort the old soldiers out to the Burying Ground, a mile from town, where they put flags on the graves of their comrades among the Sunmore men who, like them, had been soldiers in the Revolution.

Nearly everybody in town marched in this procession, carrying flags and flowers and keeping step with the music of the town drum and fife corps. "Whee-dee-deedle-dee" went the high thin voices of the fifes, and "boom-boom-boom" went the deep voices of the drums. Tramp! tramp! tramp! went the feet of the Sunmore men and women and children—especially boys.

The boys looked forward to this celebrating from one year to the next chiefly, of course, because to share in the firing of the cannon marked a long step forward in growing up. The cannon was generally

A Beautiful World, 1948, GRANDMA MOSES.

said to have been in the Battle of Bennington in 1777. Ordinary people said yes, of course it was. But more careful folks said this was not sure. As the years went by after that battle, twenty, forty, fifty; and finally by the time of this story, in 1848, seventy years, fewer and fewer people could remember it. Also, of course, there were fewer and fewer old Sunmore men who had been Revolutionary soldiers.

Until they were past eighty, they had walked in the procession like everybody else. After that, Dr. White, who of course took care of them all when they were sick, said their joints were too stiff. He took them out in his own chaise, behind his slow, ancient roan horse. Dick was rather stiff in his joints too, and was glad to walk with ceremonial slowness.

Dr. White knew more about medicine

than anyone else in town. This was to be expected because nobody else knew anything at all about it. But on the subject— local history—of which many people knew a great deal, he was also the local specialist. On the shelves of his library, mixed up with his medical books, stood more histories of Vermont than the rest of Sunmore people had, all put together. When anyone wanted to find out something about what had happened in the past, Dr. White was asked. He always knew the answer.

When May and June came in, people began to plan for the Fourth of July celebration. But there were no old soldiers left. For four or five years there had been only two. Both of them were very old, of course, for the year 1848 was seventy-one years after the Battle of Bennington. One had been ninety, and the other eighty-six. Now both were gone. The older one had died in the winter, and the family of the other one had moved away out west into York State and taken the old man with them.

It was too bad. Everybody was saying that the celebration wouldn't be much without old soldiers in it, to connect the town with the Revolution. Without them, how would people remember what the Fourth of July was really about? The ancients had always sat on the platform of the Town Hall, while the singing and speech-making went on, their long fire-arms across their knees, their soldier's leather belts strapped on over their Sunday coats. Of course what uniforms they had had, had gone all to pieces, if they'd ever had any, which was unlikely, buckskin being the wear in those early days. They had ridden in Dr. White's chaise, just behind the fife and drum corps and the little girls in white dresses carrying the bouquets, ahead of the marching men and women, four abreast in the road. When the procession reached the cemetery, the little girls handed the flowers to the big boys, and they passed them out to the hobbling old soldiers, who laid them on the graves of their comrades in the Revolution. The smaller boys had the honor of planting fresh American flags on the graves, waving above the flowers.

One of the boys in town, one of the Bostwick family, heard his folks lamenting that the celebration would not seem right with no old soldiers at all. He was the third child; Andrew was his name. He was about ten years old when this happened. He went to the nearby district school and read in the fourth reader, but long before he knew his alphabet, he knew about the Battle of Bennington and the Revolutionary War.

He was just getting to be old enough to help fire off the cannon, and to hand the flowers to the old soldiers in the cemetery. And now they were all gone.

One day in June, when he was sent out to look for a cow which, the night before, hadn't come back to the barn from the mountain pasture, he met a schoolmate up there, Will Hunter. Will's mother had sent him out to pick wild strawberries on that sloping clearing. After the two boys met, the cow and the strawberries were forgotten. They sat down on a ledge to have a talk. Before long, Andrew said something about the Fourth of July celebration with no old soldier left, not a single one.

The other boy said, "There's an old fellow lives with the Hawleys, 'way up Hawley Hollow from our house. He's their great-grandfather, I think. Maybe he was a soldier in the Revolution. He's old enough. They say he's ninety. More."

Andrew's ten-year-old mind was already firmly lodged behind the tight narrow wall of the idea of the Town. "They don't live in Sunmore," he said. "We have to have a Sunmore old soldier for our Fourth."

"Yes, they do too, live in Sunmore," said the other boy. "They don't trade at the Sunmore stores much, because from that end of the Hollow where their house is, it's easier to go out the far end to Canbury. But they vote in our Town Meeting.[1]"

The two boys looked at each other. Thinking no more of the cow and the

strawberries, they set out for Hawley Hollow.

So there *was* to be a Revolutionary soldier after all for the Fourth of July celebration! Everybody was talking about the old man, eighty-nine years, or maybe ninety, maybe more, back up on the far side of Westward Mountain, who had been remembered just in time.

When the two boys told their fathers about him, two of the Selectmen of the town had gone over the mountain to see him. They said his back was bent with rheumatism, he was almost stone deaf, and he hobbled along with two canes to steady him. But he still had his old rifle, and even his cracked leather soldier's belt, just as the others had. And they reported that when, shouting loudly in his ear, they had asked him if he had fought in the Revolutionary War, he had nodded his head. Then they asked had it been in the Battle of Bennington? When he finally heard what they were asking, he nodded his head and told them, "Yes, yes, *sir,* it certainly was."

They said the Hawleys up there, for all he was so old, thought a great deal of him. It was his great-grandson's family he was with—young people they were, had been married only five or six years. When the last of his grandchildren had died, these young people had left their little cottage in Canbury and gone up to take care of him. An arrangement often made, in our coun-

---

1. **Town Meeting**–In New England, an annual meeting of citizens 18 years and older. They vote on issues affecting the town. The town is an area larger than a village, much like the Midwest township.

try—he was to leave them his house and farm and they were to provide for his old age. They had never heard, naturally, what he had been doing seventy years ago—neither of them was over twenty-five—but they had always seen the old long gun, laid on the pegs over the fireplace, and the old belt hung with it.

Wasn't it remarkable, Sunmore people said, that just that very year when the last of the old heroes had gone, this other old Revolutionary soldier had been found. And who had found him? Why, Andrew Bostwick and William Hunter, two little boys. They were bright little boys to have known enough history to understand about the Fourth of July. Patriotic too. The program committee arranged that they were to stand on the platform during the meeting on each side of the old soldier, and to march in the procession just in front of Dr. White's chaise, each one carrying an American flag. They were to be called the "Young Guard of Honor." You don't need anyone to tell you that those boys could hardly wait for the Fourth of July to come.

On the morning of the Fourth, Andrew's father got up early, took the boys, and drove his farm wagon all the way around the mountain and up into the Hollow to bring the old man back. It was ten o'clock when they came back into Sunmore Street. A crowd was waiting in front of the Town Hall. They began to clap their hands and cheer when Mr. Bostwick helped lift the bent old man out of the wagon and led him into the Hall. Andrew and Will, the Young Guard of Honor, carried his ancient gun in and put it across his knees. He had his rusty belt strapped on over his coat.

When they took his gun to carry, he gave them such a pleasant smile of thanks that they understood why his great-grandchildren thought so much of him. He was a very nice-looking old man, everybody thought, clean and neat, with quiet, gentle eyes; and although he hadn't a tooth left, his mouth still looked as though he liked jokes.

The people came into the Town Hall, took their seats, and began fanning themselves. It was a hot day, as the Fourth often is. The speaker was there, a lawyer from Canbury. The chorus of local singers stood below the platform, facing the audience. Their leader rapped his stick. They stood at attention. But they did not begin to sing. For at this point Dr. White, who always sat on the platform with the Selectmen and the speaker, called out to Andrew, "Here! Let me look at that gun! Pass it over to me."

Andrew was surprised. He put his hand on the gun and, leaning down to the old man's ear, said to him as loudly as he could, "Dr. White wants to see your gun."

He shouted with all his might but he could not make himself heard. The old soldier was almost stone deaf. But he was willing to do anything that was wanted.

His cheerful old face was bright. He felt the friendliness all around him. He smiled and nodded and passed his gun to Andrew.

The doctor took one sharp look at it and motioned to the singers in the chorus. "Wait a minute!" he told them.

Then he put on his glasses (he was the first person in Sunmore to have spectacles) and looked very carefully at a certain place near the trigger. Everybody kept still, wondering what was in his mind.

When he looked up, his face was all astonishment. He spoke so loudly that everybody in the whole Town Hall could hear him. "This is a Hessian[2] gun! The old man must have been one of the Hessians who fought against the Americans."

There was such a silence in the Town Hall you could hear a wasp buzzing at one of the windows.

He was a Hessian! He had fought on the other side. People's mouths dropped open, they were so taken back.

The old man hadn't heard any of this because he was so deaf. He sat quietly there, between the two little boys, his gentle old eyes looking around at the people in the hall.

For a minute nobody said a word. Nobody could think of what to say. Or what to do.

Then Andrew ran out to the front of the platform and began to talk very fast. "Listen," he said. "That was a hundred years ago. Well, more than seventy years, anyhow. No matter how mad you are at somebody, you don't keep it up forever. The Bible says not to. He's lived close to us all that time, and farmed it like anybody, and had his family, and paid his taxes. He's old, so old—it would be *mean* of us to——"

Andrew had never even spoken a piece in school. He had forgotten where he was. When he realized what he was doing, he stopped talking and hung down his head. He went back and put one hand on the old man's shoulder. The wrinkled face lifted to smile at him. Andrew smiled back. But his lips were trembling.

People began to rustle and move their feet. But when Dr. White stood up as if to say something, they were still again, to listen.

He said, "I remember now, when I came to Sunmore to practice medicine and first began to be interested in Vermont history, I did hear some very old people talk about a young Hessian soldier who had been wounded in the Battle of Bennington, and was picked up unconscious, in the woods, the day after. One of the old history books in my Vermont collection says that he was carried to a farmhouse and taken care of there. By the time he was well enough to get around, many

---

2. **Hessians**—Well-trained soldiers from Hesse-Kassel, Germany, hired by the British to fight the colonists during the Revolutionary War.

months afterward, there were no more soldiers or armies around. He was only nineteen by that time, and he had come to live the way of life he saw around him. He wanted to be an American and live here.

"That history book didn't say anything more about him. But I heard something else from old Mr. Hale." The doctor looked down into the audience at a middle-aged man in the second row. "He was your grandfather, Jim Hale. He was sort of connected, in-laws somehow, with the Bennington family that took in the Hessian boy. He told me they always liked him, the young soldier, I mean. When he learned enough English, he told them his story. He had always had it hard in the Old Country, he said. He was an orphan, very poor, seventeen years old, when a recruiting gang picked him up off the street and carried him off to the barracks in Brunswick. He never liked soldiering, he

Colonel Glover's Fishermen Leaving Marblehead for Cambridge, 1775, painted about 1920, J.O.J. FROST. New York Historical Association, Cooperstown.

said. He never understood what the fighting was about, because he never knew any English till he learned it from the Vermont family who took care of him."

The doctor still held the old rifle in his hands. He turned around now and laid it back on the old man's knees. Then he said to the audience, "I rather think Andrew Bostwick was right. Seventy years is too long to go on being mad. I think our celebration would better go on. Maybe the

COL. GLOVE
FISHERM
MARBLEHEAD
1775— 21st OF JUNE
FOR CAMBRIDGE

Reverend Hardwick might have something to say to us about this."

The minister stood up, stooped in his black clergyman's clothes.

The old man from Hawley Hollow had evidently thought the program was going on, and that the doctor had been making one of the planned-for speeches. Now, seeing the minister stand up and step forward, he thought that the prayer was to be said. He composed his face, leaned forward in his chair in the respectful position you take when somebody is praying in public, and dropped his eyes to the ground.

As a matter of fact, the Reverend Hardwick did pray. He stood silent a long time. Then he said, "May war pass and peace be with us. Amen."

He sat down. The Moderator of the Town stood up. He was a burly, powerful, middle-aged man, with a serious, responsible face. He said, soberly, "I think this is something we ought to take a vote on. Don't you think so, Mr. Hardwick?"

The minister nodded. "Yes. It is something for each of us to decide. But before we vote, I think we ought to sit quiet for a moment. And think."

The Moderator reached for the clergyman's cane, and with it struck a gavel-like blow on the table. In his Moderator's voice, he said, "The question before this House is whether we can live in peace when war has long gone by."

They all sat still.

The deaf ears of the old soldier had, of course, not heard any of this. It looked all right to him. He was very much bent with rheumatism. His hands lay thin and knotted on the arms of his chair. His clean old face was calm. In the silence, he looked from one person to another in the audience. He smiled a little. After a moment, he turned his white head to look back at his little-boy guard of honor. There they were, one on each side of his chair. He nodded and leaned back as if to say, "It's all right, if you are there."

The water came into Andrew's eyes.

The people in the rows of chairs on the floor were all looking up at the old soldier and the little boys.

A man stood up and said, "Mr. Moderator, I move that our celebration proceed."

Several voices said, "I second the motion."

Then the vote was taken. Everybody voted "aye."

So that afternoon, after the usual speaking and singing had been done, and the picnic lunch eaten out on the Common, the procession formed as usual, to march out to the cemetery.

The old soldier looked very tired by this time, but still cheerful. He came out of the Town Hall on Dr. White's arm, and was helped up into the chaise. The Young Guard of Honor held their flags high, so that they stirred in the breeze. The little girls in white dresses were pushed by their mothers into line, two by two. They carried the flowers—lilies, roses, carnation pinks.

The men and women formed, four by four. The doctor slapped the reins over the old horse's back. The leader of the band lifted his hand and said, commandingly, "A—a—ll ready!"

The marchers held their flags straight, ready to go.

"Forward, *march!*" cried the bandmaster.

The fifes sang out, "Whee-dee-deedle-dee" in thin high voices.

In a deep roar, the drums said, "Boom! boom! boom!"

And away they all went.

Dorothy Canfield *(1879–1958)* was born in Kansas, the daughter of a teacher and an artist. She attended college in Ohio, New York, and France, but felt most at home in rural Vermont. Canfield wrote short stories and novels, some of them under her married name of Dorothy Canfield Fisher. Two of her popular books are *The Bent Twig* and *Understood Betsy.*

Developing Comprehension Skills

1. When and where does the main event in the story take place? When did the event that is being celebrated take place?

2. What has happened in the previous year that changes the usual celebration? When does Andrew learn of the old soldier in Hawley Hollow?

3. Why is it important to the people of Sunmore to have an old soldier for the celebration? How do they get one?

4. Why does the fact that the old man was a Hessian disturb the ceremony? How does voting to continue the celebration show that the town is ready to "live in peace when war has long gone by"?

5. What does the Fourth of July seem to mean to the people of Sunmore in 1848? Do you think this holiday means something different to people today? Explain.

Reading Literature: Short Stories

1. **Understanding Exposition.** The exposition of "The Old Soldier" is contained in the first ten paragraphs. For each of the following topics, find out what is said in the exposition and tell how the information is necessary for understanding the main event in the story:
   a. Sunmore's usual way of celebrating the Fourth
   b. Dr. White
   c. events in the past year
   d. Andrew Bostwick

2. **Identifying the Narrator.** A first-person narrator should not be confused with the writer of a story. In fact, in many stories, the writer creates a specific character for the first-person narrator. Reread the first paragraph of this story. What kind of impression do you get of the narrator?

Does the narrator seem friendly or impersonal? Does the narrator take part in the plot once the story begins? Does the narrator seem to be limited in how much he or she knows about the events?

3. **Recognizing Theme.** As you know, the **theme** is the message that the writer wants you to understand from the story. In a fable or a parable, this message is stated directly in the form of a moral. In the first paragraph, the narrator assures the reader that this story is not a fable. In Andrew's speech on page 227, however, he makes a statement that does directly state the theme of the story. Find the statement. How does it relate to what happens in the story?

4. **Thinking About Characterization.** Sometimes writers include details about physical appearance that help develop a certain feeling or understanding of a character. Find passages that describe the old soldier. What kind of person do these details suggest he is?

Vocabulary

Identifying Homographs. In a dictionary you may find two or three entry words that look the same. For example, three words are spelled *r-o-w*. Read these dictionary entries:

row[1] (rō), a line or rank
row[2] (rō), to move by oars
row[3] (rou), a noisy quarrel

Words such as *row* are **homographs.** They are spelled the same, but their meanings are completely different. These words often have the same pronunciation, but sometimes, as in *row*, they do not. Each homograph has a separate dictionary entry and definition.

The following sentences are based on stories you have read. Each underlined word is a homograph. Find each homograph in a dictionary. On a sheet of paper, write the definition that fits the context of the sentence.

1. The young woman had a lovely smile, and her rounded cheeks were a <u>tender</u> pink.
2. "The other hand is engaged at <u>present</u>," he told Miss Fairchild.
3. He would write for a long time and then <u>tear</u> it all up.
4. He could hear the steady dripping sound of a leaky <u>tap</u>.
5. Several voices said, "I <u>second</u> the motion."

Study and Research

Using an Encyclopedia. Sometimes a great deal of information is presented about a subject in an encyclopedia. So much information is presented that it is necessary to divide or outline the subject. Boldface headings or titles are used to introduce the different sections within an article.

In your school or local library, select an encyclopedia. Find the volume that has the article on the American Revolution or the Revolutionary War. On a sheet of paper, list the boldface headings or titles that are used to organize the information in the article. Then describe the types of organization used. Is it chronological? Are certain periods discussed separately? Are the periods broken down further by topics or themes? Are the same topics or themes discussed for each time period?

Developing Writing Skills

Writing a Character Sketch. A **character sketch** is a brief description of a person, highlighting aspects of the person's behavior and personality. Think of someone interesting whom you know or have heard stories about. Write a character sketch of that person, making up another name.

Prewriting. Think of specific details about the character. Make notes about the following: details of appearance such as age, the color of the person's hair and eyes, and how the person dresses; his or her most striking personality traits; and typical actions and expressions. Select two or three main characteristics you want to write about. Then go through your notes and choose details that illustrate those characteristics. Decide the order of ideas you will use to write your character sketch.

Drafting. In your opening sentence, introduce the person you are writing about. Then follow the organization you developed in prewriting. Make sure you include details to illustrate each characteristic.

Revising and Sharing. Work with a partner to check how clearly a reader can picture the person you are writing about. Does your character sketch give a sense of the main characteristics of the person? Have you made your subject interesting? After you have written your final draft, share your character sketch with the class.

Runaway Rig

CARL HENRY RATHJEN

A runaway truck is careening downhill at more than a hundred miles an hour. The driver must try to save not only himself but others on the road. Can he avoid a deadly crash?

 The kid burned out the rig's brakes on The Corkscrew grade at eleven-thirty that night. Then, panicking as the ten-wheel combo—tractor and semitrailer—sucked in momentum, he raced the diesel, double-clutched, and tried to jam into a lower gear ratio. The stripping grind from the transmission jarred up into the bunk behind him. Barney Conners came awake fast.

"Easy, kid!" he yelled even before he got his eyes open. But he knew it was too late. He also knew, without seeing, but just by feel, that they were rolling unchecked downgrade. And that could only mean The Corkscrew, the truckers' graveyard.

"Lay on the horns!" he shouted, so Joel Nichols and the other highway troopers stationed on the grade would be alerted to the emergency. He swung out of the bunk, the dull sheen of sleep snapping clear of his wide brown eyes. Ahead, sharp red clusters of taillights and beady truck markers brokenly traced the dropping twists of the divided highway. It was The Corkscrew, all right. And worse, they were already past the patrol-car spot!

Fingers of fear squeezed his stomach. It was a sickness more than the indigestion he'd been trying to sleep off, the only reason he'd let the kid drive up The Hill, with a strict admonition to wake him at the top. But the kid hadn't obeyed. He'd boomed across the ridge's level four miles. Now The Corkscrew had him.

But this was no time for jawing. Not with five miles of murderous downgrade ahead of the runaway rig loaded with tons of machine parts.

Barney angled out chunky arms to the wheel and slammed his rump against his helper. "Let me have it!"

"Barney, I didn't mean to take her down. But you looked so comfortable I thought I'd take her across the top and then——"

Barney jammed his left forearm on the wheel ring. He hoped the blasting air horns would carry back to the patrol-car station. Ahead, the driver of a hay rig heard it and changed his mind abruptly about cutting out to pass a tanker.

That's what the kid had probably done. Swung out to pass a box or something big enough to hide the large illuminated sign warning about the downgrade, ordering trucks to use low gear. Then he was into it, burned out his brakes trying to check her, and then stripped her because he was going too fast for the next lower ratio.

Barney, leaning on the horns, thought of how Flo had wanted him to give up this mountain run after Billy and Joanie were born.

"Look, Florence," he'd retorted—funny how he always used her full name when he was mad or annoyed. "You're forgetting something else I never had before I got a family. The top safety award for five years straight!"

That had been years ago. But now he was in the worst jam he'd ever been in, and it wasn't his own doing. . . .

"Barney!" the kid shouted above the horns as the rig's headlights plowed faster and faster in the darkness.

"Shut up!" Barney snapped. The kid's hands fluttered as though to help with the wheel. Barney elbowed them away, then shot a glance in the big outside mirror. Not a sign of a police car coming to assist them down to the emergency escape ramp for runaway trucks. The one night when he needed some citation-happy trooper like Joel Nichols breathing into his rear-view mirror!

"Better get out, kid," Barney yelled through the clamoring horns. The kid stared down at the streaming blur of the divider. Then he turned back, a white mask punched with wide holes for eyes and mouth. Barney didn't give him a chance to protest. "Jump while you've got the chance. I don't want to shove you out, but I need room." He reached over, grabbed the door handle, and crowded the kid's trembling body. "Out! Break it with your feet. Relaxed. Then double. Knees over stomach. Arms around head. Don't try to stop it. Here you go, kid!"

Barney rumped him out to the step, but the kid hung onto the door. Wind roared into the cab. Cold. Slicing up Barney's trouser legs, pressing his shirt. The rig's heavy treads machine-gunned the pavement. Barney slid solidly behind the big wheel, his fists at ten o'clock and two. Inching as close as he dared to the streaking edge, he kicked on the far beams. Weeds waved in the night wind, leaning away from the onrushing rig. Glass and beer cans glinted among them. The kid was in for a cutting up, but that was better than being mashed to a pulp. Willowy bushes swept into view.

"The bushes, kid!" Barney shouted. "Hit 'em!"

He didn't wait for the kid to find his

nerve. He hammered his fist on the fingers hooked over the windowsill. From the corner of his eye he saw the kid sail out of the cab. He twitched the wheel, angling away, then gave a sharp but smooth swing back to whip the trailer box away from the rolling body. He played the wheel to get that whipsawing trailer in line again.

His glance darted side to side to the mirrors again. In the left one he vaguely glimpsed the kid staggering to his feet. In the right one he hoped to spot a highway patrol booming around a curve after him. But all he saw was the glare of truck headlights.

Where the devil were the troopers tonight? Joel Nichols, he remembered now from the grapevine, was probably off duty to stand by his wife, who expected her first baby. But usually there was someone riding Barney's tail in this sector because years ago, wheeling a rush shipment, he'd gone overboard telling off Joel Nichols for delaying him with a truck inspection. After that he figured he'd better watch his driving, his gross axle loads, his lights, everything. So maybe, in a way, he could thank Joel and the others for the way he began winning safety awards.

But he didn't feel like a safety-award driver now, at the wheel of a runaway monster on The Corkscrew. He squinted ahead, the wheel trembling in his fists. Even if those two gear shifts just under his right hand had anything left beneath them, it was no good to him now. He was going too fast to mesh anything. He flicked his far beams on and off as a warning to other drivers.

Just stay out of my way, boys, he prayed. *Let me look good, like a reckless driver who only gets by because the other guys have sense enough to let him through. Give me a chance to get down to the emergency turn-off ramp.*

Rocketing down the dark grade, horns blasting, lights flashing, muscles and nerves feeling and anticipating the wild whims of the berserk life under his hands, under the seat of his pants, he rubber-burned around a curve and spotted the twin bull's-eye taillights of a car. A half mile ahead on the straightaway, and in his lane!

His forearm jostled the ring. His foot beat a frantic tattoo on the light button. Words that might have been a prayer or a curse burst up from deep in his chest. But he never knew what they were. They jammed in panic in his throat. The driver didn't hear or see him coming. That driver was doing a legal fifty-five, but this juggernaut didn't know any of the rules. Barney welded his forearm to the ring.

Come on, come on, guy! For the luvva Pete! Don't those lights blazing in and out of your rear mirror mean anything?

Barney's eyes searched desperately. To his left was the divider, sort of hollowed like a shallow gully. He couldn't take the rig in there. But he couldn't go to the right either. Not with that line of hay haulers, pole dollies, tankers, boxes, and stakers creeping down The Corkscrew. But the guy ahead could slip in between them. He would burn rubber, slide onto the shoulder maybe, go into the ditch, but wasn't that better than what could happen?

Hadn't he been reading the papers lately? Hadn't he seen the pictures of what happened to a guy like himself? The big wheeler went right over that other guy, flattened him and his passengers and the new car right down to a fourteen-inch pancake and kept on going.

Barney held the wheel steady, locked in position like his teeth as he bore down on the ranch wagon's taillights. Then, at the same instant the driver must have become aware of him, Barney saw the tousled little head lift just inside the rear window, a pink blanket draped around the tiny shoulders.

Barney winced. This was like his family traveling at night because it was cooler and the kids could sleep—and because he knew he could count on the nighttime wheelers to give him a break if anything

Route 40, 1987, MICHAEL WRIGHT. Photograph: Sena Galleries, East, Santa Fe, New Mexico.

went wrong.

Yeah, he'd have to play along. Looming down on that ranch wagon with his runaway rig crammed with machine parts, he knew he could never wipe out this family and then face Flo and his own kids. He eased the combo toward the sunken divider.

But then the ranch wagon began frantically seeking an escape niche in the wall of trucks to the right. Barney shook his head. There wasn't time or room enough for him to get by. The box would careen the rig over. He'd lose control completely, go gouging on his box sides right across the divider into the oncoming upgrade lanes. A nightmarish shambles. He wasn't too sure he could prevent it by deliberately swinging in the sunken divider. But maybe, at least, he could keep it all for himself right there in the weeds between the strips of pavement.

Then blue smoke burst from the wagon as the driver gunned her. Barney nodded grimly, holding his thundering rig steady. Maybe this was an out. Maybe not. But he wasn't thinking just about himself. It was that guy ahead.

Watch yourself, mister. You ain't geared for this. You've been driving easy back and forth to work every day, Sunday picnics. You can't suddenly come out here and let all those horses run wild with you. I've picked up too many of you guys who thought they could.

Barney sucked breath through his teeth as the light car, matching his own speed, slewed on a turn and threatened to sideswipe a semi inching down in creeper gear. Barney took his heavy rig around as though he were on tracks. But even so, he was scared, wondering if all the pushing weight in the trailer would jackknife his unit.

His eye caught a flash of red from the big outside mirror. He waited until he had the rig lined up smoothly on the straightaway, a hundred feet behind that fleeing ranch wagon. Then he whipped a glance toward the mirror. That red light came from a pursuing police car. At last!

Barney smiled tightly. Then he heard the siren undulating in the surging rhythm that was the distinctive style of Joel Nichols. Barney shook his head. He'd been right in telling Joel he took his job too seriously. Out here chasing a truck instead of standing by his wife in the hospital.

The police car closed in behind Barney's trailer, bobbing over a rough dip in the pavement. The siren screamed to give warning ahead. Barney, going downgrade faster than he'd ever driven in gear under control, began overtaking the ranch wagon. But why? That job had more soup than that packed under her hood. And the guy should be able to hold her on this straightaway. Then, looking over and beyond the car, Barney saw that the driver was planning to swing into a long gap in the trucks in the right lane.

"No!" Barney shouted, blasting his horns, flicking his lights. "Keep going!" he yelled, waving his right arm. Behind him the siren shrilled frantically. Ahead, a hay hauler whipped off onto the shoulder in a cloud of dust. Two hundred feet farther on, a flat-bedder with a tarped load shot a plume of black smoke toward the stars as the wheeler spurted ahead to clear the entrance to the emergency ramp, a strip of pavement that gradually angled from the highway, and went up a hill that would slow a runaway truck and then bog it in soft sand.

But the ranch wagon swerved into the right lane, blocking Barney's chance to ease into the escape route. The bull's-eye stoplights blazed, the guy's tires smoked to keep from rear-ending the flatbedder. His arm came out, waving Barney on by.

Barney's locked teeth combed his curse into explosive hisses. Why shouldn't he try to hit that ramp? His life was just as important as that guy's. But Barney held his runaway rig straight on its way down The Corkscrew. He flicked his markers off and on twice to the white-faced driver of the ranch wagon. That's the way you usually thanked a guy for giving you a chance to keep rolling. But thanks for what now? Just a chance to live a little longer and wonder if he could somehow manage to die alone.

The police car shrieked right after him. Tailgating. A sure citation if Joel caught somebody else doing it. Not a chance to stay out of it now if Barney hit something or piled over. "Cut it out, you fool," Barney muttered.

He fought the swaying combo around into another straightaway, surprised that his rear tractor wheels were still in contact with the pavement. If you could call it contact at better than a hundred miles an hour. He didn't have to look at the speedometer to know that. Even with the far beams on, there wasn't a chance to see the details of anything on the highway or beside it. Like that fifteen-foot smear where a drum of white paint had tumbled off a staker a week ago. Tonight it was just a speck of white that zoomed out of the darkness and whisked right under him. And under that sirening fool behind him. Barney put his foot on the useless air brake, dabbed it on and off to flash his stoplights, trying to tell Joel to drop back and stay out of the inevitable pile-up.

Another curve. This one to his left. Thank God there was nothing on it, because he couldn't hold her in his lane. She screamed rubber across the white line and kept on scorching toward the shoulder. One arching fist high, one low on the racking wheel, he wondered how much he dared tighten his arc without jackknifing or rolling over. But if one of those burning doughnuts—just one!—sneaked off the pavement——

As he leaned left, bracing into the wheel, fighting to hold her on the last inch, the corner of his eye caught the police car squalling by on the inside of the turn. Its black top tilted toward him like a gleaming ebony table reflecting his markers. She slewed right in front of him. Joel corrected, fought the counter-skid, fishtailing. Then he must have rammed his foot through the floor boards, squatting the rear end to scoot ahead, red light stabbing from mountain shoulder to divider trees, siren caterwauling through the dark canyon.

Faster, faster, faster they went down through The Corkscrew, the black-and-white police car screaming interference for the rocketing runaway. But Barney felt no elation, no triumph, no hope. What good was this going to do with that final spine-busting *S* a mile ahead? Neither of them could take it at this speed. And they would take a lot of other guys with them. Downgraders and upgraders. Because there wasn't any divider in there. Too nar-

Down Grade, 1987, MICHAEL WRIGHT. Photograph: Sena Galleries East, Santa Fe, New Mexico.

row. Just a little hump of concrete between the opposing lanes of traffic.

Barney wished he had thought of that sooner. Why had he let Joel lead him into this trap? He should have piled her up before he caught other wheelers and people in private cars in a rending, smashing tornado of impact. He desperately sought some way to do it now. But how in this canyon, with rigs and cars lining both shoulders? It would be just as horrible as in the *S*.

Wait a minute. Both shoulders? Yeah. Nothing moving on either side of the highway. Nothing except a police car on the upgrade side. It swung into a turnoff, made a wild *U* turn and began to race down on the wrong side, trying to pace him, like Joel ahead of him.

That could mean only one thing. Joel had been shouting into his radio on the way up, and back there on the way down; maybe almost from the moment he spotted the runaway. He'd gotten them on the job down here. They'd stopped traffic, got it off the pavement. But what could anybody do about that *S*?

Barney saw he was creeping up on Joel. Creeping? He was catching up as if Joel had his brakes on. Barney began flicking his lights. An arm reached gingerly out of the police car into the blast of wind. It waved for him to come on. Then the car spat exhaust smoke and barely held its lead.

Bewilderedly, Barney tracked after it.

Here came the *S*. Joel and the others were fools to think he could make that first swing to the right. Never. Not even at half this speed. Then he sensed, rather than saw—because his eyes were on that police car—there were no trucks or cars in here! Both sides, both shoulders were clear! Joel's car didn't even try to take the start of the curve. It went straight over the six-inch hump as though it weren't there, to the far side of the road.

"OK. Gotcha!" Barney muttered, eyes unblinking. Maybe he could straighten this thing out enough to get through. It was his only chance. At sight-blurring speed, he never felt his left tires cross the hump. And he didn't unfreeze the wheel until he was sure the right trailer wheels were over too. That hard little wrinkle could flip him into a turnover.

He swerved a bit, then held her straight to streak across the far shoulder, skinning by the canyon wall and the drainage ditch. Back on the pavement. Over the divider hump again. Then the other shoulder.

Hitting the pavement again, the tractor cab began to yaw, tugged side to side by the semibox behind him. If he didn't keep the razor-edge of control she'd pull him over. Or jackknife and crush him in the cab. Or ram the tractor into the rocks while tons of machine parts crashed through the bulkhead behind him.

In the mirror he caught the markers of the trailer box swinging far out to the left. Yeah, this was it! Then the skidding duals hit the hump. For an instant they held, smoking along it. Now they would lash back to the right and—But he wheeled the tractor to the right too. He picked up that skidding box, checked it, lined it up, and waited for a head-on smash because most of his attention had been focused rearward.

He winced expectantly, focusing fully dead ahead. All he saw was straightaway. He yelled. No words. No meaning. Just a bottled pressure that had to get out of him, and it came as a yell. He would bet they could hear it way ahead. Even beyond Joel's police car shrieking yards in advance of his front bumper. They could probably hear it way down there in the valley, that valley with the parkway divider looking lush green under the highway fluorescents. Someday soon he was going to lie on that grass and let its coolness kiss his hot face. No, he was going to do the kissing!

Far ahead down there, red lights winked on police cars. Minutes later he waved as he flashed by them. On past drive-in eateries, people out of their cars, staring, holding half-eaten burgers, bottles of pop. To his left the big screen of a drive-in movie swept by, but slow enough so he could glance at the picture. A guy in a cowboy hat pointing a rifle at horsemen dust-clouding down a rough slope. Barney shook his head. How come those guys never broke their necks riding like that?

Seven miles farther down the valley, where it leveled off, he scraped his sidewalls screechingly along a curb. The rig slowed, but still rolled across an intersection against a red light. But Joel was holding back traffic while another police car leapfrogged ahead to the next intersection.

Finally the rig stopped.

Barney sat on the running board. Nothing would hold still in him. His clothes stuck and dragged with sweat. His hands were all fingers that wouldn't behave. Joel came back, his boots glistening. His face had a grin that looked as sickish as Barney felt.

"Hi," Barney managed to say. It was silly, crazy, but it was enough. Joel sat down beside him. Barney stretched his legs out, then drew them back. Everything shook, no matter what, even his left hand gripping the edge of the running board.

"Nice wheeling, Barney."

"The other guys, you mean. The ones who got out of my way. Except one darn fool."

Joel looked at him. "Why didn't you jump, after you got the kid safely out?"

"Why didn't you stay at the hospital?" Barney retorted. He stood up. "Before you write out a citation, I better set out my flares and reflectors."

His legs felt wobbly, but the rest of him began to feel good. Real good.

Carl Henry Rathjen *(1909–1984)* wrote stories to entertain himself when he was a boy. As an adult, he returned to writing as a career after years of working at a variety of jobs. Rathjen graduated from New York University in 1931. Because of the Depression he had to take any jobs he could find. During this time, he worked as a camp counselor, copywriter, laborer, and cutter in a rubber factory. "Runaway Rig" was first published in *The Saturday Evening Post* in 1957 and was selected as one of the year's twenty best.

Developing Comprehension Skills

1. Describe the "runaway rig." What has happened to the brakes? to the gears?

2. List in order the things Barney does to protect others as he tries to keep the truck in control. Once he misses the emergency ramp, what dangers does Barney face?

3. What is the relationship between Barney and Joel? What does Joel do to make it possible for Barney to get the runaway rig safely down the hill?

4. Study the following list of facts. Explain the part each plays in Barney's getting the runaway rig safely down The Corkscrew.

   a. Barney has won top safety awards for his driving.

   b. Barney does not panic, but keeps planning what to do.

   c. Barney has driven down The Corkscrew many times and knows exactly how it looks even though it is dark.

   d. Joel is working even though his wife is expecting their first baby.

   e. Joel clears the road of all other traffic.

5. Do Barney and Joel just do their jobs or should they be considered heroes? Explain.

Reading Literature: Short Stories

1. **Examining Point of View.** This story is told from a **third-person limited point of view.** The narrator tells only what one character thinks, feels, and sees. The writer lets you inside Barney's mind, so you know all of his thoughts and feelings. Find one example of each of the following ways the writer develops the point of view in the story:

   a. The reader does not find out that something is about to happen until Barney begins to realize it.

b. The narrator uses slang words that a truck driver would say to describe actions or objects.

c. The story uses phrases and sentences that sound like Barney is talking to himself.

2. **Developing Suspense.** **Suspense** is a feeling of growing tension and excitement felt by a reader. What does the writer do to create a strong feeling of suspense in this story? For example, what details make the reader feel that Barney is in real danger? How does the speed of the runaway truck add to the suspense? What are the different problems that develop as the rig rushes down The Corkscrew? How does the point of view used in the story help create suspense?

3. **Understanding Conflict.** What external conflict or problem does Barney face? What internal conflict must he deal with?

Vocabulary

Using Context to Understand Figurative Expressions. The writer of "Runaway Rig" frequently uses words that create clear images, or pictures, in the reader's mind. These words, which are figurative expressions, make actions or sounds sharp and vivid. Answer the following questions about the figurative expressions in this story. Find the sentence in the story and then use context clues to see what the underlined word means in the situation being described. If necessary, consult a dictionary.

1. What kind of sound was made when "The rig's heavy treads machine-gunned the pavement"? (page 235, col. 2, paragraph 2)

2. What kind of movement does a "whipsawing trailer" make? (page 236, near top of page).

3. When Barney plans to "burn rubber, slide onto the shoulder maybe," what part of the truck is he referring to? (page 237, near top of page)

4. How close does Barney come to the wall when he is "skinning by the canyon wall and drainage ditch"? (page 241, col. 2, paragraph 3)

5. How do Joel and the other police car leapfrog the intersections down the valley? (page 242, col. 2, paragraph 1)

Critical Thinking

Evaluating Author's Purpose. Some stories are clearly meant to teach a lesson about life. Others are written more as exciting adventures. Still others are meant to amuse and entertain. Some stories serve more than one of these purposes. For example, a story may be amusing but may also make a point about life or human nature at the same time.

Write down the purpose each author had in writing the great modern short stories you have read in this chapter. When everyone in the class has finished, compare your lists to see how many agreed about each author's purpose. If there is disagreement, discuss the suggested purposes. Be prepared to support your choices.

Developing Writing Skills

Writing About Minor Characters. As you may remember, **minor characters** are the characters in a story who help to carry out the action and help to develop or support the main character. Barney is clearly the main character in this story. What part do minor characters like Joel and "the kid" play in "Runaway Rig"? Write one or two paragraphs explaining how either one of them is important.

Prewriting. Decide which of the two minor characters you will write about. Then list actions by the character that are important for the plot of the story. Next note ways in which the character helps you understand Barney. For example, in what ways does the kid contrast with Barney? In what ways are Joel and Barney alike? Is the minor character equally important for developing plot and character, or is he more important for one or the other of the two elements?

Drafting. Write a topic sentence that summarizes the importance of the character in "Runaway Rig." Be sure to support your main idea with specific examples from the story. You may want to devote one paragraph to discussing plot and one paragraph to characterization. If you use a word processor, write your draft on the processor. Make changes and add details as you draft.

Revising and Sharing. Allow some time between writing and revising your draft. Carefully read through your draft, making sure you can answer "yes" to the following questions:

Do I have a clear main idea?
Does every point I make help develop the main idea?
Are my references to the story accurate?
Do the characters do and say the things that I say they do?
Have I written in complete sentences?
Is it clear whom I am talking about when I use *he* and *him*?

If you are using a word processor, make your revisions, and then print out a final copy.

Adjö Means Goodbye

CARRIE ALLEN YOUNG

The friends in this story share many interests and good times. They never actually quarrel. So why does the friendship die?

It has been a long time since I knew Marget Swenson. How the years have rushed by! I was a child when I knew her, and now I myself have children. The circle keeps turning, keeps coming full.

The mind loses many things as it matures, but I never lost Marget. She has remained with me like the first love and the first hurt. The mind does not lose what is meaningful to one's existence. Marget was both my first love and first hurt. I met her when she joined our sixth-grade class.

She stood before the class holding tightly to the teacher's hand, her blue, frightened eyes sweeping back and forth across the room until they came to rest on my face. From that very first day, we became friends. Marget, just fresh from Sweden, and I, a sixth generation American. We were both rather shy and quiet and perhaps even lonely, and that's why we took to each other. She spoke very little English, but somehow we managed to understand each other. We visited one another at home practically every day. My young life had suddenly become deliciously complete. I had a dear friend.

Sometimes we talked and laughed on the top of the big, dazzling green hill close to the school. We had so much to talk about. So many things were new to her. She asked a thousand questions and I—I, filled to bursting with pride that it was from me that she wished to learn, responded eagerly and with excesses of superlatives.

Now, sometimes, when I drive my children to school and watch them race up the walks to the doors, I wonder what lies ahead in the momentary darkness of the hall corridors and think of Marget once more. I think of how she came out of a dark corridor one day, the day she really looked at my brother when she was visiting me. I saw her following him with new eyes, puzzled eyes, and a strange fear gripped me. "Your brother," she whispered to me, "is African?"

"No, silly."

"He looks different from you."

"He should," I said, managing to laugh. My brother *was* darker than anyone else in the family. "He's a boy and I'm a girl. But we're both black, of course."

She opened her mouth to say something else, then closed it and the fear slipped away.

Marget lived up on the hill. That was the place where there were many large and pretty houses. I suppose it was only in passing that I knew only white people lived there. Whenever I visited, Marget's mother put up a table in their garden, and Marget and I had milk and *kaka,* a kind of cake. Mrs. Swenson loved to see me eat. She was a large, round woman with deep blue eyes and very red cheeks. Marget, though much smaller, of course, looked quite like her. We did our homework after we had the cake and milk, compositions or story reading. When we finished, Mrs. Swenson hugged me close and I knew I was loved in that home. A child knows when it is loved or only tolerated. But I was loved. Mrs. Swenson thanked me with a thick, Swedish accent for helping Marget.

Marget and I had so much fun with words, and there were times when we sat for hours in my garden or hers or on the hilltop, surrounded by grass and perhaps the smell of the suppers being prepared for our fathers still at work downtown. Her words were Swedish; mine, English. We were surprised how much alike many of them sounded, and we laughed at the way each of us slid our tongues over the unfamiliar words. I learned the Swedish equivalents of *mother, father, house, hello, friend,* and *goodbye.*

One day Marget and I raced out of school as soon as the ringing bell released us. We sped down the hill, flashed over gray concrete walks and green lawns dotted with dandelions and scattered daisies, our patent leather buckled shoes slapping a merry tattoo as we went, our long stockings tumbling down our legs. We were going to Marget's to plan her birthday party. Such important business for ten-year-olds!

Eventually, after much planning and waiting, the day of the party came. I put on my pink organdy dress with the Big Bertha collar and a new pair of patent leather shoes that tortured my feet unbearably.

Skipping up the hill to Marget's, I stopped at a lawn which looked deserted. I set down my gift and began to pick the wild flowers that were growing there. Suddenly, from out of nowhere, an old man appeared. "What do you think you're doing pulling up my flowers?" he shouted. Once again I held myself tightly against the fear, awaiting the awful thing that I felt must come. "I wanted to take them to my friend," I explained. "She's having a birthday today."

The old man's eyes began to twinkle. "She is, is she? Well, you just wait a minute, young lady." He went away and came back with garden shears and cut a handful and then an armful of flowers, and with a smile sent me on my way. My childish fears had been ambushed by a kindness.

I arrived at the party early and Marget and I whizzed around, putting the finishing touches on the decorations. There were hardly enough vases for all the flowers the old man had given me. Some fifteen minutes later the doorbell rang, and Marget ran around to the front saying, "Oh, here they come!"

But it was Mary Ann, another girl in our class, and she was alone. She put her present for Marget on the table, and the three of us talked. Occasionally, Marget got up and went around to the front to see who had come unheralded by the doorbell. No one.

"I wonder what's taking them so long?" Mary Ann asked.

Growing more upset by the minute, Marget answered, "Maybe they didn't remember what time the party was."

How does a child of ten describe a sense of foreboding, the feeling that the bad things have happened because of herself? I sat silently, waiting.

When it got to be after five, Mrs. Swenson called Marget inside; she was there for a long time, and when she came out, she looked very, very sad. "My mother does not think they are coming," she said.

"Why not?" Mary Ann blurted.

"Betty Hatcher's mother was here last night, and she talked a long time with my mother. I thought it was about the party. Mother kept saying, 'Yes, yes, she is coming.'"

I took Marget's hand. "Maybe they were talking about me," I said. Oh! I remember so painfully today how I wanted her quick and positive denial to that thrust of mine into darkness where I knew something alive was lurking. Although she did it quite casually, I was aware that Marget was trying to slip her hand from mine, as though she might have had the same thought I had voiced aloud. I opened my hand and let her go. "Don't be silly," she said.

No one came. The three of us sat in the middle of rows and rows of flowers and ate our ice cream and cake. Our pretty dresses, ribbons, and shoes were dejected blobs of color. It was as if the world had swung out around us and gone past, leaving us whole, but in some way indelibly stamped forever.

It was different between Marget and me after her birthday. She stopped coming to my house, and when at school I asked her when she would, she looked as though she would cry. She had to do something for her mother was her unvarying excuse. So, one day, I went to her house, climbed up the hill where the old man had picked the flowers, and a brooding, restless thing grew within me at every step, almost a *knowing*. I had not, after all, been invited to Marget's. My throat grew dry and I thought about turning back, and for the first time the hill and all the homes looked alien, even threatening to me.

Marget almost jumped when she opened the door. She stared at me in shock. Then, quickly, in a voice I'd never heard before, she said, "My mother says you can't come to my house any more."

I opened my mouth, and closed it without speaking. The awful thing had come; the knowing was confirmed. Marget, crying, closed the door in my face. When I turned to go down the stairs and back down the hill to my house, my eyes, too, were filled with tears. No one had to tell me that the awful thing had come because Marget was white and I was not. I just *knew it* deep within myself. I guess I expected it to happen. It was only a question of when.

June. School was coming to a close. Those days brimmed with strange, uncomfortable moments when Marget and I looked at each other and our eyes darted quickly away. We were little pawns, one white, one black, in a game over which we had no control then. We did not speak to each other at all.

On the last day of school, I screwed up a strange and reckless courage and took my autograph book to where Marget was sitting. I handed it to her. She hesitated, then took it, and without looking up, wrote words I don't remember now. They were quite common words, the kind everyone was writing in everyone else's book. I waited. Slowly, she passed her book to me and in it I wrote with a slow, firm hand some of the words she had taught me. I wrote *Adjö min vän.* Goodbye, my friend. I released her, let her go, told her not to worry, told her that I no longer needed her. *Adjö.*

Whenever I think of Marget now, and I do at the most surprising times, I wonder if she ever thinks of me, if she is married and has children, and I wonder if she has become a queen by now, instead of a pawn.

Carrie Allen Young *(born 1913)* is a writer, a former social worker, and a retired professor of sociology. Young was born in Lynchburg, Virginia, and was educated at Talladega College in Alabama, where she later taught. "Adjö Means Goodbye" was her first published story.

Developing Comprehension Skills

1. How do the narrator and Marget meet? How old are they?

2. What activities do the two girls enjoy doing together?

3. What happens at Marget's birthday party that affects the friendship of the two girls?

4. Why did Marget and the narrator stop being friends? Was the problem something that either girl could control?

5. What would you have done if you were Marget? if you were the narrator?

Reading Literature: Short Stories

1. **Comparing and Contrasting Characters.** People often become friends because they have something in common. How are Marget and the narrator alike? In what ways are the two girls different? How might the fact that both are lonely bring them together?

2. **Thinking About Point of View.** Who is the narrator in this story? What is the point of view? Reread the five opening paragraphs and the final paragraph. How are these comments important to the story? Could the writer have conveyed the same ideas through a third-person narrator? Could she if she had made the narrator a sixth grader who was experiencing only the events in the flashback?

3. **Understanding Symbols.** A **symbol** is a person, place, or thing that stands for something beyond itself. In the last sentence of the story, the writer uses symbols from the game of chess. The queen is the most powerful piece. She can move freely, while a pawn has very limited movement and is easily captured. However, if a pawn does make it to the opposite side of the board, it can become a queen. In what way does the story show that Marget was a pawn? How could she become a queen?

4. **Recognizing Foreshadowing. Foreshadowing** occurs when a writer drops hints about what will happen. In this story, the writer hints at how the story will turn out when she says in the second paragraph that "Marget was both my first love and first hurt." Find two other places where the narrator is afraid that something will interfere with her friendship with Marget, even though there are no outward signs of conflict.

Vocabulary

Recognizing Different Pronunciations of a Word. Sometimes a word that can be pronounced two different ways has only one dictionary entry. The accent in this word may change from one syllable to another, depending on its part of speech. Read these sentences:

Owen's *present* was a ten-speed bike. (pres′ent)
The drama class will *present* a play tonight. (pre sent′)

In the first sentence, *present* is accented on the first syllable and is used as a noun. In the second, *present* is accented on the second syllable and is used as a verb. The dictionary gives both pronunciations for the word. It also indicates which definitions fit each of the pronunciations.

Read each of these sentences concerning stories you have read. Find the underlined word in a dictionary. On a sheet of paper, write the following:

    a. the underlined word separated into syllables with the correct accent marked
    b. the part of speech of the word as it is used in the sentence
    c. the meaning of the word as it is used in the sentence

1. The girl never thought her friend would <u>desert</u> her.
2. When she spoke, her voice was full, sweet, and <u>deliberate.</u>
3. He said with a smile, "Will you please <u>excuse</u> the other hand?"
4. Then, rain or shine, the procession would <u>escort</u> the old soldiers out to the Burying Ground.
5. During the lawyer's fifteen years in prison, they did <u>permit</u> him to have musical instruments.

Critical Thinking

Making Inferences. In this story, the writer often relies on the reader's ability to **infer.** In other words, the reader must use evidence in the story and knowledge from his or her own experience to figure out exactly what is happening. For example, the narrator relates that "It was different between Marget and me after her birthday." It is up to the reader to infer exactly what destroyed the friendship and how the conflict was caused by the difference in race. At the beginning of the story, does Marget understand how different races might feel about each other in the United States? What can you infer about the discussion between Betty Hatcher's mother and Marget's mother the night before the party?

Developing Writing Skills

Defending an Opinion. The narrator says that the event she describes in the story hurt her. She also shows that Marget was upset by what happened. Do you agree that prejudice does not hurt just those who are discriminated against—that it also hurts and limits the people who act prejudiced? Write a paragraph expressing your opinion.

Prewriting. Begin by thinking of specific examples of prejudice from your experience or from the story. How does this behavior hurt the people who are discriminated against? What effects does it have on the people who are prejudiced? Do those who act prejudiced cut themselves off from something they might enjoy or learn from?

Drafting. Develop a topic sentence that you can use to organize your draft. Be sure to give at least two specific examples and explanations in support of your main idea.

Revising and Sharing. As you reread your draft, make sure that you have included specific examples. Also check to be sure that each supporting idea develops your main idea. Before turning in your paragraph, proofread for punctuation and spelling. Be prepared to share your writing with the class and to discuss the ideas expressed by your classmates.

As Kids Go II, 1987, SAM GILLIAM. Photograph: Klein Gallery, Chicago.

The Medicine Bag

VIRGINIA DRIVING HAWK SNEVE

Martin is embarrassed by his Sioux grandfather. He is ashamed to wear the gift he will inherit from him. What makes him appreciate both his grandfather and the gift?

My kid sister Cheryl and I always bragged about our Sioux (sōō) grandpa, Joe Iron Shell. Our friends, who had always lived in the city and knew about Indians only from movies and TV, were impressed by our stories. Maybe we exaggerated and made Grandpa and the reservation sound glamorous, but when we'd return home to Iowa after our yearly summer visit to Grandpa, we always had some exciting tale to tell.

We always had some authentic Sioux article to show our listeners. One year Cheryl had new moccasins that Grandpa had made. On another visit he gave me a small, round, flat, rawhide drum that was decorated with a painting of a warrior riding a horse. He taught me a real Sioux chant to sing while I beat the drum with a leather-covered stick that had a feather on the end. Man, that really made an impression.

We never showed our friends Grandpa's picture. Not that we were ashamed of him, but because we knew that the glamorous tales we told didn't go with the real thing. Our friends would have laughed at the picture because Grandpa wasn't tall and stately like TV Indians. His hair wasn't in braids but hung in stringy, gray strands on his neck, and he was old. He was our great-grandfather, and he didn't live in a tepee, but all by himself in a part log, part tar-paper shack on the Rosebud Reservation in South Dakota. So when Grandpa came to visit us, I was so ashamed and embarrassed I could've died.

There are a lot of yippy poodles and other fancy little dogs in our neighborhood, but they usually barked singly at the mailman from the safety of their own yards. Now it sounded as if a whole pack of mutts were barking together in one place.

I got up and walked to the curb to see

what the commotion was. About a block away I saw a crowd of little kids yelling, with the dogs yipping and growling around someone who was walking down the middle of the street.

I watched the group as it slowly came closer and saw that in the center of the strange procession was a man wearing a tall black hat. He'd pause now and then to peer at something in his hand and then at the houses on either side of the street. I felt cold and hot at the same time as I recognized the man. "Oh, no!" I whispered. "It's Grandpa!"

I stood on the curb, unable to move even though I wanted to run and hide. Then I got mad when I saw how the yippy dogs were growling and nipping at the old man's baggy pant legs and how wearily he poked them away with his cane. "Stupid mutts," I said as I ran to rescue Grandpa.

When I kicked and hollered at the dogs to get away, they put their tails between their legs and scattered. The kids ran to the curb where they watched me and the old man.

"Grandpa," I said and felt pretty dumb when my voice cracked. I reached for his beat-up old tin suitcase, which was tied shut with a rope. But he set it down right in the street and shook my hand.

"Hau, Takoza, Grandchild," he greeted me formally in Sioux.

All I could do was stand there with the whole neighborhood watching and shake the hand of the leather-brown old man. I saw how his gray hair straggled from under his big black hat, which had a drooping feather in its crown. His rumpled black suit hung like a sack over his stooped frame. As he shook my hand, his coat fell open to expose a bright red satin shirt with a beaded bolo tie under the collar. His get-up wasn't out of place on the reservation, but it sure was here, and I wanted to sink right through the pavement.

"Hi," I muttered with my head down. I tried to pull my hand away when I felt his bony hand trembling, and looked up to see fatigue in his face. I felt like crying. I couldn't think of anything to say so I picked up Grandpa's suitcase, took his arm, and guided him up the driveway to our house.

Mom was standing on the steps. I don't know how long she'd been watching, but her hand was over her mouth and she looked as if she couldn't believe what she saw. Then she ran to us.

"Grandpa," she gasped. "How in the world did you get here?"

She checked her move to embrace Grandpa and I remembered that such a display of affection is unseemly to the Sioux and would embarrass him.

"Hau, Marie," he said as he shook Mom's hand. She smiled and took his other arm.

As we supported him up the steps, the door banged open and Cheryl came bursting out of the house. She was all smiles and was so obviously glad to see Grandpa that I was ashamed of how I felt.

"Grandpa!" she yelled happily. "You came to see us!"

Grandpa smiled, and Mom and I let go of him as he stretched out his arms to my ten-year-old sister, who was still young enough to be hugged.

"*Wicincala,* little girl," he greeted her and then collapsed.

He had fainted. Mom and I carried him into her sewing room, where we had a spare bed.

After we had Grandpa on the bed, Mom stood there helplessly patting his shoulder.

"Shouldn't we call the doctor, Mom?" I suggested, since she didn't seem to know what to do.

"Yes," she agreed with a sigh. "You make Grandpa comfortable, Martin."

I reluctantly moved to the bed. I knew

Horse Capturing Scene, 1982, RANDY LEE WHITE. Collection of the Artist.

Grandpa wouldn't want to have Mom undress him, but I didn't want to, either. He was so skinny and frail that his coat slipped off easily. When I loosened his tie and opened his shirt collar, I felt a small leather pouch that hung from a thong around his neck. I left it alone and moved to remove his boots. The scuffed old cowboy boots were tight, and he moaned as I put pressure on his legs to jerk them off.

I put the boots on the floor and saw why they fit so tight. Each one was stuffed with money. I looked at the bills that lined the boots and started to ask about them, but Grandpa's eyes were closed again.

Mom came back with a basin of water. "The doctor thinks Grandpa is suffering from heat exhaustion," she explained as she bathed Grandpa's face. Mom gave a big sigh, *"Oh, hinh,* Martin. How do you suppose he got here?"

We found out after the doctor's visit. Grandpa was angrily sitting up in bed while Mom tried to feed him some soup.

"Tonight you let Marie feed you, Grandpa," spoke my dad, who had gotten home from work just as the doctor was leaving. "You're not really sick," he said as he gently pushed Grandpa back against the pillows. "The doctor said you just got too tired and hot after your long trip."

Grandpa relaxed, and between sips of soup, he told us of his journey. Soon after our visit to him, Grandpa decided that he would like to see where his only living descendants lived and what our home was like. Besides, he admitted sheepishly, he was lonesome after we left.

I knew that everybody felt as guilty as I did—especially Mom. Mom was all Grandpa had left. So even after she married my dad, who's a white man and teaches in the college in our city, and after Cheryl and I were born, Mom made sure that every summer we spent a week with Grandpa.

I never thought that Grandpa would be lonely after our visits, and none of us noticed how old and weak he had become. But Grandpa knew, and so he came to us. He had ridden on buses for two and a half days. When he arrived in the city, tired and stiff from sitting so long, he set out, walking, to find us.

He had stopped to rest on the steps of some building downtown, and a policeman found him. The cop, according to Grandpa, was a good man who took him to the bus stop and waited until the bus came and told the driver to let Grandpa out at Bell View Drive. After Grandpa got off the bus, he started walking again. But he couldn't see the house numbers on the other side when he walked on the sidewalk, so he walked in the middle of the street. That's when all the little kids and dogs followed him.

I knew everybody felt as bad as I did. Yet I was so proud of this eighty-six-year-old man who had never been away from the reservation, having the courage to travel so far alone.

"You found the money in my boots?" he asked Mom.

"Martin did," she answered, and roused herself to scold. "Grandpa, you shouldn't have carried so much money. What if someone had stolen it from you?"

Grandpa laughed. "I would've known if anyone had tried to take the boots off my feet. The money is what I've saved for a long time—a hundred dollars—for my funeral. But you take it now to buy groceries so that I won't be a burden to you while I am here."

"That won't be necessary, Grandpa," Dad said. "We are honored to have you with us, and you will never be a burden. I am only sorry that we never thought to bring you home with us this summer and spare you the discomfort of a long trip."

Grandpa was pleased. "Thank you," he answered. "But do not feel bad that you didn't bring me with you, for I would not have come then. It was not time." He said this in such a way that no one could argue with him. To Grandpa and the Sioux, he once told me, a thing would be done when it was the right time to do it, and that's the way it was.

"Also," Grandpa went on, looking at me, "I have come because it is soon time for Martin to have the medicine bag."

We all knew what that meant. Grandpa thought he was going to die, and he had to follow the tradition of his family to pass the medicine bag, along with its history, to the oldest male child.

"Even though the boy," he said still looking at me, "bears a white man's name, the medicine bag will be his."

I didn't know what to say. I had the same hot and cold feeling that I had when I first saw Grandpa in the street. The medicine bag was the dirty leather pouch I had found around his neck. "I could never wear such a thing," I almost said aloud. I thought of having my friends see it in gym class or at the swimming pool and could imagine the smart things they would say. But I just swallowed hard and took a step toward the bed. I knew I would have to take it.

But Grandpa was tired. "Not now, Martin," he said, waving his hand in dismissal. "It is not time. Now I will sleep."

So that's how Grandpa came to be with us for two months. My friends kept asking to come see the old man, but I put them off. I told myself that I didn't want them laughing at Grandpa. But even as I made excuses, I knew it wasn't Grandpa that I was afraid they'd laugh at.

Nothing bothered Cheryl about bringing her friends to see Grandpa. Every day after school started, there'd be a crew of giggling little girls or round-eyed little boys crowded around the old man on the patio, where he'd gotten in the habit of sitting every afternoon.

Grandpa would smile in his gentle way and patiently answer their questions, or he'd tell them stories of brave warriors, ghosts, and animals; and the kids listened in awed silence. Those little guys thought Grandpa was great.

Finally, one day after school, my friends came home with me because nothing I said stopped them. "We're going to see the great Indian of Bell View Drive," said Hank, who was supposed to be my best friend. "My brother has seen him three times so he oughta be well enough to see us."

When we got to my house, Grandpa was sitting on the patio. He had on his red shirt, but today he also wore a fringed leather vest that was decorated with beads. Instead of his usual cowboy boots, he had solidly beaded moccasins on his feet that stuck out of his black trousers. Of course, he had his old black hat on—he was seldom without it. But it had been brushed, and the feather in the beaded headband was proudly erect, its tip a brighter white. His hair lay in silver strands over the red shirt collar.

I stared just as my friends did, and I heard one of them murmur, "Wow!"

Grandpa looked up, and, when his eyes met mine, they twinkled as if he were laughing inside. He nodded to me, and my face got all hot. I could tell that he had known all along I was afraid he'd embarrass me in front of my friends.

"*Hau, hoksilas,* boys," he greeted and held out his hand.

My buddies passed in a single file and shook his hand as I introduced them. They were so polite I almost laughed.

"How, there, Grandpa," and even a "How-do-you-do, sir."

"You look fine, Grandpa," I said as the guys sat on the lawn chairs or on the patio floor.

"*Hanh,* yes," he agreed. "When I woke up this morning, it seemed the right time to dress in the good clothes. I knew that my grandson would be bringing his friends."

"You guys want some lemonade or something?" I offered. No one answered. They were listening to Grandpa as he started telling how he'd killed the deer from which his vest was made.

Grandpa did most of the talking while my friends were there. I was so proud of him and amazed at how respectfully quiet my buddies were. Mom had to chase them home at supper time. As they left, they shook Grandpa's hand again and said to me,

"Martin, he's really great!"

"Yeah, man! Don't blame you for keeping him to yourself."

"Can we come back?"

But after they left, Mom said, "No more visitors for a while, Martin. Grandpa won't admit it, but his strength hasn't returned. He likes having company, but it tires him."

That evening Grandpa called me to his room before he went to sleep. "Tomorrow," he said, "when you come home, it will be time to give you the medicine bag."

I felt a hard squeeze from where my

heart is supposed to be and was scared, but I answered, "OK, Grandpa."

All night I had weird dreams about thunder and lightning on a high hill. From a distance I heard the slow beat of a drum. When I woke up in the morning, I felt as if I hadn't slept at all. At school it seemed as if the day would never end and, when it finally did, I ran home.

Grandpa was in his room, sitting on the bed. The shades were down, and the place was dim and cool. I sat on the floor in front of Grandpa, but he didn't even look at me. After what seemed a long time, he spoke.

"I sent your mother and sister away. What you will hear today is only for a man's ears. What you will receive is only for a man's hands." He fell silent, and I felt shivers down my back.

"My father in his early manhood," Grandpa began, "made a vision quest to find a spirit guide for his life. You cannot understand how it was in that time, when the great Teton Sioux were first made to stay on the reservation. There was a strong need for guidance from *Wakantanka,* the Great Spirit. But too many of the young men were filled with despair and hatred. They thought it was hopeless to search for a vision when the glorious life was gone and only the hated confines of a reservation lay ahead. But my father held to the old ways.

"He carefully prepared for his quest with a purifying sweat bath, and then he went alone to a high butte top to fast and pray. After three days he received his sacred dream—in which he found, after long searching, the white man's iron. He did not understand his vision of finding something belonging to the white people, for in that time they were the enemy. When he came down from the butte to cleanse himself at the stream below, he found the remains of a campfire and the broken shell of an iron kettle. This was a sign that reinforced his dream. He took a piece of the iron for his medicine bag, which he had made of elk skin years before, to prepare for his quest.

"He returned to his village where he told his dream to the wise old men of the tribe. They gave him the name *Iron Shell,* but neither did they understand the meaning of the dream. The first Iron Shell kept the piece of iron with him at all times and believed it gave him protection from the evils of those unhappy days.

"Then a terrible thing happened to Iron Shell. He and several other young men were taken from their homes by the soldiers and sent far away to a white man's boarding school. He was angry and lonesome for his parents and the young girl he had wed before he was taken away. At first Iron Shell resisted the teacher's attempts to change him, and he did not try to learn. One day it was his turn to work in the school's blacksmith shop. As he walked into the place, he knew that his medicine had brought him there to learn and work with the white man's iron.

"Iron Shell became a blacksmith and worked at the trade when he returned to the reservation. All of his life he treasured the medicine bag. When he was old, and I was a man, he gave it to me, for no one made the vision quest any more."

Grandpa quit talking, and I stared in disbelief as he covered his face with his hands. His shoulders were shaking with quiet sobs, and I looked away until he began to speak again.

"I kept the bag until my son, your mother's father, was a man and had to leave us to fight in the war across the ocean. I gave him the bag, for I believed it would protect him in battle, but he did not take it with him. He was afraid that he would lose it. He died in a faraway place."

Again Grandpa was still, and I felt his grief around me.

"My son," he went on after clearing his throat, "had only a daughter, and it is not proper for her to know of these things."

He unbuttoned his shirt, pulled out the leather pouch, and lifted it over his head. He held it in his hand, turning it over and over as if memorizing how it looked.

"In the bag," he said as he opened it and removed two objects, "is the broken shell of the iron kettle, a pebble from the butte, and a piece of the sacred sage." He held the pouch upside down and dust drifted down.

"After the bag is yours, you must put a piece of prairie sage within and never open it again until you pass it on to your son." He replaced the pebble and the piece of iron, and tied the bag.

I stood up, somehow knowing I should. Grandpa slowly rose from the bed and stood upright in front of me holding the bag before my face. I closed my eyes and waited for him to slip it over my head. But he spoke.

"No, you need not wear it." He placed the soft leather bag in my right hand and closed my other hand over it. "It would not be right to wear it in this time and place where no one will understand. Put it safely away until you are again on the reservation. Wear it then, when you replace the sacred sage."

Grandpa turned and sat again on the bed. Wearily he leaned his head against the pillow. "Go," he said. "I will sleep now."

"Thank you, Grandpa," I said softly and left with the bag in my hands.

That night Mom and Dad took Grandpa to the hospital. Two weeks later I stood alone on the lonely prairie of the reservation and put the sacred sage in my medicine bag.

Virginia Driving Hawk Sneve *(born 1933)* grew up on the Rosebud Sioux reservation in South Dakota. She received a bachelor's and a master's degree from South Dakota State University. While working as a teacher and school guidance counselor, she has also found time to write historical books and fiction. "In my writing," she says, "I try to present an accurate portrayal of American Indian life as I have known it. I also attempt to interpret history from the viewpoint of the American Indian." Her books include *Jimmy Yellow Hawk, When Thunder Spoke,* and *Betrayed.*

Developing Comprehension Skills

1. Name the members of Martin's family. Where do they live? What is Grandpa's name and where is his home?

2. How does Martin feel when he first sees his grandfather? Does his sister Cheryl feel the same way? How do you know?

3. Why does Grandpa make the long trip to Iowa? What does he sense about what is happening to his life? What tradition does he want to carry on?

4. Describe Grandpa's medicine bag. What is the Sioux tradition of the medicine bag?

5. What is the history of Grandpa's medicine bag? Why does Grandpa feel it so important to give the bag to Martin?

6. What happens to Grandpa at the end of the story? What does Martin do? Why does Martin do what he does?

7. Is it fair for Grandpa to expect Martin to carry on his family traditions? Why or why not? Does Grandpa recognize that Martin is living in a different world from that of the traditional Sioux? Give examples from the story to support your answer.

Reading Literature: Short Stories

1. **Examining Conflict.** As you know, **internal conflict** is a struggle that takes place within a character. The internal conflict that Martin faces comes from the fact that he is half Sioux, half white. Explain Martin's internal conflict. How does Martin solve the conflict? Does the struggle change Martin in some way? Explain.

2. **Understanding Background.** The background of this story is the Sioux culture. Identify at least two details of Sioux life

that are mentioned in the story. How do these details help you understand the action and characters in the story?

3. **Analyzing Plot.** What happens at the climax of this short story? In other words, what event is the turning point for Martin?

Vocabulary

Recognizing Words Borrowed from Other Languages. English includes a number of words and place names taken from Native American languages. On a separate sheet of paper, list three cities or rivers that have Native American names. Use a map or atlas if necessary. Then use a dictionary to find which of the following words are taken from Native American languages:

moccasin	tepee
cardigan	squash
coffee	hut

Study and Research

Researching Sioux Culture. This story contains some specific information about Sioux customs. Do research to find out more about the traditions and customs of the Sioux. Begin with the card or computer catalog and with the reference material in your school or local library. Look up at least two sources to find out more about the meaning of a medicine bag, the vision quest tradition, and the history that led to Native Americans living on reservations. Write a brief summary of what you learn. List the sources you used.

Developing Writing Skills

Describing a Tradition. Write a description of a tradition in your family. Perhaps there is some object that has been passed from one generation to the next. Maybe your family celebrates a special occasion or has a special way of celebrating a holiday.

Prewriting. List details that will help a stranger understand the tradition you are describing. What does the object look like, or what specific things are done at the celebration? Where does the tradition come from? Is the tradition part of a particular culture? For whom is the tradition important—for your grandparents? for your parents? for you?

Drafting. Begin your draft by clearly stating what tradition you are describing. As you write, make clear connections between ideas. Include details that will make your description come alive for the reader.

Revising and Sharing. Work with a partner to revise your writing. Have your partner tell you what points about the tradition he or she had difficulty understanding. Are there enough details about exactly what the object looks like or what the celebration involves? Are there interesting questions about the tradition that you could add? When final drafts are completed, spend class time discovering the cultural traditions of your classmates.

The Long Way Around

JEAN McCORD

...her mother's death, a young ...o longer feels part of her ... Will she ever accept the ...es in her life?

I hadn't spoken to my step-mother in three days. I was absorbed by an inner grief and anger because she had given away my mother's dresses to the Salvation Army.

I could still feel my mother around the house. Sometimes I'd come bursting in from school with some important piece of news that I wanted to share immediately, and coming through the door, I'd shout, "Mother, I'm home. Where are you?" and instantly, before the echo had died, I'd remember, too late.

My stepmother had answered once, the first time, coming out from her bedroom with a smile on her face, thinking I was calling her, saying, "Yes, Patty, what is it?" But my face was set in a frozen scowl, and I was standing there rigid, unyielding and furious at myself for such a mistake. She understood and, turning away without pressing me any further, she went back into her room and closed her door.

My mother had died two years before when I was twelve, and even though I knew better, sometimes in the middle of the night I'd awake in a terrible fear and to comfort myself back to sleep, I'd whisper into the pillow, "She's only gone away on a trip. And she'll be back." In the morning I had to face my own lie.

My father had married again last year and though my two little brothers, Jason and Scott, called this new woman "Mother," my father told me I didn't have to do so. I called her Alice even though sometimes it felt strange to call a grown woman by her first name. This Alice wasn't anything at all like my own mother. For one thing, she couldn't cook. My mother had been the best cook in the whole neighborhood. Even the other mothers around us used to say that and would come over for coffee and butter scones and things that my mother would just whip up on a moment's notice. This

Alice . . . well, sometimes our whole supper ended up in the garbage can, and my father would take us out to a restaurant. I thought it was pretty stupid and expensive, but of course Jason and Scott loved it.

To make things even worse, so it seemed to me, my father had taken a new job, and we had moved away from the town and the neighborhood where I'd spent my whole life with kids I knew and had grown up with and gone to school with and graduated with.

Now I was in junior high with a whole new batch of kids and I didn't like any of them. They didn't like me, either. I kept my distance and when school was over, I walked home alone, carrying my books with my head down and hurrying by the groups of girls laughing and giggling over some private joke. I could feel them looking at my back, and the talk always hushed a little until I was by, then they'd break out into silly, stifled snickers when I was down the street a ways.

Actually I hated them all. I hated the teachers and the new school and my new stepmother and my father, who seemed a new person too. Even my little brothers seemed to deserve a good slap for the way they had forgotten and called this Alice "Mother" as if they had never had a mother of their own.

The only one who hadn't changed, who was still the way he had always been, was Rufus, our old Samoyed. Rufus is as old as I am, and in his way he understood. After my mother died, he'd lain on his braided rag rug and refused to move for over two weeks. He wouldn't eat because he was used to my mother fixing him up a strange mixture of dog food with raw egg and bacon drippings, and nobody else seemed to know just how to do it. Finally I tried, and after a while he ate while looking at me from the corner of his eyes and seeming to apologize for it. I sat down beside him and cried into his neck, and he stopped eating long enough to lick my face which only made me cry harder.

Now the only reason I had for getting up in the morning was to greet Rufus and give him an egg. After school the only reason I came home was to take Rufus for a walk, and together we had covered most of this new town. The only trouble was that the town stayed new. Somehow no matter how often we walked down the same streets, the houses always seemed strange. Rufus would plod along at my side, his head just at the reach of my hand. He stumbled once in a while over a curb, but that was because his eyesight wasn't too good any more. My own eyesight seemed slightly affected too because there was a gray film between me and everything I looked at.

We walked all over town after school, my feet just leading the two of us. Finally I knew we had tromped over every square inch of all the streets, but still nothing looked familiar. Sometimes, returning home, I wouldn't even know we had reached the end of the walk until Rufus turned off the sidewalk and went up our front steps.

One Saturday morning I woke up very early. This was about a month ago, I think, or maybe two months. I had lain awake a long time that night watching the shadow patterns change on the ceiling when the wind tossed the big snowball bush outside my window. It seemed like the night was trying to tell me something, but I couldn't quite make out what it was. Out in the kitchen I could hear that Rufus was awake too, because every time he left his rug and walked across the floor, his toenails clicked on the linoleum. He seemed to be pacing the floor as if he wanted to go out into the night. Maybe he sensed something waiting out there for him. If my mother had been here, she'd know . . . she would have known. . . .

Somewhere there in the middle of the night, I must have made up my mind what I was going to do. When the dawn came, I just rose and dressed and without even consciously thinking about it, I packed my small overnight case, putting in my parents' wedding picture which I had retrieved from a trunk in the attic, all the socks I had, two books from the library which were due in three days, one book of my own, and a little stuffed felt doll which I had given to Jason and then taken back from him. I rolled up my printed-rose quilt and tied it in several places with my

belts. Then in blue jeans and a ski jacket I tiptoed out to the kitchen with my belongings and looked down at Rufus, who thumped his tail hard against the floor and got up. He stood with his chin over his dish waiting for me to break his egg into it. I saw then that I couldn't leave him behind, so while he slurped his egg, I rolled his rug around the outside of my quilt. Now it was a big sloppy bundle, but I didn't care.

Just as I was easing open the kitchen door I remembered I had no money, so I had to carefully put everything down and return to my bedroom. I had had a dollar put away for a long time because there was nothing I wanted to spend it on. Outside in the snowball bush the birds were beginning to cheep and call with a tremendous clatter. They were so noisy I wondered how anyone could sleep through that, and I knew I had to get away quickly.

Rufus was waiting with his head leaning against the kitchen door. He knew we were going for a walk. I wanted to take his dish, but didn't see how I could carry everything. We'd manage somehow. I stepped out into the cool grayness with those birds still clattering and the eastern sky beginning to flag out in streaks of red. It was going to be a warm day, and I knew I wouldn't need the ski jacket. Still, I thought . . . at night. . . .

Rufus and I headed toward what I hoped was south. This was vaguely the direction where our old town and old friends were. I had looked at it often enough on the map, but I wasn't sure of just what road to go along. And besides I wanted to stay off the roads. I could picture my father driving along looking for us soon enough, right about breakfast time, I thought, when they would first miss me.

But they wouldn't know anything for sure, I told myself, until I remembered I was carrying Rufus's rug.

"That was very stupid of you," I told Rufus severely, "to let me take your old rug when you knew it would give us away."

The Imminent, 1985, DUNCAN HANNAH. Photograph: Phyllis Kind Gallery, Chicago and New York City.

I walked a few swift steps ahead of him.

"Just for that, I ought to make you go back alone. Without me. Serve you right."

I was very angry. Rufus was hanging his head. The tone of my voice told him he'd done something really bad, but I finally had to forgive him. After all, it had been my own idea.

We used the road only far enough to get us out of town, then I decided we'd better strike across country even though it would be harder traveling, and we would have to climb a lot of fences. It would be safer that way. I soon found out I was right about one thing; it was a lot harder going. We walked through pasture where the ground was spongy and wet and my shoes became waterlogged. We fought our way through brush that kept trying to tear my bundles away from me, and by this time, they really felt heavy. I gave Rufus a sour look, wishing he could carry his own rug at least. We puffed up hills that gave me a stitch in the side, and I noticed that Rufus wasn't holding up too well. He was panting and beginning to lag behind.

By the time the sun was high, I was starving to death. Rufus, at least, had eaten an egg for breakfast, but I hadn't had a bite. And of course by now, I had lost my sense of direction completely. I had no idea which way was south although I had been keeping my eyes open looking for the moss that is supposed to grow on the north side of trees. I hadn't found any.

Every once in a while we would come close to a farmhouse, and there was always trouble. Farmers must keep the meanest dogs in the world. At each place a big shrieking dog would come bounding out at us, and try to pick a fight with Rufus just because we were walking nearby. Rufus would say, "Urrgghh," and show all his teeth with his black lips drawn so far back he looked like a snarling wolf and the farm dogs would back off towards home, but never shut up. I was afraid the farmers might call the police, so we would hurry on.

It was a long time before I saw a country road which I figured was safe enough to walk on. In a couple of miles we came up to a crossroads and a store with one red gas pump squatting to one side and looking like it never had any customers.

I dropped my bundles outside and went into darkness and unfamiliar smells, and there was this old farmer-type man dressed in striped overalls sitting on a sack of something. I didn't know what I wanted to buy, but anything would do. He had a small candy counter, so I bought three chocolate bars. I decided that canned dog food would keep the best for Rufus, so I got seven cans which took all the rest of my money.

"Stranger round here, aren't you, Miss?" the storekeeper said.

I mumbled something and waved backwards, because my mouth was full of stale-tasting candy. He put the cans in a sack and I left, but he followed me to the door and watched very slyly as I had to pick up my suitcase and rolled quilt which left me no way to carry the dog food. I struggled to force it under my arm, but the sack broke and the cans rolled all over the ground. In desperation I knelt and shoved them into my suitcase, and Rufus and I marched down the road with the striped overalls watching us all the way.

I could just almost hear him on the telephone, if he had such a thing, saying, "Sheriff, there's a strange gal going down the road with a big old dog and a suitcase full of dog food. Looks mighty suspicious to me." So there was no choice; we had to leave the road and go back to the pastures and farmhouses.

In the middle of the day, I knew I couldn't carry that terribly heavy suitcase any farther, so I said to Rufus, "You are going to carry some of your own food inside of you."

We sat down in the shade of some bushes, and I opened the suitcase to get out a couple of the cans. Then I broke into tears from sheer rage. I had forgotten to bring along a can opener.

I cried a long time while Rufus looked at me sadly, laying his heavy head on my knee, and banging his tail, which was full of burrs and briars, against the stony ground.

My vaguely formed idea when we first started out was that we'd make our way back to our old town and maybe one of the old neighbors or even my favorite teacher,

Miss Virginia Townsend, would take us in and keep us both if I worked for our board and room. Now I saw clearly that we weren't going to make it. It was over two hundred miles back there, and without even a can opener, well. . . .

We rested for an hour or so while I talked it over with Rufus, who was a good listener and always agreed with me.

"You knew it was a long way when you started out with me, didn't you?"

He thumped his tail once. I guess he was too tired to argue.

"I always understood that dogs knew their own way back to their old homes. Why didn't you lead?"

He looked away down the hill as if he were searching for the right direction.

"If we go back, you know what it means, don't you? They'll all be against us, and you'll certainly have to mind your P's and Q's from here on in!"

He hung his head in shame, but how can you ask a fourteen-year-old dog to walk two hundred miles when he was all worn out from doing about ten?

We stood up and looked out over a valley that faded into a blue haze in the far distance. I picked up the luggage, and we went back down the hill towards the country store. By the time we got there, Rufus was limping.

I went into that dim interior again, and the man was back on his sack, just resting and waiting with his legs crossed.

"Thought you'd be back," he said with

a snort of choked laughter.

"Could I please use your telephone?" I asked with great dignity.

"In the back there. Ask the Missus." He jerked his head.

I had to go into their living quarters. It seems they lived right there surrounded by all those groceries and hardware and chicken feed and medicine for cows and horses. His Missus was a pleasant, stumpy woman with square glasses, and after I'd called home, she gave me a glass of lemonade. I had to ask her where we were, and she took the telephone to give my father directions. He was really boiling mad and hollered over the phone at me, "Swanson's Corner! Where is that?"

I went outside to call Rufus, and she let him come into the kitchen for a drink of cold water. While we waited for my father, I tried to think how to explain all those cans of dog food and the quilt and Rufus's rug, but there didn't seem to be any way. When my father drove up, we climbed in and rode all the way home in guilty silence. My stepmother, Alice, must have told him not to say a word.

When we got home my little brothers looked at me fearfully and my father said with a glint in his eye, "Go to your room and stay there. I'll deal with you later."

Nothing more ever came of it which surprised me no end because I waited all week for punishment.

So now it was a month later, or maybe more.

I still kept to myself at school and if a person talked to me, I just turned away because I had nothing to say to any of them.

On the fifth of November it was my birthday. I woke up with poison in my heart and an ache in my throat that I had to keep swallowing because I was remembering my twelfth birthday when my mother had made a dress for me and also bought me *Tales of Robin Hood,* which I don't read anymore, but it was the book I had taken with me when Rufus and I ran away.

Breakfast seemed strangely quiet, all the more so because nobody said a thing, not even "Happy Birthday." I knew they had forgotten.

At school, like always, I answered if I was called on, but not otherwise. I ate my lunch by myself and passed most of the day thinking of how many birthdays I would have to live through before Rufus and I could leave again for good. About four more, I decided, then knew with a deep sorrow that Rufus wouldn't last to be eighteen.

When school was out, I turned in the wrong direction from home and headed for a park up on a high bluff. It was pleasant and empty. The trees were dropping their leaves in little piles, and a couple of squirrels chased each other around tree trunks like they were on a merry-go-round. I wanted to stay there forever. I wanted the leaves to cover me like little

Hansel and Gretel when they were lost in the woods. I wondered if they had had a stepmother who drove them off, and then I said aloud, "No, that isn't fair. You know it isn't Alice's fault. I don't know whose fault it is for feeling so left out of things."

I looked again at the fallen leaves and thought that my family was like the strong tree that would survive the winter, but I was probably one of the lost leaves.

"I didn't expect them to give me any presents," I kicked at the leaves. I propped my chin on my knees and sat for a long time, thinking and because it was getting late, I read my next day's history lesson. Finally it was too hard to read, and looking up, I saw it was almost dark, and it was a long way home.

I walked home like I always walked, neither slow nor hurrying. It was just too bad if I was late for supper. I didn't want any anyhow.

When I opened the door the house felt strange. My father was sitting in the front room behind his paper which he put aside for a moment, looked at me and said, "Humph!"

Jason came dancing up to me and grabbed me by the hands pulling me into the dining room.

"Where you been, Patty?" he said. "Everybody waited and waited."

Rufus rushed out from the kitchen to greet me as always, but he was wearing a silly little paper hat tied under his chin. I stood in the brightly lighted room and looked around confused. There had obviously been a party. Used paper plates lay all over and the remains of a big frosted cake was crumpled in the center of the table which had a good linen cloth on it. A pile of wrapped presents lay on the sideboard. In the kitchen I could hear Scott chattering to Alice like a little parakeet and Jason, still clutching my hand, was trying to tell me something.

"All your classmates, Patty," he was saying. "All of them. When you dint come home, we had to have the party without you. Your presents are here."

He tried to drag me towards them, but I shucked him off and rushed to my room.

I was pretty shamefaced when Alice came in to see if I wanted supper. She sat beside me on the bed and patted me on the back.

"It was my fault," she said. "I shouldn't have tried to surprise you. Anyway, come on out and feed Rufus. I think he's going to be sick from all that cake he was given."

So that's how matters stand now.

Nothing is going to change very much. I don't feel quite so mad at the whole world, and I notice my actions toward Alice are a lot friendlier. It doesn't bother me any when the boys call her "Mother." Maybe, sometime, a long time from now, I might start calling her that myself. Maybe, by spring or so, I might start growing myself back on that family tree.

Jean McCord *(born 1924)* brings many experiences to her writing. She lists forty-five different occupations in her biography, including time served in the Women's Army Corps. Her novels include *Deep Where the Octopi Lie* and *Bitter Is the Hawk's Path.* Her short stories have been published in *Seventeen* magazine and have been included in *Best American Short Stories.*

Developing Comprehension Skills

1. How is Patty related to Alice? to Jason and Scott?

2. What three major events or changes have happened to Patty in the past two years? Did Patty want these things to happen? Did she have any control over them?

3. How did Patty get along with her real mother?

4. Where does Patty plan to go? Who does she think will take her in? Are her plans realistic?

5. Why is Patty's journey more difficult than she thought it would be? How do her father and Alice respond?

6. How is Patty's birthday different from what she expected?

7. What is meant at the end of the story when Patty thinks, "Maybe, by spring or so, I might start growing myself back on that family tree"? Do you think Patty will succeed? Explain.

Reading Literature: Short Stories

1. **Identifying Conflict.** As you know, **external conflict** often involves a clash between two characters while **internal conflict** is a struggle that goes on within a character. Give an example of both types of conflict in "The Long Way Around."

2. **Comparing Narrators.** How is the narrator in this story like the narrator in "Adjö Means Goodbye"? Name two ways in which they or their experiences are similar. Are they different in any important ways?

3. **Examining Moods.** **Mood** is the feeling created by a piece of writing. "The Long Way Around" creates different moods,

depending on what the narrator is feeling or doing. Identify two passages with different moods. What are the moods? What details help to create the moods?

Vocabulary

Understanding Meaning from Related Words. Sometimes you can figure out what an unfamiliar word means because you know how another form of the word is used. For each set of sentences below, use the clues you get from the related word form in the second sentence to explain the underlined word in the first sentence.

1. a. "I was absorbed by an inner grief and anger. . . ."
   b. Sponges are used to clean up spills because they are very absorbent.

2. a. ". . . I was standing there rigid, unyielding and furious at myself for such a mistake."
   b. At a yield sign, a driver should pause and look for other traffic.

3. a. "When the dawn came, I just rose and dressed and without even consciously thinking about it, I packed my small overnight case. . . ."
   b. Tim was unconscious for a few minutes after hitting his head.

4. a. ". . . I packed my small overnight case, putting in my parents' wedding picture which I had retrieved from a trunk in the attic. . . ."
   b. The library offers computerized information-retrieval service.

5. a. "At each place a big shrieking dog would come bounding out at us. . . ."
   b. The last point in the basketball game was scored on a rebound.

Developing Writing Skills

Analyzing a Character. Write a paragraph telling whether Patty has good reason to feel unfriendly toward her stepmother, Alice.

Prewriting. The story offers two different kinds of information about Alice. Patty tells why she dislikes her stepmother. The reader also learns of some of the things her stepmother does and says. Take notes on what you learn about Alice in each way. What does Alice do that you think would be upsetting? What do Alice's actions and words suggest about the kind of person she is and how she feels about Patty?

Drafting. Begin with a topic sentence that tells whether Patty is justified in being so unfriendly to Alice. In the body of the paragraph, be sure you include evidence both from what Patty says and from what Alice herself does and says.

Revising and Sharing. Break the class into small groups. Each person should read aloud his or her draft. Discuss whether anyone feels differently about Alice after listening to what others have to say.

Home

GWENDOLYN BROOKS

Have you ever realized how much you loved something just when you were in danger of losing it? Read how this family faces the threat of having to leave their home.

What had been wanted was this always, this always to last, the talking softly on this porch, with the snake plant in the jardiniere in the southwest corner and the obstinate slip from Aunt Eppie's magnificent Michigan fern at the left side of the friendly door. Mama, Maud Martha, and Helen rocked slowly in their rocking chairs and looked at the late afternoon light on the lawn and at the emphatic iron of the fence and at the poplar tree.

These things might soon be theirs no longer. Those shafts and pools of light, the tree, the graceful iron, might soon be viewed possessively by different eyes.

Papa was to have gone that noon, during his lunch hour, to the office of the Home Owners' Loan. If he had not succeeded in getting another extension, they would be leaving this house in which they had lived for more than fourteen years. There was little hope. The Home Owners' Loan was hard. They sat, making their own plans.

"We'll be moving into a nice flat somewhere," said Mama. "Somewhere on South Park, or Michigan, or in Washington Park Court." Those flats, as the girls and Mama knew well, were burdens on wages twice the size of Papa's. This was not mentioned now.

"They're much prettier than this old house," said Helen. "I have friends I'd just as soon not bring here. And I have other friends that wouldn't come down this far for anything, unless they were in a taxi."

Yesterday, Maud Martha would have attacked her. Tomorrow she might. Today she said nothing. She merely gazed at a little hopping robin in the tree, her tree, and tried to keep the fronts of her eyes dry.

"Well, I do know," said Mama, turning her hands over and over, "that I've been getting tireder and tireder of doing that firing. From October to April, there's firing to be done."

Old Houses, 1943, JOHN ROBINSON. Private Collection.

"But lately we've been helping, Harry and I," said Maud Martha. "And sometimes in March and April and in October, and even in November, we could build a little fire in the fireplace. Sometimes the weather was just right for that."

She knew, from the way they looked at her, that this had been a mistake. They did not want to cry.

But she felt that the little line of white, somewhat ridged with smoked purple, and all that cream-shot saffron, would never drift across any western sky except that in back of this house. The rain would drum with as sweet a dullness nowhere but here. The birds on South Park were mechanical birds, no better than the poor caught canaries in those "rich" women's sun parlors.

"It's just going to kill Papa!" burst out

Maud Martha. "He loves this house! He *lives* for this house!"

"He lives for us," said Helen. "It's us he loves. He wouldn't want the house, except for us."

"And he'll have us," added Mama, "wherever."

"You know," Helen sighed, "if you want to know the truth, this is a relief. If this hadn't come up, we would have gone on, just dragged on, hanging out here forever."

"It might," allowed Mama, "be an act of God. God may just have reached down, and picked up the reins."

"Yes," Maud Martha cracked in, "that's what you always say—that God knows best."

Her mother looked at her quickly, decided the statement was not suspect, looked away.

Helen saw Papa coming. "There's Papa," said Helen.

They could not tell a thing from the way Papa was walking. It was that same dear little staccato walk, one shoulder down, then the other, then repeat, and repeat. They watched his progress. He passed the Kennedys', he passed the vacant lot, he passed Mrs. Blakemore's. They wanted to hurl themselves over the fence, into the street, and shake the truth out of his collar. He opened his gate—the gate—and still his stride and face told them nothing.

"Hello," he said.

Mama got up and followed him through the front door. The girls knew better than to go in too.

Presently Mama's head emerged. Her eyes were lamps turned on.

"It's all right," she exclaimed. "He got it. It's all over. Everything is all right."

The door slammed shut. Mama's footsteps hurried away.

"I think," said Helen, rocking rapidly, "I think I'll give a party. I haven't given a party since I was eleven. I'd like some of my friends to just casually see that we're homeowners."

Gwendolyn Brooks *(born 1917)*, Poet Laureate of Illinois, grew up in a black community in Chicago. Her experiences as a child have inspired much of her writing. She has earned many literary prizes, including the Pulitzer Prize. Brooks is the author of several books of poetry, including *Annie Allen* and *The Bean Eaters*. She has also written a novel, *Maud Martha,* and a book of children's verse, *Bronzeville Boys and Girls.* She has taught at many colleges in the Chicago area as well as at the University of Wisconsin and the City College of New York. Brooks's readings from her work are popular throughout the United States.

Developing Comprehension Skills

1. Name the characters who speak in this story. How are they related?

2. Where did Papa go at noon? What are Mama and the girls waiting for?

3. Do Mama and Helen really think that the new place will be better than their old home? If not, why do they talk about the advantages of moving?

4. At one point in their discussion, Helen and Mama suggest that it is the family being together that is important, rather than the familiar house. Do you agree that it is the way the people in a family feel about each other that makes a house a home? Explain.

Reading Literature: Short Stories

1. **Examining Suspense.** Suspense is the feeling of growing excitement and uncertainty about what will happen. Do the characters in the story share their uncertainty about Papa's success with the reader? How does the description of Papa's walk help build suspense?

2. **Understanding Characterization.** Read again what Maud Martha says and thinks. Then review Helen's remarks. In what ways are the two girls different? Which sister tries to cover up her emotions? How does she disguise her feelings? Which one seems to appreciate more the small details of the way things look and feel?

3. **Thinking About Setting.** Where does the story take place? How is this setting related to the problem the characters discuss?

Vocabulary

Using Context Clues. The following sentences are based on stories you have read. For each, use a context clue to figure out the meaning of the underlined word. Identify key words that indicate the following context clues: example, comparison, contrast, or words in a series.

1. Barney was as <u>obstinate</u> as a child who refuses to eat lima beans even if it means missing his favorite dessert.

2. Eddy joined the other boys for games of skill, <u>wit</u>, and cleverness.

3. Grandpa was <u>emphatic</u> about how he wanted to do things, unlike Martin, who was uncertain in his behavior toward Grandpa.

4. The sky was an unusual yellow, closer to <u>saffron</u> than to a dark mustard color.

Developing Writing Skills

Explaining an Opinion. Think about something in your life that you take for granted but would miss terribly if it were taken away from you. Write a paragraph explaining why the place, object, or activity is so important to you.

Prewriting. Spend some time deciding on what you want to write about: Is there a place that is especially important? a possession that you have had for a long time or that you associate with a member of your family? Is there something that you often do with a friend or relative that you would miss doing?

Once you have decided on your topic, list details about what you would miss if the thing or experience were taken away.

Drafting. As you work on your draft, try to make the reader both see and feel what it is that you would miss.

Revising and Sharing. Read over your paragraph and ask yourself the following questions: Did you use specific words and phrases that will help a reader feel how important the place, object, or activity is to you? Could you add a comparison that explains its meaning or that suggests how you would feel if it were gone? When you have made a final draft, share your paragraph with the class.

Sixteen

MAUREEN DALY

Maureen Daly wrote this story in 1937, when she herself was sixteen. In it, a girl remembers a special night. How did she feel then? How does she feel now?

Now don't get me wrong. I mean, I want you to understand from the beginning that I'm not really dumb. I know what a girl should do and what she shouldn't. I get around. I read. And I have two older sisters. So, you see, I know what the score is. I know that anyone who orders a strawberry sundae in a drugstore instead of a lemon Coke would probably be dumb enough to wear colored ankle socks with high heeled pumps or use "Evening in Paris" with a tweed suit. But I'm sort of drifting. This isn't what I wanted to tell you. I just wanted to give you the general idea of how I'm not so dumb. It's important that you understand that.

You see, it was funny how I met him. It was a winter night like any other winter night. And I didn't have my Latin done,

Jenny at Mountain Ridge, 1987, DOUG BREGA.
Photograph: Alexander Gallery, New York City.

either. But the way the moon made the twigs lash and silver-plated the snowdrifts, I just couldn't stay inside. The skating rink isn't far from our house—you can make it in five minutes if the sidewalks aren't slippery—so I went skating. I remember it took me a long time to get ready that night because I had to darn my skating socks first. I don't know why they always wear out so fast—just in the toes, too. And then I brushed my hair—hard, so hard it clung to my hand and stood up around my head in a hazy halo.

My skates were hanging by the back door all nice and shiny, for I'd just gotten them for Christmas and they smelled so strange—like fresh-smoked ham. My dog walked with me as far as the corner. She's a red chow, very polite and well mannered. She panted along beside me, and her hot breath made a frosty little balloon bouncing on the end of her nose. My skates thumped me good-naturedly on the back as I walked. The night was breathlessly quiet and the stars winked down like a million flirting eyes. It was all so lovely.

I had to cut across someone's back garden to get to the rink and last summer's grass stuck through the thin ice, brown and discouraged. Not many people came through this way and the crusted snow broke through the little hollows between corn stubbles frozen hard in the ground. I was out of breath when I got to the shanty—out of breath with running and

with the loveliness of the night. Shanties are always such friendly places—the floor all hacked to wet splinters from the skate runners and the wooden wall marked with signs of forgotten love affairs. There was a smell of singed wool as someone got too near the iron stove. Girls burst through the door laughing, with snow on their hair, and tripped over shoes scattered on the floor. A pimply-faced boy grabbed the hat from the frizzled head of an eighth-grade blonde and stuffed it into an empty galosh to prove his love and then hastily bent to examine his skate strap with innocent unconcern.

It didn't take me long to get my own skates on and I stuck my shoes under the bench—far back where they wouldn't get knocked around and would be easy to find when I wanted to go home. I walked out on my toes and the shiny runners of my new skates dug deep into the sodden floor.

It was snowing a little outside—quick, eager little Lux-like flakes that melted as soon as they touched your hand. I don't know where the snow came from for there were stars out. Or maybe the stars were in my eyes and I just kept seeing them every time I looked up into the darkness. I waited a moment. You know, to start to skate at a crowded rink is like jumping on a moving merry-go-round. The skaters go skimming round in a colored blur like gaudy painted horses and the shrill musical jabber re-echoes in the night from a hundred human calliopes. Once in, I went all right. At least after I found out exactly where that rough ice was. It was "round, round, jump the rut, round, round, jump the rut, round, round——"

And then he came. All of a sudden his arm was around my waist so warm and tight, and he said very casually, "Mind if I skate with you?" and then he took my other hand. That's all there was to it. Just that and then we were skating. It wasn't that I'd never skated with a boy before. Don't be silly. I told you before I get around. But this was different. He was a smoothie. He was a big shot up at school, and he went to all the big dances, and he was the best dancer in town except for Harold Wright who didn't count because he'd been to college in New York for two years. Don't you see? This was different.

At first I can't remember what we talked about. I can't even remember if we talked at all. We just skated and skated and laughed every time we came to that rough spot and pretty soon we were laughing all the time at nothing at all. It was all so lovely.

Then we sat on the big snowbank at the edge of the rink and just watched. It was cold at first even with my skating pants on, sitting on that hard heap of snow, but pretty soon I got warm all over. He threw a handful of snow at me and it fell in a little white shower on my hair and he leaned over to brush it off. I held my breath. The night stood still.

The moon hung just over the warming shanty like a big quarter slice of muskmelon and the smoke from the pipe chimney floated up in a sooty fog. One by one the houses around the rink twinkled out their lights and somebody's hound wailed a mournful apology to a star as he curled up for the night. It was all so lovely.

Then he sat up straight and said, "We'd better start home." Not "Shall I take you home?" or "Do you live far?" but "We'd better start home." See, that's how I know he wanted to take me home. Not because he *had* to but because he *wanted* to. He went to the shanty to get my shoes. "Black ones," I told him. "Same size as your pet movie star's." And he laughed again. He was still smiling when he came back and took off my skates and tied the wet skate strings in a soggy knot and put them over his shoulder. Then he held out his hand, and I slid off the snowbank and brushed off the seat of my pants, and we were ready.

It was snowing harder now. Big, quiet flakes that clung to twiggy bushes and snuggled in little drifts against the tree trunks. The night was an etching in black and white. It was all so lovely I was sorry I lived only a few blocks away. He talked softly as we walked, as if every little word were a secret. Did I like band music, and did I plan to go to college next year and had I a cousin who lived in Appleton and knew his brother? A very respectable Emily Post sort of conversation and then finally—how nice I looked with snow in my hair and had I ever seen the moon so—close? For the moon was following us as we walked and ducking playfully behind a chimney every time I turned to look at it. And then we were home.

The porch light was on. My mother always puts the porch light on when I go away at night. And we stood there a moment by the front steps, and the snow turned pinkish in the glow of colored light, and a few feathery flakes settled on his hair. Then he took my skates and put them over my shoulder and said, "Good night now. I'll call you." "I'll call you," he said.

I went inside then and in a moment he was gone. I watched him from my window as he went down the street. He was whistling softly and I waited until the sound faded away so I couldn't tell if it was he or my heart whistling out there in the night. And then he was gone, completely gone.

I shivered. Somehow the darkness seemed changed. The stars were little hard chips of light far up in the sky, and the moon stared down with a sullen yellow glare. The air was tense with sudden cold, and a gust of wind swirled his footprints into white oblivion. Everything was quiet.

But he'd said, "I'll call you." That's what he said—"I'll call you." I couldn't sleep all night.

And that was last Thursday. Tonight is Tuesday. Tonight is Tuesday, and my homework's done, and I darned some socks that didn't really need it, and I worked a crossword puzzle, and I listened to the radio, and now I'm just sitting. I'm just sitting because I can't think of anything else to do. I can't think of anything, anything but snowflakes and ice skates and yellow moons and Thursday night. The telephone is sitting on the corner table with its old black face turned to the wall so I can't see its leer. I don't even jump when it rings any more. My heart still prays, but my mind just laughs. Outside the night is still, so still I think I'll go crazy, and the white snow's all dirtied and smoked into grayness, and the wind is blowing the arc light so it throws weird, waving shadows from the trees onto the lawn—like thin, starved arms begging for I don't know what. And so I'm just sitting here, and I'm not feeling anything. I'm not even sad because all of a sudden I know. All of a sudden I know. I can sit here now forever and laugh and laugh and laugh while the tears run salty in the corners of my mouth. For all of a sudden I know, I know what the stars knew all the time—he'll never, never call—never.

Maureen Daly *(born 1921),* who grew up in Fond du Lac, Wisconsin, wrote her short story "Sixteen" at the age of sixteen. The story was selected for the O. Henry Memorial Award volume in 1938. When Daly was seventeen, her first novel, *Seventeenth Summer,* was published. This, too, was praised by the critics and is now considered a classic in teen-age fiction. Daly has also worked as a reporter for the *Chicago Tribune,* as an associate editor for the *Ladies Home Journal,* and as a consultant to the editors of *The Saturday Evening Post.* She continues to write travel books and stories for children and recently published a book on her daughter's battle with cancer.

Developing Comprehension Skills

1. Why does the narrator decide to go skating?

2. How much time passes between the evening the narrator tells about and the night on which she is telling the story?

3. Is this a story about something that happened—the experience of the moonlit evening? Or is it about something that didn't happen—what the narrator experiences after the evening? Or is it about both? Explain.

Reading Literature: Short Stories

1. **Analyzing Description.** In this story, the writer uses many **images,** words and phrases that appeal to the reader's senses. She includes many details that appeal to sight, hearing, touch, and smell. Choose one paragraph of description and list the images, the most vivid words and phrases, as well as the senses that they appeal to.

2. **Examining Point of View.** From whose point of view is the story told? What kind of person is she? Does the narrator seem involved or removed from what happens? Note that the opening paragraph sounds like conversation. How does the language of the story reflect the age of the speaker?

3. **Understanding Title and Purpose.** What does the title "Sixteen" refer to? What is the main point of the story? Does the writer

want to create an exciting adventure? teach a lesson? re-create an experience? The writer wrote this story when she herself was sixteen. How does this information affect your understanding of the story?

Vocabulary

Using Specific Words. The writer's use of specific terms makes this story seem realistic, set in a particular time and place. For example, instead of saying that someone has no sense of fashion, she talks about someone who "would probably be dumb enough to wear colored ankle socks with high-heeled pumps. . . ." It is clear from the context that "high-heeled pumps" are a kind of shoe. Following is a list of other specific terms from the story. For each term, tell what general kind of item is referred to and then list another specific term for an item from the same category. Use terms that a modern teen-ager from your school might use.

1. lemon Coke   3. red chow
2. Latin   4. "Evening in Paris"

Speaking and Listening

Preparing a Dramatic Reading. The opening paragraph of this story sounds as if it is being spoken directly to someone who is the same age as the narrator. Prepare this opening paragraph as a dramatic reading. Read it to yourself several times so that you can present it smoothly. Then plan where and how you can use your voice, a facial expression, or a gesture to help create a sense of the personality of the narrator.

Developing Writing Skills

Evaluating Meaning. This story was written more than fifty years ago. Write a paragraph that tells whether or not you think the story describes something a teenager today might experience.

Prewriting. You may find it helpful to meet with a small group to discuss ideas and opinions. Talk about the following points. Exactly what happens in the story? How does the girl feel at the end? Could the same kind of situation occur today? If you were in the girl's position, might you react in the same way?

Drafting. As you draft your paragraph, be sure that you focus on the assigned topic. Remember that you are not evaluating whether or not the narrator should give up hope of getting a phone call. You are discussing whether or not things have changed so much that teen-agers no longer have the type of experience described in the story.

Revising and Sharing. Have someone else read your paragraph to see if you have clearly stated a main idea and have given specific examples or evidence that support your idea.

Science Fiction and Fantasy

All of the stories you have read so far have been set in the real world. In contrast, the next few selections represent a special group of stories—science fiction and fantasy. In these stories, the feelings and personalities of the characters may seem familiar. The settings, however, are different from your ordinary, familiar world. Science fiction and fantasy are always set, at least in part, in the future or in an imaginary world.

Ricochet, 1986, RICHARD LOVING. Photograph: Roy Boyd Gallery, Chicago and Santa Monica.

The Fun They Had

ISAAC ASIMOV

Two children of the future learn about the schools of today. What do they think of your schools? What do you think of theirs?

Margie even wrote about it that night in her diary. On the page headed May 17, 2157, she wrote, "Today Tommy found a real book!"

It was a very old book. Margie's grandfather once said that when he was a little boy, *his* grandfather told him that there was a time when all stories were printed on paper.

They turned the pages, which were yellow and crinkly; and it was awfully funny to read words that stood still instead of moving the way they were supposed to—on a screen, you know. And then, when they turned back to the page before, it had the same words on it that it had had when they read it the first time.

"Gee," said Tommy, "what a waste. When you're through with the book, you just throw it away, I guess. Our television screen must have had a million books on it, and it's good for plenty more. I wouldn't throw *it* away."

"Same with mine," said Margie. She was eleven and hadn't seen as many tele-books as Tommy had. He was thirteen.

She said, "Where did you find it?"

"In my house." He pointed without looking, because he was busy reading. "In the attic."

"What's it about?"

"School."

Margie was scornful. "School? What's there to write about school? I hate school."

Margie always hated school, but now she hated it more than ever. The mechanical teacher had been giving her test after test in geography, and she had been doing worse and worse until her mother had shaken her head sorrowfully and sent for the County Inspector.

He was a round little man with a red face and a whole box of tools with dials and wires. He smiled at Margie and gave her an apple, then took the teacher apart. Margie had hoped he wouldn't know how to put it together again, but he knew how all right; and after an hour or so, there it was again, large and black and ugly, with a big screen on which all the lessons were shown and the questions were asked. That wasn't so bad. The part Margie hated most was the slot where she had to put homework and test papers. She always had to write them out in a punch code they made her learn when she was six years old, and the mechanical teacher calculated the mark in no time.

The Inspector had smiled after he was finished and patted Margie's head. He said to her mother, "It's not the little girl's fault, Mrs. Jones. I think the geography sector was geared a little too quick. Those things happen sometimes. I've slowed it up to an average ten-year level. Actually, the overall pattern of her progress is quite satisfactory." And he patted Margie's head again.

Margie was disappointed. She had been hoping they would take the teacher away altogether. They had once taken Tommy's teacher away for nearly a month because the history sector had blanked out completely.

So she said to Tommy, "Why would anyone write about school?"

Tommy looked at her with very superior eyes. "Because it's not our kind of school, stupid. This is the old kind of school that they had hundreds and hundreds of years ago." He added loftily, pronouncing the word carefully, "*Centuries* ago."

Margie was hurt. "Well, I don't know what kind of school they had all that time ago." She read the book over his shoulder for a while, then said, "Anyway, they had a teacher."

"Sure they had a teacher, but it wasn't a *regular* teacher. It was a man."

"A man? How could a man be a teacher?"

"Well, he just told the boys and girls things and gave them homework and asked them questions."

"A man isn't smart enough."

"Sure he is. My father knows as much as my teacher."

"He can't. A man can't know as much as a teacher."

"He knows almost as much, I betcha."

Margie wasn't prepared to dispute that. She said, "I wouldn't want a strange man in my house to teach me."

Tommy screamed with laughter. "You don't know much, Margie. The teachers didn't live in the house. They had a special building, and all the kids went there."

"And all the kids learned the same things?"

"Sure, if they were the same age."

"But my mother says a teacher has to be adjusted to fit the mind of each boy and girl it teaches and that each kid has to be taught differently."

"Just the same, they didn't do it that way then. If you don't like it, you don't have to read the book."

"I didn't say I didn't like it," Margie

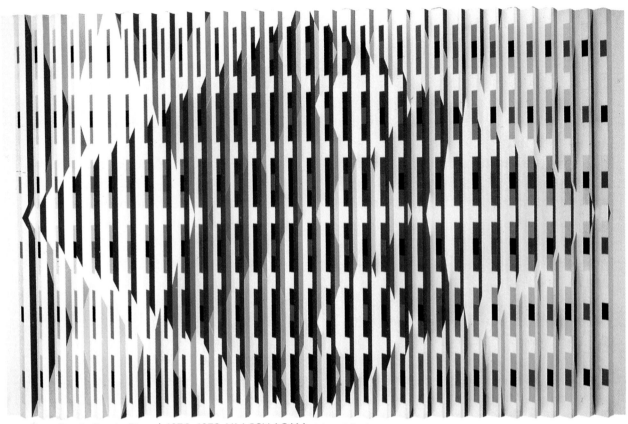

From Day to Day to Eternal, 1976–1978, YAACOV AGAM. Private Collection.

said quickly. She wanted to read about those funny schools.

They weren't even half-finished when Margie's mother called, "Margie! School!"

Margie looked up. "Not yet, Mamma."

"Now!" said Mrs. Jones. "And it's probably time for Tommy, too."

Margie said to Tommy, "Can I read the book some more with you after school?"

"Maybe," he said nonchalantly. He walked away whistling, the dusty old book tucked beneath his arm.

Margie went into the schoolroom. It was right next to her bedroom, and the mechanical teacher was on and waiting for her. It was always on at the same time every day except Saturday and Sunday, because her mother said little girls learned better if they learned at regular hours.

The screen was lit up, and it said,

"Today's arithmetic lesson is on the addition of proper fractions. Please insert yesterday's homework in the proper slot."

Margie did so with a sigh. She was thinking about the old schools they had when her grandfather's grandfather was a little boy. All the kids from the whole neighborhood came, laughing and shouting in the schoolyard, sitting together in the schoolroom, going home together at the end of the day. They learned the same things, so they could help one another with the homework and talk about it.

And the teachers were people. . . .

The mechanical teacher was flashing on the screen, "When we add the fractions ½ and ¼——"

Margie was thinking about how the kids must have loved it in the old days. She was thinking about the fun they had.

Isaac Asimov (*born 1920*) came with his family to the United States from Russia at the age of three. As a boy, he loved reading science fiction magazines. This reading stimulated Asimov's interest in science. He studied at Columbia University and then became a professor at Boston University School of Medicine. Asimov has written hundreds of books and articles on scientific and other subjects. He is best known, though, for his science fiction stories.

Developing Comprehension Skills

1. The following events are given in the order in which they are told in the story. List them in the order in which they actually took place. In other words, tell what happened first, second, and so forth.

   a. Margie writes in her diary.

   b. Tommy finds the real book.

   c. Margie's mother sends for the County Inspector.

   d. Tommy explains to Margie about old schools.

   e. Margie has her arithmetic lesson.

2. Identify at least two ways in which Margie's schooling is like yours. Then think of the ways in which it is different. Name two or more things that Margie thinks are better about your school.

3. Good science fiction carries the reader into a believable future. In many cases science fiction seems to predict the future. Find several events and things in the story that are not yet possible in today's world. Then tell whether or not you think these things or events are believable or could happen some day.

Reading Literature: Short Stories

1. **Identifying Irony.** As you know, **irony** can be a contrast between what a character believes to be true and what actually is true. Think about your own attitude toward school and the attitude other students have. What is ironic about the end of the story?

2. **Understanding Theme.** As you know, **theme** is the message in a piece of writing. A science fiction writer may set a story in the future in order to raise questions about something in today's world. In "The Fun They Had," what kind of warning might Asimov be giving about the limitations of using computers?

Vocabulary

Using the Prefix *Tele-*. In this story, the word *telebook* is used to describe a book seen on a television screen. Some other common words containing the prefix *tele-* are *telephone* and *telegraph*. *Tele-* means "far" or "at a distance." Match the words with the definitions that follow. Check a dictionary if necessary.

a. telephonic   d. telephotography
b. telethon   e. telepathy
c. telescope   f. telethermometer

1. method of photographing distant objects with camera

2. an instrument used to make distant objects appear nearer and larger

3. having the ability to convey sound across a distance

4. an apparatus for indicating the temperature of a distant point

5. a long television program, usually to ask for money for a charity

6. apparent communication from one mind to another without speech or signs

Look up the *tele-* words in a dictionary and write the respelling of each word. Note that *tele-* in the word *telepathy* is pronounced differently from *tele-* in the other words.

Speaking and Listening

Reading Dialogue. A **dialogue** is a conversation between two or more people. While writers often use speech tags such as "he said" or "she asked," sometimes dialogue is written without them. The reader is expected to recognize when one speaker stops speaking and another starts by noticing the indentations and quotation marks. With a partner, read aloud the dialogue between Margie and Tommy on page 287. Notice how accurately the writer captures the way quarreling children speak to each other. Try to use a realistic tone of voice as you read.

Developing Writing Skills

Writing Science Fiction. Choose an ordinary place in your world, such as a zoo, a library, a museum, or a restaurant. Write a description of this place as it might be in two hundred years.

Prewriting. List eight to ten details describing how the place might be different in two hundred years. Include specific ways the location might look, smell, sound, or feel. Decide how you want to organize your description. For example, you might want to follow an imaginary visitor through a museum or library and report on the things he or she does. Or, you could tell what happens from the minute you enter a restaurant until you leave.

Drafting. Follow the organization you decided on during prewriting. Include details to make the place you are describing seem interesting and realistic. Make sure each part of your description is clear.

Revising and Sharing. Collect the descriptions in a Book of the Future to keep in the classroom. Provide illustrations or diagrams that will help your readers picture the future you describe.

The Dragon

RAY BRADBURY

On a mysterious moor, two knights attempt to slay a dragon. What is surprising about this beast?

The night blew in the short grass on the moor. There was no other motion. It had been years since a single bird had flown by in the great blind shell of sky. Long ago a few small stones had simulated life when they crumbled and fell into dust. Now only the night moved in the souls of the two men bent by their lonely fire in the wilderness. Darkness pumped quietly in their veins and ticked silently in their temples and their wrists.

Firelight fled up and down their wild faces and welled in their eyes in orange tatters. They listened to each other's faint, cool breathing and the lizard blink of their eyelids. At last, one man poked the fire with his sword.

"Don't, idiot; you'll give us away!"

"No matter," said the second man. "The dragon can smell us miles off anyway. God's breath, it's cold. I wish I was back at the castle."

"It's death, not sleep, we're after. . . ."

"Why? Why? The dragon never sets foot in the town!"

"Quiet, fool! He eats men traveling alone from our town to the next!"

"Let them be eaten and let us get home!"

"Wait now. Listen!"

The two men froze.

They waited a long time, but there was only the shake of their horses' nervous skin like black velvet tambourines jingling the silver stirrup buckles, softly, softly.

"Ah." The second man sighed. "What a land of nightmares. Everything happens here. Someone blows out the sun; it's night. And then, and *then*, oh, sweet mortality, listen! This dragon—they say his eyes are fire, his breath a white gas. You can see him burn across the dark lands. He runs with sulfur and thunder and kindles the grass. Sheep panic and die insane. Women deliver forth monsters. The dragon's fury is such that tower walls shake back to dust. His victims, at sunrise, are strewn hither thither on the hills. How many knights, I ask, have gone for this monster and failed, even as we shall fail?"

"Enough of that!"

"More than enough! Out here in this desolation I cannot tell what year this is!"

"Nine hundred years since the Nativity."[1]

"No, no," whispered the second man, eyes shut. "On this moor is no Time, is only Forever. I feel if I ran back on the road the town would be gone, the people yet unborn, things changed, the castles unquarried from the rocks, the timbers still uncut from the forests. Don't ask how I know. The moor knows and tells me. And here we sit alone in the land of the fire dragon. God save us!"

"Be you afraid, then gird on your armor!"

"What use? The dragon runs from nowhere. We cannot guess its home. It vanishes in fog. We know not where it goes. Aye, on with our armor—we'll die well dressed."

Half into his silver corselet, the second man stopped again and turned his head.

Across the dim country, full of night and nothingness from the heart of the moor itself, the wind sprang full of dust from clocks that used dust for telling time. There were black suns burning in the heart of this new wind and a million burnt leaves shaken from some autumn tree beyond the horizon. This wind melted landscapes, lengthened bones like white wax, made the blood roil and thicken to a muddy deposit in the brain. The wind was a thousand souls dying and all time confused and in transit. It was a fog inside of a mist inside of a darkness. This place was no man's place and there was no year or hour at all, but only these men in a faceless emptiness of sudden frost, storm and white thunder which moved behind the great falling pane of green glass that was the lightning. A squall of rain drenched the turf. All faded away until there was unbreathing hush and the two men waiting alone with their warmth in a cool season.

"There," whispered the first man, "Oh, *there* . . ."

Miles off, rushing with a great chant and a roar—the dragon.

In silence the men buckled on their armor and mounted their horses. The midnight wilderness was split by a monstrous gushing as the dragon roared nearer, nearer. Its flashing yellow glare spurted above a hill and then, fold on fold of dark body, distantly seen, therefore indistinct, flowed over that hill and plunged vanishing into a valley.

"Quick!"

They spurred their horses forward to a small hollow.

"This is where it passes!"

---

1. **Nativity**–The birth of Christ.

They seized their lances with mailed fists and blinded their horses by flipping the visors down over their eyes.

"Lord!"

"Yes, let us use His name."

On the instant, the dragon rounded a hill. Its monstrous amber eye fed on them, fired their armor in red glints and glitters. With a terrible wailing cry and a grinding rush it flung itself forward.

"Mercy, mercy!"

The lance struck under the unlidded yellow eye, buckled, tossed the man through the air. The dragon hit, spilled him over, down, ground him under. Passing, the black brunt of its shoulder smashed the remaining horse and rider a hundred feet against the side of a boulder, wailing, wailing, the dragon shrieking, the fire all about, around, under it, a pink, yellow, orange sun-fire with great soft plumes of blinding smoke.

"Did you *see* it?" cried a voice. "Just like I told you!"

"The same! The same! A knight in armor, by the Lord Harry! We *hit* him!"

"You goin' to stop?"

"Did once; found nothing. Don't like to stop on this moor. I get the willies. Got a *feel*, it has."

"But we hit *something!*"

"Gave him plenty of whistle. Chap wouldn't budge!"

A steaming blast cut the mist aside.

"We'll make Stokely on time. More coal, eh, Fred?"

Another whistle shook dew from the empty sky. The night train, in fire and fury, shot through a gully, up a rise, and vanished away over cold earth toward the north, leaving black smoke and steam to dissolve in the numbed air minutes after it had passed and gone forever.

Untitled (Tunnels and Trains), about 1953, MARTIN RAMIREZ. Collection of Gladys Nilsson and Jim Nutt. Photograph by William H. Bengtson, Phyllis Kind Galleries, Chicago and New York City,

Developing Comprehension Skills

1. Where are the two characters who speak at the beginning of the story? What are they waiting for?

2. What evidence is there that the two characters are knights from the Middle Ages?

3. Are the two men hopeful that they will be successful in their fight with the dragon? Are they successful?

4. Are the two speakers at the end of the story the same or different characters from the two at the beginning? What form of transportation does the dragon turn out to be? What is happening to time in this story?

5. Could the events in this story really happen? Do the emotions and reactions the characters show seem like feelings real people might have? Explain.

Reading Literature: Short Stories

1. **Evaluating Setting.** Through description of the setting, the writer of this story builds a feeling of wild emptiness. Look up *moor* in the glossary or a dictionary. What kind of landscape does a moor have? How does having the story take place at night add to the feeling of uneasiness and uncertainty?

2. **Understanding Science Fiction. Science fiction** is writing based on real or imagined scientific developments and often set in an imaginary past or future. To understand "The Dragon," the reader must recognize

that two time periods are mixed. What are the two time periods? What clues are given to help the reader identify them? Do the characters in the story fully understand that they have been caught in a time warp, or mixing of times? Do they suspect that something makes the sense of time very strange and frightening in this setting? Find a passage that indicates the characters' sense of time in the story.

3. **Examining Description.** Review the descriptions of the "dragon." How does a locomotive on a steam train look as it passes in the night? How do the details describing the dragon also describe the locomotive?

Vocabulary

Recognizing Archaic Words. Archaic words are words that are no longer in common use. Some expressions simply stop being used over time. Other terms drop out of everyday vocabulary because they refer to items that are no longer used. Often you can get a general sense of what an archaic word means from the context in which it appears. For example, in this story, one of the knights gets ready by putting on his *corselet*. While you may not know exactly what it is, the context makes it clear that a *corselet* is part of a knight's armor.

Locate each of the following archaic words or terms in "The Dragon." Look for clues in the context that will help you determine at least the general meaning of the word. Then check the meaning by looking in a dictionary.

hither thither (page 293, column 1, near top of page

gird on your armor (page 293, column 1, paragraph 5)

made the blood roil (page 293, column 2, paragraph 1)

mailed fists (page 294, column 1, paragraph 1)

visors (page 294, column 1, near top of page)

Developing Writing Skills

1. **Analyzing Mood.** Write a paragraph in which you explain what techniques the writer uses to create a mood, or feeling, of fear and uncertainty in this story.

   Prewriting. Make notes as you answer the following questions: How does the setting help set up the mood? How do the characters feel about what is happening? What effect does their attitude have on the mood? What specific details and words used in the descriptions add to the mood?

   Drafting. Begin with a topic sentence that indicates the kind of mood or feeling that is created. Then give specific examples, using the notes you have made.

   Revising and Sharing. Work with a partner to evaluate how well your draft develops your main idea. Also proofread each other's work for spelling and punctuation mistakes.

2. **Creating a Time Warp.** Write a description of a person from a previous century who sees a twentieth-century invention for the first time. Your approach can be serious or humorous. Write down several kinds of details. First list details of how the object looks to the person. Next list comparisons the person makes between what he or she is familiar with and the unfamiliar object. Then list the feelings the person has about the object. Organize these details. Try writing your description without naming the object. When you have finished your description, meet with a small group and read your paragraphs to one another. Try to guess the object each person is describing.

The Gift-Giving

JOAN AIKEN

A special tradition is in danger of being lost. How do two children try to restore it?

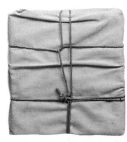

The weeks leading up to Christmas were always full of excitement, and tremendous anxiety too, as the family waited in suspense for the Uncles, who had set off in the spring of the year, to return from the summer's traveling and trading: Uncle Emer, Uncle Acraud, Uncle Gonfil, and Uncle Mark. They always started off together, down the steep mountainside, but then, at the bottom, they took different routes along the deep, narrow valley, Uncle Mark and Uncle Acraud riding eastward, toward the great plains, while Uncle Emer and Uncle Gonfil turned west, toward the towns and rivers and the western sea.

Then, before they were clear of the mountains, they would separate once more, Uncle Acraud turning south, Uncle Emer taking his course northward, so

that, the children occasionally thought, their family was scattered over the whole world, netted out like a spider's web.

Spring and summer would go by in the usual occupations: digging and sowing the steep hillside garden beds, fishing, hunting for hares, picking wild strawberries, making hay. Then, toward St. Drimma's Day, when the winds began to blow and the snow crept down, lower and lower, from the high peaks, Grandmother would begin to grow restless.

Silent and calm all summer long she sat in her rocking chair on the wide wooden porch, wrapped in a patchwork comforter, with her blind eyes turned eastward toward the lands where Mark, her dearest and firstborn, had gone. But when the winds of Michaelmas began to blow, and the wolves grew bolder, and the children dragged in sacks of logs day after day, and the cattle were brought down to the stable under the house, then Grandmother grew agitated indeed.

When Sammle, the eldest granddaughter, brought her hot milk, she would grip the girl's slender brown wrist and demand: "Tell me, child, how many days now to St. Froida's Day?" (which was the first of December).

"Eighteen, Grandmother," Sammle would answer, stooping to kiss the wrinkled cheek.

"So many, still? So many till we may hope to see them?"

"Don't worry, Granny, the Uncles are *certain* to return safely. Perhaps they will be early this year. Perhaps we may see them before the feast of St. Melin" (which was December the fourteenth).

And then, sure enough, sometime during the middle weeks of December, their great carts would come jingling and trampling along the winding valleys. Young Mark (son of Uncle Emer), from his watchpoint up a tall pine over a high cliff, would catch the flash of a baggage-mule's brass brow-medal, or the sun glancing off the barrel of a carbine, and would come joyfully dashing back to report.

"Granny! Granny! The Uncles are almost here!"

Then the whole household, the whole village, would be filled with as much turmoil as that of a kingdom of ants when the spade breaks open their hummock. Wives would build the fires higher and fetch out the best linen, wine, dried meat, pickled eggs; set dough to rising, mix cakes of honey and oats, and bring up stone jars of preserved strawberries from the cellars. And the children, with the servants and half the village, would go racing down the perilous zigzag track to meet the cavalcade at the bottom.

The track was far too steep for the heavy carts, which would be dismissed and the carters paid off to go about their business. Then with laughter and shouting, amid a million questions from the children, the loads would be divided and carried up the mountainside on muleback or on human shoulders. Sometimes the Uncles came home at night, through falling snow, by the smoky light of torches. But the children and the household always knew of their arrival beforehand and were always there to meet them.

"Did you bring Granny's Chinese shawl, Uncle Mark? Uncle Emer, have you the enameled box for her snuff that Aunt Grippa begged you to get? Uncle Acraud, did you find the glass candlesticks? Uncle Gonfil, did you bring the books?"

"Yes, yes, keep calm, don't deafen us! Poor tired travelers that we are, leave us in peace to climb this devilish hill! Everything is there, set your minds at rest—the shawl, the box, the books—besides a few other odds and ends, pins and needles and fruit and a bottle or two of wine, and a few trifles for the village. Now, just give us a few minutes to get our breath, will you, kindly——"as the children danced round them, helping each other with the smaller bundles, never ceasing to pour out questions: "Did you see the Grand Cham? the Akond of Swat? the Fon of Bikom? the Seljuk of Rum? Did you go to Cathay? to Muskovy? to Dalai? Did you travel by ship, by camel, by llama, by elephant?"

And, at the top of the hill, Grand-mother would be waiting for them, out on her roofed porch, no matter how wild the weather or how late the time, seated in majesty with her furs and patchwork quilt around her, while the Aunts ran to and fro with hot stones to place under her feet. And the Uncles always embraced her first, very fondly and respectfully, before turning to hug their wives and sisters-in-law.

Grandmother and Grandson, 1910, SUZANNE VALADON. Musée Nationale d'Art Moderne. Centre d'Art et de Culture Georges Pompidou, Paris.

Then the goods they had brought would be distributed through the village—the scissors, tools, medicines, plants, bales of cloth, ingots of metal, cordials, firearms, and musical instruments. After that there would be a great feast.

Not until Christmas morning did Grandmother and the children receive the special gifts that had been brought for them by the Uncles. This giving always took the same ceremonial form.

Uncle Mark stood behind Grandmother's chair, playing on a small pipe that he had acquired somewhere during his travels. It was made from hard black polished wood, with silver stops, and it had a mouthpiece made of amber. Uncle Mark invariably played the same tune on it at these times, very softly. It was a tune that he had heard for the first time, he said, when he was much younger, once when he had narrowly escaped falling into a crevasse on the hillside, and a voice had spoken to him, as it seemed, out of the mountain itself, bidding him watch where he set his feet and have a care, for the family depended on him. It was a gentle, thoughtful tune, which reminded Sandri, the middle granddaughter, of springtime sounds, warm wind, water from melted snow dripping off the gabled roofs, birds trying out their mating calls.

While Uncle Mark played on his pipe, Uncle Emer would hand each gift to Grandmother. And she—here was the strange thing—she, who was stone-blind all the year long, could not see her own hand in front of her face, she would take the object in her fingers and instantly identify it. "A mother-of-pearl comb, with silver studs, for Tassy . . . it comes from Babylon. A silk shawl, blue and rose, from Hind, for Argilla. A wooden game, with ivory pegs, for young Emer, from Damascus. A gold brooch, from Hangku, for Grippa. A book of rhymes, from Paris, for Sammle, bound in a scarlet leather cover."

By stroking each gift with her old, blotched, clawlike fingers, frail as quills, Grandmother, who lived all the year round in darkness, could discover not only what the thing was and where it came from, but also the color of it, and that in the most precise and particular manner, correct to a shade. "It is a jacket of stitched and pleated cotton, printed over with leaves and flowers. It comes from the island of Haranati, in the eastern ocean. The colors are leaf-brown and gold and a dark, dark blue, darker than mountain gentians——" for Grandmother had not always been blind. When she was a young girl, she had been able to see as well as anybody else.

"And this is for you, Mother, from your son Mark," Uncle Emer would say, handing her a tissue-wrapped bundle, and she would exclaim, "Ah, how beautiful! A coat of tribute silk, of the very palest green, so that the color shows only in the folds, like shadows on snow. The buttons and the button-toggles are of worked silk, lavender-gray, like pearl, and the stiff collar is embroidered with white roses."

"Put it on, Mother!" her sons and daughters-in-law would urge her, and the children, dancing 'round her chair, clutching their own treasures, would chorus, "Yes, put it on, put it on! Ah, you look like a queen, Granny, in that beautiful coat! The highest queen in the world! The queen of the mountain!"

Those months after Christmas were Grandmother's happiest time. Secure, thankful, with her sons safe at home, she would sit in the warm fireside corner of the big wooden family room. The wind might shriek, the snow gather higher and higher out of doors, but that did not concern her, for her family and all the village were well supplied with flour, oil, firewood, meat, herbs, and roots. The children had their books and toys. They learned lessons with the old priest or made looms and spinning wheels, carved stools and chairs and chests with the tools their uncles had brought them. The Uncles rested and told tales of their travels. Uncle Mark played his pipe for hours together, Uncle Acraud drew pictures in charcoal of the places he had seen, and Granny, laying her hand on the paper covered with lines, would expound while Uncle Mark played: "A huge range of mountains, like wrinkled brown lines across the horizon; a wide plain of sand, silvery blond in color,

with patches of pale, pale blue—I think it is not water but air the color of water. Here are strange lines across the sand where men once plowed it, long, long ago; and a great patch of crystal green, with what seems like a road crossing it. Now here is a smaller region of plum-pink, bordered by an area of rusty red. I think these are the colors of the earth in these territories. It is very high up, dry from height, and the soil glittering with little particles of metal."

"You have described it better than I could myself!" Uncle Acraud would exclaim, while the children, breathless with wonder and curiosity, sat cross-legged 'round her chair. And she would answer, "Yes, but I cannot see it at all, Acraud, unless your eyes have seen it first, and I cannot see it without Mark's music to help me."

"How does Grandmother *do* it?" the children would demand of their mothers, and Argilla, or Grippa, or Tassy would answer, "Nobody knows. It is Grandmother's gift. She alone can do it."

The people of the village might come in, whenever they chose, and on many evenings thirty or forty would be there, silently listening, and when Grandmother retired to bed, which she did early for the seeing made her weary, the audience would turn to one another with deep sighs, and murmur, "The world is indeed a wide place."

With the first signs of spring the Uncles

would become restless again and begin looking over their equipment, discussing maps and routes, mending saddlebags and boots, gazing up at the high peaks for signs that the snow was in retreat.

Then Granny would grow very silent. She never asked them to stay longer. She never disputed their going. But her face seemed to shrivel; she grew smaller, wizened and huddled inside her quilted patchwork.

And on St. Petrag's Day, when the Uncles set off, when the farewells were said and they clattered off down the mountain through the melting snow and the trees with pink luminous buds, Grandmother would fall into a silence that lasted, sometimes, for as much as five or six weeks. All day she would sit with her face turned to the east, wordless, motionless, and would drink her milk and go to her bed-place at night still silent and dejected. It took the warm sun and sweet wild hyacinths of May to raise her spirits.

Then, by degrees, she would grow animated and begin to say, "Only six months, now, till they come back."

But young Mark observed to his cousin Sammle, "It takes longer, every year, for Grandmother to grow accustomed."

And Sammle said, shivering though it was warm May weather, "Perhaps one year, when they come back, she will not be here. She is becoming so tiny and thin; you can see right through her hands, as if they were leaves." And Sammle held up her own thin brown young hand against the sunlight to see the blood glow under the translucent skin.

"I don't know how they would bear it," said Mark thoughtfully, "if when they came back we had to tell them that she had died."

But that was not what happened.

One December the Uncles arrived much later than usual. They did not climb the mountain until St. Misham's Day, and when they reached the house it was in silence. There was none of the usual joyful commotion.

Grandmother knew instantly that there was something wrong. "Where is my son Mark?" she demanded. "Why do I not hear him among you?" And Uncle Acraud had to tell her: "Mother, he is dead. Your son Mark will not come home, ever again."

"How do you *know?* How can you be *sure?* You were not there when he died."

"I waited and waited at our meeting place, and a messenger came to tell me. His caravan had been attacked by wild tribesmen, riding north from the Lark Mountains. Mark was killed, and all his people. Only this one man escaped and came to bring me the story."

"But how can you be *sure?* How do you know he told the *truth?*"

"He brought Mark's ring."

Emer put it into her hand. As she turned it about in her thin fingers, a long moan went through her.

"Yes, he is dead. My son Mark is dead."

"The man gave me this little box," Acraud said, "which Mark was bringing for you."

Emer put it into her hand, opening the box for her. Inside lay an ivory fan. On it, when it was spread out, you could see a bird, with eyes made of sapphires, flying across a valley, but Grandmother held it listlessly, as if her hands were numb.

"What is it?" she said. "I do not know what it is. Help me to bed, Argilla. I do not know what it is. I do not wish to know. My son Mark is dead."

Her grief infected the whole village. It was as if the keystone of an arch had been knocked out. There was nothing to hold the people together.

That year spring came early, and the three remaining Uncles, melancholy and restless, were glad to leave on their travels. Grandmother hardly noticed their going.

Sammle said to Mark: "You are clever with your hands. Could you not make a pipe—like the one my father had?"

"*I?*" he said. "Make a pipe? Like Uncle Mark's pipe? Why? What would be the point of doing so?"

"Perhaps you might learn to play on it. As he did."

"*I?*" Play on a pipe?"

"I think you could," she said. "I have heard you whistle tunes of your own."

"But where would I find the right kind of wood?"

"There is a chest, in which Uncle Gonfil once brought books and music from Leiden. I think it is the same kind of wood. I think you could make a pipe from it."

"But how can I remember the shape?"

"I will make a drawing," Sammle said, and she drew with a stick of charcoal on the whitewashed wall of the cowshed. As soon as Mark looked at her drawing he began to contradict.

"No! I remember now. It was not like that. The stops came here—and the mouthpiece was like this."

Now the other children flocked 'round to help and advise.

"The stops were farther apart," said Creusie. "And there were more of them and they were bigger."

"The pipe was longer than that," said Sandri. "I have held it. It was as long as my arm."

"How will you ever make the stops?" said young Emer.

"You can have my silver bracelets that Father gave me," said Sammle.

"I'll ask Finn the smith to help me," said Mark.

Once Mark had got the notion of making a pipe into his head, he was eager to begin. But it took him several weeks of difficult carving. The black wood of the chest proved hard as iron. And when the pipe was made, and the stops fitted, it would not play. Try as he would, not a note could he fetch out of it.

Mark was dogged, though, once he had

set himself to a task. He took another piece of the black chest and began again. Only Sammle stayed to help him now. The other children had lost hope, or interest, and gone back to the summer occupations.

The second pipe was much better than the first. By September, Mark was able to play a few notes on it. By October he was playing simple tunes made up out of his head.

"But," he said, "if I am to play so that Grandmother can see with her fingers—if I am to do *that*—I must remember your father's special tune. Can *you* remember it, Sammle?"

She thought and thought. "Sometimes," she said, "it seems as if it is just beyond the edge of my hearing—as if somebody were playing it, far, far away, in the woods. Oh, if only I could stretch my hearing a little farther!"

"Oh, Sammle! Try!"

For days and days she sat silent or wandered in the woods, frowning, knotting her forehead, willing her ears to hear the

Child and Seeing Hands, about 1950, HANS BELLMER. Collection of Joseph and Jory Shapiro. Photograph by Sheldan Collins.

tune again; and the women of the household said, "That girl is not doing her fair share of the task."

They scolded her and set her to spin, weave, milk the goats, throw grain to the hens. But all the while she continued silent, listening, listening, to a sound she could not hear. At night, in her dreams, she sometimes thought she could hear the tune, and she would wake with tears on her cheeks, wordlessly calling her father to come back and play his music to her, so that she could remember it.

In September the autumn winds blew cold and fierce. By October snow was piled around the walls and up to the windowsills. On St. Felin's Day the three Uncles returned, but sadly and silently, without the former festivities; although, as usual, they brought many bales and boxes of gifts and merchandise. The children went down, as usual, to help carry the bundles up the mountain. The joy had gone out of this tradition, though, and they toiled silently up the track with their loads.

It was a wild, windy evening. The sun set in fire, the wind moaned among the fir trees, and gusts of sleet every now and then dashed in their faces.

"Take care, children!" called Uncle Emer as they skirted along the side of a deep gully, and his words were caught by an echo and flung back and forth between the rocky walls: "Take care—care—care—care—care. . . ."

"*Oh!*" cried Sammle, stopping precipitately and clutching the bag that she was carrying. "I have it! I can remember it! *Now* I know how it went!"

And, as they stumbled on up the snowy hillside, she hummed the melody to her cousin Mark, who was just ahead of her.

"Yes, that is it, yes!" he said. "Or, no, wait a minute, that is not *quite* right—but it is close, it is very nearly the way it went. Only the notes were a little faster, and there were more of them—they went up, not down—before the ending tied them in a knot———"

"No, no, they went down at the end, I am almost sure———"

Arguing, interrupting each other, disputing, agreeing, they dropped their bundles in the family room and ran away to the cowhouse where Mark kept his pipe hidden.

For three days they discussed and argued and tried a hundred different versions. They were so occupied that they hardly took the trouble to eat. But at last, by Christmas morning, they had reached agreement.

"I *think* it is right," said Sammle. "And if it is not, I do not believe there is anything more that we can do about it."

"Perhaps it will not work in any case," said Mark sadly. He was tired out with arguing and practicing.

Sammle was equally tired, but she said, "Oh, it *must* work. Oh, let it work! Please let it work! For otherwise I don't think I can bear the sadness. Go now, Mark, quietly and quickly, go and stand behind Granny's chair."

The family had gathered, according to Christmas habit, around Grandmother's rocking chair, but the faces of the Uncles were glum and reluctant, their wives dejected and hopeless. Only the children showed eagerness, as the cloth-wrapped bundles were brought and laid at Grandmother's feet.

She herself looked wholly dispirited and cast down. When Uncle Emer handed her a slender, soft package, she received it apathetically, almost with dislike, as if she would prefer not to be bothered by this tiresome gift ceremony.

Then Mark, who had slipped through the crowd without being noticed, began to play on his pipe just behind Grandmother's chair.

The Uncles looked angry and scandalized. Aunt Tassy cried out in horror: "Oh, Mark, wicked boy, how *dare* you?" but Grandmother lifted her head, more alertly than she had done for months past and began to listen.

Mark played on. His mouth was quivering so badly that it was hard to grip the amber mouthpiece, but he played with all the breath that was in him. Meanwhile, Sammle, kneeling by her grandmother, held, with her own warm young hands, the old, brittle ones against the fabric of the gift. And, as she did so, she began to feel what Grandmother felt.

Grandmother said softly and distinctly: "It is a muslin shawl, embroidered in gold thread, from Lebanon. It is colored a soft brick red, with pale roses of sunset pink, and thorns of silver-green. It is for Sammle. . . ."

Joan Aiken (*born 1924*) has been writing stories and poems since she was five years old. She grew up in England, the daughter of American poet Conrad Aiken. Her writing career includes working for a magazine and a radio station. Aiken has a rich imagination and uses fantasy, mystery, and humor in her writing. *The Whispering Mountain* and *The Wolves of Willoughby Chase* are two of her popular books.

Developing Comprehension Skills

1. Name Grandmother's sons. Name the eldest grandchild. Who is her father? Who is young Mark's father?

2. What schedule did the Uncles follow every year? Explain where they spent each season of the year.

3. Describe the ceremony of the gift-giving. What effect did Uncle Mark's special tune have on Grandmother?

4. What changes did Uncle Mark's death cause in the Uncles' yearly schedule? How did it change Grandmother?

5. Why does Sammle want Mark to make a musical pipe?

6. At the end of the story, as Sammle helps her grandmother hold the gift while Mark plays, "she began to feel what Grandmother felt." What does Sammle feel?

7. Much of this story seems like a description of life in a small mountain village in Europe a hundred years ago or so. Are there any parts of the story that you think could not have happened? Explain.

Reading Literature: Short Stories

1. **Thinking About Characters.** Who do you think are the main characters and who are the minor characters in this story? Is the sense of the family as a closely knit and loving group important to the story? Describe the respect all of the family members give the grandmother. How might the reader's sense of the family be changed if only a few members were mentioned?

2. **Understanding Conflict.** What big problem do Sammle and Mark struggle with? What smaller problems must they overcome as they work on the major problem?

3. **Examining Description.** The many details in the story help create a sense of the happy, active world in which the family lives. Find at least three examples of passages that list a series of specific items or activities. How does the mood change at the news of Uncle Mark's death? Are there any lively descriptive passages in this part of the story?

Vocabulary

Understanding Words in Context. Use context clues to match each underlined word below with its definition. The sentences are based on those in "The Gift-Giving."

1. The ants escaped when the spade broke open their hummock.

2. Uncle Mark almost fell into a crevasse in the hillside.

3. The uncles brought back bales of cloth and ingots of metal.

4. After the uncles left, Grandmother sat silent and dejected.

5. Young Mark was dogged; when the first pipe didn't work, he immediately began to carve another.

   a. sad, depressed
   b. molded bars
   c. very small hill
   d. stubborn
   e. deep crack in the earth

Developing Writing Skills

Exploring Theme. This story tells about more than one kind of gift-giving. Write two to four paragraphs explaining at least two meanings of gift-giving as they are brought out in the story.

Prewriting. As you think about the gifts and the people who give them, you may want to use a chart like the one below. Consider not only the presents that people give to each other, but also the actions and special abilities of the characters. What meanings of *gift* does the story express? What are some of the ways people give gifts? What part do gifts play in helping the family carry on after Uncle Mark's death? Then decide which kinds of gift-giving you want to write about.

Drafting. In your opening sentence, briefly state that *gift-giving* has more than one meaning and that you are writing about two (or more) of them. Then introduce the first one. Use details and examples from the story to illustrate the idea that you are writing about. Write a separate paragraph for each meaning of gift-giving. End your composition by summarizing the meanings you have explained.

Revising and Sharing. As you reread your draft, consider the following questions. Does your opening sentence give clear direction? Are your main ideas easy to follow? Do you include specific examples for each idea? Does your conclusion tie your ideas together? When you have finished your final draft, read it to the class.

	Characters		
Gifts	Those Who Give	Those Who Receive	Those Who Give and Receive
shawl			
respect			
music			
making flute			

Chapter 4 Review

Using Your Skills in Reading Short Stories

The following paragraph is from "Last Cover," a short story about a wild fox by Paul Annixter. Read the paragraph carefully. Then answer these questions: From what point of view is the story being told? What is the setting? What do you learn about the narrator?

> I was helping Father with the planting now, but Colin managed to be in the woods every day. By degrees, he learned Bandit's range, where he drank and rested, and where he was likely to be according to the time of day. One day he told me how he had petted Bandit again, and how they had walked together a long way in the woods. All this time we had kept his secret from Father.

Using Your Comprehension Skills

Read the following lines from the poem "Casey at the Bat" by Ernest Lawrence Thayer. Identify one example of cause and effect. Then identify any clue words that helped you, and explain how they helped.

> Then from the gladdened multitude went up a joyous yell—
> It rumbled in the mountaintops, it rattled in the dell;
> It struck upon the hillside and rebounded on the flat;
> For Casey, mighty Casey, was advancing to the bat.

Using Your Vocabulary Skills

Use a context clue to figure out the meaning of each underlined word in the following sentences based on stories in this chapter. Identify the key word or words that helped you recognize the type of clue: comparison, contrast, example, or words in a series.

1. The banker <u>groped</u> for the door in the darkness, just as a blind man might feel around for a glass to drink from.

2. Some townspeople <u>lamented</u> that there were no old soldiers for the Fourth; Andrew, for example, was so sorry and upset he could not think of anything else.

3. Matilda lived in <u>poverty</u> unlike her former classmate, who had enough money to buy jewelry.

4. Patty was <u>despondent</u>, sad, and lonely in the new town.

Using Your Skills in Critical Thinking

Classify the stories you have read in this chapter according to the kind of conflict they show. Make one list of the stories that involve an external conflict. Make a second list of stories that involve an internal conflict. How many stories involve both kinds of conflict?

Using Your Writing Skills

Choose one of the writing assignments below.

1. Choose, from any story in this chapter, the character whom you could picture the best. In one to three paragraphs, explain why you chose this character. Did the writer describe him or her at length? Did the character's words or actions tell a great deal about him or her? Did you feel strongly about the character, either for or against? Use details from the story to support your statements.

2. You have learned that in the exposition of a short story, the writer usually describes the setting. Imagine that you are going to write a mystery story set in your own home or school. Write one or more paragraphs of exposition, concentrating only on the setting. Provide details that describe the setting exactly. Use words that appeal to the senses.

CHAPTER FIVE

Poetry

Equinox, 1968, JOAN MIRÓ. Etching and aquatint,
41 1/16″ x 29″. Collection Museum of Modern Art,
New York City, Gift of Studebaker Worthington, Inc.

Reading Literature

Poetry

Poetry is a form of writing that is closely related to music. Like music, poetry appeals to your senses and to your imagination. Like music, it is meant to be heard. Poets choose words for their sounds as well as for their meanings. They combine these words to create vivid pictures and to express deep feelings.

The History of Poetry

The connection between poetry and music goes back to earliest times. Songs, chants, prayers, and stories were all poems. Most cultures have used poetry to tell their **epics**, stories about great heroes and their adventures. The ancient Greeks and Romans wrote plays in poetry. In the early 1600's, the great English playwright, William Shakespeare, also wrote plays in poetry. Today, poets write in many forms and deal with a variety of subjects.

The Elements of Poetry

The Shape of a Poem.   The **shape** of a poem is the pattern or arrangement of the words on the page. All poems are written in **lines,** which may contain several words or even one word. In many poems, lines are grouped into **stanzas**. Each stanza is a separate unit of thought, similar to a paragraph.

Certain types of poems have special shapes. For example, the Japanese **haiku** has only seventeen syllables. They are arranged in three lines with five syllables in the first and third lines and seven in the second.

Concrete poems also have distinctive shapes. A **concrete poem** visually presents something important about the poem's meaning. For example, the words in a poem about a kite might be arranged in the shape of a kite.

Sounds in a Poem. Often the words in a poem are chosen to create a special sound effect. For example, many poems have **end rhyme.** The words at the ends of lines end with the same sound. Poetry also has **rhythm**—regular or varying patterns of stressed and unstressed syllables. **Alliteration** is the repetition of consonant sounds at the beginnings of words. **Assonance** is the repetition of vowel sounds within words.

Sensory Images. By using **sensory images,** or words and phrases that appeal to the five senses, a poet re-creates an experience. The reader can then imagine just how things look, sound, feel, smell, and taste.

Speaker. All poems have a **speaker**, the voice that talks to the reader. In some poems the speaker has a clear identity, using *I* and *me*. In other poems the speaker remains in the background. The speaker is not necessarily the same as the poet. For example, in "Hockey," a poem in this chapter, the speaker is a hockey player in the middle of a game.

How to Read a Poem

1. Read each poem aloud. Hearing the sounds of a poem makes the meaning clearer and adds to your enjoyment.
2. Identify the speaker. Does the speaker use *I* and *me* or remain a general voice speaking to the reader?
3. Take time to imagine, to see, hear, touch, taste, and smell what the poet is describing.
4. Give each poem a chance. Remember that each poem has something to give you if you want to take it.

Comprehension Skills

Inferences

In order to understand poetry, you must look beyond what is said directly to see all levels of meaning. In other words, you will have to make inferences. To make an **inference**, or to **infer,** you must think about all the information available and come to a conclusion. When you are reading poetry, you often will have to think about several kinds of information at the same time. For instance, the words are arranged in lines and stanzas. Words are often put together to create rhyme, rhythm, and other patterns of sound. You will also need to consider what you already know about the subject of the poem.

The following is the opening stanza of the poem "Casey at the Bat" by Ernest Lawrence Thayer:

> The outlook wasn't brilliant for the Mudville nine that day;
> The score stood two to four, with but one inning more to play.
> And so, when Cooney died at first, and Burrows did the same,
> A sickly silence fell upon the patrons of the game.

These four lines contain the information necessary to infer the answers to the following questions:

1. What game is being played? *Since there are nine team members, an inning left to play, and players are out at first, the game is baseball.*
2. Which team was losing? by what score? *Since the outlook wasn't brilliant, or good, for Mudville, Mudville is the team that is losing two to four.*

Notice that the conclusions reached are based on details given in the stanza and on the reader's general knowledge about baseball.

Exercises: Understanding Inferences

A. Below is the first stanza from the poem "Hockey" by Scott Blaine. Following the stanza are two sets of statements. One of the statements in each set is an inference that can be made from the poetry. Identify each inference and tell what words or details you used to make your choice.

> The ice is smooth, smooth, smooth.
> The air bites to the center
> Of warmth and flesh, and I whirl.
> It begins in a game . . .
> The puck swims, skims, veers,
> Goes leading my vision
> Beyond the chasing reach of my stick.

1. a. The air temperature is very cold.
   b. The air temperature is comfortable.

2. a. The speaker is watching a hockey game.
   b. The speaker is playing hockey.

B. The following lines are from the poem "Catalog" by Rosalie Moore. Which lines tell you that cats can get through tight places? Explain.

> A cat condenses.
> He pulls in his tail to go under
>   bridges,
> And himself to go under fences.

Scat (detail), 1986, JANET FISH. Photograph: Robert Miller Gallery, New York City.

Vocabulary Skills

Multiple Meanings and Levels of Language

A word can have more than one meaning. Some words have developed several meanings over a long period of time. Meaning can also be affected by the level of language being used by a writer or speaker.

Multiple Meanings

Can potatoes see with their *eyes?* If you're *bright*, does a person need sunglasses to look at you? Each underlined word has more than one meaning. Many other words in English have multiple meanings. For example, here are four dictionary definitions for *back:*

1. *n.,* the part of the body opposite to the front
2. *adj.,* at the rear
3. *adv.,* to or toward a former position
4. *vt.,* to support or help

The dictionary presents all the meanings of a word. However, in order to know exactly which definition is correct, you need to read the word in **context**—in a line or a stanza. Which definition of *back* is meant in each line below?

> If I cannot carry forests on my <u>back</u>,
> —Ralph Waldo Emerson, "The Mountain and the Squirrel"

> Poised between going on and <u>back</u>, pulled
> —Robert Francis, "The Base Stealer"

Standard and Nonstandard English

English is divided into categories called standard English and nonstandard English. **Standard English** follows accepted grammatical rules. It includes two levels, formal and informal. **Formal English** is used in academic writing and in speaking that is dignified or ceremonial. **Informal English,** or colloquial English, is used in everyday conversation and in newspapers and magazines. Informal English includes **colloquialisms,** words or phrases commonly used in informal speech. Examples are *make tracks, fix up,* and *posh.*

Nonstandard English does not follow accepted grammatical rules. Nonstandard English is used only in the most informal conversation and in writing mainly to create dialogue.

Exercises: Using Multiple Meanings and Levels of Language

A. Choose the correct definition for each underlined word in these lines from "Paul Revere's Ride" by Henry Wadsworth Longfellow.

1. Just as the moon <u>rose</u> over the bay
   a. pinkish red or purplish red
   b. moved upward

2. Wrapped in silence so deep and <u>still</u>
   a. nevertheless, yet
   b. calm, tranquil

3. Under the trees at the <u>turn</u> of the road
   a. rotation, as of a wheel
   b. place where a change in direction occurs

B. Identify the underlined word in each line below from "Casey at the Bat" as either informal or nonstandard.

1. They thought, if only Casey could but get a <u>whack</u>. . . .

2. "That <u>ain</u>'t my style," said Casey. "Strike one," the umpire said.

Poems About Nature

The world of nature is full of details you can observe: the precise way animals move, the sounds of weather or insects, and the cycle of a day from dawn to dusk. Poetry provides different ways of seeing these details. The poems in this section describe the humorous antics of animals, the quietness of early morning, and the powerful flight of an eagle.

Endangered Species: Bald Eagle, 1983, ANDY WARHOL.
Photograph by D. James Dee, Ronald Feldman Fine Arts, New York City.

Seal

Have you ever watched a seal at the zoo? How well does this poem capture the way a seal moves?

WILLIAM JAY SMITH

See how he dives
From the rocks with a zoom!
See how he darts
Through his watery room
Past crabs and eels   5
And green seaweed,
Past fluffs of sandy
Minnow feed!
See how he swims
With a swerve and a twist,   10
A flip of the flipper,
A flick of the wrist!
Quicksilver-quick,
Softer than spray,
Down he plunges   15
And sweeps away;
Before you can think,
Before you can utter
Words like "Dill pickle"
Or "Apple butter,"   20
Back up he swims
Past Sting Ray and Shark,
Out with a zoom,
A whoop, a bark;
Before you can say   25
Whatever you wish,
He plops at your side
With a mouthful of fish!

© Layle Silbert

William Jay Smith (*born 1918*) is known for his humorous poetry as well as plays, reviews, and translations. Smith was born in Winnfield, Louisiana, and claims one-sixteenth Cherokee heritage from his mother. He has been a college professor and educational consultant and has served as a member of the Vermont House of Representatives.

Developing Comprehension Skills

1. Where does the seal begin his dive? Where does he go? What does he catch?

2. Read the poem and list at least six words that show movement. What can you infer about how quickly or slowly the seal moves?

3. Reread lines 17–20. Why do you think the writer used the phrases "Dill pickle" and "Apple butter"? How do these phrases match or contrast with the rest of the poem? Are the words humorous?

4. Is this poem serious or light-hearted? Which words or phrases helped you decide?

Reading Literature: Poetry

1. **Examining a Concrete Poem.** The shape of a **concrete poem** reminds a reader of its subject. "Seal" is a concrete poem. The way it looks on the page reminds the reader of something about the seal. Explain what the shape reminds you of.

2. **Recognizing Assonance.** Many different effects can be created in poetry by repeat- ing sounds. **Assonance** is the repetition of vowel sounds within words. How many times is the long *e* sound repeated in lines 5–8? What vowel sound is repeated in lines 9–13? Do these repeated sounds help you see or hear the seal? Explain.

3. **Understanding Rhythm.** One of the most important features of the sound in a poem is **rhythm,** the pattern of unstressed and stressed syllables. In a poem with regular rhythm, the words form a regular pattern of stressed and unstressed syllables. This pattern can be shown by marking each stressed syllable with / and each unstressed syllable with ˘. For example:

$$\text{Sĕe hŏw hĕ dives}$$
$$\text{Frŏm thĕ rocks wĭth ă zoom!}$$

Continue marking the stressed and unstressed syllables of lines 2–7. You will find that the number and position of the unstressed syllables vary. How many stressed syllables are there in each line? How closely does the rhythm match the movements of the seal?

Poem

Imagine a cat walking on a narrow, cluttered shelf. Watch how the poet captures the careful movements of the cat.

WILLIAM CARLOS WILLIAMS

As the cat
climbed over
the top of

the jamcloset
first the right   5
forefoot

carefully
then the hind
stepped down

into the pit of   10
the empty
flowerpot

Meditation and Minou, 1980, WILL BARNET. Copyright © 1980 Will Barnet.

William Carlos Williams *(1883–1963)* was born in Rutherford, New Jersey. He was a practicing physician who wrote forty-nine books. These include novels, collections of essays, short stories, plays, and poems. Williams wrote of everyday life in a style that is easy to relate to. Among his works are *Paterson,* a long poem set in Paterson, New Jersey, and *Pictures from Breughal,* which won the Pulitzer Prize for 1963.

Developing Comprehension Skills

1. What part of the cat moves first into the flowerpot? What part follows after?

2. How do you picture the cat moving—fast or slowly? On what words or details in the poem do you base your inference?

3. In what ways is this poem similar to a slow-motion film? What picture is left in your mind at the end of the poem?

Reading Literature: Poetry

Appreciating the Shape of a Poem. Poets can suggest new impressions of ordinary sights just by the way they arrange the words in poems. How many lines are there in "Poem"? Write the poem out as a sentence and read it aloud. How does the arrangement of words in lines help you to picture the movement of the cat?

Catalog

ROSALIE MOORE

The title of this poem is a pun. Look up the meaning of the word catalog. *Then read the poem and find the double meaning in its title.*

Cats sleep fat and walk thin.
Cats, when they sleep, slump;
When they wake, stretch and begin
Over, pulling their ribs in.
Cats walk thin.   5

Cats wait in a lump,
Jump in a streak.
Cats, when they jump, are sleek
As a grape slipping its skin—
They have technique   10
Oh, cats don't creak.
They sneak.

Cats sleep fat.
They spread out comfort underneath
      them
Like a good mat,   15
As if they picked the place
And then sat;
You walk around one
As if he were the City Hall
After that.   20

If male,
A cat is apt to sing on a major scale;
This concert is for everybody, this
Is wholesale.
For a baton, he wields a tail.   25

(He is also found,
When happy, to resound
With an enclosed and private sound.)

A cat condenses.
He pulls in his tail to go under
      bridges,   30
And himself to go under fences.
Cats fit
In any size box or kit,
And if a large pumpkin grew under one,
He could arch over it.   35

When everyone else is just ready to
      go out,
The cat is just ready to come in.
He's not where he's been.
Cats sleep fat and walk thin.

Rosalie Moore *(born 1910)* has had a varied career. After graduating from the University of California, she worked at a radio station as a writer and announcer. She has lectured to college students at universities in the United States and in Mexico and has conducted poetry workshops. In 1977 Moore won an award for *Year of the Children,* a collection of her poems.

Developing Comprehension Skills

1. Name four actions of a cat that are mentioned in this poem.

2. What two cat sounds are described in the poem? what changes in a cat's shape?

3. Is this poem humorous or serious? Does the speaker admire cats or dislike them? Tell what evidence you use to make inferences.

4. Both "Poem" and "Catalog" are about cats. Which one is about cats in general and which is about a specific cat? Are the descriptions of cats in the two poems similar in any way? Explain.

5. Did you like one of the poems better than the other? Why? Did you like the sound of the poem better? Did one create more vivid images? Explain your answer.

Reading Literature: Poetry

1. **Examining Rhyme. Rhyme** is the repetition of syllable sounds at the ends of words. Rhyme that occurs at the ends of lines of poetry is called **end rhyme.** Sometimes end rhyme is in a regular pattern, and sometimes it changes from stanza to stanza. Look at the end rhyme in this poem. Is it regular or irregular? Are any rhymes from the beginning of the poem repeated later? How is the fifth stanza different from all the rest?

2. **Understanding Similes.** A **simile** is a comparison that uses *like* or *as*. A simile points out how two things are alike in some way. Find the similes in the second and third stanzas. Explain each comparison.

3. **Evaluating Word Choice.** This poem uses words in unusual ways to create images, or pictures, for the reader. Choose two phrases from the list below. Explain what each phrase is describing.

> sleep fat
> wait in a lump
> sing on a major scale
> walk thin
> jump in a streak
> wields a tail

New World

N. SCOTT MOMADAY

The title suggests that this poem describes a new world. Can this new world still be seen?

1.

First Man,
behold:
the earth
glitters
with leaves;   5
the sky
glistens
with rain.
Pollen
is borne   10
on winds
that low[1]
and lean
upon
mountains.   15
Cedars
blacken
the slopes—
and pines.

2.

At dawn   20
eagles
hie[2] and
hover
above
the plain   25
where light
gathers
in pools.
Grasses
shimmer   30
and shine.
Shadows
withdraw
and lie
away   35
like smoke.

3.

At noon
turtles
enter
slowly   40
into
the warm
dark loam.
Bees hold
the swarm.   45
Meadows
recede
through planes
of heat
and pure   50
distance.

4.

At dusk
the gray
foxes
stiffen   55
in cold;
blackbirds
are fixed
in the
branches.   60
Rivers
follow
the moon,
the long
white track   65
of the
full moon.

---

1. **low**–Make a mournful cry or sound.
2. **hie**–Hasten.

N. Scott Momaday *(born 1934)* is a Kiowa Indian who was born in Lawton, Oklahoma, and was raised on reservations in the Southwest. Momaday studied literature at the University of New Mexico and at Stanford University, where he received his doctorate. He has taught at the University of California and Stanford University. "I am an American Indian," says Momaday, "and am vitally interested in American Indian art, history, and culture." This interest is seen in his poems, stories, and novels. His writing tells about his people, their land, and a time gone forever. Momaday's novel, *House Made of Dawn,* won the Pulitzer Prize for 1969.

Developing Comprehension Skills

1. What three times of day does the speaker describe? What creatures are associated with each time?

2. Identify one detail about the world at dawn, noon, and dusk from stanzas two, three, and four.

3. To whom does the speaker address the poem?

4. What kind of place does this poem describe? How would the place be different if there were many people in it?

5. Think of the area in which you live. Can you see any of the sights described in the poem?

Reading Literature: Poetry

1. **Recognizing Alliteration.** In the poem "New World," Momaday uses **alliteration,** in which the same consonant sound is

repeated at the beginning of words. For example, in lines 30–32, three of the four words begin with *sh: shimmer, shine, shadows.* Find two other examples of alliteration in the poem. What connection do you see between the sounds of the words and the subjects being described?

2. **Identifying Sensory Images. Sensory images** are words and phrases that appeal to the senses: sight, hearing, touch, taste, and smell. This poem is made up of a series of sensory images. Tell which of the senses each of the following images appeals to. Some images may appeal to more than one sense.
   a. "earth glitters with leaves"
   b. "winds that low and lean"
   c. "light gathers in pools"
   d. "lie away like smoke"
   e. "the warm dark loam"
   f. "recede through planes of heat"

3. **Interpreting Descriptions.** In order to fully appreciate the images in this poem, you must make some inferences. In what way could shadows that disappear as the sun grows brighter seem like smoke? Do you get a picture of a fast or a slow movement? In lines 61–67, in what way might the light of the full moon seem like a track?

4. **Understanding Theme.** A poem, like a short story, has a **theme**, a message about life or experience. Reread "New World." What time period is covered in the second, third, and fourth stanzas? Can the sights of the poem be repeated every day? What does the poem suggest about the cycle of nature and a person's response to it?

Vocabulary

Using Parts of Speech to Determine Meanings. Many words in English can be used as more than one part of speech. For example, the word *rocks* is used as a noun in the first sentence and as a verb in the second.

He swam for the rocks.
Every time you move, the boat rocks.

Several words in the poems you have read may be used as more than one part of speech. Find the following words in a dictionary: *darts* and *twist* in "Seal"; *slump* and *scale* in "Catalog"; *slopes* and *plain* in "New World." Read the entry for each word. On a sheet of paper, write the part of speech that fits the context of the word in the poem. Then write the correct definition.

Speaking and Listening

Reading a Poem. As you know, most poems are meant to be heard. Choose one of the four poems you have just read and prepare to present it to the class. Practice reading the poem aloud so that your audience will appreciate sound patterns such as rhythm and rhyme. Pay special attention to your timing. What kind of pauses will bring out meaning? Don't stop automatically at the ends of lines. Pay attention to meaning and punctuation. Should the poem be read quickly or slowly? What kind of tone of voice is suited to the poem—good-humored, solemn, matter-of-fact? Your teacher may schedule a class reading session. Listen for the way different readings suggest different interpretations of the poems.

Developing Writing Skills

1. **Writing a Poem About an Animal.** Write a poem in which you describe the way an animal moves. Use at least one simile in your poem.

   Prewriting. Decide on the animal that you want to write about. Close your eyes and picture the animal moving. Make a list of verbs that describe the animal's movement. Then imagine to what you might compare the movement: to a waterfall? smoke? a car? Develop at least one clear simile.

   Drafting. Writing a poem is different from writing a composition. You may try several completely different drafts before you come up with something you want to revise. As you work on your poem, do not feel that you must use rhyme.

   Revising and Sharing. Begin revising by reading your draft aloud. Does it read smoothly? Can you use alliteration or asso-nance? Did you include a simile using *like* or *as*? Will readers be able to see the point of the comparison? Does the comparison give a clear impression that fits with the rest of the poem? Should you change some of the verbs to more specific words?

   When you are satisfied with your poem, read it to your classmates.

2. **Explaining the Author's Purpose.** Poems, like stories, can be written for different reasons. The writer may want to amuse the reader, to make a serious point, to create a picture, or to share a feeling or an impression. Think about "New World," "Cata-log," and "Seal." Write one paragraph explaining which two poems seem to have a similar purpose and which has a different purpose. State the purpose clearly and give examples from the poems to support your conclusions. Follow the steps in the process of writing: prewriting, drafting, revising, and sharing. Refer to the handbook for more help.

As you read this haiku, what picture do you see?

Fall

SALLY ANDRESEN

The geese flying south
In a row long and V-shaped
Pulling in winter.

The Twelve Months (detail), 1823–31,
KATSUSHIKA HOKUSAI. Freer Gallery of Art,
Smithsonian Institution, Washington, D.C.

Developing Comprehension Skills

1. What shape does the flock of geese form?

2. In order to understand this poem, you must know something about geese. What does the phrase "pulling in winter" refer to? Use what you know about geese and the title "Fall" to help you infer what the poet means.

3. What feeling does the phrase "pulling in winter" give you? How do you feel when you see a flock of geese flying south? Does this poem express your emotions?

Reading Literature: Poetry

Understanding Haiku. A **haiku** is a Japanese form of poetry. A haiku written in Japanese is exactly seventeen syllables long. Usually the syllables are arranged in three lines, with five syllables in the first and third lines and seven in the second. A haiku describes a single experience. Traditionally, a haiku presents an image from nature, but uses that image to suggest a feeling. How does "Fall" fit the form and definition of a haiku?

Sally Andresen (*born 1947*) was raised on a farm in Iowa. After graduating from Iowa State University, she became a junior high school teacher. Andresen wrote the poem "Fall" when she was in the ninth grade, for an English assignment.

Flowers of Four Seasons (detail), 17th century. SOSEN. The Philadelphia Museum of Art, Gift of Mrs. John C. Atwood.

Four Haiku

JULIUS LESTER

The following four poems are variations on traditional haiku. In what ways are they like haiku?

1.

On this summer day
I have no doubt that
I will live forever.

2.

Autumn afternoon:
Drinking tea,
I listen to the rain.

3.

Ah! The cawing of
The crows at dawn
This winter morning.

4.

I tried
to hear the silence:
Spring morning.

Julius Lester *(born 1939)* writes about the heritage of black Americans. His folktale collections, *Black Folktales* and *The Knee-High Man,* contain stories based on Afro-American folklore and on black history. Lester's nonfiction work, *The Long Journey Home,* is a collection of slave narratives, accounts of the experiences of American slaves. He recently published *The Tales of Uncle Remus: The Adventures of Brer Rabbit,* a retelling of the Uncle Remus tales. A professional musician as well as a writer, Lester has coauthored a book titled *The 12-String Guitar as Played by Leadbelly.* Lester was born in St. Louis and attended Fisk University.

Developing Comprehension Skills

1. At what time of year is each haiku set?

2. What sense do the second, third, and fourth haiku appeal to? Does the first haiku appeal to the senses? Explain your answer.

3. Which of the four haiku creates the strongest image or impression for you? Try to explain why the haiku you chose has the strongest appeal for you.

Reading Literature: Poetry

1. **Examining Haiku.** These four haiku are variations of the traditional Japanese form.

Do they strictly follow the form of seventeen syllables and three lines? Do they all present an image from nature?

2. **Recognizing Mood.** As you know, **mood** is the feeling created in the reader by a literary work. How would you describe the mood of each of the four poems? Which one seems more peaceful than the others? What gives it a tranquil feeling? What images create a livelier mood in the other poems?

3. **Identifying the Speaker.** The **speaker** is the voice that talks to the reader. What pronoun in these haiku identifies the speaker? Is the speaker closely involved

with the subjects in the poems? To whom does the speaker seem to be speaking?

Vocabulary

Completing Analogies. As you know, an analogy consists of two pairs of words that are related in the same way. Here is an example:

Cow is to herd as bird is to flock.

The second term in each pair, *herd* and *flock*, is the group name for the animal named in the first term, *cow* and *bird*. You can put the words into sentences to figure out this analogy.

A cow belongs to a herd.
A bird belongs to a flock.

Other relationships include synonyms and antonyms.

Each incomplete analogy below uses some words from the prose and poetry selections you have already read in this book. For each, choose the word that will complete the relationship and write it on a separate sheet of paper. Be able to explain why you chose that word. Use a dictionary if necessary.

1. Tired is to weary as brave is to _____.

   excited   tranquil
   valiant   severe

2. Caw is to crow as bark is to _____.

   bear   horse
   eagle   seal

3. Shout is to whisper as celebrate is to
   _____.

   lament   yell
   laugh   finish

4. Lag is to stall as zoom is to _____.

   hesitate   dart
   ask   move

5. Happy is to joyful as worried is to _____.

   anxious   late
   dull   bored

6. Reed is to grass as stingray is to _____.

   beaver   glass
   fish   danger

7. Ship is to captain as rig is to _____.

   road   truck
   tires   driver

8. Morning is to dawn as evening is to _____.

   afternoon   midday
   dusk   suppertime

Study and Research

Learning More About Haiku. Haiku has become a popular form for modern English-speaking poets. Check the card catalog or computer catalog of your local library to see if the library has any books specifically on haiku. Look up one of the books or consult an encyclopedia to find the answers to the following questions.

1. When did haiku develop in Japan?

2. Who are the best-known Japanese writers of haiku?

3. When was haiku introduced into Western poetry?

4. What are the rules for forms related to haiku such as *tanka* and *cinquain*?

Developing Writing Skills

Writing a Haiku. Write a haiku of your own. It may be either a traditional seventeen-syllable haiku or a variation like the haiku of Julius Lester.

Prewriting. Think of experiences you have had outdoors. Try to remember a particular sight, sound, smell, or touch. Choose a single, vivid experience for the topic of your poem. List words and phrases that describe the experience. Be as specific as possible. For example, do you associate the experience with a particular time or place? What adjectives suggest the experience? What verbs re-create the sight, sound, smell, or touch?

Drafting. Draw on your list of words and phrases as you write your haiku. Remember that a haiku is like a sketch rather than a detailed drawing. In seventeen or fewer syllables you cannot give a full description. Instead select single words or one or two details that suggest the experience you are writing about. Also remember that your three lines can be written as phrases rather than as a grammatically complete sentence.

Revising and Sharing. If you are writing a traditional haiku, count your syllables—can you change some words to end up with seventeen syllables, arranged five, seven, five? Will the reader be able to identify what experience you have in mind? Is there a more precise word or phrase that will make the description sharper? When you have revised, share your haiku with the class. You may want to help make a class book of haiku. Consider drawing a picture or looking for a photo to go with your haiku.

Wallowa Lake, 1927–28, STEVE HARLEY.
Abbey Aldrich Rockefeller Folk Art Center, Williamsburg, Virginia.

The Eagle

ALFRED, LORD TENNYSON

As you read this poem, discover the images that capture the dignity and power of the eagle.

He clasps the crag with crooked hands;
Close to the sun in lonely lands,
Ring'd with the azure world, he stands.

The wrinkled sea beneath him crawls;
He watches from his mountain walls,   5
And like a thunderbolt he falls.

Alfred, Lord Tennyson *(1809–1892)* was a shy man who tried to deal positively with the unhappiness he encountered in his life. His long poem *In Memoriam* was written over a seventeen-year period and was about his attempts to deal with the death of a close friend. Tennyson lived in England and was made Poet Laureate by Queen Victoria. He became one of the best-known poets in the English-speaking world. His famous works include "The Lady of Shalott."

Developing Comprehension Skills

1. Where is the eagle at the beginning of the poem?

2. The speaker says the eagle has "crooked hands." What part of the eagle is being described by this image?

3. What can you infer from lines 5 and 6 about what the eagle is doing? What kind of movement does the comparison "like a thunderbolt he falls" suggest?

4. Do you think the poet succeeds in creating a picture of the eagle as powerful and majestic? Explain why or why not.

Reading Literature: Poetry

1. **Identifying Rhythm.** Copy the first stanza of this poem, leaving a line of space above each line. Mark the stressed and unstressed syllables with these marks: /, ˘. Is the rhythm regular or irregular? Do the lines seem to move quickly or slowly? How does the pace of the rhythm fit the subject?

2. **Recognizing Alliteration.** Which sounds are repeated at the beginnings of words in lines 1 and 2? Which repeated sound stresses the harshness of the setting? Which repeated sound stresses the tightness of the eagle's grasp? Which repeated sound in line 2 stresses the emptiness of the setting?

3. **Understanding Word Choice.** The sensory images in this poem are clear because each word is precise. Look up the three words that follow. Note the specific meaning of each word. Keeping in mind the meanings of the words, describe the setting in the first stanza of the poem.

crag   crawls   azure

The Mountain and the Squirrel

RALPH WALDO EMERSON

This poem is very much like some of the fables you have read. Look for a moral stated in two words.

The mountain and the squirrel
Had a quarrel,
And the former called the latter
    "Little Prig";
Bun replied,
"You are doubtless very big;   5
But all sorts of things and weather
Must be taken in together,
To make up a year
And a sphere.

And I think it no disgrace   10
To occupy my place.
If I'm not so large as you,
You are not so small as I,
And not half so spry.
I'll not deny you make   15
A very pretty squirrel track;
Talents differ; all is well and wisely put;
If I cannot carry forests on my back,
Neither can you crack a nut."

Ielerang or Javan Squirrel,
1850, EDWARD LEAR. Hand-
colored lithograph after the
artist's drawing. Field Museum of
Natural History, Chicago.

Ralph Waldo Emerson *(1803–1882)* was born into a family of ministers. After working his way through Harvard University, he became the pastor of a Boston church. He gave up that vocation, however, because he wanted to write and lecture. Two of Emerson's prose works are *The Conduct of Life* and *Essays. Poems* and *May-Day* are collections of his best-known poetry.

Developing Comprehension Skills

1. Who was called "Little Prig"? Who did the name-calling?

2. Who speaks most of the time in this poem—the mountain or the squirrel?

3. Is the squirrel upset at not being as big as the mountain? What is one advantage the squirrel has over the mountain?

4. What is the squirrel's viewpoint about different talents? Do you agree with this viewpoint? Which of the squirrel's arguments are convincing?

Reading Literature: Poetry

Understanding Purpose. This poem tells a **fable**, a story that teaches a lesson. Read the last three lines carefully. What phrase expresses the moral? What example supports the moral?

The Panther

OGDEN NASH

Ogden Nash likes to play with words and sounds. Watch how he creates humor in "The Panther" and "The Hippopotamus."

The panther is like a leopard,
Except it hasn't been peppered.
Should you behold a panther crouch,
Prepare to say Ouch.
Better yet, if called by a panther,   5
Don't anther.

Ogden Nash *(1901–1971)* worked as a salesman in an advertising firm and for a book publisher before becoming a full-time writer. He was amused by the way misspelled words made a story or an article funny by chance. These entertaining observations led him to write poems with unusual rhymes, often using irregular spellings. Nash became one of America's best-known writers of humorous poetry.

The Hippopotamus

OGDEN NASH

Behold the hippopotamus!
We laugh at how he looks to us,
And yet in moments dank and grim
I wonder how we look to him.
Peace, peace, thou hippopotamus!   5
We really look all right to us,
As you no doubt delight the eye
Of other hippopotami.

Hippopotamus from the Egyptian tomb of Senbi. The Metropolitan Museum of Art, New York City, Gift of Edward S. Harkness, 1917.

Developing Comprehension Skills

1. Identify three animals named in these two poems.

2. Is the problem described in lines 3–6 of "The Panther" likely to happen?

3. The speaker addresses two audiences in "The Hippopotamus." Name these audiences. At what line does the change from one to the other take place?

4. Is "The Hippopotamus" only about an animal? Or is the poem also saying something about human life? What do you think is the main point of the poem?

5. Is "The Hippopotamus" serious, humorous, or both? Explain.

Reading Literature: Poetry

1. **Examining Patterns of Rhythm.** "The Hippopotamus" is written in a regular rhythm; every other syllable is stressed.

‿ / ‿ ‿ / ‿ / ‿ /
Behold the hippopotamus!

Reread the poem, noting the regular rhythm. Then reread "The Panther." Copy this poem on a sheet of paper and mark the stressed and unstressed syllables. Which line has a pattern of rhythm like "The Hippopotamus"? What is the rhythm like in the other lines? How do the different patterns of rhythm fit the subjects of the poems?

2. **Understanding Humor.** In these poems, the poet creates humor by using expressions that would seem out-of-place in the real world. For example, when does someone say "Ouch"? Would a person say "Ouch" after being attacked by a panther? Words such as *behold* and *thou* and phrases such as "Peace, peace" usually suggest a solemn address. Do they in "The Hippopotamus"? Which rhymes in the two poems do you find unexpected and amusing?

Vocabulary

Understanding Homographs and Homonyms. You have already learned about **homographs**: words that are spelled the same but are used in different ways. In addition, you should be aware of **homonyms:** words that sound the same but are spelled differently and have different meanings. For example, *eye* and *I* are pronounced exactly the same way but have different spellings and meanings. Each of the poems or set of poems below is followed by four words. Choose two words from each group. For each word give a defini-

tion that fits the way the word is used in the poem. Then give a homograph or homonym for the word. (Some words may have both a homograph and a homonym.) Use the dictionary if necessary.

1. "The Eagle": close, sea, watches, like
2. "The Mountain and the Squirrel": weather, so, track, well
3. "The Panther" and "The Hippopotamus": pepper, peace, right, to

Study and Research

Becoming Familiar with Library Resources. In your school or local library, find the record and tape collection. Also, locate the section of the card catalog or computer catalog in which these resources are listed. Notice that there are recordings of poetry and other literature as well as of music.

Find out if your library has any records or tapes of the poems in this chapter. List the title of the record or tape and the name of the person who did the reading.

Your library may have no records or tapes of poems in this book. However, it may have recordings of other poems by the poets you have studied. If so, list those records and tapes.

Ogden Nash wrote funny poems to be read to the music of *Carnival of the Animals* by the French composer Camille Saint-Saëns. Does your library have a recording of the music along with the poems? If so, list both the conductor and the narrator.

Developing Writing Skills

Comparing and Contrasting. Write two paragraphs in which you compare and contrast the way two of the poems you have read use animals.

Prewriting. Choose the two poems you want to write about. Think about the following questions and then make a chart like the one below to compare the details in the poems. (If you have a computer, you may want to use it to set up your chart.)

1. What details are given about the animal's physical appearance? about the animal's actions?

2. Does the poem use the animal to make some point about humans or human behavior? If so, what is that point?

3. Does the poem use humor in the way the animal is presented? If so, give examples.

4. Which of the animal's characteristics seem real?

5. What unusual or impossible things can the animal do?

Drafting. Use the chart to help you draft a topic sentence. In this sentence, identify the animals and the poems you are comparing and contrasting. Then present your ideas. You can talk about each poem in one paragraph. Or you can discuss the similarities of the poems in one paragraph and the differences in another paragraph.

Revising and Sharing. When revising your draft, think about the following questions. Are your comparisons clearly organized? Have you included the most important points? Are there any ideas you should add or drop? Have you included specific examples? When you have finished your draft, choose a partner and read each other's drafts. How are your ideas similar? How are they different?

	Animal's physical appearance?	Actions?	Point about humans?	Humor?	Animal real or imaginary?	Unusual or impossible behavior
Poem 1						
Poem 2						

Poems About Sports

Most people enjoy taking part in sports. They like the activity, the challenge, and the feeling of excitement. They also enjoy going to sporting events. The power and grace of an athlete are a pleasure to watch.

The poems in this section try to put into words what people feel as they take part in sports or attend games. As you read these poems, notice how the figures of speech, as well as the rhythms, images, and sounds, make the sports action come alive.

Sandlot Game, 1964, RALPH FASANELLA. Private Collection.

Reading Literature

More About Poetry

You have already learned that a poet uses shape, sounds, and sensory images to express meaning. This page and the next will tell you about a few more techniques a poet uses.

Figurative Language

As you know, poets often use figurative language to express meaning in new and unexpected ways. Figurative language includes these four figures of speech.

1. **Simile:** a comparison using *like* or *as*
2. **Metaphor:** a comparison between two unlike things that have something in common. A metaphor does not use *like* or *as.*
3. **Personification:** the technique of giving human qualities to an object, animal, or idea
4. **Hyperbole:** an exaggeration of some quality for emphasis

You have studied these figures of speech in Chapter Three, How Writers Write. Review the terms as you read the poems in the rest of this chapter.

Rhyme Scheme

In poems with rhyme, the rhyming words usually form a pattern. As you know, this pattern is called the **rhyme scheme.** To chart the rhyme scheme of a poem, you use a different letter of the alphabet to represent each rhyming sound. Look at the following example from "All But Blind" by Walter de la Mare.

```
All but blind            a
   In the burning day     b
The Barn-Owl blunders     c
   On her way.            b
```

Many different rhyme schemes are possible. Look for variations in the poems that rhyme.

Mood

Mood is the feeling created in the reader by a work of literature. Poets create mood in part by choosing the right words. The poet takes into account both the denotation and the connotation of a word. The **denotation** of a word is its dictionary definition. The **connotation** includes all the feelings and ideas associated with a word.

Poets also create mood by the level of language they use. The informal language of a poem such as "Seal" creates a casual, friendly, down-to-earth feeling. In contrast, the more formal language of a poem such as "New World" can make you feel serious and respectful.

Narrative and Lyric Poems

A poem can be either a narrative poem or a lyric poem. A **narrative poem** tells a story. Narrative poems are often long. The epic poems of long ago that told of courageous adventures were narratives. So are a few of the poems you will read in the next section.

In a **lyric poem**, the poet expresses his or her emotions. A lyric poem seems almost like a song. It does not tell a story. Many examples of lyric poems are in this chapter, including several you have read, such as "New World" and "Fall."

The Base Stealer

ROBERT FRANCIS

Try to picture a player stealing bases in a ball game. Notice how the comparisons and many specific verbs in this poem sharpen your picture.

Poised between going on and back, pulled
Both ways taut like a tightrope-walker,
Fingertips pointing the opposites,
Now bouncing tiptoe like a dropped ball
Or a kid skipping rope, come on, come on,   5
Running a scattering of steps sidewise,
How he teeters, skitters, tingles, teases,
Taunts them, hovers like an ecstatic bird,
He's only flirting, crowd him, crowd him,
Delicate, delicate, delicate, delicate—now!   10

Pinky Pettinger Stealing Home,
1986, LANCE RICHBOURG.
Private Collection. O. K. Harris, New York
City.

Robert Francis *(1901–1987)* devoted his life to writing and teaching. In his home on the outskirts of Amherst, Massachusetts, Francis lived a quiet life, gardening, reading, and writing. His award-winning works include fiction, essays, autobiography, and poetry. Francis's many collections of published poems include *Come Out into the Sun, The Orb Weaver,* and *The Sound I Listened For.*

Developing Comprehension Skills

1. Name two ways the base stealer moves.

2. Who is the speaker in this poem, the base stealer or someone watching him? How did you infer who the speaker is?

3. Is the poem successful in helping you picture a player trying to steal a base? Give examples of images that seem especially effective.

Reading Literature: Poetry

1. **Examining Similes.** As you know, a **simile** is a comparison that uses *like* or *as.* Find four similes in "The Base Stealer." To what four things is the base stealer compared? Which of the four creates the clearest picture in your mind?

2. **Understanding Connotations of Words.** Poets choose words for their connotative as well as for their denotative, or dictionary, meanings. **Connotation** refers to the way different words that have the same general meaning bring different feelings and thoughts to the reader's mind. For example, *daring* has a positive connotation while *reckless* is negative.

In lines 7–9, two sets of words have the same general meaning. Each word in the set, though, has a slightly different connotation. What is the difference between *teeters* and *skitters?* between *teases, taunts,* and *flirts?* Use a dictionary if you need help.

3. **Recognizing Mood.** As you know, the **mood** of a poem is the feeling the poem creates in the reader. As you read "The Base Stealer," what kind of feeling builds? one of relaxation and amusement? of calm and peacefulness? of tension and excitement?

Hockey

SCOTT BLAINE

This poem captures the speed and excitement of a hockey game. Watch the action move from the smooth ice of the first line to the wild drive at the end.

The ice is smooth, smooth, smooth.
The air bites to the center
Of warmth and flesh, and I whirl.
It begins in a game . . .
The puck swims, skims, veers,   5
Goes leading my vision
Beyond the chasing reach of my stick.

The air is sharp, steel-sharp.
I suck needles of breathing,
And feel the players converge.   10
It grows to a science . . .
We clot, break, drive,
Electrons in motion
In the magnetic pull of the puck.

The play is fast, fierce, tense.   15
Sticks click and snap like teeth
Of wolves on the scent of a prey.
It ends in the kill . . .
I am one of the pack in a mad,
Taut leap of desperation   20
In the wild, slashing drive for the goal.

At the Crease, 1972, KEN DANBY. Private Collection. Photograph: Gallery Moos, Toronto.

Developing Comprehension Skills

1. At what point in the game does the poem begin?

2. Is the speaker a player or someone who is watching the game? What lines in the first stanza make it clear which the speaker is?

3. Copy the fourth line of each stanza. Look at the verb used in each line. How do the verbs signal the stages of the game?

4. The fourth line of each stanza also uses a noun. How do these words convey the buildup of suspense in the poem? How does each word connect to the rest of the stanza?

5. How does this poem affect you? Do you feel drawn into what is happening in the poem? Does the poet make the game come alive for you? Explain your answers.

6. "Hockey" and "The Base Stealer" describe the action of specific sports. Do you think the reader has to be familiar with each sport to appreciate each poem? Explain why you think as you do.

Reading Literature: Poetry

1. **Understanding Metaphor.** As you know, a **metaphor** is a comparison between two unlike things that have something in common. However, the comparison is not expressed directly with *like* or *as*. Instead the comparison is suggested and you must read carefully to understand what the comparison means. As you read lines 8–9, you probably realized that they could not be describing something real. What is being compared in this metaphor? What is the metaphor in lines 12–14?

2. **Recognizing Extended Metaphor.** The final stanza is an extended metaphor. The players are compared to a pack of wolves in several different ways. To what are their sticks compared? To what is making a goal compared? What mood, or feeling, does the entire comparison create? Support your answers with phrases and lines from the poem.

Casey at the Bat

ERNEST LAWRENCE THAYER

This is one of the best known poems about sports that has ever been written. As you read, consider what has made this poem so popular.

The outlook wasn't brilliant for the Mudville nine that day;
The score stood four to two, with but one inning more to play;
And so, when Cooney died at first, and Barrows did the same,
A sickly silence fell upon the patrons of the game.

A straggling few got up to go in deep despair. The rest   5
Clung to the hope which springs eternal in the human breast;
They thought, if only Casey could but get a whack; at that,
They'd put up even money now, with Casey at the bat.

But Flynn preceded Casey, as did also Jimmy Blake;
And the former was a pudding,[1] and the latter was a fake;   10
So upon that stricken multitude grim melancholy sat,
For there seemed but little chance of Casey's getting to the bat.

But Flynn let drive a single, to the wonderment of all,
And Blake, the much despisèd, tore the cover off the ball;
And when the dust had lifted, and they saw what had occurred,   15
There was Jimmy safe on second, and Flynn a-hugging third.

Then from the gladdened multitude went up a joyous yell;
It bounded from the mountaintop and rattled in the dell;
It struck upon the hillside and recoiled upon the flat,
For Casey, mighty Casey, was advancing to the bat.   20

The Autograph, 1980, OSCAR de MEJO.
20"x 16". From the book, *My America,*
Harry N. Abrams, Inc., New York City.

There was ease in Casey's manner as he stepped into his place;
There was pride in Casey's bearing and a smile on Casey's face;
And when, responding to the cheers, he lightly doffed his hat,
No stranger in the crowd could doubt 'twas Casey at the bat.

Ten thousand eyes were on him as he rubbed his hands with dirt;   25
Five thousand tongues applauded when he wiped them on his shirt;
Then, while the writhing pitcher ground the ball into his hip,
Defiance gleamed in Casey's eye, a sneer curled Casey's lip.

And now the leather-covered sphere came hurtling through the air,
And Casey stood a-watching it in haughty grandeur there;   30
Close by the sturdy batsman the ball unheeded sped.
"That ain't my style," said Casey. "Strike one," the umpire said.

From the benches, black with people, there went up a muffled roar,
Like the beating of the storm waves on a stern and distant shore;
"Kill him! Kill the umpire!" shouted someone in the stand.   35
And it's likely they'd have killed him had not Casey raised his hand.

With a smile of Christian charity great Casey's visage[2] shone;
He stilled the rising tumult; he bade the game go on;
He signaled to the pitcher, and once more the spheroid[3] flew;
But Casey still ignored it, and the umpire said, "Strike two."   40

"Fraud!" cried the maddened thousands, and the echo answered, "Fraud!"
But one scornful look from Casey, and the audience was awed;
They saw his face grow stern and cold; they saw his muscles strain;
And they knew that Casey wouldn't let that ball go by again.

The sneer is gone from Casey's lips; his teeth are clenched in hate;   45
He pounds with cruel violence his bat upon the plate;
And now the pitcher holds the ball, and now he lets it go,
And now the air is shattered by the force of Casey's blow.

Oh, somewhere in this favored land the sun is shining bright;
The band is playing somewhere, and somewhere hearts are light,   50
And somewhere men are laughing, and somewhere children shout;
But there is no joy in Mudville—mighty Casey has struck out!

---

1. **pudding**–A stupid person.
2. **visage** (viz'ij)–Face.
3. **spheroid** (sfir'oid)–A body that is almost, but not quite a sphere.

Ernest Lawrence Thayer *(1863–1940)* was born in Worcester, Massachusetts. He attended Harvard University, where he was the editor-in-chief of the student humor magazine, *Lampoon.* He joined his classmate William Randolph Hearst as a journalist on the *San Francisco Examiner.* Thayer wrote a number of poems for newspapers and is most noted for his poem "Casey at the Bat."

Developing Comprehension Skills

1. Name two members of the Mudville team—other than Casey—who come to bat in the last inning. What does each do?

2. The first stanza says the fans felt their team was sure to lose. Later the fans' feelings begin to change. Find the lines that indicate when the change begins. What causes the change?

3. How does Casey act when he first comes up to bat? How does his attitude change after the second strike?

4. The poem doesn't reveal what happens until the last two words. How does the repetition of *somewhere* in the last stanza give a warning that something is wrong?

5. Even though the poem is about baseball, the experience described in this poem—hope turning to disappointment—is a common one. In fact, the sentence "There is no joy in Mudville" is sometimes used as a shortcut for saying an expected victory did not take place. Can you think of any experience you have had similar to the one in the poem?

Reading Literature: Poetry

1. **Recognizing Narrative.** "Casey at the Bat" is a **narrative poem**—it tells a story. What event does the poem narrate? Who is the main character in the story? What is the conflict or problem he faces?

2. **Identifying Rhyme Scheme.** As you know, the rhyme scheme shows the pattern of end rhymes in a poem. Look at the end rhymes in "Casey at the Bat." What is the rhyme scheme? Does every stanza have the same pattern?

3. **Examining Hyperbole.** This poem frequently uses **hyperbole,** or exaggeration. Note that the exaggeration often results in humor. Find three examples of hyperbole in the poem. For each example, explain what is actually happening and what is exaggerated.

4. **Understanding Irony.** **Irony** is a contrast between what is expected and what actually exists or happens. What does the crowd expect of Casey? What does Casey expect of himself? Tell what actually happens and how this outcome is ironic.

Vocabulary

Recognizing Levels of Language. This poem mixes three levels of language. Formal words, such as *stricken multitude,* are mixed with informal words, such as *whack*, and baseball jargon, such as *hugging third.* **Jargon** is the specialized vocabulary of those in the same profession or work. Jargon may be formal or informal. In sports it is usually informal.

Make two lists. For the first, write at least five words or phrases from the poem that are more formal than are usually found in conversation. For the second, write at least five terms or phrases from the poem that are either informal or sports jargon. Give a definition for each word or phrase in both lists. Notice how mixing the levels of language creates humor in the poem.

Speaking and Listening

Interpreting a Humorous Poem. You might like to present this poem with classmates as a choral reading. Or you might want to perform it alone. In either case, look for places where pauses or changes in tone of voice would be effective. Use gestures or facial expressions when appropriate. For a choral reading, different students could read just the words spoken by Casey or the umpire while two or three students read the crowd's comments.

Developing Writing Skills

Writing a Poem About Sports. Write a poem that tells about an exciting moment in a sporting event. The sport may be a team or individual competition. You may write a lyric or narrative poem. It may be humorous.

Prewriting. Decide what moment in sports you want to write about. Also decide what type of poem you want to write and whether it will be serious or humorous. Make a list of details to describe the incident. Then list words and phrases that you might use. Consider techniques you have studied in the poems you have read so far. You can use figures of speech, rhyme, rhythm, and careful word choice to create your poem.

Drafting. As you begin your draft, decide if you want to try for a fixed stanza length and regular rhyme pattern. Remember a draft can always be changed. In fact, in writing poetry, sometimes the best ideas come as you try to improve something that didn't turn out the way you wanted it to.

Revising and Sharing. Ask a partner to read your draft aloud and mark places where it seems the rhythm or rhyme (if you are using rhyme) could be improved. Also check places where a more specific word or clearer comparison could be used. Can the reader follow the action in the poem? Are there any humorous effects that don't quite work? Ask your partner for suggestions. After you have made the suggested revisions, write out a clean copy to share with the class at a reading or on a bulletin board display. Or, your school newspaper might want to print the best poems.

The Women's 400 Meters

LILLIAN MORRISON

This poem describes racers as they prepare for and begin their run. Listen for the rhythm of the lines.

Skittish,
they flex knees, drum heels and
shiver at the starting line

waiting the gun
to pour them over the stretch   5
like a breaking wave.

Bang! they're off
careening down the lanes,
each chased by her own bright tiger.

Photograph by John Kelly, The Image Bank, Chicago.

Lillian Morrison *(born 1917)* writes about subjects that interest her—jazz, dance, and sports. She was born in New Jersey and eventually moved to New York City. There she worked in the public library, where she was interested mainly in improving services to young people. Morrison is known for *The Ghosts of Jersey City,* a collection of her own poems, and *Sprints and Distances,* an anthology of sports poems that she edited.

Developing Comprehension Skills

1. Are the runners starting or finishing the race?

2. What can you infer about the racers' feelings from the first three lines?

3. What does "careening down the lanes" mean?

4. The poem does not tell who wins the race. What part of the experience of racing is the poem about? Have you had similar feelings as you have prepared for a big event or contest?

Reading Literature: Poetry

1. **Examining Figurative Language: Simile and Metaphor.** Explain the simile in lines 5 and 6. How are the runners like a wave? Is each racer really being chased by a tiger? What is the speaker trying to say in the last line?

2. **Identifying Type of Poetry.** Is this poem narrative or lyrical? That is, does it tell a story? Or does it emphasize a mood or experience? Refer to the poem in giving reasons for your answer.

Pole Vault

SHIRO MURANO

In a competition, an athlete concentrates on the track, mat, or other space in which he or she must perform. That space becomes the athlete's whole world. What is the horizon in the pole vaulter's world?

He is running like a wasp,
Hanging on a long pole.
As a matter of course he floats in the sky,
Chasing the ascending horizon.
Now he has crossed the limit,   5
    And pushed away his support.
For him there is nothing but a descent.
Oh, he falls helplessly.
Now on that runner, awkwardly fallen on the ground,
Once more   10
    The horizon comes down,
Beating hard on his shoulders.

Developing Comprehension Skills

1. Name three movements of the pole vaulter.

2. What part or parts of the competition does "Pole Vault" describe? Does "Pole Vault" focus on the same part as "The Women's 400 Meters"?

3. At the beginning of the poem, the pole vaulter is aiming for his "horizon," the crossbar, over which he jumps. What happens when he meets this horizon? What lines lead you to the answer?

4. Is this poem only about pole vaulting? Could the experience described here relate to a person's efforts in other parts of life? Explain.

Reading Literature: Poetry

1. **Recognizing Mood.** Both "Pole Vault" and "The Women's 400 Meters" are about participants in a competition. The **mood**, or feeling, the reader gets from each poem is not the same, however. Reread the poems and pay attention to your feelings as you read. Which poem seems to emphasize more the tension and excitement? Which one creates a more negative, anxious mood? Find at least one phrase in each poem to support your answers.

2. **Examining Rhythm.** Mark the stressed syllables in the first three lines. Do you see a regular pattern? Or does the rhythm vary from line to line? How does the rhythm fit the action in the poem? Find the longest line in the poem. Notice how it interrupts the flow of the rhythm in the poem. What adverb in the line describes the effect the line has on the rhythm?

Vocabulary

Choosing the Correct Meaning for the Context. Read the following pairs of sentences. One sentence in each pair is based on the poems. Choose the correct meaning for the underlined word in each sentence.

1. Bob will stretch the tent over its wobbly frame.

2. The runners waited for the signal to spread out over the stretch.
   a. extend one's body or limbs; *stretch one's legs*
   b. draw out to great length or size
   c. a straight section of a race course or track
   d. pull or spread out to full extent

3. He slashed at the puck with his stick.

4. The electronics store slashed the price of computers.
   a. cut with a sweeping stroke of a knife or sword
   b. reduced prices drastically
   c. cleared a path in the forest
   d. made a strong sweeping stroke

5. The runners <u>drummed</u> their heels on the ground.

6. In the fourth grade, I had the multiplication tables <u>drummed</u> into me.
   a. beat or played a drum
   b. beat or sounded like a drum
   c. wound in a machine on a thick bar
   d. taught by repeating over and over

7. Marcia designed the homecoming <u>float</u>.

8. The pole vaulter seemed for a moment to <u>float</u> in the air.
   a. drift or move slowly or easily
   b. cork on a fishing line
   c. flood with a liquid
   d. decorated vehicle for carrying exhibits in a parade

9. Don traced his <u>descent</u> from a family who came to America in the 1600's.

10. For the pole vaulter there is nothing but a <u>descent</u>.
    a. coming or going down
    b. downward slope
    c. ancestry
    d. sudden attack

Critical Thinking

Classifying Poems. In this book, the poems have been grouped, or classified, according to themes or subjects. The same poems could have been grouped according to other categories, such as short poems and long poems, rhymed and unrhymed poems, humorous and serious poems. Choose your own system of classifying the poems you have read in the first two sections of poems. List the names of your categories. Then, under each name, list the titles of the poems that fit in the category. Use two to four categories. Be sure to find a category for each poem.

Study and Research

Finding Books About Sports Figures. On a sheet of paper, list the number or numbers assigned to biographies and autobiographies in the classification system used by your library. Then use the card catalog or computer catalog to locate a biography or autobiography of a sports figure you admire. Write the title, author, and the Dewey Decimal or other number assigned to the book.

Developing Writing Skills

1. **Evaluating a Poem.** Consider the five poems about sports that you have just read. Which one do you think does the best job of re-creating an experience? In one paragraph explain why you chose the poem.

   Prewriting. Reread the poem you have chosen to write about. As you think about what makes the poem work well, look at the experiences it suggests. Does it capture something you yourself have felt while playing? Does it present new experiences for you to imagine? Take notes on how the poet makes the experiences come to life for you. Include such things as figures of speech and sounds of language.

   Drafting. Build your paragraph around a topic sentence. State which poem you think is best. Be sure to offer several specific points in support of your statement. Include details of the poet's technique as well as details about the experiences described.

   Revising and Sharing. Break into small groups. Each group should include class-mates who wrote about different poems. Have each member of the group read his or her paragraph aloud. Then discuss what you learned from others about the various ways you can appreciate a poem.

2. **Writing a Paragraph About Sports.** You have been reading poems about athletes, their skill and grace, their courage and determination.

   Choose one sport you know something about, either as a participant or as a spectator. Make a list of at least ten words and phrases that describe the sport. Include some words and phrases that show your attitude toward the sport also.

   Using your list as a starting place, write a paragraph in which you share just one feeling or idea about the subject you chose. Be sure to describe one event, and be sure to suggest feelings or attitudes. The speaker may be either a participant or a spectator. Follow the steps in the process of writing: prewriting, drafting, revising, and sharing. See Guidelines for the Process of Writing on page 623 of the handbook for further help.

Poems About the Individual

Who are you? What kinds of things do you feel strongly about? Whom do you admire? What do you dream of doing? The poems you are about to read all deal with questions like these. The theme in each of them should make you think about what it means to grow as an individual.

Portrait of Mademoiselle Violette Heymann, 1909, ODILON REDON. The Cleveland Museum of Art, Ohio, Honmun B. Hurlbut Collection.

All But Blind

WALTER de la MARE

Being blind usually means not being able to see physically. In what other ways can a person be blind?

All but blind
   In his chambered hole
Gropes for worms
   The four-clawed Mole.

All but blind   5
   In the evening sky,
The hooded Bat
   Twirls softly by.

All but blind
   In the burning day   10
The Barn-Owl blunders
   On her way.

And blind as are
   These three to me,
So, blind to Someone   15
   I must be.

Walter de la Mare *(1873–1956)* was raised and educated in London, England. He began writing at the age of seventeen, when he founded a high school newspaper. Later, while working as a bookkeeper, he devoted his spare time to writing. Eventually, he received a government grant, which allowed him to write full-time. He is known for his poems, nursery rhymes, and stories. In 1953, he earned the Order of Merit from Queen Elizabeth II.

Developing Comprehension Skills

1. Which three animals are described in the poem?

2. How well can the animals see? How can you tell?

3. Reread lines 13 and 14. How are the three animals blind to the speaker ("me")? Are they unable to see, or are they simply unaware of the speaker? Could both meanings apply?

4. What do you think the speaker means in the lines "So, blind to Someone / I must be"? Who is the Someone? Can you infer anything from the fact that *Someone* is capitalized?

5. What kinds of blindness are possible? Do you think you are blind in any way?

Reading Literature: Poetry

1. **Understanding Lyric Poetry.** The word *lyric* comes from the Greek word for music. This poem is a good example of a lyric. Notice how the poem uses many pleasing sound patterns. Identify examples of the following techniques of sound: rhyme (give the rhyme scheme), alliteration, repetition of words and phrases.

   Review the definition of a lyric poem on page 347. Does the treatment of the subject of "All But Blind" fit the idea of a lyric poem?

2. **Recognizing Inverted Sentence Patterns.** What is the subject of the sentence that makes up the first stanza? In ordinary speech, the subject usually comes before the verb. Change the order of the words in the sentence to follow the usual pattern. Now reread the stanza as the poet wrote it. What does the inverted sentence pattern emphasize?

3. **Identifying Theme.** As you know, the **theme** is the poet's message about life. What is the theme of "All But Blind"? You may find it helpful to review your answers to Developing Comprehension Skills questions 3–5.

Way Down in the Music

How do you feel when you listen to music? Does it make you want to "get down" and dance? What meaning does the poem give to the phrase "get down"?

ELOISE GREENFIELD

I get way down in the music
Down inside the music
I let it wake me
       take me
Spin me around and make me   5
Uh-get down

Inside the sound of the Jackson Five[1]
Into the tune of Earth, Wind and Fire[2]
Down in the bass where the beat comes from
Down in the horn and down in the drum   10
I get down
I get down

I get way down in the music
Down inside the music
I let it wake me   15
       take me
Spin me around and shake me
I get down, down
I get down

---

1. **Jackson Five**–A popular young singing group, all brothers, of the 1970's.
2. **Earth, Wind and Fire**–A rhythm-and-blues band, popular in the 1970's and early 1980's.

Eloise Greenfield (*born 1929*) grew up in North Carolina and attended Miner Teachers College. For twelve years she worked at the U.S. Patent Office in Washington, D.C. She then joined the Black Writers Workshop, first as co-director of adult fiction, then as director of children's literature. Greenfield's work was first published in 1970. She has produced picture books, novels, biographies, short stories, and poems. She has also written about her childhood with the help of her mother, Lessie Jones Little.

Developing Comprehension Skills

1. What musical instruments does the speaker mention?

2. Is the speaker playing the music or listening to the music? How do you know?

3. What does the speaker mean by "I get down"? How is the meaning of "I get down" different from the meaning of the expression "I feel down"?

4. What kind of music do you think the speaker is talking about? What feelings do you have about your favorite kinds of music? Does this poem express any of those feelings?

Reading Literature: Poetry

1. **Recognizing Repetition.** The meaning of this poem is suggested through the repetition of words and lines. What phrase is repeated most often in the poem? What single word? What lines are repeated? Notice how the repeated parts of the poem point to the meaning and help to unify the poem.

2. **Understanding Rhythm.** Does this poem have a regular pattern of stressed and unstressed syllables? Do you hear a strong or a weak beat when you read the poem aloud?

The Dream Keeper

LANGSTON HUGHES

Have you ever given up a dream because someone told you it wasn't practical? Read to find out what the speaker in this poem would do with dreams.

Bring me all of your dreams,
You dreamers,
Bring me all of your
Heart melodies
That I may wrap them   5
In a blue cloud-cloth
Away from the too-rough fingers
Of the world.

The Sign of the Mermaid, 1980, ROBERT MOTHERWELL.
Private Collection. Photograph: John Berggruen Gallery, San Francisco.

Langston Hughes *(1902–1967)* was a playwright, poet, song writer, and lecturer as well as an author of short stories and novels. He worked at many jobs before he won recognition for his writing talent. Hughes wrote about many aspects of life, drawing on his own experience, including travel to Africa. Many of Hughes's works reflect the speech patterns and jazz rhythms he heard on the streets of Harlem.

Developing Comprehension Skills

1. To whom is the poem addressed?

2. Reread the title. Who is the speaker, and what does the speaker offer to do?

3. Does the speaker consider dreams strong or fragile? How do you know?

4. What general idea about dreams do you get from the poem? How important are dreams? Do you agree with the point that the poet is making?

Reading Literature: Poetry

1. **Understanding Personification. Personification** is the technique of giving human qualities to an object, animal, or idea. Explain the personification in lines 7 and 8. Whose fingers are referred to? What can a person's "too-rough" fingers do to a delicate object?

2. **Evaluating Word Choice.** In "Dream Keeper" the poet combines familiar words that are not usually used together. An

example is the phrase "heart melodies." The word *heart* is associated with personal things; the word *melodies* suggests songs of beauty or happiness. Putting together these two meanings, how would you define "heart melodies"? What two ideas are combined in the phrase "dream keeper"? What image does the phrase "cloud-cloth" suggest?

Vocabulary

Understanding Connotations. As you know, poets pay close attention to **connotation**, to the feelings and thoughts associated with a word. Each set of words below consists of three **synonyms**—words that have similar dictionary definitions. Below these words are three sentences with one word missing. Decide which of the three synonyms has the connotation that fits each sentence. Be prepared to explain the connotation of each word.

1. groped   fumbled   explored
   a. I was so late that I _____ nervously trying to find my keys.
   b. No lights were on, so I _____ under the rug looking for the spare key.
   c. Since I knew the key was somewhere in the room, I _____ every possible hiding place.

2. melody   chant   tune
   a. It began as an advertisement, and soon everyone was humming the catchy _____.

   b. The beauty of the _____ brought tears to Mrs. Truesdale's eyes.
   c. The steady drumbeat helped emphasize the rhythm of the _____.

3. spin   rotate   turn
   a. You should _____ right at the first stop sign.
   b. The planets _____ around the sun.
   c. As the beat got faster and faster, the dancers began to _____ around.

Study and Research

Finding an Anthology. An **anthology** of poetry is a collection of poems written by one or more poets. Look up *Poetry, Anthologies* or *Poetry, Collections* in the card catalog or computer catalog at your school or local library. Find an anthology that has poems by many poets. Answer the following questions about the anthology.

1. What is the title?

2. Who edited the anthology?

3. How many poets are included? List any whose poems you have read.

4. What is the main focus? a time period, subject, place, type of poetry, group of poets?

5. How are the poems arranged? alphabetically by title or author? according to when they were written? by subject or theme?

6. Are biographies of the poets included?

Developing Writing Skills

1. **Applying a Definition.** In one paragraph show how one of the first three poems in this section fits the definition of a lyric.

   Prewriting. Review the discussions of *lyric poem* given on pages 347 and 366. On a sheet of paper, list the elements that are important to a lyric, including a theme that expresses personal feelings or impressions and the use of specific sound effects. Then go through the poem you have chosen and identify specific examples. Review the study questions for ideas.

   Drafting. Be sure to give the title of the poem you are discussing in your opening sentence. Then describe the characteristics of a lyric. Keep in mind that you are showing how the poem fits the definition of a lyric. Do not stray from the main point by giving your opinions about the ideas in the poem.

   Revising and Sharing. Work with a partner to evaluate how clearly your paragraph is organized. Make sure that the title of the poem is mentioned. Is there a clear definition of *lyric*? Have you included specific examples of each major characteristic?

2. **Using Personification.** Think of a familiar object that seems to have a personality; for example, a house with windows that look like eyes or a radio that seems like a friend who's always ready to talk to you. Write a short poem giving your impression of the way the object seems alive. Follow the steps in the process of writing: prewriting, drafting, revising, and sharing. For more help, refer to Guidelines for the Process of Writing on page 623 of the handbook.

The Courage That My Mother Had

EDNA ST. VINCENT MILLAY

The courage that my mother had
Went with her, and is with her still:
Rock from New England quarried;
Now granite in a granite hill.

The golden brooch my mother wore   5
She left behind for me to wear;
I have no thing I treasure more:
Yet, it is something I could spare.

Oh, if instead she'd left to me
The thing she took into the grave!—   10
That courage like a rock, which she
Has no more need of, and I have.

Mathilde and Robert, about 1882, MARY CASSATT. Newark Museum, Felix Fuld Bequest Fund.

Edna St. Vincent Millay *(1892–1950)* won fame at the age of nineteen for her poem "Renascence." After graduating from Vassar College, she moved to New York City. There she lived and worked in Greenwich Village among other noted writers of the 1920's and 1930's. Millay continued to write poetry, as well as stories and plays. She was awarded a Pulitzer Prize for *The Harp-Weaver and Other Poems.*

Developing Comprehension Skills

1. What piece of jewelry did the mother leave to the speaker? What quality did the mother take into the grave?

2. To what does the speaker compare her mother's courage?

3. What does the poet say she has need of in the last line?

4. Do you agree that a quality such as courage is more valuable than a possession? Can qualities be passed on from parents to children in the way that possessions can? Explain.

Reading Literature: Poetry

1. **Analyzing Stanzas.** As you know, a **stanza** is a group of lines in a poem. How many stanzas make up this poem? How many lines are in each stanza? Do the stanzas use fairly regular patterns of rhythm and rhyme? Identify one example of each.

   A poet can organize stanzas so that they work like paragraphs—that is, each stanza develops one main idea. What is the main idea of each stanza in this poem?

2. **Understanding Figurative Language.** In line 11, the poet uses a simile to describe her mother's courage. Find a metaphor that uses the same comparison earlier in the poem. What specific kind of rock does the poet talk about? What specific qualities does this type of rock suggest?

Magic Words to Feel Better

NETSILIK ESKIMO

As you read this poem, decide what the speaker wants. The title gives you a clue.

SEA GULL
who flaps his wings
over my head
        in the blue air,

you GULL up there   5
dive down
        come here
take me with you
        in the air!

Wings flash by   10
my mind's eye
and I'm up there sailing
in the cool air,
      a–a–a–a–a–ah,
           in the air.   15

Multi-Feathered Bird, 1961, KENOJUAK.
Reproduced with the Permission of the West Baffin Eskimo Cooperative.

Developing Comprehension Skills

1. Where is the sea gull? What does the speaker ask?

2. Which one of the first two stanzas is spoken directly to the gull? Which is a description of the gull?

3. Does the speaker actually fly at the end of the poem? What feeling is he describing? Find a line in the poem that supports your conclusion.

4. How does the title of this poem relate to the experience described in the poem? Could you understand the poem as well without the title?

Reading Literature: Poetry

1. **Examining Free Verse: Rhythm and Rhyme.** A poem written in **free verse** does not usually have a regular pattern of rhyme and rhythm. However, a poet still may use rhyme and rhythm when writing free verse. What rhymes occur in "Magic Words to Feel Better"? What phrase is repeated at the end of each stanza? Is this phrase exactly the same in each stanza?

   The poet varies the length of the lines and the pattern of stressed and unstressed syllables. How many stressed syllables do most lines have? Notice that in some lines all the syllables are stressed.

2. **Recognizing Onomatopoeia.** As you know, **onomatopoeia** occurs when a writer uses words that sound like what they are describing. The word *a–a–a–a–a–ah* in this poem is an example of onomatopoeia. What action or feeling does the word bring to your mind? How would the impression created by the poem change if the line were dropped?

The Duel

EMILY DICKINSON

Little David, the Bible says, killed the giant Goliath with just a small stone thrown by David's slingshot. Is the speaker in this poem as successful as David?

I took my Power in my Hand—
And went against the World—
'Twas not so much as David—had—
But I—was twice as bold—

I aimed my Pebble—but Myself   5
Was all the one that fell—
Was it Goliah[1]—was too large—
Or was myself—too small?

---

1. **Goliah**–Goliath.

Emily Dickinson *(1830–1886)* lived in Amherst, Massachusetts. She led an average life until the age of twenty-six, when she began to spend most of her time alone. Dickinson stayed indoors and had few visitors. Secretly, she wrote more than a thousand poems—most reflected deep feelings about life, love, and nature. Only seven of Emily Dickinson's poems were published while she was alive. The rest were discovered after her death, written on scraps of paper and hidden away in her bedroom.

Developing Comprehension Skills

1. Whom does the speaker fight against?

2. Does the speaker in the poem win this duel? What happens when the speaker takes aim?

3. The last two lines suggest that there are two viewpoints toward losing. You can lose because the problem or enemy is too big. Or you can lose because you are too weak or powerless to overcome the problem. Do you think one viewpoint is better than another or can both be true? Give examples that will explain and support your answer.

Reading Literature: Poetry

Understanding Allusions. Writers sometimes **allude,** or refer, to a literary person, place, or event. These references are called **allusions.** When you know something about the person, place, or event to which the writer alludes, you often understand more about the point that is being made. "The Duel" is built around an allusion to the Biblical story of David and Goliath. Who does the speaker say is like David? What is the difference between David and this person? Who is like Goliath? What did David use in his battle against Goliath? What is the weapon in this poem? (Reread the first line of each stanza if you need help.)

I Was Born Today

AMADO NERVO

In this poem, each day is a new beginning, full of possibilities. Each day offers opportunities for creating happiness and peace.

Every day that dawns, you must say to yourself,
"I was born today!
The world is new to me.
This light that I behold
Strikes my unclouded eyes for the first time;   5
The rain that scatters its crystal drops
Is my baptism!

"Then let us live a pure life,
A shining life!
Already, yesterday is lost. Was it bad? Was it beautiful?   10
. . . Let it be forgotten.
And of that yesterday let there remain only the essence,
The precious gold of what I loved and suffered
As I walked along the road . . .

"Today, every moment shall bring
      feelings of well being and cheer.   15
And the reason for my existence,
My most urgent resolve,
Will be to spread happiness all over the world,
To pour the wine of goodness into the
      eager mouths around me . . .

"My only peace will be the peace of others;   20
Their dreams, my dreams;
Their joy, my joy;
My crystal tear,
The tear that trembles on the eyelash of another;
My heartbeat,   25
The beat of every heart that throbs
Throughout worlds without end!"

Every day that dawns, you must say to yourself,
"I was born today!"

Take-Off, 1983, JOANNE CULVER.
Computer-generated art.

Amado Nervo *(1870–1919)* studied for the priesthood in his native Mexico. He gave up that vocation to become a journalist, novelist, and poet. Nervo served as a diplomat in Madrid, Spain, for more than eighteen years. He enjoyed the friendships of many writers, who encouraged him to pursue a literary career.

Developing Comprehension Skills

1. What are the first words the speaker tells you to say each day?

2. What part should the past play in each new day, according to the speaker?

3. Not every day is peaceful and joyful. What lines show that the speaker knows this?

4. The speaker in this poem says the reason for existence is to "spread happiness." What does this goal suggest about his feelings toward other people?

5. Would it be easy or difficult to put the ideas of this poem into practice? Give a reason for your answer.

Reading Literature: Poetry

1. **Recognizing Repetition.** You have seen examples of how poets repeat words and phrases to create sound effects and to sug-

gest meaning. In "I Was Born Today," how is repetition used in the fourth stanza? List the five examples.

The poet also repeats ideas to create emphasis. For example, in the first stanza, the idea of the phrase "I was born today" is restated in the line "The world is new to me." What other two images in the stanza suggest a new birth?

2. **Understanding the Speaker.** Notice that most of this poem is shown as a direct quotation. Only the first line and the second to the last line are shown outside of quotation marks. Who is supposed to be speaking these two lines? Who is supposed to be speaking the lines in quotations?

Vocabulary

Inferring Meaning from Context. Frequently you can figure out the meaning of a word from the sentence or passage in which it appears, even though there are no specific context clues. This process is called inferring the meaning. For example, read this sentence:

Joan's reason for being late seemed *plausible,* so the teacher excused her.

From the meaning of the sentence as a whole, you can guess that *plausible* means "believable" or "apparently acceptable."

The underlined words in the sentences below are taken from poems in this section. Use the information in the sentences to figure out the meaning of each word. On a sheet of paper, copy the word and write the definition you have inferred from the context.

1. The building was covered with a hard, polished rock that could only be granite.
2. In the picture of my great-grandmother as a girl, she has her hair in braids and is wearing a silver brooch pinned to her dress.
3. Nico had no reason to feel sad or worried; his future was unclouded.
4. Once I make up my mind to do something, nothing can change my resolve.
5. I felt very bold as I fearlessly marched up to the movie star and asked for his autograph.

Speaking and Listening

Listening to Poetry. You have learned that in a poem every word is important. Therefore, when you listen to a poem, it is important to listen carefully. The following activity will help you think about and improve your listening habits.

Work in groups of three to five. Each group should choose one of the poems in this section, Poems About the Individual. One person in the group should prepare to read the entire poem. The other members should each choose and prepare one stanza.

Two or more groups should join to listen to each other's presentations. First, each poem should be read by the students who prepared one stanza each. Then have the entire group discuss these questions:

1. Does the speed at which poetry is read change with the reader?
2. What effect does a change in reading speed have on the listener?
3. What might help a listener adjust to different reading speeds?
4. Does hearing someone read a poem make it easier to understand the poem? Why or why not?

Second, those students who prepared entire poems should present these poems. Then the entire group should discuss these questions:

5. Is it easier to listen to a poem of four or more stanzas when it is read by one person or when it is read by several persons? Are there some advantages to each way? What are those advantages?
6. Is it easier to listen to a short poem, of three stanzas or fewer, read by one person or by more than one person? What are the advantages and disadvantages of each way?
7. What should a listener do to develop listening skills for all poems?

Developing Writing Skills

Describing an Experience in a Poem. "Magic Words to Feel Better" tells about a simple experience. The speaker sees a soaring gull and feels like flying with it. "I Was Born Today" says that every moment of a day can bring "feelings of well being and cheer." Think of some simple, natural thing that has cheered you up or made you feel excited. Write a poem about it.

Prewriting. Allow yourself enough time to come up with a subject that you can write about comfortably. When you have chosen an animal, an object, or an activity, make up a list of verbs and comparisons that describe it. Go through your list to choose the verbs and comparisons that create the sharpest picture and that suggest how you feel about the experience.

Drafting. Try to include some section in the poem where you directly address the animal or object, as the speaker does in "Magic Words to Feel Better." Repeat words, phrases, or lines if possible. Do you want to end by telling how you feel? If you are comfortable using a rhyme or rhythm pattern, do so. You can also write in free verse.

Revising and Sharing. Put your poem aside for a time. Then reread it aloud. Will someone else get a clear sense of the feeling you are trying to suggest? If you wrote in free verse, did you use spacing to emphasize your meaning? Have you chosen words that are specific and have the correct connotations? Would onomatopoeia add to the effect you want to create?

Poems About America

The poems in this section are about people and events from America's past. Notice how the poets picture these people and events as clearly as if they were part of the present. Notice, too, that each poet leaves you with a feeling about the person or event in the poem. Do you think you would like to meet these people? Would you like to share in their adventures?

Three Flags, 1958, JASPER JOHNS. Encaustic on canvas, 30⅞"x 45½"x 5". Whitney Museum of American Art, New York City, 50th Anniversary Gift of the Gilman Foundation, Inc., The Lauder Foundation, A. Alfred Taubman, (and purchase) (80.32).

The Flower-Fed Buffaloes

VACHEL LINDSAY

This poem is about a sight that no longer can be seen. What lines make it easy to imagine how the buffaloes must have looked?

The flower-fed buffaloes of the spring
In the days of long ago,
Ranged where the locomotives sing
And the prairie flowers lie low:—
The tossing, blooming, perfumed grass   5
Is swept away by the wheat,
Wheels and wheels and wheels spin by
In the spring that still is sweet.
But the flower-fed buffaloes of the spring
Left us, long ago.   10
They gore no more, they bellow no more,
They trundle around the hills no more:—
With the Blackfeet, lying low,
With the Pawnees, lying low,
Lying low.   15

Vachel Lindsay (*1879–1931*) studied art when he was young and then later became a poet. He left his hometown of Springfield, Illinois, to travel around the country reading his poems. These readings were actually performances, in which he combined music, poetry, and elements of dance. Lindsay's readings became popular, though he later became disillusioned and eventually stopped giving them.

Developing Comprehension Skills

1. What food did the buffaloes eat? What machine can now be found where the buffaloes once were?

2. What now grows where the grass once was? What brought about the change? (In order to answer you will have to use what you know about pioneers.)

3. The Blackfeet and Pawnees are Native Americans. The speaker says that, like the buffalo, these people are now "lying low." Tell what you think the speaker is suggesting.

4. How does the speaker seem to feel about the way pioneers changed the prairies?

5. How do you feel as you read this poem? Do you think the poet wanted to create these feelings in the reader? Explain.

Reading Literature: Poetry

1. **Recognizing Sound Patterns.** The poet repeats certain sounds in this poem. Find at least three examples of repeated sounds, such as $\bar{o}$, l, $\bar{e}$, *sp*, and so forth. (The same sound may be spelled different ways.) Are these sounds soft and flowing or harsh and sharp?

2. **Identifying Rhyme Scheme.** Use letters to identify the rhyme scheme. Is it the same throughout the poem? Does the rhyme scheme help to unify the poem in any way? Explain.

Paul Revere's Ride

HENRY WADSWORTH LONGFELLOW

This long poem narrates the exciting events of the night of April 18, 1775. As you read, watch for words that make you feel the excitement of that long-ago night.

Listen my children, and you shall hear
Of the midnight ride of Paul Revere,
On the eighteenth of April, in seventy-five;
Hardly a man is now alive
Who remembers that famous day and year.   5

He said to his friend, "If the British march
By land or sea from the town tonight,
Hang a lantern aloft in the belfry arch
Of the North Church tower as a signal light,—
One, if by land, and two, if by sea;   10
And I on the opposite shore will be,
Ready to ride and spread the alarm
Through every Middlesex village and farm,
For the country folk to be up and to arm."

Then he said, "Good-night!" and with muffled oar   15
Silently rowed to the Charlestown shore.
Just as the moon rose over the bay,
Where swinging wide at her moorings lay
The *Somerset,* British man-of-war;
A phantom ship, with each mast and spar   20
Across the moon like a prison bar,
And a huge black hulk, that was magnified
By its own reflection in the tide.

Meanwhile, his friend, through alley and street,
Wanders and watches with eager ears,   25
Till in the silence around him he hears
The muster of men at the barrack door,
The sound of arms, and the tramp of feet,
And the measured tread of the grenadiers,
Marching down to their boats on the shore.   30

Then he climbed the tower of the Old North Church,
By the wooden stairs, with stealthy tread,
To the belfry-chamber overhead,
And startled the pigeons from their perch
On the somber rafters, that round him made   35
Masses and moving shapes of shade,—
By the trembling ladder, steep and tall,
To the highest window in the wall,
Where he paused to listen and look down
A moment on the roofs of the town,   40
And the moonlight flowing over all.

Beneath, in the churchyard, lay the dead,
In their night-encampment on the hill,
Wrapped in silence so deep and still
That he could hear, like a sentinel's tread,   45
The watchful night-wind, as it went
Creeping along from tent to tent,
And seeming to whisper, "All is well!"
A moment only he feels the spell
Of the place and the hour, and the secret dread   50
Of the lonely belfry and the dead;
For suddenly all his thoughts are bent
On a shadowy something far away,
Where the river widens to meet the bay,—
A line of black that bends and floats   55
On the rising tide, like a bridge of boats.

Meanwhile, impatient to mount and ride,
Booted and spurred, with a heavy stride
On the opposite shore walked Paul Revere.
Now he patted his horse's side,   60
Now gazed at the landscape far and near,
Then, impetuous, stamped the earth,
And turned and tightened his saddle-girth;
But mostly he watched with eager search
The belfry-tower of the Old North Church,   65
As it rose above the graves on the hill,
Lonely and spectral and somber and still.

The Paul Revere Event—Four Views (detail), 1968, LARRY RIVERS. Jason McCoy, Inc., New York City.

And lo! as he looks, on the belfry's height
A glimmer, and then a gleam of light!
He springs to the saddle, the bridle he turns,   70
But lingers and gazes, till full on his sight
A second lamp in the belfry burns!

A hurry of hoofs in a village street,
A shape in the moonlight, a bulk in the dark,
And beneath, from the pebbles, in passing, a spark   75
Struck out by a steed flying fearless and fleet:
That was all! And yet, through the gloom and the light
The fate of a nation was riding that night;
And the spark struck out by that steed, in his flight,
Kindled the land into flame with its heat.   80

He has left the village and mounted the steep,
And beneath him, tranquil and broad and deep,
Is the Mystic,[1] meeting the ocean tides;
And under the alders that skirt its edge,
Now soft on the sand, now loud on the ledge,   85
Is heard the tramp of his steed as he rides.

It was twelve by the village clock,
When he crossed the bridge into Medford town.
He heard the crowing of the cock,
And the barking of the farmer's dog,   90
And felt the damp of the river fog
That rises after the sun goes down.

It was one by the village clock,
When he galloped into Lexington.
He saw the gilded weathercock   95
Swing in the moonlight as he passed.
And the meeting-house windows, blank and bare,

---

1. **Mystic**–A river that flows into Boston harbor.

Gaze at him with a spectral glare,
As if they already stood aghast
At the bloody work they would look upon.   100

It was two by the village clock,
When he came to the bridge in Concord town.
He heard the bleating of the flock,
And the twitter of birds among the trees,
And felt the breath of the morning breeze   105
Blowing over the meadows brown.
And one was safe and asleep in his bed
Who at the bridge would be first to fall,
Who that day would be lying dead,
Pierced by a British musket-ball.   110

You know the rest. In the books you have read,
How the British Regulars fired and fled,—
How the farmers gave them ball for ball,
From behind each fence and farm-yard wall,
Chasing the red-coats down the lane,   115
Then crossing the fields to emerge again
Under the trees at the turn of the road,
And only pausing to fire and load.

So through the night rode Paul Revere;
And so through the night went his cry of alarm   120
To every Middlesex village and farm,—
A cry of defiance and not of fear,
A voice in the darkness, a knock at the door,
And a word that shall echo forevermore!
For, borne on the night-wind of the Past,   125
Through all our history, to the last,
In the hour of darkness and peril and need,
The people will waken and listen to hear
The hurrying hoof-beats of that steed,
And the midnight message of Paul Revere.   130

Henry Wadsworth Longfellow *(1807–1882)* was one of the most popular and respected poets of his time. One of his narrative poems, *The Song of Hiawatha,* sold more than a million copies in his lifetime. Longfellow was born in Portland, Maine, and graduated from Bowdoin College. He traveled and studied in Europe and then returned to the United States to teach college. Much of his life was spent at Harvard University, where he inspired students in their creative writing. Other well-known poems by Longfellow are *Evangeline* and "The Village Black-smith."

Developing Comprehension Skills

1. What were the date and time of Paul Revere's ride?

2. What were the signals Revere and his friend agreed on? Where did Revere watch for the signals? How did he feel as he watched?

3. Which signal was given? Did the British go by land or by sea?

4. Starting with Paul Revere's conversation with his friend, list the events of the poem in order.

5. What do you think is the purpose of this poem? Is it to teach history or to tell an exciting story? Explain your answer.

6. How well does the poem achieve its purpose? Support your opinion with examples.

Reading Literature: Poetry

1. **Recognizing Narrative Poetry.** "Paul Revere's Ride" has the elements of a short story: setting, character, plot, and conflict. What period of time is covered in the poem? Who is the main character? What conflict does the main character face?

2. **Identifying Setting.** The poem is particularly specific in terms of setting. Use the information in the poem to tell what route Paul Revere followed and what time he reached each place.

3. **Understanding Rhythm.** Choose any four lines in the poem. Copy them, leaving space between lines, and mark the stressed syllables. Count the stressed syllables in each line. Is the pattern regular? Would you describe the rhythm as slow or fast?

How does the rhythm reflect the subject of the poem?

4. **Examining Form.** The lengths of stanzas and the patterns of rhyme change throughout this poem. Examine the first, second, fourth, fifth, and sixth stanzas. For each stanza, tell the following:

a. the number of lines

b. the rhyme scheme, using letters of the alphabet

Look at how the form relates to what is happening in each stanza. For example, the first stanza has the fewest lines because it is the introduction. Give one more example that shows the connection between the form and the subject.

Vocabulary

Inferring Word Meaning. Some sentences contain context clues that provide clear and fairly exact meanings for unfamiliar words. Other sentences do not have context clues. The general context, though, can steer you in the right direction—you can tell which meanings do not fit, at least. Read each of the following excerpts from "Paul Revere's Ride." From the possible definitions after each excerpt, choose the definition for the underlined word that seems most reasonable to you.

1. Just as the moon rose over the bay,
   Where swinging wide at her moorings lay
   The *Somerset*, British man-of-war;

   a. a tract of open land with poor drainage

   b. something by which a ship is fixed in place, such as a cable

2. Till in the silence around him he hears
   The muster of men at the barrack door,
   The sound of arms, and the tramp of feet,
   And the measured tread of the grenadiers,

   a. soldiers   b. weapons

3. That he could hear, like a sentinel's tread,
   The watchful night-wind, as it went
   Creeping along from tent to tent,

   a. one who keeps watch   b. the wind

4. And the spark struck out by that steed, in his flight,
   Kindled the land into flame with its heat.

   a. made friendly   b. started a fire

5. Chasing the red-coats down the lane,
   Then crossing the fields to emerge again
   Under the trees at the turn of the road,

   a. exit   b. come into view

6. And so through the night went his cry of alarm
   To every Middlesex village and farm,—
   A cry of defiance and not of fear,

   a. joy   b. resistance

Critical Thinking

Distinguishing Facts. "Paul Revere's Ride" is a narrative poem, not an eyewitness account. Longfellow imagined some of the details about what people said and did and how they looked. Look up a factual account of Paul Revere's ride in an encyclopedia or history book. Then make a list of major events mentioned in the poem that in fact actually happened. Next, list five details that could have happened but that were probably made up by the poet.

Developing Writing Skills

1. **Comparing Poems.** You have read two long narrative poems, "Casey at the Bat" and "Paul Revere's Ride." Write a composition of two to four paragraphs comparing and contrasting the two poems.

   Prewriting. Choose two or three points from the following list to focus your discussion:

subject	mood
rhyme	rhythm
figurative language	theme
word choice	

   For each point, make notes on how it is used in each poem. Read your notes and decide whether the poems have more similarities or more differences.

   Drafting. Your topic sentence should indicate whether your composition will emphasize ways the poems are alike or ways they differ. Make sure that you have a clear focus for each paragraph as well as for the composition as a whole.

   Revising and Sharing. Find a classmate who wrote about at least one of the same points that you discussed. Read each other's compositions and discuss what kinds of ideas each of you had and how you supported your conclusions.

2. **Developing a Speaker in a Poem.** Write a short poem of four to twenty lines, rhymed or unrhymed, in which the speaker is Paul Revere's friend. Base your poem on "Paul Revere's Ride." You may use an incident mentioned in the original poem or focus on the friend's attitudes and feelings. The speaker should use "I" and "me." The following are three possibilities for your poem.

   a. a suspense-filled poem about sneaking up to the window of the British officers' meeting room to listen to their plans

   b. a humorous poem about being jealous of Paul for getting a long poem written about him, while your name isn't mentioned

   c. a proud poem about your part in the adventure

   Follow the steps in the process of writing: prewriting, drafting, revising, and sharing.

Western Wagons

STEPHEN VINCENT BENÉT
and ROSEMARY BENÉT

This poem captures the spirit of the men and women who settled the American West in the mid-to-late 1800's. Did they consider themselves heroic? As you read decide whether you would have wanted to join them.

They went with axe and rifle, when the trail was still to blaze,
They went with wife and children, in the prairie-schooner days,
With banjo and with frying pan—Susanna, don't you cry!
For I'm off to California to get rich out there or die![1]

We've broken land and cleared it, but we're tired of where we are.   5
They say that wild Nebraska is a better place by far.
There's gold in far Wyoming, there's black earth in Ioway,
So pack up kids and blankets, for we're moving out today!

The cowards never started and the weak died on the road,
And all across the continent the endless campfires glowed.   10
We'd taken land and settled—but a traveler passed by—
And we're going West tomorrow—Lordy, never ask us why!

We're going West tomorrow, where the promises can't fail.
O'er the hills in legions, boys, and crowd the dusty trail!
We shall starve and freeze and suffer. We shall die, and tame the lands.   15
But we're going West tomorrow, with our fortune in our hands.

---

1. **Susanna . . . die!**—An adaptation of words from the song "Oh, Susanna" by Stephen Foster.

Settlers moved West in great numbers after the Homestead Act of 1862. Denver Public Library.

Developing Comprehension Skills

1. What four states does the speaker say attracted the pioneers? Name two things those states were supposed to have.

2. What qualities does the poem suggest the pioneers showed? What two groups never made it to the West?

3. Does the poem show the pioneers move to the West in a positive or a negative way?

4. How does the attitude toward the move to the West in "Western Wagons" compare with the attitude expressed in "The Flower-Fed Buffaloes"?

Reading Literature: Poetry

1. **Identifying Speakers.** In the first three lines of the first stanza, the speaker uses "they" to talk about the pioneers. Who

seem to be the speakers in the rest of the poem?

2. **Analyzing Rhythm and Rhyme.** Copy the first stanza, leaving space between the lines. Mark the stressed and unstressed syllables in each line. How many stresses are in each line? Note any places where the pattern changes. Now write out the rhyme scheme that is used. Do the other stanzas use the same rhyme scheme? What is the overall effect of the rhythm and rhyme? If you know the song "Oh, Susanna," compare its rhythm with the rhythm in this poem.

Stephen Vincent Benét *(1898–1943)* was born in Bethlehem, Pennsylvania, to a family of famous writers. He studied literature at Yale University and then traveled to Paris to study and write. There he met his future wife, Rosemary, who was working as a newspaper reporter. Benét's works include novels, short stories, and poetry, as well as radio and film scripts. He won fame for the short story "The Devil and Daniel Webster" and a short novel in ballad form, *John Brown's Body.*

Rosemary Benét *(1900–1962)* worked as a journalist in Paris, France. In addition to writing newspaper stories, Benét wrote poetry and coauthored *A Book of Americans* with her husband.

Women

ALICE WALKER

This poem tells about the black women of the past who worked for a better future for their children. How does the speaker feel toward these women?

They were women then
My mama's generation
Husky of voice—Stout of
Step
With fists as well as   5
Hands
How they battered down
Doors
And ironed
Starched white   10
Shirts
How they led
Armies
Headragged Generals
Across mined   15
Fields
Booby-trapped
Ditches
To discover books
Desks   20
A place for us
How they knew what we
Must know
Without knowing a page
Of it   25
Themselves.

Mrs. Lucy Jefferson of Fort Scott, Kansas, 1949,
GORDON PARKS. Copyright © 1949 Gordon Parks.

Alice Walker (*born 1944*) was raised on a small farm in Georgia. She worked her way through college to become a teacher, lecturer, and award-winning writer. Walker, who has taught at several colleges, won an award in 1973 for *In Love and Trouble,* a collection of stories. *Revolutionary Petunias and Other Poems* was a National Book Award nominee in the same year. Her novel *The Color Purple* won the Pulitzer Prize and was made into an award-winning movie.

Developing Comprehension Skills

1. Are the women in the poem the same age as the speaker? What line in the poem gives the answer?

2. Throughout the poem the speaker is describing the strength of the women. Identify three phrases or lines that suggest this strength. What kinds of strength did these women have?

3. How does the speaker feel toward the women? Describe the speaker's feelings.

4. The speaker says that the older, uneducated women battled to get their children books and education. The speaker goes on to say that the women knew what the children "*must* know." Why did the women view education as so important?

Reading Literature: Poetry

1. **Recognizing Free Verse.** As you know, **free verse** does not usually have regular rhyme or rhythm. Does this poem have any regular rhyme or rhythm? Does it have rhyme at all? How is repetition used to establish a pattern in the poem?

   Notice that the poem is made up of short lines punctuated by only one period at the end of the last line. Describe the pace, or speed, of the lines. For example, are they slow and hesitating? Do they march? How does the pace of the lines fit the women described in the poem?

2. **Understanding Extended Metaphor.** As you have learned, an **extended metaphor** compares two unlike things in several ways. In lines 12 to 18 the metaphor of a battle is used to talk about the women's struggle. List the words and phrases that create the metaphor. What is the battle the women are fighting? How difficult does the battle seem to be? Does the speaker consider the women war heroes?

America the Beautiful

KATHARINE LEE BATES

Listen to the patterns of rhythm and rhyme in this poem. Try to picture the scenes the words create.

O beautiful for spacious skies,
   For amber waves of grain,
For purple mountain majesties
   Above the fruited plain!
     America! America!   5
   God shed His grace on thee
And crown thy good with brotherhood
   From sea to shining sea!

O beautiful for pilgrim feet,
   Whose stern, impassioned stress   10
A thoroughfare for freedom beat
   Across the wilderness!
     America! America!
   God mend thine every flaw,
Confirm thy soul in self-control,   15
   Thy liberty in law!

O beautiful for heroes proved
   In liberating strife,
Who more than self their country loved,
   And mercy more than life!   20
     America! America!
   May God thy gold refine
Till all success be nobleness
   And every gain divine!

O beautiful for patriot dream   25
   That sees beyond the years
Thine alabaster cities gleam
   Undimmed by human tears!
     America! America!
   God shed His grace on thee   30
And crown thy good with brotherhood
   From sea to shining sea!

The Grand Canyon of the Yellowstone, 1893–1901, THOMAS MORAN. National Museum of American Art, Smithsonian Institution, Washington, D.C., Gift of George G. Pratt.

Developing Comprehension Skills

1. This poem can be seen as an answer to the question, "What makes America beautiful?" Use the first line of each stanza to complete the following sentence: America is beautiful for _____.

2. Reread the third stanza. Based on your knowledge of American history, what can you infer about the kind of wars the heroes fought in? In the final stanza, what kind of society do the patriots dream about?

3. This poem was written to be set to music as a patriotic song. How are feelings of patriotism expressed in the poem? Identify three examples.

4. Do you think "America the Beautiful" describes America the way it once was, the way it actually is now, or the way it should be but is not yet?

Reading Literature: Poetry

1. **Understanding Metaphor.** Explain what is meant by each of these excerpts:
   a. A thoroughfare for freedom
   b. May God thy gold refine
      Till all success be nobleness

2. **Identifying Rhyme Scheme.** Each stanza has the same rhyme scheme. Using letters, tell what it is. (In the first stanza, consider

the words *skies* and *majesties* as rhymes.) Notice that the fifth line in each stanza does not rhyme with any other line. Why is this line important in each stanza?

3. **Recognizing Internal Rhyme.** When two words in the same line rhyme, the poet is using **internal rhyme.** Find four examples of internal rhyme in this poem. What pattern do you notice?

Vocabulary

1. **Understanding Multiple Meanings.** As you know, a single word can have several different meanings. Usually the general context of a line or stanza will indicate the part of speech and the correct meaning. Each of the words given below has a different meaning when used as a noun than it does when used as a verb. Look up each word in a dictionary and read the definitions. Then locate the word in the poem, and tell which of the definitions applies.

a. "Western Wagons": blaze, place
b. "Women": step
c. "America the Beautiful": shed, crown, beat

2. **Analyzing a Concept.** Many of the poems in this chapter deal with important concepts. The poets have used specific words and techniques to express those concepts. Listed below are several concepts you have read about in the poems. Choose one concept and analyze what it means. Look up the word in a dictionary. Then read the poem or poems that talk about the concept. You might want to meet with two or three classmates to discuss the concept. Finally, make a list of all the aspects you have thought about. Be prepared to explain your analysis in a class discussion.

happiness   courage   patriotism
beauty   hope

Katharine Lee Bates *(1859–1929)* was born in Massachusetts and graduated from Wellesley College, where she later taught. Bates became famous for writing the words for the patriotic song "America the Beautiful." The melody for the song was written by Samuel A. Ward. Bates was also known for her short stories and travel books.

Developing Writing Skills

1. **Analyzing a Poem.** "America the Beautiful" praises Americans who worked and sacrificed to create a better country. Several other poems have described the actions and courage of some of those people. Choose "Paul Revere's Ride," "Western Wagons," or "Women." Write a paragraph discussing how the poet presents the heroes or heroines of the poem.

   Prewriting. Think about the answers to questions such as these: Does the poem tell about a short period in the person's life or the person's entire life? Does it describe a single heroic act or a pattern of behavior? Does it focus on specific places and actions or suggest a general pattern of activity? What quality or qualities of the character does the poem concentrate on? How does the poet seem to feel toward the subject? admiring, amused, matter-of-fact?

   Drafting. As you write your paragraph, be sure that you focus on how the poet presents the main character or characters. Avoid discussing the history you know or your reaction to the poem.

   Revising and Sharing. Reread your draft. You should be able to answer "yes" to the following questions. If you cannot, revise your draft.

   a. Do I clearly state the main point I want to make?
   b. Have I included enough details about the way the character is presented in the poem?
   c. Does every sentence in the draft develop the main idea?

2. **Writing About a Hero.** Who is one of your personal heroes or heroines? What specific quality or qualities do you admire in him or her? Write a short tribute to that person. You may use any form: paragraph, rhymed poem, free verse. Include details that will show clearly what makes the person special. Follow the steps in the process of writing: prewriting, drafting, revising, and sharing. For more help refer to page 623 in the handbook, Guidelines for the Process of Writing.

Chapter 5 Review

Using Your Skills in Reading Poetry

Read the following lines from the poem "City" by Langston Hughes. Then follow these directions.

1. Using letters of the alphabet, chart the rhyme scheme of the poem.
2. Mark the stressed syllables in the poem. Is the poem written in a regular, steady rhythm or in free verse?
3. Identify one metaphor in the poem. To what is the city being compared? How are the two things alike?
4. What five words in the poem are alliterative?

> In the morning the city
> Spreads its wings
> Making a song
> In stone that sings.

Using Your Comprehension Skills

Read this paragraph from "Langston Terrace" by Eloise Greenfield and Lessie Jones Little. Then answer the following questions. Use inferences based on details in the paragraph. What do the writers value most about a place to live? Did the writers have an easy life? Do the writers relate well to other people?

> For us, Langston Terrace wasn't an in-between place. It was a growing-up place, a good growing-up place. Neighbors who cared, family and friends, and a lot of fun. Life was good. Not perfect, but good. We knew about problems, heard about them, saw them, lived through some hard ones ourselves, but our community wrapped itself around us, put itself between us and the hard knocks, to cushion the blows.

Using Your Vocabulary Skills

Read the following sentences based on selections in Chapter Six. Then use context to decide which meaning of the underlined word is being used.

1. Colonel Carter gave me an <u>unbroken</u> horse to train.
   a. uninterrupted   b. not tamed

2. My experience showed me that <u>nature</u>, the world of animals and plants, is not always kind.
   a. all things except those made by human beings
   b. a natural desire or function

3. Others noticed how the youth <u>conducted</u> himself during the recital.
   a. transmitted   b. behaved

Using Your Skills in Study and Research

As you know, an **anthology** is a collection of poems by one or more poets. Use the card or computer catalog in your school or local library to find an anthology of poetry by one of the poets in this chapter. Does the anthology include all of the poet's works or only some? Are the poems arranged according to when they were written, by subject, or in some other way? Is there any information about the poet included? List the titles of three poems in the anthology.

Using Your Writing Skills

Choose one of the writing assignments below.

1. Select the poem in this chapter that you liked best. Write one paragraph giving three reasons for your choice. Present your reasons in increasing order of importance.

2. Write a poem about something you especially enjoy or especially hate to do. Use free verse or a regular rhythm and rhyme scheme. Your poem may be serious or humorous. Make your poem no longer than twelve lines. Be sure to include at least one figure of speech.

CHAPTER SIX

Nonfiction

Reading Literature

Nonfiction

Nonfiction is writing that tells about real people, places, and events. Nonfiction is based on facts. In this important way it is different from fiction, which comes from the writer's imagination.

The History of Nonfiction

Nonfiction has existed as long as people have had news to tell or important facts to remember. Before writing was invented, listeners had to depend on the person reporting the news or facts. The first purpose of writing was to put news and facts into a more permanent form.

Nonfiction includes every kind of writing that has not come from imagination. Whenever people have needed to record, explain, or inform, they have written nonfiction. Here are some kinds of nonfiction:

1. Records of the lives, work, and words of famous and not-so-famous people
2. Accounts of a person's own life
3. Letters telling news and private thoughts
4. Important speeches given by talented speakers
5. Essays telling the writer's thoughts and opinions
6. Reports about ideas and information from research
7. Newspaper and magazine articles recording important events and giving useful information
8. Special reports for television and radio

The first section of this chapter includes selections from two forms of nonfiction, the autobiography and the biography.

An **autobiography** is the story of a person's life written by that person. In an autobiography, the writer shares the most important people, events, and feelings in his or her life.

A **biography** is the story of a person's life written by someone else. A biographer gathers information from letters, diaries, articles, and books. A good biographer tries to be fair in writing about his or her subject. The biographer presents both weaknesses and strengths.

The Elements of Nonfiction

Point of View. Some works of nonfiction are written from the **first-person point of view.** The writers take part in the action. They use pronouns such as *I, we,* and *me.* Other works are written from the **third-person point of view**. The writers do not take part in the action. They use pronouns such as *he* and *she.*

Tone. The **tone** of a piece of writing is the writer's attitude toward his or her subject. For example, a writer's tone might be admiring or angry, sad or amused.

Style. **Style** is the way in which a work of literature is written. Choice of words, length of sentences, and use of repetition help to make a writer's style. Style varies according to a writer's subject and purpose.

How to Read Nonfiction

1. Decide who is speaking. Is the piece written from the first-person or the third-person point of view?
2. What is the writer's attitude toward the subject? Is the writer admiring? critical?
3. Make use of your own experience with the topic. What you know will help you understand what you read.

Comprehension Skills

Opinions and Slanted Writing

When people feel strongly about a topic, they often include their opinions in their writing. Sometimes they identify their opinions. Other times, though, they mix their opinions with the facts. Watch for the ways in which writers try to persuade readers to agree with their opinions.

Fact and Opinion. An opinion is one person's belief. It may or may not be based on facts. Opinions are often stated as if they were facts. For example, "February is the shortest month" is a fact. "December is the most dreary month" is an opinion.

If a statement is really a fact, it can be proved to be true. You can check it in a source such as an encyclopedia. Sometimes you can observe that it is true.

Slanted Writing. Sometimes it may seem as if a writer is reporting only facts. Even facts, however, can be presented so that they favor one side of a topic. A writer who enjoys football, for example, may report only the exciting moments of a game. A writer who does not like the sport may report that the weather was cold and wet and that the crowd was rude.

When writing "leans" to one side of an argument or shows only one view of an event, the writer has used **slanted writing**. Slanted writing is also called **biased writing**.

Connotation and Denotation. Writers can slant their writing not only through their choice of facts but through their choice of words with desired connotations. The **connotation** of a word is the combination of ideas and emotions that the word brings to your mind. A word's connotation is not the same as its dictionary meaning, or **denotation**.

Connotations can be positive (good), negative (bad), or neutral (neither good nor bad). Even when words are close in meaning, their connotations can differ widely. The underlined words in the following sentences are similar in denotative meaning. Notice how the picture in your mind changes with each sentence.

1. The child <u>put</u> the toys on the table. (Neutral)
2. The child <u>arranged</u> the toys on the table. (Positive)
3. The child <u>threw</u> the toys on the table. (Negative)

Exercises: Identifying Opinions and Slanted Writing

A. Decide which sentences state facts and which state opinions.

1. December goes by too quickly.
2. Abraham Lincoln was our sixteenth President.
3. Training a horse takes care and effort.
4. Rick was a star that day.

B. Match each sentence with a positive slant to a similar sentence with a negative slant. Choose two words from each sentence and identify each word as having a positive, negative, or neutral connotation.

Sentences with a Positive Slant
1. Concerned citizens visited the judge's home.
2. The children loved to make up wonderful stories.
3. Helen's teacher was ready to work hard and try new ideas.

Sentences with a Negative Slant
1. The children told lies all the time.
2. Helen's new teacher was inexperienced.
3. A gang of rebels attacked the judge's home.

$\mathcal{V}$ocabulary Skills

Reference Sources

When you come across an unfamiliar word, you should first try to figure out its meaning from context clues or word parts. If this approach does not help, turn to a reference source. The dictionary and the glossary are two reference sources that will help you find the meaning of a new word. Another reference source, the thesaurus, will help you find words that are close in meaning to a given word.

The Dictionary. The **dictionary** lists words in alphabetical order and gives useful information about them. Each word that is listed is called an **entry word**. For each entry word, the dictionary gives some or all of the following information.

1. **How to divide the word into syllables.** The syllables may be separated by a space or by a centered dot: for est, for·est.

2. **How to pronounce the word.** The pronunciation is usually given in parentheses: (fôr′ist). The **respelling** identifies the sounds in the word. Each dictionary has a pronunciation key that helps you pronounce each sound correctly. **Accent marks** (′), (′) within a respelling show which syllables to stress.

3. **The part of speech of the word.** The **parts of speech** are abbreviated as follows:

n.	noun	*pro.*	pronoun	*prep.*	preposition
v.	verb	*adv.*	adverb	*conj.*	conjunction
		adj.	adjective	*interj.*	interjection

4. **The origin of the word.** The word may have come into the English language in one of a number of different ways. Its **origin**, or source, is given within brackets such as these: [ ].

5. **The definition of the word.** If there is more than one **definition**, each definition is assigned a number.

The Glossary.   A **glossary** in the back of the book lists all the words in that book that may be unfamiliar. The glossary lists words in alphabetical order and gives pronunciations and definitions.

The Thesaurus.   A **thesaurus** lists groups of words with similar meanings. A thesaurus may give synonyms for a word, or it may list words and phrases related to one subject. Before using a thesaurus, read the directions in the front of the book.

Exercises: Using Reference Sources

A. Use this entry from *Webster's New World Dictionary, Student Edition* to answer the questions below.

> **en·gaged** (in gājd'), *adj.* [Fr. and OFr. *engagier*] **1.** pledged. **2.** pledged in marriage. **3.** occupied; employed; busy. **4.** involved in combat, as troops. **5.** attached to or partly set into (a wall, etc.): as engaged columns. **6.** interlocked; meshed; in gear.

1. How is *engaged* divided into syllables?

2. Is the accent on the first or the second syllable?

3. What part of speech is *engaged*?

4. What is the meaning of *engaged* in each of these sentences?
   a. Now we are engaged in a great civil war.
   b. The couple was engaged for six months before the wedding.

B. Copy these sentences. Fill in each blank with the word *dictionary, glossary,* or *thesaurus*.

1. A _____ lists words in alphabetical order and gives pronunciations, parts of speech, origins, and definitions.

2. A _____ lists groups of related words.

3. A _____ lists and defines the new or unfamiliar words in one book in alphabetical order.

Autobiographies

An **autobiography** is the story a person writes about his or her own life. An autobiography may tell a person's whole life story up to the point of writing, or only parts of it. Most autobiographies are written from the first-person point of view.

An autobiography can give you information you cannot find anywhere else. You learn about the subject's feelings and reasons for certain actions. You also get a glimpse of how the person thought and expressed himself or herself.

Rhododendron Bower, 1920, CHARLES C. CURRAN. Collection of Fred and Maureen Radl, Cragsmoor, New York.

I Get a Colt to Break In

LINCOLN STEFFENS

In this selection, Lincoln Steffens describes an enjoyable time in his boyhood. He also tells some of his private thoughts and feelings. What are some of these thoughts and feelings? Do you sometimes feel the same way?

Colonel Carter gave me a colt. I had my pony, and my father meanwhile had bought a pair of black carriage horses and a cow, all of which I had to attend to when we had no "man." And servants were hard to get and keep in those days; the women married, and the men soon quit service to seize opportunities always opening. My hands were pretty full, and so was the stable. But Colonel Carter seemed to think that he had promised me a horse. He had not; I would have known it if he had. No matter. He thought he had, and maybe he did promise himself to give me one. That was enough. The kind of man that led immigrant trains across the continent and delivered them safe, sound, and together where he promised, would keep his word. One day he drove over from Stockton, leading a two-year-old which he brought to our front door and turned over to me as mine. Such a horse!

She was a cream-colored mare with a black forelock, mane, and tail and a black stripe along the middle of her back. Tall, slender, high-spirited, I thought then—I think now that she was the most beautiful of horses. Colonel Carter had bred and reared her with me and my uses in mind. She was a careful cross of a mustang mare and a thoroughbred stallion, with the stamina of the wild horse and the speed and grace of the racer. And she had a sense of fun. As Colonel Carter got down out of his buggy and went up to her, she snorted, reared, flung her head high in the air, and, coming down beside him, tucked her nose affectionately under his arm.

"I have handled her a lot," he said. "She is as kind as a kitten, but she is as sensitive as a lady. You can spoil her by one mistake. If you ever lose your temper, if you ever abuse her, she will be ruined forever. And she is unbroken. I might have had her broken to ride for you, but I didn't want to. I want you to do it. I have taught her to lead, as you see; had to, to get her over here. But here she is, an unbroken colt; yours. You take and you break her. You're only a boy, but if you break this colt right, you'll be a man—a young man, but a man. And I'll tell you how."

Now, out West, as everybody knows, they break in a horse by riding out to him in his wild state, lassoing, throwing, and saddling him; then they let him up, frightened and shocked, with a yelling bronco-buster astride of him. The wild beast bucks, the cowboy drives his spurs into him, and off they go, jumping, kicking, rearing, falling, till by the weight of the man, the lash, and the rowels, the horse is broken—in body and spirit. This was not the way I was to break my colt.

"You must break her to ride without her ever knowing it," Colonel Carter said. "You feed and you clean her—you, not the stable man. You lead her out to water and to walk. You put her on a long rope and let her play, calling her to you and gently pulling on the rope. Then you turn her loose in the grass lot there and, when she has romped till tired, call her. If she won't come, leave her. When she wants water or food, she will run to your call, and you will pet and feed and care for her." He went on for half an hour, advising me in great detail how to proceed. I wanted to begin right away. He laughed. He let me lead her around to the stable,

water her, and put her in the stable and feed her.

There I saw my pony. My father, sisters, and Colonel Carter saw me stop and look at my pony.

"What'll you do with him?" one of my sisters asked. I was bewildered for a moment. What should I do with the little red horse? I decided at once.

"You can have him," I said to my sisters.

"No," said Colonel Carter, "not yet. You can give your sisters the pony by and by, but you'll need him till you have taught the colt to carry you and a saddle— months; and you must not hurry. You must learn patience, and you will if you give the colt time to learn it, too. Patience and control. You can't control a horse unless you can control yourself. Can you shoot?" he asked suddenly.

I couldn't. I had a gun and I had used it some, but it was a rifle, and I could not bring down with it such game as there was around Sacramento—birds and hares. Colonel Carter looked at my father, and I caught the look. So did my father. I soon had a shotgun. But at the time Colonel Carter turned to me and said:

"Can't shoot straight, eh? Do you know what that means? That means that you can't control a gun, and that means that you can't control yourself, your eye, your hands, your nerves. You are wriggling now. I tell you that a good shot is always a good man. He may be a 'bad man' too, but he is quiet, strong, steady in speech, gait, and mind. No matter, though. If you break in this colt right, if you teach her her paces, she will teach you to shoot and be quiet."

He went off downtown with my father, and I started away with my colt. I fed, I led, I cleaned her, gently, as if she were made of glass; she was playful and willing, a delight. When Colonel Carter came home with my father for supper, he questioned me.

"You should not have worked her today," he said. "She has come all the way from Stockton and must be tired. Yes, yes, she would not show fatigue; too fine for that, and too young to be wise. You have got to think for her, consider her as you would your sisters."

Sisters! I thought; I had never considered my sisters. It was just as if he had read my thought. But he went on to draw on my imagination a centaur; the colt as a horse's body—me, a boy, as the head and brains of one united creature. I liked that. I would be that. I and the colt: a centaur.

After Colonel Carter was gone home, I went to work on my new horse. The old one, the pony, I used only for business: to go to fires, to see my friends, run errands, and go hunting with my new shotgun. But the game that had all my attention was the breaking in of the colt, the beautiful cream-colored mare, who soon knew me—and my pockets. I carried sugar to reward her when she did right, and she discovered where I carried it; so did the pony, and when I was busy they would push their noses into my pockets, both of which were torn down a good deal of the time. But the colt learned. I taught her to run around a circle, turn and go the other way at a signal. My sisters helped me. I held the long rope and the whip (for signaling), while one of the girls led the colt; it was hard work for them, but they took it in turns. One would lead the colt round and round till I snapped the whip; then she would turn, turning the colt, till the colt did it all by herself. The colt was very quick. She shook hands with each of her four feet. She let us run under her, back and forth. She was slow only to carry me. Following Colonel Carter's instructions, I began by laying my arm or a surcingle over her back. If she trembled, I drew it slowly off. When she could abide it, I tried buckling it, tighter and tighter. I laid over her, too, a blanket, folded at first, then open, and, at last, I slipped up on her myself, sat there a second, and, as she trembled, slid off. My sisters held her for me, and when I could get up and sit there a moment or two, I tied her at a block, and we, my sisters and I, made a procession of mounting and dismounting. She soon got used to this and would let us slide off over her rump, but it was a long, long time before she would carry me.

That we practiced by leading her along a high curb where I could get on as she walked, ride a few steps, and then, as she felt me and crouched, slip off. She never did learn to carry a girl on her back; my sisters had to lead her while I rode. This was not purposeful. I don't know just how it happened, but I do remember the first time I rode on my colt all the way around the lot and how, when I put one of the girls up, she refused to repeat. She shuddered, shook, and frightened them off.

While we were breaking in the colt, a circus came to town. The ring was across the street from our house. Wonderful! I lived in that circus for a week. I saw the show but once, but I marked the horse-trainers, and in the mornings when they were not too busy, I told them about my colt, showed her to them, and asked them how to train her to do circus tricks. With their hints I taught the colt to stand up on her hind legs, kneel, lie down, and balance on a small box. This last was easier than it looked. I put her first on a low, big box and taught her to turn on it; then got a little smaller box upon which she repeated what she did on the big one. By and by we had her so that she would step on a high box so small that her four feet were almost touching, and there also she would turn.

The circus man gave me one hint that was worth all the other tricks put together. "You catch her doing something herself that looks good," he said, "and then you keep her at it." It was thus that I taught her to bow to people. The first day I rode her out on to the streets was a proud one for me and for the colt, too, apparently.

She did not walk, she danced; perhaps she was excited, nervous; anyhow I liked the way she threw up her head, champed at the bit, and went dancing, prancing down the street. Everybody stopped to watch us, and so, when she began to sober down, I picked her up again with heel and rein, saying, "Here's people, Lady," and she would show off to my delight. By constant repetition I had her so trained that she would singlefoot, head down, along a country road till we came to a house or a group of people. Then I'd say, "People, Lady," and up would go her head, and her feet would dance.

But the trick that set the town talking was her bowing to anyone I spoke to. "Lennie Steffens' horse bows to you," people said, and she did. I never told how it was done; by accident. Dogs used to run out at us, and the colt enjoyed it; she kicked at them sometimes with both hind hoofs. I joined her in the game, and being able to look behind more conveniently than she could, I watched the dogs until they were in range, then gave the colt a signal to kick. "Kick, gal," I'd say, and tap her ribs with my heel. We used to get dogs together that way; the colt would kick them over and over and leave them yelping in the road. Well, one day when I met a girl I knew, I lifted my hat, probably muttered a "Good day," and I must have touched the colt with my heel. Anyway, she dropped her head and kicked—not much; there was no dog near, so she had

Street scene in Sacramento, 1878. Culver Pictures, New York.

responded to my unexpected signal by what looked like a bow. I caught the idea and kept her at it. Whenever I wanted to bow to a girl or anybody else, instead of saying "Good day," I muttered "Kick, gal," spurred her lightly, and—the whole centaur bowed and was covered with glory and conceit.

Yes, conceit. I was full of it, and the colt was quite as bad. One day my chum Hjalmar came into town on his Black Bess, blanketed. She had had a great fistula cut out of her shoulder, and she had to be kept warm. I expected to see her weak and dull, but no, the good old mare was champing and dancing, like my colt.

"What is it makes her so?" I asked, and Hjalmar said he didn't know, but he thought she was proud of her blanket. A great idea. I had a gaudy horse blanket. I put it on the colt and I could hardly hold her. We rode down the main street together, both horses and boys so full of vanity that everybody stopped to smile. We thought they admired us, and maybe they did. But some boys on the street gave us another angle. They, too, stopped and looked, and as we passed, one of them said, "Think you're something, don't you?"

Spoilsport!

We did, as a matter of fact; we thought we were something. The recognition of it dashed us for a moment; not for long, and the horses paid no heed.

We pranced, the black and the yellow, all the way down J Street, up K street, and agreed that we'd do it again, often. Only, I said, we wouldn't use blankets. If the horses were proud of a blanket, they'd be proud of anything unusually conspicuous. We tried a flower next time. I fixed a big rose on my colt's bridle just under her ear and it was great—she pranced downtown with her head turned, literally, to show off her flower. We had to change the decoration from time to time, put on a ribbon, or a bell, or a feather, but really, it was not necessary for my horse. Old Black Bess needed an incentive to act up, but all I had to do to my horse was to pick up the reins, touch her with my heel, and say, "People"; she would dance from one side of the street to the other, asking to be admired. As she was. As we were.

I would ride down to my father's store, jump off my prancing colt in the middle of the street, and run up into the shop. The colt, free, would stop short, turn, and follow me right up on the sidewalk, unless I bade her wait. If anyone approached her while I was gone, she would snort, rear, and strike. No stranger could get near her. She became a frightened, frightening animal, and yet when I came into sight she would run to me, put her head down, and as I straddled her neck, she would throw up her head and pitch me into my seat, facing backward, of course. I whirled around right, and off we'd go, the vainest boy and the proudest horse in the state.

"Hey, give me a ride, will you?" some boy would ask. "Sure," I'd say, and jump down and watch that boy try to catch and mount my colt. He couldn't. Once a cowboy wanted to try her, and he caught her; he dodged her forefeet, grabbed the reins, and in one spring was on her back. I never did that again. My colt reared, then bucked, and, as the cowboy kept his seat, she shuddered, sank to the ground, and rolled over. He slipped aside and would have risen with her, but I was alarmed and begged him not to. She got up at my touch and followed me so close that she stepped on my heel and hurt me. The cowboy saw the point.

"If I were you, kid," he said, "I'd never let anybody mount that colt. She's too good."

That, I think, was the only mistake I made in the rearing of Colonel Carter's gift-horse. My father differed from me. He discovered another error or sin, and thrashed me for it. My practice was to work hard on a trick, privately, and when it was perfect, let him see it. I would have the horse out in our vacant lot doing it as he came home to supper. One evening, as he approached the house, I was standing, whip in hand, while the colt, quite free, was stepping carefully over the bodies of a lot of girls, all my sisters and all their girl friends. My father did not express the admiration I expected; he was frightened and furious. "Stop that," he called, and he came running around into the lot, took the whip, and lashed me with it. I tried to explain; the girls tried to help me explain.

I had seen in the circus a horse that stepped thus over a row of prostrate clowns. It looked dangerous for the clowns, but the trainer had told me how to do it. You begin with logs, laid out a certain distance apart; the horse walks over them under your lead, and whenever he touches one you rebuke him. By and by he will learn to step with such care that he never trips. Then you substitute clowns. I had no clowns, but I did get logs, and, with the girls helping, we taught the colt to step over the obstacles even at a trot. Walking, she touched nothing. All ready thus with the logs, I had my sisters lie down in the grass, and again and again the colt stepped over and among them. None was ever touched. My father would not listen to any of this. He just walloped me, and, when he was tired or satisfied and I was in tears, I blubbered a short excuse: "They were only girls." And he whipped me some more.

My father was not given to whipping; he did it very seldom, but he did it hard when he did it at all. My mother was just the opposite. She did not whip me, but she often smacked me, and she had a most annoying habit of thumping me on the head with her thimbled finger. This I resented more than my father's thorough-going thrashings, and I can tell why now. I would be playing Napoleon and, as I was reviewing my Old Guard, she would crack my skull with that thimble. No doubt I was in the way; it took a lot of furniture and sisters to represent properly a victorious army; and you might think as my mother did that a thimble is a small weapon. But imagine Napoleon at the height of his power, the ruler of the world on parade, getting a sharp rap on his crown from a woman's thimble. No. My father's way was more appropriate. It was hard. "I'll attend to you in the morning," he would say, and I lay awake wondering which of my crimes he had discovered. I know what it is to be sentenced to be shot at sunrise. And it hurt in the morning, when he was not angry but very fresh and strong. But, you see, he walloped me in my own person; he never humiliated Napoleon or my knighthood, as my mother did. And I learned something from his discipline, something useful.

I learned what tyranny is and the pain of being misunderstood and wronged, or, if you please, understood and set right. They are pretty much the same. He and most parents and teachers do not break in their children as carefully as I broke in my colt.

They haven't the time that I had, and they have not some other incentives I had. I saw this that day when I rubbed my sore legs. He had to explain to my indignant mother what had happened. When he had told it his way, I gave my version: how long and cautiously I had been teaching my horse to walk over logs and girls. And having shown how sure I was of myself and the colt, while my mother was boring into his silence with one of her reproachful looks, I said something that hit my father hard.

"I taught the colt that trick, I have taught her all that you see she knows, without whipping her. I have never struck her; not once. Colonel Carter said I mustn't, and I haven't."

And my mother, backing me up, gave him a rap: "There," she said, "I told you so." He walked off, looking like a thimble-rapped Napoleon.

Lincoln Steffens (*1866–1936*) wrote his autobiography in 1931, when he was sixty-five years old. By that time, he had achieved fame as a writer, lecturer, and editor. Steffens was born in San Francisco. He attended the University of California and continued his studies in Europe. His special interests were politics and the problems of business and labor.

Developing Comprehension Skills

1. Why did Colonel Carter give Lennie a colt?

2. How did Lennie teach the colt to balance and turn on a small box?

3. On page 416, paragraph 2, you learned how most horses were broken to ride in the Old West. Compare that way of breaking a horse to the way Colonel Carter told Lennie to break his new colt. What is the difference in the trainers' attitudes? How does the effect on the horse differ?

4. Why did Lennie tell his parents how he taught his colt to step over the girls?

5. Lennie's father whipped him for having his colt step over his sisters. Lennie defended himself by saying, "They were only girls." On the same page (page 421), Lennie described how it shamed him to get "a sharp rap on [his] crown from a woman's thimble." From these two examples, what can you tell about Lennie's opinion about girls and women when he was young?

6. In telling about his parents' ways of disciplining him, Lennie says, "My father's way was more appropriate." Is this statement a fact or an opinion? How do you know? Do you agree with Lennie? Why or why not?

Reading Literature: Nonfiction

1. **Identifying Point of View.** In **first-person point of view,** the narrator takes part in the action. In **third-person point of view,** the narrator is outside the action. Is this selection narrated from the first-person or the third-person point of view? Is the narrator taking part in the action or not? How does the point of view help you know whether the selection is from a biography or an autobiography?

2. **Examining Nonfiction Writing.** This selection is presented in the nonfiction chapter, so you know it is based on real happenings. Can you tell from the selection itself that it is nonfiction rather than fiction? How is the selection similar to fiction? How is it different from fiction?

3. **Describing Tone.** **Tone** refers to a writer's attitude toward his or her subject. In the introduction to this chapter, you read that nonfiction writings can have different tones. The tone can be serious—admiring, for instance, or angry. Or it can be carefree and relaxed. How would you describe the tone of this selection? Give examples from the selection to support your answer.

Vocabulary

1. **Choosing the Correct Respelling.** You know that a dictionary and a glossary show how words are pronounced. The words are respelled with special symbols to stand for certain sounds. The pronunciation key in the dictionary or glossary explains these respelling symbols by using key words. Here is the pronunciation key from the glossary of this book.

---

at, āte, fär; pen, ēqual; sit, mīne; sō, côrn, join;
took, fool, our; us, turn; chill, shop, thick,
they, sing; zh *in* measure; 'l *in* idle;
ə *in* alive, cover, family, compare, circus.

Use the key to help you pronounce each respelling in the following list. Then read the following sentences based on the selection. Choose the respelling of the word that would make sense in each sentence. Write the word that the respelling stands for.

(1) (sen′sə tiv) (4) (sen′tôr)
(2) (stal′yən) (5) (shoog′ər)
(3) (pā′shəns)

a. The horse was a cross of a mustang mare and a thoroughbred _____.

b. The horse and I were like one united creature. We were a _____.

c. Colonel Carter warned that if I lost my temper and abused the _____ horse, she would be ruined forever.

d. Colonel Carter said that training the colt would take much _____.

e. Lennie carried _____ to reward Lady.

2. **Accent Marks and the Schwa.** Each of the words in exercise 1 has one accent mark. The respellings of some words found in the selection have more than one accent. Here is an example:

(ad′mə rā′shən)

The heavier accent is called the **primary accent**. That syllable gets the most stress. The lighter accent is called the **secondary accent**. That syllable gets a lighter stress.

Look again at the words in exercise 1. In some of them you see this symbol: ə. This is called the **schwa**. It represents the sound of the vowel heard in the unaccented syllable.

Find these words in a dictionary. Write them in syllables. Mark the primary and

secondary accents. Underline any syllables that have schwa sounds.

a. decoration d. imagination
b. thoroughbred e. repetition
c. opportunity

Critical Thinking

Understanding Connotation. In the introduction to this chapter, you learned that the connotations of words can be positive (good), negative (bad), or neutral (neither bad nor good). In the following sentence from the selection, the writer tells the reader how bad it feels to be misunderstood. Read the sentence. List the words with positive connotations and the words with negative connotations. Then tell what the writer means in the sentence.

I learned what tyranny is and the pain of being misunderstood and wronged, or, if you please, understood and set right; they are pretty much the same.

Study and Research

Taking Notes. Go to the library. Use the card catalog or computer system to find at least one book on training a horse or some other animal. Take notes on one important part of training: for instance, teaching the animal tricks. Be sure to record the title of the book, the author, and the chapter and page from which you take your notes. You may take your notes on notebook paper.

Developing Writing Skills

1. **Understanding the Author's Purpose.** This selection is mostly about training a colt. However, at the end, Steffens also tells his opinions about disciplining a child. Write a paragraph explaining his views about this subject. Include what he thought of his mother's method and his father's method.

    Prewriting. Arrange your prewriting notes in three columns. In the first column, list words and phrases that describe Lennie's method of disciplining his colt. In the other two columns, list words and phrases describing his parents' methods of discipline and Steffens's feelings about these methods.

    Drafting. When drafting your paragraph, be sure to include a topic sentence, an explanation of each method of discipline, and reasons for Steffens's view toward each method.

    Revising and Sharing. Proofread your draft. Then share it with a classmate. Ask if any sentences are unclear. Revise, using your classmate's comments as guidelines.

2. **Inferring from a Character's Words and Actions.** In this selection, the reader learns about the writer from the writer's words and actions. Write a paragraph describing in your own words what Lincoln Steffens was like as a boy. Use passages from the story to support your description. Follow the steps in the process of writing: prewriting, drafting, and revising and sharing.

3. **Writing Autobiography.** Lincoln Steffens was proud of his accomplishment in training his colt. Write a story about something you have done that you are proud of. Your story should be at least two paragraphs long. Remember to complete the steps in the process of writing.

Reb Asher the Dairyman

ISAAC BASHEVIS SINGER

Sometimes, a family needs a friend. Read to find out what makes the writer's friend so special.

There are some people in this world who are simply born good. Such was Reb Asher the dairyman. God had endowed him with many, many gifts. He was tall, broad, strong, had a black beard, large black eyes, and the voice of a lion. On the New Year and the Day of Atonement[1] he served as cantor[2] of the main prayer for the congregation that met in our house, and it was his voice that attracted many of the worshippers. He did this without payment, although he could have commanded sizable fees from some of the larger synagogues.[3] It was his way of helping my father earn a livelihood for the holidays. And as if this were not enough, Reb Asher was always doing something for us in one way or another. No one sent my father as generous a Purim[4] gift as did Reb Asher the dairyman. When Father found himself in great straits and could not pay the rent, he sent me to Reb Asher to borrow the money. And Asher never said no, nor did he ever pull a wry face. He simply reached into his pants pocket and pulled out a handful of paper money and silver. Neither did he limit himself to helping out my father. He gave charity in all directions. This simple Jew, who with great difficulty plowed through a chapter of the Mishnah,[5] lived his entire life on the highest ethical plane. What others preached, he practiced.

He was no millionaire, he was not even wealthy, but he had a "comfortable income," as my father would put it. I myself often bought milk, butter, cheese, clabber, and cream in his shop. His wife and their eldest daughter waited on customers all day long, from early in the

---

1. **Day of Atonement**—One of the Jewish High Holidays, observed with fasting and prayer.
2. **cantor**—A singer who leads the congregation in a synagogue.
3. **synagogue** (sin′ə gäg′)—A building used by Jews for worship.
4. **Purim** (poor′im)—A Jewish holiday commemorating the deliverance of the Jews from a massacre.
5. **Mishnah** (mish nä′)—The first part of the Talmud, the writings that constitute Jewish law.

morning till late at night. His wife was a stout woman, with a blond wig, puffy cheeks, and a neck covered with freckles. . . .

Just as our house was always filled with problems, doubts, and unrest, so everything in Asher's house was whole, placid, healthy. Every day Asher went to bring the cans of milk from the train. He rose at dawn, went to the synagogue, and after breakfast drove to the railroad depot. He worked at least eighteen hours every day, yet on the Sabbath,[6] instead of resting, he would go to listen to a preacher or come to my father to study a portion of the Pentateuch[7] with the commentary of Rashi.[8] Just as he loved his work, so he loved his Judaism. It seems to me that I never heard this man say no. His entire life was one great yes.

Asher owned a horse and wagon, and this horse and wagon aroused a fierce envy in me. How happy must be the boy whose father owned a wagon, a horse, a stable! Every day Asher went off to distant parts of the city, even to Praga![9] Often I would see him driving past our building. He never forgot to lift his head and greet whomever he saw at the window or on the balcony. Often he met me when I was running about the streets with a gang of boys or playing with those who were not "my kind," but he never threatened to tell my father, nor did he try to lecture me. He did not, like the other grown-ups, pull little boys by the ear, pinch their noses, or twist the brims of their caps. Asher seemed to have an innate respect for everyone, big or small.

Once when I saw him driving by in his wagon I nodded to him and called out, "Reb Asher, take me along!"

Asher immediately stopped and told me to get on. We drove to a train depot. The trip took several hours and I was overjoyed. I rode amid trolley cars, droshkies,[10] delivery vans. Soldiers marched; policemen stood guard; fire engines, ambulances, even some of the automobiles that were just beginning to appear on the streets of Warsaw rushed past us. Nothing could harm me. I was protected by a friend with a whip, and beneath my feet I could feel the throbbing of the wheels. It seemed to me that all Warsaw must envy me. And indeed people stared in wonderment at the little Hasid[11] with the velvet cap and the red earlocks who was riding in a milk wagon and surveying the city. It was evident that I did not really belong to this wagon, that I was a strange

---

6. **Sabbath** (sab′əth)—The seventh day of the week observed by Jews from Friday evening to Saturday evening as a day of rest and worship.
7. **Pentateuch** (pen′tə to͞ok′)—The first five books of the Bible.
8. **Rashi** (rä′shē)—Rabbi Solomon ben Isaac, a scholar who lived in France during the 1000's.
9. **Praga** (prä′gä)—Prague, the capital of Czechoslovakia.
10. **droshkies** (dräsh′kēz)—Low, open, four-wheeled carriages.
11. **Hasid** (has′id)—A member of a sect of Jewish mystics that emphasizes joyful worship.

kind of tourist. . . .

From that day on, a silent pact existed between me and Reb Asher. Whenever he could, he would take me along as his passenger. Fraught with danger were those minutes when Reb Asher went off to fetch the milk cans from the train, or to attend to a bill, and I remained alone in the wagon. The horse would turn his head and stare at me in astonishment. Asher had given me the reins to hold, and the horse seemed to be saying silently, "Just look who is my driver now. . . ." The fear that the horse might suddenly rear up and run off gave to these moments the extra fillip of peril. After all, a horse is not a child's plaything but a gigantic creature, silent, wild, with enormous strength. Occasionally a Gentile[12] would pass by, look at me, laugh, and say something to me. I did not understand his language, and he cast the same sort of dread upon me as did the horse: he too was big, strong, and incomprehensible. He too might suddenly turn on me and strike me. . . .

When I thought the end had come— any moment now the Gentile would strike me, or the horse would dash off and smash into a wall or a street lamp—then Reb Asher reappeared and all was well again. Asher carried the heavy milk cans with the ease of a Samson.[13] He was stronger than the horse, stronger than the Gentile, yet he had mild eyes and spoke my language, and he was my father's friend. I had only one desire: to ride with this man for days

and nights over fields and through forests, to Africa, to America, to the ends of the world, and always to watch, to observe all that was going on around me. . . .

How different this same Asher seemed on the New Year and the Day of Atonement! Carpenters had put up benches in my father's study, and this was where the women prayed. The beds had been taken out of the bedroom, a Holy Ark[14] brought in, and it had become a tiny prayer house. Asher was dressed in a white robe, against which his black beard appeared even blacker. On his head he wore a high cap embroidered with gold and silver. At the beginning of the Additional Service, Reb Asher would ascend to the cantor's desk and recite in a lion's roar: "Behold me, destitute of good works . . ."

Our bedroom was too small for the bass voice that thundered forth from this mighty breast. It was heard halfway down the street. Asher recited and chanted. He knew every melody, every movement. The twenty men who made up our congregation were all part of his choir. Asher's deep masculine voice aroused a tumult in the women's section. True, they all knew him well. Only yesterday they had bought from him or from his wife a saucepan of milk, a pot of clabber, a few

---

12. **Gentile** (jen'tīl)–Any person not a Jew.
13. **Samson** (sam's'n)–An Israelite judge noted for his great strength.
14. **Holy Ark**–An enclosure for the scrolls of the Torah, the first five books of the Bible.

ounces of butter, and had bargained with him for a little extra. But now Asher was the delegate who offered up the prayers of the People of Israel directly to the Almighty, before the Throne of Glory, amid fluttering angels and books that read themselves, in which are recorded the good deeds and the sins of every mortal soul . . . When he reached the prayer "We will express the might," and began to recite the destinies of men—who shall live and who shall die, who shall perish by fire and who by water—a sobbing broke out among the women. But when Asher called out triumphantly: "But repentance, prayer, and charity can avert the evil decree!"—then a heavy stone was taken from every heart. Soon Asher began to sing of the smallness of man and the greatness of God, and joy and comfort enveloped everyone. Why need men—who are but passing shadows, wilting blossoms—expect malice from a God who is just, revered, merciful? Every word that Asher called out, every note he uttered, restored courage, revived hope. We indeed are nothing, but He is all. We are but as dust in our lifetime, and less than dust after death, but He is eternal and His days shall never end. In Him, only in Him, lies our hope . . .

One year, at the close of the Day of Atonement, this same Asher, our friend and benefactor, saved our very lives. It happened in this way. After the daylong fast, we had eaten a rich supper. Later a number of Jews gathered in our house to dance and rejoice. My father had already put up, in the courtyard, the first beam of the hut for the coming Feast of Tabernacles. Late that night the family had at last fallen asleep. Since benches and pews had been set up in the bedroom, and the entire house was in disorder, each of us slept wherever he could find a spot. But one thing we had forgotten—to extinguish the candles that were still burning on some of the pews.

Late that night Asher had to drive to the railroad station to pick up milk. He passed our building and noticed that our apartment was unusually bright. This was not the glow of candles or a lamp, but the glare of a fire. Asher realized that our house must be burning. He rang the bell at the gate but the janitor did not rush to open it. He too was asleep. Then Asher set to ringing the bell and beating on the door, making such a commotion that at last the janitor awoke and opened the gate. Asher raced up the stairs and banged on our door, but no one answered. Then Asher the Mighty hurled his broad shoulders against the door and forced it open. Bursting into the apartment, he found the entire family asleep, while all around benches, prayer stands, and prayer books were aflame. He began to shout in his booming cantorial voice and finally roused us, and then he tore off our quilts and set to smothering the conflagration.

I remember that moment as though it

was yesterday. I opened my eyes and saw many flames, large and small, rolling about and dancing like imps. My brother Moshe's blanket had already caught fire. But I was young and was not frightened. On the contrary, I liked the dancing flames.

After some time the fire was put out. Here indeed something had happened that might well be called a miracle. A few minutes more, and we all would have been taken by the flames, for the wood of the benches was dry and they were saturated with the tallow of the dripping candles. Asher was the only human being awake at that hour, the only one who would ring the bell so persistently and risk his own life for us. Yes, it was fated that this faithful friend should save us from the fire.

We were not even able to thank him. It was as though we had all been struck dumb. Asher himself was in a hurry and left quickly. We wandered about amid the charred benches, tables, prayer books, and prayer shawls, and every few minutes we discovered more sparks and smoldering embers. We all might easily have been burned to cinders.

The friendship between my father and Reb Asher grew ever stronger, and during the war years, when we were close to starvation, Asher again helped us in every way he could.

After we had left Warsaw (during the First World War), we continued to hear news of him from time to time. One son died, a daughter fell in love with a young man of low origins and Asher was deeply grieved. I do not know whether he lived to see the Nazi occupation of Warsaw. He probably died before that. But such Jews as he were dragged off to the death camps. May these memoirs serve as a monument to him and his like, who lived in sanctity and died as martyrs.

© Layle Silbert

Isaac Bashevis Singer (*born 1904*) grew up in Poland. He was the son and grandson of rabbis. He studied to become a rabbi also but eventually made writing his career. Although Singer has lived in the United States since 1935, he still writes in Yiddish, the language of his youth. Much of Singer's writing is set in nineteenth-century Polish villages. In 1978, he received the Nobel Prize in literature for his work, which includes stories, novels, and tales for children. "Reb Asher the Dairyman" is from his memoir, *A Day of Pleasure: Stories of a Boy Growing Up in Warsaw*.

Developing Comprehension Skills

1. On the New Year and the Day of Atonement, what attracts many worshippers to the writer's house?

2. What details suggest that Reb Asher is generous with his money?

3. In the following sentence about Reb Asher, is the writer stating facts or opinions? "He rose at dawn, went to the synagogue, and after breakfast drove to the railroad depot."

4. What does the writer mean by saying that Reb Asher's "life was one great yes"?

5. What details suggest Reb Asher's strength? his gentleness?

6. How might the writer's life have been different if Reb Asher had not been a family friend?

Reading Literature: Autobiography

1. **Examining Allusion.** An **allusion** is a reference to another work of literature or to a famous person, place, or event outside of literature. In this selection, the following sentence alludes to Samson: "Asher carried the heavy milk cans with the ease of a Samson." Samson was the Biblical strongman who saved his people. How is Reb Asher like Samson?

2. **Comparing Tones.** **Tone** is the attitude a writer takes toward his or her subject. What is the tone of "Reb Asher the Dairyman"? How is the tone similar to or different from that of "I Get a Colt to Break In"?

3. **Analyzing Theme.** The **theme** of a literary work is the message about life or human nature that the writer shares with the reader. What message about the way to live does the writer share in this selection?

4. **Understanding Autobiography.** Autobiographies often suggest how people's early experiences shape their later attitudes and interests. What qualities does Singer respect in Reb Asher?

Vocabulary

Learning the Meanings of Words. Read each sentence below. First, try to figure out the meaning of the underlined word from the general context of the sentence. If you can't figure out the meaning, look up the word in a dictionary. Then write each underlined word, its definition, and the way you arrived at the definition.

1. "When Father found himself in great straits and could not pay the rent, he sent me to Reb Asher to borrow the money."

2. "Asher seemed to have an innate respect for every one, big or small."

3. "I was protected by a friend with a whip, and beneath my feet I could feel the throbbing of the wheels."

4. "From that day on, a silent pact existed between me and Reb Asher."

5. "The horse would turn his head and stare at me in astonishment."

6. "One year, at the close of the Day of Atonement, this same Asher, our friend and benefactor, saved our very lives."

Critical Thinking

Recognizing Opinions and Slanted Language. Read the following pairs of sentences from the selection. In each pair, one sentence states a fact and the other states an opinion. The sentence stating an opinion contains slanted language, one or more words that have a strong positive or negative connotation. For each pair, copy the sentence that states an opinion. Explain why it is an opinion and not a fact. Next, underline any word in the sentence with a positive or negative connotation.

Finally, tell how the underlined words affect your view of Reb Asher.

1. a. "Every day Asher went to bring the cans of milk from the train."
    b. "Asher carried the heavy milk cans with the ease of a Samson."

2. a. "This simple Jew . . . lived his entire life on the highest ethical plane."
    b. "Asher immediately stopped [his wagon] and told me to get on."

Developing Writing Skills

Describing a Person. Write a paragraph describing a friend you had when you were a young child. Tell how your friend looked and acted, and explain why you were drawn to each other. If your friendship ended, explain the reason.

Prewriting. Think about your friend for a few moments. Note details as you remember them. Consider the person's appearance, important qualities, and favorite activities. Then organize these details into groups.

Drafting. Write a draft of your paragraph, using your prewriting notes as a guide.

Revising and Sharing. Revise your draft adding or taking out details to create a vivid picture of your friend. Make sure that your paragraph is well organized. Form small groups and take turns reading your descriptions aloud.

From
The Story of My Life

HELEN KELLER

Helen Keller's childhood was very different from yours. Her autobiography can help you understand experiences you have not had yourself.

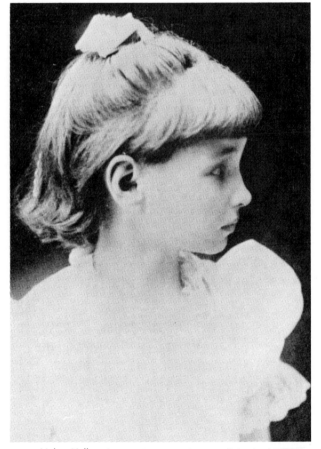

Helen Keller at age seven. American Foundation for the Blind, New York City. Photograph by Ira F. Collins.

I was born on June 27, 1880, in Tuscumbia, a little town of Northern Alabama. . . .

The beginning of my life was simple and much like every other little life. I came, I saw, I conquered, as the first baby in the family always does. . . .

I am told that while I was still in long dresses I showed many signs of an eager, self-asserting disposition. Everything that I saw other people do I insisted upon imitating. At six months, I could pipe out "How d'ye," and one day I attracted everyone's attention by saying "Tea, tea, tea" quite plainly. Even after my illness I remembered one of the words I had learned in these early months. It was the word *water*, and I continued to make some sound for that word after all other speech was lost. I ceased making the sound "wah-wah" only when I learned to spell the word.

They tell me I walked the day I was a

year old. My mother had just taken me out of the bathtub and was holding me in her lap, when I was suddenly attracted by the flickering shadows of leaves that danced in the sunlight on the smooth floor. I slipped from my mother's lap and almost ran toward them. The impulse gone, I fell down and cried for her to take me up in her arms.

These happy days did not last long. One brief spring, musical with the song of robin and mockingbird, one summer rich in fruit and roses, one autumn of gold and crimson sped by and left their gifts at the feet of an eager, delighted child. Then, in the dreary month of February, came the illness which closed my eyes and ears and plunged me into the unconsciousness of a newborn baby. They called it acute congestion of the stomach and brain. The doctor thought I could not live. Early one morning, however, the fever left me, as suddenly and mysteriously as it had come. There was great rejoicing in the family that morning, but no one, not even the doctor, knew that I should never see nor hear again.

I fancy I still have confused recollections of that illness. I especially remember the tenderness with which my mother tried to soothe me in my waking hours of fret and pain, and the agony and bewilderment with which I awoke after a tossing half sleep, and turned my eyes, so dry and hot, to the wall, away from the once-loved light, which came to me dim and yet more dim each day. But, except for these fleeting memories, if, indeed, they be memories, it all seems very unreal, like a nightmare. Gradually I got used to the silence and darkness that surrounded me and forgot that it had ever been different, until she came—my teacher—who was to set my spirit free. But during the first nineteen months of my life I had caught glimpses of broad, green fields, a luminous sky, trees and flowers which the darkness that followed could not wholly blot out. If we have once seen, "the day is ours, and what the day has shown."

Night

I cannot recall what happened during the first months after my illness. I only know that I sat in my mother's lap or clung to her dress as she went about her household duties. My hands felt every object and observed every motion, and in this way I learned to know many things. Soon I felt the need of some communication with others and began to make crude signs. A shake of the head meant "No" and a nod, "Yes"; a pull meant "Come" and a push, "Go." Was it bread that I wanted? Then I would imitate the acts of cutting the slices and buttering them. If I wanted my mother to make ice cream for dinner, I made the sign for working the freezer and shivered, indicating cold. My mother, moreover, succeeded in making me understand a good deal. I always knew when she wished me to bring her something, and I would run upstairs or any-where else she indicated. Indeed, I owe to her loving wisdom all that was bright and good in my long night.

I understood a great deal of what was going on about me. At five I learned to fold and put away the clean clothes when they were brought in from the laundry, and I distinguished my own from the rest. I knew by the way my mother and aunt dressed when they were going out, and I invariably begged to go with them. I was always sent for when there was company, and when the guests took their leave, I waved my hand to them, I think with a vague remembrance of the meaning of the gesture. . . .

I do not remember when I first realized that I was different from other people; but I knew it before my teacher came to me. I had noticed that my mother and my friends did not use signs as I did when they wanted anything done, but talked with their mouths. Sometimes I stood between two persons who were conversing and touched their lips. I could not understand and was vexed. I moved my lips and ges-ticulated frantically without result. This made me so angry at times that I kicked and screamed until I was exhausted.

I think I knew when I was naughty, for I knew that it hurt Ella, my nurse, to kick her, and when my fit of temper was over, I had a feeling similar to regret. But I cannot remember any instance in which this feel-ing prevented me from repeating the naughtiness when I failed to get what I wanted. . . .

Many incidents of those early years are fixed in my memory, isolated, but clear and distinct, making the sense of that silent, aimless, dayless life all the more intense.

One day I happened to spill water on my apron, and I spread it out to dry before the fire which was flickering on the sitting-room hearth. The apron did not dry quickly enough to suit me, so I drew nearer and threw it right over the hot ashes. The fire leaped into life; the flames encircled me so that in a moment my clothes were blazing. I made a terrified noise that brought Viny, my old nurse, to the rescue. Throwing a blanket over me, she almost suffocated me, but she put out the fire. Except for my hands and hair I was not badly burned.

About this time I found out the use of a key. One morning I locked my mother up in the pantry, where she was obliged to remain three hours, as the servants were in a detached part of the house. She kept pounding on the door, while I sat outside on the porch steps and laughed with glee as I felt the jar of the pounding. This most naughty prank of mine convinced my parents that I must be taught as soon as possible. . . .

The Search for Help

Meanwhile the desire to express myself grew. The few signs I used became less and less adequate, and my failures to make myself understood were invariably followed by outbursts of passion. I felt as if invisible hands were holding me, and I made frantic efforts to free myself. I struggled—not that struggling helped matters, but the spirit of resistance was strong within me; I generally broke down in tears and physical exhaustion. If my mother happened to be near, I crept into her arms, too miserable even to remember the cause of the tempest. After awhile, the need of some means of communication became so urgent that these outbursts occurred daily, sometimes hourly.

My parents were deeply grieved and perplexed. We lived a long way from any school for the blind or the deaf, and it seemed unlikely that anyone would come to such an out-of-the-way place as Tuscumbia to teach a child who was both deaf and blind. Indeed, my friends and relatives sometimes doubted whether I could be taught. My mother's only ray of hope came from Dickens's "American Notes." She had read his account of Laura Bridgman, and she remembered vaguely that Laura was deaf and blind, yet had been educated. But she also remembered with a hopeless pang that Dr. Howe, who had discovered the way to teach the deaf and blind, had been dead many years. His methods had probably died with him; and, if they had not, how was a little girl in a far-off town in Alabama to receive the benefit of them?

When I was about six years old, my father heard of an eminent eye doctor in Baltimore, who had been successful in many cases that had seemed hopeless. My parents at once determined to take me to Baltimore to see if anything could be done for my eyes. . . .

When we arrived in Baltimore, Dr. Chisholm received us kindly, but he could do nothing. He said, however, that I could be educated. He advised my father to consult Dr. Alexander Graham Bell, of Washington, who would be able to give him information about schools and teachers of deaf or blind children. Acting on the doctor's advice, we went immediately to Washington to see Dr. Bell, my father with a sad heart and many misgivings, I wholly unconscious of his anguish, finding pleasure in the excitement of moving from place to place. Child as I was, I at once felt the tenderness and sympathy which endeared Dr. Bell to so many hearts. He held me on his knee while I examined his watch, and he made it strike for me. He understood my signs, and I knew it and loved him at once. But I did not dream that that interview would be the door through which I should pass from darkness into light, from isolation to friendship, companionship, knowledge, love.

Dr. Bell advised my father to write to Mr. Anagnos, director of the Perkins Institution in Boston, the scene of Dr. Howe's great labors for the blind, and ask him if he had a teacher competent to begin my education. This my father did at once. In a few weeks there came a kind letter from Mr. Anagnos with the comforting assurance that a teacher had been found. This was in the summer of 1886, but Miss Sullivan did not arrive until the following March. . . .

Miss Sullivan Comes

The most important day I remember in all my life is the one on which my teacher, Anne Mansfield Sullivan, came to me. I am filled with wonder when I consider the immeasurable contrasts between the two lives that it connects. It was the third of March, 1887, three months before I was seven years old.

On the afternoon of that eventful day, I stood on the porch, expectant. I guessed vaguely from my mother's signs and from the hurrying to and fro in the house that something unusual was about to happen, so I went to the door and waited on the steps. The afternoon sun penetrated the mass of honeysuckle that covered the porch and fell on my upturned face. My fingers lingered almost unconsciously on the familiar leaves and blossoms which had just come forth to greet the sweet Southern spring. I did not know what the future held of marvel or surprise for me. Anger and bitterness had preyed upon me continually for weeks and a deep languor had succeeded this passionate struggle.

Have you ever been at sea in a dense

Helen Keller and Annie Sullivan, 1890. American Foundation for the Blind, New York City.

fog, when it seemed as if a tangible white darkness shut you in, and the great ship, tense and anxious, groped her way toward the shore with plummet and sounding-line, and you waited with beating heart for something to happen? I was like that ship before my education began, only I was without compass or sounding-line and had no way of knowing how near the harbor was. "Light! give me light!" was the wordless cry of my soul, and the light of love shone on me in that very hour.

I felt approaching footsteps. I stretched out my hand as I supposed to my mother. Someone took it, and I was caught up and held close in the arms of her who had come to reveal all things to me and, more than all things else, to love me.

The morning after my teacher came, she led me into her room and gave me a doll. The little blind children at the Perkins Institution had sent it and Laura Bridgman had dressed it; but I did not know this until afterward. When I had played with it a little while, Miss Sullivan slowly spelled into my hand the word *d-o-l-l*. I was at once interested in this finger play and tried to imitate it. When I finally succeeded in making the letters correctly, I was flushed with childish pleasure and pride. Running downstairs to my mother, I held up my hand and made the letters for *doll*. I did not know that I was spelling a word or even that words existed; I was simply making my fingers go in monkey-like imitation. In the days that followed, I learned to spell in this uncomprehending way a great many words, among them *pin, hat, cup*, and a few verbs like *sit, stand*, and *walk*. But my teacher had been with me several weeks before I understood that everything has a name.

One day, while I was playing with my new doll, Miss Sullivan put my big rag doll into my lap also, spelled *d-o-l-l* and tried to make me understand that *d-o-l-l* applied to both. Earlier in the day we had had a tussle over the words *m-u-g* and *w-a-t-e-r*. Miss Sullivan had tried to impress it upon me that *m-u-g* is *mug* and that *w-a-t-e-r* is *water*, but I persisted in confounding the two. In despair she had dropped the subject for the time, only to renew it at the first opportunity. I became impatient at her repeated attempts and, seizing the new doll, I dashed it upon the floor. I was keenly delighted when I felt the fragments of the broken doll at my feet. Neither sorrow nor regret followed my passionate outburst. I had not loved the doll. In the still, dark world in which I lived there was no strong sentiment or tenderness. I felt my teacher sweep the fragments to one side of the hearth, and I had a sense of satisfaction that the cause of my discomfort was removed. She brought me my hat, and I knew I was going out into the warm sunshine. This thought, if a wordless sensation may be called a thought, made me hop and skip with pleasure.

We walked down the path to the well-house, attracted by the fragrance of the honeysuckle with which it was covered. Someone was drawing water, and my teacher placed my hand under the spout. As the cool stream gushed over one hand, she spelled into the other the word *water*, first slowly, then rapidly. I stood still, my whole attention fixed upon the motions of the fingers. Suddenly I felt a misty consciousness as of something forgotten—a thrill of returning thought; and somehow the mystery of language was revealed to me. I knew then that *w-a-t-e-r* meant the wonderful cool something that was flowing over my hand. That living word awakened my soul, gave it light, hope, joy, set it free! There were barriers still, it is true, but barriers that could in time be swept away.

I left the well-house eager to learn. Everything had a name, and each name gave birth to a new thought. As we returned to the house, every object which I touched seemed to quiver with life. That was because I saw everything with the strange, new sight that had come to me. On entering the door, I remembered the doll I had broken. I felt my way to the hearth and picked up the pieces. I tried vainly to put them together. Then my eyes filled with tears; for I realized what I had done. For the first time I felt repentance and sorrow.

I learned a great many new words that day. I do not remember what they all were; but I do know that *mother, father, sister, teacher* were among them—words that were to make the world blossom for me, "like Aaron's rod, with flowers." It would have been difficult to find a happier child than I was as I lay in my crib at the close of that day and lived over the joys it had brought me, and for the first time longed for a new day to come.

Nature

I recall many incidents of the summer of 1887 that followed my soul's sudden awakening. I did nothing but explore with my hands and learn the name of every object that I touched; and the more I handled things and learned their names and uses, the more joyous and confident grew my sense of kinship with the rest of the world.

When the time of daisies and buttercups came, Miss Sullivan took me by the hand across the fields, where men were preparing the earth for the seed, to the banks of the Tennessee River. There, sitting on the warm grass, I had my first lessons in the beneficence of nature. I learned how the sun and the rain make to grow out of the ground every tree that is pleasant to the sight and good for food; how birds build their nests and live and thrive from land to land; how the squirrel, the deer, the lion, and every other creature finds food and shelter. As my knowledge of things grew, I felt more and more the delight of the world I was in. Long before I learned to do a sum in arithmetic or describe the shape of the earth, Miss Sullivan had taught me to find beauty in the fragrant woods, in every blade of grass, and in the curves and dimples of my baby sister's hand. She linked my earliest thoughts with nature and made me feel that "birds and flowers and I were happy peers."

But about this time I had an experience which taught me that nature is not always kind. One day my teacher and I were returning from a long ramble. The morning had been fine, but it was growing warm and sultry when at last we turned our faces homeward. Two or three times we stopped to rest under a tree by the wayside. Our last halt was under a wild cherry tree a short distance from the house. The shade was grateful, and the tree was so easy to climb that with my teacher's assistance I was able to scramble to a seat in the branches. It was so cool up in the tree that Miss Sullivan proposed that we have our luncheon there. I promised to keep still while she went to the house to fetch our lunch.

Suddenly a change passed over the tree. All the sun's warmth left the air. I knew the sky was black, because all the heat, which meant light to me, had died out of the atmosphere. A strange odor came up from the earth. I knew it. It was the odor that always precedes a thunderstorm, and a nameless fear clutched at my heart. I felt absolutely alone, cut off from my friends and the firm earth. The immense, the unknown, enfolded me. I remained still and expectant; a chilling terror crept over me. I longed for my teacher's return; but above all things I wanted to get down from that tree.

There was a moment of sinister silence, then a multitudinous stirring of the leaves. A shiver ran through the tree, and the

I left the well-house eager to l(ea)r n . Every th ing
had a name, and each name gave bir th to a
new th ou gh t . As we r e t u r n ed to the h ou s e ,
every o b j e c t I t ou ch ed s e e m ed to q u i v er with l i f e .

Above is the Braille writing for the first three sentences of paragraph two in column one on page 439. Helen Keller wrote her autobiography this way. The dots are raised on paper with a special machine much like a typewriter. The writing is read by touch.

wind sent forth a blast that would have knocked me off had I not clung to the branch with might and main. The tree swayed and strained. The small twigs snapped and fell about me in showers. A wild impulse to jump seized me, but terror held me fast. I crouched down in the fork of the tree. The branches lashed about me. I felt the intermittent jarring that came now and then, as if something heavy had fallen and the shock had traveled up till it reached the limb I sat on. It worked my suspense up to the highest point, and just as I was thinking the tree and I should fall together, my teacher seized my hand and helped me down. I clung to her, trembling with joy to feel the earth under my feet once more. I had learned a new lesson—that nature "wages open war against her children, and under softest touch hides treacherous claws."

After this experience, it was a long time before I climbed another tree. The mere thought filled me with terror. It was the sweet allurement of the mimosa tree in full bloom that finally overcame my fears. One beautiful spring morning when I was alone in the summerhouse reading, I became aware of a wonderful, subtle fragrance in the air. I started up and instinctively stretched out my hands. It seemed as if the spirit of spring had passed through the summerhouse. "What is it?" I asked, and the next minute I recognized the odor of the mimosa blossoms. I felt my way to the end of the garden, knowing that the mimosa tree was near the fence, at the turn of the path. Yes, there it was, all quivering in the warm sunshine, its blossom-laden branches almost touching the long grass. Was there ever anything so exquisitely beautiful in the world before! Its delicate blossoms shrank from the slightest earthly touch; it seemed as if a tree of paradise had been transplanted to earth.

I made my way through a shower of petals to the great trunk and for one minute stood irresolute; then, putting my foot in the broad space between the forked branches, I pulled myself up into the tree. I had some difficulty in holding on, for the branches were very large and the bark hurt my hands.

I had a delicious sense that I was doing something unusual and wonderful, so I kept on climbing higher and higher, until I reached a little seat which somebody had built there so long ago that it had grown part of the tree itself. I sat there for a long, long time, feeling like a fairy on a rosy cloud. After that I spent many happy hours in my tree of paradise, thinking fair thoughts and dreaming bright dreams.

Love

I had now the key to all language, and I was eager to learn to use it. Children who hear acquire language without any particular effort; the words that fall from others' lips they catch on the wing, as it were, delightedly, while the little deaf child must trap them by a slow and often painful process. But whatever the process, the result is wonderful. Gradually, from naming an object, we advance step by step until we have traversed the vast distance between our first stammered syllable and the sweep of thought in a line of Shakespeare.

At first, when my teacher told me about a new thing, I asked very few questions. My ideas were vague, and my vocabulary was inadequate; but as my knowledge of things grew and I learned more and more words, my field of inquiry broadened, and I would return again and again to the same subject, eager for further information. Sometimes a new word revived an image that some earlier experience had engraved on my brain.

I remember the morning that I first asked the meaning of the word *love*. This was before I knew many words. I had found a few early violets in the garden and brought them to my teacher. She tried to kiss me, but at that time I did not like to have anyone kiss me except my mother. Miss Sullivan put her arm gently round me and spelled into my hand, "I love Helen."

"What is love?" I asked.

She drew me closer to her and said, "It is here," pointing to my heart, whose beats I was conscious of for the first time. Her words puzzled me very much because I did not then understand anything unless I touched it.

I smelled the violets in her hand and asked, half in words, half in signs, a question which meant, "Is love the sweetness of flowers?"

"No," said my teacher.

Again I thought. The warm sun was shining on us.

"Is this not love?" I asked, pointing the direction from which the heat came. "Is this not love?"

It seemed to me that there could be nothing more beautiful than the sun, whose warmth makes all things grow. But Miss Sullivan shook her head, and I was greatly puzzled and disappointed. I thought it strange that my teacher could not show me love.

A day or two afterward, I was stringing beads of different sizes in symmetrical groups—two large beads, three small ones, and so on. I had made many mistakes, and Miss Sullivan had pointed them out again and again with gentle patience.

Finally I noticed a very obvious error in the sequence, and for an instant I concentrated my attention on the lesson and tried to think how I should have arranged the beads. Miss Sullivan touched my forehead and spelled with decided emphasis, "Think."

In a flash I knew that the word was the name of the process that was going on in my head. This was my first conscious perception of an abstract idea.

For a long time I was still—I was not

thinking of the beads in my lap, but trying to find a meaning for *love* in the light of this new idea. The sun had been under a cloud all day, and there had been brief showers; but suddenly the sun broke forth in all its Southern splendor.

Again I asked my teacher, "Is this not love?"

"Love is something like the clouds that were in the sky before the sun came out," she replied. Then in simpler words than these, which at the time I could not have understood, she explained: "You cannot touch the clouds, you know; but you feel the rain and know how glad the flowers and the thirsty earth are to have it after a hot day. You cannot touch love either; but you feel the sweetness that it pours into everything. Without love, you would not be happy or want to play."

The beautiful truth burst upon my mind—I felt that there were invisible lines stretched between my spirit and the spirits of others.

From the beginning of my education Miss Sullivan made it a practice to speak to me as she would speak to any hearing child; the only difference was that she spelled the sentences into my hand instead of speaking them. If I did not know the words and idioms necessary to express my thoughts she supplied them, even suggesting conversation when I was unable to keep up my end of the dialogue.

This process was continued for several

Iris and Wild Roses, 1887, JOHN LA FARGE. The Metropolitan Museum of Art, New York City, Gift of Priscilla A. B. Henderson, 1950.

years; for the deaf child does not learn in a month, or even in two or three years, the numberless idioms and expressions used in the simplest daily conversations. The little hearing child learns these from constant repetition and imitation. The conversation he hears in his home stimulates his mind and suggests topics and calls forth the spontaneous expression of his own thoughts. This natural exchange of ideas is denied to the deaf child. My teacher, realizing this, determined to supply the kinds of stimuli I lacked. This she did by repeating to me as far as possible, verbatim, what she heard, and by showing me how I could take part in the conversation. But it was a long time before I ventured to take the initiative and still longer before I could find something appropriate to say at the right time.

The deaf and the blind find it very difficult to acquire the amenities of conversation. How much more this difficulty must be augmented in the case of those who are both deaf and blind! They cannot distinguish the tone of the voice or, without assistance, go up and down the gamut of tones that give significance to words; nor can they watch the expression of the speaker's face, and a look is often the very soul of what one says.

Helen Keller (*1880–1968*) overcame the loss of sight, hearing, and speech caused by a childhood illness. Her teacher, Anne Sullivan, taught her to communicate through touch, to write and read Braille, and eventually to speak. Keller graduated with honors from Radcliffe College. She mastered several languages and lectured throughout the world. Her speaking tours helped in raising money to improve conditions for blind people.

Developing Comprehension Skills

1. How did Helen Keller become deaf and blind?

2. Here are five quotations from the selection. Tell whether each one states a fact or an opinion.

   a. "I was born on June 27, 1880, in Tuscumbia."

   b. "I owe to her loving wisdom all that was bright and good in my long night."

   c. "One morning I locked my mother up in the pantry."

   d. "Dr. Bell advised my father to write to Mr. Anagnos."

   e. "It would have been difficult to find a happier child than I was as I lay in my crib at the close of that day."

3. How did Helen learn that everything has a name? Compare this process with the way children who are not deaf and blind learn the same thing.

4. Reread the section on "Love" beginning on page 441. Why did Helen have trouble understanding the meaning of the word *love*? How did her teacher successfully explain the meaning of the word?

5. Do you think a blind person can understand how things look? Give examples from the selection to support your opinion.

6. Helen describes her temper tantrums when she was young. What does she say caused her to act that way? What was her world like in the years before Anne Sullivan came? Try to imagine the frustration and confusion she experienced. Do you think her temper tantrums were understandable behavior under the circumstances?

Reading Literature: Nonfiction

1. **Examining Autobiography.** Autobiographies give firsthand information about the writer. Give one example from the story for each of these categories:

   a. the reasons why Helen acted in a particular way

   b. one of Helen's personal, secret feelings

2. **Understanding the Author's Purpose.** Helen Keller did not have sight or hearing, two senses that most people take for granted. How does her autobiography help you understand what it is like to be deaf and blind? What problems are shared by both deaf and blind people and people without these handicaps? What special problems are faced only by deaf and blind people? Refer to the selection to support your answer.

3. **Identifying Tone.** You have read three selections of autobiography. Are the tones of the three selections alike or different? Give examples to support your answer.

4. **Thinking About Time and Place.** Autobiography reflects the time and place in which it was written. Name at least two facts you learned about what life was like a hundred years ago from this selection.

5. **Recognizing Style.** Every writer will in time develop a personal style. That person's writing becomes different from everyone else's. Even though the writer might not sign every page, a good reader can tell whether two pages were written by the same person.

   One mark of Helen Keller's style is the

use of paired words and phrases. Here are some examples:

> My hands <u>felt every object</u> and <u>observed every motion</u>.

> Early one morning, the fever left me as <u>suddenly</u> and <u>mysteriously</u> as it had come.

> Then, in the dreary month of February, came the illness that <u>closed</u> my <u>eyes</u> and <u>ears</u> and <u>plunged</u> me into the unconsciousness of a newborn baby.

> My parents were deeply <u>grieved</u> and <u>perplexed</u>.

Identify at least five other sentences containing paired words and phrases.

6. **Appreciating Word Choice.** In spite of being blind and deaf, Helen Keller often used vivid sensory words in her writing. Find three examples of clear descriptive words or phrases in this selection.

Vocabulary

Recognizing Base Words and Affixes. Several words found in the story of Helen Keller contain affixes you learned in Chapter 2. Other words contain the same letters as an affix, but the letters are part of the base word. For example, in the word *rewrite, re* is a prefix. However, in *read, re* is part of the base word.

Each of the following words contains the letters of an affix. If the letters are an affix added to a base word, write the definition of the word. Use the affix as a clue to meaning. If the letters are part of the base word, write the dictionary or glossary definition.

1. imitate
2. image
3. unconsciousness
4. discomfort
5. immeasurable
6. invisible
7. renew
8. impatient

Critical Thinking

Analyzing Slanted Writing. Helen Keller used words and phrases with positive connotations to describe herself as a child. Find two descriptions that make little Helen seem good or cute. Rewrite the sentences with words having neutral connotations (neither good nor bad). Do you think Helen Keller was unfair to write about herself with a positive slant? If writing is slanted, does that mean it is not true?

Speaking and Listening

Interpreting and Using Gestures. At the beginning of her autobiography, Helen Keller describes several ways she communicated before she knew any language. People who can see and hear often use "body language," too. Observe yourself and others for a few days. Take notes on ways that people communicate without spoken language. Then show the class some of the body language you noticed. See if your classmates can tell what your motions mean.

Developing Writing Skills

1. **Contrasting Two Autobiographies.** *The Story of My Life* and "Reb Asher the Dairyman" are both examples of autobiography. Write a paragraph contrasting the two.

   Prewriting. Decide on the focus of your contrast. For example, you may contrast the main characters, the writers' purposes, the settings, or the tones of the selections. After choosing your focus, make notes on similarities and differences between the selections.

   Drafting. Begin your draft with a topic sentence that briefly states the main point of contrast between the two selections. Develop this main idea in your supporting sentences.

   Revising and Sharing. Share your draft with a partner. Ask him or her if all your sentences are easily understood and if they are linked to your main idea. Revise sentences that are unclear.

2. **Writing a Description.** Helen Keller describes vividly how she felt sitting in a tree during a thunderstorm. Write a description of an experience that frightened you. Use specific details and descriptive words to tell what the experience was like. Appeal to as many senses as you can, including sight, hearing, touch, and smell. Remember to follow the steps in the process of writing: prewriting, drafting, revising, and sharing. If you need help, refer to the handbook at the back of the book.

Baseball in April

GARY SOTO

Gary Soto, a Mexican-American poet, recalls playing baseball as a child in Fresno, California. Are his memories good ones?

 For three springs my brother and I walked to Romain playground to try out for Little League, and year after year we failed to impress the coaches. The night of the last year we tried out, we sat in our bedroom listening to the radio and pounding our fists into gloves and talked of how we would bend to pick up grounders, stand at the plate, wave off another player to say we got the pop-up. "This is the year," Rick said with confidence as he pretended to backhand a ball and throw out the man racing to first. He pounded his glove and looked at me, "How'd you like that?"

At the tryouts there were a hundred kids. After asking around, we were pointed to lines by age group: nine, ten, and eleven. Rick and I stood in our respective lines, gloves limp as dead animals hanging from our hands, and waited to have large paper numbers pinned to our backs so that field coaches with clipboards propped on their stomachs would know who we were.

Nervous, I chewed at my palm as I moved up in the line, but when my number was called I ran out onto the field to the sound of my sneakers smacking against the clay. I looked at the kids still in line, then at my brother who was nodding his head yes. The first grounder—a three-bouncer that spun off my glove into center field. Another grounder cracked off the bat, and I bent down to gobble it up. The ball fell from my glove like food from a sloppy mouth. I stared at the ball before I picked it up to hurl it to first base. The next one I managed to pick up cleanly, but my throw made the first baseman leap into the air with an exaggerated grunt that had him looking good while I looked bad. Three more balls were hit to me, and I came up with one.

So it went for me, my number flapping

like a single, broken wing as I ran off the field to sit in the bleachers and wait for Rick to trot onto the field.

He was a star that day. With the first grounder he raced for it and threw on the run. With the next ball he lowered himself on one knee and threw nonchalantly to first. His number flapped on his back, a crooked seventeen, and I saw a coach make a check on his board. He then looked serious as he wet his lips and wrote something that demanded thought, for his brow furrowed and darkened.

Rick lunged at the next hit and missed it as it skidded into center field. With the next hit he shaded his eyes, for it was a high pop-up, something that he was good at, even graceful, and when the ball fell earthward he slapped it with his toe and looked pleased as his mouth grew fat from trying to hold back a smile. Again the coach wet his lips and made a check on his clipboard.

Rick did well at fielding. When the next number was called, he jogged off the field with his head high, and both of us sat in the bleachers, dark and serious as we watched the others trot on and off the field.

Finally the coaches told us to return after lunch to take batting practice. Rick and I ran home to fix sandwiches and talk about the morning, then what to expect in the afternoon.

"Don't be scared," he said with his mouth full of sandwich. He was thinking of my batting. He demonstrated how to stand. He spread his legs, worked his left foot into the carpet, and looked angrily at where the ball would be delivered, some twenty feet in front of him at the kitchen table. He swung an invisible bat, choked up, and swung again.

He turned to me. "You got it?" I told him I thought I did and imitated his motion as I stepped where he was standing to swing once, then again and then again, until he said, "Yeah, you got it."

We returned to the playground, and I felt proud walking to the diamond because smaller kids were watching us in awe, some of them staring at the paper number on my back. It was as if we were soldiers going off to war.

"Where you goin'?" asked Rosie, sister of Johnnie Serna, the playground terrorist. She was squeezing the throat of a large bag of sunflower seeds, her mouth rolling with shells.

"Tryouts," I said, barely looking at her as I kept stride with Rick.

At the diamond I once again grew scared and apprehensive. I got into the line of nine-year-olds to wait for my turn at bat. Fathers clung to the fence, chattering last-minute instructions to their kids who answered with, "OK, yes, all right, OK, OK," because they were also wide-eyed and scared when the kid in the batter's box swung and missed.

By the time it was my turn I was shivering unnoticeably and trying to catch

Rick's eyes for reassurance. When my number was called I walked to the plate, tapped the bat on the ground—something I had seen many times on television—and waited. The first pitch was outside and over my head. The coach who was on the mound laughed at his sorry pitch.

At the next pitch I swung hard, spinning the ball foul. I tapped my bat again, kicked at the dirt, and stepped into the batter's box. I swung stupidly at a low ball. I wound up again and sliced the ball foul, just at the edge of the infield grass, which surprised me because I didn't know I had the strength to send it that far.

I was given ten pitches and managed to get three hits, all of them grounders on the right side. One of them kicked up into the face of a kid trying to field. He tried to hang tough as he walked off the field, head bowed and quiet, but I knew tears were welling up in his eyes.

I handed the bat to the next kid and went to sit in the bleachers to wait for the ten-year-olds to come up to bat. I was feeling better after that morning's tryout at fielding because I had three hits. I also thought I looked good standing cocky at the plate, bat high over my shoulder.

Rick came up to the plate and hit the first pitch on the third base side. He sent the next pitch into left field. He talked to himself as he stood in the box, slightly bouncing before each swing. Again the coaches made checks on their clipboards,

heads following the ball each time it was smacked to the outfield.

When the ten hits were up, he jogged off the field and joined me in the bleachers. His mouth was again fat from holding back a smile, and I was jealous of his athletic display. I thought to myself, Yeah, he'll make the team and I'll just watch him from the bleachers. I felt bad—empty as a Coke bottle—as I imagined Rick running home with a uniform under his arm.

We watched other kids come to the plate and whack, foul, chop, slice, dribble, beeline, and hook balls to every part of the field. One high foul ball bounced in the bleachers and several kids raced to get it, but I was the first to latch a hand onto it. I weighed the ball in my palm, like a pound of baloney, and then hurled it back onto the field. A coach watched it roll by his feet, disinterested.

After tryouts were finished we were told—or retold, because it had been announced in the morning—that we would be contacted by phone late in the week.

We went home and by Monday afternoon we were already waiting for the phone to ring. We slouched in the living room after school, with the TV turned on and loud as a roomful of people: *Superman* at three o'clock and *The Three Stooges* at three-thirty. Every time I left the living room for the kitchen, I stole a glance at the telephone and once when no one was looking I picked it up to see if it was working: a long buzz.

By Friday when it was clear that the call would never come, we went outside to the front yard to play catch and practice bunting.

"I should have made the team," Rick said as he made a stab at my bunt. He was particularly troubled because if anyone should have made the team it was him, since he was better than most that day.

We threw grounders at one another. A few of them popped off my chest while most of them disappeared neatly into my glove. "Why couldn't I do it like this last Saturday?" I thought. I was mad at myself, then sad and self-pitying. We stopped playing and returned inside to watch *The Three Stooges.* Moe was reading from a children's storybook, his finger following the words with deliberation.

"Does the doe have a deer?" read Moe.

"Yeah, two bucks," laughed Larry.

Moe pounded him on top of the head

Photograph by Norma Morrison, Glenview, Illinois.

and called him a knucklehead. Larry rolled his eyes and looked dizzy.

We didn't make Little League that year, but we did join a team of school chums that practiced at Hobo Park near downtown Fresno. Pete, the brother of Mary Palacio, a girl who was head-over-heels for me, told us about the team, and after school Rick and I raced our bicycles to the park. We threw our bikes aside and hit the field. While Rick went to the outfield, I took second base to practice grounders.

"Give me a baby roller," Danny Lopez, the third baseman, called. I sidearmed a roller and he picked it up on the third bounce. "Good pickup," we told him. He looked pleased, slapping his glove against his pants as he hustled back to third, a smile cutting across his face.

Rick practiced pop-ups with Billy Reeves. They looked skyward with each throw in the air, mouths hanging open as if God were making a face between clouds.

When Manuel, the coach, arrived in his pickup, most of the kids ran to meet him and chatter that they wanted to play first, to play second, to hit first, to hit third. Rick and I went quiet and stood back from the racket.

Manuel shouldered a duffel bag from the back of his pickup and walked over to the palm tree that served as a backstop. He let the bag drop with a grunt, clapped his hands, and pointed kids to positions. We were still quiet, and when Pete told Manuel that we wanted to play, I stiffened up and tried to look tough. I popped my glove with my fist and looked about me as if I were readying to cross a road. Because he was older, Rick stood with his arms crossed over his chest, glove at his feet. "You guys in the outfield," he pointed as he turned to pull a bat and ball from the bag.

Manuel was middle-aged, patient, and fatherly. He bent down on his haunches to talk to kids. He spoke softly and showed interest in what we had to say. He cooed "good" when we made catches, even routine ones. We all knew he was good to us because most of the kids on the team didn't have fathers or, if they did, the fathers were so beaten from hard work that they never spent time with them. They came home to open the refrigerator for a cold drink and then to plop in front of the TV. They didn't even have the energy to laugh when something was funny. Rick and I saw this in our stepfather. While we might have opened up with laughter at a situation comedy, he just stared at the pictures flashing before him—unmoved, eyes straight ahead.

We practiced for two weeks before Manuel announced that he had scheduled our first game.

"Who we playing?" someone asked.

"The Red Caps," he answered. "West Fresno boys."

By that time I had gotten better. Rick had quit the team because of a new girlfriend, a slow walker who hugged her schoolbooks against her chest while looking like a dazed boxer at Rick's equally dazed face. Stupid, I thought, and rode off to practice.

Although I was small, I was made catcher. I winced behind my mask when the ball was delivered and the batter swung because there was no chest protector or chin guards—just a mask. Balls skidded off my arms and chest, but I didn't let on that they hurt—though once I doubled over after having the breath knocked out of me. Manuel hovered over me while rubbing my stomach and cooing words that made me feel better.

My batting, however, did not improve, and everyone on the team knew I was a "sure out." Some of the older kids tried to give me tips—how to stand, follow through, push weight into the ball. . . . Still, when I came up to bat, everyone moved in, like soldiers edging in for the attack. A slow roller to short, and I raced to first with my teeth showing. Out by three steps.

The day of the first game some of us met early at Hobo Park to talk about how we were going to whip them and send them home whining to their mothers. Soon others showed up to practice fielding grounders while waiting for the coach to pull up in his pickup. When we spotted him coming down the street, we ran to him and before the pickup had come to a stop we were already climbing the sides.

The coach stuck his head from the cab to warn us to be careful. He idled the pickup for a few minutes to wait for the others, and when two did come running, he waved for them to get in the front with him. As he drove slowly to the West Side, our hair flicked about in the wind, and we thought we looked neat.

When we arrived, we leaped from the back but stayed close by the coach who waved to the other coach as he pulled the duffel bag over his shoulder. He then scanned the other team: Like us, most were Mexican, although there were a few blacks. We had a few Anglos on our team—Okies, as we called them.

The coach shook hands with the other coach and talked quietly in Spanish, then opened up with laughter that had them patting one another's shoulder. Quieting, they turned around and considered the field, pointed to the outfield where the sprinkler heads jutted from the grass. They scanned the infield and furrowed their brows at where the shortstop would stand: it was pitted from a recent rain. They parted talking in English and our coach returned to tell us the rules.

We warmed up behind the backstop, throwing softly to one another and trying to look calm. We spied the other team and they, in turn, spied us. They seemed bigger and darker, and wore matching T-shirts and caps. We were mismatched in jeans and T-shirts.

At bat first, we scored one run on an

error and a double to left field. When the other team came up, they scored four runs on three errors. With the last one, I stood in front of the plate, mask in hand, yelling for the ball.

"I got a play! I got a play!" The ball sailed over my head and hit the backstop, only to ricochet in foul ground on the first base side. The runner was already sitting on the bench, breathing hard and smiling, by the time I picked up the ball. I walked it to the pitcher.

I searched his face, and he was scared. He was pressed to the wall, and he was falling apart. I told him he could do it. "C'mon, baby," I said, arm around his shoulder, and returned to behind the plate. I was wearing a chest protector that reached almost to my knees and made me feel important. I scanned the bleachers—a sad three-row display case—and Mary Palacio was talking loudly with a friend, indifferent to the game.

We got out of the first inning without any more runs. Then, at bat, we scored twice on a hit and an error that felled their catcher. He was doubled over his knees, head bowed like someone ready to commit hara-kiri,[1] and rocking back and forth, smothering the small bursts of yowls. We went on to add runs, but so did they; by the eighth inning they were ahead, sixteen to nine.

As the innings progressed, our team started to argue with one another. Our play was sloppy, nothing like the cool rou-

tines back at Hobo Park. Flyballs that lifted to the outfield dropped at the feet of open-mouthed players. Grounders rolled slowly between awkward feet. The pitching was sad.

"You had to mess up, *menso,*[2]" Danny Lopez screamed at the shortstop.

"Well, you didn't get a hit, and *I* did," the shortstop said, pointing to his chest.

The coach clung to the screen as if he were hanging from a tall building, and the earth was far below. He let us argue and only looked at us with a screwed-up face when he felt we were getting out of hand.

I came up for the fourth time that day in the eighth with two men on. My teammates were grumbling because they thought I was going to strike out, pop-up, roll it back to the pitcher, anything but hit the ball. I was scared because the other team had changed pitchers and was throwing "fire," as we described it.

"Look at those fireballs," the team whispered in awe from the bench as player after player swung through hard strikes, only to return to the dugout, head down and muttering. "What fire," we all agreed.

I came up scared of the fast ball and even more scared of failing. Mary looked on from the bleachers with a sandwich in her hands. The coach clung to the screen,

---

1. **hara-kiri** (hä′rə kir′ē)–Ritual suicide done by plunging a sword or knife into the abdomen. Once high-ranking Japanese chose death in this manner rather than life in disgrace.
2. **menso** (men′sō)—Stupid.

cooing words. The team yelled at me to hit it hard. Dig in, they suggested, and I dug in, bat high over my shoulder as if I were really going to do something. And I did. With two balls and a strike, the pitcher threw "fire" that wavered toward my thigh. Instead of jumping out of the way I knew I had to let the ball hit me because that was the only way I was going to get on base. I grimaced just before it hit with a thud and grimaced even harder when I went down holding my leg and on the verge of crying. The coach ran from the dugout to hover over me on his haunches and rub my leg, coo words, and rub again. A few team members stood over me with their hands on their knees, with concerned faces but stupid questions: "Does it hurt?" "Can I play catcher now?" "Let me run for him, coach!"

But I rose and limped to first, the coach all along asking if I was OK. He shooed the team back into the dugout, then jogged to stand in the coach's box at first. Although my leg was pounding like someone at the door, I felt happy to be on first. I grinned, looked skyward, and adjusted my cap. "So this is what it's like," I thought to myself. I clapped my hands and encouraged the batter, our leadoff man. "C'mon, baby, c'mon, you can do it." He hit a high fly ball to center, but while the staggering player lined up to pick it from the air, I rounded second on my way to third, feeling wonderful that I had gotten that far.

We lost nineteen to eleven and would go on to lose against the Red Caps four more times because they were the only team we would ever play. A two-team league. But that's what it was that spring.

The sad part is that I didn't know when the league ended. As school grew to a close, fewer and fewer of the players came to play, so that there were days when we were using girls to fill the gaps. Finally one day Manuel didn't show up with his duffel bag over his shoulder. On that day I think it was clear to us—the three or four who remained—that it was all over, though none of us let on to the others. We threw the ball around, played pickle, and then practiced pitching. When dusk began to settle, we lifted our bicycles and rode home. I didn't show up the next day for practice but instead sat in front of the television watching Superman bend iron bars.

I felt guilty, though, because I was thinking that one of the players might have arrived for practice only to find a few sparrows hopping about on the lawn. If he had, he might have waited on the bench or, restless and embarrassed, he may have practiced pop-ups by throwing the ball into the air, calling "I got it," and trying it again all by himself.

Gary Soto (*born 1952*) is a talented poet and a professor of Chicano studies and English. His poetry is praised for its simple style and its sympathetic descriptions of poor people in California's San Joaquin Valley. Also praised is Soto's volume of boyhood remembrances, *Living Up the Street*, which received an American Book Award in 1985. "Baseball in April" is a chapter from this book.

Developing Comprehension Skills

1. What do the writer and his brother want to do at the beginning of the selection?

2. What are the differences between the Little League team and the neighborhood team? Does each have advantages and disadvantages?

3. What is the writer's attitude toward his brother? What makes you think so?

4. What does the writer do when he comes up to bat for the fourth time in the game against the Red Caps? What reason does he give for doing this?

5. What is Manuel's relationship to the boys on the Hobo Park team? How does he treat them? How does the writer feel about Manuel?

6. In what ways were their experiences playing baseball enjoyable for the writer and his brother? In what ways were their experiences painful? In your opinion, were the boys helped more than harmed by playing baseball? Give reasons for your answer.

Reading Literature: Nonfiction

1. **Thinking About Character.** The writer tells two different stories in this selection—one about trying out for Little League and one about playing on a team with schoolmates. What happens to the writer in each story? What qualities does he show in each? What strengths does he have? weaknesses?

2. **Identifying Mood. Mood** is the feeling the writer creates for the reader of a literary work. A mood can be one of joy, uneasiness, or sadness, for example. A writer's choice of words and sensory

images helps establish mood. Reread the last paragraph of "Baseball in April." What mood is created? What are the words and images that help create this feeling?

3. **Comparing Writing Styles.** **Style** refers to the way in which a literary work is written. One element of a writer's style may be his or her use of simile. A simile is a comparison that uses the word *like* or *as*. Here are examples of similes found in the selection by Helen Keller:

> I was like that ship before my education began.
>
> . . . words that were to make the world blossom for me, "like Aaron's rod, with flowers."
>
> It seemed as if a tree of paradise had been transplanted to earth.

Here are three similes found in "Baseball in April":

> I weighed the ball in my palm, like a pound of baloney.
>
> The ball fell from my glove like food from a sloppy mouth.
>
> I felt bad—empty as a Coke bottle.

How are these similes different from those in the Helen Keller autobiography? How do they "fit" the main character? What other differences do you see in the writers' styles?

Vocabulary

Using Field Labels in a Dictionary. A word may have a special meaning in a particular field. The dictionary indicates such a definition with a **field label**, printed in italics and sometimes abbreviated. Specialized definitions usually follow the general definitions of a word. Read the following entry from *Webster's New World Dictionary, Student Edition* for the word *staff*. There is a field label before definition 5, which explains the meaning of *staff* in the field of music.

> **staff** (staf) **n., pl. staffs**; also, for senses 1 & 5, **staves** [OE. *stæf* < IE. base *stebb-*, pole] **1.** a stick, rod, or pole used as a support in walking, or as a weapon, a symbol of authority, a measure, etc. **2.** a group of people assisting a leader **3.** a group of military or naval officers serving a commanding officer as advisers and administrators **4.** a specific group of workers [a teaching *staff*] **5.** *Music* the five horizontal lines and four spaces between them on which music is written —*adj.* of, by, for, or on a staff —*vt.* to provide with a staff, as of workers

Following is a list of words from "Baseball in April." Look up each word in a dictionary and write both its baseball definition and one of its more general definitions.

plate	foul
diamond	slice
error	strike

Critical Thinking

Inferring a Writer's Opinion. Sometimes it is difficult to tell whether an opinion expressed in a work of literature belongs to the writer or to a character. For example, in this selection, when Rick realizes that the coaches will never call him, he becomes troubled. The selection states that Rick is upset because "if anyone should have made the team it was him, since he was better than most that day." It is unclear whether it is Rick who believes this, or the writer as well. The writer's opinion must be inferred from the descriptive language he uses and the factual details he includes in other parts of the selection. Do you think the writer believes that Rick should have made the team? What might have been a reason for Rick's rejection? Find evidence in the selection to support your answers.

Developing Writing Skills

1. **Narrating a Personal Experience.** Write about an experience you had during a tryout for a sports team, a play, a musical group, or another activity.

   Prewriting. Make an informal outline of your narrative by answering the following questions: What was the tryout for? Why did you want to be chosen? What did you have to do? How did you feel? What was the outcome?

   Drafting. Write a draft, presenting events in time order. As you write, you will probably remember more details to include. For example, you may want to describe your competitors or the judge.

   Revising and Sharing. Revise your draft, adding or omitting details if necessary. Explain special terms that may not be familiar to your audience. Share your narrative with the class.

2. **Analyzing a Character.** The coach, Manuel, is an important character in this selection. What kind of person is he? Write a paragraph stating your opinion of him. List incidents from the story that support your opinion. Follow the steps in the process of writing: prewriting, drafting, revising, and sharing. Refer to the handbook at the back of the book if you need help.

Biographies

A **biography** is a true story of a real person's life. The story may tell about the person's entire life or about one small part of it. Unlike an autobiography, a biography is written by another person, usually from the third-person point of view.

Biographers research their subjects thoroughly. If their subjects are still living, biographers may interview them. Skilled biographers tell both the good and less admirable qualities of their subjects. Wherever possible, the writers use the subjects' own words.

Icon-Ero, 1980, ED PASCHKE. Photograph: Phyllis Kind Gallery, New York and Chicago.

From
Mumbet: The Story of Elizabeth Freeman

HAROLD W. FELTON

Elizabeth Freeman was born a slave in the eighteenth century. She showed courage and resourcefulness by suing in court for her freedom. Here she displays these same traits as she confronts a band of armed men.

Hard times came. Many workmen were without jobs. Money was scarce. Farmers found it difficult to pay their debts and taxes. It was 1786. The United States had won the war and was independent of England. But the states were loosely organized. The Federal Government had only limited powers under Articles of Confederation. The Congress was struggling to create a stable government. The Federal Constitution would not be ratified until 1789.

Rebellion against the Government smoldered in the hearts of men who, a half dozen years before, had won a war of rebellion against a king.

Daniel Shays led the rebellion in Massachusetts. Unfortunately, as is often the case, mob action took the place of protest and discussion. Unruly men took to the roads intent on plunder. Mortgages had been foreclosed. Property had been sold to collect debts. The rebels made for the courts and for the homes of the wealthy. Columns of black smoke pushing into the sky, like dark exclamation points, punctuated the horizon and told of fires that sometimes came with the rebels.

Judge Theodore Sedgwick had been elected to the Congress and was away from home on government business. He had been in active opposition to Shays's followers and the rebels had often threatened his life.

Mumbet was in the house alone with Mrs. Sedgwick and the children. Mrs. Sedgwick was ill, in bed.

Mumbet saw a column of smoke far up the road. She saw people hurry past the house. The news spread. A gang of Shays's men was coming.

She called the children and they came running. "Come on, now. I want you to go to your mother's room. You go along too,

Little Bet. Shays's men are comin'." She followed them as they trooped up the stairs.

"What is it, Bet?" Mrs. Sedgwick asked as they filed into her room.

"Shays's rebels are comin'. I think the children should stay with you."

"Oh, dear," Mrs. Sedgwick moaned helplessly. "What will we do?"

"Jes' leave it to me. I'll try to take care of 'em. I hope I can keep their minds away from settin' fire to anything, or breakin' or stealin' anything."

Mrs. Sedgwick's eyes opened wide with fear and burned dark against her pale face. Her hands fluttered helplessly above the sheets.

"Don't you worry." Mumbet's calmness and her proven ability to take care of things quieted the ill woman.

"Now you children, you jes' stay right here. Don't leave the room, and don't you be scared."

After she closed the door she moved quickly through the house. She hid the wine and the spirits in a dark corner of the cellar but left the porter stacked in neat rows on a shelf in the pantry. Smiling grimly, she selected the bottles of porter that had gone flat and put them in the front row. Flat porter was very bitter and she hoped its bitterness might discourage drinking, if the men found it.

Returning upstairs, she gathered up the silver, stuffing it into pillow cases. Then she carried the heavy load to her room on the top floor. There, she put it all in a large pine chest that stood by the wall near her sewing table. She covered the silver with blankets and quilts she had made and piled her winter clothes on top.

Satisfied that she had done the best she could, she locked the pine chest and stuffed the key beneath the handkerchief in the bottom of one of her apron's big pockets. She gave it a firm pat as though the treasure were safely stowed away in a bank vault.

Then Mumbet moved to the window and peered out. She had finished her work just in time. A group of men on horseback were coming down the road toward the house.

As she went rapidly down the stairs she heard loud voices in the yard. "I've got to be as nice to 'em as I can," she muttered softly to herself. "But—" She picked up the long, heavy kitchen fireplace shovel she had brought from the back of the house and gripped it firmly.

The voices were louder now. She heard the tramp of hard-soled shoes coming across the porch. Mumbet stood silently in the hall, waiting.

The front door trembled under heavy blows. Mumbet stiffened. Her porch floor was being scuffed, her door was being marked—the floor and the door she had polished and cleaned so carefully.

She strode to the door, opened it wide, and stood squarely in the frame, the long shovel held solidly in her hand. A dozen

Elizabeth Freeman, 1811, SUSAN SEDGWICK (daughter of Judge Sedgwick). Massachusetts Historical Society, Boston.

rough men stood before her. "What do you mean by knockin' your gun butt against my door?" she demanded. "No use in that! There's a knocker. Next time, use it!"

The mob standing before her had not expected so firm a response. None of them seemed to have a voice. "What do you want?" she asked sternly.

The leader, a tall man with a dark beard, found words. "Where's Judge Sedgwick?" he asked in a rough voice.

"He's not here," Bet said with a scowl.

"He's here all right," one of the men insisted.

"Yeah. An' we want him," another said.

Bet's shovel moved slightly, but dangerously. "I said he's not here, an' I mean what I say," she said firmly.

"Search the house," came a voice from the crowd. "Search it for arms and ammunition too!"

"Yeah. Search it. If we can't find no guns or the judge, there's always the silver."

"Let's search it."

"Yeah. Get goin'."

"Push her out of the way."

"Don't you dare touch me!" Mumbet said defiantly. "Don't you dare strike a woman, not even a poor old black woman!"

There was a long silence. Then feet scuffled against the floor as the crowd pushed toward her.

"We came here to find the judge," a voice insisted from the rear of the crowd.

"We got to search, ma'am," the leader said.

Ma'am! That was a good sign. At least they had not knocked her aside. Her firmness had prevented that. And at least one of them had some small courtesy in him. She would not retreat. She would show no fright. She would control them. At least, if a show of courage and firmness would control them, she would do it.

"Well," she said as she looked calmly at

the hard faces. "I tell you Judge Sedgwick is not here. He's off, tryin' to make a better government for us, while you're here tryin' to tear it down. Nobody's here except me and the children and Mrs. Sedgwick, and she's sick. I'll show you around and you can search all you want to. But don't you go and do any damage and don't you get Mrs. Sedgwick upset or she'll get real sick, real bad again." The quick sentences were firm commands. The shovel danced slightly, but menacingly.

Mumbet stood aside as the men moved into the wide hall. She noticed that some of them took off their hats and stuffed them in their pockets. Humph! Some of them have at least got a little bit of gentleman in them, she thought. But they were hard, rough men and they had only started their search. She still had a far distance to go with them.

"Where's the guns an' ammunition?" the leader asked.

"There's none that I know of here," said Mumbet. "The judge took all that stuff to his office, or somewhere."

"Where's the silver?" he demanded as he saw the bare shelves and sideboard.

"Put away somewhere," Mumbet answered. She was glad he didn't ask her where it had been put. Why was it that these people felt they had to fight and destroy and steal things? There were better ways to right wrongs and correct injustices. She had proven that by going to

court to get her freedom. But her thoughts were quickly interrupted.

"Look in the drawers for the silver. Look in all the closets. Look under everything." The leader's commands were brisk.

"I jest want to get my hands on that silver," one of the men said as he pushed his hands into a big drawer.

"Sure. The judge is loaded with it," another said.

The men went quickly through the first floor. In the cellar one of them paused in the pantry. "Hey, look at this!" He reached for a bottle among the many stacked on the shelf before him.

"Bottles! Let me have one!"

"Me too!"

The man who held the bottle struck its neck against a stone in the wall of the pantry.

Bet heard the voice and the crash of glass. This was a dangerous moment. If they found the spirits, such men would be very difficult. She must act. "Wait a minute!" she cried as she shouldered her way through the crowd. Her shovel pointed the way. She glared at the man holding the broken bottle.

"That's porter. If you want some, I'll fetch a corkscrew and draw the cork. I'll give you some—in a glass. Then you can drink it like you were a gentleman!"

She took the broken bottle from the speechless man. Then, picking up one of the bottles with flat porter, she moved toward the glasses.

Carefully Mumbet put a few glasses on a tray, opened the bottle of flat porter, poured some of it into a glass, and offered it to the rowdy who had broken the bottle. "We always entertain everybody who comes to this house, and we offer them what we have—whether they know how to act like gentlemen or not. If you are thirsty, you are more than welcome to a drink."

The man took the glass and tasted the liquid. "Phew! That's bitter stuff!" he exclaimed. "If gentlemen drink such cursed sour stuff, they can keep it. If that's what gentlemen drink, I'm glad I ain't one."

"You've got no problems about that," Mumbet sniffed. "Is anyone else thirsty?" Her dark, flashing eyes moved over the crowd.

A few of the men tasted the flat porter, but it was a drink they were not familiar with and they found it much too bitter for their taste.

"Now, you are welcome to search the cellar—but don't you damage anything, or I'll skin you alive!" The shovel moved menacingly.

After all the men came up from the cellar, she stopped them in the kitchen. "Like I told you, only Mrs. Sedgwick and the children are upstairs."

"The judge is in the closet in her room, eh?" the leader said.

"Along with the silver," another added.

"No he's not and it's not. But if you think you jes' have to take a look, two of you can do it. There's no reason for all of you to go traipsin' around in her room and disturbin' a poor sick woman."

"All right," the leader said. "Let's go upstairs. Only two of us will search her room."

"This way then. Be quiet—and don't scuff my floors! Pick up your feet when you walk!" She glared at them and the rough men followed her meekly as she led the way.

She stopped in front of Mrs. Sedgwick's door as the other rooms were searched. When they returned to the hall, Mumbet said, "Excuse me. I'll be right back." She opened the door and entered the room.

"They want to search the room, but only two of them will come in," she said.

"Oh my! Oh dear!" Mrs. Sedgwick said, pulling the bedclothes up closely around her.

"They won't cause trouble. Not so long as I've got breath in my body," Bet said quietly and with a firmness that did not permit of doubt. "Children, you stand close to your mother. You too, Little Bet. Don't be afraid." She shepherded them to the bed.

"Come in," she said, opening the door.

Two men entered, embarrassed, trying not to see Mrs. Sedgwick and the children. After a quick look in the closets and the bureau drawers, they turned toward the door. "Aren't you goin' to look under the bed?" Mumbet asked, her voice dripping with sarcasm.

They paused, looked at each other, and finally stooped down to peer under the bed. Then they went out, Mumbet following them.

"Now where's the silver?" the leader demanded, turning to face the black woman.

"The judge knew Shays's men were on the loose in the country before he went away. No doubt he hid it or had someone hide it," she replied.

"What's on the top floor?" the leader asked, looking up the stairway.

"My room and the children's playroom," Mumbet answered.

"Come on. Let's take a look."

Mumbet led them up the stairs and quickly the closets and the drawers in the children's playroom were searched. When she went into her own room, she sank down on the pine chest with a heavy sigh, and as she sat, she began to wipe her face with her handkerchief and fan herself with it.

Her closet suffered the indignity of search. "What's in the chest?" the leader asked.

"This is my chest," Mumbet said.

"We'll jest take a look."

"Sure. Take a look. You been takin' plenty of looks, scuffin' my floors an' makin' a nuisance of yourselves. Now you want to look in a poor old black lady's pine chest." Her voice was sharp.

"Why—"

Mumbet didn't know what the man was going to say, but she didn't give him a chance to finish or to think.

"What kind of men are you anyway? Pretty small, I can see that. Why you haven't even looked under my bed yet. It's right there. Why don't you look underneath it? The silver might be there. Or even the judge might be there," she scoffed.

"Here I've been escortin' you all through this house, showin' you everything you want to see, lettin' you search your way from the cellar to the attic to your hearts' content, with you messin' up my floors and things that I work so hard to keep smooth and shinin' an' clean." She breathed a huge sigh that seemed a part of her long speech.

She didn't stop talking. "Now you've got me all tuckered out. And here I am, a poor old black woman, poorer than any of you, if the truth was known, probably. All worn out from watchin' you do all your foolishness." She sighed at the distress of it all, but the high note of scorn never left her voice.

"I told you in the beginning you wouldn't find the judge and that you wouldn't find any silver. But no. You wouldn't believe me. And now, the first time I get a chance to catch my breath, you want to go pokin' around in a poor old lady's pine chest. I declare, I never— What big, brave men you are! Real heroes,

I bet. Why don't you look under my bed first?" she repeated. "Very likely you'll find the judge. Then you can go pokin' around in my pine chest among my winter petticoats!"

She did not pause often, but when she did, the very silence in the pauses carried contempt that cut deep. But no matter how much she talked, Mumbet did not move from her place on the pine chest. It seemed clear that she would talk all the rest of the day and all night if the men who faced her would stand and listen.

"Come on, let's go," someone of the crowd said.

"Sure. Come on."

The leader paused. Mumbet held her breath, but she had stored up within her another torrent of reason, of words, of argument, and still more scorn.

"All right," the man said. "Come on. Why do we want to go pokin' around through her things?"

Mumbet remained firmly on her pine chest until the last of the men trailed out of the room. Then she followed them downstairs, her fire shovel still waving like a rattlesnake ready to strike.

In the lower hall, she passed ahead and courteously held the door open. Her face was stern, and she had not dropped the firm pose that had held them under control. She smiled inwardly when some of the men touched their foreheads and muttered, "Thank you, ma'am" as they filed out before her.

Harold W. Felton (*born 1902*) was a writer and a lawyer. His lifelong interests in folklore and biography led him to write many books on tall-tale heroes, such as Paul Bunyan and Pecos Bill, and on real-life heroes, such as Jim Beckwourth and Nat Love. Felton was inspired to write about Elizabeth Freeman after touring the home of her former master, Colonel John Ashley, at Ashley Falls, Massachusetts.

Developing Comprehension Skills

1. What does Mumbet do when she hears that Shays's men are coming?

2. Do you think Mumbet takes foolish risks when she offers Shays's men a drink and when she allows them to enter Mrs. Sedgwick's room?

3. When Shays's men enter Mumbet's room, she makes a long speech to them while sitting on her pine chest. Why does she do this?

4. Think about Mumbet's conduct with Shays's men. What qualities does she seem to have? Do you think that most people would have been able to handle the situation as well as she did?

Reading Literature: Nonfiction

1. **Recognizing Point of View.** As you recall, in **first-person point of view**, the narrator takes part in the action. In **third-person point of view**, the narrator is outside the action. Is this biographical selection narrated from the first-person or third-person point of view? How is the point of view different from that used in the autobiographies that you have read?

2. **Identifying Dialect.** A **dialect** is a variety of language spoken by the people of a region or social group. In the following sentence, one of Shays's men speaks in a dialect.

   If gentlemen drink such cursed sour stuff, they can keep it. If that's what gentlemen drink, I'm glad I ain't one.

In this sentence Mumbet speaks in a dialect.

   Here I've been escortin' you all through this house, showin' you everything you want to see, lettin' you search your way from the cellar to the attic to your hearts' content, with you messin' up my floors and things that I work so hard to keep smooth and shinin' an' clean.

   Find two more examples of dialect in the selection. Why might a writer use dialect?

3. **Learning About History Through Literature.** What historical facts and details does the writer include in this selection?

4. **Understanding Biography.** Biographers do a great deal of research. Often, they talk to people who knew the subject. The author of "Mumbet," however, wrote about someone who lived long ago. How might he have gotten his information? Would he have had any way of knowing Mumbet's exact words?

Vocabulary

Comparing a Dictionary with a Glossary. Here are three words from the selection: *indignity, sarcasm,* and *scorn.* Look up each of these words in a dictionary and in the glossary of this book. Compare the information in the two entries. What information do you find in both entries? What information do you find in the dictionary but not in the glossary?

Critical Thinking

Identifying Slanted Writing. In this selection, is the description of events slanted, or one-sided? Consider the writer's choice of facts. What kinds of facts are reported about Shays's men? Do these facts give you a positive or negative opinion of them? What kinds of facts are given about Mumbet? How do these facts influence your opinion of her? Do you think the writer has presented a fair picture of both Mumbet and Shays's men? If not, what reason might he have had for slanting his writing?

Study and Research

Planning a Biography. Pretend that you are going to write a biography about any two of the following: a historical character, a famous living person, or someone you know. Draw up a plan for each biography. Each plan should list your subject and the sources that you would use to find information about that person. For the famous subjects, make a trip to the library. In the reference section, find three sources that you could use. List these sources. For the subject who is not famous, list the writings, objects, people, and places you could examine or interview to gather information.

Developing Writing Skills

1. **Analyzing a Character.** Mumbet is both clever and courageous. In one paragraph, explain how she shows these two qualities.

   Prewriting. Divide a sheet of paper into two columns labeled *Cleverness* and *Courage*. In the first column, write ways in which Mumbet outwits Shays's men. In the second column, note ways in which she faces danger.

   Drafting. Draft your paragraph, using your prewriting notes as an outline. Begin your draft with a clear topic sentence.

   Revising and Sharing. Check your draft to make sure that your ideas are well organized and your sentences are complete and clear. Revise where necessary, then proofread.

2. **Describing Events from a Different Point of View.** Imagine that you are one of Shays's men. Give yourself a name and an occupation. Describe the events of that day from your point of view. Make sure that you describe Mumbet. Follow the steps in the process of writing: prewriting, drafting, revising, and sharing. Refer to the handbook at the back of this book if you need help with the writing process.

The Dark Secret of Captain Flood:
Part One

A. B. C. WHIPPLE

Captain Flood once terrorized the high seas. As you read, ask yourself how this real pirate differs from pirates in storybooks.

Captain James Flood had a secret. He kept it well, so well that when he died his secret almost died with him. In all his life Captain Flood revealed his secret to only one man, the first mate of his pirate ship. If he had not told his first mate, we would not know his strange, evil story. But we do, and here it is—the dark secret of Captain Flood.

He came from Jamaica, one of the major islands of the Caribbean Sea. Nothing else is known about his background. His story has come down to us through a legend of the islands, passed on by generation after generation. No one has ever found out what kind of life he led as a child or how he came to be a pirate. All that anyone knows is that his pirate ship suddenly appeared in the Caribbean in the early years of the eighteenth century. The ship's name, the *Shark*, was well chosen, because Captain Flood was one of the most bloodthirsty pirates of the Spanish Main.

He was also one of the smartest. The *Shark* was a small sloop, but that did not keep Captain Flood from attacking the great thirty-gun French frigate *L'Oriflamme* one night. He found her in the harbor of Petit Goâve, at the western end of the island of Hispaniola, the area now known as Haiti.

Captain Flood sailed up to the harbor entrance in the dark of the night. Inside the harbor he could see the lights of his prize as she lay tied to a wharf. Two boats slid away from the *Shark*, their oars muffled with cloth to prevent any splashing. The faces of the men were blackened to hide them in the darkness. Silently they rowed into the harbor and under the towering stern of the big French frigate.

Luck was with Captain Flood and his men that black night. The big frigate's guns were unmanned. Most of the crew were ashore. Only one watchman paced the wide deck. It took scarcely more than a few minutes for Flood's men to slip up behind the sailor, put a knife into him, and kill him before he could cry out the warning. His body still lay on the deck of the French frigate as the pirates cast off the lines, shook out her mainsail, and swung her away from the wharf.

There were other watchmen in the harbor, and big guns guarded the entrance. But so swiftly and silently did Flood's men work that no one saw the frigate's tall masts sweep across the bay and out to the open sea.

As the ship caught the wind in the rest of her sails outside the harbor, she picked up speed. Captain Flood, who had waited aboard the *Shark* near the harbor entrance, now sent her after his prize. Together the two vessels swept out into the Windward Passage, between the islands of Hispaniola and Cuba. There Flood went aboard the frigate and ordered his men to undo the locks they had clamped on her hatches. The sailors below were hauled on deck, a few at a time, and invited to join the crew of pirates. Some accepted. The rest were put over the side into two of the frigate's boats, to row off over the horizon to shore if they could.

They did, finding a beach at Cape Tiburon, on the western tip of Hispaniola. But apparently these were the last victims of Captain Flood to live to tell the tale.

In fact, in the next battle even some of Flood's own pirates were sacrificed. The *Shark* and the captured frigate, which Flood had renamed *Le Moustique (The Mosquito)*, had crossed the Atlantic Ocean looking for prizes. Off the island of Madeira they attacked a huge, heavily-armed East Indiaman. This time Flood tried a frontal attack. And it failed. But he was still too smart to pay for his mistake. He sent the little *Shark* in against the huge ship but stayed out of range himself in his frigate. The *Shark* was pounded to pieces. If Flood had attacked with both his ships, he might have won the battle. Evidently the captain of the East Indiaman thought so. At least he ran off as soon as he had shot up the *Shark* enough to outdistance her. Waiting out of range aboard his frigate, Flood watched his prize go without trying to catch her. Then he went over to the *Shark* and transferred all her treasure and able-bodied men to his frigate.

The injured he simply left aboard the sinking *Shark*. As he sailed away, the men aboard the frigate could hear the screams of the wounded on the *Shark*, unable to escape the water slowly creeping over them.

Now there was only the frigate. Back across the Atlantic she sailed, this time to the Bahamas, a string of islands and keys off the east coast of Florida. And in among the Bahamas, Captain Flood and his crew had a remarkable run of luck.

In fact, so many prizes did *Le Moustique* capture that within a few weeks her hold was loaded down with gold and jewels and coins. Captain Flood began to worry about the frigate. How could she maneuver well in battle, with her hull settled so low in the water?

That was when he dreamed up his secret. That was also when he told the one man with whom he shared his secret, his first mate. Little is known about this man except his nickname, "Caesar." Flood had no choice but to bring Caesar into his plot, because he could not handle it all by himself.

He had made his preparations, though. For many years he had searched out the loneliest islands of the Caribbean, going ashore on one after another until he had found just the island he had wanted. He now set the course of the pirate ship for this spot—Lotus Island, off the east coast of Hispaniola.

This end of Hispaniola is now the Dominican Republic, and the island is now Catalina. Then it was a wild and desolate place, the home of nothing more than a few goats, some great lumbering turtles and thousands of sea birds wheeling and squawking over the island's steep cliffs.

The birds swirled angrily about the intruding frigate as she eased through the narrow passage into the harbor. It was noon when *Le Moustique* swung to her anchor in the deepest part of the bay. And all that afternoon the boats went back and forth to the shore. They carried the chests of silver and gold and jewels to be buried in the dense jungle back of the beach. By sundown the work was done, and the rum was broken out for the celebration.

For most of that night raucous laughter and singing echoed across the bay as the pirates celebrated their good luck. It was nearly dawn when the last man had fallen into a dead sleep, and the ship rode quietly at her anchor with no one stirring aboard. Now it was time for Captain Flood and First Mate Caesar to go to work.

While Caesar got a boat ready, Flood hoisted up three chests, which he had carefully hidden in his cabin. The two men lowered the chests into the boat, climbed down and pushed off, rowing toward the highest cliff on the shore.

It seemed to rise straight into the sky from the beach, where rocks and coral ledges showed above the low tide. Around the side of the great cliff, the jungle crowded down to the water's edge. There was one break in the wall of trees and underbrush, where a stream trickled into the bay. Flood and Caesar made for this spot.

As the boat grounded on the pebbles of the beach, the two men jumped out and lifted the chests onto the bank. Then came the difficult part.

There was of course no way up the face of the cliff. But back in the jungle behind the beach there was a path. It was not much more than a faint trail worn many years before, probably by some of the herds of goats which roamed about the island. It was narrow and blocked in many places by vines and underbrush. As it climbed the hill, it became steep, twisting, and dangerous. But Flood and Caesar made it to the top, lugging one of the chests with them. Down the back of the cliff they went. Twice more they staggered up the steep trail, lifting and dragging the other two chests with them. It was almost noon by the time they had the last chest on the peak of the cliff. They rested, wiping the sweat from their faces and necks, swatting at the insects that swarmed around them in clouds, and looking out across the bay that stretched away from them far below.

Captain Flood rose and walked over to a tiny cave back of the edge of the cliff. He poked about in the cave and came out with a block and tackle—a pulley which was caked with rust and loops of what seemed like miles of rope. After some yanking and grunting, he had the pulley working again. He fastened it to a stubby tree which grew at the cliff's edge. He tied one end of the rope to the first chest and swung it over the ledge.

Slowly, with the rope creaking through the rusted pulley, the chest went down the sheer side of the cliff. About halfway down, it rested on a tiny ledge. This was the only place where the cliff did not appear to be like the side of a wall, going straight down hundreds of feet to the coral ledges and rocks which now looked so small, far below them. Here and there a bush stuck out of the cliffside, but there were no other ledges. This one was directly below the edge of the cliff where Flood and Caesar stood; and as they watched, the first chest came to rest on it.

Flood tied down the end of the rope

So the Treasure Was Divided. 1905, HOWARD PYLE. Delaware Art Museum, Wilmington.

which he had been paying out. One after the other he and Caesar slid down the rope and landed on the ledge. Cut into the side of the cliff was a fair-sized cave. Together the men untied the chest and shoved it into the cave. Then, at Flood's direction, Caesar climbed back up the rope, hand over hand. He pulled up the rope, tied it to the second chest, and lowered it slowly to the ledge where Flood waited. Sliding down after it, he helped Flood push it into the cave. Once more he pulled himself hand over hand back up to the top of the cliff. He tied on the third chest and lowered it to Flood. Sliding down the rope, he helped the captain hide this last chest.

So it was that Captain Flood and his first mate hid away for themselves the choicest part of the pirate ship's loot. In those three chests, they had a treasure worth perhaps more than all the gold and silver and jewels they had buried in the jungle the day before. The rest of the crew would know nothing about it. Whenever they wanted, Flood and Caesar could return, help themselves to whatever they needed, and be rich for the rest of their lives.

But that was not all of Captain Flood's secret.

The two men had stuffed their pockets with gold and were about to climb back up the rope, when Flood looked out across the bay and shouted, "The ship! Look!"

Thereupon Caesar made his mistake. He turned his back to Flood as he looked across the bay. At the same moment that he saw the ship riding quietly and safely at anchor, he was pushed off the ledge.

Caesar had time only to wave his arms in the air and scream before he was gone. Captain Flood leaned back against the cliffside, panting and listening. The scream died in a crashing thud. Flood waited a moment to catch his breath, then grabbed the rope and climbed hand over hand to the top of the cliff.

After he had hidden the block and tackle, he looked over the edge to see if Caesar's body was in sight. It was not—only the jagged coral ledges and rocks could be seen, with the water snarling among them.

It had worked exactly as Captain Flood had planned. Now he had the treasure of the three chests to himself. He would have to explain to the crew that Caesar had fallen into the water and drowned. But once he had done that, the three rich chests would be all his, and no one would know the murder he had committed to keep them to himself. That was Captain Flood's secret.

He did convince his crew. The few who were awake when he returned to the ship believed his story. With no questions asked, Flood ordered the anchor up. *Le Moustique* rode the tide out of the bay and into the open sea.

Developing Comprehension Skills

1. Captain Flood does many evil deeds. Some are listed below. Put these deeds in the order that they occurred.

   a. Captain Flood and his pirates unload their loot and hide it in the jungles of Lotus Island.

   b. Captain Flood and his men from the *Shark* capture the frigate *L'Oriflamme*.

   c. Captain Flood pushes Caesar over the cliff.

   d. *Le Moustique* and the *Shark* attack a heavily-armed East Indiaman off the island of Madeira.

   e. Captain Flood and Caesar carry three chests of gold and jewels up Lotus Island's steepest cliff.

2. Why do you think Caesar went along with Flood's plan? Why didn't he ever consider that he too could be in danger?

3. Captain Flood was not only evil, but he was also clever. List three examples from the selection that show his cleverness.

4. Think about the pirates you have read about in stories and seen in movies. Their way of life is often shown as exciting and glamorous. Does Captain Flood differ from fictional pirates? Would you want to join his crew? Why or why not?

5. Examine the following sentences. Indicate whether each states a fact or an opinion.

   a. "The ship's name, the *Shark*, was well chosen. . . ."

   b. "As the ship caught the wind in the rest of her sails outside the harbor, she picked up speed."

   c. "If Flood had attacked with both his ships, he might have won the battle."

   d. "At the same moment that he saw the ship riding quietly and safely at anchor, he was pushed off the ledge."

Reading Literature: Nonfiction

1. **Identifying Tone.** Tone can be described as admiring, angry, carefree, amused, sad, or serious. Tone is neutral, or objective, when the writer relates the actions of a subject without showing approval or disapproval. Look over this selection. Is Flood's biographer objective? Does he praise Flood? Does he condemn him? Explain your answer.

2. **Analyzing Organization.** Look at the first paragraph of the selection. When is this information being given: before or after Flood's death? Where does the writer jump back in time? Are the events after this point narrated in chronological order, the order in which they happened?

The Dark Secret of Captain Flood:
Part Two

A. B. C. WHIPPLE

What happens to Captain Flood?
Does he return for the treasure?
Does anyone learn his secret?
Read and find out.

Strangely, Captain Flood's luck turned against him. It took a while for him to know it. But after a few weeks he began to realize that no matter where he went, there were no prizes to be had. It was as if the Caribbean had been swept clean of merchant ships.

Captain Flood took *Le Moustique* out onto the Atlantic. Still no luck. He decided to give his men a much-needed vacation, and put into the harbor at New Providence, the beautiful island now called Nassau. Then it was the rough, tough, brawling frontier town of the Caribbean. Flood's men could hardly wait to swarm ashore.

It took them only a few days to spend everything they had not buried—days which Captain Flood spent out in the harbor aboard the frigate, fretting to be away.

He was not going to take the chance of liquor loosening his tongue in one of those waterfront taverns. The secret was all his now; he shared it with no one. So he spent his time in the loneliness of his cabin, itching to haul up anchor and sail away.

When finally his men had returned aboard ship, exhausted and penniless, all agreed that it was time to return to Lotus Island and dig up those chests. A few days later *Le Moustique* was again slipping slowly into the almost landlocked bay. The anchor had hardly taken hold in the harbor bottom when the crew was crashing through the jungle to the hiding place of their loot.

The chests were still there and still heavy. They were brought back to the ship, and the rusted locks were broken open. The gold had turned green; the silver was black with tarnish; the jewels were covered with a slimy mold. But all were as valuable as before, and the men chattered excitedly about the heaps of treasure as they thought again of those taverns and gaming tables of New Providence.

Later when the pirates were in a deep sleep, Flood dropped a boat over the side. By the faint light of a rising moon, he started rowing for the shore. As he rowed, he looked over his shoulder at the great cliff rising into the sky above him, black and menacing.

By the time the boat crunched onto the shore, Flood was so excited that he set out on the run for the path behind the cliff. He was panting heavily when he reached the top, but he did not wait to rest before digging into the little cave for the block and tackle. It was there, apparently untouched. He quickly rigged it to the tree stump and swung himself off the edge, dropping hand over hand to the tiny ledge halfway down the cliff.

The chests were still in the cave, jammed with gold and jewels and precious stones. Captain Flood fondled them greedily and stuffed his pockets with all he could carry. From inside his shirt he pulled a bag, which he filled with more loot and hung around his neck, buttoning his shirt over it again. It would be impossible for him to shove the chest out onto the ledge and haul it to the top of the cliff by himself. He had to be satisfied with what his pockets and the bag would carry. He took a last loving look at what he was leaving behind until the next visit, closed the chests, and went out of the cave.

The ledge was bathed in the light of the moon, which now hung out over the bay. The whole island lay beneath him, with a fringe of white sand shining between the jungle and the water's edge. The ripples of the harbor glinted in the moonlight and the dark hulk of the ship squatted in the middle of the bay. Captain Flood stood admiring the sight for a moment and then reached for the rope.

It was gone.

For a minute or two he fumbled about, not realizing what had happened. But then he heard a sound that made his blood run cold. It started like a low chuckle, rising into a cackling laugh. But it was more the hysterical cry of a madman.

Somehow Flood knew, even before he looked to the top of the cliff, what was silhouetted against the moonlit sky. He was right. There was no mistaking the outline of the head. It was Caesar.

What Flood could not understand was how it had happened. How had Caesar lived? How could anyone have fallen off that ledge and survived? In a mad, gloating singsong, Caesar explained. He had struck against a bush growing out of the side of the cliff. He had bounced into a spreading tree at the bottom. He had broken an arm and a leg in the fall, and he had been knocked unconscious. But the bush and the tree had saved his life. The rising tide had brought him to, and he had dragged himself up onto the beach beside the foot of the cliff. And then, as if sent by Providence, a merchantman had put into the harbor for wood and water and had rescued him. He had pretended to be a marooned sailor and had been taken to Kingston, Jamaica, with no further questions.

It had taken Caesar a few months to recover. But as soon as he was well again, he had shipped out on another merchantman and had deserted at San Domingo. There he had hired a sloop and made his way back to Lotus Island. He had had to wait for more months than he could remember. But through it all, he had known that there was one thing of which he could be sure. Captain Flood would return to the island and to the cave on the ledge. Now he had. Caesar laughed again—a laugh that brought goose flesh to Captain Flood's skin.

But despite his mad cackle, Caesar had a plan, which he now offered to Flood. It was a scheme which he had thought out during the many months while he had waited and nursed his revenge. If Flood would fasten the rope to each of the three chests, one by one, Caesar would then let down the rope for a fourth time for Flood—after he had hidden the chests.

Flood did not reply immediately. He settled down on the ledge to consider some other way out. After what he had done to Caesar, he could expect the same kind of treatment. Once he had helped Caesar hoist the three chests to the top of the cliff, he would be left to starve. Flood decided to wait until dawn, which he estimated was about three hours off. Perhaps he could find a way of escape from the ledge.

So he waited, while the moon slowly crossed the sky, while the pirate frigate below him swung around on her anchor with the changing tide, and while the muffled, impatient stamping of Caesar could be heard above him. In the stillness of the night, Flood could hear the water sucking angrily among the jagged coral formations below. Far off in the jungle behind the cliff a bird shrieked in the night. Out at sea the moon glinted off a breaker. Thus the hours dragged by.

The faint light of dawn had just begun to spread across the sky when the whole harbor seemed to explode. Below, in the middle of the bay, the pirate ship suddenly erupted in one great ball of flame. Probably a drunken crewman had lit a match in the powder magazine. Whatever the cause, *Le Moustique* blew into bits that soared into the air and fell hissing back into the water. One minute the frigate lay quietly at anchor; the next minute she was nothing more than a few big chunks of wood burning to the water's edge. As the last flame was quenched, Flood searched the moonlit water for a sign of some survivor swimming for the shore. There was none.

With the full light of dawn, he studied the bay more carefully. Except for a

Burning of the Frigate Philadelphia *in the Harbor of Tripoli on February 4* (detail), 1804,
ED MORAN.   United States Naval Academy Museum, Annapolis, Maryland.

charred timber or two, it was as if there had been no ship in the harbor a few hours before.

And now that there was light, Flood looked for a way up or down from his ledge. He could find nothing but sheer precipice, broken only here and there by a projecting bush or stub of a tree.

Then he thought of a plan. It was desperate, almost suicidal. But it was the only way.

Looking up, he saw that Caesar's head had disappeared from the edge of the cliff. A call brought him back. Flood said that he gave up. He was ready to tie on the chests if Caesar would send down the rope. He agreed that all three chests belonged to Caesar.

He had barely finished his promise when the block and tackle creaked and the rope started swinging down toward the ledge. Meanwhile, Flood climbed back

into the cave and hauled out the first chest. The rope was waiting for him when he emerged.

He grabbed the rope, wound it around the chest, tied it firmly, tested the knot, and yelled to Caesar to haul away. The line went taut. The chest bumped along the ledge and swung away. As it swung back toward Flood, it was at about shoulder height. Flood took a breath and jumped for it.

Apparently Caesar was too busy hauling the rope to realize that he had a double load. Perhaps he figured that only now had the chest swung free. In any case, the combined weight of the chest and Flood, who now hung onto the rope at the bottom, was almost more than the tackle and the tree trunk could bear. There was a creaking and a snapping, but somehow everything held. Gradually the chest, with Captain Flood still out of sight below it, rose alongside the sheer face of the cliff.

Inch by inch it came to the top. Sweating and swearing, Caesar hauled away until he had it high enough to swing in toward him. That was when he spotted Flood.

In dumb amazement he let the rope slip through his hands. At the same moment Flood jumped again, this time swinging himself the few inches to the edge of the cliff, where he grabbed hold of a rock and hung there. The chest, missing him by little more than an inch, plummeted past his shoulders.

Caesar caught himself and grabbed at the rope. It was whirring too fast through the tackle. He tried to take a turn around the tree stump. The rope jerked free. Seconds later the crash echoed up the side of the cliff as the chest struck the rocks below.

The two panting men stared at each other. Flood tried to haul himself up over the rock, but he was too exhausted for the moment. Now Caesar came slowly and menacingly toward him.

He tried to stomp Flood's fingers loose. He mashed one, but Flood managed to shift his hand out of the way in time to save the others. Caesar then raised his boot, took careful aim and brought it down on Flood's head.

In the same moment Flood ducked and reached out with one hand. He caught Caesar by the ankle.

Kicking angrily, Caesar tried to free himself. But Flood was hanging on for his life. Caesar could only grab at a bush, haul himself away from the edge and watch his enemy come slowly up after him. Then, as Flood let go and clambered to his feet, Caesar plunged at him. The two men went into a clinch and wrestled at the brink of the cliff, silently, desperately, murderously. Then it was over.

Flood reeled back, seemed to hang in mid-air for a moment, flailing his arms. Then he was gone.

Caesar lay on the grass away from the edge of the cliff for fully half an hour

before he could recover his strength. Without looking over the side, he secreted the block and tackle for a future visit. Carefully he made his way down the narrow trail on the back side of the cliff and climbed over the rocks to where the mashed corpse of Captain Flood lay wedged between two coral shelves. The clothes had been ripped from the body, but Caesar found some of the best jewels scattered nearby. He stuffed them in his pockets. The bag around Flood's neck had broken open. It was still usable though. The remains of the chest lay a few hundred feet away. From the jumble of doubloons and silver pieces, Caesar selected the best and filled the bag. He did not look back at the body, already being submerged by the rising tide, as he picked his way back to the beach.

He could not recall, as he told the story later, how many weeks he had to wait before a passing ship spotted his distress signal flying atop the great cliff. But again he was lucky, and again he was rescued within a few weeks from the time he had fashioned his signal. In those few weeks the tides and the ravenous fish had wiped out all evidence of Captain Flood.

Caesar of course said nothing then about the hidden chests or the dramatic fight on the top of the cliff. Many years later he made his way back to Lotus Island. The chests were gone.

Then he told his story. No one ever did find out who made off with the chests. But even today, when heavy winds drive the tide far out of the bay, the natives of the island can sometimes pick up a few pieces that still remain of the rich, once-secret treasure of Captain Flood.

A. B. C. Whipple (*born 1918*) has always loved the sea. He has explored Long Island Sound in a search for Captain Kidd's treasure, and he has also traveled to the Bahamas, the West Indies, and the waters off England, Japan, and Hong Kong. "The Dark Secret of Captain Flood" is from Whipple's book *Famous Pirates of the New World*. His other works include *Yankee Whalers of the South Seas* and *The Mysterious Voyage of Captain Kidd*.

Developing Comprehension Skills

1. The first line of Part Two reads: "Strangely, Captain Flood's luck turned against him." Is this statement a fact or an opinion? Defend your answer.

2. When Captain Flood returns to the high cliff on Lotus Island, what surprise awaits him?

3. What offer does Caesar make to Captain Flood?

4. What risks are involved in Captain Flood's plan of escape?

5. Caesar waited many months to seek his revenge on Captain Flood. He devised a careful plan. Why do you think he devised such a plan? Why didn't he tell someone else about the treasure and then just haul the chests away? Is Caesar as evil and cruel as Captain Flood? Give reasons for your answers.

Reading Literature: Nonfiction

1. **Examining Nonfiction Writing.** This selection has a setting and characters and tells a story. These elements are generally found in fiction. What, then, makes this selection nonfiction?

2. **Interpreting Character.** The writer describes Flood's actions. He also describes Flood's thoughts and feelings. Find three sentences in Part Two that describe Flood's actions and three sentences that describe his thoughts and feelings. What do the sentences suggest about Flood?

3. **Analyzing Organization.** Review the early events of Part Two, ending with Caesar's offer to Flood. How is the order in which these events are presented different from the order in which they actually happened? Why would it be difficult to describe the events in strict time order?

Vocabulary

Using a Dictionary to Identify Parts of Speech. Many words in this selection can be used as different parts of speech. *Harbor, swarm, sail, ship, loot, tackle, block, chuckle, cry, hoist,* and *escape* are some examples. Using your dictionary, look up five of these words. Write down the parts of speech that each can be used for. Then write two sentences for each word, using the word as a different part of speech in each sentence.

Critical Thinking

1. **Recognizing the Effect of Connotations.** The words used to describe a character are often meant to influence the reader's opinion of the character. Read this description of Caesar's laugh after he has trapped Captain Flood.

> It started like a low chuckle, rising into a cackling laugh. But it was more the hysterical cry of a madman.

Does this description create a positive, negative, or neutral impression of Caesar? What are the connotations of the words *cackling, hysterical, cry,* and *madman*? What images and feelings do they bring to

your mind? Create a different impression of Caesar by replacing these four words with words having other connotations.

2. **Supporting a Generalization.** The writer states: "Flood was one of the most blood-thirsty pirates of the Spanish Main." This statement is a generalization, a conclusion based on facts. List the facts in the selection that support this generalization. Do these facts support the generalization, or is more information needed?

Study and Research

Finding Facts in an Encyclopedia. Look up *Piracy* or *Pirate* in an encyclopedia. Read the general article and look over the titles of related articles that may be listed at the end. In the general article or one of the related articles, find the name of another pirate and a description of one of his or her deeds. Write this information on an index card or a sheet of notebook paper. Is the deed of this pirate similar to any of Captain Flood's deeds? Share your ideas with a classmate.

Developing Writing Skills

1. **Comparing Characters.** In two paragraphs, compare Captain Flood and Caesar. Explain how they are alike and how they are different.

   Prewriting. First, jot down words and phrases describing qualities the two characters share. For example, you might note that both men were greedy. After listing each word or phrase, give an example of how each man reveals the quality. Consider not only their actions, but also their feelings and their reasons for actions. In the same way, make notes about the differences between the characters.

   Drafting. Use your prewriting notes as a guide when drafting your paper. Begin your draft with a clear topic sentence that states whether the two characters are mainly alike or mainly different.

   Revising and Sharing. Share your draft with a small group of classmates. Ask them to suggest ways to improve the paragraphs. You may want to change the order of your statements or choose different supporting examples. Use the suggestions as guidelines for revision.

2. **Using Chronological Order in a Story.** Choose a modern-day villain from a movie, a TV show, or a book. Imagine her or him in the same situation as Captain Flood. What would the villain do? Tell a brief story in chronological order. Use words with negative connotations. Remember to follow the steps in the process of writing: prewriting, drafting, revising, and sharing.

Peculiarsome Abe

CARL SANDBURG

This selection from a biography of Abraham Lincoln tells about Abe's boyhood. As you read, see if you can explain the title, "Peculiarsome Abe."

The farm boys in their evenings at Jones's store in Gentryville talked about how Abe Lincoln was always reading, digging into books, stretching out flat on his stomach in front of the fireplace, studying till midnight and past midnight, picking a piece of charcoal to write on the fire shovel, shaving off what he wrote, and then writing more—till midnight and past midnight. The next thing Abe would be reading books between the plow handles, it seemed to them. And once, trying to speak a last word, Dennis Hanks said, "There's suthin' peculiarsome about Abe."

He wanted to learn, to know, to live, to reach out; he wanted to satisfy hungers and thirsts he couldn't tell about, this big boy of the backwoods. And some of what he wanted so much, so deep down, seemed to be in the books. Maybe in books he would find the answers to dark questions pushing around in the pools of his thoughts and the drifts of his mind. He told Dennis and other people, "The things I want to know are in books; my best friend is the man who'll git me a book I ain't read." And sometimes friends answered, "Well, books ain't as plenty as wildcats in these parts o' Indianny."

This was one thing meant by Dennis when he said there was "suthin' peculiarsome" about Abe. It seemed that Abe made the books tell him more than they told other people. All the other farm boys had gone to school and read "The Kentucky Preceptor," but Abe picked out questions from it, such as "Who has the most right to complain, the Indian or the Negro?" Abe would talk about it, up one way and down the other, while they were in the cornfield pulling fodder for the winter. When Abe got hold of a storybook and read about a boat that came near a magnetic rock, and how the magnets in the rock pulled all the nails out of the boat

Boyhood of Lincoln, 1868, EASTMAN JOHNSON. Oil on canvas. The University of Michigan Museum of Art; Bequest of Henry C. Lewis.

so it went to pieces and the people in the boat found themselves floundering in water, Abe thought it was funny and told it to other people. After Abe read poetry, especially Bobby Burns's poems, Abe began writing rhymes himself. When Abe sat with a girl, with their bare feet in the creek water, and she spoke of the moon rising, he explained to her it was the earth moving and not the moon—the moon only seemed to rise.

John Hanks, who worked in the fields barefooted with Abe, grubbing stumps, plowing, mowing, said: "When Abe and I

came back to the house from work, he used to go to the cupboard, snatch a piece of corn bread, sit down, take a book, cock his legs up high as his head, and read. Whenever Abe had a chance in the field while at work, or at the house, he would stop and read."

Abe liked to explain to other people what he was getting from books; explaining an idea to someone else made it clearer to him. The habit was growing on him of reading out loud; words came more real if picked from the silent page of the book and pronounced on the tongue; new balances and values of words stood out if spoken aloud. When writing letters for his father or the neighbors, he read the words out loud as they got written. Before writing a letter, he asked questions such as: "What do you want to say in the letter? How do you want to say it? Are you sure that's the best way to say it? Or do you think we can fix up a better way to say it?"

As he studied his books, his lower lip stuck out. Josiah Crawford noticed it was a habit and joked Abe about the "stuck-out lip." This habit too stayed with him. . . .

What he got in the schools didn't satisfy him. He went to three different schools in Indiana, besides two in Kentucky—altogether about four months of school. He learned his A,B,C's, how to spell, read, and write. And he had been with the other barefoot boys in butternut jeans learning "manners" under the school teacher,

Andrew Crawford, who had them open a door, walk in, and say, "Howdy do?" Yet what he tasted of books in school was only a beginning, only made him hungry and thirsty, shook him with a wanting and a wanting of more and more of what was hidden between the covers of books.

He kept on saying, "The things I want to know are in books; my best friend is the man who'll git me a book I ain't read." He said that to Pitcher, the lawyer over at Rockport, nearly twenty miles away, one fall afternoon, when he walked from Pigeon Creek to Rockport and borrowed a book from Pitcher. Then when fodder-pulling time came a few days later, he shucked corn from early daylight till sundown along with his father and Dennis Hanks and John Hanks, but after supper he read the book till midnight, and at noon he hardly knew the taste of his corn bread because he had the book in front of him. It was a hundred little things like these which made Dennis Hanks say there was "suthin' peculiarsome" about Abe.

Besides reading the family Bible and figuring his way all through the old arithmetic they had at home, he got hold of *Aesop's Fables, Pilgrim's Progress, Robinson Crusoe,* and Weems's *The Life of Francis Marion.* The book of fables, written or collected thousands of years ago by the Greek slave known as Aesop, sank deep in his mind. As he read through the book a second and third time, he had a feeling there were fables all around him, that everything he touched and handled, everything he saw and learned had a fable wrapped in it somewhere. . . .

The style of the Bible, of Aesop's fables, the hearts and minds back of those books, were much in his thoughts. His favorite pages in them he read over and over. Behind such proverbs as, "Muzzle not the ox that treadeth out the corn," and "He that ruleth his own spirit is greater than he that taketh a city," there were the music of simple wisdom and the mysteries of common everyday life that touched deep spots in him, while out of the fables of the ancient Greek slave he came to see that cats, rats, dogs, horses, plows, hammers, fingers, toes, people, all had fables connected with their lives, characters, places. There was, perhaps, an outside for each thing as it stood alone, while inside of it was its fable. . . .

Such book talk was a comfort against the same thing over again, day after day, so many mornings the same kind of water from the same spring, the same fried pork and cornmeal to eat, the same drizzles of rain, spring plowing, summer weeds, fall fodder-pulling, each coming every year, with the same tired feeling at the end of the day, so many days alone in the woods or the fields or else the same people to talk with, people from whom he had learned all they could teach him. Yet there ran through his head the stories and sayings of other people, the stories and sayings of books, the learning his eyes had caught from books; they were a comfort; they were good to have because they were good by themselves; and they were still better to have because they broke the chill of the lonesome feeling.

He was thankful to the writer of Aesop's fables because that writer stood by him and walked with him, an invisible companion, when he pulled fodder or chopped wood. Books lighted lamps in the dark rooms of his gloomy hours. . . . Well—he would live on; maybe the time would come when he would be free from work for a few weeks, or a few months, with books, and then he would read. . . . God, then he would read. . . . Then he would go and get at the proud secrets of his books.

His father—would he be like his father when he grew up? He hoped not. Why should his father knock him off a fence rail when he was asking a neighbor, passing by, a question? Even if it was a smart question, too pert and too quick, it was no way to handle a boy in front of a neighbor. No, he was going to be a man different from his father. The books—his father hated the books. His father talked about "too much eddication"; after readin', writin', 'rithmetic, that was enough, his father said. He, Abe Lincoln, the boy, wanted to know more than the father, Tom Lincoln, wanted to know. Already, Abe knew more than his father; he was writing letters for the neighbors; they hunted out the Lincoln farm to get young

A reconstruction of Lincoln's boyhood home at Knob Creek, Kentucky. Photograph by W. L. McCoy, Hodgenville, Kentucky.

Abe to find his bottle of ink with blackberry brier root and copperas in it, and his pen made from a turkey buzzard feather, and write letters. Abe had a suspicion sometimes his father was a little proud to have a boy that could write letters, and tell about things in books, and outrun and outwrestle and rough-and-tumble any boy or man in Spencer County. Yes, he would be different from his father; he was already so; it couldn't be helped.

In growing up from boyhood to young manhood, he had survived against lonesome, gnawing monotony and against floods, forest and prairie fires, snakebites, horse-kicks, ague, chills, fever, malaria, "milk-sick."

A comic outline against the sky he was, hiking along the roads of Spencer and other counties in southern Indiana in those years when he read all the books within a fifty-mile circuit of his home. Stretching up on the long legs that ran from his moccasins to the body frame with its long, gangling arms, covered with linsey-woolsey, then the lean neck that carried the head with its surmounting coonskin cap or straw hat—it was, again, a comic outline—yet with a portent in its shadow. His laughing "Howdy," his yarns and drollery, opened the doors of men's hearts.

Carl Sandburg *(1878–1967)* was the son of Swedish immigrants who settled in Illinois. Sandburg held a variety of jobs, served in the army, and traveled around the country. He sang and played his guitar, collected folk music, and listened to folk tales. Those experiences are reflected in his poetry, fiction, and nonfiction. Sandburg's use of free verse, slang, dialect, and street talk makes his writing come alive with the sights and sounds of America's past. Sandburg's biography of Abraham Lincoln, which won a Pulitzer Prize in 1940, is still popular reading.

Developing Comprehension Skills

1. How much time did Abe Lincoln spend in school? Was he satisfied with what he learned in school?

2. Why did Abe like to read?

3. Where does the title "Peculiarsome Abe" come from? Is the phrase a good choice for the title? Why or why not?

4. The writer says that Abe was bored with "the same people to talk with, people from whom he had learned all they could teach him." The phrase "all they could teach him" is a generalization. Does the writer have enough information to make this statement? What is he trying to say? Can you think of a different way to express the idea?

Reading Literature: Nonfiction

1. **Identifying Style.** One mark of Carl Sandburg's style in this biography is the use of parallel constructions. Here is an example:

> . . . Abe Lincoln was always <u>reading</u>, <u>digging</u> into books, <u>stretching</u> out flat on his stomach in front of the fireplace, <u>studying</u> till midnight and past midnight, <u>picking</u> a piece of charcoal to write on the fire shovel, <u>shaving</u> off what he wrote, and then <u>writing</u> more. . . .

The underlined words all have the same grammatical form (present participle) and are used in the same way (part of compound verb). Therefore, they are parallel.

Identify at least two other sentences in which you find parallel constructions.

2. **Comparing Characters.** Compare what you have read about Lincoln Steffens, Gary Soto, and Abe Lincoln when they were boys. List two ways they were different and two ways they were similar. Consider questions such as these. Who had confidence? Who was thoughtful? What were each boy's favorite activities? Who related well to people?

3. **Evaluating Biographies.** The selection about Elizabeth Freeman covers a single incident in her life. This selection about Abe Lincoln covers several years of his boyhood. Which approach do you think works better in helping you know about the subject of the biography? Or do you think that the approaches are equally good? Give a reason for your answer.

Vocabulary

Using a Thesaurus. A thesaurus lists groups of words that are similar in meaning. When you are writing, you can use a thesaurus to find a synonym for a word. You must be careful when choosing among the synonyms listed, however, because they will have different connotations. Use a dictionary to check the exact meanings of words listed in the thesaurus.

1. Imagine that for a paper about Abraham Lincoln you have written the sentence, "Abraham Lincoln lived in the boondocks of Indiana." You think that *boondocks* is too informal, and you would like to replace it with another word. Among the words you might find grouped with *boondocks* in a thesaurus are *wilds, sticks, outback,* and *backwoods.* Test each of these four words in the sentence. Which would you choose to replace *boondocks*? Why?

2. Use a thesaurus to replace the word *nosy* in the sentence, "Abraham Lincoln was very nosy; he read books to find answers to his many questions."

Study and Research

Scanning, Skimming, and In-Depth Reading. Your reason for reading influences how quickly you read. When reading for fun, you read at a different speed than when you are trying to find specific information.

In **scanning**, you look for specific information. To scan, move your eyes quickly down the page. Look for key words or phrases that point to the information you need. When you find a key word or phrase, stop scanning and read slowly. Scanning is faster than skimming or in-depth reading.

In **skimming**, you look over the page quickly to see what information is there. You skim to get a general idea of the content. You look at the titles, headings, and words in dark type to find out whether anything on the page interests you. Skimming is not as fast as scanning.

In **in-depth reading** you go even more slowly than in skimming. Now you read for understanding. First you read the boldface type to identify the important ideas on the page. You also notice how the material is organized. Then you read the material carefully, looking up unfamiliar words in the glossary or a dictionary. You read slowly enough to understand the ideas in each paragraph.

Selections by or about the following people are included in this chapter. Look up one of these people in an encyclopedia.

Benjamin Franklin
Abraham Lincoln
Helen Keller
Eleanor Roosevelt
John F. Kennedy
Martin Luther King, Jr.

First, scan the article to find the following information:

1. The date of birth
2. The date of death

Next, skim the article. On a sheet of paper, note three interesting facts about the person.

Finally, do an in-depth reading of the article. Determine how the article is organized. On a sheet of paper, copy any boldface heads and write the main idea of each paragraph.

Developing Writing Skills

1. **Writing Biography.** Try writing a short biography of someone you know, someone your age or a little older. The person you choose must be someone you can interview.

   Prewriting. Before you interview your subject, prepare questions about his or her birth date, schools attended, jobs, and hobbies. Also include questions about feelings and opinions, such as favorite songs or sports or classes, and most important memories. Write out the questions beforehand. During the interview, take notes on the subject's answers. Write down the main ideas, not every word.

   Drafting. After the interview, use the subject's answers to help you write about that person's life. Include details of daily life as in Carl Sandburg's biography of Lincoln. Write so that someone reading your biography could learn something about life in the twentieth century.

   Revising and Sharing. Review your draft and revise sections that are unclear. Share the biography with the class.

2. **Learning About Human Experience Through Nonfiction.** Nonfiction writing reflects the culture, or way of life, of a certain time and place. Write a paragraph telling what you learned from this selection about life in Indiana in Abe Lincoln's time. What things were different from life today? What things were the same? Follow the steps in the process of writing: prewriting, drafting, revising, and sharing. If you need help with the writing process, refer to the handbook, page 623, Guidelines for the Process of Writing.

Day of Light and Shadow

GENEVIEVE FOSTER

This selection describes Abraham Lincoln's last day. As you read, separate provable facts from the writer's imagined details. Does the author's opinion of Lincoln show through?

April 14, 1865, was a great day for the United States and a happy one for Abraham Lincoln. For that day, almost exactly four years after it had been fired upon, the Stars and Stripes were raised again above Fort Sumter! War was over! The Union had been saved. Slavery had been abolished. All, and more, that Lincoln had pledged himself to do had been accomplished.

His work was done. The care that had weighed so heavily upon him for the last four years seemed to have slipped now from his shoulders. His lined face, which had grown so drawn and haggard, was almost radiant.

The last day he began, as usual, working at his desk, and then had breakfast at eight. Robert, his oldest son, now twenty-one, was with him. Just returned from camp, he was full of news from the army at City Point. He had a picture of Robert E. Lee to show his father. Lincoln looked at it earnestly. "It is a good face," he said.

After breakfast came several interviews and letters to write before the Cabinet meeting which was called for eleven o'clock.

"Today," said the President, "General Grant will be with us."

Frederick Seward, acting for his father who was then dangerously ill, was the first to arrive. One by one, the others came in, entering into casual conversation over the day's news and speculating as to where the leaders of the rebel government had now gone.

"I suppose, Mr. President," said the Postmaster General, "you would not be sorry to have them escape out of the country."

"Well, I should be for following them up pretty close to make sure of their going," answered Lincoln in a comical tone.

There was some further speculation as to how soon word could be expected from General Sherman in North Carolina.

Then a half cloud passed over Lincoln's face, and he told of a strange dream that he had had the previous night. The dream itself was not so strange, he said, as the fact that he had had it several times before— and each time it had preceded some great victory or disaster. . . .

It was a vague feeling of being on a strange phantom ship, sailing, or floating toward some vast, indefinite, unknown shore. . . .

Someone ventured the suggestion that the anxiety in his mind each time over what might happen may have led to the dream.

"Perhaps," said Lincoln, thoughtfully, "that may be the explanation."

And here Stanton burst in—carrying a large roll of papers, and the group around the table was complete. General Ulysses S. Grant was then cordially introduced. Grant nodded and told in the fewest possible words the incidents of the surrender at Appomattox.

"And what terms did you give the common soldier?" asked Lincoln.

"I told them to go back to their homes and families, and that they would not be molested if they did nothing more," said Grant.

The President's face lighted with approval. That was right. There must be no hate shown or vindictiveness. Now that the war was over, everything must be done to help the bankrupt people of the South back to prosperity. So the talk turned to postwar plans. Stanton spread out his big roll of paper, showing charts for reconstruction. These were discussed until the meeting broke up at two o'clock.

As they were leaving, Lincoln spoke of going to the theater that evening to see "The American Cousin." Turning to General Grant, he said that he hoped that he and Mrs. Grant would accompany them. But there seemed to be some misunderstanding, because, though it had been advertised in the papers, General Grant said that they were to leave town that evening. Lincoln, himself, was not too eager about going, but since it had been announced, he thought he'd better go.

He made an appointment for the following day, and then went to lunch, from which his next callers saw him return munching an apple.

Then followed a talk with Vice-President Andrew Johnson, the man who was so soon to be faced with an overwhelming task. For now the time was growing short; it was past three o'clock. Lincoln could not stay much longer. There were only a few last things for him to do.

Towards late afternoon, for a short rest he put on his high black hat and went for a drive with Mrs. Lincoln, alone. No, "just ourselves," he had told her when she had suggested guests. It was a fresh spring day, the lilacs were in blossom, the willows along the river were green, the dogwood was opening. Lincoln's face glowed.

"I never felt so happy in my life," he

The last portrait of Abraham Lincoln, April 11, 1865. ALEXANDER GARDNER.
National Portrait Gallery, Smithsonian Institution, Washington, D.C.

said, drawing a deep breath.

Returning, he walked across the gravel path to the War Department and "was more cheerful and happy," Stanton thought, "than he had ever seen him." But to the guard who walked back to the White House with him in the gathering dusk, he spoke of men who, he believed, would take his life. And when they reached the steps it was "Good-bye, Crooks," that he said, for the first time, and not "Good night."

The strands of happiness and tragedy that made Abraham Lincoln's life were twisting closely now . . . for in the next moment, seeing two friends from Illinois, the governor and a congressman, he called to them in the cheeriest tone. Laughing and chatting, he led them to his office, and there read them one ridiculous story after another. His son Tad came to call him to supper, and he said he'd be right there. But first he wanted them to hear just one more story, the one perhaps in which the author poked fun at the "Goriller Linkin, whuz rane he had hoped wood be a short wun."

Then the author said, "The Confederacy is ded. It's gathered up its feet, sed its last words, and deceest . . . Linkin will serve his term out—our leaders will die off uv chagrin and inability to live long out uv offis. And so, Farewell, vane world!" And Lincoln left them laughing.

After dinner the Speaker of the House came for a few minutes, to say that, if there was to be no special session of Congress during the summer, he would take a trip to the West Coast—where, by the way, the transcontinental railroad was now being built.

The clock ticked on; it was just time to go to the theater, if they must, when the congressman from Massachusetts was announced. After a few words Lincoln arranged to see him in the morning. Taking a small card he wrote a few words on it, and then he signed his name—for the last time.

They were now at the door. Outside, the carriage was waiting. A breath of fresh cool air came in as the door was opened, and they walked out onto the portico in the moist spring night. Abraham Lincoln stood for a moment, then stepped into the carriage. Its door closed behind him, the horses started, the carriage rolled down the driveway, the sound of the wheels on the gravel grew fainter and then died away—and he was gone. Abraham Lincoln was gone.

And only then could the people of Abraham Lincoln's world realize how great he was. He was too tall when he walked beside them.

Genevieve Foster *(1893–1979)* was inspired to write by her grandparents, who had a deep interest in history. Her favorite subjects were historical figures, such as Columbus, the Pilgrims, and Abraham Lincoln. Born in New York City, Foster grew up and attended college in Wisconsin. She studied art and worked in advertising for a few years before choosing writing as a career.

Developing Comprehension Skills

1. List at least five of Abraham Lincoln's activities on his last day.

2. President Lincoln liked what General Grant told the common soldiers from the South. What does Lincoln's reaction suggest about his feelings toward these people?

3. What dream did Lincoln have the night before his death? What connection do you see between the events in the dream and Lincoln's death?

4. The writer says that only after Lincoln died did people realize how great he was. What exaggeration does she use in the last sentence to make this point? Is this exaggeration an appropriate one to use about Lincoln?

5. Why is the title "Day of Light and Shadow" a fitting one for this selection?

Reading Literature: Nonfiction

1. **Identifying Biography.** Review the explanations of a biography on pages 409 and 459. What makes this selection biographical and not fictional?

2. **Recognizing Foreshadowing.** Although the writer of this selection reports historical facts, she develops suspense by dropping hints about what will happen. Such use of hints in literature is called **foreshadowing**. Find the first hint that this day will be Lincoln's last. Then locate three other examples of foreshadowing in this selection.

Vocabulary

Reviewing Context Clues and Word Parts. Read these sentences from the selection. Try to figure out the meaning of each underlined word by using context clues or word parts. On a sheet of paper, write your own definition of the word. Then tell whether you used context clues or word parts to figure out the meaning.

1. "The Union had been saved. Slavery had been abolished."

2. "[Lincoln's] lined face, which had grown so drawn and haggard, was almost radiant."

3. "It was a vague feeling of being on a strange phantom ship, sailing, or floating towards some vast, indefinite, unknown shore."

4. "Everything must be done to help the bankrupt people of the South back to prosperity."

5. "Stanton spread out his big roll of paper, showing charts for reconstruction."

6. "But there seemed to be some misunderstanding, because . . . [the Grants] . . . were to leave town that evening."

Critical Thinking

1. **Separating Fact and Opinion.** Tell which of the following sentences state facts and which state opinions:

   a. War was over!
   b. "It is a good face."
   c. There must be no hate shown. . . .
   d. Returning, he walked across the gravel path to the War Department. . . .

2. **Recognizing Words with Positive Connotations.** Even though the writer of "Day of Light and Shadow" reports facts, she also suggests her opinions. In the following sentences, she uses words with positive connotations to depict Lincoln. Examine these sentences. What is the effect of each underlined word? What opinion of Lincoln does the writer give to the reader in these sentences?

a. "Lincoln looked at it earnestly." (page 491, paragraph 3)

b. " 'Perhaps,' said Lincoln thoughtfully, 'that may be the explanation.' " (page 492, paragraph 4)

c. "Lincoln's face glowed." (page 492, paragraph 12)

Study and Research

Scanning and Skimming for Specific Information. Go to the library and find at least three biographies of Abraham Lincoln. On a sheet of paper, write the title and author of each biography. Then look inside each book. Scan the table of contents and index. Identify those pages that concern Lincoln's reading as a boy. Skim only these pages from each of three books.

After you have completed this skimming, put the three books in order according to the amount of information each has. The first book should be the one that contains the most details about Lincoln's early reading. The last book should be the one that contains the fewest details. Write a few notes about each book to explain your ranking.

Developing Writing Skills

1. **Explaining Metaphor.** A **metaphor** is a direct comparison between two unlike things that have something in common. Metaphor is used in this sentence from the selection: "The strands of happiness and tragedy that made Abraham Lincoln's life were twisting closely now." Write a paragraph telling what this sentence means.

   Prewriting. In your prewriting notes, answer the following questions. What is Lincoln's life being compared to? What is the strand of happiness? the strand of tragedy? How are they being twisted?

   Drafting. Begin your draft with a clear topic sentence that states what the com-

parison is. Develop your ideas with examples from the selection.

   Revising and Sharing. Read your draft to a classmate and ask if your explanation is clear. Revise unclear sections.

2. **Supporting an Opinion.** Some people think that nonfiction is read only for information, not for enjoyment. What do you think? In a paragraph explain your opinion about nonfiction. Your first sentence should state your opinion. Then you should give reasons to support your view. Follow the steps in the process of writing. If you need help, refer to the Guidelines for the Process of Writing on page 623 in the handbook.

Personal Writings, Anecdotes, and Speeches

The following section includes two letters and a farewell speech written by Abraham Lincoln. The section also contains humorous stories about Lincoln and great words from famous Americans. These selections are a sample of the many forms that nonfiction can take. Like biographies and autobiographies, they will help you understand what people think and feel.

The Right to Know (detail), 1968, NORMAN ROCKWELL. Printed by Permission of the Estate of Norman Rockwell; Copyright © 1968 Estate of Norman Rockwell.

Reading Literature

Types of Nonfiction

You have learned that nonfiction includes all writing that is based on facts rather than on imagination. In general, there are two types of nonfiction.

In the first type of nonfiction, a writer gives a true account of a subject's life. Autobiographies and biographies are examples of this type of nonfiction. So are anecdotes, which are a kind of biography, and letters which tell events.

Speeches, essays, and letters of opinion are examples of another type of nonfiction. In this writing, the author discusses ideas and opinions. The reader learns what the writer thinks and feels about one or more topics.

In both types of nonfiction, writers use both fact and opinion. In the first type, the writer is giving information about people and events. However, in order to make a subject come alive, he or she often includes opinions.

In the second type, the writers tell what they believe and why. They base their opinions on facts and use facts to support their statements. Frequently, writers try to persuade their readers to agree with them.

Anecdotes

An anecdote is a brief account of some happening in a subject's life. Not every anecdote is entirely true. For example, the anecdotes about Abraham Lincoln in this section may or may not tell about events exactly as they happened. However, each anecdote shows some quality that the people of Lincoln's time valued and talked about.

Letters

The letter is one of the oldest and most popular forms of nonfiction writing. Letters are written to describe a trip, to tell news and to make business arrangements. A writer also can write a letter to explain what he or she thinks. In the letter to his stepbrother in this section, for example, Abraham Lincoln presents his opinions and gives reasons for these opinions.

Speeches

A speech is a form of nonfiction written to be read aloud. Speech writers must be able to tell how their words will sound to a crowd of people. They must capture the listeners'—or readers'—interest quickly and hold their attention. Well-written speeches sound both important and sincere. The ideas are well organized and are important. The speech by Abraham Lincoln in this chapter has these qualities.

Essays

The essay is a type of nonfiction in which a writer states an opinion and explains his or her reasons for this opinion. A good essay is well organized. The line of thought is clear. The tone of an essay can range from serious to humorous, depending on the writer's purpose.

Almost any topic can be the subject of an essay. Some writers speak of ordinary happenings and everyday life. The three essays in this chapter are of this kind. Other writers use the essay form to discuss serious topics, such as peace, truth, and freedom.

Lawyer Lincoln Turns Down a Case

ABRAHAM LINCOLN

Lincoln wrote this note when he was a lawyer. A man had died, leaving a widow, six children, and a debt of $600. The man to whom the debt was owed asked Lincoln to help him collect it. What advice did Lincoln give?

Yes, we can doubtless gain your case for you; we can set a whole neighborhood at loggerheads; we can distress a widowed mother and her six fatherless children, and thereby get for you six hundred dollars to which you seem to have a legal claim, but which rightfully belongs, it appears to me, as much to the woman and her children as it does to you. You must remember, however, that some things legally right are not morally right. We shall not take your case, but we will give you a little advice for which we will charge you nothing. You seem to be a sprightly, energetic man. We would advise you to try your hand at making six hundred dollars in some other way.

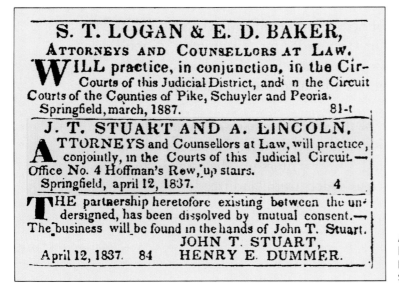

Announcement of Lincoln's first law partnership in Springfield, Illinois. Illinois State Historical Library, Springfield.

Abraham Lincoln (*1809–1865*) was a self-educated man who grew up on the frontier of Kentucky and Indiana. He held jobs as postmaster and lawyer and served as a member of the Illinois legislature. Lincoln was elected President in 1860. He remained in office until his assassination in 1865. As leader of the North during the Civil War, he was an inspiration to people all over the world. Lincoln's literary style in his speeches and letters was clear and sincere. His sense of humor still amuses readers today.

Developing Comprehension Skills

1. What did the man want to hire Lincoln to do?

2. Why didn't Lincoln want to take the case?

3. How can something be legally right but not morally right?

Reading Literature: Nonfiction

1. **Learning About a Character.** This note gives a reader insight into Lincoln's personality. What quality or qualities do you become aware of?

2. **Recognizing Style.** **Style** refers to the way that a literary work is written. This excerpt from a letter contains five sentences. The first sentence is as long as the other four combined. This sentence is also complex. It is made up of several shorter clauses. What emotional effect is created by joining these clauses in one sentence? Try to imagine Lincoln reading this sentence to the man. What tone of voice do you think he would use?

The second sentence is short and direct. Following such a long first sentence, what is the effect of a short sentence here? What tone of voice do you imagine Lincoln using for this sentence?

Letter to His Stepbrother

ABRAHAM LINCOLN

Here is a personal letter from Lincoln to his stepbrother. Read it carefully to understand Lincoln's reasoning. Do you think it was easy for him to write what he did?

Dec. 24, 1848

Dear Johnston:

Your request for eighty dollars, I do not think it best to comply with now. At the various times when I have helped you a little, you have said to me, "We can get along very well now," but in a very short time I find you in the same difficulty again. Now this can only happen by some defect in your conduct. What that defect is, I think I know. You are not *lazy*, and still you *are* an *idler*. I doubt whether since I saw you, you have done a good whole day's work, in any one day. You do not very much dislike to work, and still you do not work much, merely because it does not seem to you that you could get much for it.

This habit of uselessly wasting time is the whole difficulty; it is vastly important to you, and still more so to your children, that you should break this habit. It is more important to them, because they have longer to live, and can keep out of an idle habit before they are in it, easier than they can get out after they are in.

You are now in need of some ready money; and what I propose is, that you shall go to work, "tooth and nail," for somebody who will give you money for it.

Lincoln's desk from his house, now a museum, in Springfield, Illinois. Copyright © Erich Hartmann/Magnum Photos, Inc., New York City.

Let father and your boys take charge of your things at home—prepare for a crop, and make the crop, and you go to work for the best money wages, or in discharge of any debt you owe, that you can get. And to secure you a fair reward for your labor, I now promise you that for every dollar you will, between this and the first of May, get for your own labor either in money or in your own indebtedness, I will then give you one other dollar.

By this, if you hire yourself at ten dollars a month, from me you will get ten more, making twenty dollars a month for your work. In this, I do not mean you shall go off to St. Louis, or the lead mines, or the gold mines, in California, but I mean for you to go at it for the best wages you can get close to home—in Coles County.

Now if you will do this, you will soon be out of debt, and what is better, you will have a habit that will keep you from getting in debt again. But if I should now clear you out, next year you will be just as deep in as ever. You say you would almost give your place in Heaven for $70 or $80. Then you value your place in Heaven very cheaply, for I am sure you can with the offer I make you get the seventy or eighty dollars for four or five months' work. You say if I furnish you the money you will deed me the land, and if you don't pay the money back, you will deliver possession—

Nonsense! If you can't now live *with* the land, how will you then live without it? You have always been kind to me, and I do not now mean to be unkind to you. On the contrary, if you will but follow my advice, you will find it worth more than eight times eighty dollars to you.

Affectionately,
Your brother,

A. Lincoln

Developing Comprehension Skills

1. What is the purpose of the letter? Is Lincoln merely refusing to lend money, or does he have some other purpose?

2. What promise does Lincoln make to his stepbrother?

3. Do you think Abraham Lincoln had a fairly close relationship with his stepbrother? Give reasons for your answer.

4. Do you believe Lincoln was right to respond to his stepbrother as he did? Explain.

Reading Literature: Nonfiction

Examining a Letter. Lincoln expresses his opinions with considerable detail in this letter. What is the tone of the letter? Is the letter personal or impersonal?

Vocabulary

Using a Thesaurus. Use a thesaurus to find synonyms that could replace the underlined words in the following sentences from the selection. Choose the words that are similar in connotation to the words they replace and that also can be used as the same part of speech.

1. "Now this can only happen by some <u>defect</u> in your conduct."

2. "This habit of uselessly wasting time is the whole <u>difficulty</u>. . . ."

3. "You are now in need of some ready money; and what I <u>propose</u> is, that you shall go to work. . . ."

4. "You say if I <u>furnish</u> you the money you will deed me the land. . . ."

Critical Thinking

Analyzing Organization. Lincoln begins his letter to his stepbrother by saying that he is refusing to send the $80. He then presents his reasons. Write down the reasons from Lincoln's argument. Here are the first three.

1. I have helped you before, but you soon had money problems again.

2. You are not lazy, but you are an idler.

3. You have a habit of wasting time.

Developing Writing Skills

Writing a Personal Letter. Write a letter to a real or imaginary person. The letter should be at least three paragraphs long and should deal with a serious topic.

Prewriting. Select a person to write to and a topic to write about. For example, you might write to a friend who has moved away and suggest ways that the friend can become part of his or her new community. Describe your feelings about the topic. Determine what you want the person to do after reading the letter.

Drafting. Write a draft of your letter, expanding the ideas in your prewriting notes. Carefully choose words that express your feelings and that will produce the response you want.

Revising and Sharing. Share your draft with a classmate. Ask her or him to pretend to be the person to whom you wrote the letter. Ask what feelings the letter communicates and what her or his response would be. Revise parts that do not give the right message.

Farewell Address:
Delivered at Springfield, Illinois, February 11, 1861

ABRAHAM LINCOLN

When Lincoln was elected President, he had to move from Illinois to Washington, D.C. This is how he said goodbye to his friends and neighbors.

Abraham Lincoln when he first arrived in Washington in February, 1861, ALEXANDER GARDNER. National Portrait Gallery, Smithsonian Institution, Washington, D.C.

My Friends:

No one, not in my situation, can appreciate my feeling of sadness at this parting. To this place, and the kindness of these people, I owe everything. Here I have lived a quarter of a century, and have passed from a young to an old man. Here my children have been born, and one is buried. I now leave, not knowing when or whether ever I may return, with a task before me greater than that which rested upon Washington. Without the assistance of that Divine Being who ever attended him, I cannot succeed. With that assistance, I cannot fail. Trusting in Him who can go with me, and remain with you, and be everywhere for good, let us confidently hope that all will yet be well. To His care commending you, as I hope in your prayers you will commend me, I bid you an affectionate farewell.

Developing Comprehension Skills

1. To what or whom did Lincoln feel he owed everything?

2. Did Lincoln think he was becoming President at an important time in history? Give a reason for your answer.

3. This speech was written before the start of the Civil War. What did Lincoln mean by saying he hoped "that all will yet be well"?

4. Sometimes a person elected to office delivers a speech just to get publicity. Was this Lincoln's goal? If not, what do you think was his purpose in giving this speech? Explain your answer.

Reading Literature: Nonfiction

1. **Identifying Tone in a Speech.** How do you think Lincoln felt when he gave this speech? Is he being honest about his feelings? Give reasons for your answers.

2. **Understanding a Speech.** A good speech should leave you with ideas to think about. What ideas does Lincoln leave with his listeners? Name at least two.

3. **Recognizing Style.** Lincoln composed effective speeches by using several methods, or techniques, in writing. One technique was balancing words within a sentence or in sentences close together. In the third sentence, for example, he uses two related verb phrases, "have lived" and "have passed." Other examples are "born" and "buried," and "when or whether." Find in the "Farewell Address" two additional examples of this technique.

Vocabulary

Completing Analogies. One kind of analogy contains two pairs of words related in the same way; for example, the two words in the pair might be synonyms or antonyms. Look at this analogy:

East is to west as morning is to _____.

Because east and west are opposites, the correct answer to this analogy must be the opposite of morning. The correct answer is evening or night. Complete the following analogies on a separate sheet of paper. The answers are words from selections in this chapter.

1. Book is to title as person is to _____.
   subject   name
   idea   page

2. Strength is to weakness as courage is to _____.
   love   doubt
   bravery   cowardice

3. Class is to student as crowd is to _____.
   individual group
   teacher   leader

4. Infant is to adult as kitten is to _____.
   baby   person
   cat   pet

5. Energetic is to lazy as busy is to _____.
   difficult   quiet
   hurried   idle

Speaking and Listening

Delivering a Speech. Choose the speech by Lincoln or one you have written. Prepare to present it to a group. For your speech to be effective, you must be sure that you understand exactly what you are saying. As you practice, follow the points in this checklist.

1. Vary the pitch, or level, of your voice. Do not speak in a monotone.
2. Speak slowly and clearly. Pronounce words carefully.
3. Keep eye contact with your audience.
4. Speak with feeling in your voice. Sound as if you mean what you say. Speak as if your topic is important to you, and it will be important to your audience.

When you deliver your speech to the group, speak slowly. Say the words as if you mean them. Make sure that you stand straight, speak clearly, and look directly at your audience.

Developing Writing Skills

1. **Writing A Speech.** Imagine that you are giving a farewell address at your graduation ceremony. Write a brief speech, no longer than Lincoln's, in which you express your feelings upon leaving your friends and classmates for high school.

    Prewriting. Make notes on your feelings about leaving; the people, activities, and things you will miss; and what you will look forward to doing in high school.

    Drafting. Begin your draft with an opening sentence that summarizes your feelings and sets the tone of the speech. When choosing words, consider how they sound when read aloud.

    Revising and Sharing. Read your speech to a small group. Ask your listeners to state the feelings they were left with and the details they remember. Use their comments to revise parts that are not clear or memorable.

2. **Evaluating the Effectiveness of a Speech.** Lincoln's "Farewell Address" is very short. It probably took a minute or two to deliver. Did this shortness make the speech more effective or less effective? Would the speech have been better if it had been longer? Write a paragraph explaining your opinion. Follow the steps in the process of writing: prewriting, drafting, revising, and sharing. If you need help with the process of writing, refer to Guidelines for the Process of Writing on page 623 in the handbook.

Horse Trade

BEATRICE SCHENK de REGNIERS

Before there were cars, horses provided fast transportation. A horse trade was an important event. What do you learn about Abraham Lincoln from this anecdote?

Lincoln and the judge were joking about who could make the better horse trade. At last they agreed to meet in the morning to swap horses. Lincoln would not see the judge's horse beforehand. And the judge would not see Lincoln's horse.

The next morning a crowd gathered. Who would get the better of the trade?

The judge came first, dragging behind him the oldest, sorriest, boniest nag that ever managed to stand on four feet.

While the crowd was still laughing, Lincoln came along, carrying a carpenter's wooden saw horse. For a full minute Lincoln stared at the judge's horse without saying a word.

"Judge," said Lincoln at last, "this is the first time I ever got the worst of it in a horse trade."

Developing Comprehension Skills

1. Lincoln brought a horse to the horse trade. What kind of horse did he bring?

2. Why did Lincoln decide that he had gotten the worst of the trade?

3. What was Lincoln trying to do at the horse trade? What do you think his attitude was toward the horse trade?

Reading Literature: Nonfiction

Inferring Character. Lincoln's sense of humor comes through in his bringing a saw horse to the trade. He is playing a joke on the judge. After it is all over with, at whom else is he laughing? What does this tell you about his personality?

Lincoln Tells a Story About the King, the Farmer, and the Donkey

BEATRICE SCHENK de REGNIERS

Abraham Lincoln was a humorous man. Yet he had a serious job, and there was a war going on. See how he used humor to help solve a real problem.

One day President Lincoln found twenty men in his office waiting to see him. They all wanted jobs in the government. And they all had letters and other papers with them saying what smart men they were—what good work they could do.

These men didn't seem to understand that the President did not have time to give to the many, many people who came to him for jobs. There was a civil war going on. How could the President turn these job-hunters away without hurting their feelings? Maybe he could do it with a story.

"Gentlemen," said President Lincoln, "let me tell you a story I read long ago."

There was once a King who wanted to go hunting. He called the man who was Chief Weatherman and Court Minister.

"Tell me," said the King, "will it rain today?"

"No, your Majesty," said the Chief Weatherman and Court Minister. "The weather is clear. It won't rain. Good hunting to you!"

The King set out with his hunting party. On the way they met a farmer riding on a donkey. "Don't try to go hunting today, Your Majesty," said the farmer. "It is going to rain."

The King laughed and rode on. Surely the Court Minister knew better than a simple farmer!

But just as the King reached the forest, it began to rain. Oh, how it poured! The King and everyone with him were soaked to the skin.

When the King got home, he fired the

Court Minister. Then he sent for the farmer.

"From now on," said the King, "you will have the job of Chief Weatherman and Court Minister. Now tell me, how did you know it would rain?"

"I didn't," said the farmer. "It's my donkey who knows when it is going to rain. He puts his ears forward when wet weather is coming; he puts them back when it's going to be dry. So you see, Your Majesty, I cannot take the job."

The King sent the farmer away and sent for the donkey. And the King gave the donkey the job of Chief Weatherman and Court Minister.

"And that," said Lincoln, "is when the King made a great mistake."

"Why do you say that?" asked one of the job-hunters.

"Why, ever since that time," said Lincoln, "every donkey wants a job with the government."

The men couldn't help laughing. And then Lincoln told them, "Gentlemen,

Abraham Lincoln, L.G. WRIGHT. Collection of Kirby Rodriguez.

leave your letters and papers with me, and when the war is over, you will hear from me."

Beatrice Schenk de Regniers grew up in Crawfordsville, Indiana. She was active in a theatre-dance group in Chicago and then began writing books for young people. *The Snow Party, The Shadow Book,* and *May I Bring a Friend?* have won book awards. Regniers has served as editor of a book club.

Developing Comprehension Skills

1. Who told the King that it would rain? How did this person know what the weather would be?

2. What is Lincoln's attitude toward the men waiting to see him? Does he respect them? How do you know?

3. Why did President Lincoln tell his story? Do you think that he accomplished what he intended?

Reading Literature: Nonfiction

1. **Understanding Organization.** This anecdote contains two stories. How are they connected? In other words, how is the anecdote organized?

2. **Comparing Anecdotes.** Both of the stories in this anecdote teach a lesson. What is the moral, or lesson, of each? How does the lesson of the story about the king and the donkey help the men understand and remember Lincoln's point? What does the lesson of the anecdote tell the reader about how to work well with people?

Developing Writing Skills

Writing an Anecdote. The two anecdotes that you have read about Lincoln show one of his qualities—his sense of humor. Choose someone, either famous or not, whom you admire. Write an anecdote about that person, highlighting one of his or her qualities. The anecdote may be made up, but it must highlight a quality that the person really has.

Prewriting. After choosing the person you want to write about, list several of the person's admirable qualities. Choose the quality you want to highlight and list two or three situations that would make good anecdotes. Decide on one situation and write several details that would make an interesting story.

Drafting. As you write, make sure the events in the anecdote follow time order. Use specific details that will enable the reader to understand and appreciate the quality you want to emphasize. Keep your sentences brief and to the point.

Revising and Sharing. Read your anecdote to a classmate. Ask whether or not the parts of the story flow together smoothly. Have you included any material that interferes with the anecdote? Do you need to add any details? After you have made any necessary revisions, practice reading your anecdote aloud in preparation for sharing it with the class.

The Words of Famous Americans

These statements by famous Americans had meaning for the people of their times and for people of later generations. As you read, try to see what makes these quotations memorable.

A little neglect may breed great mischief . . . for want of a nail the shoe was lost; for want of a shoe the horse was lost; and for want of a horse the rider was lost.

—Benjamin Franklin, *Poor Richard's Almanack* (1758)

These are times in which a genius would wish to live. It is not in the still calm of life, or in the repose of a pacific station, that great challenges are formed. . . . Great necessities call out great virtues.

—Abigail Adams, Letter to John Quincy Adams (January 19, 1780)

You can fool all of the people some of the time, and some of the people all of the time, but you cannot fool all of the people all of the time.

—Abraham Lincoln, Speech (1858)

You gain strength, courage, and confidence by every experience in which you really stop to look fear in the face. You are able to say to yourself, "I lived through this horror. I can take the next thing that comes along." . . . You must do the thing you think you cannot do.

—Eleanor Roosevelt, *You Learn by Living* (1960)

And so, my fellow Americans, ask not what your country can do for you; ask what you can do for your country.

—John F. Kennedy, *Inaugural Address* (January 20, 1961)

I have a dream that my four little children will one day live in a nation where they will not be judged by the color of their skin, but by the content of their character.

—Martin Luther King, Jr., Speech at Civil Rights March on Washington (August 28, 1963)

Freedom to Dream, 1985, CAROL WAGNER. Made for the Great American Quilt Festival in 1986. Collection of the Artist, Minnesota.

Developing Comprehension Skills

1. What does Lincoln say that it is impossible to do? What is the question that John F. Kennedy wants Americans to ask themselves? By what does Martin Luther King, Jr., dream that his children will be judged?

2. State in your own words the main idea of each quotation. Which two quotations seem to express the same idea?

3. Which of these quotations most appeals to you, either in message or style? Give reasons for your answer.

Reading Literature: Nonfiction

Recognizing Techniques of Style. All writers use a variety of techniques to present their ideas clearly and powerfully. They may repeat words or phrases for emphasis. They may also balance words or phrases that have the same grammatical form, as Lincoln did in his "Farewell Address." Reread the quotations and find examples of repetition and balance.

Vocabulary

Using a Thesaurus. In the quotation by Abigail Adams, the idea of one phrase, "the still calm of life," is repeated in the following phrase, "the repose of a pacific station." The words *still, calm, repose,* and *pacific* are similar in meaning and are grouped in the thesaurus under the heading *calmness*. Use the thesaurus to select two words that could replace *repose* and *pacific* in the second phrase. Choose words that are the same part of speech as the words they replace and that also have similar connotations. Does changing the two words change the feeling of Adams's statement in any way?

Developing Writing Skills

Applying Literature to Life. Choose one of the quotations and write a paragraph explaining how it applies to life today. Use an incident from your own experience or from current events to show why the saying is still meaningful.

Prewriting. Write down the point that is being made by the quotation. Recall an event that seems to illustrate this point, and note how the event does this.

Drafting. Use your prewriting notes to compose a draft of your paragraph. You may want to restate and explain the meaning of the quotation at the beginning of the paper. Or, you may first want to relate the incident and then show how the quotation is linked to it.

Revising and Sharing. Check your draft to be sure that you have made clear connections between the incident and the quotation. After making the revisions needed, share your paragraph with the class.

Essays

Most readers like to read about famous and important people. However, they also like to read about people and things closer to their own lives. The selections in this section challenge readers to take a closer look at the world around them.

Woman with Plants, 1929, GRANT WOOD. Collection of the Cedar Rapids Museum of Art, Iowa.

April and Robins

HAL BORLAND

In this essay, the writer tells of a bird whose song signals the coming of spring. As you read, see why the robin is special to the writer.

Robin, 1971, SALLIE MIDDLETON. Foxfire Fine Arts, Inc., Charlotte, North Carolina.

April 2

People who can't tell a bald eagle from a vulture know what a robin looks like, and they know that when robins strut the lawn, April must be here. April just isn't April, in this part of the world, without robins. Spring couldn't come without them.

The robin long ago became a kind of national bird without a shred of legal backing. It didn't need legal proclamations, for the robin is one of the best known and widely distributed birds in all these United States. Perhaps most important of all, it is a cosmopolitan bird, equally at home in a city park, on a suburban lawn, and in the open country. Unlike most other thrushes, it prefers to nest near a house. Being a comparatively large bird, big as a blue jay, and a conspicuous bird with its black head and cinnamon-red breast, the robin simply can't be overlooked. Besides, robins love to strut. And to sing, preferably from a street-side tree.

The robin's song is often underrated, probably because the robin is so common and so vocal. But the robin, after all, is a thrush, and the thrushes are accomplished songsters. The robin sings long, loudly, and rather deliberately. Its notes are clear and rich in tone. And no two robins sing exactly the same way; they vary their songs, put the phrases together differently. An individual robin may sing as many as ten different songs, varying with the time of day.

Robins are already singing in many places. Their chorus will increase day by day. After all, it is April, even to a robin.

Hal Borland *(born 1900)* grew up on the American frontier. He was greatly influenced by his childhood experiences. After completing high school, he worked his way through the University of Colorado by taking a job as a newspaper correspondent. Borland lived on a farm and developed a deep interest in nature. His essays about outdoor life appeared in *The New York Times* for more than twenty years.

Shortest Month

HAL BORLAND

You have read Mr. Borland's comments on April. Now find out how he feels about a winter month.

December 4

December is the shortest month of the year. No argument will be accepted, if it is to the contrary; and those who point to February are merely making gestures. True, December does have thirty-one days, such as they are. But can you really call days those hurried little spans that come zipping past, once Thanksgiving is behind and Christmas lies just ahead? Certainly not. Why, if you even pause to check them off on the calendar, you have no time for anything else! The Thanksgiving turkey vanishes, and you turn around, and there is the Christmas tree waiting to be decorated. New Year's Day is here, and January. December is gone again.

There is no illusion about it, except for those who are innate sticklers. In round figures, December has only 288 hours of daylight; and that counts in even those dreary times when the sun sulks behind a mass of clouds all day. Even March, of evil reputation, can muster that many hours of daylight in twenty-four days. And June, magnificent June, does as well by us in only nineteen days.

What is a December day, anyway? Nine hours of daylight, with a few minutes left over at each end to turn the lights on and off. And fifteen hours of darkness. With a moon, to be sure, and a great many stars. But darkness, just the same. You eat breakfast by lamplight, hurry to work in half-light, and get home in darkness. You have four weekends in which to watch the sun scurry across the southern quadrant of the sky.

December? By sundown tonight we will have had just a little over thirty-seven hours of December daylight. Enough said?

Arctic Owl and Winter Moon,
1960, CHARLES BURCHFIELD.
Private Collection. Photograph: Kennedy Galleries, New York.

Developing Comprehension Skills

1. What two things does the writer say almost everyone knows about robins? Look at the opening paragraph of the first essay to find out.

2. Read each statement below and decide whether it is a fact or an opinion. Give a reason for your decision.

a. "April just isn't April . . . without robins."

b. "But the robin, after all, is a thrush. . . ."

c. "[T]he robin simply can't be overlooked."

d. "An individual robin may sing as many as ten different songs. . . ."

3. The writer says that spring couldn't come without robins. What does he mean? What experience is he trying to convey? Can you think of similar experiences?

4. What does December have less of than March or June?

5. Do you agree with the writer's opinion of December? Explain your reasons.

Reading Literature: Nonfiction

1. **Analyzing Organization of an Essay.** Reread each paragraph in the essay on robins. Then in your own words identify the main idea of each paragraph. What is the connection between the main ideas?

2. **Identifying Mood.** The **mood** of a work of literature is the feeling it gives the reader. How would you describe the mood of "April and Robins"?

3. **Recognizing Personification. Personification** is the giving of human qualities to an object, an animal, or an idea. An example is "the great ship, tense and anxious, groped her way toward the shore" from *The Story of My Life* by Helen Keller. Find three examples of personification in "Shortest Month."

4. **Understanding Theme.** In these essays the writer conveys a **theme**, or message, to you. What is the theme of "Shortest Month"? How does this theme differ from that of "April and Robins"?

Vocabulary

1. **Reviewing Context Clues.** In each sentence below, the underlined word is from an essay by Hal Borland. You can determine the meaning of each word by using a context clue. On a sheet of paper, write each underlined word, its definition, and the key words that helped you discover the meaning.

   a. "The robin is a <u>cosmopolitan</u> bird. For instance, it is at home in a city park, on a suburban lawn, and in the open country."

   b. "Like other thrushes that are <u>accomplished</u> songsters, the robin sings long, loudly, and rather deliberately."

   c. "Being a large bird, and a <u>conspicuous</u> bird with its black head and cinnamon-red breast, the robin simply can't be overlooked."

2. **Reviewing Word Parts.** In Chapter Two, you learned the meanings of several Greek and Latin prefixes. Another Latin prefix used in some English words is *quadra,* or *quadri,* meaning *four.* For example, in "Shortest Month" this phrase appears: "across the southern quadrant of the sky." A *quadrant* is one-fourth of a circle.

   Read the following sentences. Choose the correct prefix to fill in the blank before each base word. Choose from among *quadri* and the other Latin and Greek prefixes listed on page 75. If necessary, check your answers in a dictionary.

a. A __lingual person speaks three languages, and a __lingual person speaks four.

b. A __cycle has one wheel and a __cycle has four wheels.

c. A celebration marking the end of two hundred years is a __centennial, and one marking the end of four hundred years is a __centennial.

d. A __syllabic word has many syllables, and a __syllablic word has four.

e. A __gon is a figure with many sides, and a __agon has ten sides.

Developing Writing Skills

Writing an Essay. Write a brief essay that expresses your opinion about a particular month.

Prewriting. Choose one month and think of two or three reasons for liking or disliking it. Put your reasons in order of importance, beginning with either the most important or the least important.

Drafting. Draft your essay, using your prewriting notes as a guide. As you write, think of ways to connect your ideas and of examples to illustrate them.

Revising and Sharing. Share your draft with a partner. Ask if your ideas are presented in an orderly way and your reasons are convincing. Use your partner's comments as guidelines for revision.

Langston Terrace

ELOISE GREENFIELD *and*
LESSIE JONES LITTLE

In this essay, a woman speaks about her childhood home. What feelings does she express about her home? Does your definition of "home" match hers?

I fell in love with Langston Terrace the very first time I saw it. Our family had been living in two rooms of a three-story house when Mama and Daddy saw the newspaper article telling of the plans to build it. It was going to be a low-rent housing project in northeast Washington, and it would be named in honor of John Mercer Langston, the famous black lawyer, educator, and congressman.

So many people needed housing and wanted to live there, many more than there would be room for. They were all filling out applications, hoping to be one of the 274 families chosen. My parents filled out one, too.

I didn't want to move. I knew our house was crowded—there were eleven of us, six adults and five children—but I didn't want to leave my friends. I didn't want to go to a strange place and be the new person in a neighborhood and a school where most of the other children already knew each other. I was eight years old, and I had been to three schools. We had moved five times since we'd been in Washington, each time trying to get more space and a better place to live. But rent was high so we'd always lived in a house with relatives and friends and shared the rent.

One of the people in our big household was Lillie, Daddy's cousin and Mama's best friend. She and her husband also applied for a place in the new project. During the months that it was being built, Lillie and Mama would sometimes walk fifteen blocks just to stand and watch the workmen digging holes and laying bricks. They'd just stand there watching and wishing. And at home, that was all they could talk about. "When we get our new place. . . ." "If we get our new place. . . ."

Lillie got her good news first. I can still see her and Mama standing at the bottom of the hall steps, hugging and laughing and crying, happy for Lillie, then sitting on the steps, worrying and wishing again for Mama.

Finally, one evening, a woman came to the house with our good news, and Mama and Daddy went over and picked out the house they wanted. We moved on my ninth birthday. Wilbur, Gerald, and I went to school that morning from one house, and, when Daddy came to pick us up, he took us home to another one. All the furniture had been moved while we were in school.

Langston Terrace was a lovely birthday present. It was built on a hill, a group of tan brick houses and apartments with a playground as its center. The red mud surrounding the concrete walks had not yet been covered with black soil and grass seed, and the holes that would soon be homes for young trees were filled with rainwater. But it still looked beautiful to me.

We had a whole house all to ourselves. Upstairs and downstairs. Two bedrooms, and the living room would be my bedroom at night. Best of all, I wasn't the only new person. Everybody was new to this new little community. By the time school opened in the fall, we had gotten used to each other and had made friends with other children in the neighborhood, too.

I guess most of the parents thought of the new place as an in-between place. They were glad to be there, but their dream was to save enough to pay for a house that would be their own. Saving was hard, though, and slow, because each time somebody in a family got a raise on the

job, it had to be reported to the manager of the project so that the rent would be raised, too. Most people stayed years longer than they had planned to, but they didn't let that stop them from enjoying life.

They formed a resident council to look into any neighborhood problems that might come up. They started a choral group and presented music and poetry programs on Sunday evenings in the social room or on the playground. On weekends, they played horseshoes and softball and other games. They had a reading club that met once a week at the Langston branch of the public library, after it opened in the basement of one of the apartment buildings.

The library was very close to my house. I could leave by my back door and be there in two minutes. The playground was right in front of my house, and after my sister Vedie was born and we moved a few doors down to a three-bedroom house, I could just look out of my bedroom window to see if any of my friends were out playing.

There were so many games to play and things to do. We played hide-and-seek at the lamppost, paddle tennis and shuffleboard, dodge ball and jacks. We danced in fireplug showers, jumped rope to rhymes, played "Bouncy, Bouncy, Bally," swinging one leg over a bouncing ball, played baseball on a nearby field, had parties in the social room, and bus trips to the beach. In the playroom, we played Ping-Pong and pool, learned to sew and embroider and crochet.

For us, Langston Terrace wasn't an in-between place. It was a growing-up place, a good growing-up place with neighbors who cared, family and friends, and a lot of fun. Life was good. Not perfect, but good. We knew about problems, heard about them, saw them, lived through some hard ones ourselves; but our community wrapped itself around us, put itself between us and the hard knocks, to cushion the blows.

It's been many years since I moved away, but every once in a long while I go back just to look at things and remember. The large stone animals that decorated the playground are still there: a walrus, a hippo, a frog, and two horses. They've started to crack now, but I remember when they first came to live with us. They were friends, to climb on or to lean against, or to gather around in the evening. You could sit on the frog's head and look way out over the city at the tall trees and rooftops.

Nowadays, whenever I run into old friends, mostly at a funeral or maybe a wedding, after we've talked about how we've been and what we've been doing, and how our children are, we always end up talking about our childtime in our old neighborhood. And somebody will say, "One of these days we ought to have a Langston reunion." That's what we always called it, just "Langston," without the "Terrace." I guess because it sounded more homey. And that's what Langston was. It was home.

Eloise Greenfield *(born 1929)* was born in North Carolina and grew up in Washington, D.C. She has written many picture books, novels, and short stories. She has also written a collection of poetry titled *Honey, I Love* and biographies of Rosa Parks and Paul Robeson. "Langston Terrace" is taken from *Childtimes: A Three Generation Memoir*, a book Greenfield wrote with her mother, Lessie Jones Little. This book compares the childhoods of Greenfield, her mother, and her grandmother.

Lessie Jones Little *(1906–1986)* was born in North Carolina and attended North Carolina State Normal School. She began writing when she was sixty-seven and a great-grandmother. Before becoming a writer, she worked as an elementary school teacher.

Developing Comprehension Skills

1. At first, the writer has mixed feelings about moving to Langston Terrace. What advantages does she see? What disadvantages is she worried about?

2. How does the writer feel when her family actually moves to Langston Terrace? What makes her feel this way?

3. Explain what the writer means by this sentence: "Our community wrapped itself around us, put itself between us and the hard knocks, to cushion the blows."

4. The writer says that life was good at Langston Terrace. She says that Langston was "home." What is most important in making a place a home? List the feelings, qualities, people, activities, and things you associate with the idea of home. How does your list compare with the writer's description of Langston Terrace?

Reading Literature: Nonfiction

1. **Evaluating an Essay.** As you know, an essay can be about ordinary events and everyday life. What kinds of everyday events and experiences are included in this essay? Why are these experiences worth writing about? How do the events in the essay relate to the writer's life? How important were these events and experiences to the writer?

2. **Identifying Tone.** As you know, **tone** is the writer's attitude toward the subject. In this essay, the writer says, "I fell in love with Langston Terrace the very first time I saw it" and "It [Langston Terrace] was a growing-up place, a good growing-up place." What tone do these sentences have? Can you find other statements that have the same tone?

3. **Making Inferences About Character.** The writer does not directly describe herself in this essay. What can you infer, or what conclusions can you draw, about her? What do you think her relations with her family were like? How do you think she got along with other people? Did she have many friends? Be sure to support your inferences with details from the essay.

Vocabulary

Identifying the Correct Respelling, Part of Speech, and Definition. Read the following sentences based on the nonfiction selections you have read. Each of the underlined words can be pronounced two different ways. Each word also can be used as more than one part of speech. Decide how each word is used in the sentence. Then look up the word in the dictionary. On a sheet of paper, write the following information for each word:

    a. The correct respelling
    b. The part of speech
    c. The correct definition

1. If you abuse the horse, she will be ruined forever.

2. My father's way of discipline was more appropriate.

3. I am filled with wonder when I consider the contrasts between the two lives which that day connects.

4. I returned again and again to the subject, eager for more information.

5. I explored with my hands and learned the name of every object that I touched.

6. Lincoln refused his stepbrother eighty dollars because of a defect in the stepbrother's conduct.

7. The defect was that his stepbrother didn't do a day's work in a day.

8. Langston Terrace was a low-rent housing project in northeast Washington.

Study and Research

Locating Information. You have learned to use the dictionary to find the meanings of unfamiliar words. The dictionary also contains entries for the names of famous people or groups of people, places, and events. For example, you can find Helen Keller and Warsaw entered in most dictionaries. However, the dictionary will give only a brief explanation of these entries. The encyclopedia will provide much more information.

The following words and names appear in the nonfiction selections. Locate each item in the dictionary and write the definition. Then locate each item in the encyclopedia. Write two facts not given in the dictionary.

1. Dr. Alexander Graham Bell
2. Little League
3. Daniel Shays or Shays's Rebellion
4. Spanish Main
5. Civil War
6. Washington, D.C.

Developing Writing Skills

Writing About a Place. Think about a place that was important to you when you were younger. It might be your home, a place in your neighborhood, a friend's or relative's house, a classroom, a secret hiding place, a park, or a vacation spot. Write an essay of two to four paragraphs explaining why this place was important to you.

Prewriting. List as many details as you can about the place. First, list the sights, sounds, smells, and even tastes that you associate with the place. Then list the people, events, and activities that were important. Finally, write down the feelings you had about the place and your experiences there. Decide how you want to organize the details. In what order do you want to present them to the reader?

Drafting. Follow the organization that you have developed. In your first paragraph, introduce the place and the aspect of it that you have decided to write about first. In the following paragraphs, develop the rest of your ideas in the order you have chosen.

Revising and Sharing. As you revise your draft, consider the following questions: Have I used clear, vivid words to describe the place? Do the sentences flow smoothly from one to the other? Are the paragraphs clearly connected? Can the reader follow the ideas?

After you have finished the final draft, work with your classmates to make a class book of favorite places. You may want to add photos, drawings, or pictures from magazines to illustrate each place.

Chapter 6 Review

Using Your Skills in Reading Nonfiction

The following paragraphs are from *A Portrait of Myself* by Margaret Bourke-White, a famous photographer for *Life* magazine. Read them. Then answer these questions: From what point of view are the paragraphs written? Are they biographical or autobiographical? How would you describe the writer's tone?

> A few months later, in the spring of 1929, I received a telegram from a man I had never met: HAVE JUST SEEN YOUR STEEL PHOTOGRAPH. CAN YOU COME TO NEW YORK AT OUR EXPENSE? Signed: HENRY R. LUCE, TIME, THE WEEKLY NEWS MAGAZINE.
>
> When I arrived, Mr. Luce and his associates explained that they were planning to launch a new magazine, which they hoped to illustrate with the most dramatic photographs of industry that had ever been taken. Did I think this was a good idea, he asked?
>
> A good idea? I went back to Cleveland to pick up my belongings. Before I left again for New York, I wrote my mother: "I feel as if the world has been opened up and I hold all the keys."

Using Your Comprehension Skills

The following dialogue is from a play you will read in Chapter Seven. In it, Professor Pierson states both facts and opinions. Identify which statements are facts and which are opinions. Explain how each fact can be proved.

Phillips. Professor, would you please tell our radio audience what you see as you observe the planet Mars through your telescope?

Pierson. Nothing unusual at the moment, Mr. Phillips. A red disk swimming in a blue sea. Stripes across the disk. The stripes are merely the result of atmospheric conditions peculiar to the planet.

Phillips. Then you are quite convinced that living intelligence does not exist on Mars?

Pierson. I should say that chances against it are a thousand to one.

Using Your Vocabulary Skills

The following sentences are from the plays you will read in Chapter Seven. Look up each underlined word in a dictionary. On a sheet of paper, write the part of speech and the definition that fits the context. Be prepared to pronounce the word correctly.

1. "Her beauty is certainly <u>elusive</u>, Your Majesty."
2. "I never heard anything less <u>cryptic</u>."
3. "I wish I could <u>convey</u> the atmosphere of this fantastic scene."
4. "As a scientist, he will give you his explanation of the <u>calamity</u>."

Using Your Skills in Critical Thinking

List all the people about whom you have read in this chapter. Note which ones overcome obstacles and achieve great things. What qualities, or personality traits, do these people share? What does it take for them to meet the problems and challenges they face? What generalization can you make about these people? Be sure to support your generalization with facts from the selections.

Using Your Writing Skills

Complete one of the writing assignments below, using the process of writing: prewriting, drafting, revising, and sharing.

1. From the selections in this chapter, choose the person you found most admirable. Explain, in two or three paragraphs, why you admire that person. Be sure to include specific examples to support your reason.

2. Choose a famous person who interests you. Write two paragraphs about one incident that involves the person. Write the first paragraph as if you were the biographer of the person. Write the second paragraph as if you were the person. Remember to use the appropriate point of view.

CHAPTER SEVEN

Drama

Deep Bait, 1980, RICHARD HULL.
Photograph by William H. Bengtson, Phyllis Kind
Gallery, Chicago and New York.

Reading Literature

Drama

Drama is a form of literature in which a story is told through the words and actions of characters. Most literature is meant to be read. A drama, or **play,** is meant to be performed. It can be acted out on a stage or on film, radio, or television.

The History of Drama

People staged dramas long before they began to write them. The oldest known written plays came from ancient Greece around 500 B.C. The Greeks staged plays before large crowds in outdoor theaters. They also gave prizes for the best plays.

Hundreds of years later, in countries such as Germany, France, and England, plays based on stories from the Bible were acted out. Much later, around A.D. 1500, people enjoyed morality plays. In these plays, characters had to choose between good and evil.

In the late 1500's people felt great excitement about drama. The best-known playwright of that time was William Shakespeare. His plays told stories about kings and soldiers and common people. Shakespeare wrote serious plays called **tragedies.** He also wrote **comedies** that have happier endings.

In the twentieth century, plays have been written for radio and television as well as for the stage. In this chapter you will read two types of plays, a radio drama and a play written for the stage.

The Elements of Drama

The Form of Written Drama. The written form of a play, or **script**, lists the characters. The script also identifies the characters as they speak, as in these lines from *The Ugly Duckling*:

Queen. How old is he?

Chancellor. Five-and-twenty, I understand.

Most plays are divided into short sections called **scenes.** When the time or place changes, a new scene begins. Long plays are divided into **acts,** which are made up of scenes.

Characteristics of Drama. When you read a play, you should try to see it and hear it in your mind. The following elements of drama help you to do so. **Dialogue** refers to the conversations between characters in a play. The dialogue tells the story. **Stage directions** are instructions to the director and to the actors. These tell the actors how to enter, speak, and behave on the stage. They also explain what the audience should see and hear. In most plays stage directions are printed in parentheses.

Some stage directions describe **sound effects.** These are the sounds that are to be heard as part of a play. In radio plays, sound effects may include directions to **fade in, fade,** or **fade out.** These words mean that voices, music, or sounds get louder or softer.

How to Read a Play

Picture the play being acted out. Pay special attention to the stage directions. Try to enter into the world of the play. For a radio play, imagine the voices and the sound effects.

Comprehension Skills

Author's Purpose

As writers prepare to write, they think about what they want their writing to do. Their purpose, or reason for writing, could be one or more of the following: to entertain, to teach, to persuade, to express feelings, or to make people think about a social problem. A writer's purpose affects the many choices that need to be made. These include choices of topic, form, characters, setting, and plot.

To understand an author's purpose, study your own reactions. Ask yourself: Were you entertained? Did you learn something? Did you gain an understanding of other people's problems?

Writers do not always achieve their purposes. Sometimes they intend their work to be funny, but readers don't laugh. Some writing is meant to teach, but all it does is bore readers. Only the audience can tell if the writer has succeeded.

Author's Choice of Words

Suppose a play is set in colonial times in America. You would expect the characters to sound as if they lived in those times. Perhaps they would use words such as *thee, doth,* and *oft.*

Suppose another play is set in modern times. An army officer is reporting to the nation. You would not expect him to say, "Don't worry, folks. No problem." Instead, you would expect him to speak like the captain in *Invasion from Mars:* "Situation arising from reported presence of certain individuals of unidentified nature is now under complete control." His words sound stiff and formal, as you would expect.

A writer must choose words carefully, so that the characters always sound real. You, as a reader, can decide whether a writer has chosen the characters' words well.

Exercises: Understanding the Author's Purpose and Choice of Words

A. Identify what the writer's purpose appears to be in each of the following excerpts.

1. "To Matt Henson, Peary gave the honor of planting the American flag at the North Pole while he stood in salute. It was April 6, 1909."

    —Langston Hughes, "Matthew A. Henson"

    a. to inform you
    b. to persuade you
    c. to shock you

2. "My grandmothers were strong.
    Why am I not as they?"   —Margaret Walker, "Lineage"

    a. to make you laugh
    b. to express feelings
    c. to teach

B. For each character below, choose the fitting line of dialogue.

1. **Chancellor.** (*The Ugly Duckling*)

    a. "As your majesty is aware, the young prince Simon arrives today to seek her Royal Highness's hand in marriage."
    b. "Hey King, don't forget the prince is coming by today to pop the question."

2. **Radio Announcer.** (*Invasion from Mars*)

    a. "Ladies and gentlemen, due to circumstances beyond our control, we are unable to continue the broadcast."
    b. "We've been cut off! Oh, no! What'll I do?"

Vocabulary Skills

Inferring Word Meanings

What do you do when you are reading and you come to a word you don't understand? Do you stop reading and look up the word in a dictionary? That's not a bad idea, but you may not always have a dictionary close at hand. Also, looking up every unfamiliar word as you read can slow you down. Another way to figure out meaning is to look for clues in the general context.

When you have to guess at the meaning of a word, you may find a clue to the meaning in the sentence where you found the word. Here is an example. In these lines from *The Ugly Duckling*, the unfamiliar word is underlined.

> **King.** It is our . . . plan that at the first meeting she should pass herself off as the Princess—a harmless <u>ruse</u>, of which you will find frequent record in the history books.

What could *ruse* mean? To figure it out, first ask yourself what part of speech the word could be. *Ruse* is probably a noun because it follows the word *a* and the adjective *harmless*. Also, the plan calls for someone to pretend that she is the Princess. From this clue, you can guess that the plan involves a trick. *Ruse* probably means "trick." Note that *trick* makes sense in the sentence. As you read on, you will know more surely whether your guess is correct.

This way of figuring out the meaning of an unfamiliar word from its context is called inferring the meaning. **Inference** means using what the writer has told you in order to figure out what the writer has not told you.

Here is another example of a word whose meaning can be inferred from context. This time the context is more than one sentence. This passage is from *Invasion from Mars*. Martians have killed at least forty people. The radio announcer is trying to keep the audience informed.

> **Announcer.** Ladies and gentlemen, I have just been informed that we have finally established communication with an eyewitness of the tragedy. Professor Pierson . . . will give you his explanation of the calamity.

What does *calamity* mean? First, decide what part of speech it is. If you reread the sentence, you will see that *calamity* must be a noun, because the phrase "of the" needs a noun to complete it.

Now look for other clues. Professor Pierson saw a tragedy. You can guess that the thing he will explain will be that tragedy, or disaster. *Calamity* must mean "disaster."

Exercise: Inferring Word Meanings

Use context to figure out the meaning of each underlined word. Choose from the definitions following each quotation.

1. **King.** My dear Chancellor, we are not considering her Royal Highness's character, but her chances of getting married. You observe that there is a distinction.
   a. a good chance   b. an argument   c. a difference

2. **Announcer two.** The gas seems to be moving toward the earth with enormous velocity.
   a. silence   b. speed   c. restraint

3. **Announcer two.** Ladies and gentlemen, I have a grave announcement to make. Incredible as it may seem, those strange beings who landed in the Jersey farmlands tonight are the vanguard of an invading army from the planet Mars.
   a. the soldiers at the front of an army
   b. a kind of vehicle
   c. a kind of guard

The Ugly Duckling

A. A. MILNE

Can you judge a person's character from his or her appearance? As you read, think about how appearances can be deceiving.

CHARACTERS

A Voice	The Chancellor
The King	Dulcibella
The Queen	Prince Simon
The Princess Camilla	Carlo

SCENE. *The Throne Room of the Palace; a room of many doors, or, if preferred, curtain-openings; simply furnished with three thrones for* Their Majesties *and* Her Royal Highness The Princess Camilla—*in other words, with three handsome chairs. At each side is a long seat: reserved, as it might be, for his Majesty's Council (if any), but useful, as today, for other purposes. The* King *is asleep on his throne with a handkerchief over his face. He is a king of any country from any storybook, in whatever costume you please. But he should be wearing his crown.*

A Voice *(Announcing).* His Excellency the Chancellor! *(The* Chancellor, *an elderly man in horn-rimmed spectacles, enters, bowing. The* King *wakes up with a start and removes the handkerchief from his face.)*

King *(With simple dignity).* I was thinking.

Chancellor *(Bowing).* Never, Your Majesty, was greater need for thought than now.

King. That's what I was thinking. *(He struggles into a more dignified position.)* Well, what is it? More trouble?

Chancellor. What we might call the old trouble, Your Majesty.

King. It's what I was saying last night to the Queen. "Uneasy lies the head that wears a crown" was how I put it.

Illuminated manuscript leaf from *The History of Alexander the Great,* after 1474. The J. Paul Getty Museum, Santa Monica, California.

Chancellor. A profound and original thought, which may well go down to posterity.

King. You mean it may go down well with posterity. I hope so. Remind me to tell you some time of another little thing I said to Her Majesty: something about a fierce light beating on a throne. Posterity would like that, too. Well, what is it?

Chancellor. It is in the matter of Her Royal Highness's wedding.

King. Oh . . . yes.

Chancellor. As Your Majesty is aware, the young Prince Simon arrives today to seek her Royal Highness's hand in marriage. He has been traveling in distant lands and, as I understand, has not—er—has not——

King. You mean he hasn't heard anything.

Chancellor. It is a little difficult to put this tactfully, Your Majesty.

King. Do your best, and I will tell you afterwards how you got on.

Chancellor. Let me put it this way. The Prince Simon will naturally assume that Her Royal Highness has the customary—so customary as to be in my own poor opinion, slightly monotonous—has what one might call the inevitable—so inevitable as to be, in my opinion again, almost mechanical—will assume, that she has the, as *I* think of it, faultily faultless, icily regular, splendidly——

King. What you are trying to say in the fewest words possible is that my daughter is not beautiful.

Chancellor. Her beauty is certainly elusive, Your Majesty.

King. It is. It has eluded you, it has eluded me, it has eluded everybody who has seen her. It even eluded the Court Painter. His last words were, "Well, I did my best." His successor is now painting the view across the water-meadows from the West Turret. He says that his doctor has advised him to keep to landscape.

Chancellor. It is unfortunate, Your Majesty, but there it is. One just cannot understand how it can have occurred.

King. You don't think she takes after *me*, at all? You don't detect a likeness?

Chancellor. Most certainly not, Your Majesty.

King. Good. . . . Your predecessor did.

Chancellor. I have often wondered what happened to my predecessor.

King. Well, now you know. (*There is a short silence.*)

Chancellor. Looking at the bright side, although Her Royal Highness is not, strictly speaking, beautiful——

King. Not, truthfully speaking, beautiful——

Chancellor. Yet she has great beauty of character.

King. My dear Chancellor, we are not considering Her Royal Highness's character, but her chances of getting married. You observe that there is a distinction.

Chancellor. Yes, Your Majesty.

King. Look at it from the suitor's point of view. If a girl is beautiful, it is easy to assume that she has, tucked away inside her, an equally beautiful character. But it is impossible to assume that an unattractive girl, however elevated in character, has, tucked away inside her, an equally beautiful face. That is, so to speak, not where you want it—tucked away.

Chancellor. Quite so, Your Majesty.

King. This doesn't, of course, alter the fact that the Princess Camilla is quite the nicest person in the Kingdom.

Chancellor *(Enthusiastically).* She is indeed, Your Majesty. *(Hurriedly)* With the exception, I need hardly say, of Your Majesty—and Her Majesty.

King. Your exceptions are tolerated for their loyalty and condemned for their extreme fatuity.

Chancellor. Thank you, Your Majesty.

King. As an adjective for your King, the word "nice" is ill-chosen. As an adjective for Her Majesty, it is—ill-chosen.

(At which moment Her Majesty *comes in. The* King *rises. The* Chancellor *puts himself at right angles.)*

Queen *(Briskly).* Ah. Talking about Camilla? *(She sits down.)*

King *(Returning to his throne).* As always, my dear, you are right.

Queen *(To* Chancellor*).* This fellow, Simon—What's he like?

Chancellor. Nobody has seen him, Your Majesty.

Queen. How old is he?

Chancellor. Five-and-twenty, I understand.

Queen. In twenty-five years he must have been seen by somebody.

King *(To the* Chancellor*).* Just a fleeting glimpse.

Chancellor. I meant, Your Majesty, that no detailed report of him has reached this country, save that he has the usual personal advantages and qualities expected of a Prince and has been traveling in distant and dangerous lands.

Queen. Ah! Nothing gone wrong with his eyes? Sunstroke or anything?

Chancellor. Not that I am aware of, Your Majesty. At the same time, as I was venturing to say to His Majesty, Her Royal Highness's character and disposition are so outstandingly——

Queen. Stuff and nonsense. You remember what happened when we had the Tournament of Love last year.

Chancellor. I was not myself present,

Your Majesty. I had not then the honor of—I was abroad, and never heard the full story.

Queen. No; it was the other fool. They all rode up to Camilla to pay their homage—it was the first time they had seen her. The heralds blew their trumpets and announced that she would marry whichever Prince was left master of the field when all but one had been unhorsed. The trumpets were blown again, they charged enthusiastically into the fight, and— (*The* King *looks non-chalantly at the ceiling and whistles a few bars.*)—don't do that.

King. I'm sorry, my dear.

Queen (*To* Chancellor)*.* And what happened? They all simultaneously fell off their horses and assumed a posture of defeat.

King. One of them was not quite so quick as the others. I was very quick. I proclaimed him the victor.

Queen. At the Feast of Betrothal held that night——

King. We were all very quick.

Queen. The Chancellor announced that by the laws of the county the successful suitor had to pass a further test. He had to give the correct answer to a riddle.

King. There are times for announcing facts and times for looking at things in a broad-minded way. Please remember that, Chancellor.

Chancellor. Yes, Your Majesty.

Queen. I invented the riddle myself. Quite an easy one. What is it which has four legs and barks like a dog? The answer is, "A dog."

King (*To* Chancellor)*.* You see that?

Chancellor. Yes, Your Majesty.

King. It isn't difficult.

Queen. He, however, seemed to find it so. He said an eagle. Then he said a serpent; a very high mountain with slippery sides; two peacocks; a moonlight night; the day after tomorrow——

King. Nobody could accuse him of not trying.

Queen. *I* did.

King. I *should* have said that nobody could fail to recognize in his attitude an appearance of doggedness.

Queen. Finally he said "Death." I nudged the King——

King. Accepting the word *nudge* for the moment, I rubbed my ankle with one hand, clapped him on the shoulder with the other, and congratulated him on the correct answer. He disappeared under the table, and, personally, I never saw him again.

Queen. His body was found in the moat next morning.

Chancellor. But what was he doing in the moat, Your Majesty?

King. Bobbing about. Try not to ask needless questions.

Chancellor. It all seems so strange.

Queen. What does?

Chancellor. That Her Royal Highness, alone of all the Princesses one has ever heard of, should lack that invariable attribute of Royalty, supreme beauty.

Queen (*To the* King). That was your Great-Aunt Malkin. She came to the christening. You know what she said.

King. It was cryptic. Great-Aunt Malkin's besetting weakness. She came to *my* christening—she was one hundred and one then, and that was fifty-one years ago. (*To the* Chancellor) How old would that make her?

Chancellor. One hundred and fifty-two, Your Majesty.

King (*After thought*). About that, yes. She promised me that when I grew up I should have all the happiness which my wife deserved. It struck me at the time—well, when I say "at the time," I was only a week old—but it did strike me as soon as anything could strike me—I mean of that nature—well,

work it out for yourself, Chancellor. It opens up a most interesting field of speculation. Though naturally I have not liked to go into it at all deeply with Her Majesty.

Queen. I never heard anything less cryptic. She was wishing you extreme happiness.

King. I don't think she was *wishing* me anything. However.

Chancellor (*To the* Queen). But what, Your Majesty, did she wish Her Royal Highness?

Queen. Her other godmother—on my side—had promised her the dazzling beauty for which all the women in my family are famous— (*She pauses, and the* King *snaps his fingers surreptitiously in the direction of the* Chancellor.)

Chancellor (*Hurriedly*). Indeed, yes, Your Majesty. (*The* King *relaxes.*)

Queen. And Great-Aunt Malkin said— (*To the* King)—what were the words?

King. I give you with this kiss
A wedding-day surprise.
Where ignorance is bliss
'Tis folly to be wise.

I thought the last two lines rather neat. But what it *meant*——

Queen. We can all see what it meant. She was given beauty—and where is it?

Great-Aunt Malkin took it away from her. The wedding-day surprise is that there will never be a wedding day.

King. Young men being what they are, my dear, it would be much more surprising if there *were* a wedding day. So how——

(*The* Princess *comes in. She is young, happy, healthy, but not beautiful. Or let us say that by some trick of make-up or arrangement of hair she seems plain to us: unlike the Princess of the storybooks.*)

Princess (*To the* King). Hello, darling! (*Seeing the others*) Oh, I say! Affairs of state? Sorry.

King (*Holding out his hand*). Don't go, Camilla. (*She takes his hand.*)

Chancellor. Shall I withdraw, Your Majesty?

Queen. You are aware, Camilla, that Prince Simon arrives today?

Princess. He has arrived. They're just letting down the drawbridge.

King (*Jumping up*). Arrived! I must—

Princess. Darling, you know what the drawbridge is like. It takes at *least* half an hour to let it down.

King (*Sitting down*). It wants oil. (*To the* Chancellor) Have *you* been grudging it oil?

Princess. It wants a new drawbridge, darling.

Chancellor. Have I Your Majesty's permission——

King. Yes, yes. (*The* Chancellor *bows and goes out.*)

Queen. You've told him, of course? It's the only chance.

King. Er—no. I was just going to, when——

Queen. Then I'd better. (*She goes to the door.*) You can explain to the girl; I'll have her sent to you. You've told Camilla?

King. Er—no. I was just going to, when——

Queen. Then you'd better tell her now.

King. My dear, are you sure——

Queen. It's the only chance left. (*Dramatically to heaven*) My daughter! (*She goes out. There is a little silence when she is gone.*)

King. Camilla, I want to talk seriously to you about marriage.

Princess. Yes, father.

King. It is time that you learnt some of the facts of life.

Princess. Yes, father.

King. Now the great fact about marriage is that once you're married you live happy ever after. All our history books affirm this.

Princess. And your own experience too, darling.

King (*With dignity*). Let us confine ourselves to history for the moment.

Princess. Yes, father.

King. Of course, there *may* be an exception here and there, which, as it were, proves the rule; just as—oh, well, never mind.

Princess (*Smiling*). Go on, darling, you were going to say that an exception here

May (detail) from *Très Riches Heures du Duc de Berry,* 15th century, LIMBOURG BROTHERS.
Musée Condé, Chantilly, France. Giraudon/Art Resource, New York City.

and there proves the rule that all princesses are beautiful.

King. Well—leave that for the moment. The point is that it doesn't matter *how* you marry, or *who* you marry, as long as you *get* married. Because you'll be happy ever after in any case. Do you follow me so far?

Princess. Yes, father.

King. Well, your mother and I have a little plan——

Princess. Was that it, going out of the door just now?

King. Er—yes. It concerns your waiting-maid.

Princess. Darling, I have several.

King. Only one that leaps to the eye, so to speak. The one with the—well, with everything.

Princess. Dulcibella?

King. That's the one. It is our little plan that at the first meeting she should pass herself off as the Princess—a harmless ruse, of which you will find frequent record in the history books—and allure Prince Simon to his—that is to say, bring him up to the—In other words, the wedding will take place immediately afterwards, and as quietly as possible—well, naturally in view of the fact that your Aunt Malkin is one hundred and fifty-two; and since you will be wearing the family bridal veil—which is no doubt how the custom arose—the surprise after the ceremony will be his. Are you following me at all? Your attention seems to be wandering.

Princess. I was wondering why you needed to tell me.

King. Just a precautionary measure, in case you happened to meet the Prince or his attendant before the ceremony; in which case, of course, you would pass yourself off as the maid——

Princess. A harmless ruse, of which, also, you will find frequent record in the history books.

King. Exactly. But the occasion need not arise.

A Voice (*Announcing*). The woman Dulcibella!

King. Ah! (*To the* Princess) Now Camilla, if you will just retire to your own apartments, I will come to you there when we are ready for the actual ceremony. (*He leads her out as he is talking, and as he returns calls out:*) Come in, my dear! (Dulcibella *comes in. She is beautiful, but dumb.*) Now don't be frightened, there is nothing to be frightened about. Has her Majesty told you what you have to do?

Dulcibella. Y-yes, Your Majesty.

King. Well now, let's see how well you can do it. You are sitting here we will say. (*He leads her to a seat.*) Now imagine that I am Prince Simon. (*He curls his moustache and puts his stomach in. She giggles.*) You are the beautiful Princess Camilla whom he has never seen. (*She giggles again.*) This is a serious moment in your life, and you will find that a giggle will not be helpful. (*He goes to the door.*) I am announced: "His Royal Highness Prince Simon!" That's me being announced. Remember what I said about giggling. You should have a faraway look upon the face. (*She does her best.*) Farther away than that. (*She tries again.*) No, that's too far. You are sitting there, thinking beautiful thoughts—in maiden meditation, fancy-free, as I remember saying to Her Majesty once . . . speaking of somebody else . . . fancy-free, but with the mouth definitely shut—that's better. I advance and fall upon one knee. (*He does so.*) You extend your hand graciously—*graciously*; you're not trying to push him in the face—that's better, and I raise it to my lips—so—and I kiss it—(*He kisses it warmly.*)—no, perhaps not so ardently as that, more like this (*He kisses it again.*) and I say, "Your Royal Highness, this is the most—er—Your Royal Highness, I shall ever be—no—Your Royal Highness, it is the proudest—" Well, the point is that *he* will say it, and it will be something com-plimentary, and then he will take your hand in both of his and press it to his heart. (*He does so.*) And then—what do you say?

Dulcibella. Coo!

King. No, not Coo.

Dulcibella. Never had anyone do *that* to me before.

King. That also strikes the wrong note. What you want to say is, "Oh, Prince Simon! . . ." Say it.

Dulcibella (*Loudly*). Oh, Prince Simon!

King. No, no. You don't need to shout until he has said "What?" two or three times. Always consider the possibility that he *isn't* deaf. Softly, and giving the words a dying fall, letting them play around his head like a flight of doves.

Dulcibella (*Still a little over-loud*). O-o-o-o-h, Prinsimon!

King. Keep the idea in your mind of a flight of *doves* rather than a flight of panic-stricken elephants, and you will be all right. Now I'm going to get up, and you must, as it were, *waft* me into a seat by your side. (*She starts wafting.*) Not rescuing a drowning man, that's another idea altogether, useful at times, but at the moment inappropriate. Wafting. Prince Simon will put the necessary muscles into play—all you're required to do is to indicate by a gracious movement of the hand the seat you require him to take. Now! *(He gets up, a little stiffly, and sits next to her.)* That was better. Well, here we are. Now, I think you give me a look: something let us say, halfway between the breathless adoration of a nun and the voluptuous abandonment of a woman of the world; with an undertone of regal dignity, touched, as it were, with good comradeship. Now try that. *(She gives him a vacant look of bewilderment.)* Frankly, that didn't quite get it. There was just a little something missing. An absence, as it were, of all the qualities I asked for, and in their place an odd resemblance to an unsatisfied fish. Let us try to get it another way. Dulcibella, have you a young man of your own?

Dulcibella *(Eagerly, seizing his hand).* Oo, yes, he's ever so smart, he's an archer, well not as you might say a real archer, he works in the armory, but old Bottlenose *you* know who I mean, the Captain of the Guard, says the very next man they ever has to shoot, my Eg shall take his place, knowing Father and how it is with Eg and me, and me being maid to Her Royal Highness and can't marry me till he's a real soldier, but ever so loving, and funny like, the things he says. I said to him once, "Eg," I said—

King *(Getting up).* I rather fancy, Dulcibella, that if you think of Eg all the time, *say* as little as possible, and, when

thinking of Eg, see that the mouth is not more than partially open, you will do very well. I will show you where you are to sit and wait for His Royal Highness. *(He leads her out. On the way he is saying:)* Now remember—*waft*—*waft*—*not hoick*.[1]

(Prince Simon wanders in from the back unannounced. He is a very ordinary-looking young man in rather dusty clothes. He gives a deep sigh of relief as he sinks into the King's throne . . . . Camilla, a new and strangely beautiful Camilla, comes in.)

Princess *(Surprised).* Well!

Prince. Oh, hello!

Princess. Ought you?

Prince *(Getting up).* Do sit down, won't you?

Princess. Who are you, and how did you get here?

Prince. Well, that's rather a long story. Couldn't we sit down? You could sit here if you liked, but it isn't very comfortable.

Princess. That is the King's Throne.

Prince. Oh, is that what it is?

Princess. Thrones are not meant to be comfortable.

---

1. **hoick** (hoik)–To move or pull abruptly.

Prince. Well, I don't know if they're meant to be, but they certainly aren't.

Princess. Why were you sitting on the King's Throne, and who are you?

Prince. My name is Carlo.

Princess. Mine is Dulcibella.

Prince. Good. And now couldn't we sit down?

Princess (*Sitting down on the long seat to the left of the throne, and, as it were, wafting him to a place next to her*). You may sit here, if you like. Why are you so tired? (*He sits down.*)

Prince. I've been taking very strenuous exercise.

Princess. Is that part of the long story?

Prince. It is.

Princess (*Settling herself*). I love stories.

Prince. This isn't a story really. You see, I'm attendant on Prince Simon, who is visiting here.

Princess. Oh? I'm attendant on Her Royal Highness.

Prince. Then you know what he's here for.

Princess. Yes.

Prince. She's very beautiful, I hear.

Princess. Did you hear that? Where have you been lately?

Prince. Traveling in distant lands—with Prince Simon.

Princess. Ah! All the same, I don't understand. Is Prince Simon in the palace now? The drawbridge *can't* be down yet!

Prince. I don't suppose it is. And what a noise it makes coming down!

Princess. Isn't it terrible?

Prince. I couldn't stand it any more. I just had to get away. That's why I'm here.

Princess. But how?

Prince. Well, there's only one way, isn't there? That beech tree, and then a swing and a grab for the battlements, and don't ask me to remember it all ——(*He shudders.*)

Princess. You mean you came across the moat by that beech tree?

Prince. Yes. I got so tired of hanging about.

Princess. But it's terribly dangerous!

Prince. That's why I'm so exhausted. Nervous shock. (*He lies back and breathes loudly.*)

Princess. Of course, it's different for *me*.

Prince (*Sitting up*). Say that again. I must have got it wrong.

Princess. It's different for me, because I'm used to it. Besides, I'm so much lighter.

Prince. You don't mean that *you*——

Princess. Oh yes, often.

Prince. And I thought I was a brave man! At least, I didn't until five minutes ago, and now I don't again.

Princess. Oh, but you are! And I think it's wonderful to do it straight off the first time.

Prince. Well, *you* did.

Princess. Oh no, not the first time. When I was a child.

Prince. You mean that you crashed?

Princess. Well, you only fall into the moat.

Prince. Only! Can you *swim*?

Princess. Of course.

Prince. So you swam to the castle walls and yelled for help, and they fished you out and walloped you. And next day you tried again. Well, if *that* isn't pluck——

The Idealization of Courtly Love, 15th century. From a French illuminated manuscript. The Granger Collection, New York City.

Princess. Of course I didn't. I swam back and did it at once; I mean I tried again at once. It wasn't until the third time that I actually did it. You see, I was afraid I might lose my nerve.

Prince. Afraid she might lose her nerve!

Princess. There's a way of getting over from this side, too; a tree grows out from the wall and you jump into another tree—I don't think it's quite so easy.

Prince. Not quite so easy. Good. You must show me.

Princess. Oh, I will.

Prince. Perhaps it might be as well if you taught me how to swim first. I've often heard about swimming, but never——

Princess. You can't swim?

Prince. No. Don't look so surprised. There are a lot of other things which I can't do. I'll tell you about them as soon as you have a couple of years to spare.

Princess. You can't swim and yet you crossed by the beech tree! And you're *ever* so much heavier than I am! Now who's brave?

Prince (*Getting up*). You keep talking about how light you are. I must see if there's anything in it. Stand up! (*She stands obediently and he picks her up.*) You're right, Dulcibella. I could hold you here forever. (*Looking at her*) You're very lovely. Do you know how lovely you are?

Princess. Yes. (*She laughs suddenly and happily.*)

Prince. Why do you laugh?

Princess. Aren't you tired of holding me?

Prince. Frankly, yes. I exaggerated when I said I could hold you for ever. When you've been hanging by the arms for ten minutes over a very deep moat, wondering if it's too late to learn how to swim—(*He puts her down.*)—what I meant was that I should *like* to hold you forever. Why did you laugh?

Princess. Oh, well, it was a little private joke of mine.

Prince. If it comes to that, I've got a private joke too. Let's exchange them.

Princess. Mine's very private. One other woman in the whole world knows, and that's all.

Prince. Mine's just as private. One other man knows, and that's all.

Princess. What fun. I love secrets. . . . Well, here's mine. When I was born, one of my godmothers promised that I should be very beautiful.

Prince. How right she was.

Princess. But the other one said this:

I give you with this kiss
A wedding-day surprise.
Where ignorance is bliss
'Tis folly to be wise.

And nobody knew what it meant. And I grew up very plain. And then, when I was about ten, I met my godmother in the forest one day. It was my tenth birthday. Nobody knows this—except you.

Prince. Except us.

Princess. Except us. And she told me what her gift meant. It meant that I *was* beautiful—but everybody else was to go on being ignorant, and thinking me plain, until my wedding day. Because, she said, she didn't want me to grow up spoilt and willful and vain, as I should have done if everybody had always been saying how beautiful I was; and the best thing in the world, she said, was to be quite sure of yourself, but not to expect admiration from other people. So ever since then my mirror has told me I'm beautiful, and everybody else thinks me ugly, and I get a lot of fun out of it.

Prince. Well, seeing that Dulcibella is the result, I can only say that your god-mother was very, very wise.

Princess. And now tell me *your* secret.

Prince. It isn't such a pretty one. You see, Prince Simon was going to woo Princess Camilla, and he'd heard that she was beautiful and haughty and imperious—all *you* would have been if your godmother hadn't been so wise. And being a very ordinary-looking fellow himself, he was afraid she wouldn't think much of him, so he suggested to one of his attendants, a man called Carlo, of extremely attractive appearance, that *he* should pretend to be the Prince, and win the Princess's hand; and then at the last moment they would change places——

Princess. How would they do that?

Prince. The Prince was going to have been married in full armor—with his visor down.

Princess (*Laughing happily*). Oh what fun!

Prince. Neat, isn't it?

Princess (*Laughing*). Oh, very . . . very . . . very.

Prince. Neat, but not so terribly *funny.* Why do you keep laughing?

Princess. Well, that's another secret.

Prince. If it comes to that, *I've* got another one up my sleeve. Shall we exchange again?

Princess. All right. You go first this time.

Prince. Very well. . . . I am not Carlo. (*Standing up and speaking dramatically*)

I am Simon!—*ow!* (*He sits down and rubs his leg violently.*)

Princess (*Alarmed*). What is it?

Prince. Cramp. (*In a mild voice, still rubbing*) I was saying that I was Prince Simon.

Princess. Shall I rub it for you? (*She rubs.*)

Prince (*Still hopefully*). I am Simon.

Princess. Is that better?

Prince (*Despairingly*). I am Simon.

Princess. I know.

Prince. How did you know?

Princess. Well, you told me.

Prince. But oughtn't you to swoon or something?

Princess. Why? History records many similar ruses.

Prince (*Amazed*). Is that so? I've never read history. I thought I was being profoundly original.

Princess. Oh, no! Now I'll tell you my secret. For reasons very much like your own the Princess Camilla, who is held to be extremely plain, feared to meet Prince Simon. Is the drawbridge down yet?

Prince. Do your people give a faint, surprised cheer every time it gets down?

Princess. Naturally.

Prince. Then it came down about three minutes ago.

Princess. Ah! Then at this very moment your man Carlo is declaring passionate love for my maid, Dulcibella. That, I think, is funny. (*So does the* Prince. *He laughs heartily.*) Dulcibella, by the way, is in love with a man she calls Eg, so I hope Carlo isn't getting carried away.

Prince. Carlo is married to a girl he calls "the little woman," so Eg has nothing to fear.

Princess. By the way, I don't know if you heard, but I said, or as good as said, that I am the Princess Camilla.

Prince. I wasn't surprised. History, of which I read a great deal, records many similar ruses.

Princess (*Laughing*). Simon!

Prince (*Laughing*). Camilla! (*He stands up.*) May I try holding you again? (*She nods. He takes her in his arms and kisses her.*) Sweetheart!

Princess. You see, when you lifted me up before, you said, "You're very lovely," and my godmother said that the first person to whom I would seem lovely was the man I should marry; so I knew then that you were Simon and I should marry you.

Prince. I knew directly I saw you that I should marry you, even if you were Dulcibella. By the way, which of you *am* I marrying?

Princess. When she lifts her veil, it will be Camilla. (*Voices are heard outside.*) Until then it will be Dulcibella.

Prince (*In a whisper*). Then goodbye, Camilla, until you lift your veil.

Princess. Goodbye, Simon, until you raise your visor.

(*The* King *and* Queen *come in arm-in-arm, followed by* Carlo *and* Dulcibella, *also arm-in-arm. The* Chancellor *precedes them, walking backwards, at a loyal angle.*)

Prince (*Supporting the* Chancellor *as an accident seems inevitable*). Careful! (*The* Chancellor *turns indignantly round.*)

King. Who and what is this? More accurately who and what are all these?

Carlo. My attendant, Carlo, Your Majesty. He will, with your Majesty's permission, prepare me for the ceremony. (*The* Prince *bows.*)

King. Of course, of course!

Queen (*To* Dulcibella). Your maid, Dulcibella, is it not, my love? (Dulcibella *nods violently.*) I thought so. (*To* Carlo) *She* will prepare Her Royal Highness. (*The* Princess *curtsies.*)

King. Ah, yes. Yes. *Most* important.

Princess (*Curtsying*). I beg pardon, Your Majesty, if I've done wrong, but I found the gentleman wandering——

King (*Crossing to her*). Quite right, my dear, quite right. (*He pinches her cheek, and takes advantage of this kingly gesture to say in a loud whisper:*) We've pulled it off!

(*They sit down; the* King *and* Queen *on their thrones,* Dulcibella *on the* Princess's *throne.* Carlo *stands behind* Dulcibella, *the* Chancellor *on the right of the* Queen, *and* Prince *and* Princess *behind the long seat on the left.*)

Chancellor (*Consulting documents*). H'r'm! Have I Your Majesty's authority to put the final test to His Royal Highness?

Queen (*Whispering to* King). Is this safe?

King (*Whispering*). Perfectly, my dear. I told him the answer a minute ago. (*Over his shoulder to* Carlo) Don't forget. Dog. (*Aloud*) Proceed, Your Excellency. It is my desire that the affairs of my country should ever be conducted in a strictly constitutional manner.

Chancellor (*Oratorically*). By the constitution of the country, a suitor to Her Royal Highness' hand cannot be deemed successful until he has given the correct answer to a riddle. (*Conversationally*) The last suitor answered incorrectly, and thus failed to win his bride.

King. By a coincidence he fell into the moat.

Chancellor (*To* Carlo). I have now to ask Your Royal Highness if you are prepared for the ordeal?

Carlo (*Cheerfully*). Absolutely.

Chancellor. I may mention, as a matter, possibly, of some slight historical interest to our visitor, that by the constitution of the country the same riddle is not allowed to be asked on two successive occasions.

King (*Startled*). What's that?

Chancellor. This one, it is interesting to recall, was propounded exactly a century ago, and we must take it as a fortunate omen that it was well and truly solved.

King (*To* Queen). I want my sword directly.

Chancellor. The riddle is this. What is it which has four legs and mews like a cat?

Carlo (*Promptly*). A dog.

King (*Still more promptly*). Bravo, bravo! (*He claps loudly and nudges the* Queen, *who claps too.*)

Chancellor (*Peering at his documents*). According to the records of the occasion to which I referred, the correct answer would seem to be——

Princess (*To* Prince). Say something, quick!

Chancellor. —not dog, but——

Prince. Your Majesty, have I permission to speak? Naturally His Royal Highness could not think of justifying himself on such an occasion, but I think that with Your Majesty's gracious permission, I could——

King. Certainly, certainly.

Prince. In our country, we have an animal to which we have given the name "dog," or, in the local dialect of the more mountainous districts, "doggie." It sits by the fireside and purrs.

Carlo. That's right. It purrs like anything.

Prince. When it needs milk, which is its staple food, it mews.

Carlo (*Enthusiastically*). Mews like nobody's business.

Prince. It also has four legs.

Carlo. One at each corner.

Prince. In some countries, I understand, this animal is called a "cat." In one distant country to which His Royal Highness and I penetrated it was called by the very curious name of "hippo-potamus."

Carlo. That's right. *(To the* Prince*)* Do you remember that ginger-colored hippopotamus which used to climb on my shoulder and lick my ear?

Prince. I shall never forget it, sir. *(To the* King*)* So you see, Your Majesty——

King. Thank you. I think that makes it perfectly clear. *(Firmly to the* Chancellor*)* You are about to agree?

Chancellor. Undoubtedly, Your Majesty. May I be the first to congratulate His Royal Highness on solving the riddle so accurately?

King. You may be the first to see that all is in order for an immediate wedding.

Chancellor. Thank you, Your Majesty. *(He bows and withdraws. The* King *rises, as do the* Queen *and* Dulcibella.*)*

King *(To* Carlo*)*. Doubtless, Prince Simon, you will wish to retire and prepare yourself for the ceremony.

Carlo. Thank you, sir.

Prince. Have I Your Majesty's permission to attend His Royal Highness? It is the custom of his country for Princes of the royal blood to be married in full armor, a matter which requires a certain adjustment——

King. Of course, of course. *(Carlo bows to the* King *and* Queen *and goes out. As the* Prince *is about to follow, the* King *stops him.)* Young man, you have a quality of quickness which I admire. It is my pleasure to reward it in any way which commends itself to you.

Prince. Your Majesty is ever gracious. May I ask for my reward after the ceremony? *(He catches the eye of the* Princess, *and they give each other a secret smile.)*

King. Certainly. *(The* Prince *bows and goes out. To* Dulcibella*)* Now, young woman, make yourself scarce. You've done your work excellently, and we will see that you and your what was his name?

Dulcibella. Eg, Your Majesty.

King. ——that you and your Eg are not forgotten.

Dulcibella. Coo! *(She curtsies and goes out.)*

Princess *(Calling)*. Wait for me, Dulcibella!

King *(To* Queen*)*. Well, my dear, we may congratulate ourselves. As I remember saying to somebody once, "You have not lost a daughter, you have gained a son." How does he strike you?

Queen. Stupid.

King. They made a very handsome pair, I thought, he and Dulcibella.

Queen. Both stupid.

King. I said nothing about stupidity. What I *said* was that they were both extremely handsome. That is the important thing. *(Struck by a sudden idea)* Or isn't it?

Queen. What do you think of Prince Simon, Camilla?

Princess. I adore him. We shall be so happy together.

King. Well, of course you will. I told you so. Happy ever after.

Queen. Run along now, and get ready.

Princess. Yes, mother. *(She throws a kiss to them and goes out.)*

King *(Anxiously).* My dear, have we been wrong about Camilla all this time? It seemed to me that she wasn't looking quite so plain as usual just now. Did you notice anything?

Queen *(Carelessly).* Just the excitement of the marriage.

King *(Relieved).* Ah, yes, that would account for it.

May "Hawking" from *The Playfair Hours* (detail), late 15th century.
Victoria and Albert Museum, London.

A. A. Milne *(1882–1956)* was born in London, England, and educated at Trinity College in Cambridge. He wrote nearly thirty plays, mostly comedies, as well as books of fiction, nonfiction, and poetry. Several generations of children and adults have been charmed by his Winnie-the-Pooh books, which he wrote for his son, Christopher Robin.

Developing Comprehension Skills

1. Why do the king and queen feel that they have to trick Prince Simon into marrying their daughter?

2. Why does Princess Camilla's godmother want the Princess to grow up looking plain?

3. *The Ugly Duckling* is also the title of a fairy tale written by Hans Christian Andersen. In this tale, a duckling is treated cruelly because of his ugly appearance. One day, however, he discovers that he has turned into a beautiful swan. What do the two stories have in common besides their titles?

4. What do you think was the author's purpose in writing this play? Was it simply to entertain or does it have another purpose? If the play has a message, what is it?

5. How well do you think Princess Camilla and Prince Simon will get along? Explain your answer.

Reading Literature: Drama

1. **Making a Time Line.** You have learned that a **time line** is a way of showing the important events that make up the plot of a story. Complete a time line for this play by adding two or three other important events.

    1. The King tells the Princess about the plan to trick Prince Simon.

1	2	3	4

    2. Prince Simon and Princess Camilla meet.

2. **Understanding Stage Directions.** Stage directions tell the actors how to behave on the stage and how to speak the words. Stage directions also help the reader understand what the characters are like. For example, one stage direction in this play tells Dulcibella to give the King "a vacant look of bewilderment." This suggests the idea that she is too dumb to understand what the King is asking her to do. Explain what the following stage directions show about the character for whom they are intended.

> (*The* Chancellor . . . *enters, bowing.*)
> (*The* Chancellor *precedes them, walking backwards, at a loyal angle.*)

3. **Appreciating Differences in Dialogue.** The characters in this play use more than one level of language. Sometimes they speak in an official manner or in a formal, dignified way as if they were in a fairy tale. At other times their speech is quite informal and down-to-earth. Here are examples from this play of formal and informal dialogue:

> **King.** Your exceptions are tolerated for their loyalty and condemned for their extreme fatuity.
>
> **Princess.** Hello, darling! Oh, I say! Affairs of state? Sorry.

Find two examples each of formal and informal language in this play. For each situation briefly note the following: Who is speaking? What is the situation? What does the speech suggest about the character?

4. **Understanding a Character.** A **stereotype** is a character whose ideas, actions, and words fit with a widely-held idea of what that type of person is like. A stereotype has no individuality and does not change or grow. He or she does only what is expected of that certain type of person.

A fairy-tale king, according to one popular stereotype, is a dignified, powerful, and wise ruler. He rules his kingdom with a firm hand and demands complete loyalty and obedience from his subjects.

In what ways does the King in this play fit the stereotype of a fairy-tale king? In what ways does he differ from the stereotype? Find specific details to support your answers.

5. **Recognizing Irony.** Sometimes a writer lets the reader know more than the characters themselves know. The result is **irony**. In this play, for example, the audience, along with Princess Camilla and Prince Simon, knows that the Princess is beautiful, even though she appears plain to everyone else.

On page 556, the King makes the following statement to Princess Camilla, "We've pulled it off!" What does the King think is true? What do the princess and the reader know to be true?

6. **Appreciating Parody.** A **parody** is a humorous imitation of a serious work. This play is in some ways a parody of traditional fairy tales, such as *Cinderella* and *Sleeping Beauty*. These stories have kings and queens, moats and castles, beautiful princesses and fairy godmothers. In fairy tales,

difficult riddles often must be answered and heroic deeds must be performed before people can get married and live happily ever after.

What elements of parody do you find in this play? List incidents, speeches, and characters that imitate traditional fairy tales. Explain how this play makes fun of fairy tales in a good-natured way.

Vocabulary

Inferring Meaning from Context. As you have learned, you sometimes must infer the meaning of an unfamiliar word from the general context of the passage in which it appears. Sometimes a single sentence will be enough; other times you must examine the entire paragraph or several paragraphs around the word.

Find the words listed below in *The Ugly Duckling*. For each word, read as many sentences or paragraphs as you need to determine the meaning. On a sheet of paper, write the word and your definition. Then look up the word in a dictionary. After your definition, write the dictionary definition that best fits the context.

1. tactfully (page 542, column 1, the Chancellor's 2nd speech)

2. simultaneously (page 544, column 1, the Queen's 2nd speech)

3. affirm (page 547, column 1, the King's 1st speech)

4. ardently (page 549, column 1, the King's 1st speech)

5. strenuous (page 551, column 1, the Prince's 4th speech)

6. pluck (page 552, column 2, the Prince's last speech)

7. imperious (page 554, column 2, lines 1–2, the Prince's 1st speech)

8. swoon (page 555, column 1, the Prince's 5th speech)

9. deemed (page 557, column 1, line 1, the Chancellor's 1st speech)

10. successive (page 557, column 1, the Chancellor's 3rd speech)

Critical Thinking

Comparing and Contrasting Characters. Review the description you wrote of Princess Camilla. (See the first exercise under Developing Writing Skills.) Next, make a list of words and phrases that describe Prince Simon. Compare the two characters. In what ways are the Prince and Princess alike? In what ways are they different? Which person do you find more interesting? Why?

Speaking and Listening

Giving a Dramatic Reading. Work with a group to present a portion of *The Ugly Duckling*. Each group member should select a role, study that character, and practice reading that character's lines aloud. The group should practice reading the selection together at least once. Make sure that every speaker talks loudly enough to be heard. Try to make your dialogue sound as much like natural conversation as possible. Finally, present your reading to the other groups in your class.

Developing Writing Skills

1. **Analyzing a Character.** Write a description of Princess Camilla. Discuss whether being considered plain was an advantage or disadvantage to her as she grew up.

    Prewriting. List words and phrases that describe Camilla's character and personality. Make notes about how "growing up plain" has affected the kind of person she is.

    Drafting. Describe Princess Camilla in your first paragraph. In your second paragraph, discuss how her character and personality are affected by the fact that everyone considers her plain.

    Revising and Sharing. Skim the play to make sure that your description of Camilla is accurate and complete. Check your second paragraph to make sure that you have supported your statements with evidence from the play. Make any necessary revisions.

2. **Explaining the Theme.** In one paragraph, explain the message that the writer of this play wants to share with the reader. Make prewriting notes about what the writer seems to be saying about physical beauty and beauty of character. Then in your topic sentence, state what you think is the theme of the play. In your other sentences, explain how the writer develops this theme. Share the first draft of your paragraph with a partner. Discuss whether the theme and its development are clearly explained.

From The War of the Worlds
Invasion from Mars

H. G. WELLS
Adapted by Howard Koch

This science fiction radio play uses radio-news techniques to tell its story. As you read, think about why the original broadcast had such an impact upon those who were listening.

CHARACTERS

Announcer	Gunner
Orson Welles	Observer
Announcer two	Commander
Phillips	Operator one
Pierson	Operator two
Wilmuth	Operator three
Captain	Voices
Officer	Stranger

October 30, 1938: Shortly after 8 P.M., more than a million Americans, just tuning in their radios, heard a "news commentator" report that Martian invaders had landed in New Jersey. The monsters were reported armed with flames and poison gas and were marching toward New York. In a wave of mass hysteria, thousands of citizens fled to the highways. Churches overflowed. Soldiers and nurses volunteered for duty. A few of the terrified listeners tried to commit suicide; many had to be treated for shock.

The following selection is condensed and adapted from that famous radio broadcast. Announcements before, during, and after the show told listeners that the program was a regular Mercury Theatre presentation, starring Orson Welles. Perhaps, as you read, you'll understand the reactions of those who tuned in late—and didn't wait for the next announcement.

ACT ONE

Sound. *Theme.*

Announcer. Ladies and gentlemen: the director of the Mercury Theatre on the Air, Orson Welles. . . .

Orson Welles. We know now that in the early years of the twentieth century this world was being watched closely by beings more intelligent than man and yet as mortal. We know now that, as human beings busied themselves about their various concerns, they were scrutinized and studied, perhaps almost as narrowly as a man with a microscope might scrutinize the tiny creatures that swarm and multiply in a drop of water.

Across an immense ethereal gulf, intellects vast, cool, and unsympathetic regarded this earth with envious eyes and slowly drew their plans against us. . . .

In the thirty-ninth year of the twentieth century, in the year 1938, came the great awakening.

It was near the end of October. Business was better. The war scare was over. On this particular evening thirty-two million people were listening in on radios. . . .

Fade in . . .

Announcer two. We now take you to the Meridian Room in the Hotel Park Plaza in downtown New York, where you will

Actor Orson Welles reading from *Invasion from Mars,* 1938. Culver Pictures, New York City.

be entertained by the music of Ramon Raquello (rä mōn' rä kāl'yō) and his orchestra.

Sound. *Spanish theme song . . . fades.*

Announcer two. Ladies and gentlemen, we interrupt our program of dance music to bring you a special bulletin from the Intercontinental Radio News.

At twenty minutes before eight, Central Time, Professor Farrell of the Mount Jennings Observatory, Chicago, Illinois, reported observing several explosions of incandescent gas, occurring at regular intervals on the planet Mars. The gas seems to be moving toward the earth with enormous velocity. Professor Pierson of the observatory at Princeton confirms Farrell's observation and describes the phenomenon as (quote) like a jet of blue flame shot from a gun (unquote). We now return you to Ramon Raquello, playing the ever-popular "Stardust."

Sound. *Music.*

Announcer two. Ladies and gentlemen, following on the news given in our bulletin a moment ago, the Government Meteorological Bureau has requested the large observatories of the country to keep an astronomical watch on any further disturbances occurring on the planet Mars. Due to the unusual nature of this occurrence, we have arranged an interview with the noted astronomer Professor Richard Pierson, who will give us his views on this event. We now take you to the observatory at Princeton, New Jersey, where Carl Phillips, our commentator, will interview Professor Pierson.

Sound. *Entire interview in echo chamber; faint ticking sound.*

Phillips. Good evening, ladies and gentlemen. This is Carl Phillips, speaking to you from the observatory at Princeton. I am standing in a large semicircular room, pitch black except for an oblong split in the ceiling. Through this opening I can see a sprinkling of stars that cast a kind of frosty glow over the intricate mechanism of the huge telescope. The ticking sound you hear is the vibration of the clockwork. Professor Pierson stands directly above me on a small platform, peering through the giant lens. Professor, may I begin asking you questions?

Pierson. At any time, Mr. Phillips.

Phillips. Professor, would you please tell our radio audience exactly what you see as you observe the planet Mars through your telescope?

Pierson. Nothing unusual at the moment, Mr. Phillips. A red disk swimming in a blue sea. Transverse stripes across the disk. Quite distinct now because Mars happens to be at the point nearest the earth.

Phillips. In your opinion, what do these transverse stripes signify, Professor Pierson?

Pierson. Not canals, I can assure you, Mr. Phillips, although that's the popular conjecture of those who imagine Mars to be inhabited. From a scientific viewpoint, the stripes are merely the result of atmospheric conditions peculiar to the planet.

Phillips. Then you're quite convinced that living intelligence as we know it does not exist on Mars? That there is no life on Mars?

Pierson. I should say the chances against it are a thousand to one.

Phillips. And yet how do you account for these gas eruptions occurring on the surface of the planet at such regular intervals?

Pierson. Mr. Phillips, I cannot account for them.

Phillips. By the way, Professor, for the benefit of our listeners, how far is Mars from the earth?

Pierson. Approximately forty million miles.

Phillips. Well, that seems a safe enough distance——Just a moment, ladies and gentlemen. Someone has just handed Professor Pierson a message. While he reads it, let me remind you that we are speaking to you from the observatory in Princeton, New Jersey, where we are interviewing the world-famous astronomer Professor Richard Pierson.... One moment, please. I shall read you the wire that Professor Pierson has just received from Dr. Gray of the Natural History Museum, New York.... "Seismograph registered shock of almost earthquake intensity occurring within a radius of twenty miles of Princeton. Please investigate. Signed. Lloyd Gray...." Professor Pierson, could this occurrence possibly have something to do with the disturbances observed on the planet Mars?

Pierson. Hardly, Mr. Phillips. This is probably a meteorite of unusual size, and its arrival at this particular time is merely a coincidence. However, we shall conduct a search as soon as daylight permits.

Phillips. Thank you, Professor. Ladies and gentlemen, we've just brought you a special interview with Professor Pierson, at Princeton Observatory. This is Carl Phillips speaking. We now return you to our New York studio.

Sound. *Fade in piano playing.*

Announcer two. Ladies and gentlemen, here is a special announcement from Trenton, New Jersey: "It is reported that at 8:50 P.M. a huge, flaming object, believed to be a meteorite, fell on a farm in the neighborhood of Grovers Mill, New Jersey, twenty-two miles from Trenton. The flash in the sky was visible within a radius of several hundred miles, and the noise of the impact was heard as far north as Elizabeth, New Jersey."

We have dispatched a special mobile unit to the scene, and we will have our commentator, Mr. Phillips, give you a word description as soon as he reaches the farm. In the meantime, we give you Bobby Millette and his orchestra, from the Hotel Martinet in Brooklyn.

Sound. *Swing band for twenty seconds . . . then cut.*

Announcer two. We take you now to Grovers Mill, New Jersey.

Sound. *Crowd noises . . . police sirens.*

Phillips. Ladies and gentlemen, this is Carl Phillips again, at the Wilmuth farm, Grovers Mill, New Jersey. Professor Pierson and I made the eleven miles from Princeton in ten minutes. Well, I . . . I hardly know where to begin, to paint for you a word picture of the strange scene before my eyes, like something out of a modern Arabian Nights.[1] I guess that's the—the *thing* directly in front of me, half-buried in a vast pit. Must have hit with terrific force. The ground is covered with splinters of a tree it struck on its way down. What I can see of the object itself doesn't look very much like a meteor, at least not the meteors I've seen. It looks more like a huge cylinder. It has a diameter of about thirty yards, and the metal

on the sheath is—well, I've never seen anything like it. The color is sort of yellowish-white. Curious spectators are pressing close to the object, in spite of police efforts to keep them back.

Here's Mr. Wilmuth, owner of the farm. He may have some interesting facts to add. . . . Mr. Wilmuth, would you please tell the radio audience as much as you remember of this rather unusual visitor that dropped in your backyard? Step closer, please. Ladies and gentlemen, this is Mr. Wilmuth.

Wilmuth. I was listenin' to the radio.

Phillips. Closer and louder, please.

Wilmuth. Yes, sir—while I was listenin' to the radio and kinda drowsin', that Professor fellow was talkin' about Mars, so I was half dozin' and half dreamin'——

Phillips. Yes, Mr. Wilmuth, and then you saw something?

Wilmuth. Not first off. First off, I heard something.

Phillips. And what did you hear?

Wilmuth. A hissin' sound. Like this: sssssssss . . . kinda like a Fourt' o' July rocket.

Phillips. Then what?

Wilmuth. I seen a kinda greenish streak and then zingo! Somethin' smacked the

---

1. **Arabian Nights**–A collection of fanciful Middle Eastern folk tales.

ground. Knocked me clear out of my chair!

Phillips. Thank you, Mr. Wilmuth. Thank you.

Wilmuth. Want me to tell you some more?

Phillips. No. That's quite all right, that's plenty. . . . Ladies and gentlemen, you've just heard Mr. Wilmuth, owner of the farm where this thing has fallen. I wish I could convey the atmosphere of this fantastic scene. Hundreds of cars are parked in a field in back of us. Police are trying to rope off the road leading to the farm, but cars are breaking right through. Their headlights throw an enormous spot on the pit where the object's half-buried. Some of the more daring souls are venturing near the edge. Their silhouettes stand out against the brightness of the metal.

Sound. *Faint humming.*

Phillips. One man wants to touch the thing . . . he's having an argument with a policeman. The policeman wins. . . . Now, ladies and gentlemen, there's something I haven't mentioned in all this excitement, but it's becoming more distinct. Perhaps you've caught it already on your radio. Listen: *(long pause)* . . . Do you hear it? It's a curious humming sound that seems to come from inside the object. I'll move the microphone nearer. Here. *(pause)* Now we're not more than twenty-five feet away. Can you hear it now? Oh, Professor Pierson!

Pierson. Yes, Mr. Phillips?

Phillips. Can you tell us the meaning of that noise inside the thing?

Pierson. Perhaps the unequal cooling of its surface.

Phillips. Do you still think it's a meteor, Professor?

Pierson. I don't know what to think. The metal casing is definitely not found on this earth. Friction with the earth's atmosphere usually tears holes in a meteorite. This thing is smooth and, as you can see, of cylindrical shape.

Phillips. Just a minute! Something's happening! Ladies and gentlemen, this is *terrific!* This end of the thing is beginning to flake off! The top is beginning to rotate like a screw! The thing must be hollow!

Voices. She's a-movin'!

Look, the darn thing's opening up!

Keep back there! Keep back, I tell you.

Maybe there's men in it trying to escape!

It's red hot—they'll burn to a cinder!

Keep back there! Keep those idiots back!

Creating the sound effects in a radio play. Culver Pictures, New York City.

Sound. *The clanking of a huge piece of falling metal.*

Voices. She's off! The top's loose! Look out there! Stand back!

Phillips. Ladies and gentlemen, this is the most terrifying thing I have ever witnessed. . . . Wait a minute! Someone's *crawling out of the top!* Someone or . . . *something!* I can see peering out of that black hole two luminous disks . . . are they eyes? It might be a face. It might be——

Sound. *Shout of awe from the crowd.*

Phillips. Good heavens, something's wriggling out of the shadow like a gray snake. Now it's another one, and another. They look like tentacles to me. There, I can see the thing's body. It's as large as a bear, and it glistens like wet leather. But that face. It—it's indescribable. I can hardly force myself to keep looking at it. The eyes are black and gleam like a serpent's. The mouth is V-shaped, with saliva dripping from rimless lips that seem to quiver and pulsate. The monster's rising up! The crowd falls back. They've seen enough. This is the most extraordinary experience. I . . . I'm taking a new position as I talk. Hold on, will you please? I'll be back in a minute.

Announcer two. We are bringing you an eyewitness account of what's happening on the Wilmuth farm, Grovers Mill, New Jersey. We now return you to Carl Phillips at Grovers Mill.

Phillips. Ladies and gentlemen. (Am I on?) Ladies and gentlemen, here I am, back of a stone wall that adjoins Mr. Wilmuth's garden. From here I get a sweep of the whole scene. More state police have arrived. They're drawing up a cordon in front of the pit, about thirty of them. No need to push the crowd back now. They're willing to keep their distance. The captain is conferring with someone. We can't quite see who. Oh, yes, it's Professor Pierson. Now the professor moves around one side, studying the object, while the captain and two policemen advance with something in their hands. I can see it now. It's a white handkerchief tied to a pole—a flag of truce. If those creatures know what that means—what anything means! *Wait!* Something's happening! I don't believe it——

Sound. *Hissing, followed by a humming that increases in intensity.*

Phillips. A humped shape is rising out of the pit. I can make out a small beam of light against a mirror. What's that? There's a jet of flame springing from that mirror, and it leaps right at the advancing men. It strikes them head on! Good Lord, they're turning into flame!

Sound. *Screams and unearthly shrieks.*

Phillips. Now the whole field's caught fire——

Sound. *Explosion.*

Phillips. The woods . . . the barns . . . the gas tanks of automobiles . . . it's spreading everywhere. It's coming this way. About twenty yards to my right——

Sound. *Crash of microphone . . . then dead silence. . . .*

Announcer two. Ladies and gentlemen, due to circumstances beyond our control, we are unable to continue the broadcast from Grovers Mill. Evidently there's some difficulty with our field transmission. However, we will return to that point at the earliest opportunity. In the meantime, we have a late bulletin from San Diego, California: "Professor Indelkoffer, speaking at a dinner of the California Astronomical Society, expressed the opinion that the explosions on Mars are undoubtedly nothing more than severe volcanic disturbances on the surface of the planet." We continue now with our piano interlude.

Sound. *Piano . . . then cut.*

Announcer two. Ladies and gentlemen, I have just been handed a message that came in from Grovers Mill by telephone. "At least forty people, including six State Troopers, lie dead in a field east of the village of Grovers Mill, their bodies burned and distorted beyond all possible recognition." The next voice you hear will be that of Brigadier General Montgomery Smith, commander of the State Militia at Trenton, New Jersey.

Smith. I have been requested by the governor of New Jersey to place the counties of Mercer and Middlesex under martial law. No one will be permitted to enter this area except by special pass. Four companies of State Militia will aid in the evacuation of homes within the range of military operations. Thank you.

Announcer. You have just been listening to General Montgomery Smith, commanding the State Militia at Trenton. In the meantime, further details of the catastrophe at Grovers Mill are coming in. The strange creatures, after unleashing their deadly assault, crawled back into their pit and made no attempt to prevent the efforts of firemen to recover the bodies and extinguish the fire.

We have been unable to establish any contact with our mobile unit at Grovers Mill, but we hope to be able to return you there at the earliest possible moment. In the meantime, we take you—uh, just one moment please.

Sound. *Whisper, long pause.*

Announcer. Ladies and gentlemen, I have just been informed that we have finally established communication with an eyewitness of the tragedy. Professor Pierson has been located at a farmhouse near Grovers Mill where he has established an emergency observation post. As a scientist, he will give you his explanation of the calamity. Professor Pierson.

Pierson. Of the creatures in the rocket cylinder at Grovers Mill, I can give you no authoritative information—either as to their nature, their origin, or their purposes here on earth. Of their destructive instrument I might venture some explanation. For want of a better term, I shall refer to the mysterious weapon as a heat-ray. It's all too evident that these creatures have scientific knowledge far in advance of our own. It is my guess that they are able to generate an intense heat and project it against any object they choose by means of a polished parabolic mirror of unknown composition—much as the mirror of a lighthouse projects a beam of light.

Announcer. Thank you, Professor Pierson. Ladies and gentlemen, here is a bulletin from Trenton. It is a brief statement informing us that the charred body of Carl Phillips has been identified in a Trenton hospital.

Now here's another bulletin from Washington, D.C.: "Ten units of Red Cross emergency workers have been assigned to the headquarters of the State Militia stationed outside Grovers Mill, New Jersey." Here's a bulletin from State Police, Princeton Junction: "The fires at Grovers Mill and vicinity are now under control. Scouts report all quiet in the pit and no sign of life appearing from the mouth of the cylinder. . . ." And now, ladies and gentlemen, in view of the gravity of the situation, we are turning over our entire broadcasting facilities to the State Militia at Trenton, at their request. . . . We take you now to the field headquarters of the State Militia near Grovers Mill, New Jersey.

Captain. This is Captain Lansing of the Signal Corps at Grovers Mill. Situation arising from the reported presence of certain individuals of unidentified nature is now under complete control.

The cylindrical object, which lies in a pit directly below our position, is surrounded on all sides by eight battalions of infantry, adequately armed with rifles and machine guns. All cause for alarm, if such cause ever existed, is now entirely unjustified. The things, whatever they are, do not even venture to poke their heads above the pit. I can see their hiding place plainly in the glare of the searchlights here. With all their reported resources, these creatures can scarcely stand up against heavy machine-gun fire. Anyway, it's an interesting outing for the troops. Now wait a minute! I see something on top of the cylinder. No, it's nothing but a shadow. Now the troops are on the edge of the Wilmuth farm. Seven thousand armed men closing in on an old metal tube. Wait, that wasn't a shadow! It's something moving . . . solid metal . . . kind of a shieldlike affair rising up out of the cylinder. . . . It's going higher and higher. Why, it's standing on legs— actually rearing up on a sort of metal framework. Now it's reaching above the trees and the searchlights are on it! Hold on! (*Long pause.*)

Announcer two. Ladies and gentlemen, I have a grave announcement to make. Incredible as it may seem, those strange beings who landed in the Jersey farmlands tonight are the vanguard of an invading army from the planet Mars. The battle, which took place tonight at Grovers Mill, has ended in one of the most startling defeats ever suffered by an army in modern times—seven thousand men armed with rifles and machine guns pitted against a single fighting machine of the invaders from Mars. One hundred and twenty known survivors. The rest strewn over the battle area from Grovers Mill to Plainsboro, crushed and trampled to death under the metal feet of the monster, or burned to cinders by its heat-ray. The monster is now in control of the middle section of New Jersey and has effectively cut the state through its center. Communication lines are down from Pennsylvania to the Atlantic Ocean. Railroad tracks are torn. Highways to the north, south, and west are clogged with frantic human traffic. By morning the fugitives will have swelled Philadelphia, Camden, and Trenton, it is estimated, to twice their normal population.

At this time, martial law prevails throughout New Jersey and eastern Pennsylvania. Bulletins too numerous to read are piling up in the studio here. Cables received from English, French, and German scientific bodies offer assistance. Astronomers report continued gas outbursts at regular intervals on planet Mars. Majority voice opinion that enemy will be reinforced by additional rocket machines. . . . Attempts made to locate Professor Pierson at Princeton, who has observed Martians at close range. It is feared he was lost in recent battle.

Langham Field, Virginia: "Scouting planes report three Martian machines visible above tree tops, moving north toward Somerville with population fleeing ahead of them. Heat-ray not in use. Although advancing at express-train speed, invaders pick their way carefully. They seem to be making conscious effort to avoid destruction of cities and countryside. However, they stop to uproot power lines, bridges, and railroad tracks. Their apparent objective is to crush resistance, paralyze communication, and disorganize human society." Here is a bulletin from Basking Ridge, New Jersey: "Coon hunters have stumbled on a second cylinder, similar to the first, embedded in the great swamp twenty miles south of Morristown. U.S. Army fieldpieces are proceeding from Newark to blow up second invading unit before cylinder can be opened and the fighting machines rigged. They are taking up positions in the foothills of Watchung Mountains.[2]" Another bulletin from Langham Field, Virginia: "Scouting planes report enemy machines, now three in number, increasing speed northward, kicking over houses and trees in their evident haste to form a conjunction with their allies south of Morristown. Machines also sighted by telephone operator east of Middlesex within ten miles of Plainfield." Here's a

---

2. **Watchung** (wä chung′) **Mountains**—Located in north central New Jersey.

Study and Research

Finding Facts in an Encyclopedia. Find and read an encyclopedia article about the planet Mars. Then answer the following questions.

1. About how far is Mars from Earth?

2. How long does it take Mars to orbit the sun?

3. How many moons does Mars have? What are their names?

4. Describe the surface of Mars.

5. In what year did Viking I and Viking II land on Mars? What kinds of information did these two spacecraft gather?

6. Does an invasion from Mars seem to be possible?

Developing Writing Skills

Creating an Alien. Many science fiction plays, books, and movies are based on the idea of aliens visiting Earth. There have been evil aliens, as in this play and the movie *Aliens.* There have been friendly aliens, as in the movies *Close Encounters of the Third Kind* and *E.T.*

Invent an evil or a friendly alien visiting Earth. In two paragraphs, describe your alien.

Prewriting. Make notes about your alien's size, shape, color, and type of skin or fur. Note the number of heads it has and whether its organs for seeing, smelling, hearing, and eating are all located on one head, as in humans. Make notes about the way the alien moves: does it walk, ooze, or fly? Explain how it communicates with others. List any other important facts about the alien's behavior.

Drafting. Describe your alien's physical appearance in the first paragraph. In the second paragraph, describe its behavior.

Revising and Sharing. Share the draft of your paragraphs with a partner. Discuss these points: Does the first paragraph give the reader a clear picture of the alien's appearance? Does the second paragraph clearly explain the alien's behavior? Use your partner's comments to help you in revising your paragraphs.

You may wish to compare your description with those of others in the class and then take a vote on which alien is the most interesting and which is the most repulsive. Or you might have a classmate draw a picture of your creature based on your description.

From The War of the Worlds
Invasion from Mars

It's the end of the earth as we know it. Or is it? What can possibly defeat the Martian machines?

H. G. WELLS
Adapted by Howard Koch

ACT TWO

Fade in . . .

Pierson. As I set down these notes on paper, I'm obsessed by the thought that I may be the last living man on earth. I have been hiding in this empty house near Grovers Mill—a small island of daylight cut off by black smoke from the rest of the world. All that happened before the arrival of these monstrous creatures now seems part of another life. I look down at my blackened hands, my torn shoes, my tattered clothes, and I try to connect them with a professor who lived at Princeton, and who, on the night of October 20, glimpsed through his telescope an orange splash of light on a distant planet. My wife, my colleagues, my students, my books, my observatory, my— my world . . . where are they? Did they ever exist? Am I Richard Pierson? What day is it? Do days exist without calendars? Does time pass when there are no human hands left to wind the clocks? . . . In writing down my daily life, I tell myself I shall preserve human history between the dark covers of this little book that was meant to record the movements of the stars. . . . But to write I must live, and to live I must eat. I find moldy bread in the kitchen and an orange not too spoiled to swallow. I keep watch at the window. From time to time I catch sight of a Martian above the black smoke.

The smoke still holds the house in its black coil. . . . Suddenly I see a Martian mounted on his machine, spraying the air with a jet of steam, as if to dissipate the smoke. I watch in a corner as his huge metal legs nearly brush against the house. Exhausted by terror, I fall asleep. . . . It's morning. Sun streams in the window . . . the black cloud of gas

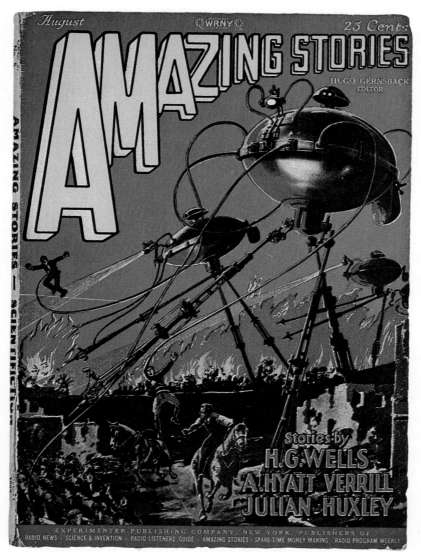

Cover: *Amazing Stories,*
illustrating *The War of the Worlds*
by H. G. Wells, 1927. The Granger
Collection, New York City.

has lifted. I venture from the house. I make my way to a road. No traffic. Here and there a wrecked car, baggage overturned, a blackened skeleton. I push on north. For some reason I feel safer trailing these monsters than running away from them. And I keep a careful watch.

I must keep alive. I come to a chestnut tree and fill my pockets. Two days I wander in a vague northerly direction through a desolate world. Finally I notice a living creature—a small red squirrel in a beech tree. I stare at him and wonder. He stares back at me. I believe at that moment the animal and I shared the same emotion—the joy of finding another living being. . . . I push on north. I find dead cows and, beyond, the charred ruins of a dairy. The silo remains standing guard over the wasteland like a lighthouse deserted by the sea. Astride the silo perches a weathercock. The arrow points north. . . . *Fade out.*

Fade in . . .

Next day I came to a city vaguely familiar in its contours, yet its buildings are strangely dwarfed and leveled off, as if a giant had sliced off its highest towers with one capricious sweep of his hand. I reached the outskirts. I found Newark, undemolished but humbled by some whim of the advancing Martians. Presently, with an odd feeling of being watched, I caught sight of something crouching in a doorway. I made a step toward it, and it rose up and became a man—a man, armed with a large knife.

Stranger. Stop! Where did you come from?

Pierson. I come from . . . many places. A long time ago from Princeton.

Stranger. Princeton, huh? That's near Grovers Mill!

Pierson. Yes.

Stranger. Grovers Mill . . . *(laughs as at great joke).* . . . There's no food here. This is my country—all this end of town down to the river. There's only food for one. . . . Which way are you going?

Pierson. I don't know. I guess I'm looking for—for people.

Stranger. Say, we're in the open here. Let's crawl into this doorway and talk.

Pierson. Have you seen any Martians?

Stranger. They've gone over to New York. At night the sky is alive with their lights. Just as if people were still living there. By daylight you can't see them. Five days ago a couple of them carried something big across the flats from the airport. I believe they're learning how to fly our airplanes.

Pierson. Then it's all over with humanity. Stranger, there's still you and I. Two of us left.

Stranger. They got themselves in solid; they wrecked the greatest country in the world. Those green stars, they're probably falling somewhere every night. They've only lost one machine. There isn't anything to do. We're licked.

Pierson. What will they do to us?

Stranger. I've thought it all out. Right now we're caught as we're wanted. The

Martian only has to go a few miles to get a crowd on the run. But they won't keep doing that. They'll begin catching us, systematic like—keeping the best and storing us in cages and things. They haven't begun on us yet!

Pierson. Not begun!

Stranger. Not begun. All that's happened so far is because we don't have sense enough to keep quiet . . . bothering them with guns and such stuff and losing our heads and rushing off in crowds. Now instead of our rushing around blind, we've got to fix ourselves up according to the way things are now.

Pierson. But what is there to live for?

Stranger. There won't be any more concerts for a million years or so, and no nice little dinners at restaurants. If it's amusement you're after, I guess the game's up.

Pierson. And what is there left?

Stranger. *Life* . . . that's what! I want to live. And so do you! We're not going to be exterminated. And I don't mean to be caught, either, and tamed and fattened and bred like an ox.

Pierson. What are you going to do?

Stranger. I'm going on . . . right under their feet. I gotta plan. We men as men are finished. We don't know enough. We gotta learn plenty before we get a chance. And we've got to live and keep free while we learn. I've thought it all out, see.

Pierson. Tell me the rest.

Stranger. Well, it isn't all of us that are made for wild beasts. That's why I watched you. All these little office workers that used to live in these houses—they'd be no good. They haven't any stuff to 'em. I've seen hundreds of 'em running wild to catch their commuters' train in the morning, for fear that they'd get fired if they didn't; running back at night, afraid they wouldn't be in time for dinner. Lives insured and a little invested in case of accidents. The Martians will be a godsend for those guys. Nice roomy cages, good food, careful breeding, no worries. After a week or so of chasing about the fields on empty stomachs, they'll come and be glad to be caught.

Pierson. You've thought it all out, haven't you?

Stranger. You bet I have! And that isn't all. These Martians will make pets of some of them, train 'em to do tricks. Who knows? Get sentimental over the pet boy who grew up and had to be killed. And some, maybe, they'll train to hunt us.

Pierson. No, that's impossible. No human being——

Stranger. Yes, they will. There's people who'll do it gladly.

Pierson. In the meantime, you and I and others like us . . . where are we to live when the Martians own the Earth?

Stranger. I've got it all figured out. We'll live underground. I've been thinking about the sewers. Then there's cellars, vaults, underground storerooms, railway tunnels, subways. And we'll get a bunch of strong men together. Get all the books we can—science books. That's where men like you come in, see? We'll raid the museums, we'll even spy on the Martians. We may not have to learn much before—just imagine this: four or five of their own fighting machines suddenly start off—and not a Martian in 'em. But *men*—men who have learned the way how. It may even be in our time. Imagine having one of them lovely things with its heat-ray wide and free! We'd turn it on Martians, we'd turn it on men. We'd bring everybody down to their knees.

Pierson. That's your plan?

Stranger. You and me and a few more of us, we'd own the world.

Pierson. I see.

Stranger. Say, what's the matter? Where are you going?

Pierson. Not to *your* world. Goodbye, Stranger. . . .

I came at last to the Holland Tunnel. I entered that silent tube, anxious to know the fate of the great city on the other side of the Hudson. Cautiously I came out of the tunnel and made my way up Canal Street.

I wandered up through the Thirties and Forties;[1] I stood alone on Times Square. I caught sight of a lean dog running down Seventh Avenue with a piece of dark brown meat in his jaws and a pack of starving mongrels at his heels. He made a wide circle around me, as though he feared I might prove a fresh competitor. I walked up Broadway past silent shop windows displaying their wares to empty sidewalks— past the Capitol Theater, silent, dark— past a shooting gallery, where a row of empty guns faced an arrested line of wooden ducks. I hurried on. Suddenly I caught sight of the hood of a Martian machine, standing somewhere in Central Park, gleaming in the late afternoon sun. An insane idea! I rushed recklessly across Columbus Circle and into the Park. I climbed a small hill above the pond at Sixtieth Street. From there I could see, standing in a silent row along the Mall, nineteen of those great metal Titans, their cowls empty, their steel arms hanging listlessly by their sides. I

---

1. **Thirties and Forties**—Street numbers in New York City.

looked in vain for the monsters that inhabited those machines.

Suddenly, my eyes were attracted to the immense flock of black birds that hovered below me. They circled to the ground, and there before my eyes, stark and silent, lay the Martians, with the hungry birds pecking and tearing shreds of flesh from their dead bodies. When their bodies were examined in laboratories, it was found that they were killed by the disease bacteria against which their systems were unprepared . . . slain after all man's defenses had failed.

Strange it now seems to sit in my peaceful study at Princeton writing down this last chapter of the record begun at a deserted farm in Grovers Mill. Strange to see from my window the university spires dim and blue through an April haze. Strange to watch children playing in the streets. Strange to see young people strolling on the green, where the new spring grass heals the last black scars of a bruised earth. Strange to watch the sightseers enter the museum where the disassembled parts of a Martian machine are kept on public view. Strange when I recall the time I first saw it, bright and clean-cut, hard and silent, under the dawn of that last unforgettable day.

Sound. *Music.*

Orson Welles at a press interview after the panic triggered by *Invasion from Mars* broadcast, 1938. Culver Pictures, New York City.

H. G. Wells (*1866–1946*) was a noted British writer who believed strongly in scientific progress. He graduated from London University where he received a science degree with honors. Wells published hundreds of books in various fields, but is best known for his science fiction. His famous works include *The War of the Worlds* and *The Time Machine*. Wells wrote of airplanes, submarines, and moon voyages long before people believed such things could become real.

Developing Comprehension Skills

1. While Act One focuses on many characters, this act concentrates almost totally on one character. Who is that person? What was his profession before the invasion? How does he "speak" to the audience?

2. Describe the Stranger's plan for hiding from the Martians and eventually conquering the world.

3. What does Pierson think of the Stranger's plan?

4. In the end the Martians are destroyed by disease bacteria, which their bodies cannot fight. Reread the end of the last speech. What does Pierson find strange about the life he sees around him? What does the speech suggest about how people have recovered from the Martian invasion?

5. Does the writer's purpose change in any way in Act Two? Explain your answer.

6. If the Martians had succeeded in conquering the Earth, do you think many humans would willingly live in comfortable cages, as the Stranger suggests? Would some people share the Stranger's ambition to "own the world"?

Reading Literature: Drama

1. **Recognizing Plot Development.** You have learned that the plot of a story includes five parts: exposition, rising action, climax, falling action, and resolution. In this play, the rising action is the landing of the Martians and the Martian attack. The resolution is Pierson's discovery of the dead Martians in Central Park

and the return to normal life. When does the **climax**, the most exciting part of the story, occur? Make a plot diagram for the play, filling in all five parts.

2. **Understanding Conflict.** In a story, the struggle between opposing forces is called the **conflict.** Is the main conflict in *Invasion from Mars* internal or external? Who or what is the source of that conflict? How is it resolved?

3. **Thinking About the Main Character.** Professor Pierson is the main character in this play. As the play progresses, he changes. How is Professor Pierson different at the end of the play than he is in the beginning? Think about how he reacts on page 567 to the question about the seismography reading. Also, think about the questions he asks himself on page 580 as he writes down notes.

4. **Examining Mood. Mood** is the feeling you get as you are reading a selection. Act One of this play has many characters and a rapid pace of events. The mood is one of fear and excitement. What is the mood of Act Two? What factors contribute to this changed mood? Is the mood hopeful at the very end of the play?

5. **Inferring Theme.** What idea comes out of Pierson's encounter with the squirrel? What is hopeful and what is frightening about the Stranger's plans? As a result, what **theme,** or message, can you infer?

6. **Recognizing Irony.** The term **irony** can be used to describe any of the following situations:

a. A character says one thing and means another.
b. The reader knows something that a character does not know.
c. What seems to be true is quite different from what really is true.
d. What happens is what seems to be the least likely to happen.

In this play, the Martian monsters in their giant machines are destroyed by one of the earth's tiniest forms of life. Which kind of irony best describes this outcome?

Vocabulary

Reviewing Context Clues. The following words are found in the given locations in the play. Read the paragraph in which each word is found. On a sheet of paper, write which context clue helped you figure out the meaning of the word. Also, write the meaning of the word.

1. hysteria (page 564, paragraph 1)
   a. antonym
   b. main idea
   c. restatement

2. wriggling (page 570, column 2, Phillips's 1st speech)
   a. main idea
   b. antonym
   c. example

3. pulsate (pages 570–571, Phillips's speech)
   a. words in a series
   b. synonym
   c. contrast

4. gravity (page 573, column 1, Announcer's 1st speech)

    a. words in a series
    b. example
    c. main idea

5. incapacitated (page 576, column 1, Operator one's 2nd speech)

    a. restatement
    b. antonym
    c. cause and effect

6. vaults (page 584, column 1, Stranger's 2nd speech)

    a. definition
    b. comparison
    c. words in a series

Critical Thinking

Evaluating Literature. Which of the two plays in this chapter did you enjoy more? What qualities contributed to your enjoyment? In considering this, think about the major elements in the play. Is the plot exciting and full of suspense? Are the characters interesting and true-to-life? Is the dialogue amusing? Is the setting carefully imagined? Is the theme thought-provoking? Does the play show weaknesses in any of these elements? List the two or three elements of the play that you feel are most effective.

Speaking and Listening

Presenting a Monologue. Sometimes in a play only one character appears in a scene. The character talks to himself or herself—and to the audience. Such a speech is called a **monologue.** At the beginning of Act Two of *Invasion from Mars,* Professor Pierson has a long monologue. At the end of the act he has another monologue.

A monologue can be tricky to present, especially in a radio play. Because there is only one person talking, the audience can become bored quickly. To avoid boring the audience, the speaker must put feeling into his or her voice. The speaker's voice must show changes in mood, even if they are slight.

Work in small groups to practice reading either of Pierson's monologues. Discuss qualities of your speech that you can change, such as the speed with which you talk, the pitch of your voice, and its loudness. Then take turns reading the monologue and applying these techniques.

Developing Writing Skills

1. **Describing Techniques of Radio Scripts.** The audience of a radio play cannot see the setting or the action of the play. A writer, though, can make up for this difficulty and even take advantage of it. In a paragraph, describe three or more ways in which the writer of *Invasion from Mars* made it possible for the audience to imagine the action. Prove your point with examples from the play.

    Prewriting. Review *Invasion from Mars* to find ways in which the writer deals with the problem of the audience not seeing the action. Be on the lookout for techniques the writer uses to help the listener imagine what is happening. Note any specific examples you find.

    Drafting. State the main idea of your paragraph in a topic sentence. Then describe techniques used by the writer of *Invasion from Mars*. Give specific examples of how those techniques are used in the play.

    Revising and Sharing. Share your draft with a partner. Ask him or her to explain the techniques you described and to discuss your examples of those techniques. If your partner has difficulty doing so, revise your draft to make your writing clearer.

2. **Presenting an Opinion.** When this radio play was first presented, some people believed that Martians really had invaded Earth. Some of these people reacted out of fright and tried to run away. Write a paragraph describing what you think would happen if this play were presented over the radio now. Do you think that people would react the way they did in 1938? Why or why not?

    In your prewriting notes, list reasons that people might react the way you think they might. Refer to your prewriting notes as you draft your paragraph. Reread your draft, asking yourself if you have solid reasons to support your argument. Make any necessary revisions.

3. **Writing a Radio Script.** For the six o'clock radio news, write a three-minute or four-minute broadcast describing the landing on Earth of a creature from another planet. If you wish, you may use the alien that you created for the Developing Writing Skills exercise on page 579.

    In your prewriting notes, list words and phrases that describe the creature. Also make notes about the creature's vehicle (if any) and the way it arrives on Earth. If you wish, you may include an eyewitness or an authority whom you can interview. As you draft your script, remember to write in the style of a radio news broadcast. If necessary, review the style used in *Invasion from Mars*. If possible, act out your script with several classmates, and make further revisions if necessary. Then share your script with the entire class.

Chapter 7 Review

Using Your Skills in Reading Plays

Read the following brief scene from a play. List the characters in the scene, and identify the stage directions. What does the dialogue tell about the setting of the play? Does the dialogue seem to suit the characters? Why or why not? What conflict exists between Arthur and Merlin?

> *(As the curtain opens, Arthur and Merlin are seated at Arthur's Round Table.)*
>
> **Arthur.** Merlin, my kingdom is in order, and all my subjects are happy. This castle's getting a little empty, though. I guess it's about time I got married.
>
> **Merlin.** Who's the lucky lady?
>
> **Arthur** *(smiling).* The most beautiful woman I've ever seen—Lady Guinevere!
>
> **Merlin** *(alarmed).* Guinevere! Oh, no! She's not right for you! Let me fix you up with someone you'd be happier with.
>
> **Arthur.** No, I've made my choice. Guinevere is the only woman I'd ever want to marry. Go see if it's OK with her father, and let's get this show on the road! *(He waves Merlin out.)*

Using Your Comprehension Skills

The passage above contains dialogue that is modern and informal. What do you suppose might have been the author's purpose in using this language? Can you suggest a reason for writing a play about King Arthur in modern speech?

Which words in the scene above are not in keeping with a formal court scene? How might you change Arthur's words to create a greater air of royalty and authority?

Using Your Vocabulary Skills

Each of these sentences is from a selection in this book. Each sentence contains an underlined word. If you did not know the meaning of any of these words, which ones would you have to look up in a dictionary? Which words might you be able to figure out? Write one of the following terms to identify how you would determine the meaning of each word: word parts, context clues, the dictionary.

1. "The farmer said he thought that was <u>unsound</u> reasoning."

2. "Robin settled down by the fire again, with the <u>exquisite</u> garments across his knees."

3. "The prisoner began <u>zealously</u> to study languages, philosophy, and history. He fell on these subjects with hunger."

4. "He set sail for England by way of Cyprus, but a <u>gale</u> blew his ships off their course and drove them to Italy."

Using Your Skills in Critical Thinking

Compare these three types of literature: short stories, nonfiction, and drama. How are the three alike? How are they different? To answer these questions, consider some of the elements of literature: plot, character, dialogue, setting, theme. On a sheet of paper, list those elements that are most important for each type and those that are sometimes absent. Then make the comparison and contrast.

Using Your Writing Skills

Choose one of the assignments below.

1. When reading a play, you should cooperate with the writer and enter his or her created world. Write from one to three paragraphs describing the world created in *The Ugly Duckling* or *Invasion from Mars*. Tell how the created world is different from your own.

2. Choose a short section of dialogue from one of the short stories, legends, or nonfiction selections in this book. Rewrite this dialogue in the same form as it would be written in a play. Add stage directions and sound effects, if appropriate.

Handbook
for Reading
and Writing

Act. An act is a major unit of action in a play. Each act may contain several scenes, and each scene may have a different setting. *The Ugly Duckling* (page 540) is a one-act play. *Invasion from Mars* (page 564) has two acts.

Alliteration. Alliteration is the repetition of consonant sounds at the beginnings of words. This type of repetition is found in prose, poetry, and everyday speech. The phrases "pen pal," "silver spoon," and "last laugh" all contain alliteration. Notice how alliteration gives the following line a musical quality:

> He clasps the crag with crooked hands;
> ("The Eagle," page 337)

For more about alliteration, see pages 118–119.

Allusion. An allusion is a reference to another work of literature or to a familiar person, place, or event outside of literature. For example, in "The Duel" (page 377), Emily Dickinson alludes to the story of David and Goliath.

For more about allusion, see page 378.

Anecdote. An anecdote is a brief story told to entertain or to make a point. "Horse Trade" (page 509) is an anecdote that shows Abraham Lincoln's sense of humor.

For more about anecdotes, see page 498.

Assonance. Assonance is the repetition of a vowel sound within words. The phrases "free and easy" and "time flies" contain this kind of repetition. Notice the repetition of the *a* and *e* sounds in these lines from the poem "Seal" (page 321).

> Past crabs and eels
> And green seaweed,
> Past fluffs of sandy
> Minnow feed!

Autobiography. An autobiography is the story of a person's life, written by that person. Although a form of nonfiction, an autobiography contains elements of fiction, such as character, setting, plot, and conflict. An example of an autobiography is "I Get a Colt to Break In" (page 415).

For more about autobiography, see pages 409 and 414.

See also *Biography* and *Nonfiction*.

Biography. A biography is the story of a person's life, written by another person.

Although a form of nonfiction, biography may contain several elements found in fiction, such as character, setting, plot, conflict, and suspense. An example of a biography is *From Mumbet: The Story of Elizabeth Freeman* (page 460).

For more about biography, see pages 409 and 459.

See also *Autobiography* and *Nonfiction.*

Character. A character is a person or animal who takes part in the action of a work of literature. Generally, the plot of a short story focuses on one character, the main character. A story may also have one or more minor characters. They keep the action moving forward and help the reader learn more about the main character. Matilda Loisel is the main character in "The Necklace" (page 176). Her husband and Madame Forestier are minor characters.

For more about character, see pages 3, 71, and 206.

See also *Characterization.*

Characterization. Characterization is the use of literary techniques to reveal the nature of a character. One important way that a writer reveals a character is through physical description. A second way to reveal a character is to present his or her speech, thoughts, and actions. A third way is through the comments, actions, and feelings of other characters. Finally, a writer may use a narrator to make direct comments about a character.

For more about characterization, see page 206.

Climax. The climax, or turning point, is the high point of interest or suspense in a story or play. Generally, at the climax, the outcome of a story becomes clear. In "The Old Soldier," for example, the climax comes when the doctor discovers that the old soldier was a Hessian (page 227).

For more about climax, see page 139.

See also *Exposition, Falling Action, Plot, Resolution,* and *Rising Action.*

Concrete Poem. A concrete poem visually presents something important about the poem's meaning. For example, in "Seal" (page 321), the lines form curves down the page. These curves suggest the shape of a seal and its movement in the water.

See also *Shape.*

Conflict. Conflict is a struggle between opposing forces. It creates the tension and suspense in a story or play. Two types of conflict are internal and external.

An internal conflict takes place inside the mind of a character. For example, in "The Medicine Bag" (page 254), Martin wants to wear his grandfather's medicine bag, but fears that his friends will laugh at him.

An external conflict takes place between a character and some outside person or force. Sometimes the external conflict is a struggle between characters.

An example is the battle between the mongoose and the cobras in "Rikki-tikki-tavi" (page 151). At other times, the struggle is between a character and an outside force. In "Runaway Rig" (page 234), Barney Conners struggles to avoid a crash as his truck hurtles downhill. Yet another kind of external conflict presents a struggle between a character and society. In "Adjö Means Goodbye" (page 246), the main character comes to grips with the prejudice in her community.

For more about conflict, see page 207.

Description. Description is writing that creates a picture of a scene, event, or character. Writers choose their details carefully to create exact descriptions. Notice how the underlined words in the following passage help the reader to see the character.

All I could do was stand there with the whole neighborhood watching and shake the hand of the leather-brown old man. I saw how his gray hair straggled from under his big black hat, which had a drooping feather in its crown. His rumpled black suit hung like a sack over his stooped frame. As he shook my hand, his coat fell open to expose a bright red satin shirt with a beaded bolo tie under the collar.
("The Medicine Bag," page 255)

A description may also provide details of sound, smell, touch, or other senses. Sometimes a description includes details about the actions or attitudes of a character.

See also *Sensory Images.*

Dialect. A dialect is a variety of language that is spoken in a certain place or among a certain group of people. Notice the dialect in the following lines from *Invasion from Mars.*

Wilmuth. I seen a kinda greenish streak and then zingo! Somethin' smacked the ground. Knocked me clear out of my chair!
(pages 568–569)

Dialogue. A dialogue is a conversation between two or more characters. Such conversations make the characters seem real and provide hints about their personalities. Dialogue is very important in drama. No quotation marks are used for dialogue in plays. In other types of writing, the exact words of a character are set off by quotation marks.

For more about dialogue, see page 535.

Drama. Drama is writing that tells a story through dialogue and action. A drama, or a play, is meant to be performed by actors and actresses. Like other types of fiction, drama has such elements as character, setting, plot, suspense, conflict, and theme.

To help performers and directors, playwrights often provide stage directions. They indicate how lines should be spoken and how characters should move. They also give information about sound effects, music, lighting, and scenery.

Plays are divided into acts. Each act may have several scenes in which the time or place changes.

For more about drama, see pages 534–535.

See also *Act, Dialogue, Scene,* and *Stage Directions*.

Episode. An episode is a self-contained section of a longer story. Arthur's pulling the sword from the stone is one episode in the Arthurian legend.

Essay. An essay is a brief nonfiction work that deals with one subject, often in a personal way. "Shortest Month" (page 520) is an essay. In it the writer shares thoughts and feelings about December.

For more about the essay, see pages 499 and 517.

Exposition. The exposition is the part of a plot that provides background information and that introduces the setting and the important characters. The following passage from "Spotted Eagle and Black Crow" contains the exposition.

> Many lifetimes ago, there lived two brave warriors. One was named *Wanblee Gleska*—Spotted Eagle. The other's name was *Kangi Sapa*—Black Crow. They were friends but, as it happened, they both loved the same girl, *Zintkala Luta Win*—Red Bird. She was beautiful, a fine tanner and

quill-worker, and she liked Spotted Eagle best, which made Black Crow very jealous. (page 22)

For more about exposition, see page 139.

See also *Plot*.

Extended Metaphor. An extended metaphor is a series of comparisons between two unlike things that have several elements in common. For example, in the poem "Women" (page 398), Alice Walker develops the comparison between the struggle of black women to have their children educated and a military battle.

See also *Metaphor*.

External Conflict. See *Conflict*.

Fable. A fable is a brief story, usually with animal characters, that teaches a lesson about human nature. The animals in fables usually act and speak like humans.

See also *Moral*.

Falling Action. The falling action is the part of a plot in which the story begins to draw to a close. The falling action comes after the climax and before the resolution. In "*From* The Chronicles of Robin Hood: How Marian Came to the Greenwood" (page 49), the climax comes when Robin and Marian recognize each other. The falling action includes their return to the cave at Dunwold Scar and Marian's introduction to the outlaw band.

For more about falling action, see page 139.

See also *Climax, Plot,* and *Resolution.*

Fantasy. A fantasy is a story that is set in an imaginary world. "The Gift-Giving" (page 298), for example, is a fantasy.

For more about fantasy, see page 285.

Fiction. Fiction is writing about imaginary people, places, and events. Some stories come totally from imagination. Other stories are based partly on facts. Such stories include some real and some imaginary people, places, and events.

For more about fiction, see page 138.

See also *Nonfiction.*

Figurative Language. Figurative language is language that communicates ideas beyond the literal, or actual, meanings of the words. For example, in the poem "Fall" on page 331, Sally Andresen writes:

> The geese flying south
> In a row long and V-shaped
> Pulling in winter.

The speaker does not mean that the geese physically pull winter across the sky, but that the sight of the geese signals the coming of winter.

Special types of figurative language, called figures of speech, are hyperbole, metaphor, personification, and simile.

For more about figurative language, see pages 125–133.

See also *Hyperbole, Metaphor, Personification,* and *Simile.*

Flashback. A flashback is a part of a story that interrupts the sequence of events to relate an earlier conversation, scene, or event. Generally, a plot moves forward in time. Sometimes, though, a writer interrupts this movement to tell the reader something that happened before the story began. This information helps explain the present actions of a character.

For example, the first paragraph of "The Bet" (page 168) describes an old banker pacing the floor of his room. In the second paragraph a flashback tells about a strange bet made by the banker fifteen years ago. The reader must know about the terms of the bet to understand why the old banker is upset.

Foreshadowing. Foreshadowing is the technique of hinting about something that will occur in a story. Foreshadowing creates suspense and makes the reader eager to find out what will happen. An example of foreshadowing occurs at the beginning of "Hearts and Hands" (page 145), when Mr. Easton uses his left, not his right, hand to clasp Miss Fairchild's fingers. This detail hints that he is the prisoner.

Free Verse. Free verse is poetry without patterns of rhyme and meter. Like most poetry, free verse generally is more rhythmic than ordinary language. Much modern poetry is written in free verse. One example is the poem "Women" (page 398).

Haiku. A haiku is a form of poetry that has seventeen syllables arranged in three lines. The first line has five syllables; the second line, seven; and the third line, five.

The haiku form comes from Japanese poetry. When haiku are translated from Japanese into other languages, however, it is almost impossible to keep the syllable count while communicating the same meanings. The poem "Fall" (page 331) is an example of haiku.

For more about haiku, see pages 314 and 332.

Humor. Humor is the quality that makes writing funny or amusing. One of the ways a writer can create humor is by using exaggeration. Another is by narrating foolish events in a serious way.

Hyperbole. Hyperbole is an exaggeration for emphasis. Examples are expressions such as "I'm dying of thirst" and "That sweater cost a fortune!" The following sentence contains hyperbole.

> I put on...a new pair of patent leather shoes that tortured my feet unbearably. ("Adjö Means Goodbye," page 248)

For more about hyperbole, see pages 132–133.
See also *Figurative Language.*

Imagery. See *Sensory Images.*

Internal Conflict. See *Conflict.*

Irony. Irony is a contrast between what is expected and what actually exists or happens. For example, in "Hearts and Hands" (page 145), it is ironic that Mr. Easton, the prisoner, looks bold, instead of glum, on his way to prison.

Legend. A legend is a story passed down through many generations and popularly believed to have a historic basis. While the main character in a legend may have lived at one time, many of the stories associated with her or him are fictitious. The legend of King Arthur is an example of an old English legend. It is probable that King Arthur did in fact live. It is highly unlikely, however, that most of the stories associated with him are true.

For more about legends, see pages 2–3 and 70–71.

Letter. A letter is a form of nonfiction usually intended to be read by one person. Letters are written for many reasons, such as to describe daily events, to express opinions, or to make business arrangements. Sometimes the private letters of an important person are later published. They allow readers to learn about the writer and the time in which he or she lived. The letters of Abraham Lincoln (pages 500 and 502) are valuable for these reasons.

For more about letters, see page 499. See also *Nonfiction*.

Line. A line is a basic unit in a poem. Lines may be very long or as short as a single word. Sometimes, lines are grouped into stanzas.

See also *Stanza*.

Lyric Poem. See *Poetry*.

Main Character. See *Character*.

Metaphor. A metaphor is a comparison between two unlike things that have something in common. Unlike a simile, a metaphor does not use the words *like* or *as*. The following lines from the poem "Hockey" (page 350) contain a metaphor.

> We clot, break, drive,
> Electrons in motion
> In the magnetic pull of the puck.

The speaker compares hockey players and electrons.

For more about metaphor, see pages 128–129.

See also *Figurative Language* and *Simile*.

Monologue. In drama, a monologue is a speech given by a character who is alone on stage. The audience listens to the character thinking out loud. An example is the speech given by Professor Pierson at the beginning of Act Two in *Invasion from Mars* (page 580).

For more about monologue, see page 588.

Mood. Mood is the feeling the writer intends the reader to get from a literary work. A writer can create this special feeling through the choice of words. In "The Dragon," Ray Bradbury creates a mood of loneliness with this description of the setting:

> The night blew in the short grass on the moor. There was no other motion. It had been years since a single bird had flown by in the great blind shell of sky. Long ago a few small stones had simulated life when they crumbled and fell into dust. Now only the night moved in the souls of the two men bent by their lonely fire in the wilderness. (page 292)

For more about mood, see page 347.

Moral. A moral is the lesson taught by a story. The lesson is a guideline for living. Examples include "Honesty is the best policy" and "Look before you leap." Most fables end with a moral, and other stories can have morals too.

See also *Fable*.

Narrative. A narrative is any writing that tells a story. The events in a narrative may be real or imaginary. Types of narrative include anecdotes, autobiographies, biographies, legends, narrative poems, novels, and short stories.

Narrative Poem. See *Poetry*.

Narrator. The narrator is the teller of a story. Sometimes the narrator is a character in the story. At other times the narrator is an outside voice created by the writer. The narrator in "The Long Way Around" (page 264), for example, is the main character, Patty.

See also *Point of View*.

Nonfiction. Nonfiction is writing about real people, places, and events. Nonfiction presents factual information. Types of nonfiction include autobiographies, biographies, letters, anecdotes, speeches, and essays.

Writers of nonfiction use such elements of fiction as characterization, setting, plot, and conflict.

For more about nonfiction, see pages 408–409 and 498–499.

See also *Anecdote, Autobiography, Biography, Essay, Fiction, Letter,* and *Speech*.

Onomatopoeia. Onomatopoeia is the use of words to imitate sounds. Words such as *bang, pop, crunch, meow, snap, babble, squeal,* and *thump* are examples of onomatopoeia. Notice the words that imitate sounds in the following lines:

Out with a zoom,
    A whoop, a bark;
("Seal," page 321)

For more about onomatopoeia, see page 124.

Oral Tradition. Oral tradition refers to the passing of stories or poems by word of mouth from generation to generation. Legends and folk tales come from oral tradition.

For more about oral tradition, see page 2.

See also *Legend* and *Tale*.

Parody. A parody is an imitation that makes fun of a story, poem, song, play, or other work. *The Ugly Duckling* (page 540) is a parody of fairy tales.

Personification. Personification is the technique of giving human qualities to an object, animal, or idea. The following lines from "Paul Revere's Ride" contain personification:

And the meeting-house windows, blank
    and bare,
Gaze at him with a spectral glare,
(pages 390–391)

For more about personification, see pages 130–131.

See also *Figurative Language*.

Play. See *Drama*.

Plot. Plot is the sequence of events in a story. It is the writer's plan for what happens, when, and to whom.

Generally, a plot includes exposition, rising action, climax, falling action, and resolution. The plot centers on a conflict—a problem or struggle faced by the main character. The actions taken by that character build toward the climax, the high point of interest. At this point or shortly after, the main character wins or loses the conflict. Then the story begins to draw to a close, and the loose ends are tied up.

For more about plot, see pages 3, 71, and 138–139.

See also *Climax, Conflict, Exposition, Falling Action, Resolution,* and *Rising Action.*

Poetry. Poetry is an expression of ideas and feelings in compact, imaginative, and musical language. Most poems are presented in lines, sometimes grouped into stanzas. Many poems depend heavily on sensory images, figurative language, and sound devices such as rhythm and rhyme. Types of poetry include lyric and narrative poems. A lyric poem expresses strong feelings. A narrative poem tells a story.

For more about poetry, see pages 314–315 and 346–347.

See also *Haiku, Rhyme, Rhyme Scheme, Rhythm,* and *Stanza.*

Point of View. Point of view is the perspective from which a story is told. Generally, a writer tells a story from the first-person or the third-person point of view.

In stories told from the first-person point of view, such as "Adjö Means Goodbye" (page 246), the narrator is a character in the story. He or she uses pronouns such as *I, me,* and *we.*

In stories told from the third-person point of view, such as "The Necklace" (page 176), the narrator is outside of the story. This narrator uses pronouns such as *he* and *she.*

If a story is told from the third-person omniscient point of view, the narrator sees into the minds of characters. "A Christmas Tree for Lydia" (page 213) is told from this point of view.

If a story is told from the third-person limited point of view, the narrator tells only what one character sees, thinks, and feels. This point of view is used in "Runaway Rig" (page 234).

For more about point of view, see pages 139 and 409.

See also *Narrator.*

Prose. Prose is writing organized into paragraphs. Prose includes fiction and nonfiction writing except for poetry and drama.

Repetition. Repetition is the technique of using a sound, a word, a phrase, or a line again for emphasis. In "All But Blind" (page 365), the repetition of the word *blind* emphasizes the similarity between the Mole, the Bat, the Barn-Owl, and the speaker.

See also *Alliteration* and *Rhyme.*

Resolution. The resolution is the point in a plot at which the loose ends are tied up. The resolution comes after the falling action. In "The Long Way Around" (page

264), the resolution comes when Patty admits that she no longer feels "so mad at the whole world."

For more about resolution, see page 139.

See also *Conflict* and *Plot*.

Rhyme. Rhyme is the repetition of syllable sounds at the ends of words. In the following lines from "The Courage That My Mother Had" (page 373), the first line rhymes with the third, and the second line rhymes with the fourth.

> The golden brooch my mother wore
> She left behind for me to wear;
> I have no thing I treasure more:
> Yet, it is something I could spare.

For more about rhyme, see pages 120–121 and 315.

See also *Rhyme Scheme*.

Rhyme Scheme. The rhyme scheme of a poem is the pattern of rhymes at the ends of lines. You can chart this pattern by using letters of the alphabet to show which lines end with the same sounds. Notice the rhyme scheme in these lines from "Paul Revere's Ride":

> He said to his friend, "If the British march   *a*
> By land or sea from the town tonight,   *b*
> Hang a lantern aloft in the belfry arch   *a*
> Of the North Church tower as a signal light,—   *b*
> One, if by land, and two, if by sea;   *c*
> And I on the opposite shore will be,   *c*

> Ready to ride and spread the alarm   *d*
> Through every Middlesex village and farm,   *d*
> For the country folk to be up and to arm." (page 387)   *d*

For more about rhyme scheme, see pages 121 and 346–347.

See also *Rhyme*.

Rhythm. Rhythm is the pattern of stressed and unstressed syllables in a sentence, a paragraph, or a line of poetry. Stressed syllables may be marked with /, and unstressed syllables with ˘. Notice the rhythm in these lines from "Casey at the Bat":

> The outlook wasn't brilliant for the
> Mudville nine that day;
> The score stood four to two, with but
> one inning more to play;   (page 353)

For more about rhythm, see pages 28 and 122–123.

Rising Action. The rising action is the part of a plot that introduces and develops the conflict, or struggle. The rising action builds toward the climax. In "*From* The Legend of Robin Hood: How Marian Came to the Greenwood" (page 49), the rising action begins when Peterkin the Juggler reveals that Marian, Robin's love, will soon marry another man.

For more about rising action, see page 139.

See also *Climax, Conflict, Exposition, Falling Action,* and *Plot.*

Scene. A scene is a unit of action that takes place in one setting. Most plays consist of several scenes.

For more about scene, see page 535.
See also *Act.*

Science Fiction. Science fiction is writing based on real or imagined scientific developments. Science fiction often presents an imagined view of the future or the past. "The Fun They Had" (page 286) is a science fiction story. The movies *Star Wars* and *The Empire Strikes Back* are examples of science fiction.

Sensory Images. Sensory images are words and phrases that appeal to the five senses: sight, hearing, touch, taste, and smell. Another term for sensory images is *imagery.* Notice how the words and phrases in the following passage appeal to the senses:

> The tennis shoes silently hushed themselves in the carpet, sank as in a jungle grass, in loam and resilient clay. He gave one solemn bounce of his heels in the yeasty dough, in the yielding and welcoming earth.
> ("The Sound of Summer Running," page 200).

For more about sensory images, see page 315.
See also *Description.*

Setting. Setting is the time and place of the action of a story. The setting includes descriptions of customs, manners, clothing, scenery, weather, buildings, rooms, furnishings, and methods of transportation. Sometimes the setting of a story is rather unimportant, as in "Southpaw" (page 208). In other stories the setting is important. For example, in "Sixteen" (page 279), the setting reflects the feelings of the narrator.

For more about setting, see pages 3 and 71.

Shape. Shape is the way that words look on the page. Sometimes the arrangement of words suggests something about the subject of a poem. For example, the short lines in "Poem" (page 323) suggest a cat's slow, careful movement.

For more about shape, see page 314.
See also *Concrete Poem.*

Short Story. A short story is a work of fiction that generally can be read in one sitting. A short story usually develops one major conflict, or struggle, and produces a single effect on the reader. Elements of the short story include setting, character, plot, and theme. "Hearts and Hands" (page 145) is an example of a short story.

For more about the short story, see pages 138–139 and 206–207.
See also *Fiction.*

Simile. A simile is a comparison using *like* or *as.* Examples include "pretty as a picture," "nutty as a fruitcake," and "strong as an ox." The first lines from "The Base Stealer" (page 348) contain a simile.

> Poised between going on and back, pulled
> Both ways taut like a tightrope-walker,

For more about simile, see pages 126–127.

See also *Figurative Language* and *Metaphor*.

Sound Effects. Sound effects are sounds made as part of a play. In a radio play, sound effects help listeners picture events that they cannot see. Instructions for sound effects are given in the stage directions. They may include directions to fade in, fade, fade out, or cut. *Fade in* means that voices, music, or other sounds get gradually louder. *Fade* or *fade out* means to get gradually softer, and *cut* means to stop abruptly.

Speaker. The speaker in a poem is the voice that talks to the reader. The speaker is not necessarily the poet. In "New World" (page 327), the speaker is the first human being seeing the world.

For more about speaker, see page 315.

Speech. A speech is a form of nonfiction written to be read before an audience. Abraham Lincoln's "Farewell Address" (page 506) is an example of a speech.

For more about speeches, see page 499.

Stage Directions. Stage directions are notes included in plays to help readers picture the action. Stage directions can describe stage sets, lighting, music, and sound effects. Stage directions also can tell the actors and actresses how to move and speak their lines. Generally stage directions are given in parentheses and printed in italics. Notice the following stage directions from *The Ugly Duckling* (page 540):

> **A Voice** *(Announcing).* His Excellency the Chancellor! *(The Chancellor, an elderly man in horn-rimmed spectacles, enters, bowing. The King wakes up with a start and removes the handkerchief from his face).*

For more about stage directions, see page 535.

Stanza. A stanza is a group of lines that form a unit in a poem. Stanzas are like paragraphs in prose selections. "All But Blind" (page 365) is an example of a poem with four stanzas.

For more about stanzas, see page 314.

Stereotype. A stereotype is an oversimplified view of what members of a particular group are like. In "Southpaw" (page 208), Richard believes that girls should learn to knit rather than play baseball. This stereotype brings about a conflict with Janet, who wants to join his team.

For more about stereotypes, see page 212.

Style. Style is the way in which a work of literature is written. Some elements that make up a writer's style are sentence length, vocabulary, imagery, and figurative language.

For more about style, see page 409.

Surprise Ending. A surprise ending is an unexpected twist in plot at the end of a story. For example, in "The Necklace" (page 176), Matilda Loisel finds out that the lost necklace was not made of diamonds.

Suspense. Suspense is a feeling of growing tension and excitement felt by a reader. A writer creates suspense by raising questions in the reader's mind. In "Runaway Rig" (page 234), for example, the reader wonders whether the runaway truck will crash.

Symbol. A symbol is a person, place, or object that stands for something outside of itself. Many symbols can be found in everyday life. For example, the bald eagle and Uncle Sam stand for the United States.

In literature, symbols often reinforce ideas. In "Adjö Means Goodbye" (page 246), the detail about pawns in a chess game suggests the powerlessness of the two little girls.

Tale. A tale is a simple story told in prose or poetry. Examples include folk tales, fairy tales, and legends. Many tales were passed down orally from generation to generation. "Lazy Peter and His Three-Cornered Hat" (page 42) is a tale.

See also *Legend*.

Theme. The theme is the message about life that the writer shares with the reader. Sometimes the writer states the theme directly. At other times, the reader must infer it. In "The Old Soldier" (page 222), one theme is that after a time hatred becomes pointless.

For more about theme, see pages 3 and 207.

Tone. Tone is the writer's attitude toward a subject. The tone can be serious, bitter, humorous, sympathetic, or angry. The tone of "Adjö Means Goodbye" (page 246) is serious. The tone of "The Panther" (page 341), on the other hand, is humorous.

Analysis. Analysis involves breaking down something into its elements and examining each one. Many elements make up a literary work. When you analyze, you focus on each element individually.

For example, when you analyze a poem, you look at elements such as rhyme, rhythm, imagery, figurative language, and theme. As you study each element, you understand the entire work better.

Throughout this book, study questions in Developing Comprehension Skills, Reading Literature, and Developing Writing Skills focus on elements in literary works. In addition, questions under Critical Thinking develop skills of analysis.

Cause and Effect. Cause and effect describes the relationship between some events in a story, poem, or play. In this relationship, one event brings about a second event. The first event is the cause, and the second event is the effect.

Sometimes clue words signal cause-and-effect relationships. Some clue words are *because, since, so that, in order that,* and *if/then.*

For more about cause and effect, see pages 140–141.

Classification. Classification involves the grouping of ideas, people, or objects on the basis of something that they have in common. For example, you might classify characters in a story using the categories of age, personality, or appearance. You might classify poems according to rhyme, rhythm, or figurative language.

For more about classification, see pages 47, 166, and 362.

Comparison. Comparison is the act of pointing out that different people, places, or things have something in common. This technique can make ideas clear or stimulate the imagination. For example, in "I Get a Colt to Break In" the writer compares the training given to his colt with the training given to most children (page 421–422).

As a reader, you can make comparisons within a work or among several works. For example, you may determine the ways in which characters within a work are alike or the ways in which characters from different works are alike.

See also *Contrast.*

Conclusions. See *Inferences.*

Connotation. The connotation of a word is its suggested meaning. The connotations of words can make readers feel positively or negatively about a subject.

For more about connotation, see pages 347 and 410–411.

See also *Connotation* and *Slanted Writing.*

Contrast. Contrast means pointing out differences. In "The Necklace," for example, the writer contrasts Matilda's real world and her dream world (page 176).

Sometimes, as a reader, you contrast elements within a work or in several works. For example, you might notice the differences between two settings in a story or between the images in two poems.

See also *Comparison.*

Deductive Reasoning. Deductive reasoning involves applying a general statement to a specific case. For example, you may begin with a general statement such as, "In the summer, it never snows in Florida." From that statement, you can deduce that if you are in Florida on August 10, you won't see snow.

See also *Inductive Reasoning.*

Denotation. Denotation is the dictionary meaning of a word.

See also *Connotation* and *Slanted Writing.*

Evaluation. To evaluate means to judge the worth of something. When you evaluate a work of literature, you apply standards by which to judge it.

To evaluate a work of literature, examine the elements one by one. Then judge how well the elements work together.

Support your judgments with evidence from the work.

See also *Analysis, Comparison, Contrast,* and *Standards.*

Fact and Opinion. A fact is a statement that can be proved, such as "September has thirty days." An opinion, on the other hand, is a statement that cannot be proved, such as "September is the most beautiful month." Generally, writers present facts to support an opinion, as in the following example. The opinion is underlined. Supporting the opinion are sentences that state facts.

> Some of the most unusual scenery in the world is in our national parks. The borders of Grand Canyon Park include most of the mile-deep canyon. In Yellowstone Park, visitors can see numerous geysers. Petrified Forest Park holds both ancient trees that have changed to rock and a brightly colored desert. Hawaii Volcanoes Park has two active volcanoes.

When you read, decide which statements are facts and which are opinions. Watch for opinions that are not supported. Be aware of slanted writing. Remember that a writer's opinions may influence his or her choice of details. Also remember that a writer may state facts with words having positive or negative connotations.

For more about fact and opinion, see page 410.

See also *Slanted Writing.*

Figurative Language. Figurative language is language that communicates ideas beyond the literal meanings of the words. By using figurative language, writers suggest new ways of looking at things.

For example, when people tell you to take a statement with a grain of salt, they don't want you to sprinkle salt on words. The expression "with a grain of salt" means you should not take something seriously. To understand this example of figurative language, you have to go beyond the actual meaning of the words.

For more about figurative language, see pages 125 to 133.

Generalizations. A generalization is a statement made about a group. An example is "All plays are written in dialogue."

Sometimes generalizations are too broad, as in the following example: "All trees lose their leaves in the fall." In reality, some trees keep their leaves in the fall. The word *all* makes this statement too broad.

You can correct this faulty generalization by using a qualifier such as *some, often, many,* or *most.* The statement "Many trees lose their leaves in the fall" is a true generalization.

For more about generalizations, see page 102.

See also *Inductive Reasoning.*

Inductive Reasoning. Inductive reasoning involves drawing general conclusions from specific facts. Here is an example:

Facts
Amusement Park A has a roller coaster.
Amusement Park B has a roller coaster.
Amusement Park C has a roller coaster.

General conclusion
Most amusement parks have roller coasters.

In using inductive reasoning, make sure that the facts support the conclusion.

See also *Deductive Reasoning, Generalizations,* and *Inferences.*

Inferences. An inference is a logical conclusion based on evidence. As you read, you often make inferences. You infer, or figure out, more than the words say. The evidence may be facts that the writer gives or your own experiences. For example, a writer could describe this situation: A girl walks down a school hall past a boy who says "Hello." The girl doesn't answer. From this information, the reader might infer either that the girl did not hear the boy or that she didn't want to speak to him.

For more about inferences, see pages 72–73 and 316–317.

Logical Order Logical order refers to a way of presenting information in writing. In logical order, one detail leads to the next, and the connection between the details is clear. Logical order may be used in stories to explain why a character acts in a certain way. For example, Spotted Eagle states his reasons for forgiving Black Crow in logical order (page 26).

Logical order also is used frequently in essays. It helps the reader understand what the writer believes or feels. For example, the logical order used in the third paragraph of "April and Robins" (page 519) explains the writer's feelings about the robin's song.

See also *Time Order*.

Main Idea. The main idea is the one idea to which the sentences in a paragraph relate. Sometimes, the main idea is stated in a topic sentence, which may come at the beginning, middle, or end of a paragraph. A paragraph may not have a topic sentence. In this case, you must infer the main idea.

In the following paragraph, the topic sentence is underlined:

> <u>Software for word processing can speed up your writing.</u> If you misspell a word, you can make the correction cleanly. If you are on your fifth sentence and want to add words to the first sentence, you can move everything else to fit in the new words. If you decide to change the order of sentences, you can rearrange your words without retyping them.

The topic sentence states the main idea. The other sentences give supporting details.

For more about main idea, see pages 4 and 5.

Opinions. See *Fact and Opinion*.

Outcomes. When you use what you know to infer what will happen, you are predicting an outcome.

Some outcomes are easy to predict. For example, when you hear the band at a ball game play "The Star-Spangled Banner," you can predict that the game will start soon. Predicting other outcomes is not so simple. For example, you would not know at the beginning of the ball game which team will win.

When you predict outcomes in a story or play, consider the clues the writer gives you. Use what you know about the character, the plot, the setting, and human behavior to help you in your inferences.

For more about outcomes, see page 73.

Paragraphs. See *Main Idea*.

Purpose. Some purposes, or reasons for writing, are to entertain, to express feelings, to inform, and to persuade. Writers may combine these purposes, but generally one is more important. A writer's purpose in treating the subject guides him or her in selecting the form for the writing.

For more about purpose, see pages 536–537.

Slanted Writing. Slanted writing presents only one side of an issue or one view of an event. Although slanted writing appears to report facts, it actually presents the writer's opinions.

One way to slant writing is to mix opinions with fact, as in the following example:

The custom of summer vacation from school started at a time when students were needed for farm work. Since students are no longer needed on farms, we no longer need summer vacation.

Another way to slant writing is to select only those facts that support a particular opinion. For example, a writer might try to convince someone that a certain actor was the best by mentioning only the successful movies in which he appeared.

A writer also can use words that lead the reader to feel a particular way about the facts. The writer will carefully choose words with the connotations, or suggestions, that he or she wants. For example, both sentences below report the same fact. One does it in a favorable way; the other strongly suggests disapproval.

The school has invested in a new, more efficient copying machine.

The school has thrown away more money on a newfangled copying machine that's supposed to be faster than the one we already have.

For more about slanted writing, see pages 64 and 410.

See also *Connotation* and *Fact and Opinion*.

Standards. Standards are measures of quality or value. They are the yardsticks according to which people make judgments. To establish standards for judging a literary work, you first must decide what qualities are important. If you want to set standards for judging a short story, for example, think about what makes a good short story. Do you look for believable characters? a carefully developed plot? powerful descriptions? an exciting climax? natural-sounding dialogue? Establishing standards guides you in judging the worth of what you have read.

See also *Evaluation*.

Time Order. Time order is the presentation of events in the order in which they take place. Writers sometimes use words or phrases to signal the order of events. These words and phrases include *then, next, gradually, while, finally,* and *the following day*.

For more about time order, see page 140.

See also *Cause and Effect* and *Logical Order*.

Topic Sentence. See *Main Idea*.

Word Choice. A writer's choice of words depends on many influences. These include the writer's purpose and his or her audience. In a story, the setting also influences the choice of words. Characters must sound as if they belong to the time and place described. For example, if the story takes place in modern times, a character might use terms based on space travel, such as *liftoff* and *touchdown*.

For more about word choice for characters, see pages 536–537.

Summary of Vocabulary Skills

1. Word Parts

Studying word parts can help you figure out the meanings of unfamiliar words. The two kinds of word parts are base words and affixes. Two kinds of affixes are prefixes and suffixes. Many word parts are based on Greek and Latin words.

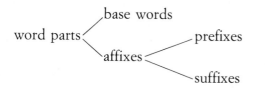

Base Word. A word to which word parts are added is called a base word. For example, in *careless* the base word is *care*. The base word in *reappear* is *appear*. Sometimes the spelling of a base word changes when a word part is added. For example, the *n* in *win* is doubled when *er* is added, as in *winner*.

For more about changes in base words, see *Spelling Changes*.

Prefix. A word part added to the beginning of a base word is called a prefix. Adding a prefix changes the meaning of the word.

Prefix	+	Base Word	=	New Word
in-	+	correct	=	incorrect

For a list of prefixes, see page 74.

Suffix. A word part added to the end of a base word is called a suffix. Adding a suffix changes the meaning of the word.

Base Word	+	Suffix	=	New Word
hope	+	-ful	=	hopeful

For a list of suffixes, see page 74.

Spelling Changes. Before suffixes can be added, one of the following changes may be needed.

1. When a suffix beginning with a vowel is added to a word ending in silent *e*, the *e* is usually dropped.

    write + -er = writer

    The *e* is not dropped when a suffix begins with a consonant.

    late + -ly = lately

2. When a suffix is added to a word ending in *y* preceded by a consonant, the *y* usually becomes an *i*.

    happy + -ness = happiness

    The *y* does not change when preceded by a vowel.

    joy + -ous = joyous

3. Words of one syllable, ending in one consonant preceded by one vowel, double the final consonant before adding *-ing, -ed,* or *-er.*

swim + -ing = swimming

When two vowels appear in a one-syllable word, the final consonant is not doubled.

clean + -er = cleaner

Word Parts from Greek and Latin. Many Greek and Latin words are shortened and used as prefixes and suffixes in English.

Knowing the meanings of these word parts will help you understand many English words. For example, the Greek prefix *tele-* means "far off," and the word part *-gram* means "something written." These two word parts are found in the word *telegram*.

For more about Greek and Latin word parts, see page 75.

2. Context Clues and Inferring Meaning

Context refers to the sentence or paragraph in which you find a word. Sometimes the context gives clues about the meaning of a new word. Look for the following kinds of context clues.

Antonyms. An antonym, or a word opposite in meaning to a new word, may be given in the same or a nearby sentence. Often the antonym appears in the same position in its sentence as the new word.

The group's decision on the date of the picnic was equivocal. However, their decision on the menu was clear and firm.

The antonyms *clear and firm* and *equivocal* both appear after the verb *was*. *Equivocal* means "the opposite of clear and firm."

For more about antonyms, see page 7.

Comparison and Contrast. Writers often compare ideas. One part of the comparison may give you a clue to the meaning of a new word. Signal words are *like, as, similar to,* and *than.*

Here is an example of a comparison clue:

Among people in our city, the diversity in languages is even more noticeable than the differences in foods.

The comparison suggests that *diversity* means "difference."

Contrast clues also give hints about the meanings of new words. A contrast clue suggests what the new word is not. The following words signal contrast clues: *although, but, however, yet, on the other hand, different from,* and *in contrast.*

Many of Karen's ideas are irrational, but her idea for a new city park certainly is sensible.

The contrast suggests that *irrational* is the opposite of *sensible.*

For more about comparison and contrast clues, see pages 142–143.

Definition or Restatement. A definition or restatement tells the meaning of a new word. Look for these key words and punctuation marks: *is, who is, which is, that is, in other words, or,* dashes, commas, and parentheses.

> The plans for the trip were <u>nebulous</u>. That is, they were not clear.
> Next on the <u>itinerary</u>, or route, was a visit to the aquarium.

For more about definition or restatement, see page 6.

Example Clue. In an example clue, a new word is related to a familiar word. The new word may be an example of a familiar term, or the familiar term may be an example of the new word.

Key words and phrases alert you to look for examples in a sentence. Some words and phrases that signal example clues are *an example, for example, one kind, for instance, some types, such as.*

> Ancient musical instruments, such as the <u>psaltery</u>, were displayed at the museum.

For more about examples, see page 142.

Inferring Meaning. Sometimes, even without specific clues, you can infer the meaning of a word from other words in a sentence or paragraph. For example, clues to the meaning of the word *serape* are in the following sentence:

> The <u>serape</u> that the farmer wore was made of a bright red and yellow wool.

You can infer that a serape is a brightly colored garment.

The following paragraph suggests the meaning of the word *lacrosse.*

> This was Jan's first game of <u>lacrosse</u>. The other nine players on her team had all played before. She had a difficult time hitting the small rubber ball with the long-handled racket. To everyone's surprise, she was the first player to score a goal.

From the paragraph, you can infer that lacrosse is a game played by two teams of ten players each. The object of the game is to hit the ball into the goal by using a long-handled racket.

For more about inferring meaning from context, see pages 538–539.

Words in a Series. In a sentence, a series of words may belong to the same group. If one of the words is unfamiliar to you, you might guess its meaning by relating it to the familiar words. From the following example, you can guess that *tatting* is similar to sewing and embroidery.

> Monica was very eager to learn sewing, embroidery, and <u>tatting</u>.

For more about words in a series, see page 143.

3. Denotation, Connotation, and Multiple Meanings

Denotation and Connotation. Denotation refers to the dictionary meaning of a word. **Connotation** refers to the suggested meanings of a word. For example, the denotations of *clever* are "bright, intelligent, or skillful in doing some particular thing." However, the connotations may suggest trickery, as in the following sentence:

> Josh always has a <u>clever</u> way of getting out of his chores.

In order to understand most directions, explanations, and statements of fact, you need to know only the denotations of words. However, to understand most literature, you also need to consider the connotations of words.

For more about denotation and connotation, see pages 347 and 410–411.

Multiple Meanings. Many words have more than one meaning. To choose the denotation that the writer intended, read the words in context. Try out different meanings and choose the best one.

Use the context of the following sentence to figure out the best meaning of *knot*:

> The ship's speed was twenty <u>knots</u>.

The dictionary gives several definitions for *knot*:

1. a tying or twining together
2. a unit of speed used on ships
3. a joint on the stem of a plant

Clearly, the second meaning works best in the sentence.

For more about multiple meanings, see page 318.

4. Levels of Language

Standard English describes language that follows all grammatical rules and guidelines. Standard English can be formal or informal.

Formal standard English is used in speeches and in most serious literature.

Informal standard English is used in conversations, personal letters, diaries, magazines, and newspapers. It is casual and friendly. Informal standard English may include **idioms,** expressions that mean something different from the literal meaning, and **slang,** expressions that are popular for a while.

Nonstandard English describes language that does not always follow these rules. Writers use nonstandard English for special effects. For example, characters who are close friends might speak to each other in nonstandard English.

For more about levels of language, see pages 318–319.

5. Reference Books: The Dictionary, Glossary, and Thesaurus

Dictionary. Sometimes context clues and word parts do not give enough information about unfamiliar words. Then you should use a dictionary, an alphabetical listing of words and their meanings.

The different definitions, or meanings, of a word will be listed. These denotations will probably be grouped by parts of speech. To choose the right meaning, test each definition in the sentence in which you found the word.

Glossary. The glossary is often found in the back of a nonfiction book. It contains an alphabetical listing of new or unfamiliar words that are used in the book.

The definition given for a glossary word explains its meaning in a particular selection.

Thesaurus. Some dictionaries give information about the connotations of a word. Another book that gives information about connotations is the thesaurus. In a thesaurus, a word is listed with other words similar in meaning.

For more about the dictionary, see pages 412–413; the glossary, page 413; and the thesaurus, page 413.

See also *The Dictionary* and *Thesaurus* under Guidelines for Study and Research.

1. Using the Library

Arrangement of Books

Books in a library are divided into two groups: fiction and nonfiction.

Fiction books are stories about imaginary happenings. They are arranged alphabetically according to the last name of the author. This name is generally shown on the spine of the book.

Nonfiction books contain factual information. Most libraries arrange these books according to the **Dewey Decimal System.** Every book is assigned a number in one of ten categories. This **call number** is printed on the spine of the book. The books are then arranged on the shelves in numerical order.

The Dewey Decimal System		
000–099	General Works	encyclopedias, almanacs, handbooks
100–199	Philosophy	conduct, ethics, psychology
200–299	Religion	the Bible, mythology, theology
300–399	Social Science	law, education, government, folklore, legend
400–499	Language	languages, grammar, dictionaries, almanacs
500–599	Science	mathematics, chemistry, physics
600–699	Useful Arts	farming, cooking, sewing, radio, nursing, engineering, television, business, gardening, cars
700–799	Fine Arts	music, painting, drawing, acting, games, sports
800–899	Literature	poetry, plays, essays
900–999	History	biography, travel, geography

The Card Catalog

The best way to locate a book in the library is to use the **card catalog.** The card catalog is a cabinet of narrow drawers filled with cards for each book in the library. The cards are arranged alphabetically according to the words on the top line of each card. On the top left corner of the cards for nonfiction books, you will find the call number. Using the call number, you can locate the book.

Generally, the card catalog provides three cards for every nonfiction book in the library: an author card, a title card, and a subject card. Each of the three cards contains the same information, but in a different order. The **author card** lists the author's name on the top line. The **title card** lists the title on the top line. The **subject card** lists the subject or topic of the book on the top line.

If you know the author of a book, use the author card to look up the book. If you know the title, use the title card. If you are looking for books about a particular topic, use the subject cards.

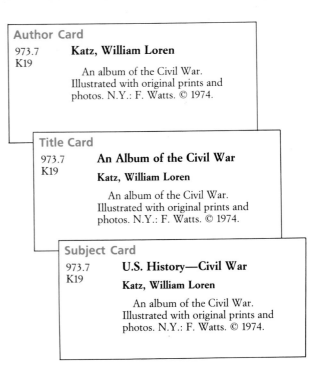

Many libraries now have their card catalogs entered on a computer. The type of computer varies with the library. You can use the computer to find books listed by authors, titles, or subjects. Usually there are directions near the computer that show how to use it. Ask a librarian to help you with the computer if you are unfamiliar with it.

2. Using Reference Materials

The Nonfiction Book

When you are looking for detailed information about a topic, your best source may be a nonfiction book. To decide whether the book will be useful to you, examine these parts:

The title page. Does the title mention your topic?

The copyright page. If you need up-to-date information, is the copyright date a recent one?

The table of contents. Is the organization of the book clear? Do any sections or chapters concern your topic?

The index. Does the index list terms or names that you need information about?

The Encyclopedia

An **encyclopedia** is a collection of factual articles on a wide variety of topics. The articles are arranged in alphabetical order according to their titles. Generally, if an encyclopedia is several volumes long, an index appears in the last volume. The index lists volumes and pages that give information on various topics.

For more about the encyclopedia, see page 84.

The Dictionary

A **dictionary** is an alphabetical listing of words, called entry words, and their meanings. The **glossary** of a nonfiction book is a dictionary limited to difficult terms from that book.

How to Find a Word. In order to find a word in the dictionary, look first at the **guide words.** Generally, two guide words are printed at the top of every page. They show the first and last words on the page.

Keep looking until you find the guide words between which your word falls.

For example, here are the guide words for two pages of a dictionary. On which page will *radiant* appear?

radial—radium   radius—railway

You need to compare the guide words to the sixth letter in the first pair and the fifth letter in the second pair in order to find the answer. *Radiant* will appear on the first page, between *radial* and *radium*.

What the Entry Word Tells You. Use the **entry word** itself, printed in **boldface** (dark) type, to see how the word is spelled and where to break it into syllables.

How to Find the Pronunciation. Use the **respelling** that follows the entry word to determine the pronunciation of the word. The respelling appears within parentheses. It uses letters and symbols to stand for the sounds of the spoken word. To find out what each letter and symbol stands for, you must refer to the **pronunciation key.**

entry word   respelling   part of speech

ra·di·ant (rā′dē ənt) *adj.* **1.** shining brightly. **2.** showing pleasure. **3.** coming from the sun or other source in rays.

meanings

Accent marks in the respelling indicate which syllable to stress when you say the word. If the word has more than two syllables, it may have more than one accent. The heavy accent is called the **primary accent.** The lighter one is called the **secondary accent.**

secondary accent   primary accent

Mississippi (mis′ə sip′ē)

How to Find the Part of Speech and the Meaning. Immediately following the respelling is an abbreviation that tells the **part of speech** of the word. Then you will find the **definition,** or statement of meaning. All the definitions for one part of speech are grouped together.

After some entries, you will find subentries listed in dark, or bold, type. **Subentries** are familiar phrases in which the entry word appears. The special meaning of the phrase is then listed.

For more on the use of the dictionary, see pages 412–413.

Other Reference Sources

Almanac. An almanac is a book that is published yearly. It gives up-to-date information and statistics about many subjects.

Atlas. An atlas is a book of maps. An index at the front or the back lists countries, cities, and physical features such as rivers, deserts, and mountain ranges alphabetically. Some atlases give additional information such as the populations and capital cities.

To find a specific place, first look it up in the index. The index will tell you which page contains the map that you need. After you have turned to that page, use the coordinates listed in the index to pinpoint the location.

For more about atlases, see page 40.

Magazines. Magazines offer current information about many topics. To locate magazine articles about a topic, look in the *Readers' Guide to Periodical Literature.* It lists topics in alphabetical order and articles that deal with them.

Nonprint Resources. These resources include films, slides, records, tapes, compact discs, and computer software. In some libraries, **picture files** contain posters, photos, and copies of works of art. These resources are often catalogued separately from the rest of the library's collection.

Thesaurus. A thesaurus is a book of synonyms and antonyms. It can help you find an exact or lively word to express an idea. For example, if you need another word for *worried,* the thesaurus would provide synonyms such as *anxious* or *troubled* from which to choose. Look in the front of the thesaurus for directions. The index at the back of the book also will help you find particular words.

For more about the thesaurus, see page 413.

3. Studying

Three Types of Reading

When you study or do research, you can use different methods of reading. Each is suited for a particular purpose.

Skimming. This is one type of fast reading. It gives you a quick overview of the material you are about to read. Skimming also helps you become familiar with the most important facts. To skim, move your eyes rapidly over the material. Look for titles, subtitles, and illustrations that will give you clues about the content of the material.

Scanning. Another type of fast reading is scanning. It allows you to locate a piece of information quickly. To scan, move your eyes quickly over the page. Look for key words that will lead you to the facts and ideas you need.

In-depth Reading. This third type of reading is slower than scanning or skimming. When you want to understand and remember what you read, you must do in-depth reading. To read this way, first look for main ideas in titles, subheadings, and first sentences of paragraphs. Then, carefully read about each one, noting details such as names, dates, numbers, and reasons. Try to make connections between facts and ideas.

The SQ3R Study Method

The SQ3R study method is a sure way to improve reading and study skills. SQ3R stands for five steps: Survey, Question, Read, Record, and Review.

Survey. Look over the material to get a general idea of what it is about. Read the titles and subtitles. Look at the pictures, maps, graphs, or tables. Read the introduction or first few paragraphs.

Question. Read any study questions provided in the book or by your teacher. They will help you identify important points to look for when you read.

Read. Read the material. Identify main ideas. Keep the study questions in mind.

Record. After reading, write the answers to the study questions. Make brief notes to help you remember any other important ideas.

Review. Look back at the study questions and try to answer them without using your notes. You may need to review the material to find the answers. Last, study your notes so that you will be able to remember the information later.

4. Organizing Information

Note-Taking

As you read, you will probably recognize some main ideas and important facts. Write them down in a notebook.

Notes do not have to be written in sentences. They should be in your own words. Write them clearly so that when you read them later, they will still make sense.

Taking notes helps you understand the material since you are always looking for the most important facts. Besides, notes are useful for later review.

Outlining

One way of organizing your notes for study or research is to outline them. An outline helps you identify the main ideas and highlight the important facts. It also provides a visual summary of the information.

When you make an outline, label the main ideas with Roman numerals. Indent and label important facts or ideas with capital letters. These are subtopics. Use the format below when you outline.

    I. (First main topic)
        A. (Subtopic)
        B. (Subtopic)

    II. (Second main topic)
        A. (Subtopic)
        B. (Subtopic)

Name of encyclopedia | Volume number

World Book Encyclopedia, Volume 15

Title of article | Page numbers

"George Brinton McClellan" pages 266-267

Fact

McClellan became general in chief of all Union armies in 1861. Lincoln removed him in 1862 because of his delay in pursuing the Confederates.

Whenever you write, you should follow certain steps essential for good writing. These steps belong to the **process of writing.** This process includes **prewriting, drafting, revising,** and **sharing.**

Prewriting

Prewriting includes the planning that writers do before beginning to write. During the prewriting stage, writers make several important choices.

Choosing a Subject. Think about subjects that interest you. List any ideas and then go over them carefully. Choose the idea that interests you most or that you want to explore. That idea then becomes your subject.

For example, if you are interested in legends, you might choose one or two legends, such as "Richard the Lion-Hearted: Saved by a Song," or "The Pied Piper of Hamelin: The Broken Bargain" as your subject.

Selecting a Form. Sometimes, a writing assignment will specify the form. For example, you might be asked to write a paragraph, a fable, a poem, a short story, or an essay. Other times, you may select the form for your writing. Let your purpose guide you in your choice. For example, if you want to point out a characteristic of certain legends, you might choose to write a paragraph.

Limiting the Subject. Limit the subject to a topic, or one guiding idea. Think about the aspects of the subject that you can cover. Then consider which aspect will be most interesting.

For example, if you want to compare the legends about King Richard and the Pied Piper, you first might list the following aspects:

mood	events	characters
setting	details	use of music

Then you might narrow the subject to one aspect, such as the use of music in the legends.

Considering the Audience. Decide who will read your writing. When you know whom you are writing for, you will be better able to decide which details to include. For example, if your audience knows little about your topic, you may have to provide some background information.

Gathering Supporting Information. List everything you know about the topic and the questions that you must answer. At this point, you may need to use reference sources such as encyclopedias. Take notes on the information you find.

In gathering information about music in the legends of King Richard and the Pied Piper, you might reread both selections and take notes similar to the following.

Prewriting Notes

Specific details

"Richard"

Richard lived in the twelfth century.

Richard was hidden in a dungeon.

Blondel was a minstrel.

Blondel was offered large sums of money to stay at many a palace.

Outside a prison, Blondel sang a song and Richard sang back.

Richard and Blondel made up tunes and songs together.

"Pied Piper"

"A certain power—call it music or call it magic."

The Pied Piper wore a yellow and red coat.

The Piper's music led the children to the hills.

The Piper's music told of a magic land.

The Piper played on a pipe, led rats to the river.

Organizing Ideas. Reread your list of details, and cross out any that now seem unrelated to the topic. Then choose an order for presenting the remaining details.

For example, you may choose time order for events from a story. For a description, you may list details in the order you might notice them. Make a plan, or outline, showing the order for your ideas.

Here is a plan for a paragraph comparing the use of music in the two legends.

The main idea, or purpose, has been included in the plan to make sure that all the sentences relate to the topic.

Prewriting Notes—Revision

"Richard"

~~Richard lived in the twelfth century.~~

Richard was hidden in a dungeon.

Blondel was a minstrel.

~~Blondel was offered large sums of money to stay at many a palace.~~

Outside a prison, Blondel sang a song and Richard sang back.

Richard and Blondel made up tunes and songs together.

"Pied Piper"

"A certain power—call it music or call it magic."

The Pied Piper wore a yellow and red coat.

The Piper's music led the children to the hills.

The Piper's music told of a magic land.

The Piper played on a pipe, led rats to the river.

Purpose: to compare how music is important to the plots of two legends

Audience: classmates

Drafting

Drafting means putting words on paper or into a word processor. Try to get all your thoughts down in sentence form. Don't worry about errors in spelling and punctuation. You can correct them later in revising the draft. Follow your prewriting plan, but change it if you think of better ideas. Leave space between the lines of your draft for corrections and changes.

Notice how rough the writing is in the following first draft of a paragraph.

First Draft

Music in Two Legends

When I read "Richard the Lion Hearted: Saved by a Song" I enjoyed reading about how music saved king Richards life. He is hidden in a dungeon. However, the minstrel Blondel finds him. When Blondel sings a song, the king answers him. In "the Pied Piper Of Hamlin: The Broken Bargain," music gets rid of the rats. Also it leads the children into a hill, from which they never return. Although the legends are very diffrent music is used in both.

Revising

After you have written the first draft, you are ready to revise it to make your writing clearer and smoother. Ask yourself these questions:

1. Is the topic well developed? Should any details be added or dropped?
2. Is the organization clear?
3. Are the words exact?
4. Is the writing interesting and enjoyable?

Mark any corrections and notes on your draft. Cross out the words that you drop. Write in the words that you want to add. If you are using a word processor, revise your work on the screen. You may need to write several drafts before you are satisfied.

Proofreading. Your writing should be correct as well as clear and interesting. After you have rewritten the draft, read it over again, this time looking for errors in grammar, usage, capitalization, punctuation, and spelling. Use the proofreading

First Draft — Revision

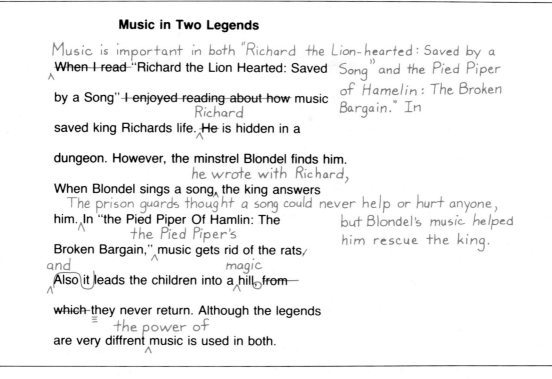

Music in Two Legends

Music is important in both "Richard the Lion-hearted: Saved by a
~~When I read~~ "Richard the Lion Hearted: Saved Song" and the Pied Piper
by a Song" ~~I enjoyed reading about how~~ music of Hamelin: The Broken
Richard Bargain." In
saved king Richards life. ~~He~~ is hidden in a
dungeon. However, the minstrel Blondel finds him.
                                        he wrote with Richard,
When Blondel sings a song, the king answers
          The prison guards thought a song could never help or hurt anyone,
him. In "the Pied Piper Of Hamlin: The   but Blondel's music helped
          the Pied Piper's   him rescue the king.
Broken Bargain," music gets rid of the rats,
and   magic
Also it leads the children into a hill, from—
which they never return. Although the legends
          the power of
are very diffrent music is used in both.

symbols below to correct your errors. You may find a dictionary and a grammar book helpful at this stage.

Study the revised draft on page 628. Notice how the writer has improved the paragraph by dropping unnecessary

Proofreading Symbols

Symbol	Meaning	Example
∧	insert	diffrent
≡	capitalize	king
/	make lower case	Of
∼	transpose (trade positions)	Also it
ℓ	omit letters, words	they
¶	make new paragraph	¶Music
⊙	insert a period	both⊙

Second Draft—Proofreading

Music in Two Legends

¶ Music is important in both "Richard the Lion-hearted:

Saved by a Song" and the Pied Piper of Hamelin: The

Broken Bargain." In "Richard the Lion-Hearted: Saved

by a Song" music saved king Richards life. Richard

is hidden in a dungeon. However, the minstrel Blondel

finds him. When Blondel sings a song he wrote with

Richard, the king answers him. The prison guards

thought a song could never help or hurt anyone,

but Blondel's music helped him rescue the king.

In "the Pied Piper Of Hamlin: The Broken Bargain,"

the Pied Piper's music gets rid of the rats and it

also leads the children into a magic hill. They

never return. Although the legends are very

diffrent the power of music is used in both.

---

words and adding precise ones. The connections between ideas are now smoother. The writer has also corrected errors in capitalization, punctuation, grammar, and spelling. First study this revised draft. Then compare it with the final draft on page 629. The final draft reflects the changes that were marked on the revised draft.

Preparing the Final Copy. When you are satisfied that your writing is clear, smooth, and correct, write or type the draft one last time. If you have used a word processor, look over your writing, make a printout, and then proofread the final copy.

Final Copy

Music in Two Legends

Music is important in both "Richard the Lion-Hearted:

Saved by a Song" and "The Pied Piper of Hamelin: The

Broken Bargain." In "Richard the Lion-Hearted: Saved

by a Song," music saves King Richard's life. Richard

is hidden in a dungeon. However, the minstrel Blondel

finds him. When Blondel sings a song he wrote with

Richard, the king answers him. The prison guards

thought a song could never help or hurt anyone,

but Blondel's music helped him rescue the king.

In "The Pied Piper of Hamelin: The Broken Bargain,"

the Pied Piper's music gets rid of the rats, and it

also leads the children into a magic hill. They

never return. Although the legends are very

different, the power of music is used in both.

Sharing. Sharing involves showing your writing to others and having them comment on it. Share your writing with your family, friends, and teachers. If you put care and effort into your work, others are sure to enjoy it. You also might consider displaying your writing on a bulletin board or in a booklet.

Checklist for the Process of Writing

Prewriting

1. Choose a subject.
2. Select a form.
3. Limit the subject.
4. Consider the audience.
5. Gather supporting information.
6. Organize ideas.

Drafting

1. As you write, keep your topic, purpose, and audience in mind.
2. Write your thoughts and feelings in sentence form.
3. Let your writing flow. Do not worry about errors at this time.

Revising

1. Read your draft. Ask yourself these questions:
   a. Is your writing interesting? Will others want to read it?
   b. Is your writing organized well? Are the details arranged in a sensible order?
   c. Should any details be left out? Should any be added?
   d. Is every word the best possible choice?

2. Proofread your draft. Consider these questions as you look for errors:

   Grammar and Usage
   a. Is every word group a sentence rather than a fragment?
   b. Does every verb agree with its subject?
   c. Is the form of each pronoun, adjective, and adverb correct?

Capitalization
a. Is the first word in every sentence capitalized?
b. Are all proper nouns and proper adjectives capitalized?
c. Are titles capitalized correctly?

Punctuation
a. Does each sentence have the correct end mark?
b. Are marks such as commas, apostrophes, hyphens, colons, semicolons, question marks, quotation marks, and underlining used correctly?

Spelling
a. Have unfamiliar words been checked in a dictionary?
b. Are plural and possessive forms spelled correctly?

3. Prepare the final copy. Make all changes and correct all errors. Finally, proofread your writing again and read it aloud as a final check.

Sharing

Let your family, friends, and teachers read your writing. Make your writing available on a bulletin board or in a booklet.

Glossary

The **glossary** is an alphabetical listing of words from the selections, along with their meanings. The glossary gives the following information:

un·err·ing (un ur′ iŋ, -er′-) *adj.* making no mistake; without error; certain; sure. —**un·erring· ly** *adv.*

1. **The entry word broken into syllables.**

2. **The pronunciation of each word.** The **respelling** is shown in parentheses. The most common way to pronounce a word is listed first. The Pronunciation Key below shows the symbols for the sounds of letters and key words that contain those sounds. A key is repeated on every second page.

   A **primary accent** ′ is placed after the syllable that is stressed the most when the word is spoken. A **secondary accent** ′ is placed after a syllable that has a lighter stress.

3. **The part of speech of the word.** The following abbreviations are used: *n.* noun   *v.* verb   *adj.* adjective   *adv.* adverb

4. **The meaning of the word.** The definitions listed in the glossary apply to selected ways a word is used in these selections.

5. **Related forms.** Words with suffixes such as *-ing, -ed, -ness,* and *-ly* are listed under the base word.

Pronunciation Key

Symbol	Key Words	Symbol	Key Words	Symbol	Key Words	Symbol	Key Words
a	fat	ō	go	ou	out	ch	chin
ā	ape	ô	law, horn	u	up	sh	she
ä	car, lot	ōō	tool	ur	fur, bird	th	thin
e	elf, ten	oo	look			*th*	then
ē	even	yōō	use, cute, few			zh	leisure
i	hit	yoo	united, cure	ə	a in ago	ŋ	ring
ī	bite, fire	oi	oil		e in agent	′	able (ā′b'l)
					i in sanity		
					o in comply		
					u in focus		
				ər	perhaps, murder		

From *Webster's New World Dictionary, Student Edition*, Copyright © 1981 by Simon & Schuster, Inc.

A

a·ban·don (ə ban′dən) *n.* unrestrained freedom of action or emotion. —**abandonment** *n.*

ab·bey (ab′ē) *n.* a monastery.

a·bide (ə bīd′) *v.* to put up with; to submit to.

a·breast (ə brest′) *adv.* side by side.

a·broad (ə brôd′) *adv.* in a foreign land.

a·byss (ə bis′) *n.* a deep crack in the earth.

ac·count (ə kount′) *n.* business.

a·cute (ə kyo͞ot′) *adj.* very serious; critical.

ad·mo·ni·tion (ad′mə nish′ən) *n.* a warning.

a·dorn (ə dôrn′) *v.* to put decorations on.

af·firm (ə fʉrm′) *v.* to declare positively; assert to be true.

a·ghast (ə gast′) *adj.* feeling great horror or distress.

a·gue (ā′gyo͞o) *n.* a fever, marked by chills.

al·a·bas·ter (al′ə bas′tər) *n.* a translucent, whitish, fine-grained variety of gypsum, used for making plaster of Paris.

al·der (ôl′dər) *n.* a tree or bush belonging to the birch family.

al·fal·fa (al fal′fə) *n.* a deep-rooted plant grown in the United States, used for food for cattle and horses.

al·ien (āl′yən *or* āl′ē ən) *adj.* strange; not natural.

a·light (ə līt′) *v.* to come down after flight; settle. *adj.* lighted up; glowing.

al·lure·ment (ə lo͞or′mənt) *n.* an attraction or fascination.

a·loft (ə lôft′) *adv.* far above the ground; in the air.

am·bas·sa·dor (am bas′ə dər) *n.* the highest-ranking diplomat representing a government in another country.

am·ber (am′bər) *n.* a yellow or brownish-yellow translucent fossil substance used in jewelry. *adj.* brownish-yellow color.

am·bi·tion (am bish′ən) *n.* the thing strongly desired.

a·men·i·ty (ə men′ə tē *or* ə mē′nə tē) *n.* pleasant quality.

a·miss (ə mis′) *adj.* wrong; improper; gone astray.

an·cient (ān′shənt) *n.* an aged person.

an·i·mate (an′ə māt′) *v.* to cause to act; inspire.

an·te·cham·ber (an′ti chām′bər) *n.* a smaller room leading into a larger or main room.

an·vil (an′vəl) *n.* an iron or steel block on which metal objects are hammered into shape.

anx·i·e·ty (aŋg zī′ə tē) *n.* the state of being uneasy or worried about what may happen.

ap·a·thet·ic (ap′ə thet′ik) *adj.* not interested; indifferent. —**apathetically** *adv.*

ap·pa·ra·tus (ap′ə rat′əs *or* ap′ə rāt′əs) *n.* instruments or equipment for a specific use.

ap·par·ent (ə per′ənt *or* ə par′ənt) *adj.* appearing to be true.

ap·pease (ə pēz′) *v.* to make peaceful; to satisfy or relieve. —**appeased** *adj.*

ap·pre·hen·sive (ap′rə hen′siv) *adj.* uneasy or fearful about the future.

apt (apt) *adj.* tending or inclined; likely.

A·ra·bi·an Nights (ə rā′bē ən nīts′) *n.* A collection of ancient tales from Arabia, India, and Persia.

arc (ärk) *n.* the band of sparks formed by an electric current.

---

at, āte, fär; pen, ēqual; sit, mīne; sō, côrn, join, to͝ok, fo͞ol, our; us, tʉrn; chill, shop, thick, *th*ey, siŋ; zh *in* measure; ′l *in* idle; ə *in* alive, cover, family, robot, circus.

ar·dent (är'd'nt) *adj.* passionate. —**ardently** *adv.*

ar·is·toc·ra·cy (ar'ə stäk'rə sē) *n.* a privileged ruling class; nobility.

ar·mor·y (är'mər ē) *n.* a place where firearms are made and stored.

as·ton·ish·ment (ə stän'ish mənt) *n.* great surprise or amazement.

a·stride (ə strīd') *adv.* with one leg on either side of a horse.

as·tro·nom·i·cal (as'trə näm'i k'l) *adj.* having to do with the science of the stars, planets, and other heavenly bodies.

at·mos·pher·ic (at'məs fer'ik *or* at'məs fir'ik) *adj.* of or in the air surrounding the earth.

aug·ment (ôg ment') *v.* to make or become greater; increase.

au·then·tic (ô then'tik) *adj.* genuine; real.

a·wry (ə rī') *adj.* untidy; messy.

az·ure (azh'ər) *adj.* like the color of a clear sky; sky-blue.

B

back·woods (bak'woodz') *n.pl.* heavily wooded areas far from centers of population.

bade (bad) *v.* commanded; told; asked.

bai·ley (bā'lē) *n.* outer court of a castle.

ban·tam (ban'təm) *n.* a small domestic bird.

bap·tism (bap'tiz'm) *n.* any experience that initiates or purifies.

ba·rom·e·ter (bə räm'ə tər) *n.* an instrument used in measuring the air pressure.

bat·tal·ion (bə tal'yən) *n.* a large group of soldiers.

bat·ter·ing ram (bat'ər ing ram') *n.* an ancient military machine having a heavy wooden beam for breaking down gates or walls: its iron end was sometimes shaped like a ram's head.

bat·ter·y (bat'ər ē *or* bat'rē) *n.* an emplacement equipped with heavy guns, rockets, and other artillery.

bat·tle·ment (bat''l mənt) *n.* a low wall on top of a tower, with openings for shooting.

bau·ble (bô'b'l) *n.* a showy but worthless thing; trinket.

bay (bā) *v.* to make a sharp, abrupt cry.

bear·ing (ber'ing) *n.* way of carrying and conducting oneself; manner.

be·drag·gle (bi drag''l) *v.* to make wet, limp, and dirty, as by dragging through mud or mire. —**bedraggled** *adj.*

bel·fry (bel'frē) *n.* the part of a steeple that holds the bell.

bel·low (bel'ō) *v.* to roar with a loud sound.

ben·e·fac·tor (ben'ə fak'tər) *n.* a person who has given help, especially financial help.

be·nef·i·cence (bə nef'ə s'ns) *n.* the quality of being kind or doing good.

ber·serk (bər surk' *or* bər zurk' *or* bur'sərk) *adj.* violent; destructive.

be·set·ting (bi set'ing) *adj.* constantly harassing.

be·wil·der (bi wil'dər) *v.* to confuse hopelessly; puzzle. —**bewilderment** *n.*

birth·right (burth'rīt') *n.* the rights that a person has because he was born in a certain family.

black (blak) *adj.* evil; wicked.

blaze (blāz) *v.* to mark a trail by cutting off pieces of bark from trees along the way.

bleak (blēk) *adj.* not cheerful; gloomy.

blithe (blī*th*) *adj.* cheerful; carefree.

blub·ber (blub'ər) *v.* to weep loudly.

blun·der (blun'dər) *v.* to move clumsily; flounder; stumble.

bod·y (bäd'ē) *n.* group of people regarded as a unit.

bog (bäg *or* bôg) *v.* to sink or become stuck.

bolt (bōlt) *n.* a roll of cloth of a given length.

boom (bōōm) *v.* to move at top speed.

boon (bōōn) *adj.* pleasant; merry; sociable.

bore (bôr) *v.* to make a hole in or through.

borne (bôrn) *v.* carried; transported.

bow·er (bou′ər) *n.* a place enclosed by overhanging branches or by vines on a trellis.

brack·en (brak′′n) *n.* large, coarse fern.

brawl (brôl) *v.* to quarrel or fight noisily.

break·er (brāk′ər) *n.* a wave that breaks into foam.

breed (brēd) *v.* to be the source of; produce.

bri·ar (brī′ər) *n.* a thorny bush, such as a bramble or wild rose.

bri·er·root (brī′ər rōōt′) *n.* the root wood of a thorny bush, such as a bramble or wild rose.

broad·sword (brôd′sôrd′) *n.* a sword with a broad blade, for slashing rather than thrusting.

bro·ken (brō′k′n) *adj.* trained; tamed.

bron·co·bust·er (brä̃ng′kō bus′tər) *n.* a person who tames wild horses.

brooch (brōch *or* brōōch) *n.* a large ornamental pin with a clasp.

brunt (brunt) *n.* the heaviest or hardest part.

buck·ler (buk′lər) *n.* a small, round shield worn on the arm for protection.

buck·skin (buk′skin′) *n.* clothes of soft yellowish-gray leather made from the skins of deer or sheep.

bulk·head (bulk′hed′) *n.* an upright partition dividing a tractor-trailer for protection in case of an accident.

bun·ga·low (bung′gə lō′) *n.* a thatched house or cottage.

bunt (bunt) *v.* to hit a pitched ball lightly so that it does not go beyond the infield, usually in a sacrifice play. —**bunting** *n.*

bu·reau (byōōr′ō) *n.* a chest of drawers for storing clothing.

bur·nish (bur′nish) *v.* to make shiny by rubbing; polish.

burr (bur) *n.* the rough, prickly seedcase or fruit of certain plants.

bur·row (bur′ō) *n.* a hole or tunnel dug in the ground by an animal for shelter and protection.

butte (byōōt) *n.* a steep hill standing alone on a plain.

but·tress (but′ris) *n.* a support or prop built against a wall to strengthen it.

C

cack·le (kak′′l) *v.* to make the shrill, broken vocal sounds of a hen. *n.* cackling laughter or chatter.

ca·lam·i·ty (kə lam′ə tē) *n.* any great misfortune that brings loss and suffering; disaster.

cal·cu·late (kal′kyə lāt′) *v.* to determine; compute.

cal·li·o·pe (kə lī′ə pē) *n.* a keyboard instrument like an organ, having a series of steam whistles.

can·ton·ment (kan tän′mənt *or* kan tōn′mənt) *n.* the place to which troops are assigned.

ca·per (kā′pər) *v.* to skip or jump in a playful manner.

ca·pri·cious (kə prish′əs) *adj.* likely to change suddenly and for no apparent reason.

cap·size (kap′sīz *or* kap sīz′) *v.* to overturn or upset.

cap·tain·cy (kap′tən sē) *n.* leadership.

---

at, āte, fär; pen, ēqual; sit, mīne; sō, côrn, join,
took, fōōl, our; us, turn; chill, shop, thick, they,
sing; zh *in* measure; ′l *in* idle;
ə *in* alive, cover, family, robot, circus.

cap·u·chin (kap′yoo shin *or* kə pyoo′shin) *n.* a woman's cloak with a hood.

car·bine (kär′bīn *or* kär′bēn) *n.* a rifle with a short barrel.

ca·reen (kə rēn′) *v.* **1.** to lurch from side to side while moving rapidly. **2.** to tip; tilt.

caste (kast) *n.* an exclusive social group or class.

ca·tas·tro·phe (kə tas′trə fē) *n.* a terrible disaster.

cat·er·waul (kat′ər wôl′) *v.* to make a shrill, howling sound like that of a cat; wail; scream.

cat·kin (cat′kin) *n.* a drooping, scaly spike of small, crowded flowers, as on poplar or walnut trees.

cause·way (kôz′wā′) *n.* a raised path or road across shallow water.

cav·al·cade (kav′′l kād′ *or* kav′′l kād′) *n.* a procession.

caw (kô) *v.* to make a harsh cry like a crow.

cha·grin (shə grin′) *n.* a feeling of embarrassment and annoyance.

chaise (shāz) *n.* a lightweight carriage with a folding top and two or four wheels.

champ (champ) *v.* to bite down repeatedly and restlessly.

Champs É·ly·sées (shän zā lē zā′) *n.* a famous avenue in Paris.

chan·cel·lor (chan′sə lər) *n.* a high official or prime minister in certain countries.

char (chär) *v.* to burn; scorch.

cheep (chēp) *v.* to utter short, faint, shrill sounds like a young bird.

che·mise (shə mēz′) *n.* a woman's garment similar to a loose, short slip.

choke up (chōk up) *v.* to hold a bat toward the middle of the handle.

cho·ral (kôr′əl) *adj.* sung by, or recited by, a choir or chorus.

chow (chou) *n.* a dog, originally from China, with a thick brown or black coat and a black tongue.

ci·ta·tion (sī tā′shən) *n.* a traffic ticket or summons for breaking a traffic law.

clab·ber (klab′ər) *n.* thickly curdled sour milk.

clam·ber (klam′bər) *v.* to climb clumsily or with effort, using both hands and feet.

clar·i·fy (klar′ə fī′) *v.* to make or become easier to understand.

clinch (klinch) *n.* the act of gripping an opponent's body with the arms.

clot (klät) *v.* to form into a large mass.

coach·man (kōch′mən) *n.* the driver of a carriage.

cocks·comb (käks′kōm′) *n.* part of a jester's cap that resembles the red, fleshy growth on the head of a rooster.

coil (koil) *n.* anything wound into a series of rings or a spiral.

com·fort·er (kum′fər tər *or* kum′fə tər) *n.* a quilted bed covering.

com·men·tar·y (käm′ən ter′ē) *n.* a series of notes on a book.

com·pas·sion (kəm pash′ən) *n.* sorrow for the suffering or trouble of another.

com·pe·tent (käm′pə tənt) *adj.* well qualified; capable.

com·pet·i·tor (kəm pet′ə tər) *n.* a person who enters into a rivalry with someone else.

com·posed (kəm pōzd′) *adj.* calm; self-controlled.

com·pul·sive (kəm pul′siv) *adj.* having to do with repeated and senseless impulses to do a particular thing.

com·rade (käm′rad *or* käm′rəd) *n.* a close friend. —**comradeship** *n.*

con·ceal (kən sēl′) *v.* to hide.

con·dense (kən dens′) *v.* to compact; compress.

con·fine (kän′fīn′) *n.* a boundary or limit.

con·fla·gra·tion (kän′flə grā′shən) *n.* a big fire.

con·gest (kən jest′) *v.* **1.** to make too full; overcrowd. **2.** to cause too much blood to collect in the vessels of a part of the body. —**congestion** *n.*

con·gre·ga·tion (käng′grə gā′shən) *n.* a group of people coming together for religious worship.

con·jec·ture (kən jek′chər) *n.* a guess; judgment.

con·so·la·tion (kän′sə lā′shen) *n.* comfort; solace.

con·spic·u·ous (kən spik′yoo wəs) *adj.* attracting attention by being outstanding; striking.

con·tempt (kən tempt′) *n.* the feeling of a person toward someone or something he considers worthless; scorn.

con·tent (kən tent′) *adj.* happy enough with what one has.

con·tour (kän′toor) *n.* the outline of a figure or an area.

con·tra·dict (kän′trə dikt′) *v.* to assert the opposite of a statement.

con·verge (kən vʉrj′) *v.* to come together; to move toward the same place.

con·vey (kən vā′) *v.* to make known; communicate.

cop·per·as (käp′ər əs) *n.* a green crystalline compound used in the making of ink.

co·quette (kō ket′) *n.* a girl or woman who tries to get men to notice her; flirt. —**coquettish** *adj.*

cor·dial (kôr′jəl) *n.* a stimulating medicine, food, or drink. *adj.* warm and friendly; sincere. —**cordially** *adv.*

cor·don (kôr′d'n) *n.* a line or circle of police stationed around an area to guard it.

cor·ru·gate (kôr′ə gāt′ *or* kär′ə gāt′) *v.* to put ridges or grooves in, to make something look wavy.

corse·let (kôrs′lət) *n.* a medieval piece of body armor.

cos·mo·pol·i·tan (käz′mə päl′ə t'n) *adj.* at home in all countries or places.

coun·sel (koun′s'l) *n.* advice.

coun·te·nance (koun′tə nəns) *n.* the look on a person's face that shows his nature or feelings.

cou·pé (koo pā′) *n.* a closed carriage seating two passengers, with a seat outside for the driver.

court (kôrt) *v.* to try to win the love of.

cov·et·ous (kuv′it əs) *adj.* greedy; wanting to have what another has.

cow·er (kou′ər) *v.* to crouch or huddle up from fear.

cowl (koul) *n.* a monk's hood. —**cowlish** *adj.*

cox·comb (käks′kōm′) *n.* a silly, vain fellow.

crag (krag) *n.* a steep, rugged rock that rises above other rocks.

cran·ny (kran′ē) *n.* a small, narrow opening.

creep·er (krēp′ər) *n.* a plant whose stem puts out rootlets for creeping along a surface.

cre·vasse (kri vas′) *n.* a deep crack or opening.

crim·son (krim′z'n) *adj.* deep rich red.

cro·chet (krō shā′) *v.* to do needlework in which loops of thread or yarn are interwoven with a hooked needle.

cro·cus (krō′kəs) *adj.* deep orange yellow.

---

at, āte, fär; pen, ēqual; sit, mīne; sō, côrn, join,
took, fool, our; us, tʉrn; chill, shop, thick, *th*ey,
sing; zh *in* measure; ′l *in* idle;
ə *in* alive, cover, family, robot, circus.

crouch (krouch) *v.* to stoop low with the limbs close to the body, as an animal ready to pounce.

Cru·sade (kroo sād') *n.* a military expedition, which Christians of western Europe undertook from time to time in the eleventh through the thirteenth centuries, to capture the Holy Land from the Moslems.

cryp·tic (krip'tik) *adj.* having a hidden meaning; mysterious.

cus·tom (kus'təm) *n.* a usual practice or habit. —**customary** *adj.*

cyl·in·der (sil'ən dər) *n.* anything hollow or solid with a tubular shape. —**cylindrical** *adj.*

D

dagged (dag'əd) *adj.* with a jagged edge.

da·is (dā'is *or* dī'is) *n.* a platform raised above the floor at one end of a room.

dale (dāl) *n.* a valley.

dam·ask (dam'əsk) *n.* a durable fabric decorated with woven designs, used for table linen.

dank (dangk) *adj.* disagreeably damp; moist and chilly.

dap·ple (dap''l) *adj.* marked with spots; spotted.

darn (därn) *v.* to mend or repair by sewing a network of stitches.

dash (dash) *v.* to throw or thrust.

deem (dēm) *v.* to judge.

de·fect (dē'fekt) *n.* an imperfection; fault.

de·fi·ance (di fī'əns) *n.* the act of opposing boldly.

de·ject·ed (di jek'tid) *adj.* depressed; disheartened.

de·lib·er·a·tion (di lib'ə rā'shən) *n.* careful consideration.

delve (delv) *v.* to search.

den·si·ty (den'sə tē) *n.* the quality of being thick.

de·pos·it (di päz'it) *n.* sediment; something left lying.

de·range (di rānj') *v.* to make insane. —**derangement** *n.*

des·o·late (des'ə lit) *adj.* **1.** solitary; forlorn. **2.** uninhabited; deserted.

des·o·la·tion (des'ə lā'shən) *n.* a lonely, deserted place.

de·spair (di sper') *n.* loss of hope.

des·per·ate (des'pər it) *adj.* extreme; drastic; reckless because one has lost hope. —**desperately** *adv.*

des·tin·y (des'tə nē) *n.* a series of events that follow one another in a way that seems inevitable or unavoidable.

dis·may (dis mā') *n.* loss of courage when faced with trouble or danger; alarm.

dis·pose of (dis pōz' uv) *v.* to give away.

dis·po·si·tion (dis'pə zish'ən) *n.* one's general nature or mood.

dis·si·pate (dis'ə pāt') *v.* to scatter; disperse.

dis·tort (dis tôrt') *v.* to twist out of shape.

dis·tress (dis tres') *n.* pain; sorrow.

doc·ile (däs''l) *adj.* easy to manage.

doff (däf *or* dôf) *v.* to remove or raise.

dog·ged (dôg'id *or* däg'id) *adj.* not giving in readily; persistent; stubborn. —**doggedness** *n.*

dole·ful (dōl'fəl) *adj.* full of sorrow or sadness; mournful. —**dolefully** *adv.*

dow·ry (dou'rē) *n.* the property that a woman brings to her husband at marriage.

drag·gle (drag''l) *v.* to make or become wet and dirty by dragging in mud or water; to trail on the ground. —**draggled** *adj.*

drift (drift) *v.* to move gradually from a set position or intention.

droll·er·y (drōl'ər ē) *n.* a quaint or amusing sense of humor.

duch·y (duch'ē) *n.* the territory ruled by a duke or duchess.

E

ear·locks (ir'läks) *n.* a lock of hair hanging in front of the ear.

ec·stat·ic (ik stat'ik *or* ek stat'ik) *adj.* feeling great joy or delight.

ef·fi·cient (ə fish'ənt) *adj.* effective.

e·late (i lāt' *or* ē lāt') *v.* to raise the spirits of.

e·lu·sive (i lōō'siv) *adj.* hard to discover or understand; puzzling.

em·bel·lish (im bel'ish) *v.* to decorate; ornament; adorn.

em·broi·der (im broi'dər) *v.* to make a design on fabric with needlework.

em·i·nent (em'ə nənt) *adj.* outstanding; noteworthy; distinguished.

em·phat·ic (im fat'ik) *adj.* very striking.

em·po·ri·um (em pôr'ē əm) *n.* a store; marketplace.

en·camp·ment (in kamp'mənt) *n.* a camp or campsite.

en·chant·ment (in chant'mənt) *n.* a magic spell or charm.

en·dow (in dou') *v.* to provide with some talent or quality.

en·fold (in fōld') *v.* to wrap; envelop.

en·mi·ty (en'mə tē) *n.* bitter attitude or feeling; hostility.

e·nor·mous (i nôr'məs) *adj.* very large or very great; huge.

e·quiv·a·lent (i kwiv'ə lənt) *n.* something that is equal in meaning.

es·sence (es''ns) *n.* fundamental nature or most important quality of something.

e·the·re·al (i thir'ē əl) *adj.* very light; delicate; heavenly.

eth·i·cal (eth'i k'l) *adj.* having to do with morality; of or conforming to moral standards.

ex·cess (ik ses' *or* ek'ses') *n.* an amount or quantity greater than necessary.

ex·em·pla·ry (ig zem'plə rē) *adj.* serving as a model.

ex·ter·mi·nate (ik stur'mə nāt') *v.* to destroy or get rid of entirely; wipe out; annihilate.

ex·tin·guish (ik sting'gwish) *v.* to put out.

ex·u·ber·ant (ig zōō'bər ənt) *adj.* full of life or high spirits.

F

fan·cy (fan'sē) *v.* to imagine.

fash·ion (fash'ən) *v.* to make or form in a certain way; shape.

fat·ed (fāt'id) *adj.* decided by fate; destined.

fife (fīf) *n.* a small, shrill-toned musical instrument resembling a flute.

fil·let (fil' it) *n.* a narrow band worn around the head to hold the hair in place.

fil·lip (fil'əp) *n.* anything that stimulates or livens up.

fi·nesse (fi nes') *n.* skillfulness and ability to handle difficult situations with tact.

fis·tu·la (fis'choo lə) *n.* an abnormal passage from an abscess to the skin.

flail (flāl) *v.* to move one's arms about frantically.

flat (flat) *n.* **1.** an apartment. **2.** an area of level land.

flaunt·ing (flônt'ing) *adj.* fluttering freely; gaudy.

fledg·ling (flej'ling) *n.* a young bird.

---

at, āte, fär; pen, ēqual; sit, mīne; sō, côrn, join, took, fōōl, our; us, turn; chill, shop, thick, they, sing; zh *in* measure; 'l *in* idle; ə *in* alive, cover, family, robot, circus.

flog (fläg *or* flôg) *v.* to beat with a stick or whip.

flour·ish (flʉr'ish) *n.* a grand sweeping movement.

fod·der (fäd'ər) *n.* coarse food for cattle or horses.

foe (fō) *n.* enemy; opponent.

fon·dle (fän'd'l) *v.* to stroke lovingly; caress.

fore·close (fôr klōz') *v.* to take away the right to redeem a mortgage when regular payments have not been kept up.

fore·lock (fôr'läk') *n.* a lock of hair growing just above the forehead.

fore·stall (fôr stôl') *v.* to prevent.

fran·tic (fran'tik) *adj.* wild with worry or fear.

fraud (frôd) *n.* a person who cheats or is not what he pretends to be.

fraught (frôt) *adj.* filled, charged, or loaded.

fret (fret) *v.* worry.

frig·ate (frig'it) *n.* a fast, medium-sized sailing warship of the 18th and early 19th centuries.

frock (fräk) *n.* a dress.

fron·tal (frunt''l) *adj.* in or at the front.

G

ga·ble (gā'b'l) *n.* the triangular part of a wall between the sloping ends of a ridged roof. —**gabled** *adj.*

gait (gāt) *n.* a manner of walking or running.

gale (gāl) *n.* a strong wind ranging in speed from 32 to 63 miles per hour.

gal·lant (gal'ənt *or* gə lant') *n.* a high-spirited, stylish man.

gal·lant·ry (gal'ən trē) *n.* a polite act or remark.

ga·losh (gə läsh') *n.* an overshoe or boot.

gam·ut (gam'ət) *n.* the entire range or extent.

gan·gling (gaŋ'gliŋ) *adj.* tall, thin, and awkward.

gen·er·ate (jen'ə rāt') *v.* to produce.

gen·tian (jen'shən) *n.* a flowering plant.

ges·tic·u·late (jes tik'yə lāt') *v.* to make movements with the hands or arms.

ges·ture (jes'chər) *n.* something said or done only for effect.

gild (gild) *v.* to cover with a thin layer of gold or a gold color. —**gilded** *adj.*

gilt (gilt) *adj.* golden.

gird (gʉrd) *v.* to fasten with a belt or a band.

girth (gʉrth) *n.* a band put around the belly of a horse to hold a saddle.

glint (glint) *n.* a gleam, flash, or glitter. *v.* to gleam; flash.

gloat (glōt) *v.* to gaze or think with malicious pleasure.

gnaw (nô) *v.* to torment, as by constant fear or worry.

gore (gôr) *v.* to pierce with a horn or tusk.

gouge (gɔuj) *v.* to force or tear.

grade (grād) *n.* the slope of a road.

gran·deur (gran'jər *or* gran 'jɔɔr) *n.* great dignity; magnificence.

gran·ite (gran'it) *n.* a very hard rock consisting of feldspar and quartz.

gren·a·dier (gren'ə dir') *n.* an infantry soldier who threw grenades.

gri·mace (gri mās' *or* grim'əs) *v.* to twist the face in a look of pain.

groom (grōōm *or* grɔɔm) *n.* man or boy whose work is taking care of horses.

gross (grōs) *adj.* total weight of something.

ground·er (grɔun'dər) *n.* a batted ball that strikes the ground almost immediately after being hit and rolls or bounces along.

grub (grub) *v.* to clear the ground by digging up roots and stumps.

grudge (gruj) *v.* to give sparingly and unwillingly.

gru·el·ling (groo′əl irg *or* grool′irg) *adj.* very tiring; exhausting.

guil·der (gil′dər) *n.* the monetary unit and a coin of the Netherlands.

gulf (gulf) *n.* a wide gap or separation.

gul·ly (gul′ē) *n.* a channel or valley worn by running water; small, narrow ravine.

gyp·sy (jip′sē) *n.* a member of a wandering people with dark skin and black hair. —**gypsyish** *adj.*

H

hag·gard (hag′ərd) *adj.* having a worn look.

hag·gle (hag′′l) *v.* to argue about terms or price; bargain.

ham·let (ham′lit) *n.* a very small village.

ham·per (ham′pər) *v.* to keep from moving freely; hinder.

hap·haz·ard (hap′haz′ərd) *adj.* not planned. —**haphazardly** *adv.*

ha·ra·ki·ri (hä′rə kir′ē *or* her′ē ker′ē) *n.* suicide done as a ritual by cutting open one's abdomen; once practiced by high-ranking Japanese to avoid facing disgrace.

har·ass (hə ras′ *or* har′əs) *v.* to trouble, worry, or torment.

har·row (har′ō) *v.* to cause pain, fear, or discomfort. —**harrowed** *adj.*

Has·i·dim (has′ə dim) *n.* a sect of Jewish mystics, originating in 18th-century Poland, emphasizing joyful worship. —**Hasidic** (ha sid′ik) *adj.*

hatch (hach) *n.* a covering for a ship's opening on the floor or roof.

haugh·ty (hôt′ē) *adj.* having or showing excess pride in oneself.

haunch (hônch *or* hänch) *n.* the part of the body including the hip, buttock, and thickest part of the thigh.

hearth (härth) *n.* the stone or brick floor of a fireplace.

her·ald (her′əld) *n.* a person who announces significant news.

her·mit·age (hur′mit ij) *n.* a place where a person can live away from other people; private retreat; house of various monastic orders.

hie (hī) *v.* to hurry or hasten.

hind (hīnd) *adj.* back; rear.

hith·er (hith′ər) *adv.* to this place; here.

hob·ble (häb′′l) *v.* to walk unsteadily; limp. —**hobbling** *adj.*

hold (hōld) *n.* the interior of a ship below the deck, in which the cargo is carried.

hol·low (häl′ō) *n.* a hole; cavity; empty space.

Ho·ly Land (hō′lē land′) *n.* a portion of the land on the east coast of the Mediterranean Sea (at that time part of the Ottoman Empire) that included the city of Jerusalem.

hom·age (häm′ij *or* äm′ij) *n.* anything given or done to show respect or honor.

hon·ey·comb (hun′ē kōm′) *v.* to fill with holes like the structures made by bees.

hose (hōz) *n.* a man's tightfitting outer garment covering the hips, legs, and feet.

hov·er (huv′ər *or* häv′ər) *v.* to stay fluttering in the air near one place.

hulk (hulk) *n.* a big ship.

hull (hul) *n.* the frame or body of a ship.

hum·mock (hum′ək) *n.* a low rounded hill.

hy·a·cinth (hī′ə sinth′) *n.* a plant of the lily family, with spikes of fragrant, bell-shaped flowers.

---

at, āte, fär; pen, ēqual; sit, mīne; sō, côrn, join, took, fool, our; us, turn; chill, shop, thick, they, sing; zh *in* measure; 'l *in* idle; ə *in* alive, cover, family, robot, circus.

hys·te·ri·a (his tir′ē ə *or* his ter′ē ə) *n.* any outbreak of wild, uncontrolled excitement.

id·i·om (id′ē əm) *n.* the usual way in which words are joined together.

i·dler (īd′lər) *n.* one who loafs; lazy person.

il·lu·sion (i lōō′zhən) *n.* **1.** an unreal or misleading appearance. **2.** a false idea or mistaken belief.

im·meas·ur·a·ble (i mezh′ər ə b'l) *adj.* too large to be measured; vast.

im·mense (i mens′) *adj.* very large; vast; huge.

im·mod·er·ate (i mäd′ər it) *adj.* not kept under control; excessive.

imp (imp) *n.* an evil spirit; a small demon.

im·pas·sioned (im pash′ənd) *adj.* having or showing strong feelings; fiery; ardent.

im·pet·u·ous (im pech′ōō wəs) *adj.* **1.** moving with great force or violence; rushing. **2.** acting suddenly with little thought; impulsive.

im·press (im pres′) *v.* to arouse the interest or approval of.

im·pulse (im′puls) *n.* a sudden feeling that makes one want to act.

in·can·des·cent (in′kən des′'nt) *adj.* glowing with intense heat.

in·ca·pac·i·tate (in′kə pas′ə tāt′) *v.* to make unable or unfit; to disable.

in·cen·tive (in sen′tiv) *n.* something that makes someone want to work harder; stimulus; motive.

in·ces·sant (in ses′'nt) *adj.* never ceasing; continuing endlessly —**incessantly** *adv.*

in·com·pre·hen·si·ble (in′käm pri hen′sə b'l *or* in käm′pri hen′sə b'l) *adj.* cannot be understood.

in·del·i·ble (in del′ə b'l) *adj.* cannot be erased or blotted out; permanent. —**indelibly** *adv.*

in·dig·nant (in dig′nənt) *adj.* angry about something unjust or unfair. —**indignantly** *adv.*

in·dig·ni·ty (in dig′nə tē) *n.* something that insults or hurts one's dignity or pride.

in·dis·tinct (in′dis tiŋkt′) *adj.* not clearly seen; vague.

in·ev·i·ta·ble (in ev′ə tə b'l) *adj.* cannot be avoided; certain to happen.

in·flux (in′fluks′) *n.* a continual coming in.

in·gen·ious (in jēn′yəs) *adj.* clever, resourceful, and inventive.

in·got (iŋg′gət) *n.* a mass of metal cast into a bar or other convenient shape.

in·i·ti·a·tive (i nish′ē ə tiv *or* i nish′ə tiv) *n.* the action of taking the first step or move.

in·nate (i nāt′ *or* in′āt) *adj.* existing naturally rather than acquired.

in·quir·y (in′kwə rē *or* in′kwī′rē) *n.* an investigation or question.

in·stinc·tive (in stiŋk′tiv) *adj.* caused by a tendency to behave in a characteristic or natural way. —**instinctively** *adv.*

in·ten·si·ty (in ten′sə tē) *n.* relative strength; magnitude.

in·tent (in tent′) *adj.* firmly directed; strongly resolved.

in·ter·mit·tent (in′tər mit′'nt) *adj.* stopping and starting again at intervals; pausing from time to time.

in·tox·i·cate (in täk′sə kāt′) *v.* to make wild with excitement or happiness.

in·tri·cate (in′tri kit) *adj.* full of elaborate detail; complex.

in·var·i·a·ble (in ver′ē ə b'l) *adj.* unchanging; constant. —**invariably** *adv.*

ir·rel·e·vant (i rel′ə vənt) *adj.* having nothing to do with the subject. —**irrelevantly** *adv.*

ir·res·o·lute (i rez′ə lōōt′) *adj.* not able to

decide or make up one's mind; hesitating.

i·so·late (ī′sə lāt′) *v.* to set apart from others; place alone.

itch (ich) *v.* to have a restless desire.

J

jab·ber (jab′ər) *n.* silly, rambling talk.

jar·di·niere (jär′d'n ir′) *n.* an ornamental bowl, pot, or stand for flowers or plants.

jaw (jô) *v.* to talk.

joust (joust *or* jōōst) *n.* a combat with lances between knights on horseback.

jo·vi·al (jō′vē əl *or* jō′vyəl) *adj.* full of hearty, playful good humor. —**joviality** *n.*

jug·ger·naut (jug′ər nôt′) *n.* a terrible, destructive force.

K

keep (kēp) *n.* the heavily fortified inner tower of a castle.

key·stone (kē′stōn′) *n.* the central, topmost stone of an arch.

kin·dle (kin′d'l) *v.* to set on fire; ignite.

kin·ship (kin′ship′) *n.* a relationship; close connection.

kith and kin (kith ənd kin) *n.* friends, acquaintances, and relatives.

L

lad·en (lād′'n) *v.* loaded; burdened.

la·ment (lə ment′) *v.* to express deep sorrow.

land·locked (land′läkt′) *adj.* entirely or almost entirely surrounded by land.

lan·guor (laŋ′gər) *n.* a lack of spirit, listlessness.

lar·i·at (lar′ē it) *n.* a rope.

latch onto (lach än′tōō) *v.* to get hold of; obtain.

lec·ture (lek′chər) *v.* to scold at length.

leer (lir) *n.* a sly, sidelong look together with a suggestive or wicked smile.

le·gion (lē′jən) *n.* a large number; multitude.

lib·er·ate (lib′ə rāt′) *v.* to release or free.

li·chen (lī′kən) *n.* small simple plant growing on rocks and trees, used to make dye.

lin·ger (liŋ′gər) *v.* to continue to stay.

lin·sey-wool·sey (lin′zē wōōl′zē) *n.* a coarse cloth made of cotton and wool.

lit·er·al·ly (lit′ər əl ē) *adv.* actually; in fact.

lit·ter (lit′ər) *n.* straw or hay used as bedding for animals.

live·li·hood (līv′lē hōōd′) *n.* means of supporting life; subsistence.

loam (lōm) *n.* a rich soil of clay, sand, and organic matter.

lodge (läj) *v.* to fix firmly. —**lodged** *adj.*

loft·y (lôf′tē) *adj.* haughty; proud. —**loftily** *adv.*

(at) log·ger·heads (lôg′ər hedz′) *adv.* in disagreement.

louis (lōō′ē) *n.* a French coin of varying value.

lu·mi·nous (lōō′mə nəs) *adj.* bright; filled with light.

lurch (lurch) *v.* to jump forward suddenly.

M

mack·i·naw (mak′ə nô′) *n.* a short, double-breasted coat of heavy woolen cloth, usually plaid.

Ma·don·na (mə dän′ə) *n.* Mary, mother of Jesus.

---

at, āte, fär; pen, ēqual; sit, mīne; sō, côrn, join, took, fōōl, our; us, turn; chill, shop, thick, they, sing; zh *in* measure; 'l *in* idle; ə *in* alive, cover, family, robot, circus.

mag·a·zine (mag′ə zēn′ *or* mag′ə zēn′) *n.* the place on a warship where explosives are stored.

mag·nif·i·cence (mag nif′ə s′ns) *n.* richness and splendor.

mag·ni·tude (mag′nə to͞od′ *or* mag′nə tyo͞od′) *n.* great influence.

mailed (māld) *adj.* covered or protected with a flexible body armor.

main·sail (mān′s′l *or* mān′sāl′) *n.* sail set from the mainmast of a vessel.

ma·jes·tic (mə jes′tik) *adj.* grand; stately; dignified. —**majestically** *adv.*

man-at-arms (man′ət ärmz′) *n.* a heavily armed medieval soldier.

mane (mān) *n.* the long hair growing from the top or sides of the neck of an animal.

ma·neu·ver (mə no͞o′vər *or* mə nyo͞o′vər) *v.* move in a skillful manner.

man-of-war (man′əv wôr′ *or* man′ə wôr′) *n.* an armed naval vessel; warship.

man·sard roof (man′särd ro͞of′) *n.* a roof with two slopes on each of the four sides, the lower steeper than the upper.

man·tle (man′t′l) *n.* a loose, sleeveless cloak or cape.

marsh·mal·low (marsh′mel′ō *or* marsh′mal′ō) *n.* soft, sweet, spongy food.

mar·tial law (mär′shəl lô′) *n.* temporary rule by the military authorities over the civilians in time of war.

mar·vel (mär′v′l) *v.* to wonder about. *n.* an astonishing thing.

ma·son·ry (mā′s′n rē) *n.* brickwork or stonework.

mass (mas) *adj.* of a large number of persons or things.

mas·tiff (mas′tif) *n.* a large, powerful, smooth-coated dog.

mat·ting (mat′iṉg) *n.* a straw or hemp floor covering.

mech·a·nism (mek′ə niz′m) *n.* the working parts of a machine.

med·i·ta·tion (med′ə tā′shən) *n.* deep reflection or quiet thought.

mel·an·chol·y (mel′ən käl′ē) *adj.* sad and depressed. *n.* sadness and depression of spirit.

mem·oir (mem′wär) *n.* a record of events based on the writer's personal observation or knowledge.

men·ace (men′is) *v.* to threaten danger or harm. —**menacingly** *adv.*

mer·chant·man (mur′chənt mən) *n.* a ship used in commerce.

mer·ry·mak·ing (mer′ē mā′kiṉg) *n.* having fun; festivity.

me·te·or·ite (mēt′ē ə rīt′) *n.* a small, solid body that travels through outer space, survives passage through the atmosphere, and falls to earth as a mass of mineral material.

Mich·ael·mas (mī′k′l məs) *n.* feast of the archangel Michael, celebrated on September 29.

mi·li·tia (mə lish′ə) *n.* an army composed of citizens rather than professional soldiers, called up in time of emergency.

mi·mo·sa (mi mō′sə) *n.* a tree belonging to the legume family having heads or spikes of small white, yellow, or pink flowers.

moat (mōt) *n.* a deep, broad ditch dug around a castle, often filled with water for protection.

mod·er·a·tor (mäd′ə rāt′ər) *n.* one who serves as a chairperson.

mo·lest (mə lest′ *or* mō lest′) *v.* to annoy so as to trouble or harm.

mo·men·tar·y (mō′mən ter′ē) *adj.* lasting for only a brief time.

mon·grel (muṉg′grəl *or* mäṉg′grəl) *n.* an animal produced by crossing breeds or varieties.

mon·u·ment (män′yə mənt) *n.* a writing serving as a memorial.

moor (moor) *n.* a tract of open rolling wasteland.

moor·ing (moor′iŋ) *n.* place where a ship is held in place by cables or chains.

mor·tal (môr′t'l) *adj.* that must eventually die.

mor·tal·i·ty (môr tal′ə tē) *n.* all human beings; mankind.

moth·er-of-pearl (mu*th*′ər əv purl′) *n.* the hard, pearly layer on the inside of certain seashells, used for making buttons and jewelry.

mount (mount) *n.* a horse to ride.

mul·ti·tu·di·nous (mul′tə tood′'n əs *or* mul′tə tyood′'n əs) *adj.* very numerous; many.

musk·mel·on (musk′mel′ən) *n.* a roundish fruit growing on a vine.

mus·ter (mus′tər) *v.* to gather up; summon. *n.* an assembling of military troops.

mu·tu·al (myoo′choo wəl) *adj.* done or felt by each of two or more toward the other or others.

N

niche (nich) *n.* a recess or empty space.

noc·tur·nal (näk tur′n'l) *adj.* active during the night.

non·cha·lant (nän′shə länt′) *adj.* showing cool lack of concern; casually indifferent. —**nonchalantly** *adv.*

O

ob·jec·tive (əb jek′tiv *or* äb jek′tiv) *n.* aim; goal.

ob·liv·i·on (ə bliv′ē ən *or* ō bliv′ē ən) *n.* a state of having forgotten, not caring, or not knowing.

ob·scure (əb skyoor′ *or* äb skyoor′) *v.* to conceal from view; hide.

ob·sti·nate (äb′stə nit) *adj.* unreasonably determined to have one's own way; stubborn.

o·di·ous (ō′dē əs) *adj.* arousing or deserving hatred or disgust.

o·men (ō′mən) *n.* a thing or happening supposed to foretell a future event.

or·gan·dy (ôr′gən dē) *n.* a very sheer, crisp cotton fabric.

out·land·ish (out lan′dish) *adj.* very odd.

P

pace (pās) *n.* a horse's gait in which both legs on the same side are raised together.

pa·cif·ic (pə sif′ik) *adj.* peaceful; calm; tranquil.

pact (pakt) *n.* an agreement between persons, groups, or nations.

page (pāj) *n.* boy training for knighthood who served a person of high rank in the court.

palm·er (päm′ər *or* päl′mər) *n.* pilgrim who carried a palm leaf as a sign that he had been to the Holy Land.

pang (paŋ) *n.* a sudden feeling of pain or distress.

par·a·bol·ic (par′ə bäl′ik) *adj.* concave with the regular outline of a curve.

par·a·lyze (par′ə līz) *v.* to make powerless or helpless; bring activity to a stop.

par·lor (pär′lər) *n.* a living room set aside for guests.

---

at, āte, fär; pen, ēqual; sit, mīne; sō, côrn, join, took, fool, our; us, turn; chill, shop, thick, *th*ey, siŋ; **zh** *in* measure; **'l** *in* idle; ə *in* alive, cover, family, robot, circus.

pas·sion·ate (pash′ən it) *adj.* very strong; intense.

pa·tron (pā′trən) *n.* **1.** a regular customer. **2.** a person who regularly supports an activity.

paunch (pônch) *n.* a large belly. —**paunchy** *adj.*

pawn (pôn) *n.* a player of the lowest value or rank, as in a chess game.

pen·e·trate (pen′ə trāt′) *v.* to make one's way into or through something.

pen·sive (pen′siv) *adj.* thinking deeply of serious or melancholy things.

pep·per (pep′ər) *v.* to sprinkle thickly.

per·plex (pər pleks′) *v.* to confuse.

per·sist·ent (pər sis′tənt) *adj.* continuing, especially in the face of opposition; stubborn. —**persistently** *adv.*

pert (pʉrt) *adj.* bold or impudent in speech or behavior.

pe·so (pā′sō) *n.* monetary unit of many Spanish-American countries.

pe·ti·tion (pə tish′ən) *n.* a request.

phe·nom·e·na (fi näm′ə nə) *n., pl.* of **phenomenon** facts or experiences that can be seen, heard, and scientifically described..

pi·ous (pī′əs) *adj.* pretending to be virtuous without really being so.

plac·id (plas′id) *adj.* tranquil; calm.

plague (plāg) *n.* anything that causes suffering or trouble; calamity.

plant (plant) *v.* to make known in order to mold public opinion.

plod (pläd) *v.* to walk or move heavily; trudge.

pluck (pluk) *n.* courage to meet danger or difficulty; fortitude.

plume (plo͞om) *n.* something like a feather in shape or lightness.

plum·met (plum′it) *n.* a lead weight hung at the end of a line, used to find out how deep water is. *v.* to fall or drop straight downward.

plun·der (plun′dər) *v.* to take goods or property by force.

plunge (plunj) *v.* to move violently and rapidly forward.

poise (pɔiz) *v.* to suspend.

pop-up (päp′up) *n.* a ball popped into the infield.

por·tent (pôr′tent) *n.* a foreshadowing; something of significance.

por·ter (pôr′tər) *n.* a dark-brown beer.

por·ti·co (pôr′tə kō′) *n.* a porch or covered walk consisting of a roof supported by columns.

pos·ter·i·ty (päs ter′ə tē) *n.* all future generations.

po·tion (pō′shən) *n.* a drink or liquid dose of medicine or a substance that is supposed to do magic.

prai·rie-schoon·er (prer′ē sko͞o′nər) *n.* a large covered wagon used by pioneers to cross the American prairies.

prec·i·pice (pres′ə pis) *n.* a steep cliff; a vertical, or almost vertical, rock face.

pre·cip·i·tate (pri sip′ə tāt′) *v.* to rush headlong; move swiftly. —**precipitately** *adv.*

pred·e·ces·sor (pred′ə ses′ər) *n.* a person coming before another, as in public office.

pre·vail (pri vāl′) *v.* to exist widely.

prick (prik) *v.* to cause to point or stick up.

prig (prig) *n.* an annoying person who is very proper and acts as though he or she were better than others.

prim·rose (prim′rōz′) *adj.* light-yellow.

pri·va·tion (prī vā′shən) *n.* lack of the ordinary necessities of life.

proc·la·ma·tion (präk′lə mā′shən) *n.* something that is announced officially.

pro·found (prə found′) *adj.* showing great knowledge or thought.

pro·pri·e·tor (prə prī′ə tər) *n.* one who owns and operates a business.

pros·per·i·ty (prä sper′ə tē) *n.* good fortune or success.

pros·trate (präs′trāt) *adj.* lying flat on the ground.

prov·i·dence (präv′ə dəns) *n.* the care or help of God or nature.

pul·sate (pul′sāt) *v.* to throb; quiver.

pu·ri·fy (pyoor′ə fī′) *v.* to free from guilt, sin, or corruption by a special ceremony.

Q

quad·rant (kwäd′rənt) *n.* a fourth part of the circumference of a circle; an arc of 90°.

quag·mire (kwag′mīr′) *n.* wet, boggy ground.

quaint (kwānt) *adj.* unusual; curious.

quar·ry (kwôr′ē *or* kwär′ē) *v.* to excavate or dig up.

quest (kwest) *n.* a journey; a search.

quet·zal (ket säl′) *n.* a Central American bird, usually brilliant green and red.

quick·sil·ver (kwik′sil′vər) *n.* the metal mercury.

quill (kwil) *n.* **1.** any of the large stiff wing or tail feathers of a bird. **2.** the hollow stem of a feather.

quirk (kwʉrk) *n.* sudden twist or turn.

quiv·er (kwiv′ər) *v.* to shake or tremble.

R

ra·di·ant (rā′dē ənt) *adj.* showing joy, love, and well-being.

ra·di·us (rā′dē əs) *n.* the distance from the center to the outside of a circle.

ram·ble (ram′b'l) *n.* a stroll; walk.

rap·ture (rap′chər) *n.* great joy; ecstasy.

ras·cal (ras′k'l) *n.* a fun-loving, mischievous person.

rat·i·fy (rat′ə fī′) *v.* to approve or confirm in an official way.

rau·cous (rô′kəs) *adj.* loud and rowdy.

rav·e·nous (rav′ə nəs) *adj.* greedily hungry.

rear (rir) *v.* **1.** to raise or bring to maturity. **2.** to rise up on the hind legs.

re·cede (ri sēd′) *v.* to go or move back.

re·clothe (re klō*th*′) *v.* to get oneself back to a state of control or balance.

re·coil (ri koil′) *v.* to return to the starting point.

rec·on·cil·i·a·tion (rek′ən sil′ē ā′shən) *n.* the settlement of a quarrel.

re·con·struc·tion (rē′kən struk′shən) *n.* the period from 1867 to 1877, and the process of bringing the Southern States back into the Union after the Civil War.

red·coat (red′kōt′) *n.* in colonial times, a British soldier in a uniform with a red coat.

reel (rēl) *v.* to give way or fall back; stagger.

re·frac·tion (ri frak′shən) *n.* the bending of a ray of light as it passes on a slant from one medium to another of different density.

re·fur·bish (ri fʉr′bish) *v.* to clean or polish.

re·joice (ri jois′) *v.* to be glad or happy.

re·luc·tant (ri luk′tənt) *adj.* not wanting to do something; unwilling. **—reluctantly** *adv.*

re·pose (ri pōz′) *n.* calm; peace.

re·sist·ance (ri zis′təns) *n.* opposition.

re·solve (ri zälv′ *or* ri zôlv′) *n.* a fixed resolution or intention.

re·sound (ri zound′) *v.* to echo or be filled with sound.

---

at, āte, fär; pen, ēqual; sit, mīne; sō, côrn, join, took, fool, our; us, tʉrn; chill, shop, thick, *th*ey, sing; **zh** *in* measure; **'l** *in* idle; ə *in* alive, cover, family, robot, circus.

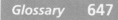

re·spec·tive (ri spek′tiv) *adj.* relating separately to each of two or more.

re·tort (ri tôrt′) *v.* to respond in a sharp, quick way.

rig (rig) *n.* a tractor-trailer.

ri·ot (rī′ət) *v.* to act in a wild way in a public disturbance with others.

roan (rōn) *adj.* a solid color, such as reddish-brown or black, with a thick sprinkling of white hairs.

roil (roil) *v.* to stir up; agitate.

row·el (rou′əl) *n.* the small wheel with sharp points forming the end of a spur.

ru·ble (rōō′b′l) *n.* monetary unit of the Soviet Union.

ruse (rōōz) *n.* a trick or plan for fooling someone.

rus·tic (rus′tik) *n.* a country person.

S

sac·ris·ty (sak′ris tē) *n.* a room in a church where the sacred vessels and robes are kept.

saf·fron (saf′rən) *adj.* orange yellow.

sa·lon (sə län′ *or* sal′än) *n.* a room where guests are received.

Sam·o·yed (sam′ə yed′) *n.* a strong Siberian dog with a thick, white coat.

sanc·ti·ty (saŋk′tə tē) *n.* holiness.

sap (sap) *n.* any fluid considered vital to life or health.

Sar·a·cen (sar′ə s′n) *n.* an Arab or Moslem, especially at the time of the Crusades.

sar·casm (sär′kaz′m) *n.* a mocking remark.

sat·u·rate (sach′ə rāt′) *v.* to cause to be thoroughly soaked.

scat·ter·ing (skat′ər iŋ) *n.* a small amount spread out here and there.

scoff (skôf *or* skäf) *v.* to show scorn or mockery.

scone (skōn) *n.* a small, flat cake.

score (skôr) *n.* twenty.

scorn (skôrn) *n.* great contempt for someone.

scru·ti·nize (skrōōt′′n īz′) *v.* to look at closely or examine carefully.

scul·lion (skul′yən) *n.* domestic servant doing the rough, dirty work in a kitchen.

scur·ry (skʉr′ē) *v.* to move quickly; scamper.

scut·tle (skut′l) *v.* to run quickly; scamper.

sec·tor (sek′tər) *n.* any of the sections into which an area is divided.

seis·mo·graph (sīz′mə graf′) *n.* an instrument that records the force and time of earthquakes and other earth tremors.

sen·ior·i·ty (sēn yôr′ə tē *or* sēn yär′ə tē) *n.* a higher rank because of age.

sen·ti·men·tal (sen′tə men′t′l) *adj.* having tender, gentle feelings.

sen·ti·nel (sen′ti n′l) *n.* a person set to guard a group; sentry.

serf (sʉrf) *n.* a person under the feudal system who was bound to his master's land.

shame·faced (shām′fāst′) *adj.* ashamed; embarrassed.

shan·ty (shan′tē) *n.* a shack; small building.

sheath (shēth) *n.* **1.** a case for the blade of a knife or sword. **2.** a covering.

sheen (shēn) *n.* brightness; luster.

sheer (shir) *adj.* extremely steep.

shle·miel (shlə mēl′) *also* **schlemiel** *n.* a bungling person who regularly fails or is easily fooled or cheated.

shuck (shuk) *v.* to cast off; push away.

side·board (sīd′bôrd′) *n.* a piece of dining-room furniture for holding table linen, silver, or china.

si·dle (sī′d′l) *v.* to move sideways.

siege (sēj) *n.* the surrounding of a city or fort by an enemy army trying to capture it by continued blockade and attack.

sim·plic·i·ty (sim plis′ə tē) *n.* the fact of being uneducated or ignorant.

sim·u·late (sim′yoo lāt′) *v.* to look or act like.

si·mul·ta·ne·ous (sī′m'l tā′nē əs) *adj.* occurring at the same time. —**simultaneously** *adv.*

sin·ew (sin′yoo) *n.* tendon.

sin·gle·foot (siṅg′g'l foot′) *n.* the manner of walking of a horse in which the legs on the same side move together, but each foot falls separately.

sin·is·ter (sin′is tər) *adj.* threatening harm or evil; ominous.

skirt (skʉrt) *n.* the outer parts or border; outskirts.

skit·ter (skit′ər) *v.* to skip or move along quickly.

skit·tish (skit′ish) *adj.* very nervous.

slice (slīs) *v.* to hit a ball so that it curves.

sloe-black eyes (slō′blak īz′) *n.* dark, almond-shaped eyes.

sloop (sloop) *n.* a fore-and-aft rigged sailing vessel with one mast.

sluice (sloos) *n.* a channel for carrying off extra water.

smol·der (smōl′dər) *v.* to be present but kept under control.

snuff (snuf) *n.* a preparation of powdered tobacco put on the gums or taken up into the nose by sniffing.

sod·den (säd′'n) *adj.* filled with moisture; soaked.

som·ber (säm′bər) *adj.* dark and gloomy.

sou (soo) *n.* a French coin no longer in use.

south·paw (south′pô′) *n.* a left-handed baseball pitcher.

Span·ish Main (span′ish mān′) *n.* the coastal region of the Americas along the Caribbean Sea; especially the north coast of South America.

spar (spär) *n.* a pole for supporting the sails on a ship.

spec·tral (spek′trəl) *adj.* ghostly.

spec·u·late (spek′yə lāt′) *v.* to think; ponder.

sphe·roid (sfir′oid) *n.* a body that is almost but not quite a sphere.

sphinx (sfiṅgks) *n.* an ancient Egyptian statue having a lion's body and the head of a human.

spit·tle (spit′'l) *n.* saliva.

spon·ta·ne·ous (spän tā′nē əs) *adj.* done in a natural way without effort or much thought.

sprat (sprat) *n.* a small fish belonging to the herring family.

spring (spriṅg) *v.* to arise as if from some source.

spurt (spʉrt) *v.* to force out suddenly.

squall (skwôl) *n.* a brief, violent windstorm, usually with rain or snow.

squat (skwät *or* skwôt) *adj.* short and thick. *v.* to crouch low.

squire (skwīr) *n.* young man of high birth who attended a knight.

sta·ble (stā′b'l) *adj.* not likely to change; lasting.

stac·ca·to (stə kät′ō) *adj.* made up of short, sharp elements.

stake (stāk) *v.* to bet; gamble.

stam·i·na (stam′ə nə) *n.* endurance.

staunch (stônch *or* stänch) *adj.* firm; loyal.

stealth·y (stel′thē) *adj.* secret; sneaky, or quiet.

steed (stēd) *n.* a high-spirited riding horse.

steep (stēp) *n.* a sharply rising slope.

---

at, āte, fär; pen, ēqual; sit, mīne; sō, côrn, join, took, fool, our; us, tʉrn; chill, shop, thick, they, siṅg; zh *in* measure; 'l *in* idle; ə *in* alive, cover, family, robot, circus.

stern (sturn) *n.* the rear portion of a boat or ship.

stick·ler (stik′lər) *n.* a person who insists on having things done in a certain way.

sti·fle (stī′f'l) *v.* to hold back; stop.

sting·ray (sting′rā′) *n.* a large ray fish having a whiplike tail with a sharp spine that can inflict painful wounds.

stitch (stich) *n.* a sudden sharp pain in the side.

stole (stōl) *v.* moved quietly or secretly.

stow (stō) *v.* to put or hide away.

strad·dle (strad′'l) *v.* to place oneself with a leg on either side of something.

strag·gle (strag′'l) *v.* to leave from time to time. —**straggling** *adj.*

strait (strāt) *n.* difficulty; distress.

strat·a·gem (strat′ə jəm) *n.* a scheme or plan for achieving some purpose.

strut (strut) *v.* to walk in a proud, swaggering manner.

stu·pe·fy (stoo′pə fī′ *or* styoo′pə fī′) *v.* to stun or astound.

sul·fur (sul′fər) *n.* a pale-yellow, solid substance, often in the form of crystals: it burns with a blue flame and choking fumes.

sul·len (sul′ən) *adj.* gloomy; depressing.

sul·try (sul′trē) *adj.* uncomfortably hot and moist; sweltering.

su·per·la·tive (sə pur′lə tiv *or* soo pur′lə tiv) *n.* something that is the highest of its kind.

sup·ple (sup′'l) *adj.* flexible; easily changed; adaptable —**suppleness** *n.*

sur·cin·gle (sur′sing′g'l) *n.* a saddle strap.

sur·coat (sur′kōt′) *n.* an outer coat; especially a short cloak worn over a knight's armor.

surge (surj) *n.* a sudden strong increase or rush.

sur·rep·ti·tious (sur′əp tish′əs) *adj.* done in a secret or sly way. —**surreptitiously** *adv.*

sur·rey (sur′ē) *n.* a carriage having four wheels, two seats, and usually a flat top.

sur·vey (sər vā′) *v.* to look at or study in a broad, general way.

sus·pect (sus′pekt) *adj.* viewed with suspicion; believed to be guilty of something.

sus·pi·cion (sə spish′ən) *n.* a very small amount; trace.

swarth·y (swôr′*th*ē) *adj.* having a dark complexion.

sys·tem·at·ic (sis′tə mat′ik) *adj.* according to a set of logical principles or rules.

T

tab·loid (tab′loid) *n.* a newspaper with pages about half the usual size, many pictures, and short, often sensational, news stories.

tan·ner (tan′ər) *n.* a person whose work is turning hides and skins into leather.

tap·es·try (tap′is trē) *n.* a heavy cloth woven with decorative designs and pictures, used as a wall hanging.

tat·ter·de·mal·ion (tat′ər di māl′yən *or* tat′ər di mal′yən) *n.* a person in torn, ragged clothing; ragamuffin.

tat·ters (tat′ərz) *n.pl.* shreds or pieces.

tat·too (ta too′) *n.* **1.** a signal. **2.** a loud drumming or rapping.

taut (tôt) *adj.* **1.** strained; tense. **2.** tightly stretched.

tem·pest (tem′pist) *n.* a violent outburst.

tem·po (tem′pō) *n.* rate of activity; pace.

tet·a·nus (tet′'n əs) *n.* an infectious, often fatal disease.

thick·et (thik′it) *n.* a thick growth of shrubs or underbrush.

thith·er (thi*th*′ər) *adv.* to that place; there.

thong (thông) *n.* a narrow strip of leather rope.

thrash (thrash) *v.* to give a severe beating to; flog. —**thrashings** *n.*

tinge (tinj) *v.* to color slightly; to give a tint to.

ti·tan (tīt''n) *n.* any person or thing of great size or power.

tog·gle (täg''l) *n.* a pin or bolt used to prevent slipping.

tongue (tuŋ) *n.* a narrow strip of land.

traipse (trāps) *v.* to walk or wander in an aimless or lazy way.

tran·quil·li·ty (traŋ kwil'ə tē *or* tran kwil'ə tē) *n.* the state of peacefulness; calmness.

trans·verse (trans vurs') *adj.* lying across; crosswise.

trav·erse (tra vurs') *v.* to pass over or through.

treach·er·ous (trech'ər əs) *adj.* not loyal or faithful; betraying or likely to betray.

tread (tred) *v.* to trample.

tri·fle (trī'f'l) *n.* something of little value or importance.

trun·dle (trun'd'l) *v.* to roll or move along with a rolling gait.

tuck·er (tuk'ər) *v.* to tire out.

tuft (tuft) *n.* a bunch of hairs, feathers, grass, etc., attached at the base.

tu·mult (tōō'mult *or* tyōō'mult) *n.* loud noise or uproar from a crowd.

tu·reen (too rēn') *n.* a large deep dish with a lid, for serving soups or stews.

turf (turf) *n.* a surface layer of earth containing grass; the ground.

tur·moil (tur'moil) *n.* a very excited or confused condition; uproar.

twang (twaŋ) *v.* to pull at and release quickly to sound tones.

tweak (twēk) *v.* to give a sudden, twisting pinch.

tyr·an·ny (tir'ə nē) *n.* very cruel and unjust use of power or authority.

U

u·biq·ui·tous (yōō bik'wə təs) *adj.* seeming to be everywhere at the same time.

un·du·late (un'joo lāt') *v.* to move in waves.

un·her·ald·ed (un her'əld əd) *adv.* not announced.

un·quar·ried (un kwôr'ēd) *v.* not excavated from the place where building stone or marble is found.

un·rul·y (un rōō'lē) *adj.* hard to control, restrain, or keep in order.

un·seem·ly (un sēm'le) *adj.* not proper or decent.

un·sound (un sound') *adj.* not sensible.

u·su·rer (yōō'zhoo rər) *n.* a person who lends money at an unreasonably high rate of interest.

V

va·grant (vā'grənt) *adj.* following no fixed direction or course; random.

vague (vāg) *adj.* not sharp, certain, or exact.

van·guard (van'gärd') *n.* the front part of an army in an advance attack.

van·i·ty (van'ə tē) *n.* a being vain, or overly proud of oneself. —**vain** *adj.*

vat (vat) *n.* a large tub or tank.

veer (vir) *v.* to change direction; shift; turn.

veil (vāl) *v.* to hide or cover up. —**veiled** *adj.*

ve·loc·i·ty (və läs'ə tē) *n.* quickness of motion; speed.

ve·ran·da (və ran'də) *n.* an open, roofed porch along the side of a building.

---

at, āte, fär; pen, ēqual; sit, mīne; sō, côrn, join, took, fool, our; us, turn; chill, shop, thick, *th*ey, siŋ; **zh** *in* measure; '**l** *in* idle; ə *in* alive, cover, family, robot, circus.

ver·ba·tim (vər bāt′əm) *adv.* word for word.

ves·sel (ves″l) *n.* **1.** a ship or large boat. **2.** a utensil for holding something.

ves·ti·bule (ves′tə byo͞ol′) *n.* a small entrance hall.

vex (veks) *v.* to disturb or irritate. —**vexation** *n.*

vin·dic·tive (vin dik′tiv) *adj.* wanting to get revenge. —**vindictiveness** *n.*

vir·tue (vur′cho͞o) *n.* general moral excellence; goodness or morality.

vis·age (viz′ij) *n.* the face.

vo·lup·tu·ous (və lup′cho͞o wəs) *adj.* physically attractive.

vow (vou) *n.* a solemn promise or pledge.

W

waft (waft *or* wäft) *v.* to move lightly.

wag·gish (wag′ish) *adj.* playful; joking; comical.

wail·ing (wāl′iṇg) *n.* a loud cry of grief or pain.

wa·ter clos·et (wôt′ər kläz′it) *n.* toilet.

wa·ver (wā′vər) *v.* to sway to and fro.

weath·er·cock (weth′ər käk′) *n.* a weather vane in the form of a rooster.

wharf (hwôrf *or* wôrf) *n.* a platform built along or out from the shore, where ships can dock and load or unload; pier; dock.

whim (hwim *or* wim) *n.* a sudden thought or wish to do something without any particular reason.

whin·ny (hwin′ē *or* win′ē) *v.* to neigh in a low, gentle way.

whir (hwur *or* wur) *v.* to fly or revolve with a whizzing or buzzing sound.

whole·sale (hōl′sāl′) *adj.* widespread or general.

wield (wēld) *v.* to handle and use a tool or weapon with skill and control.

wince (wins) *v.* to draw back slightly, usually twisting the face in pain.

wiz·ened (wiz″nd) *adj.* dried up; shriveled.

wolfs·head (wo͝olfs′hed) *n.* outlaw.

won·der·ment (wun′dər mənt) *n.* amazement.

woo (wo͞o) *v.* to try to win the love of.

wrig·gle (rig″l) *v.* to twist and turn to and fro; squirm.

writhe (rīth) *v.* to make twisting or turning movements.

wry (rī) *adj.* made by twisting or distorting the features.

Y

yaw (yô) *v.* to swing back and forth across a planned course or heading.

yeast·y (yēs′tē) *adj.* foamy; frothy.

yowl (youl) *n.* a long, mournful cry; howl.

Z

zeal·ous (zel′əs) *adj.* full of great enthusiasm; very eager. —**zealously** *adv.*

Guidelines for Capitalization, Punctuation, and Spelling

Capitalization

Punctuation

Spelling

Guidelines for Capitalization

1 Proper Nouns and Proper Adjectives

> A **common noun** is a general name of a person, place, thing, or idea.

princess   city   ship   honesty

> Capitalize proper nouns. A **proper noun** names a particular person, place, or thing.

Princess Diana   Tulsa   *Titanic*

A proper noun can be made up of one or more words. Capitalize all important words in a proper noun.

New Year's Day   Kalamazoo River   Johnny Appleseed

> Capitalize proper adjectives. A **proper adjective** is made from a proper noun.

Danish — Denmark   Portuguese — Portugal

Proper adjectives are often used with common nouns. Do not capitalize the common noun.

French dressing   Greek alphabet   Siamese cat

> Capitalize the names of people and pets.

Begin every word in a name with a capital letter. An initial stands for a name. Write initials as capital letters. Put a period after an initial.

Susan B. Anthony   A. J. Foyt   Muggins

Often, a word for a family relation is used as the name of a particular person, or as part of the name. *Mom* and *Grandpa Lewis* are two examples. Capitalize a word used in this way.

> **Capitalize a title used with a person's name.**

A **title** is a term of respect used in front of a name. Many titles have short forms called **abbreviations**. Capitalize abbreviations of titles. Follow an abbreviation with a period.

Mister — Mr.   Mistress — Mrs.   Doctor — Dr.

The title *Miss* has no abbreviated form. Do not use a period after this title. *Ms.* has no long form.

Did Mr. Lee interview Dr. Smith or Mayor Gentry?

> **Capitalize the word** *I.*

Margaret and I walked to the library.

Key to Writing

Take special care when capitalizing unusual names such as MacDonald or Rip Van Winkle.

2 More Proper Nouns

> **Capitalize the names of particular places and things.**

1. Capitalize cities, states, and countries.

   Laredo, Texas, is near Mexico.

2. Capitalize streets, bridges, parks, and buildings.

   The tour guide showed us the Empire State Building, the Brooklyn Bridge, Wall Street, and Central Park.

3. Capitalize geographical names. Do not capitalize *north*, *south*, *east*, or *west* when they refer to directions. Capitalize these words only when they refer to a particular section of the country or world.

The Millers turned south and drove to Death Valley.
In the United States, the Mississippi River is the dividing line between the East and West.
Blue Ridge Mountains extend from the North to the South.

Capitalize the names of months, days, and holidays.

Do not capitalize the seasons: spring, summer, winter, and fall.

We celebrate Father's Day and the first day of summer in June.

Capitalize the names of races, religions, nationalities, and languages.

Modern American Indian artists often use traditional designs.
Judaism, Christianity, and the Muslim religion share a belief in one God.
The Russians and the Chinese have a common border.
Does this junior high school offer French?

Capitalize words referring to God and to religious scriptures.

the Lord	the Bible	the Book of Genesis
Allah	the Talmud	the New Testament

Capitalize the names of clubs, organizations, and business firms.

Carolyn's dog is registered with the American Kennel Club.
Have you heard of the International Kitefliers Association?
Don's father works for American Plastics, Incorporated.

Key to Writing

Carefully follow capitalization rules. Incorrect capitalization can confuse meaning in your writing.

Little Rock (Arkansas)	I am going west. (direction)
little rock (pebble)	I am going out West. (area of country)

3 Outlines and Titles

> Capitalize the first word of each line of an outline.

Notice that the major divisions of an outline are marked with Roman numerals (I., II.). The next most important divisions are identified with capital letters (A., B.). After that, numerals mark the divisions.

```
Capitalization and Punctuation
 I. Use of capital letters
    A. Proper nouns and adjectives
    B. First words
       1. Sentences
       2. Poetry
       3. Outlines
       4. Titles
II. Use of periods
```

> Capitalize the first word, last word, and all important words in a title.

Do not capitalize an article (*the*, *a*, *an*), or a short preposition (*in*, *for*, *from*, *by*), unless it comes first or last.

Raiders of the Lost Ark (movie title)

Anne Morrow Lindbergh, *Gift from the Sea* (book)

Lewis Carroll, "The Walrus and the Carpenter" (poem)

Titles are also underlined or enclosed in quotation marks. Follow this general rule for punctuating titles. Place quotation marks around titles of short works such as stories, poems, newspaper articles, and reports. Underline the titles of longer works such as books, movies, magazines, newspapers, and television series. In printed works, these titles are in italics instead of underlined.

Guidelines for Punctuation

1 The Period

> Use a period at the end of a declarative sentence and most imperative sentences.

Declarative:	The next clue is hidden under that rock.
Imperative:	Look under that rock for the next clue.

> Use a period after an abbreviation. To save time and space we often use words in a shortened form. These forms are called **abbreviations**.

The names of states, days, and months are often abbreviated. Except for such abbreviations as *Mr.*, *Mrs.*, *Ms.*, A.M., and P.M., avoid using abbreviations when you write sentences. Look at these abbreviations.

P.O.	Post Office	in.	inch
U.S.A.	United States of America	doz.	dozen
St.	Street	ht.	height
Mt.	Mountain	wt.	weight
R.R.	Railroad	lb.	pound
D.C.	District of Columbia	oz.	ounce

Some special abbreviations are written without periods.

FM	frequency modulation	PBS	Public Broadcasting System
CB	citizens' band	USAF	United States Air Force
M	meter	ml	milliliter

The two-letter state abbreviations such as IL, OH, and CA are written with capital letters and no periods. If you are not sure whether an abbreviation is written with periods, look in a dictionary.

> Use a period after an initial. We often shorten a name to its first letter, which is called an initial. Always use a period after an initial.

P. Travers—Pamela Travers
J. C. Penny—James Cash Penny

> Use a period after each number or letter that shows a division of an outline or that precedes an item in a list.

Punctuation (an outline)
I. End marks
  A. The period
    1. Sentences
    2. Abbreviations and initials
    3. Outlines and lists
  B. The question mark
  C. The exclamation point

Talent Show Act (a list)
1. tumblers
2. tap dancer
3. singer
4. band

2 The Question Mark and the Exclamation Point

> Use a question mark at the end of an interrogative sentence. An **interrogative sentence** is a sentence that asks a question.

Where are we?   When do the geese migrate?

Use an exclamation point at the end of an exclamatory sentence and some imperative sentences. An **exclamatory sentence** is a sentence that expresses strong feelings.

Jackie struck out!   It's a home run!

Use an exclamation point at the end of an imperative sentence that shows surprise or other strong emotion.

Look out!   Hurry!

Use an exclamation point after an interjection. An **interjection** is a word or group of words used to express strong feeling.

Oh! How beautiful!   Wow! What an ending!

Key to Writing and Speaking

When you write dialogue, use question marks and exclamation points to show how words and sentences are spoken.

3 The Comma

Commas signal the reader to pause. This pause keeps the reader from running together words or ideas that should be separate.

Use commas to separate the items in the series. There are always three or more words in a series.

The Jungle Pet Store sells mynah birds, lizards, turtles, and tropical fish.

In a series, place commas after each word except the last. It is important to insert commas carefully when you write a series. Notice how the meaning of this sentence changes when the commas are removed.

The grocery clerk packed Anna's bag with soda, crackers, broccoli, soup, cream, cheese, and peanut butter.

The grocery clerk packed Anna's bag with soda crackers, broccoli soup, cream cheese, and peanut butter.

> If *yes*, *no*, or *well* begin a sentence, use a comma after them.

Yes, we're walking.   Well, we'll meet you there.

> When you use *and*, *but*, or *or* to combine two sentences, put a comma before these words.

We ran fast. We nearly missed the bus.
We ran fast, but we nearly missed the bus.

> Use commas to set off the name of a person spoken to.

One comma is needed when the name starts or ends the sentence. A comma is needed before and after a name in the middle of the sentence. Look at the way commas are used in these sentences.

Peter, what is your favorite color?
Mail this letter please, Joseph.
I think, Abigail, that you are taller than Sara.

> Use commas to set off an appositive. An **appositive** follows a noun and renames the noun. It is used to give more information. Notice how commas set off the appositive in this sentence.

Mr. Lopez, our swim coach, retired last week.

> Use commas to separate the parts of a date. If a date is in the middle of a sentence, use a comma after the last part.

Our field trip to the Brookfield Zoo is on Friday, May 13.
On November 7, 1962, Eleanor Roosevelt died.

> Use a comma to separate the name of a city from the name of a state or country.

We once lived near Trenton, New Jersey.
My parents traveled to Zurich, Switzerland, last year.

Key to Writing

Do not overuse commas. Too many commas make a sentence harder to read instead of easier.

4 Other Uses for Commas

> Use a comma to set off the explanatory words of a direct quotation.

Notice where the comma is placed in this direct quotation.

Courtney announced, "The movie will begin in ten minutes."

The explanatory words *Courtney announced* come before the quotation. A comma is placed after the last explanatory word. Now read this quotation.

"I want to go home," moaned Lisa.

The explanatory words come after the quotation. A comma is placed inside the quotation marks and after the last word of the quotation. Sometimes the quotation is separated into two parts.

"One of the people in this room," the detective said, "is the murderer."

A comma is used after the last word of the first part. Another comma is used after the last explanatory word. You will learn more about punctuating quotations in part 7 of this guide.

> Use a comma after the greeting of a friendly letter and after the closing of any letter.

Dear Agnes,   Sincerely yours,

> Use a comma whenever the reader might be confused.

Some sentences can be very confusing if commas are not used.

Going up the elevator lost power.

In the grocery bags were in demand.

Notice how much clearer a sentence is when a comma is used.

Going up, the elevator lost power.
In the grocery, bags were in demand.

5 The Apostrophe and the Hyphen

> Use an apostrophe to show possession. To form the possessive of a singular noun, add an apostrophe and *s* after the apostrophe.

city + 's = city's   Carlos + 's = Carlos's

To form the possessive of a plural noun that does not end in *s,* add an apostrophe and an *s* after the apostrophe.

gentlemen + 's = gentlemen's   geese + 's = geese's

To form the possessive of a plural noun that ends in *s,* add only an apostrophe.

birds + ' = birds'   cities + ' = cities'

> Use an apostrophe in a contraction. A **contraction** is a word made by joining two words and omitting one or more letters. An apostrophe replaces the missing letters.

can + not = can't	we + are = we're	they + are = they're
will + not = won't	does + not = doesn't	she + would = she'd
you + will = you'll	he + had = he'd	are + not = aren't

Use a hyphen after the first part of a word at the end of a line. When you write, you sometimes run out of room at the end of a line. Then you may have to split the word. Put a hyphen at the end of a syllable. Then write the second part of the word on the next line.

Before you choose a career, investigate many fields.

Never divide words of one syllable, such as *slight* or *bounce*. If you are in doubt about dividing a word, look it up in a dictionary.

Do not write a single letter at the end or beginning of a line. For example, these divisions would be wrong: *a- mong, inventor- y.*

Use a hyphen in compound numbers from twenty-one through ninety-nine.

seventy-six trombones   Twenty-third Psalm

6 The Colon and the Semicolon

Use a colon after the greeting in a business letter.

Dear Mrs. Winter: Dear Sir:

Use a colon between the numerals that tell hours and minutes.

8:30 A.M.   3:30 P.M.

Remember to capitalize the letters and to use periods after each letter in the abbreviations A.M. and P.M.

> Use a semicolon to combine two related sentences.

There are two ways to combine two related sentences into one. The first way is to use a conjunction such as *and*, *but*, or *or* to connect the sentences. When you write this kind of sentence, use a comma before the conjunction.

> Judge Marino announced her decision, and the courtroom emptied quickly.

The second way to combine two related sentences is to use a semicolon (;). The semicolon takes the place of both the comma and the conjunction.

> Judge Marino announced her decision; the courtroom emptied quickly.

Key to Writing

Correct use of the semicolon will help you avoid writing run-on sentences.

Incorrect: The conductor raised her baton the concert began.
Correct: The conductor raised her baton; the concert began.

7 Quotation Marks

When you write what a person has said, you are writing a **quotation**. When you write the person's exact words, you write a **direct quotation**. If you do not write the exact words, you are writing an **indirect quotation**. Study these sentences.

Direct quotation: Steven whispered, "I'm hiding."
Indirect quotation: Steven said that he was hiding.

> Put quotation marks before and after the words of a direct quotation.

Notice that Steven's exact words are set apart by quotation marks in the first sentence.

Quotation marks (" ") are two pairs of small marks that look like apostrophes. They tell the reader that the exact words of the speaker or writer are being quoted.

Separate the words of a direct quotation from the rest of the sentence with a comma or end mark in addition to quotation marks.

Julie exclaimed, "The band is marching!"
"The band is marching!" Julie exclaimed.

Notice that, in the first sentence above, the comma comes *before* the quotation marks. The second sentence starts with the quoted words. Here the end mark is placed *inside* the quotation marks.

Place question marks and exclamation points inside quotation marks if they belong to the quotation itself.

Michael asked, "Did the bird's wing heal?"
"It's perfect!" answered Marianne.

In the first sentence, the question is quoted. Therefore, the question mark is placed inside the quotation marks. In the second sentence, the speaker is showing strong emotion. The exclamation point is also placed inside the quotation marks.

Place question marks and exclamation points outside quotation marks if they do not belong to the quotation. Remember to capitalize the first word of a direct quotation.

Did Dad say, "Come home at seven o'clock"?
I was shocked to hear her say, "I'll go"!

Divided Quotations

Sometimes a quotation is divided. Explanatory words, like *she said* or *he asked*, are in the middle of the quotation.

"My favorite movie," Lewis said, "is the original *King Kong*."

Notice that two sets of quotation marks are used in this quotation. The explanatory words are followed by a comma. This sentence has a comma after the explanatory words because the second part of the quotation does not begin a new sentence. Use a period after the explanatory words if the second part of the quotation is a sentence.

"We wrote that," said the students. "It is a group poem."

Key to Writing

Said is a common explanatory word used in writing. Try to use a variety of explanatory words when you write. Try some of these.

explained	announced	exclaimed	requested
commented	expressed	asked	noted

8 Punctuating Titles

> Put quotation marks around the titles of stories, poems, reports, articles, and chapters of a book.

"Spring Song" (poem)   "The Ransom of Red Chief" (story)

> Underline the title of a book, magazine, play, motion picture, or TV series. When these titles are printed, they are in italics.

Mary Jane by Dorothy Sterling   *Mary Jane* by Dorothy Sterling

> Underline the title of a painting or the name of a ship.

Washington Crossing the Delaware (painting)
Queen Elizabeth II (ship)

Guidelines for Spelling

| Make a habit of looking at words carefully. | When you come to a new word, be sure you know its meaning. If you are not certain, look up the word in a dictionary. |

Make a habit of looking at words carefully.

When you come to a new word, be sure you know its meaning. If you are not certain, look up the word in a dictionary.

Practice seeing every letter. Many people see a word again and again but don't really look at it. When you see a new word or a tricky word, like *government*, look at all the letters. To help you remember them, write the word several times.

When you speak, pronounce words carefully.

Sometimes people misspell words because they say them wrong. Be sure that you are not blending syllables together. For example, you may write *probly* for *probably* if you are mispronouncing it.

Find out your own spelling enemies and attack them.

Look over your papers and make a list of the misspelled words. Also keep a list of new words that are difficult for you. Study these words until you can spell them correctly and easily.

Find memory devices to help with problem spellings.

Some words are difficult to remember. In these cases, a memory device may help you. A memory device is a trick, or a catchy sentence, that you can remember easily. The device tells you how to spell the word. Here are three examples:

principal The princi*pal* is my *pal*.
tragedy Every *age* has its tr*age*dy.
embarrass I turned *re*ally *red* and felt *so* silly.

Proofread what you write.

To make sure that you have spelled all words correctly, reread your work. Examine it carefully, word for word. Don't let your eyes race over the page and miss incorrectly spelled words.

Use a dictionary.

You don't have to know how to spell every word. No one spells everything correctly all the time. A good dictionary can help you to be a better speller. Use a dictionary whenever you need help with spelling.

Mastering Specific Words

When you notice that you are having trouble with a certain word, take a few minutes to study it carefully. Give it all your attention. If you spend the time and energy to learn it correctly once, you will save yourself all the trouble of correcting it many times.

Follow these steps to master a specific word.

Steps for Mastering Specific Words

1. **Look at the word and say it to yourself.**

Pronounce it carefully. If it has two or more syllables, say it again, one syllable at a time. Look at each syllable as you say it.

2. **Look at the letters. Spell the word aloud.**

If the word has two or more syllables, pause between syllables as you say the letters.

3. **Without looking at the word, write it.**

Be sure to form each letter properly. Take your time.

4. **Now look at your book or list to see if you have spelled the word correctly.**

If you have, write it once more. Compare it with the correct spelling again. For best results, repeat the process once more.

5. **If you have misspelled the word, notice where the error was.**

Then repeat steps 3 and 4 until you have spelled the word correctly three times in a row.

Rules for Spelling

Adding Prefixes and Suffixes

Prefixes

A prefix is a word part added to the beginning of a word to change its meaning. When a prefix is added to a word, the spelling of the word stays the same.

Prefix	Base Word	New Word
un- (not)	+ named	= unnamed (not named)
re- (again)	+ enter	= reenter (enter again)
dis- (not)	+ appear	= disappear (not appear)
il- (not)	+ legible	= illegible (not legible)
pre- (before)	+ set	= preset (set before)
im- (not)	+ mature	= immature (not mature)
mis- (incorrectly)	+ state	= misstate (state incorrectly)
in- (not)	+ formal	= informal (not formal)

The Suffixes *-ly* and *-ness*

A suffix is a word part added to the end of a word to change its meaning. When the suffix *-ly* is added to a word ending with *l*, both *l*'s are kept. When *-ness* is added to a word ending in *n*, both *n*'s are kept.

Base Word	Suffix	New Word
mean	+ **-ness**	= meanness
practical	+ **-ly**	= practically

The Final Silent e

When a suffix beginning with a vowel is added to a word ending with a silent *e*, the *e* is usually dropped.

make + ing = making   advise + or = advisor
confuse + ion = confusion   believe + able = believable
expense + ive = expensive   fame + ous = famous

When a suffix beginning with a consonant is added to a word ending with a silent *e*, the *e* is usually kept.

hate + ful = hateful   hope + less = hopeless
bore + dom = boredom   sure + ly = surely
safe + ty = safety   move + ment = movement

The following words are exceptions:

truly   argument   ninth   wholly   judgment

Words Ending in *y*

When a suffix is added to a word that ends with *y* following a consonant, the *y* is usually changed to *i*.

noisy + ly = noisily   fifty + eth = fiftieth
happy + est = happiest   heavy + ness = heaviness

Note this exception: When *-ing* is added, the *y* remains.

bury + ing = burying   cry + ing = crying
deny + ing = denying   apply + ing = applying

When a suffix is added to a word that ends with *y* following a vowel, the *y* usually is not changed.

joy + ful = joyful   pay + ment = payment
stay + ing = staying   annoy + ed = annoyed

The following words are exceptions: paid, said.

Words with *ie* or *ei*

When the sound is long *e* ($\bar{e}$), the word is spelled *ie* except after *c*.

The following rhyme provides some rules which will help you.

I before *e*
Except after *c*,
Or when sounded like *a*
As in n*ei*ghbor or w*ei*gh.

I before E

belief	relieve	yield	fierce	achieve
niece	brief	field	chief	shield

Except after C

receive	ceiling	perceive	deceit
conceive	conceited	receipt	

Or when sounded like A

weight   eight
neigh

These words are exceptions:

either	weird	species
neither	seize	leisure

Doubling the Final Consonant

Words of one syllable, ending with one consonant following one vowel, double the final consonant before adding *-ing*, *-ed*, or *-er*.

sit + ing = sitting	sad + er = sadder
hop + ed = hopped	stop + ing = stopping
shop + er = shopper	let + ing = letting

The final consonant is **not** doubled when it follows two vowels.

meet + ing = meeting	loan + ed = loaned
break + ing = breaking	train + er = trainer

Words with the "Seed" Sound

Only one English word ends in *sede: supersede*.
Three words end in *ceed: exceed*, *proceed*, *succeed*.
All other words ending in the sound of "seed" are spelled *cede*.

concede   precede   recede   secede

Words Often Confused

Sometimes your problems in spelling are caused by the language itself. In English there are many words that are easily confused. These words sound the same, or nearly the same, but are spelled differently and have different meanings. Words of this type are called **homophones**. Here are some examples of homophones.

horse—hoarse   pare—pear—pair   tail—tale   do—dew—due

When you have problems with homophones, general spelling rules won't help you. The only solution is to memorize which spelling goes with which meaning.

Here is a list of homophones and other words frequently used and frequently confused in writing. Study the sets of words, and try to connect each word with its correct meaning.

accept means to agree to something or to receive something willingly.
except means to keep out or leave out. As a preposition, *except* means "but" or "leaving out."

▶ My brother will *accept* the job the grocer offered him.
▶ Michelle likes every flavor of ice cream *except* pistachio.

capital means chief, important, or excellent. It also means the city or town that is the official seat of government of a state or nation.
capitol is the building where a state legislature meets.
the Capitol is the building in Washington, D.C., in which the United States Congress meets.

▶ The *capital* of Illinois is the city of Springfield.
▶ The *capitol* of Illinois is a stately building in Springfield.
▶ The senators arrived at the *Capitol* in time to vote.

hear means to listen to.
here means in this place.

▶ Every time I *hear* this song, I feel happy.
▶ Reference books are found *here* in the library.

it's is the contraction for *it is* or *it has*.
its shows ownership or possession.

▶ *It's* nearly midnight.
▶ The boat lost *its* sail during the storm.

lead (lēd) is a heavy, gray metal.
lead (lēd) means to go first, to guide.
led (lĕd) is the past tense of *lead* (lēd).

▶ Water pipes are often made of *lead*.
▶ These signs will *lead* us to the hiking trail.
▶ Bloodhounds *led* the detectives to the scene of the crime.

loose means free or not tight.
lose means to mislay or suffer the loss of something.

▶ The rider kept the horse's reins *loose*.
▶ If you *lose* your book, report the loss to the library as soon as possible.

peace is calm or stillness or the absence of disagreement.
piece means a portion or part.

▶ After two years of war, *peace* was finally achieved.
▶ This statue was carved from a *piece* of jade.

principal means first or most important. It also refers to the head of a school.
principle is a rule, truth, or belief.

▶ A *principal* export of Brazil is coffee.
▶ Our school *principal* organized a safety council.
▶ One *principle* of science is that all matter occupies space.

quiet means free from noise or disturbance.
quite means truly or almost completely.

▶ The only time our classroom is *quiet* is when it's empty.
▶ The aquarium tank is *quite* full.

their means belonging to them.
there means at that place.
they're is the contraction for *they are*.

▶ Our neighbors sold *their* house and moved to a farm.
▶ Please take the squirt guns over *there*.
▶ My sisters have never skied, but *they're* willing to try.

to means in the direction of.
too means also or very.
two is the whole number between one and three.

▶ The surgeon rushed *to* the operating room.
▶ The lights went off, and then the heat went off, *too*.
▶ Only *two* of the four mountaineers reached the peak.

weather is the state of the atmosphere referring to wind, moisture, temperature, etc.
whether indicates a choice or alternative.

▶ Australia has summer *weather* when the United States has winter.
▶ *Whether* we drive or take the train, we will arrive in three hours.

who's is the contraction for *who is* or *who has*.
whose is the possessive form of *who*.

▶ *Who's* been chosen to be a crossing guard?
▶ *Whose* skateboard was left on the sidewalk?

you're is the contraction for *you are*.
your is the possessive form of *you*.
▶ *You're* going to the costume party, aren't you?
▶ Please bring *your* sheet music to choir practice.

Index of Titles and Authors

Index of Skills

Speech, 499, 507–508

Stanza, *See* **Poetry**

Style, 409, 445–446, 457, 488–489, 501, 507, 516

Surprise Ending, *See* **Plot**

Suspense, 244, 277

Symbol, 251

Tale, 2, 46–48

Theme, 2, 3, 27, 40, 47, 102, 173–174, 203, 207, 211, 232, 290, 329, 366, 431, 522, 587

Time Order, 577
  time line, 19–20, 91, 560

Title, 283–284

Tone, 409, 423, 431, 445, 474, 507, 528

Word Choice, 326, 338, 370, 446

Comprehension and Thinking Skills

Alternatives, 12, 83, 283, 328, 378, 381, 488, 501

Analysis, 212, 446, 505

Attitude, 326, 332, 356, 396, 399, 423, 456, 495, 509, 512, 527

Audience, 342

Author's Purpose, 19, 244, 504, 507, 512, 536, 537, 560, 577, 586, 590

Cause and Effect, *See* **Relationships**

Classification, 47, 166, 311, 362

Comparison, 290, 324, 326, 361, 374, 396, 445, 456, 457, 481, 560, 562
  See also **Contrast**

Conclusions, *See* **Inference**

Connotation, *See* **Slanted Writing**

Context Clues, 6–7, 35–36, 47, 66–67, 142–143, 277–278, 308, 310, 311, 578

Contrast, 184, 272–273, 290, 326, 423, 445, 456, 474, 522, 562
  See also **Comparison**

Denotation, *See* **Slanted Writing**

Details
  recalling details, 12, 19, 27, 35, 39, 46, 63, 66, 83, 91, 101, 148–149, 164, 173, 184, 194, 202, 211, 220, 231, 243, 251, 262, 272, 277, 283, 290, 295, 308, 322, 324, 326, 328, 332, 334, 338, 340, 342, 349, 351, 356, 359, 361, 366, 368, 370, 374, 376, 378, 381, 386, 392, 396, 399, 401, 423, 431, 445, 456, 467, 474, 481, 488, 495, 501, 504, 507, 509, 512, 516, 521, 522, 527, 560, 577, 586
  supporting main idea, 4–5, 12, 19, 27, 35, 39, 46, 66, 431

Evaluating
  believability, 20–21, 27, 35, 46, 63, 202, 290, 295, 308, 342, 393
  literature, 244, 588
  tone, 63, 322, 326, 342

Fact and Opinion, 410, 411, 423, 431, 432, 445, 457–458, 474, 481, 495, 521–522, 530–531

Facts, 393, 423, 468, 482

Figurative Language, 125–133, 134, 346

Generalizations, 102, 482, 488

Inference, 72, 73, 149, 252, 316–317, 404, 431, 516
  about character, 12, 19, 27, 35, 39, 46, 63, 91, 101, 104, 148–149, 164, 165, 173, 174, 184, 202, 211, 220, 252, 295, 308, 340, 423, 445, 467, 474, 481, 488, 495, 507, 509, 512, 527, 560, 562, 577, 586
  from poetry, 322, 324, 332, 338, 349, 356, 359, 361, 366, 368, 370, 376, 381, 386, 396, 399, 401
  of opinion, 423, 457–458

Writing Skills

Study and Research Skills

Speaking and Listening Skills

Art Credits

Cover

Ano Mera, Mykonos (detail), 1984, THOMAS McKNIGHT. Collection of the Artist.

Fine Art for Selection Openers

15 *Rat IV,* 1977, MANON CLEARY. Private Collection.
37 Aztec feathered cloak from Mexico. Photo by Lee Boltin, Picture Library, Croton-on-Hudson, New York.
196 *Two Pair,* 1982, DON NICE. Etching, 32" x 42". Published by Pace Editions, Inc., New York City.
254 *Blackfoot Holy Man,* 1981, JERRY INGRAM. Private Collection.
298 *Wrapped Book,* 1972–1973, CHRISTO. © 1973 Christo. Collection of Jacob Baal-Teshuva, New York City. Photograph by Eeva-Inkeri.
426 *The Cattle Dealer* (detail), 1912, MARC CHAGALL. Public Art Collection, Basel Art Museum, Switzerland. SEF/Art Resource, New York City. Copyright © 1988 ADAGP/ARS, New York City.

Illustrations

Roberta Polfus, 42; Kinuko Y. Craft, 77, 80–81, 88, 90, 95; Allen Davis, 151, 154, 160–161; Troy Thomas, 198, 201, 213; Ron Hilmer, 247; Lubov Yegudin, 469.

Photographs

From *American Indian Painting and Sculpture,* Abbeville Press, New York City, "Blue Corn Maiden" by Gilbert Attencio of San Ildefonso Pueblo: xviii. Brandywine River Museum, Chadds Ford, Pennsylvania: 58. The Bettman Archive: 148, 164, 173, 340, 366, 370, 378, 397 (Steven), 444, 488, 586. Culver Pictures: 184, 231, 324, 341, 386, 392, 422, 560. © 1987 *Chicago Tribune,* all rights reserved, used with permission: 277. Columbia University: 220. Joan Farber: 512. Focus on Sports: 448. © 1987 Elizabeth Gilliland: 359. Sydney Rachel Goldstein: 326. Harvard University Archives: 356. Historical Pictures Service: 338. Illinois State Historical Society, 500, 504. Library of Congress: 501. © 1987 Henry Nelson: 475. *The New York Times Pictures:* 519. Dick Swanson/*People Weekly,* © 1977 Time Life: 211. Jane Scherr: 456. Bachrach/Smith College Archives: 34. Stanford University Archives: 328. UPI/Bettmann: 399. Vasser College Library: 374. Wellesley College Archives: 402. AP/Wide World Photos: 289, 349, 480, 494.

Acknowledgments

Ricardo E. Alegría: For "Lazy Peter and the Three-Cornered Hat" by Ricardo E. Alegría, from *The Three Wishes*, a Collection of Puerto Rican Folktales. Brandt & Brandt Literary Agents, Inc.: For "Western Wagons" by Stephen Vincent Benét, from *A Book of Americans* by Rosemary & Stephen Vincent Benét, Holt Rinehart and Winston, Inc.; copyright 1933 by Rosemary & Stephen Vincent Benét; copyright renewed © 1961 by Rosemary Carr Benét. Gwendolyn Brooks (The David Company, Chicago): For "Home," from *Maud Martha;* reprinted by permissions of the author. Curtis Brown, Ltd.: For *The Ugly Duckling* by A. A. Milne; copyright © 1941 by A. A. Milne. Don Congdon Associates, Inc.: For *The Dragon* by Ray Bradbury, published in *Esquire;* copyright © 1955 by Ray Bradbury, renewed 1983 by Ray Bradbury. For *The Sound of Summer Running* by Ray Bradbury, published in *The Saturday Evening Post* (as *Summer in the Air*) 1956; copyright © 1956 by Ray Bradbury; renewed 1984 by Ray Bradbury. Cooper Square Publishers, Totowa, N.J. 07512: For "Adjö Means Goodbye" by Carrie Allen Young, from *Beyond the Angry Black* by John A. Williams. Delacorte Press/Seymour Lawrence: For "Seal," excerpted from *Laughing Time* by William Jay Smith; copyright © 1953, 1955, 1956, 1957, 1959, 1968, 1974, 1977, 1980 by William Jay Smith. Dodd, Mead & Company, Inc.: For an excerpt from *Mumbet: The Story of Elizabeth Freeman* by Harold W. Felton; copyright © 1970 by University of Nebraska Foundation. Doubleday & Company, Inc.: For an excerpt from *The Story of My Life* by Helen Keller; copyright 1902, 1903, 1905 by Helen Keller. For "Six Horsemen," from *African Wonder Tales* by Frances Carpenter; copyright © 1963 by Frances Carpenter Huntington. For "Hearts and Hands," from *Waifs and Strays* by O. Henry; copyright 1917 by Doubleday & Company, Inc. For "Rikki-tikki-tavi," from *The Jungle Book* by Rudyard Kipling. For "The Fun They Had," from *Earth Is Room Enough* by Isaac Asimov; © 1957 by Isaac Asimov. E. P. Dutton: For "The Flower-Fed Buffaloes" by Vachel Lindsay, from *Going to the Stars;* copyright 1926 by D. Appleton & Co., renewed by Elizabeth C. Lindsay. For "America the Beautiful" by Katherine Lee Bates, from *Poems*. For "Four Haiku," from *Who I Am,* poems by Julius Lester; text and photographs copyright © 1974 by Julius Lester; reprinted by permission of the publisher, Dial Books for Young Readers. Education Development Center, Inc.: For "Magic Words to Feel Better," from *Songs and Stories of the Netsilik Eskimos,* translated by Edward Field from text collected by Knud Rasmussen, courtesy Education Development Center, Inc., Newton, MA. M. Evans and Company, Inc.: For excerpts from *The World's Great Stories* by Louis Untermeyer; copyright © 1964 by Louis Untermeyer. Farrar, Straus and Giroux, Inc.: For "Reb Asher the Dairyman," from *A Day of Pleasure* by Isaac Bashevis Singer; copyright © 1963, 1965, 1966, 1969 by Isaac Bashevis Singer. The Golden Quill Press: For "Puppy" by Robert L. Tyler, from *The Disposition of Don Quixote & Other Poems*. Harcourt Brace Jovanovich, Inc.: For "Summer of the Beautiful White Horse" by William Saroyan, from *My Name is Aram;* copyright 1938, 1966 by William Saroyan. For an excerpt from "I Get a Colt to Break In" by Lincoln Steffens, from *Boy on Horseback* by Lincoln Steffens; copyright 1931 by Harcourt Brace Jovanovich, Inc.; renewed 1959 by Peter Steffens. For "The Old Soldier," from *Four-Square* by Dorothy Canfield; copyright 1949 by Dorothy Canfield, renewed © 1977 by Sarah Fisher Scott. For excerpts from Chapter XVIII in *Abe Lincoln Grows Up* by Carl Sandburg; copyright 1926, 1928 by Harcourt Brace Jovanovich, Inc., renewed 1954, 1956 by Carl Sandburg. For "Women," from *Revolutionary Petunias & Other Poems* by Alice Walker; copyright © 1970 by Alice Walker. Harper & Row, Publishers, Inc.: For "Way Down in the Music," from *Honey, I Love and Other Love Poems* by Eloise Greenfield (Thomas Y. Crowell Company); copyright © 1978 by Eloise Greenfield. For "Langston Terrace," from *Childtimes: A Three Generation Memoir* by Eloise Greenfield and Lessie Jones Little (Thomas Y. Crowell Company); copyright © 1979 by Eloise Greenfield and Lessie Jones Little; copyright © 1971 by Pattie Ridley Jones. Harper & Row Publishers, Inc., and Jonathan Cape, Ltd.: For "The Gift-Giving," from *Up the Chimney Down: And Other Stories* by Joan Aiken; copyright © 1984 by Joan Aiken Enterprises, Ltd. Harvard University Press: For "The Duel" by Emily Dickinson, from *The Poems of Emily Dickinson,* ed. by Thomas H. Johnson, Cambridge, Mass.: The Belknap Press of Harvard University Press; copyright © 1951, 1955, 1979, 1983 by the President and Fellows of Harvard College, reprinted by permission of the publishers and the Trustees of Amherst College. International Creative Management, Inc.: For "Invasion from Mars," by Howard Koch, from *The Panic Broadcast;* copyright 1940 Princeton University Press, 1968 by Howard Koch. Lescher & Lescher, Ltd.: For "The Southpaw" by Judith Viorst, from *Free to Be . . . You and Me;* copyright © 1974 by Judith Viorst. Little, Brown and Company: For "The Panther," and "The Hippopotamus," from *Verses from 1929 On* by Ogden Nash; copyright 1935, 1940, 1942 by The Curtis Publishing Company, first appeared in *The Saturday Evening Post.* Jean McCord: For "The Long Way Around," from *Deep Where the Octopi Lie;* reprinted by permission of the author. Norma Millay Ellis: For "The Courage That My Mother Had" by Edna St. Vincent Millay, from *Collected Poems,* Harper & Row; copyright 1954 by Norma Millay Ellis. Modern Poetry Association: For "Pole Vault" by Shiro Murano, translated from the Japanese by Satoru Sato with the assistance of Constance Urdang, from *Poetry,* May 1956. N. Scott Momaday: For "New World," from *The Gourd Dancer* by M. Scott Momaday; reprinted by permission of the author. William Morrow & Company, Inc.: For "The Women's 400 Meters," from *The Sidewalk Racer and Other Poems of Sports and Motion* by Lillian Morrison; copyright © 1968, 1977 by Lillian Morrison, by permission of Lothrop, Lee & Shepard Books (A Division of William Morrow & Company). New Directions Publishing Corporation: For "Poem" by William Carlos Williams, from *Collected Earlier Poems of William Carlos Williams;* copyright 1938 by New Directions Publishing Corporation. The New Yorker Magazine: For "Catalogue" by Rosalie Moore, from *The New Yorker Magazine,* May 25, 1950; copyright © 1940, 1968 by The New Yorker Magazine, Inc. Oxford University Press: For "How Marian Came to the Greenwood," from *The Chronicles*

Staff Credits

Executive Editor, Literature: Susan D. Schaffrath
Senior Editor: Sherry A. Stansbury
Associate Editors: Christine M. Iversen, Ursula Y. McPike, Dennis M. Ryan,
    Linda Williams

Senior Production Coordinator: Patricia L. Reband
Production Editors: Susan V. Shorey, Julie Zink
Copyeditor: Virginia Swanton

Designer: Linda Schifano FitzGibbon